CALIFORNIA CAMPING

CALIFORNIA CAMPING

The Complete Guide
to California's
Recreation Areas

Tom Stienstra

Foghorn Press

San Francisco

Editor JOSEPH HESSION

Cover and book design by MELODY KEAN HALLER

Research by JULIE LANCELLE & CLAUDIA JANSEN

Maps by LASLO VESPREMI

Cover photo by GILBERT ROBINSON

Backcover photo by TERRY L. DUNCKEL

Library of Congress Cataloging in Publication Data

Stienstra, Tom
California Camping: The Complete Guide to California's Recreation Areas

1. Camping   2. Recreation   3. California   I. Title

GV191.42.C2S74   1987   796.54'09794   86-83284

ISBN 0-935701-20-6

Printed in the United States of America

✦ CONTENTS ✦

◆ CONTENTS ◆
continued

· JOINING THE FIVE · PERCENT CLUB

G oing on a camping trip can be like trying to put hiking boots on an octopus. You've tried it too, eh? Instead of the relaxing, exciting sojourn it was intended to be, a camping trip can turn into a scenario called "You Against The World." You want something easy? Try fighting an earthquake.

But it doesn't have to be that way, and that's what this book is all about. If you give it a chance, it can put the mystery, excitement and fun back into your camping vacations—and remove the fear of snarls, confusion and occasional temper explosions of volcanic proportions that keep people at home, locked away from the action.

Mystery? There are hundreds of hidden, rarely-used campgrounds listed and mapped in this book that you never dreamed of. Excitement? With many of these campsites comes the sizzle with the steak, the hike to a great lookout, the big fish at the end of the line. Fun? The how-to section of the book can take the futility out of your trips so you can put the fun back in. Add it up, put it in your cash register and you can turn camping into the satisfying adventure it is meant to be, whether for just an overnight quickie or for a month-long fortune hunt.

It has been documented that 95 percent of vacationers use only five percent of the available recreation areas. With this book, you can leave the herd to wander and be free. You can join the inner circle, the five percenters who know the great, hidden areas used by so few people. To join the Five Percent Club, you should take a hard look at the maps for the areas you wish to visit, and in turn, the numbered listings for the campgrounds that follow. As you study the camps, you will start to feel a sense of excitement building, a sense that you are about to unlock a door and catch a glimpse into a world that is rarely viewed. When you feel that excitement, act on it, parlay the energy into a great trip, so you can spend your time making new memories, rather than thinking of old ones.

We have tracked down and mapped more than 1,500 campgrounds in California, organized them county-by-county and then detailed each of them in the corresponding listings.

This is how the county campgrounds guide works. Each of California's 58 counties has been given a number. Locate the county you plan to visit and you will find each campground distinquished by a separate number. In addition, each campground is given a logo that refers to its level of development - Primitive; Developed for tent camping; or a motorhome park.

A primitive camp has few facilities and may not have piped water available, but it is free or very low cost. A developed camp has piped water, some facilites, and reservations are often necessary. And a motorhome park has been expressly designed for recreational vehicles, providing hookups and full amenities. Some also have spaces for tents.

The campground maps and guide lists can serve two ways: 1. If you're on the road, it's late in the day and stuck for a spot for the night, you can likely find one nearby. 2. You can custom tailor a vacation to fit exactly into your plans, rather than heading off, and hoping—maybe praying—it turns out all right.

For the latter, you may wish to obtain additional maps, particularly if you are venturing into areas governed by the U.S Forest Service or Bureau of Land Management. Both are federal agencies and have low-cost maps available that detail all hiking trails, lakes, streams and back country camps reached via logging roads. The back country camps are often in primitive and rugged settings, but provide the sense of isolation that many need on a trip. In addition, they can provide good jumpoff points for backpacking trips, if that is your calling. These camps are also often free, and we have included hundreds of them in this book.

At the other end of the spectrum are the developed parks for motorhomes, parks that offer a home away from home with everything from full hookups to a grocery store to a laundromat. These spots are just as important as the remote camps with no facilities. Instead of isolation, RV parks provide a place to shower, get outfitted for food and clean clothes. For the motorhome cruisers, they offer spots to stay in high style while touring the area. They tend to cost from $12 to $20 per night, with an advance deposit necessary in summer months.

Somewhere between the two—the remote, unimproved camps and the lavish motorhome parks—are hundreds and hundreds of campgrounds that provide a compromise; beautiful settings, some facilities, with a small overnight fee. Piped water, vault toilets and picnic tables tend to come with the territory, along with a fee of $4 to $10. Because they offer a bit of both worlds, this is where demand is highest. Reservations are usually advised, and at state parks, particularly during the summer season, you can expect company. This does not mean to abandon them in hope of a less confined environment. For one, most state parks have set up quotas so you don't feel like you've been squeezed in with a shoehorn, and secondly, the same parks often provide off-season or weekday prospects when there can be virtually no use.

Prior to your trip, you will want to get organized, and that's where you will want to start putting boots on that giant octopus. The key to organization for any task is breaking it down to its key components, then solving each element independent of the others. Remember the octopus. Grab a moving leg, jam a boot on, and make sure it's on tight before reaching for another leg. Do one thing at a time, in order, and all will get done quick and right.

As a result, we have isolated the different elements of camping, and you should do the same when planning for your trip. There are separate sections on each of the primary ingredients for a successful trip: 1. Food and cooking gear; 2. Clothes and weather protection; 3. Foot wear, leg care, and how to choose the right boots and socks; 4. Sleeping gear and how to get your rest; 5. Combatting bugs and some common-sense first-aid; 6. Fishing and recreation gear; 7. How to obtain good maps and put them to use.

Each section has a list at the end of its respective chapter. This way you can become completely organized for your trip in just one week—spending just a little time each evening, working a different section each night. In itself, getting organized is an unnatural act for many. By splitting it up, you take the pressure out and put the fun back in.

As a fulltime outdoors writer, the question I get asked more than any other is, "Where are you going this week?" All of the answers are in this book.

⋄ FOOD & COOKING ⋄ GEAR

It was a warm, crystal clear day, the kind of day when if you had ever wanted to go sky diving, you would go sky diving. That was exactly the case for my old pal Foonsky, who had never before tried the sport. But a funny thing happened after he jumped out of the plane and pulled on the ripcord for the first time: The parachute didn't open.

In total free fall, Foonsky noticed the earth below started looking bigger and bigger. Not one to panic, he calmly pulled the ripcord on the emergency parachute. But nothing happened then either. No parachute, no nothing.

The ground was getting closer and closer, and as he tried to search out for a soft place to land, Foonsky detected a small object shooting up toward him, getting larger as it approached. It looked like a camper.

Foonsky figured this could be his last chance, so as they passed in mid-flight, he shouted, "Hey, do you know anything about parachutes!"

The other fellow just shouted back as he headed off into space, "Do you know anything about lighting camping stoves!"

Well, Foonsky got lucky and his parachute opened. But as for the other fellow, well, he's probably in orbit like a NASA weather satellite. If you've ever had a mishap lighting a camping stove, you know exactly what we're talking about.

When it comes to camping, all things are not created equal. Nothing is more important than lighting your stove easily and have it reach full heat without feeling like you're playing with a short fuse to a miniature bomb. If your stove does not work right, your trip can turn into a disaster, regardless of how well you have planned the other elements. In addition, a bad stove will add an underlying feel of futility to your day, especially if you have carefully detailed your cooking gear and food for the trip. You will constantly have the inner suspicion that your darn stove is going to foul up on you again.

CAMPING STOVES

If you are buying a camping stove, remember this one critical rule: Do not leave the store with a new stove unless you have been shown exactly how to use it.

Know what you are getting. Many stores that specialize in outdoor recreation equipment now provide experienced campers/employees who will demonstrate the use of every stove they sell, and while they're at it, describe its respective strengths and weaknesses.

A second rule to remember is never buy a stove that uses kerosene for fuel. Kerosene is smelly and messy, provides low heat, needs priming, and in America, is virtually obsolete as a camp fuel. As a test experience, I tried using a kerosene stove once. It could scarcely boil a pot of water. In addition, some kerosene leaked out when the stove was packed and it ruined everything it touched. The smell of kerosene never did go away. Kerosene remains popular in Europe only because the campers haven't much heard of white gas yet. But when they do, they will demand it.

That leaves white gas or butane as the best fuels. Either can be right for you, depending on your special preferences.

White gas is the most popular, because it can be purchased at most outdoor recreation stores, at many supermarkets, and is inexpensive and effective. It burns hot, has virtually no smell, and evaporates quickly if it should spill. If you get caught in wet, miserable weather and can't get a fire going, you can use it as an emergency fire starter—though its use as such should be sparing and never on an open flame.

White gas is a popular fuel both for car campers who use the large, two-burner stoves equipped with a fuel tank and a pump, or for hikers who use one of the lightweight backpacking stoves. On the latter, lighting can require priming with a gel called priming paste, which some people dislike. Another problem with white gas is that it can be extremely explosive.

As an example, I once almost burned my beard completely off in a mini-explosion while lighting one of the larger stoves styled for car camping. I was in the middle of cooking dinner when the flame suddenly shut down. Sure enough, the fuel tank was empty, and after re-filling it, I pumped the tank 50 or 60 times to regain pressure. When I lit a match, the sucker ignited from three feet away. The concussion from the explosion was like a stick of dynamite going off, and immediately, the smell of burning beard was in the air. In the quick flash of an erred moment, my once thick, dark beard had been reduced to a mass of little, yellow burned curly cues.

My error? After filling the tank, I forgot to shut the fuel cock off while pumping up the pressure in the tank. As a result, as I pumped the tank, the stove burners were slowly producing the gas/air mixture, filling the air space above the stove. The strike of a match—even from a few feet away—and ka-boom!

That problem can be solved by using stoves that use bottled butane fuel. On the plus side, butane requires no pouring, pumping or priming, and stoves that use butane are the easiest to light of all camping stoves. Just turn a knob and light, that's it. On the minus side, because it comes in bottles, you never know precisely how much fuel you have left, and when a bottle is empty, you have a potential piece of litter. The person who tosses an empty butane cartridge on the ground and leaves it behind is perpetrating a gross insult to his camping brethren.

The other problem with butane as a fuel is that it just plain does not work well in cold weather, or when there is little fuel left in the cartridge. Since you cannot predict mountain weather in spring or fall, and most certainly will eventually use most of the fuel in the cartridge, butane can thus make a frustrating choice. If there is any chance of the temperature falling below freezing, you must sleep with your butane cartridge to keep it warm, or otherwise forget its use come morning.

Personally, I prefer using a small, lightweight stove that uses white gas so I can closely gauge fuel consumption. My pal Foonsky uses one with a butane bottle because it lights so easily. We have contests to see who can boil a pot of water faster and the difference is usually negligible. Thus, other factors are important when choosing a stove.

Of the other elements, ease of cleaning the burner is the most important. If you camp much, especially with the smaller stoves, the burner holes will eventually become clogged. Some stoves have a built-in cleaning needle; a quick twist of a knob and you're in business. On the other hand, others require disassembling and a protracted session using special cleaning tools. If a stove is difficult to clean, you will tend to put off doing it, and your stove will sputter and pant while you get humiliated watching the cold pot of water sitting atop it.

Thus, before making a purchase, require the salesman to show you how to clean the burner head. Except in the case of the large, multi-burner family camping stoves, which rarely require cleaning, this test can do more to determine the long-term value of a stove than any other factor.

BUILDING FIRES

One summer expedition took me to the Canadian wilderness in British Columbia for a 75-mile canoe trip on the Bowron Lake Circuit, a chain of 13 lakes, six rivers and seven portages. It is one of the true great canoe trips in the world, a loop trip that ends just a few hundred feet distant from the start. But at the first camp at little Kibbee Lake, my camp stove developed a fuel leak at the base of the burner and the nuclear-like blast that followed just about turned Canada into a giant crater.

As a result, the final 70 miles of the trip had to be completed without a stove, cooking on open fires each night. The problem was compounded by the weather. It rained eight of the 10 days. Rain? In Canada, raindrops the size of silver dollars fall so hard they actually bounce on the lake surface. We had to stop paddling a few times in order to empty the rain water out of the canoe. At the end of the day, we'd make camp, and then came the test. Either make a fire, or go to bed cold and hungry.

With an axe, at least we had a chance for success. As soaked as all the downed wood was, I was able to make my own fire-starting tinder from the chips of splitting logs. No matter how hard it rains, the inside of a log is always dry.

In miserable weather, matches don't stay lit long enough to get the tinder started. Instead, we used either a candle or the little, wax-like fire-starter cubes that stay lit for several minutes. From that, we could get the tinder going. Then we added small, slender strips of wood that had been axed from the interior of the logs. When the flame reached a foot high, we added the logs, with the dry interior of them facing in. By the time the inside of the logs had caught fire, the outside would be drying from the heat. It wasn't long and a royal blaze was brightening the rainy night.

That's a worst-possible case scenario and perhaps you will never face anything like it. Nevertheless, being able to build a good fire and cook on it can be one of the more satisfying elements of a camping trip. At times, just looking into the flames can provide a special satisfaction at the end of a good day.

However, never expect to build a fire for every meal, or in some cases, even build one at all. Many state and federal campgrounds have been picked clean of downed wood, or forest fire danger will force rangers to prohibit them altogether during the fire season. In either case, you either use your camp stove or go hungry.

But when you can build a fire, and the resources are available to do so, it will add depth and a personal touch to your camping trip. Of the campgrounds listed in the directory of this book, the sites that allow for fires will likely already have fire rings available. In primitive areas where you can make your own, you should dig a ring eight inches deep, line the edges with rock, and clear all the needles and twigs in a five-foot radius. The next day, when the fire is dead out, you can discard the rocks, fill over the black charcoal with dirt, then scatter pine needles and twigs over it. Nobody will even know you camped there. That's the best way I know to keep a secret spot a real secret.

When you start to build a campfire, the first thing you will notice is that no matter how good your intentions, your fellow campers will not be able to resist moving the wood around. Watch. You'll just be getting ready to add a key piece of wood at just the right spot, and your companion will stick his mitts in, quietly believing he has a better idea, shift the fire around and undermine your best thought-out plans.

So I make a rule on camping trips. One person makes the fire and everybody else stands clear, or is involved with other camp tasks, like gathering wood, getting water, putting up tents, or planning dinner. Once the fire is going strong, then it's fair game; anyone adds logs at their discretion. But in the early, delicate stages of the campfire, it's best to leave it to one person at a time.

Before a match is first struck, a complete pile of firewood should be gathered alongside. Then start small, with the tiniest twigs you can find, and slowly add in larger twigs as you go, criss-crossing them like a miniature teepee. Eventually, you will get to the big chunks that will produce high heat. The key is to get one piece of wood burning into another, which then burns to another, setting off what I call the chain of flame. Conversely, single pieces of wood, set apart from each other, will not burn.

On a dry, summer evening at a campsite where plenty of wood is available, about the only way you can blow the deal is to get impatient and try to add the big pieces too quickly. Do that and you'll just get smoke, not flames, and it won't be long before every one of your fellow campers is poking at your fire. It will drive you crazy, but they just can't help it.

COOKING GEAR

I like traveling light, and I've found all one needs is a cooking pot, small frying pan, metal pot grabber, fork, knife, cup and matches for a cook kit. In fact, I keep it all in one small bag, which fits into my pack. If I'm camping out of my 4-wheel drive rig, the little bag of cooking gear is easy to keep track of. Simple, not complicated, is the key to keeping a camping trip on the right track.

You can get more elaborate by purchasing complete cook kits with plates, a coffee pot, large pots and other cookware, but what really counts is having one single pot you're happy with. It needs to be just the right size, not too big or small, and be stable enough so it won't tip over, even if it is at a slight angle on a fire and full of water at a full boil. Mine is just 6 inches wide and 4½ inches deep, holds better than a quart of water, and has served well for several hundred camp dinners.

The rest of your cook kit is easy to complete. The frying pan should be small, light-gauge aluminum, teflon-coated, with a fold-in handle so it's no hassle to store. A pot grabber is a great addition, that is, a little aluminum gadget that will clamp to the edge of pots and allow you to lift them and pour water with total control and without burning your fingers. A fork, knife and cup are at your discretion. For cleanup, take a small bottle filled with dish cleaner and a plastic scrubber, and you're in business.

A Sierra Cup, which is a wide aluminum cup with a wire handle, is ideal because you can eat out of them as well as use them for drinking. This means no plates to clean after dinner, so cleanup is quick and easy. In addition, if you go for a hike, you can clip them to your belt with the wire handle.

If you want a more formal setup, complete with plates, glasses, silverware, and the like, you can end up spending more time preparing and cleaning up from meals than you do enjoying the country you are exploring. In addition, the more equipment you bring, the more loose ends you will have to deal with—and loose ends can cause plenty of frustration. If you have a choice, choose simple.

And remember what Thoreau said: "A man is rich in proportion to what he can do without."

FOOD AND COOKING TRICKS

On a trip to the Bob Marshall Wilderness in western Montana, I woke up one morning, yawned, and said, "What've we got for breakfast?"

The silence was ominous. "Well," finally came the response, "we don't have any food left."

"What!?"

"Well, I figured we'd catch trout for meals every other night."

On the return trip, we ended up eating wild berries, buds, and yes, even tried roots (not too tasty). When we finally landed the next day at a Kalispell pizza parlor, we nearly ate the wooden tables.

Running out of food on a camping trip can do more to turn reasonable people into violent grumps than any other event. There's no excuse for it, not when a system for figuring meals can be outlined with precision and little effort. You should not go out and buy a bunch of food, throw it in your rig and head off for yonder. That leaves too much to chance. And if you've ever been in the woods and real hungry, you'll know to take a little effort to make sure a day or two of starvation will not re-occur.

A three-step process offers a solution:

• 1. Make a general meal-by-meal plan and make sure your companions like what is on it. Never expect to catch fish for any meals.

• 2. Tell your companions to buy any speciality items on their own, and not to expect you to take care of everything, like some special brand of coffee.

• 3. Put all the food on your living room floor and literally figure every day of your trip meal-by-meal, bagging the food in plastic bags as you go. You will know exact food quotas and will not go hungry.

Fish for meals? There's a guaranteed rule for that. If you expect to catch fish for meals, you will most certainly get skunked. If you don't expect to catch fish for meals, you will probably catch so many they'll be coming out of your ears. I've seen it a hundred times.

One of the best camp dinner meals you can make is a self-designed soup/stew mix. After bringing a pot of water to a full boil, add in ramen or pasta, then cut up a potato, carrot, onion and garlic clove and let it simmer—then add in a soup mix or two. Because vegetables can take 10 minutes to cook, it is often a good idea to add in the soup mix well after the vegetables. Read the directions on the soup mix to determine cooking time. Make sure you stir it up, otherwise your concoction may fall victim to "The Clumps." That done, pull a surprise bottle of wine out of your pack and we're talking about a gourmet dinner in the outback.

If you are car camping and have a big ice chest, you can bring virtually anything to eat and drink. If you want to go on the trail, well, then the rules of the game change.

They'll be no steaks, beer, or french fries waiting in your pack when you reach the top of the mountain. But that doesn't mean you don't have to eat well. Some of the biggest advances in the outdoor industry have come in the freeze-dried dinners now available for campers. Some of them are almost good enough to serve in restaurants. Sweet-and-sour pork over rice, tostadas, burgundy chicken . . . it sure beats the poopy goop we used to eat, like the old, soupy chili mac dinners that tasted bad and looked so unlike "food" that its consumption was near impossible, even for my dog.

To provide an idea of how to plan a menu, consider what my companions and I ate while hiking 250 miles on California's John Muir Trail:

• Breakfast: Instant soup, oatmeal (never get plain), one beef jerky stick, coffee or hot chocolate.

• Lunch: One beef stick, two jerky sticks, one Granola bar, dried fruit, half cup of pistachio nuts, Tang, small bag of M&M's.

• Dinner: Instant soup, freeze-dried dinner, milk bar, rainbow trout.

What was that last item? Rainbow trout? Right! Lest you plan on it, you can catch them every night.

COOKING GEAR LIST:

Matches bagged in different zip-lock bags
Fire-starter cubes or candle
Camp stove
Camp fuel
Pot, pan, cup
Pot grabber
Knife, fork
Dish soap and scrubber
Salt, pepper, spices
Itemized food
Plastic spade

OPTIONAL:

Axe or hatchet
Wood or charcoal for barbeque
Ice chest
Spatula
Grill
Tin foil

· CLOTHING & WEATHER · PROTECTION

What started as the innocent pursuit of a perfect campground had evolved into one heck of a predicament for Foonsky and me.

We had parked at the end of a logging road and then bushwhacked our way down a canyon to a pristine trout stream. On my first cast, a little flip into the plunge pool of a waterfall, I caught a 16-inch rainbow trout, a real beauty that jumped three times. Magic stuff.

Then just across the stream, we saw it: The Perfect Camping Spot. On a sandbar on the edge of the forest, there lay a flat, high and dry spot above the river. Nearby was plenty of downed wood collected by past winter storms that we could use for firewood. And, of course, this beautiful trout stream was bubbling along just 40 yards from the site.

But nothing is perfect, right? To reach it, we had to wade across the river, though it didn't appear too difficult a task. The cold water tingled a bit, and the river came up surprisingly high, just above belt level. But it would be worth it to camp at The Perfect Spot.

Once across the river, we put on some dry clothes, set up camp, explored the woods, and fished the stream, catching several nice trout for dinner. But late that afternoon, it started raining. What, rain in the summertime? Nature makes its own rules. By next morning it was still raining, pouring like a Yosemite waterfall from a solid gray sky. We both looked skyward, and with our mouths open, almost drowned on the spot.

That's when we noticed The Perfect Camping Spot wasn't so perfect. The rain had raised the river level too high for us to wade back across. We were marooned, wet and hungry.

"Now we're in a heck of a predicament," said Foonsky, the water streaming off him.

Getting cold and wet on a camping trip—with no way to get warm—is not only unnecessary and uncomfortable, but it can be a fast ticket to hypothermia, the number one killer of campers in the woods. By definition, hypothermia is a condition where body temperature is lowered to the point that it causes illness. It is particularly dangerous because the afflicted are usually unaware it is setting in. The first sign is a sense of apathy, then a state of confusion over decisions, which can lead eventually to collapse (or what appears to be sleep), then death.

You must always have a way to get warm and dry in short order, regardless of any condition you may face. If you have no way of getting dry, then to prevent hypothermia you must take emergency steps. Those steps are detailed in the chapter on first-aid.

But you should never reach that point. For starters, always have different sets of clothes tucked away, so no matter how cold and wet you might get, you always have something dry. On hiking trips, I always carry a second set of clothes, sealed to stay dry, in a plastic garbage bag. I keep a third set waiting back at the truck.

If you are car camping, the vehicle can cause an illusionary sense of security. But with an extra set of dry clothes stashed safely away, there is no illusion. The security is real. For finishers, make sure those clothes can make you warm and keep you that way. And no matter how hot the weather is when you start on your trip, always be prepared for the worst. Foonsky and me were taught the hard way.

Both of us were soaking wet on that sandbar, so we tried holing up in the tent for the night. A sleeping bag with Quallofil, or another polyester fiber fill, can retain warmth, even when wet, because the fill is hollow and retains its loft. So as miserable as it was, we made it through the night.

The rain finally stopped the next day, and the river dropped a bit, but it was still rolling big and angry. Using a stick as a wading staff, Foonsky crossed about 80 percent of the stream before he was dumped, but he made a jump for it and managed to scramble to the river bank. He waved for me to follow. "No problem," I thought.

It took me some 20 minutes to reach nearly the same spot where Foonsky had been dumped, the heavy river current above my belt and pushing hard. Then, in the flash of an instant, my wading staff slipped on a rock. I teetered in the river current, and then was knocked over like a bowling pin, completely submerged. I went tumbling down the river, heading right toward a waterfall. While underwater, I looked up at the river surface and can remember how close it appeared, yet how out of control I was. Right then, this giant hand appeared, and I grabbed it. It was Foonsky. If it wasn't for that hand, I would have sailed right over the nearby waterfall.

My momentum drew Foonsky right into the river, and we scrambled in the current, but I suddenly sensed the river bottom under my knees. On all fours, the two of us clambered ashore. We were safe.

"Thanks 'ol buddy," I said.

"Man, we're wet," he responded. "Let's get to the rig and get some dry clothes on."

DRESSING IN LAYERS

After falling in the river, Foonsky and me looked like a couple of cold swamp rats. When we eventually reached the truck, and finally started getting into warm clothes, a strange phenomenon hit both of us—now that we were warming up, we started shivering and shaking like an old engine trying to start. It's the body's built-in heater. Shivering is how the body tries to warm itself, producing as much heat as if you were jogging.

To retain that heat, you should dress in "layers." The interior layer, what you wear closest to your skin, and the exterior layer, what you wear to repel the weather, are the most important.

In the good 'ol days, campers wore long underwear made out of wool, which was scratchy, heavy, and sometimes sweaty. Well, times have changed. You can now wear long underwear made of Polypropylene, a synthetic material that is warm, light and wicks dampness away from your skin. It's ideal to wear in a sleeping bag on cold nights, during cool evenings after the sun goes down, or for winter snow sports. Poly shirts come in three weights, light, medium and heavy, and medium can be a perfect garment for campers. The light weight seems to cling to your body. We call it Indian Underwear, because it keeps creeping up on you. The heavy weight is very warm and can be bulky. For most folks, the medium is just right.

The next layer of clothes should be a light cotton shirt or a long-sleeve cotton/wool shirt, or both, depending on coolness of the day. For pants, many just wear blue jeans when camping, but blue jeans can be hot, tight, and once wet, they tend to stay that way. Putting on wet blue jeans on a cold morning is a tortuous way to start the day. I can tell you that from experience since I have suffered that fate a number of times. A better choice are pants made from a cotton/canvas mix, which are available at outdoor shops. They are light, have a lot of give and dry quickly. If the weather is quite warm, shorts that have some room to them can be the best choice.

VESTS, PARKAS

In cold weather, you should take the layer system one step further with a warm vest and a parka jacket. Vests are especially useful because they provide warmth without the bulkiness of a parka.

The warmest vests and parkas are either filled with down, Quallofil, or are made with a cotton/wool mix. Each has its respective merits and problems. Downfill provides the most warmth for the amount of weight, but becomes useless when wet, taking a close resemblance to a wet dish rag. Quallofil keeps much of its heat-retaining qualities even when wet, but is expensive. Vests made of cotton/wool mixes are the most attractive and also are quite warm, but can be as heavy as a ship's anchor when wet.

Sometimes the answer is combining the two. One of my favorite camping companions wears a good-looking, cotton-wool vest, and a parka filled with Quallofil. The vest never gets wet, so weight is less of a factor.

RAIN GEAR

One of the most miserable nights I ever spent in my life was on a camping trip where I didn't bring my rain gear or a tent. Hey, it was early August, the temperature had been in the 90's for weeks, and if anybody told me it was going to rain, I would have asked them to consult with a brain doctor. But rain it did. And as I got more and more wet, I kept saying to myself, "Hey, it's summer, it's not supposed to rain." Then I remembered one of the Ten Commandments of camping: Forget your rain gear and you can guarantee it will rain.

To stay dry, you need some form of water repellent shell. It can be as simple as a $5 poncho made out of plastic, or as elaborate as a Gore-Tex rain jacket and pants that cost $300 a set. What counts is not how much you spend, but how dry you stay.

Some can do just fine with a cheap poncho, and note that ponchos can serve other uses in addition to that as a rain coat. Ponchos can be used as a ground tarp, a rain cover for supplies or a backpack, or in a pinch, can be roped up to trees to provide a quick storm ceiling if you don't have a tent. The problem with ponchos is that in a hard rain, you just don't stay dry. First your legs get wet, then they get soaked. Then your arms follow the same pattern. If you're wearing cotton, you'll find that once part of the garment gets wet, the water will spread until, alas, you are dripping wet, poncho and all. Before long you start to feel like a walking refrigerator.

One high-cost option is buying a Gore-Tex rain jacket and pants. Gore-Tex is actually not a fabric, as is commonly believed, but a laminated film that coats a breathable fabric. The result is a lightweight, water repellent, breathable jacket and pants. They are perfect for campers, but they cost a fortune.

Some hiking buddies of mine have complained that the older Gore-Tex rain gear loses some water repellent qualities over time. However, manufacturers insist that this is the result of water seeping through seams, not leaks in the jacket. At each seam, tiny needles will have pierced through the fabric, and as tiny as the holes are, water will find a way through. An application of Seam Lock, especially at major seams around the shoulders of a jacket, can usually end the problem.

If you don't want to spend the big bucks for Gore-Tex rain gear, but want more rain protection than a poncho affords, a coated nylon jacket is the middle road that many choose. They are inexpensive, have the highest water repellent qualities of any rain gear, and are warm, providing a good outer shell for your layers of clothing. But they are not without fault. These jackets don't breathe at all, and if you zip it up tight, you can sweat like an Eskimo.

My brother, Rambob, gave me a $20 nylon jacket prior to an expedition we took climbing Northern California's Mt. Shasta, one of America's most impressive peaks at 14,162 feet. I wore that $20 special all the way to the top and with no complaints; it's warm and 100 percent waterproof. At $20, it seems like a treasure, especially compared to the $180 Gore-Tex jackets. And its value increases every time it rains.

OTHER GEAR, AND A FEW TIPS

What are the three items most commonly forgotten on a camping trip? "A cook, a dish washer and a fish cleaner," said my pal, the Z-Man.

C'mon now, bucko, the real answers? A hat, sunglasses and chapstick. A hot day is unforgiving without them.

A hat is crucial, especially when you are visiting high elevations. Without one you are constantly exposed to everything nature can give you. The sun will dehydrate you, sap your energy, sunburn your head, and in worst cases, cause sunstroke. Start with a comfortable hat. Then finish with sunglasses, chapstick and sunscreen for additional protection. That will help protect you from extreme heat.

To guard against extreme cold, it's a good idea to keep a pair of thin ski gloves stashed away with your emergency clothes, along with a wool ski cap. The gloves should be thick enough to keep your fingers from stiffening up, but pliable enough to allow full movement, so you don't have to take them off to complete simple tasks, like lighting a stove. An option to gloves are glovelets, which look like gloves with no fingers. In any case, just because the weather turns cold doesn't mean that your hands have to.

And if you fall into a river like Foonsky and me did, well, I hope you have a set of dry clothes waiting back at your rig. And a hand reaching out for you.

CAMPING CLOTHES LIST:

Polypropylene underwear

Cotton shirt
Long sleeve cotton/wool shirt
Cotton/canvas pants
Vest
Parka
Rain jacket, pants, or poncho
Hat
Sunglasses
Chapstick
Sunscreen

OPTIONAL:

Seam Lock
Shorts
Swimming suit
Gloves
Ski cap

· HIKING & FOOT ·
CARE

We had set up a nice, little camp in the woods, and my buddy, Foonsky, sitting against a big Douglas fir, was strapping on his hiking boots.

"New boots," he said with a grin. "But they seem pretty stiff."

We decided to hoof it on down the trail for a few hours, exploring the mountain wildlands that are said to hide Bigfoot and other strange creatures. These woods are quiet and secret, and after even a short while on the trail, a sense of peace and calm seems to settle in. The forest provides the chance to be cleansed with clean air and the smell of trees, freeing you from all troubles.

But it wasn't long and the look of trouble was on Foonsky's face. And no, it wasn't from seeing Bigfoot.

"Got a hot spot on a toe," he said.

Immediately we stopped. He pulled off his right boot, then socks, and inspected the left side of his big toe. Sure enough, a blister had bubbled up, filled with fluid, but not popped. From his medical kit, Foonsky cut a small piece of moleskin to fit over the blister, then taped it to hold it in place. A few minutes later, we were back on the trail.

A half hour later, there was still no sign of Bigfoot. But Foonsky stopped again and pulled off his other boot. "Another hot spot." Another small blister had started on the little toe of his left foot, over which he taped a band-aid to keep it from further chafing against the inside of his new boot.

In just a few days, ol' Foonsky—a big, strong guy who goes 6-foot-5, 200-plus pounds—was walking around like a sore-hoofed hoss that had been loaded with a month of supplies and then ridden over sharp rocks. Well, it wasn't the distance that had done Foonsky in, it was those blisters. He had them on eight of his ten toes and was going through band-aids, moleskin and tape like he was a walking emergency ward. If he used any more tape, he was going to look like a mummy from an Egyptian tomb.

If you've ever been in a similar predicament, then you know the frustration of wanting to have a good time, wanting to hike and explore the area at which you have set up a secluded camp, only to be turned gimp legged by several blisters. No one is immune, not big, strong guys nor small, innocent-looking women. All are created equal before the blister god. You can be forced to bow to it unless you get your act together.

That means wearing the right style boots for what you have in mind—and then protecting your feet with a careful selection of socks. And then, if you are still so unfortunate as to get a blister of two, it means knowing how to treat them fast so they don't turn your walk into a sore-footed endurance test.

What causes blisters? In almost all cases, it is the simple rubbing of your foot against the rugged interior of your boot. That act can be worsened by several factors:

• 1. A very stiff boot, that is, one in which your foot moves inside the boot as you walk, instead of the boot flexing as if it was another layer of skin.

• 2. Thin, holey, or dirty socks. This is the fastest route to blister death. Thin socks will allow your feet to move inside of your boots, holey socks will allow your skin to chafe directly against the boot's interior, and dirty socks will wrinkle and fold, also rubbing against your feet instead of cushioning them.

• 3. Soft feet. By itself, soft feet will not cause blisters, but in combination with a stiff boot or thin socks, can cause terrible problems. This often afflicts men more than women because females in general go barefoot more than men, and the bottom of their feet thus become tougher. In fact, some of the biggest, toughest-looking guys you'll ever see—from Hells Angels to pro football players—have feet that are as soft as a baby's butt. Why? Because they never go barefoot and don't hike much.

SELECTING THE RIGHT BOOTS

One summer I hiked 400 miles, including 250 miles in three weeks along the crest of California's Sierra Nevada, and another 150 miles over several months in an earlier general training program. In that span, I got just one blister, suffered on the fourth day of the 250-miler. I treated it immediately, and suffered no more. One key is wearing the right boot, and for me, that means a boot that acts as a thick layer of skin that is flexible and pliable to my foot. I want my feet to fit snugly in them, with no interior movement.

There are three kinds of boots: Hiking shoes, backpacking boots, and mountaineering boots. Either select the right one for you or pay the consequences.

The stiffest of the lot is the mountaineering boot. These boots are often identified by mid-range tops, laces that extend almost as far as the toe area, and ankle areas that are as stiff as a board. The lack of "give" in them is what enamors them to mountaineers. The stiffness is preferred when rock climbing, walking off-trail on craggy surfaces, or hiking down the edge of stream beds where small rocks can cause you to turn your ankle. Because these boots don't give on rugged, craggy terrain, it reduces ankle injuries and provides better traction.

The backlash of stiff boots is that if careful selection of socks is not made, and your foot starts slipping around in them, you will get a set of blisters that would raise even Foonsky's eyebrows. But if you just want to go for a nice walk, or even a good romp with a backpack, then hiking shoes or backpacking boots are better designed for those respective uses.

Hiking shoes are the lightest of all boots, designed for day walks or short backpacking trips. Some of the newer models are like rugged tennis shoes, designed with a canvas top for lightness and a lug sole for traction. These are perfect for people who like to walk but rarely carry a backpack. Because they are flexible, they are easy to break in, and with fresh socks, rarely cause blister problems. And because they are light, general hiking fatigue is greatly reduced.

On the negative side, because they have shallow lug soles, traction can be far from good on slippery surfaces. In addition, canvas hiking shoes provide less than ideal ankle support, which can be a problem in rocky areas, such as along a stream where you might want to go trout fishing. Turn your ankle and your trip can be ruined.

My preference is for a premium backpacking boot, the perfect medium between the stiff mountaineering boots and the soft canvas hiking shoes. The deep lug bottom provides traction, high ankle coverage provides support, yet the soft, waterproof leather body gives each foot a snug fit—add it up and that means no blisters. On the negative side, they can be quite hot, weigh a ton, and if they get wet, take days to dry.

There are a zillion styles, brands and price range of boots to choose from. If you wander about, looking at them equally, you will get as confused as a kid in a toy store. Instead go into the store with your mind clear about what you want, then find it and buy it. If you want the best, expect to spend $60 to $80 for hiking shoes, from $100 to $140 and sometimes more for backpacking or mountaineering boots. This is one area you don't want to scrimp on, so try not to yelp about the high cost. Instead, walk out of the store believing you deserve the best, and that's exactly what you just paid for.

If you plan on using the advice of a shoe salesman for your purchase, first look at what kind of boots he is wearing. If he isn't even wearing boots, then any advice he might attempt to tender may not be worth a plug nickel. Most people I know who own quality boots, including salesmen, will wear them almost daily if their job allows, since boots are the best footwear available. However, even these well-meaning folks can offer skeptical advice. Every hiker I've ever met says he wears the world's greatest boot.

Instead, enter the store with a precise use and style in mind. Rather than fish for suggestions, tell the salesman exactly what you want, and try two or three different brands of the same style—and always try on the matching pair of boots simultaneously so you know exactly how they'll feel. If possible, walk up and down stairs with them. Are they too stiff? Are your feet snug yet comfortable, or do they slip? Do they have that "right" kind of feel when you walk?

If you get the right answers to those questions, then you're on your way to blister-free, pleasure-filled days of walking.

SOCKS

The poor gent was scratching his feet like ants were crawling over them. I looked closer. Huge yellow calluses had covered the bottom of his feet, and at the ball and heel, the calluses were about a quarter of an inch thick, cracking and sore.

"I don't understand it," he said. "I'm on my feet a lot, so I bought a real good pair of hiking boots. But look what they've done to my feet. My feet itch so much I'm going crazy."

People can spend so much energy selecting the right kind of boot, that they can virtually overlook wearing the right kind of socks. One goes with the other.

Your socks should be thick enough to provide a cushion for your foot, as well as a good, snug fit. Without good socks, instead you might try to get the boot laces real tight—and that's like putting a tourniquet on your feet. You should have plenty of clean socks on hand, or plan on washing what you have on your trip. As socks are worn, they become compressed, dirty and damp. Any one of those factors can cause problems.

My camping companions believe I go overboard when it comes to socks, that I bring too many, wear too many. But it works, so that's where the complaints stop. So how many do I wear? Well, would you believe three socks on each foot? It may sound like overkill, but each has its purpose, and like I said, it works.

The interior sock is thin, lightweight and made out of Polypropylene or silk, synthetic materials that actually transport moisture away from your skin. With a poly interior sock, your foot stays dry when it sweats. Without a poly sock, your foot can get damp, mix with dirt, which in turn can cause a "hot spot" to start on your foot. Eventually you get blisters, lots of them.

The second sock is for comfort, and can be cotton, but a thin wool-based composite is ideal. Some made of the latter can wick moisture away from the skin, much like the qualities of Polypropylene. If wool itches your feet, a thick cotton sock can be suitable, though cotton collects moisture and compacts more quickly than other socks. If you're on a short hike rather than a long one, though, cotton will do just fine.

The exterior sock should be made of high quality, thick wool—at least 80 percent wool. It will cushion your feet, provide that "just right" snug fit in your boot, and in cold weather, give you some additional warmth and insulation. It is critical to keep the wool sock clean. If you wear a dirty wool sock over and over again, it will compact and lose its cushion, start wrinkling while you hike, and with that chain of events, your feet will catch on fire from the blisters that start popping up.

A FEW TIPS

If you are like most folks, that is, the bottom of your feet are rarely exposed and quite soft, you can take additional steps in their care. The best tip is keeping a fresh foot pad in your boot made of sponge rubber. Another cure for soft feet is to get out and walk or jog on a regular basis prior to your camping trip.

If you plan to use a foot pad and wear three socks. you will need to use these items when sizing boots. It is an unforgiving error to wear thin cotton socks when buying boots, than later trying to squeeze all this stuff, plus your feet, into your boots. There just won't be enough room.

The key to treating blisters is fast work at the first sign of a hot spot. But before you remove your socks. first check to see if the sock has a wrinkle in it, a likely cause to the problem. If so, either change socks or get them pulled tight, removing the tiny folds, after taking care of the blister. Cut a piece of moleskin to cover the offending toe, securing the moleskin with white medical tape. If moleskin is not available, small band-aids can do the job, but have to be replaced daily, and sometimes with even more frequency. At night, clean your feet and sleep without socks.

Two other items that can help your walking is an Ace bandage and a pair of gaters.

For sprained ankles and twisted knees, an Ace bandage can be like an insurance policy to get you back on the trail and out of trouble. Over the years, I have had serious ankle problems and have relied on a good wrap with a four-inch bandage to get me home. The newer bandages come with clips permanently attached, so you don't have to worry about losing them.

Gaters are leggings made of plastic, nylon or Gore-Tex which fit from just below your knees, over your calves and attach under your boots. They are of particular help when walking in damp areas, or places where rain is common. As your legs brush against ferns or low-lying plants, gaters will deflect the moisture. Without them and your pants will be soaking wet in short order.

Should your boots become wet, a good tip is to never try to force dry them. Some well-meaning folks will try to speed dry them at the edge of a campfire or actually put the boots in an oven. While this may dry the boots, it can also loosen the glue that holds them together, ultimately weakening your shoe until one day they fall apart in a heap.

A better bet is to treat the leather so the boots become water repellent. Silicone-based liquids are the easiest to use and least greasy of the treatments available.

A final tip is to have another pair of lightweight shoes or mocassins that you can wear around camp, and in the process, give your feet the rest they deserve.

HIKING AND FOOT CARE LIST:

Quality hiking boots
Backup lightweight shoes
Polypropylene socks
Thick cotton socks
80 percent wool socks
Strong boot laces
Innersole or foot cushion
Ace bandage
Moleskin and medical tape
Band-Aids
Gaters
Water repellent boot treatment

· SLEEPING · GEAR

O ne mountain night in the pines on an eve long ago, my dad, brother and I rolled out our sleeping bags and were bedded down for the night. After the pre-trip excitement, a long drive, an evening of trout fishing and a barbecue, we were like three tired doggies who had played too much.

But as I looked up at the stars, I was suddenly wide awake. The kid was still wired. A half hour later? No change—wide awake.

And as little kids can do, I had to wake up 'ol dad to tell him about it. "Hey, dad, I can't sleep."

"This is what you do," he said. "Watch the sky for a shooting star and tell yourself that you cannot go to sleep until you see at least one. As you wait and watch, you will start getting tired and it will be difficult to keep your eyes open. But tell yourself you must keep watching. Then you'll start to really feel tired. When you finally see a shooting star, you'll go to sleep so fast you won't know what hit you."

Well, I tried it that night and I don't even remember seeing a shooting star, I went to sleep so fast.

It's a good trick, and along with having a good sleeping bag, ground insulation, maybe a tent—or a few tricks for bedding down in a pickup truck or motorhome—you can get a good night's sleep on every camping trip.

Some 20 years after that camping episode with my dad and brother, we made a trip to the Planetarium at the Academy of Sciences in San Francisco to see a show on Halley's Comet. The lights dimmed, and the ceiling turned into a night sky, filled with stars and a setting moon. Meanwhile, a scientist began explaining phenomenons of the heavens.

After a few minutes, I began to feel drowsy. Just then, a shooting star zipped across the Planetarium ceiling. I went into a deep sleep so fast it was like I was in a coma. I didn't wake up until the show was over, the lights were turned back on and people were leaving the auditorium.

Drowsy, I turned to see if 'ol Dad had liked the show. Oh yeah? He not only had gone to sleep too, but apparently had no intention of waking up. Just like a camping trip.

SLEEPING BAGS

What could be worse than trying to sleep in a cold, wet sleeping bag on a rainy night without a tent in the mountains?

Answer: Trying to sleep in a cold, wet sleeping bag on a rainy night without a tent in the mountains—when your sleeping bag is filled with down.

Water will turn a down-filled sleeping bag into a mushy heap. Many campers do not like a high-tech approach, but the state-of-the-art poly-fiber sleeping bags can keep you warm even when wet. That factor, along with temperature rating and weight are key factors when selecting a sleeping bag.

A sleeping bag is basically a shell filled with a heat-retaining insulation. By themselves, they are not warm. Your body provides the heat, and the sleeping bag's ability to retain that heat is what makes them warm or cold.

The old-styled canvas bags are heavy, bulky, cold, and when wet, useless. With other options available, their use is limited. Anybody who sleeps outdoors or backpacks should choose otherwise.

Instead, buy and use a sleeping bag filled with down or one of the quality polyfills. Down is light, warm and aesthetically pleasing to those who don't think camping and technology mix. If you like down bags, be sure to keep it double wrapped in plastic garbage bags on your trips in order to keep it dry. Once wet, you'll spend your nights howling at the moon.

The polyfiber-filled bags are not necessarily better that those filled with down, but can be. The one key advantage is that even when wet, some poly-fills can retain up to 80 to 85 percent of your body heat. This allows you to sleep and get valuable rest even in miserable conditions. And my camping experience is that no matter how lucky you may be, there comes a time when you will get caught in an unexpected, violent storm and everything you've got will get wet, including your sleeping bag. That's when the value of a poly-fill bag becomes priceless. You either have one and can sleep—or you don't have one and suffer. It is that simple. Of the synthetic fills, Quallofil made by Dupont is the leader of the industry.

But as mentioned, just because a sleeping bag uses a high-tech poly-fill doesn't necessarily make it a better bag. Other factors come into play.

The most important are a bag's temperature rating and weight. The temperature rating of a sleeping bag refers to how cold it can get before you start actually feeling cold. Many campers make the mistake of thinking, "I only camp in the summer, so a bag rated at 30 or 40 degrees should be fine." Later, they find out it isn't so fine, and all it takes is one cold night to convince them of that. When selecting the right temperature rating, visualize the coldest weather you might ever confront, and then get a bag rated for even colder weather.

For instance, if you are a summer camper, you may rarely experience a night in the low 30's or high 20's. A sleeping bag rated at 20 degrees would thus be appropriate, keeping you snug, warm and asleep. For most campers, I advise bags rated at zero or 10 degrees.

If you buy a poly-filled sleeping bag, never leave it squished in your stuff sack between camping trips. Instead keep it on a hanger in a closet or use it as a blanket. One thing that can reduce a polyfilled bag's heat-retaining qualities is if you lose the loft out of the tiny hollow fibers that make up the fill. You can avoid this with proper storage.

The weight of a sleeping bag can also be a key factor, especially for backpackers. When you have to carry your gear on your back, every ounce becomes important. To keep your weight to a minimum, sleeping bags that weigh just three pounds are available, though expensive. But if you hike much, it's worth the price. For an overnighter, you can get away with a 4 or 4 1/2-pound bag without much stress. However, bags weighing five pounds and up should be left back at the car.

I have two sleeping bags: A 7-pounder that feels like I'm sleeping in a giant sponge, and a little 3-pounder. The heavy duty model is for pick-up truck camping in cold weather and doubles as a blanket at home. The lightweight bag is for hikes. Between the two, I'm set.

INSULATION PADS

Even with the warmest sleeping bag in the world, if you just lay it down on the ground and try to sleep, you will likely get as cold as a winter cucumber. That is because the cold ground will suck the warmth right out of your body. The solution is to have a layer of insulation between you and the ground. For this, you can use a thin Insulite pad, a lightweight Therm-a-Rest inflatable pad, or an air mattress. Here is a capsule summary of them:

• Insulite Pads: They are light, inexpensive, roll up quick for transport, and can double as a seat pad at your camp. The negative side is that at night, they will compress, making it feel like you are sleeping on granite.

• Therm-a-Rest Pads: They are a real luxury, because they do everything an Insulite pad does, but also provide a cushion. The negative side to them is that they are expensive by comparison, and if they get a hole in them, become worthless unless if you have a patch kit.

• Air Mattress: OK for car campers, but their bulk, weight and the amount of effort necessary to blow them up makes them a nuisance for any other purpose.

A FEW TRICKS

When surveying a camp area, the most important consideration should be to select a good spot to sleep. Everything else is secondary. Ideally, you want a flat spot that is wind sheltered on ground soft enough to drive stakes into. Yeah, and I want to win the lottery.

Sometimes that ground will have a slight slope to it. In that case, always sleep with your head on the uphill side. If you sleep parallel to the slope, every time you roll over in your sleep, you can find yourself rolling right down the hill. If you sleep with your head on the downhill side, you can get a headache that feels like an axe is embedded in your brain.

When you have found a good spot, clear it of all branches, twigs and rocks, of course. A good tip is to then dig a slight indentation in the ground where your hip will fit. Since your body is not flat, but has curves and edges, it will not feel comfortable on flat ground. Some people even get severely bruised on the sides of their hips when sleeping on flat, hard ground. For that reason alone, they learn to hate camping. Instead, bring a spade, dig a little depression in the ground for your hip, and sleep well.

After the ground is prepared, throw a ground cloth over the spot, which will keep much of the morning dew off you. In some areas, particularly where fog is a problem, morning dew can be heavy and get the outside of your sleeping bag quite wet. In that case, you either need a tent or some kind of roof, like that of a poncho or tarp, with its ends tied to trees.

TENTS AND WEATHER PROTECTION

All it takes is to get caught in the rain once without a tent and you will never go anywhere without one again. A tent provides protection from rain, wind and mosquito attacks. In exchange, you can lose a starry night's view, though some tents now even provide moon roofs.

A tent can be as complex as a four-season, tubular-jointed dome with rain fly, or nothing more complicated than two ponchos snapped together and roped up to a tree. They can as cheap as a $10 tube tent, which is nothing more than a hollow piece of plastic, or as expensive as a $500 five-person deluxe expedition dome model. They vary greatly in size, price, and put-up time. If you plan on getting a good one, then plan on doing plenty of shopping and asking lots of questions. The key ones are: Will it keep me dry? How hard is it to put up? Is it roomy enough? How much does it weigh?

With a little bit of homework, you can get the right answers to these questions.

• Will it keep me dry? On many one and two-person tents, the rain fly does not extend far enough to keep water off the bottom sidewalls of the tent. In a driving rain, water can also drip from the rain fly and to the bottom sidewalls of the tent. Eventually the water can leak through to the inside, particularly through the seams where the tent has been sewed together. Water can sneak through the tiny needle holes.

You must be able to stake out your rain fly so it completely covers all of the tent. If you are tent shopping and this does not appear possible, then don't buy the tent. To prevent potential leaks, use seamlock, a glue-like substance, to close potential leak areas on tent seams. On the large umbrella tents, keep a patch kit handy and dig a small canal around your tent to channel rain water.

Another way to keep water out of your tent is to store all wet garments outside the tent, under a poncho. Moisture from wet clothes stashed in the tent will condense on the interior tent walls. If you bring enough wet clothes in the tent, by the next morning you can feel like you're camping in a duck blind.

• How hard is it to put up? If a tent is difficult to erect in full sunlight, you can just about forget it at night. Some tents can go up in just a few minutes without requiring help from another camper. This might be the kind of tent you want.

The way to compare put-up time of tents when shopping is to count the number of connecting points from the tent poles to the tent, and also the number of stakes required. The fewer, the better. Think simple. My tent has seven connecting points and, minus the rain fly, requires no stakes. It goes up in a few minutes. If you need a lot of stakes, it is a sure tipoff to a long put-up time. Try it at night or in the rain, and you'll be ready to cash your chips and go for broke.

Another factor are the tent poles themselves. Some small tents have poles that are broken into small sections and are connected by Bungy cords. It takes only an instant to convert it to a complete pole.

Some outdoor shops have tents on display on their showroom floor. Before buying the tent, have the salesman take the tent down and put it back up. If it takes him more than five minutes, or he says he "doesn't have time," then keep looking.

• Is it roomy enough? Don't judge the size of a tent on floor space alone. Some tents small on floor space can give the illusion of roominess with a high ceiling. You can be quite comfortable in them, snug yet not squeezed in.

But remember that a one-person or two-person tent is just that. A two-person tent has room for two people plus gear. That's it. Don't buy a tent expecting it to hold more than it is intended to.

• How much does it weigh? If you're a hiker, this becomes the pre-eminent question. If it's much more than six or seven pounds, forget it. A 12-pound tent is bad enough, but get it wet and its like carrying a pi-ano on your back. On the other hand, weight is scarcely a factor if you camp only where you can take your car. My dad, for instance, used to have this giant canvas umbrella tent that folded down to this neat little pack that weighed about 500 pounds.

AN OPTION

If you like going solo and choose not to own a tent at all, a biffy bag can provide the weather protection you require. A biffy bag is a water repel-lent shell in which your sleeping bag fits. They are light and tough, and for some, are a perfect option to a heavy tent. On the down side, howev-er, there is a strange sensation when you try to ride out a rainy night in one. You can hear the rain hitting you, sometimes even feel the pound-ing of the drops through the biffy bag. It can be unsettling to try and sleep under such circumstance.

PICKUP TRUCK CAMPERS

If you own a pick-up truck with a camper shell, you can turn it into a self-contained campground with a little bit of work. This can be an ideal way to go because it is fast, portable, and you are guaranteed a dry environment.

But that does not necessarily mean it is a warm environment. In fact, without insulation from the metal truck bed, it can feel like trying to sleep on an iceberg. That is because the metal truck bed will get as cold as the air temperature, which is often much colder than the ground temperature. Without insulation, it can be much colder in your camper shell than it would be on the open ground.

When I camp in my rig, I use a large piece of foam for a mattress and insulation. The foam measures four inches thick, is 48 inches wide and 76 inches long. It makes for a bed as comfortable as anything one might ask for. In fact, during the winter, if I don't go camping for a few weeks because of writing obligations, I sometimes will throw the foam on the living room floor, lay down the old sleeping bag, light a fire, and camp right in my living room. It's in my blood, I tell you.

If you camp in cold areas in your pick-up truck camper shell, a Coleman catalytic heater can keep you toasty. When using a catalytic heater, it is a good idea to keep ventilation windows partially open to keep the air fresh. Don't worry about how cold it is—the heater will take the snap out of it.

MOTORHOMES

The problems motorhome owners encounter come from two primary sources: Lack of privacy and light intrusion.

The lack of privacy stems from the natural restrictions of where a "land yacht" can go. Without careful use of the guide portion of this book, motorhome owners can find themselves in parking lot settings, jammed in with plenty of neighbors. Because motorhomes often have large picture windows, you lose your privacy, causing some late nights, and come daybreak, light intrusion forces an early wakeup. The result is you get short on sleep.

The answer is to always carry inserts to fit over the inside of your windows. This closes off the outside and retains your privacy. And if you don't want to wake up with the sun coming daybreak, you don't have to. It will still be dark.

GOOD NIGHT'S SLEEP LIST:

Sleeping bag
Insulite pad or Therm-a-rest
Tent
Ground tarp

OPTIONAL:

Air pillows
Mosquito netting
Foam pad for truck bed
Windshield light screen for motorhome
Catalytic heater

· FIRST AID & PROTECTION ·
AGAINST INSECTS

A mountain night could not have been more perfect, I thought as I lay in my sleeping bag.

The sky looked like a mass of jewels and the air tasted sweet and smelled of pines. A shooting star fireballed across the sky, and I remember thinking, "It just doesn't get any better."

Just then, as I was drifting into sleep, this mysterious buzz appeared from nowhere and deposited itself inside my left ear. Suddenly awake, I whacked my ear with the palm of a hand about hard enough to cause a minor concussion. The buzz disappeared. I pulled out my flashlight and shined it on my palm, and there, lit in the blackness of night, lay the squished intruder. A mosquito, dead amid a stain of blood, both his and mine.

Satisfied, I turned off the light, closed my eyes and thought of the fishing trip planned for the next day. Then I heard them. It was a squadron of mosquitos, flying landing patterns around my head. I tried to grab them with an open hand, but they dodged the assault and flew off. Just 30 seconds later another landed back in my left ear. I promptly dispatched the invader with a rip of the palm.

Now I was completely awake, so I got out of my sleeping bag to retrieve some mosquito repellent. While en route, several of the buggers swarmed and nailed me in the back and arms. Later, after application of the repellent and again snug in my sleeping bag, the mosquitos would buzz a few inches from my ear. After getting a whiff of the poison, they would fly off. It was like sleeping in a sawmill.

The next day, drowsy from little sleep, I set out to fish. I'd walked but 15 minutes when I brushed against bush and felt this stinging sensation on the inside of my arm, just above the wrist. I looked down. A tick had got his clamps into me. I ripped it out before he could embed his head into my skin.

After catching a few fish, I sat down against a tree to eat lunch, and just watch the water go by. My dog, Rebel, sat down next to me and stared at the beef jerky I was munching as if it was a T-bone steak. I finished eating, gave him a small piece, patted him on the head and said,

"Good dog." Right then, I noticed an itch on my arm where a mosquito had drilled me. I unconsciously scratched it. Two days later, in that exact spot, some nasty red splotches started popping up. Poison oak. By petting my dog and then scratching my arm, I had transferred the oil residue of the poison oak leaves from Rebel's fur to my arm.

On returning back home, Foonsky asked me about the trip.

"Great," I said. "Mosquitos, ticks, poison oak. Can hardly wait to go back."

"I'd like to go too," he said.

"On the next trip," I answered, "We'll declare war on those buggers."

MOSQUITOS, NO-SEE-UMS, GNATS AND HORSEFLIES

On a trip to Canada, Foonsky and me were fishing a small lake from the shore when suddenly a black horde of mosquitos could be seen moving across the lake toward us. It was like when the Frency Army looked across the Rhine and saw the Wehrmacht coming. There was a literal buzz in the air. We fought them off for a few minutes, then made a fast retreat to the truck and jumped in, content the buggers had been fooled. But somehow, still unknown to us, the mosquitos started gaining entry to the truck. In 10 minutes, we squished 15 of them while they attempted to plant their oil derricks in our skin. Just outside the truck, the black horde waited for us to make a tactical error, like rolling down a window. It took a sudden hailstorm to wipe out the attack.

When it comes to mosquitos, no-see-ums, gnats and horseflies, there are times when there is nothing you can do. Said episode was one of those times. However, in most situations you can muster a defense to repel the attack.

The first key with mosquitos is to wear clothing too heavy for them to drill through. Expose a minimum of skin, wear a hat, and around your neck, tie a bandana, one that has preferably been sprayed with repellent. If you try to get by with just a cotton T-shirt, you will be declared a federal mosquito sanctuary.

So first your skin must be well covered, exposing only your hands and face. Second, you should have your companion spray your clothes with repellent in an aerosol can. Third, you should dab liquid repellent directly on your skin.

Taking vitamin B1 and eating garlic are reputed to act as natural insect repellents, but I've met a lot of mosquitos that are not convinced. A better bet is to take the mystery out of the task and examine the contents of the repellent in question. The key is the percentage of the ingredient called Non-diethyl-metatoluamide. That is the poison, and the percentage of it in the container must be listed and will indicate that brand's effectiveness. Inert ingredients are just excess fluids used to fill the bottles.

At night, the easiest way to get a good night's rest without mosquitos buzzing in your ear is to sleep in a bug-proof tent. If the night's are warm and you want to see the stars, new tent models are available that have a skylight covered with mosquito netting. If you don't like tents on summer evenings, mosquito netting rigged with an air space at your head can solve the problem. Otherwise prepare to get bit, even with the use of mosquito repellent.

If your problems are with no-see-ums or biting horseflies, then you need a slightly different approach.

No-see-ums are a tiny, black insect that can look like nothing more than a sliver of dirt on your skin. Then you notice something stinging— and when you rub the area, you scratch up a little no-see-um. The results are similar to mosquito bites, making your skin itch, splotch, and when you get them bad, puffy. In addition to using the techniques described to repel mosquitos, you should go one step further.

The problem is no-see-ums are tricky little devils. Somehow they can actually get under your socks and around your ankles, where they will bite to their heart's content all night long while you sleep, itch, sleep and itch some more. The best solution is to apply a liquid repellent to your ankles, then wear clean socks.

Horseflies are another story. They are rarely a problem, but when they get their dander up, they can cause problems you'll never forget.

One such episode occurred when Foonsky and I were paddling a canoe along the shoreline of a large lake. This giant horsefly, about the size of a fingertip, started divebombing the canoe. After 20 minutes, it landed on his thigh. Foonsky immediately slammed it with an open hand—then let out a blood-curdling "yeeeee-ow" that practically sent ripples across the lake. When Foonsky whacked it, the horsefly had somehow turned around and bit him in the hand, leaving a huge, red welt.

In the next 10 minutes, that big fly strafed the canoe on several more divebomb runs. I finally got ready with my canoe paddle, swung like a baseball player, and nailed that horsefly like I'd hit a home run. It landed about 15 feet from the boat, still buzzing, and shortly thereafter was eaten by a large rainbow trout, which was comforting to Foonsky.

If you have horsefly or yellowjacket problems, you'd best just leave the area. One, two or a few can be dealt with. More than that and your fun camping trip will be about as fun as being roped to a tree and stung by an electric shock rod.

On most trips, you will spend time doing everything possible to keep from getting bit by mosquitos or no-see-ums. When that fails, you must know what to do next—and fast if you are among those ill-fated campers who get big, red lumps from a bite inflicted from even a microscopic-sized mosquito.

A fluid called "After Bite," or a dab of ammonia, should be applied immediately to the bite. To start the healing process, apply a first-aid gel, not liquid, such as Campho-Phenique.

TICKS

Ticks are a nasty, little vermin that will wait in ambush, jump on unsuspecting prey, and eventually crawl to a prime location before trying to fill his body with his victim's blood.

I call them the Dracula Bug, but by any name they can be a terrible camp pest. Ticks rest on grasses and low plants and attach themselves to those who brush against the vegetation. Dogs are particularly vulnerable. Typically, they are no more than 18 inches above ground. If you stay on the trails, you can usually avoid them.

There are two common species of ticks. The common coastal tick is larger, brownish colored, and prefers to crawl around prior to putting the clamps on you. The latter habit can give you the creeps, but when you feel it crawling, you can just pick it off and dispatch it. Their preferred destination is usually the back of your neck, just where the hairline starts. The other species, a wood tick, is small, black, and when he puts the clamps in, immediately painful. When a wood tick gets into a dog for a few days, it can cause a large, red welt.

In either case, ticks should be removed as soon as possible. If you have hiked in areas infested with them, it is advisable to shower as soon as possible, discarding and washing your clothes immediately. If you just leave your clothes in a heap, a tick can crawl from your clothes and thus invade your home. They like warmth, and one way or another, they can end up in your bed. Waking up in the middle of the night with a tick crawling across your chest can really give you the creeps.

Once a tick has the clampers on you, you must decide how long it has been there. If it has been a short time, the most painless and effective method is to just take a pair of sharp tweezers and grasp the little devil, making certain to isolate the mouth area, then pull him out.

If the tick has been in longer, you may wish to have a doctor extract it. Some people will burn it with a cigarette, or poison it with lighter fluid. In any case, you must take care to remove all of it, especially its claw-like mouth.

The wound, however small, should then be cleansed and dressed.

This is done by applying liquid peroxide, which cleans and sterilyzes the wound and then coating on a dressing such as First-Aid Cream, Campho-Pehnique gel, or Neosporin ointment.

POISON OAK

After a nice afternoon hike, about a five miler, I was concerned about possible exposure to poison oak, so I immediately showered and put on clean clothes. Then I settled into a chair with my favorite foamy body-building elixer to watch the end of a baseball game. The game went 18 innings, and meanwhile, my dog, tired from the hike, had gone to sleep on my bare ankles.

A few days later I had a case of poison oak. My feet looked like they had been on fire and put out with an ice pick. The lesson? Don't always trust your dog, give him a bath as well, and beware of extra-inning ball games.

You can get poison oak only from direct contact with the oil residue from the leaves. It can be passed in a variety of fashions, as direct as skin/leaf contact or as indirect as leaf to dog, dog to sofa, sofa to skin. Once you have it, there is little you can do but want to itch yourself to death. Applying Caladryl lotion or its equivalent can help because it contains antihistamines, which attack and dry the itch.

A tip that may sound crazy but seems to work is advised by my pal Furni. You should expose the afflicted area to the hottest water you can stand, then suddenly emerse it in cold water. The hot water opens the skin pores and gets the "itch" out. The cold water then quickly seals the pores.

In any case, you're a lot better off if you don't get poison oak to begin with. Remember the old Boy Scout saying: "Leaves of three, let them be." Also remember that poison oak can disguise itself. In the spring it is green, then gradually turns reddish in the summer. By fall, it becomes a bloody, ugly-looking red. In the winter, they lose their leaves altogether and appear to be nothing more than the barren, brown sticks of a small plant. However, at any time and in any form, skin contact can cause quick infection.

Some people are more easily afflicted than others, but if you are one of the lucky few, don't cheer too loud. While some people can be exposed to the oil residue of poison oak with little or no effect, the body's resistance can gradually be worn down by repeated exposures. At one time, I could practically play in the stuff and the only problems would be a few little bumps on the inside of my wrist. Now, some 15 years later, times have changed. My resistance has broken down. If I merely rub against poison oak now, in a few days the exposed area can look like it has been used for a track meet.

So regardless if you consider yourself vulnerable or not, you should take heed to reduce exposure. That can be done by staying on trails when you hike and making sure your dog does the same. Remember, the worst stands of poison oak are usually brush-infested areas just off the trail. It can also be done by dressing so your skin is completely protected, wearing long-sleeve shirts, long pants and boots. If you suspect you've been exposed, immediately wash your clothes, then wash yourself with with aloe vera, rinsing with a cool shower.

And don't forget to give your dog a bath as well.

SUNBURN

The most common injury suffered on camping trips is sunburn, yet some people wear it as a badge of honor, believing that it somehow enhances their virility. Well it doesn't. Neither do suntans. And too much sun can lead to serious burns or sunstroke, or at the least, result in leathery skin at an early age.

It is easy enough to avoid. Use a high-level sunscreen on your skin, chapstick on your lips, and wear sunglasses and a hat. If any area gets burned, apply First-Aid Cream, which will soothe and provide moisture for the parched, burned skin.

The best advice from Doctor Bogney is not to worry about getting a suntan. Those that do are involved in a practice that is not only one of the ultimate wastes of time, but eventually ruinous to their skins as well.

A WORD ABOUT GIARDIA

Some mountain streams may be clear, cold, free-running and taste as clean as the granite rocks they polish, but beware, because they may contain an invisible stomach killer. Giardia, a relatively new danger to mountain campers, is a microscopic organism that can cause severe diarrhea and abdominal cramps. It's a painful souvenir of your camping trip that can last for weeks.

The simplest ways to protect yourself is to drink piped water, water you carry to your camping spot, or to use one of the lightweight water filtration systems available at backpacking stores. They are fast and effective. A slower yet inexpensive route when unsure about drinking water is to boil it for at least two minutes, and at high altitudes, for at least five minutes. However, this can be frustrating since few thirsty campers like to drink hot water. In addition, boiled water can taste like ashes from the campfire.

Water purification tablets, such as iodine or chlorine, do a good job in killing bacteria, but are unreliable against Giardia. The tablets work slowly, requiring as much as 30 minutes, and even then may not be 100 percent effective.

If you are without a filtration device and are in an area where no piped water is available, such as a wilderness area, then special care must be used to determine what streams you can take water from. Michael Furniss, a hiking buddy and hydrologist, has shown me how to identify "safe" streams, but all were the headwaters of small feeder creeks in high, mountain pass areas. In many cases, we would climb high above the trail to obtain water from a source in order to be certain that no one had camped above the waterway.

"Major rivers and any creek that meanders through a meadow should be avoided at all costs," Furniss advised.

The reason is Giardia is transferred from affected individuals into a watershed through waste products. When it rains, the organism can be washed from the waste and into the river. Eventually, somewhere downstream, it can be consumed by an unsuspecting camper, and the cycle continues.

To prevent the spread of Giardia, National Park Service law mandates that waste be buried no closer than 100 yards to natural waters and at least eight inches deep.

This is dead serious business. If you have any doubts about the water you plan to drink, the purchase of a water purification unit will not only solve those doubts, but allow you to enjoy your trip free of worry.

HYPOTHERMIA

No matter how well planned your trip might be, a sudden change in weather can turn it into a puzzle for which there are few answers. Bad weather, or an accident, can result in a dangerous chain of events.

Such a chain of episodes occurred for my brother, Rambob, and myself on a fishing trip one fall day just below the snow line. The weather had suddenly turned very cold and ice was forming along the shore of the lake. Suddenly, the canoe was placed in terrible imbalance and just that quick, it flipped. The little life vest seat cushions were useless, and using the canoe as a paddle board, we tried to kick our way back to shore—where my dad was going crazy at the thought of his two sons drowning before his eyes.

It took 17 minutes in that 38-degree water, but we finally made it to the shore. When they pulled me out of the water, my legs were dead, not strong enough to even hold up my weight. In fact, I didn't feel so much cold as tired, and I just wanted to lay down and go to sleep.

I closed my eyes, and my brother-in-law, Lloyd Angal, slapped me in the face several times, then got me on my feet and pushed and pulled me about.

In the celebration over making it to shore, only Lloyd had realized that hypothermia was setting in—where the temperature of the body is lowered to the point that it causes poor reasoning, apathy and collapse. It can look like the endangered is just tired and needs to sleep, but that sleep can become a coma.

Ultimately, my brother and I shared what little dry clothing remained. We then began hiking to get muscles functioning, creating internal warmth. We shivered, another way the body creates warmth for itself. We ate whatever munchies were available because the body produces heat by digestion. And most important, we got our heads as dry as possible. More body heat is lost through wet hair than any other single factor.

A few hours later, we were in a pizza parlor replaying the incident, talking about how only a life vest can do the job of a life vest. We decided never again to rely on those little floatation seat cushions that disappear when the boat flips.

Almost by instinct we had done everything right to prevent hypothermia: Don't go to sleep, get dry clothes on, dry your head, induce shivering, start a physical activity and eat something. That's how you fight hypothermia. In a dangerous setting, whether you fall in a lake, a stream, or get caught unprepared in a storm, that's how you can stay alive.

After being in that ice-bordered lake for almost 20 minutes, and then finally pulling ourselves to the shoreline, a strange, eerie phenomenon occured. My canoe was flipped rightside up and gone was almost all of its contents; tackle box, flotation cushions and cooler. But remaining was one paddle and one fishing rod, the trout rod my grandfather had given me for my 12th birthday.

Lloyd gave me a smile. "This means that you are meant to paddle and fish again," he said with a laugh.

FIRST AID KIT LIST:

Bandaids
Sterile gauze pads
Roller gauze
Athletic tape
Moleskin
Thermometer
Aspirin
Ace bandage

SECONDARY KIT LIST:

Mosquito repellent
After Bite or ammonia
Campho-Phenique gel
First Aid cream
Sunscreen
Neosporin ointment
Caladryl
Biodegradable soap
Towelettes

OPTIONAL:

Water purification system
Coins for emergency phone call
Extra set of matches
Tweezers
Mirror for signaling

· FISHING & RECREATIONAL · EQUIPMENT

Feet tired and hot, stomachs hungry, we stopped our hike for lunch beside a beautiful little river pool that was catching the flows from a long but gentle waterfall. My brother, Rambob, passed me a piece of jerky. I took my boots off, then slowly dunked my feet into the cool, foaming water.

I was gazing at a towering peak across a canyon, when suddenly —Wham!—there was a sudden jolt at the heel of my right foot. I pulled my foot out of the water. Incredibly, a trout had bitten it.

My brother looked at me like I had antlers growing out of my head. "Wow!" he exclaimed, "that trout almost caught himself an outdoors writer!"

It's true that in remote areas trout sometimes bite on almost anything, even feet. In California's High Sierra, I have caught limits of trout using nothing but a bare hook. The only problem is the fish will often hit the splitshot sinker instead of the hook. Of course, fishing isn't usually that easy. But it gives you an idea of what is possible.

America's wildlands are home for a remarkable abundance of fish and wildlife. Deer browse with little fear of man, bear keep an eye out for your food, and little critters like squirrels and chipmunks are daily companions. Add in the fishing and you can get some real zing on your camping trip.

Your camping trips will evolve into premium outdoor experiences if you can parlay in a few good fishing trips, avoid bear problems, and occasionally add a little offbeat fun with some camp games.

TROUT AND BASS

He creeps up on the stream as quiet as an old Indian, keeping his shadow off the water. With his little spinning rod, he'll zip his lure within an inch or two of its desired mark, probing along rocks, the edges of riffles, pocket water; wherever he can find a change in river habitat. It's my brother, Rambob, trout fishing, and he's a master at it.

In most cases, he'll catch a trout on his first or second cast. After that it's time to move upriver, giving no spot much more than five minutes due. Stick and move, stick and move, stalking the stream like a bobcat zeroing in on an unsuspecting rabbit. He might keep a few trout for dinner, but mostly he releases what he catches. Rambob doesn't necessarily fish for food. It's the feeling that comes with it.

Fishing can give you a sense of exhilaration, like you've taken a good shower after being coated with dust. On your walk back to camp, the steps come easy. You suddenly understand what John Muir meant when he talked of developing a oneness with nature, because you have it. That's what fishing can help provide.

You don't need a million dollars worth of fancy gear to catch fish. What you need is the right outlook, and that can be learned. That goes regardless if you are fishing for trout or bass, the two most popular fisheries in America. Your fishing tackle selection should be as simple and as clutter-free as possible.

At home I've got every piece of fishing tackle you might imagine, more than 30 rods and many tackle boxes, racks and cabinets filled with all kinds of stuff. I've got one lure that looks like a chipmunk and another that resembles a miniature can of beer with hooks. If I hear of something new, I want to try it, and usually do. It's a result of my lifelong fascination with the sport.

But if you just want to catch fish, there's an easier way to go. And when I go fishing, I take that path. I don't try to bring everything. It would be impossible. Instead, I bring a relatively small amount of gear. At home I will scan my tackle boxes for equipment and lures, make my selections, and bring just the essentials. Rod, reel and tackle will fit into a side of my backpack or a small carrying bag.

So, what kind of rod should be used on an outdoors trip? For most camper/anglers, I suggest the use of a light, multi-piece spinning rod that will break down to a small size. One of the best deals on the fishing market is the six-piece Daiwa 6½-foot pack rod, No. 6752. It retails for as low as $30 yet is made of a graphite/glass composite that gives it qualities of much more expensive models. And it comes in a hard plastic carrying tube for protection. Other major rod manufacturers, such as Fenwick, Sabre and Contender, offer similar premium rods. It's rough to miss with any of them.

The use of graphite/glass composites in fishing rods has made them lighter and more sensitive, yet stronger. The only downside to graphite as a rod material is that it can be brittle. If you rap your rod against something, it can crack or cause a weak spot. That weak spot can eventually snap when under even light pressure, like setting a hook or casting. Of course, a small bit of care will prevent that from ever occurring.

If you haven't bought a fishing reel in some time, you will be surprised at the quality and price of micro spinning reels on the market. The reels come tiny and strong, with rear-control drag systems. Sigma, Shimano, Cardinal, Abu and others all make premium reels. They also come expensive, usually $50 to $75. They're worth it. With your purchase, you've just bought a reel that will last for years and years.

The one downside to spinning reels is that after longterm use, the bail spring will weaken. The result is that after casting and beginning to reel, the bail will sometimes not flip over and allow the reel to retrieve the line. You then have to do it by hand. This can be incredibly frustrating, particularly when stream fishing where instant line pickup is essential. The solution is to have a new bail spring installed every few years, a cheap, quick operation for a tackle expert.

You might own a giant tackle box filled with lures, but on your fishing trip you are better off to fit the essentials into a small container. One of the best ways to do that is to use the Plano Micro-Magnum 3414, a tiny two-sided tackle box for trout fishermen that fits into a shirt pocket. In mine, I can fit 20 lures in one side of the box and 20 flies, splitshot and snap swivels in the other. For bass lures, which are larger, you need a slightly larger box, but the same principle can apply.

There are more fishing lures on the market than you can imagine, but a few special ones can do the job, and I make sure they are in my box on every trip. For trout, a few of my favorites are: small black Panther Martin spinner with yellow spots, small gold Kastmaster, yellow Roostertail, gold Z-Ray with red spots, Super Duper and Mepps Lightning spinner.

You can take it a step further using an insider's wisdom. My old pal Ed the Dunk showed me his trick of taking a tiny Dardevle spoon, then spraypainting it flat black and dabbing five tiny red dots on it. It's a real killer, particularly in tiny streams where the trout are spooky.

The best trout catcher I've ever used on rivers is a small metal lure called a Met-L Fly. On days when nothing else works, it can be like going to a shooting gallery. The problem is that the lure is near impossible to find. Rambob and I consider the few we have left so valuable that if the lure is snagged on a rock, a cold swim is deemed mandatory for its retrieval. These lures are as elusive to find in tackle shops as trout can be to catch without one.

For bass you can also fit all you need into a small plastic tackle box. I have fished with many bass pros and all of them actually use just a few lures: A white spinner bait, a small jig called a Git's It, a surface plug called a Zara Spook and plastic worms. At times, like when the bass move into shoreline areas during the spring, shad minnow imitations such as those made by Rebel or Rapala can be dynamite. For instance, my favorite is the one-inch blue/silver Rapala. Every spring, as the lakes begin to warm and the fish snap out of their winter doldrums, I like to float and paddle around small lakes in my small raft. I'll cast that little Rapala along the shoreline and catch and release hundreds of bass, bluegill and sunfish. The fish are usually sitting close to the shoreline awaiting my offering.

A FEW TRICKS

There's an old angler's joke about how you need to "think like a fish." But if you're the one getting zilched, you may not think it's so funny.

The irony is that it is your mental approach, what you see and what you miss, that often determines your fishing luck. Some people will spend a lot of money on tackle, lures and fishing clothes, and that done, just saunter up to a stream or lake, cast out and wonder why they are not catching fish. The answer is their mental outlook. They are not attuning themselves to their surroundings.

You must try living on nature's level, not your own. Do the former and you will start to feel things you never believed even existed. Soon you will see things that will allow you to catch fish. You can get a head-start by reading about fishing, but to get your degree in fishing, you must attend the University of Nature.

On every fishing trip, regardless of what you fish for, try to follow three hard-and-fast rules:

• 1. Always approach the fishing spot so you will be undetected by the fish.

• 2. Present your lure, fly or bait in a manner so it appears completely natural, as if no line was attached.

• 3. Stick and move, hitting one spot, working it the best you can, then move to the next.

Here's a more detailed explanation:

1. APPROACH: No one can just walk up to a stream or lake, cast out and start catching fish as if someone had waved a magic wand. Instead, give the fish credit for being smart. After all, they live there.

Your approach must be completely undetected by the fish. Fish can sense your presence through sight and sound, though this is misinterpreted by most people. By sight, this only rarely means the fish actually see you. More likely, they will see your shadow on the water, or the movement of your arm or rod while casting. By sound, it doesn't mean they hear you talking. It means they will detect the vibrations of your footsteps along the shore, kicking a rock, or the unnatural plunking sound of a heavy cast hitting the water. Any of these elements can spook them off the bite. In order to fish undetected, you must walk softly, keep your shadow off the water, and keep your casting motion low. All of these keys become easier at sunrise or sunset, when shadows are on the water. At mid-day, a high sun causes high levels of light penetration in the water, which can make the fish skittish to any foreign presence.

Like hunting, you must stalk the spots. When my brother Rambob sneaks up on a fishing spot, he looks like a burglar sneaking through an unlocked window.

2. PRESENTATION: Your lure, fly, or bait must appear in the water as if no line was attached so it appears as natural as possible.

My pal Mo Furniss has skindived in rivers to watch what the fish see when somebody is fishing.

"You wouldn't believe it," he said. "When the lure hits the water, every trout within 40 feet, like 15, 20 trout, will do a little zig-zag. They all see the lure, they're all aware something is going on. Meanwhile, on-shore the guy casting doesn't get a bite and thinks there aren't any fish in the river."

If your offering is aimed at fooling a fish into striking, it must appear as part of its natural habitat, as if it is an insect just hatched or a small fish looking for a spot to hide. That's where you come in.

After you have sneaked up to a fishing spot, you should zip your cast upstream, then start your retrieve as soon as it hits the water. If you let the lure sink to the bottom, then start to retrieve, you have no chance. A minnow, for instance, does not sink to the bottom then start swimming. On rivers, the retrieve should be more of a drift, as if the "minnow" was in trouble and the current was sweeping it downstream.

When fishing on trout streams, always hike and cast upriver, then retrieve as the offering drifts downstream in the current. This is effective because trout will sit almost motionless, pointed upstream, finning against the current. This way they can see anything coming their direction, and if a potential food morsel arrives, all they need is to move over a few inches, open their mouths, and they've got an easy lunch. Thus you must cast upstream.

Conversely, if you cast downstream, your retrieve will bring the lure from behind the fish, where he cannot see it approaching. And I've never seen a trout that had eyes in its tail. In addition, when retrieving a downstream lure, the river current will tend to sweep your lure inshore to the rocks.

3. FINDING SPOTS: A lot of fishermen don't catch fish and a lot of hikers never see any wildlife. The key is often where they are looking.

The rule of the wild is that fish and wildlife will congregate wherever there is a distinct change in the habitat. This is where you should begin your search. To find deer, for instance, forget probing a thick forest, but look for where a forest breaks into a meadow, or a clearcut has splayed a stand of trees. That's where the deer will be. Look for the change.

In a river, it can be where a riffle pours into a small pool, a rapid that plunges into a deep hole and flattens, a big boulder in the middle of a long riffle, a shoreline point, a rock pile, a submerged tree. Look for the changes. On the other hand, long straight stretches of shoreline will not hold fish—the habitat is lousy.

On rivers, the most productive areas are often where short riffles tumble into small oxygenated pools. After sneaking up from the downstream side and staying low, you should zip your cast so the lure plops gently in the white water just above the pool. Starting your retrieve instantly, the lure will drift downstream and plunk into the pool. Bang! That's where the trout will hit. Take a few more casts, then head upstream to the next spot.

With a careful approach and lure presentation, and by fishing in the right spots, you have the ticket to many exciting days on the water.

OF BEARS AND FOOD

The first time you come nose-to-nose with a bear, it can practically make your skin quiver.

Even mild-mannered black bears, the most common bear in America, can send shockwaves through your body. They range from 250 to 400 pounds and have large claws and teeth that are made to scare campers. When they bound, the muscles on their shoulders seem to roll like ocean breakers.

Bears in camping areas are accustomed to sharing the mountains with hikers and campers. They have become specialists in the food raiding business. As a result, you must be able to make a bear-proof food hang, or be able to scare the fellow off. Many campgrounds provide bear and raccoon-proof food lockers. You can also stash your food in your vehicle, but that puts a limit on your trip.

If you are in a particularly remote area, there will be no food lockers available. Your car will not be there either. The answer is making a bear-proof food hang—suspending all of your food wrapped in a plastic garbage bag from a rope in mid-air, often 10 feet from the trunk of a tree, 20 feet off the ground. (Counter-balancing two bags with a rope thrown over a tree limb is very effective, but an extensive search must often be made to find an appropriate limb.)

This is accomplished by tying a rock to a rope, then throwing it over a high but sturdy tree limb. Next, tie your food bag to the rope and hoist it up in the air. When you are satisfied with the position of the food bag, you then tie off the end of the rope on another tree. Nothing else will do, especially for hikers in bear-troubled areas, such as Yosemite, Sequoia or Kings Canyon National Parks. One day in Yosemite near Tuolomne Meadows, I met five consecutive teams of hikers heading the other direction. Every one of them had lost their food to bears.

I've been there. On one trip, Foonsky and Rambob had left to fish and I was stoking up an evening campfire when I felt the eyes of an intruder on my back. I turned around and this big bear was heading straight for our camp. In the next half hour, I scared the bear off twice, but then he got a whiff of something sweet in my brother's pack.

In most situations you can spook a black bear by banging on a pot and shouting like a lunatic. But some bears are on to the old banging-the-pot trick. If so, and he gets a whiff of your Tang, banging on a pot and shouting can be like trying to stop a steamroller with a roadblock.

In this case, the bear rolled into camp like a semi-truck, grabbed my brother's pack, ripped it open and plucked out the Tang and the Swiss Miss. The bear, a 350-pounder, then sat astride a nearby log and lapped at the goodies like a thirsty dog finding water.

I took two steps toward the pack and that bear jumped off the log and galloped across the camp right at me. Scientists say a man can't outrun a bear, but they've never seen how fast I can go up a granite block with a bear on my tail. Once a bear get his mitts on your gear, he considers it his.

Shortly thereafter, Foonsky returned while I was still perched on top of the rock, and demanded to know how I could let a bear get our Tang. But it took all three of us, Foonsky, Rambob and myself, all charging at once and shouting like madmen to clear the bear out of the camp and send him off over the ridge. It was a lesson to never let food sit unattended again—a lesson learned the hard way.

FUN AND GAMES

You can bring an added dimension to your camping trip with a few recreational tools.

One such tool is an inexpensive star chart. They allow you to identify stars, constellations and planets on clear mountain nights. Another good addition is a pocket-size handbook on tree identification. Both of these can provide a unique perspective to your trip, and make you feel more a participant of the wild, rather than an observer.

If you want more excitement, and maybe a little competition with your companions, a good game using twigs or rocks is called "3-5-7." You set up the game by laying out three rows of twigs, with three twigs in one row, five in another, seven in the other. Alternating turns with one competitor, you are allowed to remove all or as few as one twig from a row, but from only one row per turn. You alternate turns removing twigs and whoever is left picking up the last twig is the loser.

Some folks bring a deck of cards and a tiny cribbage board, or will set up a poker game. Of the latter, I've been in a few doozies on backpacking trips. Money is meaningless in the woods, but something like penny candy has a value. Betting a pack of M&Ms and a beef stick in a poker game in the outback is like laying down a million dollars in Las Vegas.

In a game of seven-card stud, I caught a straight on the last card of the deal, but Foonsky was showing three sevens and bluffing full house. When I bet five M&Ms with nuts and two Skittles, Rambob folded. "Too much for me." But Foonsky matched my bet, and then with painful slowness, raised me a grape stick.

All was quiet. It was the highest bet ever made. I felt nervous, my heart started pounding, and again I looked hard at my cards. The decision came tough. I folded. The potential of losing a grape stick, even with a great hand like I had, was just too much to gamble.

But I still had my grape stick.

FISHING/RECREATION GEAR LIST

Fishing rod
Fishing reel with fresh line
Small tackle box with lures, splitshot, and snap swivels
Pliers
Knife
Firecrackers for bear protection

OPTIONAL:
Rope for bearproof food hang
Stargazing chart
Tree identification handbook
Deck of cards
Backpacking cribbage board

· MAPS & HOW TO ·
USE THEM

N ow you're ready to join the Five Percent Club, that is, the five percent of Californians who know the secret spots where you can camp, fish and hike and have the time of your life doing it.

To aid in that pursuit, there are a number of contacts, map sources and reservation systems available for your use. These include contacts for national forests, state parks, national parks and motorhome parks. The state and federal agencies listed can provide detailed maps at low costs and any additional information you might require.

NATIONAL FORESTS

The Forest Service provides many secluded camps and also permits camping anywhere except where it is specifically prohibited. If you ever want to clear the cobwebs and get away from it all, this is the way to go.

Many Forest Service campgrounds are quite remote, have no developed water and no reservations or check-in is possible—and there is no charge for their use. At many Forest Service campgrounds that provide piped water, the camp fee is often only a few dollars, with payment done on the honor system. Because most of these camps are in mountain areas, they are subject to closure from snow or mud during the winter.

Dogs are permitted on National Forests with no extra charge, and no hassle. Conversely, in state and national parks, dogs are not allowed on trails.

Maps for National Forests are among the best you can get, detailing all back country streams, lakes, hiking trails and logging roads for access. They cost $1 and are available by writing USDA-Forest Service, Office of Information, Pacific Southwest Region, 630 Sansome Street, San Francisco, CA 94111.

I've found the Forest Service personnel to be the most helpful of the government agencies when obtaining camping or hiking trail information. Unless you are buying a map, it is advisable to phone, not write, to get the best service. For specific information on a National Forest, write or phone at the following addresses and phone numbers:

- **Angeles National Forest,** located northeast of Los Angeles; write 701 N. Santa Anita Ave., Arcadia, CA 91006, or phone (818) 574-1613.
- **Cleveland National Forest,** located east of San Diego; write 880 Front Street, Room 5-N-14, San Diego, CA 92188, or phone (619) 557-5050.
- **Eldorado National Forest,** located east of Placerville; write 100 Forni Road, Placerville, CA 95667, or phone (916) 622-5061.
- **Inyo National Forest,** located in the eastern Sierra Nevada, north of Bishop; write 873 North Main Street, Bishop, CA 93514, or phone (714) 873-5841.
- **Klamath National Forest,** located northeast of Eureka; write 1215 South Main Street, Yreka, CA 96097, or phone (916) 842-6131.
- **Lake Tahoe Basin,** located west of Lake Tahoe; write P.O. Box 731002, 870 Emerald Bay Road, South Lake Tahoe, CA 95731, or phone (916) 573-2600.
- **Lassen National Forest,** located east of Redding; write 707 Nevada Street, Susanville, CA 96130, or phone (916) 257-2151.
- **Los Padres National Forest,** located south of Monterey; write 406 S. Mildred, King City, CA 93930, or phone (805) 963-6711.
- **Mendocino National Forest,** located northeast of Ukiah; write 420 Laurel Street, Willows, CA 95988, or phone (916) 934-3316.
- **Modoc National Forest,** located in northeast corner of state; write 441 N. Main Street, Alturas, CA 96101, or phone (916) 233-5811.
- **Plumas National Forest,** located northwest of Lake Tahoe; write P.O. Box 1500, Quincy, CA 95971, or phone (916) 283-2050.
- **San Bernardino National Forest,** located east of San Bernardino; write 1824 South Commercenter Circle, San Bernardino, CA, 92408, or phone (714) 383-5588.
- **Sequoia National Forest,** located south of Sequoia National Park; write 900 W. Grand Ave., Porterville, CA 93257, or phone (209) 784-1500.
- **Shasta/Trinity National Forest,** located north and west of Redding; write 2400 Washington Ave., Redding, CA 96001, or phone (916) 246-5222.
- **Sierra National Forest,** located south of Yosemite National Park; write Federal Building, 1130 O Street, Fresno, CA 93721, or phone (209) 487-5115.
- **Six Rivers National Forest,** located between Eureka and Crescent City; write 507 F Street, Eureka, CA 95501, or phone (707) 442-1721.
- **Stanislaus National Forest,** located east of Sonora; write 19777 Greenley Road, Sonora, CA 95370, or phone (209) 532-3671.
- **Tahoe National Forest,** located northwest of Lake Tahoe; write Highway 49, Nevada City, CA 95959 or phone (916) 265-4531.

STATE PARKS

The California State Park system provides many popular camping spots. Reservations are often a necessity during the summer months. The camps include drive-in numbered sites, tent space, picnic table, with showers and a bathroom provided nearby. Although some parks are well-known, there are still some little-known gems in the State Park system where campers can get seclusion even in summer months.

Reservations can be obtained through a reservation system called Mixtix, which can be reached with a toll-free call anywhere in California by phoning (800) 444-7275. Mistix charges $3.75 for the reservation service, a separate cost from the campsite fee. Most state parks charge $10 per night, with a $1 fee for pets.

NATIONAL PARKS

The National Parks in California are natural wonders, ranging from the spectacular yet crowded Yosemite Valley to the remote and rugged beauty of Lava Beds National Monument in northeastern California. At National Parks, reservations must be made directly through the park:

The six most popular are Yosemite (209-372-4461), Sequoia (209-565-3341), Kings Canyon (209-565-3341), Death Valley National Monument (619-786-2331), Devil's Postpile National Monument (619-934-2289), and Point Reyes National Seashore (415-556-0560).

The best of the rest are Lassen Volcanic National Park (916-595-4444), Lava Beds National Monument (916-667-2282), Whiskeytown National Recreation Area (916-241-6584), Joshua Tree National Monument (619-367-7511), and Pinnacles National Monument (408-389-4526).

MOTORHOME PARKS

Reservations for many motorhome parks can be made through Leisuretime Reservation Systems, with a toll-free line available. In California, it can be reached by phoning (800) 822-2267, and from out of state at (800) 824-2267. Leisuretime charges a $3.50 fee for reservations, which is separate from campsite charges.

The charge for hookups at motorhome parks varies from $10 to $20 per night. In remote areas of California, the charge for a space in a motorhome park is often below $10. In populated areas, the charge often climbs to the $20 range per night. Many motorhome parks, particularly those in rural counties, are not on the Leisuretime system. These must be contacted directly by phone. Many require a deposit with a reservation, which is usually just an advance payment for your first night's fee.

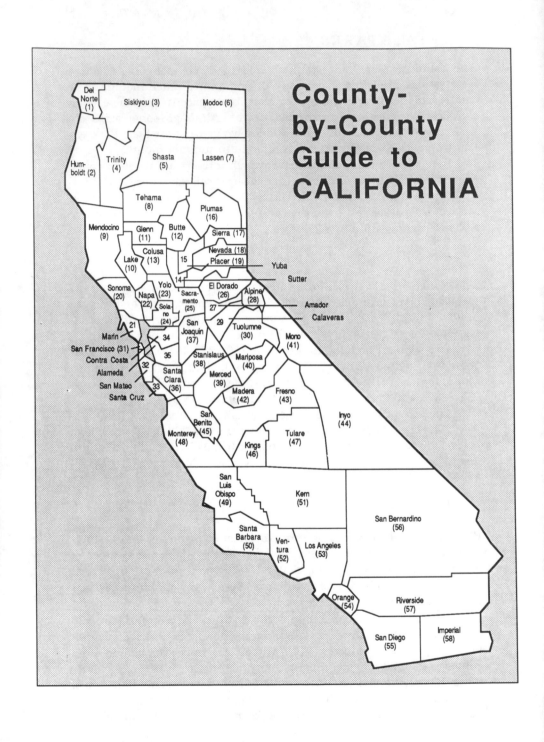

County-
by-County
Guide to
CALIFORNIA

·COUNTY GUIDE TO·
CAMPING AREAS

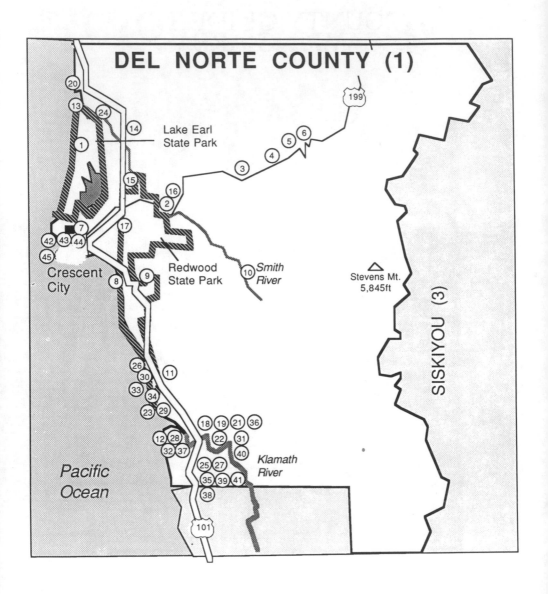

DEL NORTE COUNTY (1)

199

Lake Earl
State Park

Crescent
City

Redwood
State Park

Smith
River

Stevens Mt.
5,845ft

SISKIYOU (3)

Pacific
Ocean

Klamath
River

101

DEL NORTE COUNTY

◆

Site **1**   LAKES EARL
            AND TALAWA

Campsites, facilities: There are eight primitive campsites. No water, but environmental toilets and picnic tables are provided.

Reservations, fee: Reservations can be made through Camp Lincoln Office by phoning (707)464-9533; $3 use fee.

Who to contact: Write Camp Lincoln at 4241 Kings Valley Rd., Crescent City, CA 95531, or phone at number above.

Location: Drive half a mile north of Crescent City on Highway 101 and turn northwest on Northcrest/Lake Earl Drive. Then, go west on Old Mill Rd. and Sand Hill Rd. for trail and beach access. If gate is locked, call Camp Lincoln Office at above number.

Trip note: Lakes Earl and Talawa offer seven and a half miles of ocean frontage, more than a mile of river frontage, 20 miles of horseback riding and numerous hiking trails. Boating and fishing available.

Site **2**   JEDEDIAH SMITH
            REDWOODS STATE PARK

Campsites, facilities: There are 108 campsites for tents or motorhomes. Piped water, flush toilets, showers, handicap facilities, picnic tables, fireplaces and a sanitary disposal station are provided. Propane, groceries and a laundromat are available nearby.

Reservations, fee: Reservations advised through MISTIX by phoning (800)446-7275 (3.75 fee); campsite fee is $10.

Who to contact: (707)458-3310.

Location: Drive nine miles northeast of Crescent City on Highway 199.

Trip note: Park is set on the Smith River, where you can fish, swim and float down the river (no lifeguards). In summer, interpretive walks and talks are provided. Howland Hill Road is an unpaved, narrow, scenic alternate route to Crescent City through redwood forest. It gives you access to Stout Grove and hiking trails; trailers not recommended. Walker Road is an unpaved scenic road through redwood forest that provides access to the Smith River and short hiking trails.

Site **3**
PANTHER
FLAT
▲

Campsites, facilities: There are 10 tent spaces and 31 campsites for tents and mo-
   torhomes. Piped water, vault toilets, fireplaces and picnic tables are pro-
   vided. Propane, groceries and a laundromat are available nearby.
Reservations, fee: No reservations; $4 use fee.
Who to contact: Write Six Rivers National Forest Headquarters at 507 F Street,
   Eureka, CA 95501, or phone (707)442-1721.
Location: Drive two and a half miles east of Gasquet on Highway 199.
Trip note: Open from April through October. Camp is set on the Smith River
   where good swimming and fishing can be found.

Site **4**
GRASSY
FLAT
▲

Campsites, facilities: There are eight tent spaces and 11 campsites for tents or
   motorhomes. Piped water, vault toilets, fireplaces and picnic tables are pro-
   vided. Propane, groceries and a laundromat are available nearby.
Reservations, fee: No reservations; $3 use fee.
Who to contact: Write Six Rivers National Forest Headquarters at 507 F Street,
   Eureka, CA 95501, or phone (707)442-1721.
Location: Drive five miles east of Gasquet on Highway 199.
Trip note: Open from May through September. Camp is set on the Smith River
   which provides good swimming and fishing.

Site **5**
PATRICK
CREEK
▲

Campsites, facilities: There are five tent spaces and 12 campsites for tents and
   motorhomes. Piped water, flush toilets, picnic tables and fireplaces pro-
   vided.
Reservations, fee: No reservations; $4 use fee.
Who to contact: Write Six Rivers National Forest Headquarters at 507 F Street,
   Eureka, CA 95501, or phone (707)442-1721.
Location: Drive eight miles northeast of Gasquet on Highway 199.
Trip note: Open from May through September. Camp located on Patrick Creek,
   a feeder stream to the Smith River, which provides good swimming and
   fishing.

Site **6**
CEDAR
RUSTIC
▲

Campsites, facilities: There are four tent spaces and eight campsites for tents or motorhomes. Piped water, vault toilets, fireplaces and picnic tables are provided.

Reservations, fee: No reservations; $3 use fee.

Who to contact: Write Six Rivers National Forest Headquarters at 507 F Street, Eureka, CA 95501, or call (707)442-1721.

Location: Drive nine and a half miles northeast of Gasquet on Highway 199.

Trip note: Open from May through September. Nearby attractions include Bear Basin Butte, which abounds with unusual wildflowers and a stand of weeping (Brewer's) spruce (travel one mile northeast on Highway 199, then turn right, or southeast, and drive about seven miles). Island Lake is beautiful and secluded, about five miles southeast of Bear Basin Butte.

Site **7**   REDWOOD
                    NATIONAL PARK   ▲

Campsites, facilities: Drive through sites.

Reservations, fee: Reservations through Camp Lincoln Office by calling (707)464-9533.

Who to contact: Write Redwood National Park Headquarters at 1111 Second Street, Crescent City, CA 95531, or call (707)464-6101.

Location: Drive on Highway 101 to Crescent City.

Trip note: Information center here.

Site **8**   NICKEL
                        CREEK   ▲

Campsites, facilities: There are 10 tent spaces. No water, but picnic tables and fireplaces provided.

Reservations, fee: No reservations, no fee.

Who to contact: Write Redwood National Park Headquarters at 1111 Second Street, Crescent City, CA 95531, or phone (707)464-6101.

Location: Drive south on Highway 101 from Crescent City for 2 1/2 miles, then turn onto road to Enderts Beach and hike in a half mile to the campground.

Trip note: There is beach access, and in the summer two hour tidepool and seashore walks are conducted. Open all year.

Site **9**   MILL
                        CREEK   ▲

Campsites, facilities: There are 20 tent spaces, and 125 campsites for tents or motorhomes to 27 feet long. Piped water, a sanitary disposal station, flush toilets, showers, fireplaces and picnic tables provided.

Reservations, fee: Reservations through MISTIX by phoning (800)446-7275 (3.75 fee); $10 camp use fee.

Who to contact: Call Del Norte Redwoods State Park at (707)458-3310.

Location: Drive nine miles south of Crescent City on Highway 101.
Trip note: Open from April to October. Groves of redwoods thrive in this nurturing coastal climate and creeks criss-cross the area. Evening ranger programs conducted.

Site **10**   BIG
                                   FLAT   ▲

Campsites, facilities: There are 16 tent spaces and 14 campsites for tents or motorhomes to 22 feet long. Piped water, vault toilets, picnic tables and fireplaces provided.
Reservations, fee: No reservations or fee required.
Who to contact: Write Six Rivers National Forest Headquarters at 507 F Street, Eureka, CA 95501, or call (707)442-1721.
Location: From Highway 199, turn on South Fork Road and drive 25 1/2 miles south of Gasquet.
Trip note: Open May to September. Camp is set next to Hurdy-Gurdy Creek, and nearby is the wild and scenic South Fork of the Smith River. Both provide excellent swimming and fishing.

Site **11**   DE MARTIN   ▲

Campsites, facilities: There are 10 tent spaces here. Piped water is available.
Reservations, fee: No reservations, no fee.
Who to contact: Write 1111 Second Street, Crescent City, CA 95531, or call (707)464-6101.
Location: From Crescent City, drive south on Highway 101 for approximately 18 miles, then go east at Wilson Creek Road and walk into the campground.
Trip note: Open all year. Located on Wilson Creek. Little known spot.

Site **12**   FLINT
                                   RIDGE   ▲

Campsites, facilities: There are 10 tent spaces. Piped water is available.
Reservations, fee: No reservations, no fee.
Who to contact: Write Redwood National Park Headquarters at 1111 Second Street, Crescent City, CA 95531, or call (707)464-6101.
Location: Take Coastal Drive out of Klamath and walk into the campground.
Trip note: Exhibits available along Coastal Drive. A coastal trail leads from the campground and picks up again on the north bank of the Klamath River at the end of Requa Road. A good site for whale watching. Another hike leads south from Flint Ridge on the coastal trail into the heart of Redwood National Park, where the trail ends at Tall Trees Grove. Approximate distance fom Flint Ridge to Tall Trees Grove is 18 miles, with Gold Bluffs Campground at the halfway point.

Site **13**   SALMON HARBOR
                                    RESORT

Campsites, facilities: There are 98 campsites for tents or motorhomes, 88 with
   full hookups and cable TV. A laundromat, showers, boat rentals, and a recreation room are provided. Ice, gas, and a bait and tackle shop are available nearby.
Reservations, fee: Reservations through Camp Lincoln Office by phoning
   (707)464-9533.
Who to contact: Call (707)487-3341.
Location: Drive three miles north of the town of Smith River on Highway 101 to
   the mouth of the Smith River. Located at 200 Salmon Harbor Road, Smith
   River.
Trip note: Located on the mouth of the Smith River, overlooking the ocean. Enjoy fishing, beachcombing, and driftwood and agate hunting.

Site **14**   KINGS VALLEY
                                   RV RESORT

Campsites, facilities: There are 78 tent and motorhome campsites. A gift store,
   groceries, ice, laundromat, sanitary disposal station and firewood are avail-
   able.
Reservations, fee: Call (707)487-4831 for reservations and fee
Who to contact: Call (707)487-4831.
Location: Drive nine miles north of Crescent City on Highway 101 to one mile
   south of the Highway 199 junction. Located at 6701 Highway 101 North,
   Crescent City.
Trip note: Enjoy cool, comfortable camping in a beautiful redwood forest along
   Highway 101. Near river, beach and national forest.

Site **15**   CRESCENT CITY
                                REDWOODS KOA

Campsites, facilities: There are 44 tent spaces and 50 campsites for motorhomes
   with hookups for electricity, water and sewage. A sanitary disposal station,
   piped water, flush toilets, showers, picnic tables, a laundromat, fireplaces
   and a playground provided. Propane and groceries available nearby.
Reservations, fee: An $11 deposit required.
Who to contact: Call (707)464-5744.
Location: Drive four miles north of Crescent City on Highway 101, and one mile
   north of the junction of Highways 101 and 199. Located at 4241 Highway
   101 North, Crescent City.
Trip note: Located in the giant redwoods, this campground is one mile from
   Redwood National Park and four miles from the ocean and the river. Possible pastimes include hiking in the redwoods, salmon and steelhead fishing,
   swimming, beachcombing, crabbing, rock hounding, clamming, charter

and jet boat rental, caving and golf.

Site **16**   HIOUCHI HAMLET
                        RV RESORT

Campsites, facilities: There are 101 campsites for tents or motorhomes, 92 with
    hookups for electricity and water and 83 with hookups for sewage. Piped
    water, flush toilets, showers, a laundromat and a sanitary disposal station
    are provided. Propane, groceries and a golf course are available nearby.
Reservations, fee: A $12 deposit is required.
Who to contact: Call (707)458-3321.
Location: Drive nine miles east of Crescent City on Highway 199, to 2000 High-
    way 199, Crescent City.
Trip note: Out of the wind and fog and in the heart of the forest. Good base
    camp for steelhead trip in winter.

Site **17**   VILLAGE
                        CAMPER INN

Campsites, facilities: There are 14 tent spaces, 21 campsites for tents or motor-
    homes and 110 motorhome spaces. There are 130 spaces with hookups for
    electricity and water, and 110 with hookups for sewage. Motorhomes are al-
    lowed a maximum length of 34 feet. A sanitary disposal station, piped wa-
    ter, flush toilets and picnic tables are provided. Cable TV is available.
Reservations, fee: A $9 deposit is required.
Who to contact: Call (707)464-3544.
Location: Southbound on Highway 101, take Washington Boulevard to Parkway
    Drive. Northbound on Highway 101, take a right on Parkway Drive north
    of Crescent City. Located at 1543 Parkway Drive, Crescent City.
Trip note: Wooded spaces on twenty acres. Located near agate and driftwood
    beaches. Ocean or river fishing.

Site **18**   CHINOOK
                        RV RESORT

Campsites, facilities: There are 82 motorhome spaces, all with hookups for elec-
    tricity, water and sewage. Piped water, flush toilets, showers, a playground,
    laundromat and recreation room are provided. Propane and groceries avail-
    able nearby.
Reservations, fee: $12 deposit required.
Who to contact: Write Chinook RV Resort at P.O. Box 7, Klamath, CA 95548, or
    phone at (707)482-3511.
Location: One mile north of the Klamath River Bridge on Highway 101.
Trip note: Grassy RV spaces overlook the Klamath River, famous for salmon and
    steelhead fishing. This spot is surrounded by mountains covered with beau-
    tiful redwood trees. There is river frontage.

Site **19**
KLAMATH
CAMPER CORRAL

Campsites, facilities: There are 45 tent spaces and 100 motorhome sites, all with hookups for electricity and water, and 76 with hookups for sewage. A sanitary disposal station, water, flush toilets, showers, picnic tables, fireplaces and a playground are provided. Propane, a laundromat, cable TV, ice, and a bait and tackle shop are available.

Reservations, fee: $9 deposit required.

Who to contact: Write Klamath Camper Corral at P.O. Box 729, Klamath, CA 95548, or call (707)482-5741.

Location: Take the Terwer Valley Road exit at the north end of the Klamath River Bridge on Highway 101, and drive west one-eighth of a mile.

Trip note: Open from April 1 to November 1. This resort has 3000 feet of Klamath River frontage, grassy tent sites, salmon and steelhead fishing, berry picking, the ocean nearby and hiking trails.

Site **20**
SHIP ASHORE
RV PARK

Campsites, facilities: There are 201 motorhome sites, all with hookups for electricity, water and sewage. Piped water, flush toilets, showers, a laundromat, a recreation room, and a boat dock and ramp are provided. Propane, groceries and boat rentals are available.

Reservations, fee: A $10 deposit is required.

Who to contact: Write Ship Ashore RV Park at P.O. Box 75, Smith River, CA 95567, or call (707)487-3141.

Location: Drive Three miles north of Smith River on Highway 101.

Trip note: Park is set on five acres adjacent to the Smith River. There is a restaurant, lounge and hot tub.

Site **21**
GOLDEN BEAR
RV PARK

Campsites, facilities: There are 88 motorhomes sites with hookups for electricity, water and sewage. Piped water, flush toilets, showers, picnic tables, fireplaces and a recreation room are provided. A laundromat, ice, LP gas, a boat dock and ramp, and boat rentals are available.

Reservations, fee: A $10 deposit required.

Who to contact: Write the Golden Bear RV Park at P.O. Box 775, Klamath, CA 95548, or phone (707)482-3333.

Location: Drive one mile north of Klamath on Highway 101 at the Klamath River.

Trip note: Popular motorhome spot during fall salmon run on the Klamath River. Labor Day weekend spotlights season.

Site 22 KAMP KLAMATH

Campsites, facilities: There are 99 campsites for tents or motorhomes, all with hookups for electricity, water and sewage. Piped water, flush toilets, showers, a laundromat, cable TV and a recreation room are provided. Ice, boat rentals, and a boat dock and ramp are available.

Reservations, fee: A $10 deposit is required.

Who to contact: Write Kamp Klamath at Box 128, Klamath, CA 95548, or call (707)482-3405.

Location: Drive one and a half miles north of Klamath on Highway 101.

Trip note: This camp is level and grassy with many sites along the Klamath River, which is famous for fall salmon fishing. Relax in the hot tub after a day of travel.

Site 23 REQUA RESORT

Campsites, facilities: There are 10 campsites for tents and 44 sites for motorhomes, all with hookups for electricity and sewage. Piped water, flush toilets, showers, picnic tables and fireplaces provided. A laundromat, restaurant, boat rentals, and a boat dock and ramp are available.

Reservations, fee: Reservations not required, but a good idea; $10 deposit.

Who to contact: Write Requa Resort at Box 5, Klamath, CA 95548, or call (707)482-5432.

Location: Turn west from Highway 101 onto Requa Road and drive one mile west, then turn on Mouth of Klamath Road and drive one half mile southwest to Highway 151.

Trip note: Open from April through October. Resort is set on 75 acres at the mouth of the Klamath River, a well known salmon fishing locale.

Site 24 VALLEY VIEW MOTEL TRAILER PARK

Campsites, facilities: There are 25 campsites for tents or motorhomes, 12 with full hookups available. Flush toilets, a dump station, showers, fireplaces and picnic tables are provided. A laundromat is available.

Reservations, fee: Reservations not required; $8 use fee.

Who to contact: Write Valley View Motel Trailer Park at Rfd. 2, P.O. Box 1295, Smith River, CA 95567, or call (707)487-3472.

Location: Drive one mile north on Highway 101 from the north edge of the town of Smith River.

Trip note: Open all year.

Site **25**
BLACKBERRY
PATCH

Campsites, facilities: There are 35 campsites for motorhomes, all with hookups for electricity, water and sewage. Piped water, flush toilets, showers, and picnic tables are provided. A laundromat is available.

Reservations, fee: Call (707) 482-4782 for reservations, fee.

Who to contact: Write to 401 Terwer Riffle Rd., Klamath, CA 95548, or call (707)482-4782.

Location: From the junction of Highway 101 and Highway 169, go three and one quarter miles east on Highway 169, then one quarter of a mile west on Terwer Road.

Trip note: Open from May 15 to October 31. Good salmon fishing in September and October.

Site **26**
CAMP MARIGOLD MOTEL
AND TRAILER PARK

Campsites, facilities: There are 40 campsites for tents or motorhomes, all with hookups for electricity, water and sewage. Piped water, flush toilets, showers, picnic tables and fireplaces are provided. A laundromat is available.

Reservations, fee: Reservations not required, but a good idea; $8 deposit.

Who to contact: Write to Camp Marigold Motel and Trailer Park at 16101 Highway 101 North, Klamath, CA 95548, or call (707)482-3585.

Location: Drive three and a half miles north of the north edge of town on Highway 101.

Trip note: Open all year. Good base camp for Klamath River fishing trip during fall salmon run.

Site **27**
CRIVELLIS
TRAILER PARK

Campsites, facilities: There are 31 sites for motorhomes, all with hookups for electricity, water and sewage. Piped water, flush toilets and showers are provided. A laundromat is available.

Reservations, fee: Reservations not required, but a good idea; $8 deposit.

Who to contact: Write Crivellis Trailer Park at 4100 Highway 169, Klamath, CA 95548, or call (707)482-3713.

Location: From the junction of Highway 101 and Highway 169 (Terwer Valley Rd.), drive two and one half miles east on Highway 169.

Trip note: Open all year. Good base camp for salmon fishing trip during fall run.

Site 28   DAD'S
CAMP   ▲

Campsites, facilities: There are 100 campsites for tents or motorhomes, 30 with partial hookups. Piped water, flush toilets, showers, vault toilets, a sanitary disposal station, picnic tables and fireplaces are provided. Ice, boat rentals, a dock and a gift store are available.

Reservations, fee: Call (707) 482-3415 for reservations, fee.

Who to contact: Write Dad's Camp at P.O. Box 557, Klamath, CA 95548, or call (707)482-3415.

Location: From the junction of Highway 169 and Highway 101, drive one mile south on 101, then three and one half miles west on Klamath Beach Rd.

Trip note: Open from May 1 to October 1. Located right at the mouth of the Klamath River.

Site 29   DEL'S
CAMP   ▲

Campsites, facilities: There are 75 campsites for tents or motorhomes, 47 with hookups for electricity, water and sewage, and 12 with partial hookups. Piped water, flush toilets, showers, picnic tables and fireplaces are provided. Boat rentals and a dock are available. Hiking trails.

Reservations, fee: Reservations are not required, but are a good idea; $9 deposit.

Who to contact: Write Del's Camp at 300 Requa Road, Klamath, CA 95548, or call (707)482-4922.

Location: From the junction of Highway 169 and Highway 101, drive two and a half miles north on Highway 101, then one half mile west on Requa Road.

Trip note: Open from May 15 to October 30. Good base camp for Klamath River fishing trip during fall salmon run.

Site 30   FORTAIN
TRAILER PARK   ▲

Campsites, facilities: There are 12 campsites for tents or motorhomes, six with hookups for electricity, water and sewage, and six with partial hookups. Piped water, flush toilets and showers are provided. A laundromat is available.

Reservations, fee: Call for rates.

Who to contact: Write Fortain Trailer Park at 15875 Highway 101 North, Klamath, CA 95548, or call (707)482-4901.

Location: Drive three and three-fourth miles from the north edge of town on Highway 101.

Trip note: Open all year. Option for fall camp for salmon fishing trip.

Site **31** KING SALMON
RESORT

Campsites, facilities: There are 76 campsites for tents or motorhomes, 60 with
hookups for electricity, water and sewage. Piped water, flush toilets and
showers are provided. A laundromat, boat rentals and a dock are available.
Reservations, fee: Reservations not required, but are a good idea; $10 deposit.
Who to contact: Write King Salmon Resort at P.O. Box 327, Klamath, CA 95548,
or call (707)482-4151.
Location: From the junction of Highway 101 and Highway 169, drive one half a
mile northwest on Highway 169.
Trip note: Open from June 1 to October 15. Popular spot during salmon run.
Reservations a must when fishing is good during fall run.

Site **32** KLAMATH COVE
RV PARK

Campsites, facilities: There are 97 campsites for tents or motorhomes, 45 with
hookups for electricity, water and sewage, and 42 with partial hookups.
Piped water, flush toilets, showers, picnic tables, and a recreation room are
provided. LP gas and a boat dock are available.
Reservations, fee: Reservations not required, but are a good idea; $7 deposit.
Who to contact: Write Klamath Cove RV Park at P.O. Box 66, Klamath, CA
95548, or call (707)482-3305.
Location: From the junction of Highway 169 and Highway 101, drive one mile
south on Highway 101, then drive three and one quarter miles west on Klamath Beach Road.
Trip note: Open from May 1 to October 15. Good salmon fishing from mid-August through September.

Site **33** MYSTIC FOREST
RV PARK

Campsites, facilities: There are 35 campsites for tents or motorhomes, 30 with
hookups for electricity, water and sewage, and 15 drive through sites. Piped
water, flush toilets, showers, picnic tables, fireplaces and a playground are
provided. A laundromat is available.
Reservations, fee: Reservations are not required, but are a good idea; $8 deposit.
Who to contact: Write Mystic Forest RV Park at 15875 Highway 101 North, Klamath, CA 95548, or call (707)482-4901.
Location: From the junction of Highway 101 and Highway 169, drive three and
one quarter miles north on Highway 101.
Trip note: Open from May 15 to October 15. Lower Klamath River nearby. Numerous hiking trails in the area.

Site **34**
PANTHER CREEK
TRAILER RESORT

Campsites, facilities: There are 60 campsites for tents or motorhomes, all with hookups for electricity, water and sewage, and 30 drive through sites. Piped water, flush toilets and showers are provided. Boat rentals and a dock are available.

Reservations, fee: Reservations are not required, but are a good idea; $8 deposit.

Who to contact: Write Panther Creek Trailer Resort at 200 Hughes Road, Klamath, CA 95548, or call (707)482-9921.

Location: From the junction of Highway 101 and Highway 169, drive two and one half miles north on Highway 101. Turn west on Requa Road, then turn on Hughes Road.

Trip note: Open from June 1 to October 15.

Site **35**
REDWOOD
REST

Campsites, facilities: There are 100 campsites for tents or motorhomes, 44 with hookups for electricity, water and sewage, 56 with partial hookups and 10 drive through sites. Piped water, flush toilets, showers and picnic tables provided.

Reservations, fee: Reservations are not required, but are a good idea; $10 deposit.

Who to contact: Write to Redwood Rest at Star Route Box 67, Klamath, CA 95548, or call (707)482-5033.

Location: From the junction of Highway 101 and Highway 169 (Terwer Valley Road), drive three and one quarter miles east on Highway 169.

Trip note: Open from May 1 to November 1. Reservations advised during summer and a necessity when salmon fishing picks up in mid-August.

Site **36**
RIVERSIDE
RV PARK

Campsites, facilities: There are 92 sites for motorhomes, all with hookups for electricity, water and sewage, and 30 drive through sites. Piped water, flush toilets, showers and a recreation room are provided. A laundromat, boat rentals and a dock are available.

Reservations, fee: Reservations are not required, but are a good idea; $8 deposit.

Who to contact: Write Riverside RV Park at P.O. Box 235, Klamath, CA 95548, or call (707)482-2523.

Location: Drive one and a half miles north on Highway 101 from its junction with Highway 169.

Trip note: Open from April 15 to November 1. Good salmon fishing during fall run on Klamath River.

Site **37**   RIVERWOODS
                               CAMPGROUND

Campsites, facilities: There are 50 campsites for tents or motorhomes, 11 with
    hookups for electricity, water and sewage, and four with partial hookups.
    Piped water, flush toilets, showers, a sanitary disposal station, picnic tables
    and fireplaces are provided. Hiking trails.
Reservations, fee: Reservations not required, but are a good idea; $8 deposit.
Who to contact: Write Riverwoods Campground at Box 589, Klamath, CA 95548,
    or call (707)482-5591.
Location: Drive one mile south on Highway 101 from its junction with Highway
    169, then drive two miles west on Klamath Beach Road.
Trip note: Open from April 1 to October 15. Good salmon fishing on Klamath
    River during fall run.

Site **38**   STAR
                            MOBILE HOME PARK

Campsites, facilities: There are 11 sites for motorhomes, all with hookups for
    electricity, water and sewage. Picnic tables are provided. A laundromat is
    available.
Reservations, fee: Call for rates.
Who to contact: Write Star Mobile Home Park at Star Route Box 488, Klamath,
    CA 95548, or call (707)482-2663.
Location: Drive one block north on Arrow Mills Road from its intersection with
    Highway 169, then drive east on paved road.
Trip note: Open all year. Option for base camp for Klamath River fishing trip.

Site **39**   STEELHEAD
                                 LODGE

Campsites, facilities: There are 51 sites for motorhomes, all with hookups for
    electricity, water and sewage, and 10 drive through sites. Piped water, flush
    toilets, showers and picnic tables are provided.
Reservations, fee: Reservations not required, but are a good idea; $7 deposit.
Who to contact: Write Steelhead Lodge at 330 Terwer Riffle Road, Klamath, CA
    95548, or call (707)482-8145.
Location: Drive three and one quarter miles east on Highway 169 from its junc-
    tion with Highway 101, then one block south on Terwer Riffle Rd.
Trip note: Open all year.

Site **40**   STRAWNS
                               RV PARK

Campsites, facilities: There are 12 sites for motorhomes, all with hookups for electricity, water and sewage, and 12 drive through sites. Piped water, flush toilets and showers are provided. A laundromat is available.

Reservations, fee: No reservations are required; $5 deposit fee.

Who to contact: Write Strawns RV Park at P.O. Box 806, Klamath, CA 95548, or call (707)482-5461.

Location: Drive three-quarters of a mile north on Highway 101 from its junction with Highway 169, then one block east on Ehlers Way.

Trip note: Open all year. Small campground, option for Klamath River campers.

Site **41**   TERWER
                           PARK   ▲

Campsites, facilities: There are 98 campsites for tents or motorhomes, all with hookups for electricity, water and sewage, and 20 drive through sites. Piped water, flush toilets, showers and picnic tables are provided. LP gas, a laundromat, boat rentals and a dock are available.

Reservations, fee: Reservations are not required, but a good idea; $10 deposit.

Who to contact: Write Terwer Park at 641 Terwer Riffle Road, Klamath, CA 95548, or call (707)482-3855.

Location: Drive three and one quarter miles east on Highway 169 from its junction with Highway 101, then one half a mile west on Terwer Riffle Rd.

Trip note: Open all year. Terwer Riffle on lower Klamath River is one of the better salmon, steelhead fishing spots in the area.

Site **42**   ACI SHORELINE
                        CAMPGROUND   ▲

Campsites, facilities: There are 242 campsites for tents or motorhomes, 192 with hookups for electricity, water and sewage. Piped water, flush toilets, showers, picnic tables and handicap facilities are provided.

Reservations, fee: Reservations are not required, but are a good idea; $8 deposit.

Who to contact: Write Aci Shoreline Campground at 900 Sunset Circle, Crescent City, CA 95531, or call (707)464-2473.

Location: Drive 100 yards west on Sunset Circle from its intersection with Highway 101.

Trip note: Open all year. Good beachcombing year around. Smith River, Jed Smith Redwoods and Six Rivers National Forest are all within 10 miles.

Site **43**   CRESCENT CITY HARBOR
                         RV PARK

Campsites, facilities: There are 132 sites for motorhomes, all with hookups for electricity, water and sewage. Piped water, flush toilets, showers, a sanitary disposal station and picnic tables are provided. A laundromat is available.

Reservations, fee: Reservations are not required, but a good idea; $10 deposit.

Who to contact: Write Crescent City Harbor RV Park at 750 Highway 101 South, Crescent City, CA 95531, or call (707)464-9482.

Location: In the town of Crescent City on Highway 101 at Citizen Dock Road.

Trip note: Open all year. Good ocean beachcombing year around. Smith River, Jed Smith State Park and Six Rivers National Forest are all within 10 miles.

Site **44**   HARBOR
RV ANCHORAGE

Campsites, facilities: There are 169 sites for motorhomes, all with hookups for electricity, water and sewage, and 26 drive through sites. Piped water, flush toilets, showers, a sanitary disposal station and picnic tables are provided. A laundromat is available.

Reservations, fee: Reservations are required.

Who to contact: Write Harbor RV Anchorage at 159 Starfish Way, Crescent City, CA 95531, or call (707)464-2616.

Location: Drive one block west on Anchor Way from its intersection with Highway 101, then one block north on Starfish Way.

Trip note: Open all year. Smith River, Jed Smith State Park and Six Rivers National Forest are all within 10 miles.

Site **45**   NORTHCREST
RV PARK

Campsites, facilities: There are 14 sites for motorhomes, all with hookups for electricity, water and sewage. Piped water, flush toilets, showers and picnic tables are provided. A laundromat is available.

Reservations, fee: Reservations are not required, but a good idea; $9 deposit.

Who to contact: Write Northcrest RV Park at 1253 Northcrest Drive, Crescent City, CA 95531, or call (707)464-9291.

Location: Drive one quarter of a mile north on Northcrest Drive from its junction with Highway 101.

Trip note: Open all year. Good hiking through redwoods at Jed Smith State Park east of Crescent City off Highway 199.

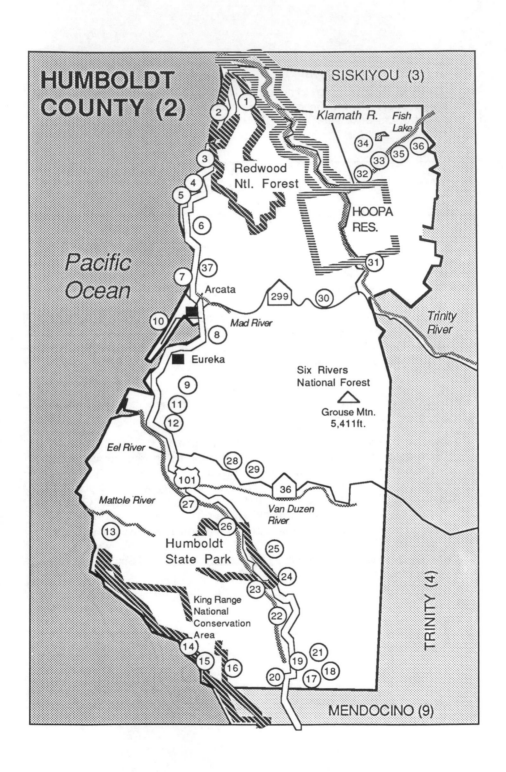

HUMBOLDT COUNTY (2)

SISKIYOU (3)

Klamath R. Fish Lake

Redwood Ntl. Forest

HOOPA RES.

Pacific Ocean

Arcata

299

Mad River

Trinity River

Eureka

Six Rivers National Forest

△ Grouse Mtn. 5,411ft.

Eel River

101

Mattole River

Van Duzen River

Humboldt State Park

King Range National Conservation Area

TRINITY (4)

MENDOCINO (9)

HUMBOLDT COUNTY

◆

Site **1** PRAIRIE
CREEK △

Campsites, facilities: There are 10 sites for tents, and 65 for tents or motorhomes
  up to 27 feet long. Piped water, flush toilets, showers, picnic tables and fire-
  places are provided. A grocery store, laundromat and propane are available.
Reservations, fee: Reservations advised through MISTIX at (800)446-7275.
  Campsite fee is $10 per night; pets $1.
Who to contact: Call Prairie Creek Redwoods State Park at (707)488-2171.
Location: Nine miles north of Orick on Highway 101.
Trip note: A remarkable park where herds of Roosevelt elk wander free. Great
  photography opportunity, good hiking in park and scenic drive through
  redwoods on unpaved Barrel Road.

Site **2** GOLD BLUFF
BEACH △

Campsites, facilities: There are 25 campsites for tents or motorhomes up to 20
  feet long. Non-piped water, flush toilets, showers, fireplaces and tables are
  available for campers' use.
Reservations, fee: Reservations not required. $6 fee per night; pets $1.
Who to contact: Phone Prairie Creek Redwoods State Park at (707)488-2171.
Location: Drive eight miles north of Orick on Highway 101, turn on Davison
  Road. Note: No trailers allowed on Davison Road, which is narrow and
  unpaved.
Trip note: Fern Canyon Trail is one of the best hikes in California, located at
  end of Davison Road. Some herds of elk in the area. Open year around,
  beach setting, heavy rain in winter.

Site **3** STONE
LAGOONS 🌲

Campsites, facilities: A primitive camp with 25 campsites for tents or motorhomes. No water, but vault toilets and fireplaces provided. A laundromat,
  grocery store and propane gas are available nearby.

Reservations, fee: No reservations; $3 fee per night.
Who to contact: Call Prairie Creek Redwoods State Park at (707)488-2171.
Location: Camp is located five miles southwest of Orick off Highway 101.
Trip note: Open year around, with canoeing potential on Stone Lagoon.

Site **4**   BIG   ▲
                                      LAGOON

Campsites, facilities: There are 11 campsites for tents or motorhomes. Piped water, pit toilets, fireplaces, picnic tables and a playground are provided. Groceries and propane gas are available nearby.
Reservations, fee: No reservations; $6 fee per night; pets $1.
Who to contact: Phone Big Lagoon County Park at (707)445-7652.
Location: Drive eight miles north of Trinidad on Highway 101.
Trip note: This is a remarkable, huge lagoon that borders the Pacific Ocean. It provides good boating, fishing, exploring, and in winter, duck hunting.

Site **5**   PATRICK'S POINT   ▲
                              STATE PARK

Campsites, facilities: There are 123 campsites for tents or motorhomes up to 31 feet long. Piped water, flush toilets, showers, fireplaces and picnic tables are provided.
Reservations, fee: Reservations are strongly advised during summer, available through MISTIX by phoning (800)446-7275. Sites are $10 per night; $1 for pets.
Who to contact: Phone Patrick's Point State Park at (707)677-3570.
Location: The park is located five miles north of Trinidad on Highway 101.
Trip note: Unique trails that probe in virtual tunnels through fern vegetation is a highlight, along with beach lookouts and common whale sightings. Often foggy and damp, but always beautiful.

Site **6**   HIDDEN   ▲
                                  CREEK

Campsites, facilities: There are 10 tent spaces, 37 motorhome spaces, and 13 sites for tents or motorhomes. Partial and full hookups are available. A sanitary disposal station and propane gas can be found in the park. A short walk will get you to a laudromat and grocery store.
Reservations, fee: Reservations advised through Leisuretime by phoning (800)822-2267. Campsite fee is $8 per night.
Location: The park is located in Trinidad at 199 North Westhaven.
Trip note: Some of California's best deep sea fishing for salmon, lingcod and rockfish is available on boats out of nearby Trinidad Harbor. Good beachcombing for agates, driftwood.

Site 7	CLAM BEACH	

Campsites, facilities: There are 100 campsites for both tents or motorhomes. Water, pit toilets, propane, a grocery store and a laundromat arc available.
Reservations, fee: Reservations not necessary. Campsite fee is $5 per night; $1 for pets.
Who to contact: Phone Clam Beach County Park at (707)445-7652.
Location: Drive two miles west of McKinleyville off Highway 101.
Trip note: Good perch fishing where the Mad River pours into the ocean. Some steelhead fishing in January, February. Open year around.

Site 8	EUREKA KOA	

Campsites, facilities: There are 25 tent sites and 140 motorhome spaces with full or partial hookups. Piped water, flush toilets, showers, fireplaces and picnic tables are provided. A grocery store, laudromat, propane and playground are nearby.
Reservations, fee: Reservations required with a $12 deposit. $12 fee per night; pets allowed.
Who to contact: Phone Eureka KOA at (707)822-4243.
Location: Eureka KOA is located four miles northeast of Eureka at 4050 North Highway 101.
Trip note: Open year around. Ocean charter boats available for salmon fishing. Good clam digging, beachcombing on local coast.

Site 9	EBB TIDE PARK	

Campsites, facilities: There are six sites for tents or motorhomes, and 76 motorhome sites with full or partial hookups. Piped water, flush toilets, showers, picnic tables, a santiary dump station and a laundromat are available.
Reservations, fee: Reservation required with a $10 deposit. Camp fee is $10 per night; pet permitted.
Who to contact: Phone Ebb Tide Park at (707)445-2273.
Location: One mile east of Eureka off Highway 101 at 2600 Sixth Street.
Trip note: Open year around. Near the Fort Humboldt State Historical Park.

Site 10	SAMOA BOAT LAUNCH	

Campsites, facilities: There are 40 motorhome spaces at this county park. Piped water and flush toiles are provided. Grocery shopping, propane gas and a laundromat are available nearby.

Reservations, fee: Reservations not required. Fee is $5 per night; $1 for pets.
Who to contact: Phone the Samoa Boat Launch at (707)445-7652.
Location: From Highway 101 in Eureka, drive on Route 255 across Humboldt
Bay to the Samoa Peninsula.
Trip note: Open year around. Near the famed all-you-can-eat logger-style Samoa
Cookhouse. Good beachcombing and clamming on low tides. Located
across the bay from Humboldt Bay National Wildlife Refuge.

Site **11**   E-Z
                                  LANDING

Campsites, facilities: There are 55 motorhome spaces with full hookups. Piped
water and flush toilets are provided. Showers and a laundromat are
available.
Reservations, fee: Reservation required with a $13.50 deposit. Site fee $13.50 per
night; pets allowed.
Who to contact: Phone E-Z Landing RV Park and Marina at (707)442-1118.
Location: Situated five miles south of Eureka on Highway 101 at 1875 Buhne
Drive.
Trip note: Good base camp for salmon trips in July and August. Boat launch
available. Ideal for ocean fishing, clamming, beachcombing and boating.

Site **12**   JOHNNY'S
                                  MARINA

Campsites, facilities: There are 53 motorhome spaces with full hookups. Piped
water, flush toilets, showers, sanitary disposal station and laundromat are all
provided.
Reservations, fee: Reservation through Leisuretime strongly advised by phoning
(800)822-2267. Camp fee is $10.95 per night.
Who to contact: Phone Johnny's Marina and RV Park at (707)442-2284.
Location: Situated along the Pacific Ocean five miles south of Eureka off King
Salmon Ave. and Highway 101 at 1821 Buhne Drive.
Trip note: Boat rentals, launching and mooring available. Beachcombing, clam-
ming, perch fishing from shore. Charter fishing trips at nearby wharf.

Site **13**   A.W. WAY
                                  PARK

Campsites, facilities: There are 30 campsites for tents or motorhomes. Piped wa-
ter, flush toilets, showers, fireplaces and picnic tables are provided. A gro-
cery store, laundromat and propane gas are available.
Reservations, fee: Reservations not required. Camp fee is $6 per night; pets $1.
Who to contact: Phone A.W. Way County Park at (707)445-7652.
Location: Drive seven and one half miles southeast of Petrolia via Mattole Road.
Trip note: A secluded, hidden camp. Steelhead fishing from mid-December to

March on Mattole River. Heavy rain area in winter, often foggy in summer.

Site **14** HORSE
MOUNTAIN

Campsites, facilities: There are nine campsites for tents or motorhomes up to 15 feet long. Piped water, vault toilets, fireplaces and tables are provided.
Reservations, fee: No reservations; $2 fee per night.
Who to contact: Phone Bureau of Land Management at (707)822-7648.
Location: Drive 20 miles west of Briceland via Shelter Cove and Kings Peak Road.
Trip note: Open year around. Elevation 2000 feet. A spot few people know about. Good hiking, and in the fall, hunting.

Site **15** TOLKAN

Campsites, facilities: There are nine campsites here for tents or motorhomes up to 15 feet long. Piped water, vault toilets fireplaces and picnic tables are provided. A grocery store is nearby.
Reservations, fee: No reservations; $2 fee per night.
Who to contact: Phone Tolkan Camp through the Bureau of Land Management at (707)822-7648.
Location: Drive 20 miles west of Briceland off Shelter Cove Road on Kings Peak Road.
Trip note: Open year around. Elevation 1840 feet. Good hiking and exploring in nearby Bear Creek.

Site **16** NADELOS

Campsites, facilities: There are 12 tent sites and two areas for tents or motorhomes up to 30 feet long. Piped water, vault toilets, fireplaces and picnic tables are provided. Groceries and propane are available nearby.
Reservations, fee: No reservations; $2 per night fee; pets allowed.
Who to contact: Call the Bureau of Land Management at (707)822-7648.
Location: Nadelos is located 18 miles southwest of Briceland off Shelter Cove Road, on Chemise Mountain Road.
Trip note: Open year around. Elevation 1840 feet. Good opportunities for hiking.

Site **17** HUCKLEBERRY

Campsites, facilities: There are 36 campsites for tents or motorhomes up to 30

feet. Piped water, flush toilets, showers, fireplaces and picnic tables are provided. A grocery store, a sanitary disposal station and propane gas are available.

Reservations, fee: Reservations a must in summer months through MISTIX by phoning (800)446-7275. $10 per night fee; pets $1.

Who to contact: Call Richardson Grove State Park at (707)946-2311.

Location: Located eight miles south of Garberville on Highway 101.

Trip note: Set in a giant grove of coastal redwoods, the tallest trees in the world. Good hiking, sight-seeing, but often crowded by tourists in summer months. Good base camp in winter months for steelhead fishing in South Fork of Eel River.

Site **18**   MADRONE   ▲

Campsites, facilities: There are 40 sites for tents or motorhome to 30 feet long. Piped water, flush toilets, showers, fireplaces and picnic tables are provided. A grocery store, sanitary disposal station and propane are available nearby.

Reservations, fee: Reservations usually necessary through MISTIX by phoning (800)446-7275. $10 per night fee; pets $1.

Who to contact: Phone Richardson Grove State Park at (707)946-2311.

Location: Park is set eight miles south of Garberville on Highway 101.

Trip note: See trip notes for No. 17, Huckleberry Camp.

Site **19**   OAK
                               FLAT   ▲

Campsites, facilities: There are 94 campsites for tents or motorhomes to 30 feet long. Piped water, flush toilets, showers, fireplaces and picnic tables are provided. Grocery Store, sanitary disposal station and propane are available nearby.

Reservations, fee: Reservations necessary is summer months through MISTIX by phoning (800)446-7275. $10 per night fee; pets $1.

Who to contact: Phone Richardson Grove State Park at (707)946-2311.

Location: Set eight miles south of Garberville on Highway 101.

Trip note: One of three campgrounds in Richardson Grove State Park. See trip note for No. 17, Huckleberry Camp.

Site **20**   BENBOW
                               LAKE   ▲

Campsites, facilities: There are 76 campsites for tents or motorhomes up to 30 feet long. Piped water, flush toilets, showers, fireplaces and picnic tables are provided. Grocery store, laundromat and propane are available nearby.

Reservations, fee: Reservations strongly suggested from May through September through MISTIX by phoning (800)446-7275. Camp fee $10; pets $1.

Who to contact: Phone Benbow Lake State Recreation Area at (707)247-3318.

Location: Drive two miles south from Garberville on Highway 101.

Trip note: Located on South Fork of the Eel River, which gets heavy use in summer. River dammed to make Benbow Lake for swimming and light boating. In winter, a good spot for steelhead fishing.

| Site 21 | BENBOW VALLEY RV PARK | |

Campsites, facilities: There are 112 paved motorhome sites with full hookups, lawns, trees and picnic tables. Cable TV, rest rooms, showers, laundromat, grocery store, gas, restaurant, playground, recreation room, 9-hole golf course and summer lake boat rentals are available.

Reservations, fee: Deposit required with reservation; camp fee $19 per night.

Who to contact: Phone Benbow Valley RV Park at (707)923-2777.

Location: Set along South Fork of Eel River two miles south of Garberville off Highway 101 at 700 Benbow Drive.

Trip note: Open year around. A home away from home. Not for those who want isolation, but a nice spot along the river with all amenities available. Leashed pets allowed.

| Site 22 | DEAN CREEK RESORT | |

Campsites, facilities: There are 40 motorhome sites, all with water, electricity, cable TV, a picnic table and barbeque. Twenty sites have sewer hookups. Available is a laundromat, store, giant spa, sauna, sanitary dump station and recreation room. In summer, innertubes and tandem bikes are available.

Reservations, fee: An $11 deposit required; $11 fee per night.

Who to contact: Phone Dean Creek Resort at (707)923-2555.

Location: Set four miles north of Garberville off Highway 101 on Redwood Drive.

Trip note: Open year around. Set on South Fork of Eel River, with good steelhead fishing in winter.

| Site 23 | GIANT REDWOODS RV PARK | |

Campsites, facilities: There are 66 sites for motorhomes to 40 feet long, each with electricity, water, cable TV, table and firepit. Thirty sites have sewer hookups. There are also 30 tent sites. A store, ice, propane, laundromat, dump station, and recreation room are available.

Reservations, fee: Reservations strongly suggested between May and September through Leisuretime Reservations by phoning (800)822-2267; $11 per night fee.

Who to contact: Phone Giant Redwoods RV Camp at (707)943-3198.

Location: The camp is set in Myers Flat on Myers Road, just off Avenue of the Giants.

Trip note: Scenic drive on Avenue of the Giants. Park has 23 acres, much of it fronting the Eel River. Open year around.

Site **24**   HIDDEN
                         SPRINGS

Campsites, facilities: There are 50 tent sites and 105 sites for tents or motorhomes to 30 feet long. Piped water, flush toilets, showers, fireplaces and picnic tables are provided. Grocery store, laundromat and propane gas are available nearby.

Reservations, fee: Reservations suggested through Mistix by phoning (800)446-7275. $6 fee; pets $1.

Who to contact: Phone Humboldt Redwoods State Park at (707)946-2311.

Location: Park is set one mile south of Myers Flat off Highway 101.

Trip note: Open from May through September, when it gets heavy use. Good hiking on redwood trails.

Site **25**   BURLINGTON

Campsites, facilities: There are 14 tent sites and 20 sites for tents or motorhomes up to 27 feet long. Piped water, flush toilets, showers, fireplaces and picnic tables are provided. Grocery store, laundromat and propane gas are available.

Reservations, fee: Reservations suggested through MISTIX by phoning (800)446-7275. $10 fee per night; pets $1.

Who to contact: Phone Humboldt Redwoods State Park at (707)946-2311.

Location: Burlington Camp is two miles south of Weott off Highway 101 on Avenue of the Giants.

Trip note: Open year around, often to capacity in summer months. Good hiking in redwoods. Winter fishing for steelhead in Eel River.

Site **26**   ALBEE
                         CREEK

Campsites, facilities: There are 14 sites for tents and 20 sites for tents or motorhomes up to 30 feet long. Piped water, flush toilets, showers, fireplaces and picnic tables are provided.

Reservations, fee: Reservations urged during summer through MISTIX by phoning (800)446-7275. $10 per night; $1 for pets.

Who to contact: Phone Humboldt Redwoods State Park at (707)946-2311.

Location: Drive eight miles northwest of Weott off Highway 101 via Bull Creek Flats Road.

Trip note: Open from May through September. One of the more secluded camp-grounds in Humboldt Redwoods State Park. Good hiking in area.

Site **27**   STAFFORD
RV PARK

Campsites, facilities: There are 40 sites for motorhomes up to 40 feet long with water and electricity. Thirteen sites have sewer hookups. There are 31 tent sites. Piped water, flush toilets, showers, fireplaces and picnic tables are provided. Playground, sanitary disposal station, satellite TV reception and gas are available.

Reservations, fee: Reservations made through Leisuretime by phoning (800)822-2267; $7 per night fee.

Who to contact: Phone Stafford RV Park at (707)764-3416.

Location: Stafford RV Park is set three miles south of Scotia off Highway 101 at 385 North Road.

Trip note: Tour of giant sawmill or drive through redwoods in Avenue of the Giants. River access.

Site **28**   VAN DUZEN
COUNTY PARK

Campsites, facilities: There are 40 sites for tents or motorhomes. Piped water, flush toilets, fireplaces and picnic tables are provided. Grocery store and laundromat are available nearby.

Reservations, fee: No reservations; $6 camp fee per night; pets $1.

Who to contact: Phone at (707)445-7652.

Location: Drive six miles east of Carlotta on State Route 36.

Trip note: Relatively hidden compared to state parks in area. Open year around, but gets heavy rain in winter.

Site **29**   GRIZZLY CREEK
REDWOODS

Campsites, facilities: There are 36 sites for tents and 30 sites for tents or motor-homes up to 30 feet long. Piped water, flush toilets, showers, fireplaces and picnic tables are provided. A laundromat and grocery store are available.

Reservations, fee: Reservations suggested through MISTIX by phoning (800)446-7275. $10 per night fee; pets $1.

Who to contact: Phone at (707)777-3683.

Location: Park is set eight miles west of Bridgeville on State Route 36.

Trip note: Open year around. Relatively secluded for a state park. Beautiful setting in redwoods.

Site 30   BOISE
                                     CREEK   ▲

Campsites, facilities: There are 10 sites for tents and two sites for tents or motor-
homes up to 22 feet long. Piped water, vault toilets, picnic tables and fire-
places are provided. Grocery store, laundromat, propane available.
Reservations, fee: No reservations; $4 per night fee.
Who to contact: Phone Six Rivers National Forest at (707)442-1721.
Location: Located two miles west of Willow Creek on State Route 299.
Trip note: During fall and winter, good salmon and steelhead fishing on nearby
Trinity River. Keep your eyes on lookout for giant footprints; this is Bigfoot
country.

Site 30   TISH
                                      TANG   ▲

Campsites, facilities: There are 28 sites for tents and 14 sites for tents or motor-
homes up to 32 feet long. Piped water, vault toilets, picnic tables and fire-
places are provided.
Reservations, fee: No reservations; $3 per night fee.
Who to contact: Phone Six Rivers National Forest at (707)442-1721.
Location: Drive eight miles north of Willow Creek on State Route 96.
Trip note: Camp set above Trinity River. Hot weather during the summer.
Highway 96 is twisty from Willow Creek to Weitchpec.

Site 32   AIKENS   ▲

Campsites, facilities: There are 29 sites for tents or motorhomes to 22 feet long.
Piped water, vault toilets, picnic tables, fireplaces and sanitary disposal sta-
tion are provided.
Reservations, fee: No reservations; $4 fee per night.
Who to contact: Phone Six Rivers National Forest at (707)442-1721.
Location: Camp is set five miles northeast of Weitchpec on State Route 96.
Trip note: Located along Klamath River, just outside edge of Indian Reservation.
Good steelhead fishing from mid-August through mid-December.

Site 33   BLUFF CREEK
                                  GROUP CAMP   ▲

Campsites, facilities: There are 12 sites for tents or motorhomes to 22 feet long.
Two of the sites are on the Klamath River and have fish smokers. Piped
water, vault toilets, picnic tables and fireplaces are provided.
Reservations, fee: No reservations; $10 group fee per night.
Who to contact: Phone Six Rivers National Forest at (707)442-1721.

Location: Camp is set 10 miles southwest of Orleans on State Route 96.

Trip note: Camp in ideal setting on Klamath River. Good steelhead fishing in the fall and winter.

Site **34**
FISH
LAKE

Campsites, facilities: There are 10 sites for tents and 13 sites for tents or motorhomes to 22 feet long. Piped water, vault toilets, picnic tables and fireplaces are provided.

Reservations, fee: No reservations; $3 per night fee.

Who to contact: Phone Six Rivers National Forest at (707)442-1721.

Location: Campground is set along Fish Lake, 16 miles southwest of Orleans off State Route 96.

Trip note: Good trout fishing for stocked rainbow trout in June and July. Gets little camping pressure in other months. Located in the heart of Bigfoot country.

Site **35**
MOUNTAIN VIEW
RANCH

Campsites, facilities: There are 28 motorhome sites, all with full hookups. Rest rooms, showers, laundromat and sanitary disposal station are available.

Reservations, fee: A $9 deposit is required; fee is $9 per night.

Who to contact: Phone at (916)627-3354.

Location: This RV park is located two miles southwest of Orleans on Redcap Road.

Trip note: Open from April to December, with good fishing in Klamath River from August to December.

Site **36**
PEARCH
CREEK

Campsites, facilities: There are nine sites for tents and two sites for tents or motorhomes to 22 feet long. Piped water, vault toilets, picnic tables and fireplaces are provided. Grocery store, laundromat and propane gas are available nearby.

Reservations, fee: No reservations; $3 per night fee.

Who to contact: Phone Six Rivers National Forest at (707)442-1721.

Location: Drive one mile northeast of Orleans on State Route 96.

Trip note: Camp is open year around and has fish smokers, which is either a sign of optimisim or tells you how good the fishing can be on the Klamath. Indeed, the fishing is excellent, especially for 18- to 22-inch steelhead from August through November.

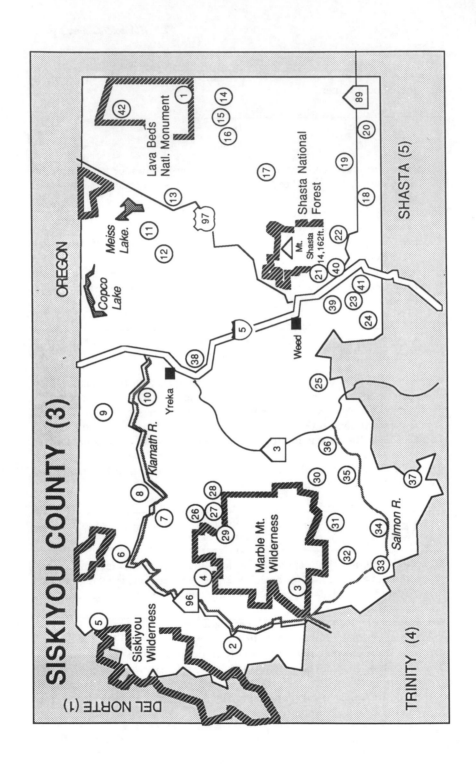

SISKIYOU COUNTY (3)

MAP THREE

SISKIYOU COUNTY

◆

Site **1**   LAVA BEDS NATIONAL MONUMENT
INDIAN WELL

Campsites, facilities: The campground at Lava Beds consists of 40 sites suitable
for tents, pickup campers or small trailers. Each site has a picnic table, fire
ring and cooking grill. During the summer season, which extends from
Memorial Day to Labor Day, water and flush toilets are available. Rangers
are also available during the summer to lead activities, including nightly
campfire programs. During the winter, the water in the campground is
turned off and only pit toilets are available. However, water and flush toilets
are always available at camp headquarters. The town of Tulelake (30 miles
north of the headquarters) is the nearest supply station.

Reservations, fee: No reservations. Winter camping is free, but in the summer, a
$5 fee is charged per night.

Who to contact: Call Lava Beds National Monument at (916)667-2282.

Location: The campground at Lava Beds is situated about 3/4 mile from the
headquarters, 30 miles south of Tulelake off Highway 139.

Trip note: See the audio-visual program at the Visitor Center, then explore one
(or more) of the 20 developed lava tube caves, climb a cinder cone, visit
Mammoth Crater, view Indian pictographs, visit the Thomas-Wright Bat-
tlefield, explore Captain Jack's stronghold, or visit the Wildlife Overlooks at
Tule Lake. Nearby Klamath National Wildlife Refuge is the Pacific
Flyway's largest bald eagle wintering spot.

Site **2**   DILLON CREEK
KLAMATH NATIONAL FOREST

Campsites, facilities: There are 10 tent sites and 11 motorhome sites. The maximum length allowed for motorhomes is 32 feet. Water, vault toilets, picnic
table and a fireplace provided.

Reservations, fee: No reservations; $4 fee per night.

Who to contact: Phone Klamath National Forest Headquarters at (916)842-6131.

Location: The camp is located 15 miles north of Somes Bar on Highway 96.

Trip note: Open year around. Elevation 800 feet. Some of the Klamath River's
best bankfishing access is along this stretch of river. Steelhead prospects are
best from mid-August through winter.

Site 3

OAK BOTTOM
KLAMATH NATIONAL FOREST

Campsites, facilities: There are 20 tent sites and 36 campsites for tents and motorhomes up to 32 feet. Water, vault toilets, picnic tables and fireplaces are provided. Grocery store nearby.
Reservations, fee: No reservations; $4 fee per night.
Who to contact: Phone Klamath National Forest Headquarters at (916)842-6131.
Location: Set three miles east of Somes Bar on Somes Bar-Etna Road.
Trip note: Elevation 700 feet. Open year around. Good steelhead fishing on Klamath River from September through December. An option for fisherman is heading up the Salmon River, which feeds into the Klamath at Somes Bar.

Site 4

SULPHUR SPRINGS
KLAMATH NATIONAL FOREST

Campsites, facilities: Walk-in tent sites with non-piped water (spring, stream), vault toilets, picnic tables and fireplaces provided.
Reservations, fee: No reservations, no fee.
Who to contact: Phone Klamath National Forest Headquarters at (916)842-6131.
Location: Set 14 miles south of Happy Camp on Elk Creek Road.
Trip note: Open May through October. Elevation 3100 feet. Located in the heart of the Klamath River Country.

Site 5

WEST BRANCH
KLAMATH NATIONAL FOREST

Campsites, facilities: There are 15 tent sites and camp spaces for tents or motorhomes up to 32 feet. Water, vault toilets, picnic tables and fireplaces provided.
Reservations, fee: No reservations, no fee.
Who to contact: Phone Klamath National Forest Headquarters at (916)842-6131.
Location: Set 14 1/2 miles northwest of Happy Camp off Indian Creek Road.
Trip note: Open May through October. Elevation 2200 feet. Located on the edge of the Siskiyou wilderness. Forest Service maps are very helpful for back country orientation and locating the region's many remote hiking trails.

Site 6

FORT GOFF
KLAMATH NATIONAL FOREST

Campsites, facilities: There are five campsites, with non-piped water (spring, stream), vault toilets, picnic tables and fireplaces. A grocery store and laundromat are nearby.
Reservations, fee: No reservations, no fee.
Who to contact: Phone Klamath National Forest Headquarters at (916)842-6131.
Location: Set five miles northwest of Seiad Valley on Highway 96.

Trip note: Open May through October. Elevation 1400 feet. Best shorefishing spots on the Klamath River are in this area. Most productive fishing is in the fall and winter for steelhead.

Site **7**
O'NEIL CREEK
KLAMATH NATIONAL FOREST

Campsites, facilities: There are 10 tent sites and 14 campsites for motorhomes up to 22 feet. Non-piped water (spring, stream), vault toilets, picnic tables and fireplaces provided. A grocery store and laundromat are nearby.
Reservations, fee: No reservations, no fee.
Who to contact: Phone Klamath National Forest Headquarters at (916)842-6131.
Location: Set five miles east of Seiad Valley on Highway 96.
Trip note: Open May through November. Elevation 1500 feet. Good shoreline access for fishermen in this area.

Site **8**
SARAH TOTTEN
KLAMATH NATIONAL FOREST

Campsites, facilities: There are 12 tent sites, five motorhome spaces and five group sites. Maximum length allowed for motorhomes is 22 feet. Piped water, vault toilets, picnic tables and fireplaces are provided. Grocery store is nearby.
Reservations, fee: No reservations; $4 fee per night.
Who to contact: Phone Klamath National Forest Headquarters at (916)842-6131.
Location: Camp is located 1/2 mile northeast of Hamburg on State Route 96.
Trip note: Open year around. Elevation 1400 feet. One of the better Klamath River Forest Service campgrounds.

Site **9**
BEAVER CREEK
KLAMATH NATIONAL FOREST

Campsites, facilities: There are eight campsites. Piped water, vault toilets, picnic tables and fireplaces provided.
Reservations, fee: No reservations, no fee.
Who to contact: Phone Klamath National Forest Headquarters at (916)842-6131.
Location: Set four miles northeast of Klamath River on Beaver Creek Road.
Trip note: Open May through October. Elevation 2400 feet. Good steelhead fishing in fall, kayaking or canoeing in summer. Kayak and canoe rentals and lessons available at Beaver Creek Lodge.

Site **10**
TREE OF HEAVEN
KLAMATH NATIONAL FOREST

Campsites, facilities: There are 10 tent sites and 11 motorhome spaces. Maximum length allowed for motorhomes is 22 feet. Piped-water, vault toilets,

picnic table and fireplace provided.
Reservations, fee: No reservations; $5 fee per night.
Who to contact: Phone Klamath National Forest Headquarters at (916)842-6131.
Location: Twelve miles northwest of Yreka on Highway 96.
Trip note: Open May through October. Elevation 2100 feet. Camp is right on the Klamath River. A prime hideaway, not far from Highway 5.

Site **11**   JUANITA
                  KLAMATH NATIONAL FOREST   ◩

Campsites, facilities: There are 12 tent sites and 11 spaces for motorhomes up to 32 feet. Piped water, vault toilets, picnic tables and fireplaces provided. Boating allowed, but no motorboats on lake.
Reservations, fee: No reservations; $4 fee per night.
Who to contact: Phone Klamath National Forest Headquarters at (916)842-6131.
Location: Set eight and a half miles west of Macdoel via Meiss Lake-Sam's Neck Road.
Trip note: Open May through October. Elevation 5100 feet. Forest Service map details nearby fishing, hiking.

Site **12**   MARTIN'S
                     DAIRY   ◩

Campsites, facilities: There are two tent sites and seven motorhome spaces. Non-piped water (spring, stream), vault toilets, picnic tables and fireplaces provided.
Reservations, fee: No reservations, no fee.
Who to contact: Phone Klamath National Forest Headquarters at (916)842-6131.
Location: Set 30 miles southwest of Macdoel off Ball Mountain and Little Shasta Roads.
Trip note: Open June through October. Elevation 6000 feet. This is a secluded, little-known campground. Before heading into the backcountry, obtain a map of Klamath National Forest.

Site **13**   SHAFTER
                  KLAMATH NATIONAL FOREST   ◩

Campsites, facilities: There are 14 camping or motorhome spaces. Maximum length allowed for motorhomes is 32 feet. Piped water, vault toilets, picnic tables and fireplaces provided. A grocery store is nearby.
Reservations, fee: No reservations; $3 fee per night.
Who to contact: Phone Klamath National Forest Headquarters at (916)842-6131.
Location: Set six and a half miles south of Mt. Hebron via Old State Highway.
Trip note: Open May through October. Elevation 4300 feet. Some good views to the south of Mt. Shasta as you drive south on Highway 97.

Site 14 | MEDICINE LAKE |

Campsites, facilities: There are 44 tent and motorhome spaces. Piped water, vault toilets, picnic tables and fireplaces provided.

Reservations, fee: No reservations; $4 fee per night.

Who to contact: Phone Modoc National Forest Headquarters at (916)233-5811.

Location: Set 31 miles northeast of Bartle off Medicine Lake Road.

Trip note: Open June through October. Elevation 6700 feet. Set along Medicine Lake. A remote camping option for car campers.

Site 15 | HEMLOCK |

Campsites, facilities: There are 22 tent and motorhome spaces. Maximum length allowed for motorhomes is 22 feet. Piped water, vault toilets, picnic tables and fireplaces provided.

Reservations, fee: No reservations; fee $4 per night.

Who to contact: Phone Modoc National Forest Headquarters at (916)233-5811.

Location: Set 31 miles northeast of Bartle off Medicine Lake Road.

Trip note: Open June through October. Elevation 6700 feet. Set along shoreline of Medicine Lake.

Site 16 | HEADQUARTERS |

Campsites, facilities: There are five tent and motorhome spaces. Piped water, vault toilets, picnic tables and fireplaces provided.

Reservations, fee: No reservations; fee $3 per night.

Who to contact: Phone Modoc National Forest Headquarters at (916)233-5811.

Location: Set 31 miles northeast of Bartle off Medicine Lake Road.

Trip note: Open June through October. Elevation 6700 feet. A little known site. It can quickly turn cold, even in summer.

Site 17 | HARRIS SPRINGS
SHASTA TRINITY NATIONAL FOREST |

Campsites, facilities: There are 15 tent and rnotorhome spaces. Maximum length allowed for motorhomes is 32 feet. Piped water, vault toilets, picnic tables and fireplaces provided.

Reservations, fee: Call for current rates.

Who to contact: Phone Shasta-Trinity National Forest Headquarters at (916)246-5222.

Location: Set 17 miles east of McCloud on Highway 89, then 17 miles north on Medicine Lake Road (Bartle turn-off).

Trip note: Open May 15 through September 15. Maps of Shasta-Trinity National Forest detail the back country roads, hiking trails and area streams.

Site **18**
FOWLER'S CAMP
SHASTA TRINITY NATIONAL FOREST

Campsites, facilities: There are 39 tent and motorhome spaces. Maximum length allowed for motorhomes is 32 feet. Piped water, vault toilets, picnic tables and fireplaces are provided.
Reservations, fee: No reservations; $4 fee per night.
Who to contact: Phone Shasta-Trinity National Forest Headquarters at (916)246-5222.
Location: Set six and a half miles east of McCloud off Highway 89.
Trip note: Open May 15 through September 15. Elevation 3500 feet. Beautiful camp set along upper McCloud River, with good trout fishing, several waterfalls and views of Mount Shasta.

Site **19**
CATTLE CAMP
SHASTA TRINITY NATIONAL FOREST

Campsites, facilities: There are two tent sites and spaces for six motorhomes up to 32 feet. No water available, but vault toilets and fireplace provided.
Reservations, fee: No reservations, no fee.
Who to contact: Phone Shasta-Trinity National Forest Headquarters at (916)246-5222.
Location: Set 11 miles east of McCloud off Highway 89.
Trip note: Open May 15 through September 15. Elevation 3800 feet. A primitive and secluded campground. Be sure to bring your own water.

Site **20**
ALGOMA
SHASTA TRINITY NATIONAL FOREST

Campsites, facilities: There are two tent and six motorhome spaces. Maximum length allowed for motorhomes is 32 feet. No water, but vault toilets, picnic tables and fireplaces provided.
Reservations, fee: No reservations, no fee.
Who to contact: Phone Shasta Trinity National Forest Headquarters at (916)246-5222.
Location: Set 14 miles east of McCloud off Highway 89.
Trip note: Open May 15 through September 15. Elevation 3800 feet. A prime spot in a primitive setting which offers excellent fishing on the McCloud River. Bring your own water.

| Site 21 | MCBRIDE SPRINGS SHASTA TRINITY NATIONAL FOREST | |

Campsites, facilities: There are six tent sites and three motorhome spaces. Maximum length allowed for motorhomes is 16 feet. Piped water, vault toilets, picnic tables and fireplaces provided. A grocery store and laundromat are nearby.

Reservations, fee: No reservations; $3 fee per night.

Who to contact: Phone Shasta-Trinity National Forest Headquarters at (916)246-5222.

Location: Set four and a half miles northeast of Mount Shasta off Highway 5 on Everitt Memorial Highway.

Trip note: Open May through October. Elevation 5000 feet. A nice spot with Lake Siskiyou, Lake McCloud and Lake Shastina not far away.

| Site 22 | PANTHER MEADOW | |

Campsites, facilities: There are four tent and motorhome spaces. Maximum length allowed for motorhomes is 16 feet. No water, but vault toilets, picnic tables and fireplaces provided.

Reservations, fee: No reservations, no fee.

Who to contact: Phone Shasta-Trinity National Forest Headquarters at (916)246-5222.

Location: Located 13 1/2 miles northeast of Mount Shasta on Everitt Memorial Highway.

Trip note: Open May 15 through September 15. Elevation 7400 feet. Very quiet site located on the slopes of Mount Shasta. A potential jump-off spot for hikes to the summit, or a one- or two-day trip for well-prepared hikers.

| Site 23 | CASTLE LAKE SHASTA TRINITY NATIONAL FOREST | |

Campsites, facilities: There are six tent sites available. No water, but vault toilets, picnic table and fireplace provided.

Reservations, fee: No reservations, no fee.

Who to contact: Phone Shasta-Trinity National Forest Headquarters at (916)246-5222.

Location: Set 11 1/2 miles southwest of Mount Shasta off Barr Road on Castle Lake Road.

Trip note: Open May 15 through September 15. Small lake provides boating in summer, ice skating in winter. Spectacular view of Mt. Shasta to the east. This site is transformed into a Nordic Ski Center in winter.

Site **24**
GUMBOOT
SHASTA TRINITY NATIONAL FOREST

Campsites, facilities: There are four tent and motorhome spaces. Maximum
   length allowed for motorhomes is 16 feet. No water, but vault toilets and
   picnic tables provided at campsites.
Reservations, fee: No reservations, no fee.
Who to contact: Phone Shasta-Trinity National Forest Headquarters at (916)246-
   5222.
Location: Set at Gumboot Lake, 17 miles southwest of Mount Shasta off Highway 5.
Trip note: Open May 15 through September 15. Elevation 6200 feet. Prime trout
   fishing lake for float tubers or from a raft. The lake is usually iced up until
   mid-June. One of many alpine lakes accessible via Forest Service roads.

Site **25**
KANGAROO
LAKE

Campsites, facilities: There are 11 tent sites at Kangaroo Lake with piped water,
   vault toilets, fireplaces and picnic tables provided.
Reservations, fee: No reservations, no fee.
Who to contact: Phone Klamath National Forest Headquarters at (916)842-6131.
Location: Head 18 1/2 miles northeast of Callahan via State Route 3 and Ga-
   zelle-Callahan Road.
Trip note: Open from June through October. Car-top boats are allowed at Kan-
   garoo Lake. Elevation 6000 feet. A prime, little-known campground.

Site **26**
BRIDGE
FLAT

Campsites, facilities: There are eight sites at Bridge Flat for tents or motorhomes
   up to 22 feet long. Piped water, vault toilets, fireplaces and picnic tables are
   provided.
Reservations, fee: No reservations; $4 fee per night.
Who to contact: Phone Klamath National Forest Headquarters at (916)842-6131.
Location: Set 21 miles west of Fort Jones on Scott River Road.
Trip note: Open May through October. Elevation 2000 feet. Backpackers might
   consider this site as a base camp for hikes into nearby Marble Mountain
   Wilderness. Access to Scott River is nearby.

Site **27**
SPRING
FLAT

Campsites, facilities: There are 16 spaces at Spring Flat for tents only. Piped water, vault toilets, fireplaces and picnic tables are provided.

Reservations, fee: No reservations; $4 fee per night.
Who to contact: Phone Klamath National Forest Headquarters at (916)842-6131.
Location: Set 20 1/2 miles west of Fort Jones on Scott River Road.
Trip note: Open from May through October. Elevation 2200 feet. A quiet and remote spot reachable by car. Good fishing in adjacent Scott River.

Site **28**   INDIAN
               SCOTTY

Campsites, facilities: This camp is made for large groups. There are 27 campsites for tents or motorhomes up to 22 feet in length. Piped water, vault toilets, fireplaces and picnic tables are provided.
Reservations, fee: Reservations made through Scott River Ranger District: (916)468-5351; $4 fee per night.
Who to contact: Phone Klamath National Forest Headquarters at (916)842-6131.
Location: Set 18 miles west of Fort Jones on Scott River Road.
Trip note: Open from May through October. Elevation 2400 feet. Good for group camps. Try fishing on Scott River.

Site **29**   LOVERS
               CAMP

Campsites, facilities: There are 10 tent-only sites. Non-piped water, vault toilets, fireplaces and picnic tables are provided. There are also facilities for stock unloading and a corral.
Reservations, fee: No reservations, no fee.
Who to contact: Phone Klamath National Forest Headquarters at (916)842-6131.
Location: Set 21 miles southwest of Scott Bar off Scott River Road.
Trip note: Open from June through October. Camp trailhead leads into the Marble Mountain Wilderness. Elevation 4300 feet. Be sure to bring water.

Site **30**   IDLEWILD

Campsites, facilities: There are nine tent-only campsites and 14 sites for tents or motorhomes up to 22 feet long. Piped water, vault toilets, fireplaces and picnic tables are provided.
Reservations, fee: No reservations; $4 fee per night.
Who to contact: Phone Klamath National Forest Headquarters at (916)842-6131.
Location: Set six miles northeast of Sawyers Bar on Sawyers Bar Road.
Trip note: Open from June through October. Camp trailhead leads into the Marble Mountains Wilderness. Elevation 2600 feet. A hidden spot that gets very cold in winter.

Site **31**   LITTLE
                              NORTH FORK

Campsites, facilities: There are four tent spaces with piped water, vault toilets,
    picnic tables and fireplaces.
Reservations, fee: No reservations, no fee.
Who to contact: Phone Klamath National Forest Headquarters at (916)842-6131.
Location: Set three and a half miles northwest of Sawyers Bar on Somes Bar -
    Etna Road.
Trip note: Open June through October. Elevation 4300 feet. Trailhead leads to
    Marble Mountains. Fishermen can hole up here during steelhead fishing
    trips on Salmon River in the fall and winter.

Site **32**   RED
                              BANK

Campsites, facilities: There are two sites for tents only and two for tents or motor-
    homes up to 16 feet long. CAUTION: There is water, but it's not piped and
    should be boiled for five minutes before use. Vault toilets, picnic tables and
    fireplaces are provided.
Reservations, fee: No reservations, no fee.
Who to contact: Phone Klamath National Forest Headquarters at (916)842-6131.
Location: Set seven and a half miles west of Sawyers Bar on Somes Bar-Etna
    Road.
Trip note: Open June through October. Elevation 1700 feet. A primitive setting,
    bring your own water. Good hiking on nearby national forest.

Site **33**   MATTHEWS
                              CREEK

Campsites, facilities: There are seven tent only sites and seven sites for tents or
    motorhomes up to 22 feet long. Piped water, vault toilets, fireplaces and
    picnic tables are provided.
Reservations, fee: No reservations, no fee.
Who to contact: Phone Klamath National Forest Headquarters at (916)842-6131.
Location: Set eight and a half miles northwest of Cecilville on Salmon River
    Road.
Trip note: Open June through October. Explore the South Fork of the Salmon
    River. Elevation 1700 feet.

Site **34**   EAST
                              FORK

Campsites, facilities: The East Fork Camp has six tent sites and three sites for
    motorhomes up to 16 feet long. Non-piped water, vault toilets, fireplaces

and picnic tables are provided.

Reservations, fee: No reservations, no fee.

Who to contact: Phone Klamath National Forest Headquarters at (916)842-6131.

Location: Set two miles northeast of Cecilville on Callahan-Cecilville Road.

Trip note: Open June through October. Elevation 2400 feet. Camp is on Salmon River. Check Department of Fish and Game regulations for closed areas on Salmon River.

Site **35**   SHADOW
                                 CREEK   🌲

Campsites, facilities: There are five tent sites and five sites for motorhomes up to 22 feet long. Piped water, vault toilets, fireplaces and picnic tables are provided.

Reservations, fee: No reservations; $4 fee per night.

Who to contact: Phone Klamath National Forest Headquarters at (916)842-6131.

Location: Set seven miles northeast of Cecilville on Callahan Road.

Trip note: Elevation 2900 feet. Open from June through October. Secluded and quiet but no fishing allowed.

Site **36**   TRAIL
                                 CREEK   ▲

Campsites, facilities: There are eight tent sites and seven sites for tents or motor-homes up to 22 feet long. Piped water, vault toilets, fireplaces and picnic tables are provided.

Reservations, fee: No reservations; $4 fee per night.

Who to contact: Phone Klamath National Forest Headquarters at (916)842-6131.

Location: Set 17 miles southwest of Callahan on Callahan-Cecilville Road.

Trip note: Open from May through October. Elevation 4700 feet. Set on upper Salmon River. Hunters welcome.

Site **37**   BIG
                                 FLAT   ▲

Campsites, facilities: There are five campsites for tents or motorhomes up to 16 feet long. Non-piped water, vault toilets, fireplaces and picnic tables are provided.

Reservations, fee: No reservations, no fee.

Who to contact: Phone Klamath National Forest Headquarters at (916)842-6131.

Location: Set 30 miles northwest of Trinity Center off State Route 3 on Coffee Creek Road.

Trip note: Open from July through October. Elevation 5000 feet. Try your hand fishing for small rainbow trout on upper Trinity River.

Site **38**
WAIIAKA
TRAILER HEAVEN

Campsites, facilities: This spot offers 50 motorhome sites, with full hookups. Water, flush toilets, showers, a playground, a laundromat and propane gas are just a few of the amenities offered.

Reservations, fee: Reservations require an $11.00 deposit; $11 fee per night.

Who to contact: Phone (916)842-4500.

Location: In Yreka on Fairlane Road.

Trip note: A good spot for motorhome campers heading up Highway 5.

Site **39**
LAKE SISKIYOU
CAMPGROUND

Campsites, facilities: There are 54 motorhome spaces with full hookups and 245 additional sites for tents or RVs. Piped water, flush toilets, fireplaces, picnic tables, showers, a playground, propane, a grocery store, a laundromat and a sanitary disposal station are all available for campers' use. There are also boat rentals.

Reservations, fee: Reservation fee of $3.50 payable to Leisuretime Reservation Systems, Inc.: (800)822-2267; $10 camping fee per night.

Who to contact: Phone (916)926-2610.

Location: Set four and a half miles southwest of Mt. Shasta off Highway 5 on W. A. Barr Road.

Trip note: Open April through October. Elevation 3200 feet. A gem of a lake set in the shadow of Mt. Shasta, it offers very good trout fishing in May. An option is heading up east fork of Sacramento River, or on nearby Forest Service road to explore several alpine lakes.

Site **40**
MT. SHASTA
KOA

Campsites, facilities: There are 41 motorhome spaces with full hookups, and 89 additional spaces for tents or motorhome (partial hookups). Water, flush toilets, fireplaces, picnic tables, a playground, sanitary disposal station, propane gas, a grocery store and laundromat are available.

Reservations, fee: Reservation fee is $11.00; camping fee $11.00 per night.

Who to contact: Phone (916)926-4029.

Location: In Mt. Shasta at 900 North Mt. Shasta Blvd.

Trip note: Open year around. Elevation 3400 feet. Good layover near Highway 5, it offers excellent fishing prospects at Lake Siskiyou or upper Sacramento River.

| Site 41 | RAILROAD PARK RESORT | ◮ |

Campsites, facilities: There are 60 motorhome sites, with full and partial hookups available. There are also 20 tent sites. A store, laundromat and hot showers are available.

Reservations, fee: Call in advance for space and rates.

Who to contact: Write Railroad Park Resort, 100 Railroad Park Road, Dunsmuir, CA 96025 or call (916)235-9983

Location: Head two miles south of Dunsmuir on Highway 5 and take the Railroad Park exit.

Trip note: Set in spirit of railroad history. Castle Crags, a series of granite spires, rises in background.

| Site 42 | SHADY LANES TRAILER PARK | ◮ |

Campsites, facilities: There are 52 motorhome sites with full hookups. Hot showers and a laundromat are provided.

Reservations, fee: Call in advance for space and rates.

Who to contact: Write Shady Lanes Trailer Park, 795 Modoc Avenue, Box 297, Tulelake, CA 96134 or call (916)667-2617

Location: From Highway 139, take south exit on Eastwest Road to Modoc Avenue, turn left to mid-block.

Trip note: Lava Beds National Monument and Tulelake Game Refuge are nearby. Open year around.

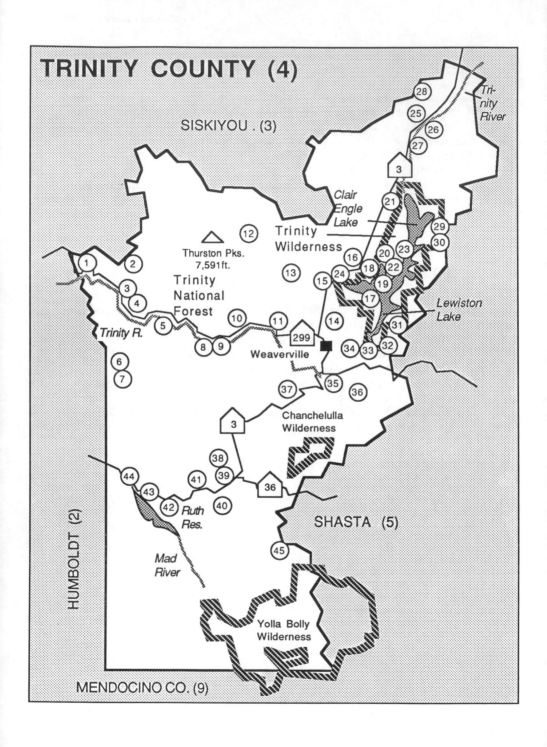

TRINITY COUNTY (4)

SISKIYOU . (3)

Tri-nity River

28

25

26

27

3

Clair Engle Lake

21

Trinity Wilderness

29

30

△
Thurston Pks.
7,591ft.

12

16

20

23

Trinity
National
Forest

13

24

18

22

15

19

Lewiston Lake

1

2

17

3

4

31

Trinity R.

5

10

11

14

299

34

33

32

8

9

Weaverville

35

6

7

37

35

36

Chanchelulla
Wilderness

3

38

39

44

41

36

43

42

40

Ruth
Res.

SHASTA (5)

45

Mad
River

HUMBOLDT (2)

Yolla Bolly
Wilderness

MENDOCINO CO. (9)

MAP FOUR

TRINITY COUNTY

◆

Site 1

LAZY DOUBLE "B"
RV PARK

Campsites, facilities: There are 19 tent sites and 46 motorhome spaces with full or partial hookups. A grocery store, laundromat, sanitary dump station, a playground, hot showers, free firewood, rest rooms, picnic tables and fireplaces are provided.

Reservations, fee: $3.50 reservation fee payable to Leisuretime Reservations Systems, Inc.: (800)822-2267; $10 fee per night.

Who to contact: Phone (916)629-2156.

Location: Set in Salyer on Highway 299, 95 miles west of Redding or 46 miles east of Eureka.

Trip note: Open year around. Elevation 600 feet. Relax on sandy beaches, or go rafting and inner tubing in the beautiful Trinity River. Good salmon fishing in fall, steelhead fishing in winter. Free instruction offered for gold panners. On-site trailer rentals.

Site 2

DENNY

Campsites, facilities: There are 10 tent sites and six campsites that will accommodate tents or motorhomes up to 22 feet long. Piped water, vault toilets, picnic tables and fireplaces provided.

Reservations, fee: No reservations, no fee.

Who to contact: Phone Shasta-Trinity National Forest at (916)246-5222.

Location: Set one and a half miles south of the town of Denny on Denny Road.

Trip note: Open year around. Elevation 2000 feet. Very secluded and quiet.

Site 3

GRAY'S
FALLS

Campsites, facilities: There are 17 tent sites and 16 campsites for tents or motorhomes up to 32 feet long. Piped water, flush toilets, picnic tables and fireplaces are provided.

Reservations, fee: No reservations; $4 fee per night.

Who to contact: Phone Six Rivers National Forest at (707)442-1721.
Location: Set six miles southeast of Salyer on Highway 299.
Trip note: Open from May through November. Elevation 1000 feet. Hike to Gray's Falls from the campground on Trinity River.

Site 4   BURNT
                                RANCH   ◬

Campsites, facilities: There are 11 tent sites and four campsites for tents or motorhomes. Piped water, vault toilets, picnic tables and fireplaces are provided. A grocery store is nearby.
Reservations, fee: No reservations, no fee.
Who to contact: Phone Shasta-Trinity National Forest Headquarters at (916)246-5222.
Location: Set 1/2 mile northwest of Burnt Ranch on Highway 299.
Trip note: Open year around. Elevation 1200 feet. Good base camp for fall or winter fishing trip on the beautiful Trinity River. Picturesque drive in summer.

Site 5   HAYDEN
                                FLAT   ◬

Campsites, facilities: There are 11 tent sites and 24 campsites for tents or motorhomes. Piped water, vault toilets, picnic tables and fireplaces are provided. A grocery store is nearby.
Reservations, fee: No reservations; $4 fee per night.
Who to contact: Phone Shasta-Trinity National Forest at (916)246-5222.
Location: Set 1/2 mile west of Del Loma on Highway 299.
Trip note: Open year around. Elevation 1200 feet. A nice riverside spot.

Site 6   BIG
                                SLIDE   ◬

Campsites, facilities: There are four tent sites and four campsites for tents or motorhomes up to 16 feet long. Non-piped water, vault toilets, picnic tables and fireplaces are provided. A grocery store and laundromat are nearby.
Reservations, fee: No reservations, no fee.
Who to contact: Phone Shasta-Trinity National Forest at (916)246-5222.
Location: Set five miles northwest of Hyampom on Lower South Fork Road.
Trip note: Open from April through November. Elevation 1200 feet. Shasta-Trinity Forest Map details the hiking trails near this little visited spot.

Site 7   SLIDE CREEK

Campsites, facilities: There are four tent spaces. Piped water, vault toilets, picnic tables and fireplaces are provided. A grocery store and laundromat are nearby.

Reservations, fee: No reservations, no fee.

Who to contact: Phone Shasta-Trinity National Forest at (916)246-5222.

Location: Set five miles northwest of Hyampom on Lower South Fork Road.

Trip note: Open from April through November. Elevation 1200 feet. Just about nobody knows about this camp site. Forest Service details back country roads for access.

Site 8   BIG BAR

Campsites, facilities: There are three tent sites here. Piped water, vault toilets, picnic tables and fireplaces are provided. A grocery store is nearby.

Reservations, fee: No reservations, no fee.

Who to contact: Phone Shasta-Trinity National Forest at (916)246-5222.

Location: Set one mile southeast of Big Bar on Highway 299.

Trip note: Open year around. Elevation 1200 feet. Prime Trinity River hideaway.

Site 9   BIG FLAT

Campsites, facilities: There are nine campsites for tents or motorhomes up to 22 feet long. Piped water, vault toilets, picnic tables and fireplaces are provided. A grocery store and laundromat are nearby.

Reservations, fee: No reservations; $4 fee per night.

Who to contact: Phone Shasta-Trinity National Forest at (916)246-5222.

Location: Set in Big Flat on Highway 299.

Trip note: Open year around. Elevation 1200 feet. An option if Site No. 8 is full.

Site 10   PIGEON POINT

Campsites, facilities: There are four tent sites and six campsites for tents or motorhomes up to 22 feet long. No water, but vault toilets, picnic tables and fireplaces provided. A grocery store is nearby.

Reservations, fee: No reservations, no fee.

Who to contact: Phone Shasta-Trinity National Forest at (916)246-5222.

Location: Set two miles west of Helena on Highway 299.

Trip note: Open from May through October. Elevation 1100 feet. Set on Trinity

River. Good salmon fishing in the fall.

Site **11**   JUNCTION
                                CITY

Campsites, facilities: There are 12 campsites for motorhomes up to 30 feet long.
   Piped water, vault toilets, picnic tables and fireplaces are provided. Grocer-
   ies and propane gas are available nearby.
Reservations, fee: No reservations; $4 fee per night.
Who to contact: Phone (916)246-5325 - A Bureau of Land Management
   Campground.
Location: Set 1 1/2 miles northwest of Junction City on Highway 299.
Trip note: Open year around. Elevation 2000 feet. Some of the Trinity River's
   best fall salmon fishing is in this area.

Site **12**   HOBO
                                GULCH

Campsites, facilities: There are 10 sites for tents or motorhomes. Non-piped wa-
   ter, vault toilets, picnic tables and fireplaces provided.
Reservations, fee: No reservations, no fee.
Who to contact: Phone Shasta-Trinity National Forest at (916)246-5222.
Location: Set 20 miles north of Helena via Hobo Gulch Road.
Trip note: Open year around. Elevation 2900 feet. Situated on North Fork of the
   Trinity in the Salmon-Trinity Alps Wilderness Primitive Area. Numerous
   trails lead out from this camp into the wilderness, one of which hooks up to
   the New River Divide Trail.

Site **13**   RIPSTEIN

Campsites, facilities: There are six tent sites and two campsites for tents or mo-
   torhomes. No water, vault toilets, picnic tables and fireplaces are provided.
Reservations, fee: No reservations, no fee.
Who to contact: Phone Shasta-Trinity National Forest at (916)246-5222.
Location: Set 15 miles north of Junction City on Canyon Creek Road.
Trip note: Open year around. Elevation 3000 feet. Good fishing in Canyon
   Creek. Backpackers will enjoy the hike up Canyon Creek Trail to Canyon
   Creek Falls and beyond to the Canyon Creek Lakes, Sawtooth Mountain,
   and the Boulder Creek Lakes. Beware of old mine sites in the area.

Site **14**   EAST
                               WEAVER

Campsites, facilities: There are eight tent sites and seven campsites for tents or mobile homes up to 16 feet long. Piped water, vault toilets, picnic tables and fireplaces are provided. A grocery store and laundromat are nearby.

Reservations, fee: No reservations; $4 fee per night.

Who to contact: Phone Shasta-Trinity National Forest at (916)246-5222.

Location: Set three and a half miles north of Weavervill off Highway 3.

Trip note: Open from May through September. Elevation 2800 feet. Hiking Trail leads to Weaver Lake, Weaver Bally Mountain and Monument Peak.

Site **15**   RUSH
                          CREEK

Campsites, facilities: There are 11 campsites for tents or motorhomes up to 22 feet long. No water, but vault toilets, picnic tables and fireplaces provided.

Reservations, fee: No reservations, no fee.

Who to contact: Shasta-Trinity National Forest at (916)246-5222.

Location: Set nine and a half miles northeast of Weaverville off Highway 3.

Trip note: Open from June through September. Elevation 2700 feet. Primitive spot that offers fishing on Rush Creek, just a few miles from Trinity Lake. Remember to bring your own water.

Site **16**   BRIDGE
                          CAMP

Campsites, facilities: There are eight campsites. Piped water, vault toilets, picnic tables and fireplaces are provided.

Reservations, fee: No reservations; $4 fee per night.

Who to contact: Phone Shasta-Trinity National Forest at (916)246-5222.

Location: Set 17 miles north of Weaverville off Highway 3.

Trip note: Open from May through September. Elevation 2700 feet. Near the south shore of Trinity Lake on Stuart Fork. A wilderness trail leads to Stuart Fork, goes past Oak Flat, Morris Meadows and up to Emerald Lake and the Sawtooth Mountains. Good fishing on Stuart Fork.

Site **17**   TANNERY
                          GULCH

Campsites, facilities: There are 49 tent sites and 20 campsites for tents or motorhomes up to 32 feet long. Piped water, vault toilets, picnic tables and fireplaces are provided. A grocery store and boat ramp are nearby.

Reservations, fee: No reservations; $6 fee per night.

Who to contact: Phone Shasta-Trinity National Forest at (916)246-5222.

Location: Set 13 1/2 miles northeast of Weaverville off Highway 3 at Trinity Lake.

Trip note: Open from May through October. Elevation 2400 feet. Popular Trinity Lake camp.

Site **18**   STONEY
                               POINT   ⛺

Campsites, facilities: There are 22 tent sites. Piped water, flush toilets, picnic ta-
    bles and fireplaces are provided.
Reservations, fee: No reservations, no fee.
Who to contact: Phone Shasta-Trinity National Forest at (916)246-5222.
Location: Set 14 miles north of Weaverville on Highway 3 at Trinity Lake.
Trip note: Open from May through October. Elevation 2400 feet. Nice lakeside
    camp.

Site **19**   MINERSVILLE   ⛺

Campsites, facilities: There are 28 tent sites and two campsites for tents or motor-
    homes up to 22 feet long. Piped water, flush toilets, picnic tables and fire-
    places are provided. A grocery store and boat ramp are nearby.
Reservations, fee: No reservations; $5 fee per night.
Who to contact: Phone Shasta-Trinity National Forest at (916)246-5222.
Location: Set 18 miles northeast of Weaverville off Route 3 at Trinity Lake.
Trip note: Open from June through October. Elevation 2500 feet. A classic shor-
    eline camp on Trinity Lake.

Site **20**   BUSHYTAIL
                               GROUP CAMP   ⛺

Campsites, facilities: There are 27 tent sites and 13 campsites for tents or motor-
    homes up to 22 feet long. Piped water, flush toilets, picnic tables and fire-
    places are provided. A grocery store and a boat ramp are nearby.
Reservations, fee: Reservation required; $30 group fee per night.
Who to contact: Phone Shasta-Trinity National Forest at (916)246-5222.
Location: Set 17 miles northeast of Weaverville off Highway 3 at Trinity Lake.
Trip note: Open from June through September. Elevation 2500 feet.

Site **21**   PREACHER
                               MEADOW   ⛺

Campsites, facilities: There are 45 campsites for tents or motorhomes up to 32
    feet long. Piped water, vault toilets, picnic tables and fireplaces are pro-
    vided. A grocery store, laundromat and boat ramp are nearby.
Reservations, fee: No reservations; $4 fee per night.
Who to contact: Phone Shasta-Trinity National Forest at (916)246-5222.
Location: Set two miles southwest of Trinity Center off Highway 3.
Trip note: Open from May through October. Elevation 2900 feet. To reach
    Salmon-Trinity Alps Primitive Area, take the Swift Creek Trail to Swift

Creek Gorge from Panther Meadows (a day hike).

Site **22**   HAYWARD   ▲
                         FLAT

Campsites, facilities: There are 75 tent sites and 33 campsites that will accomo-
date tents or motorhomes up to 32 feet. Piped water, flush toilets, picnic
tables and fireplaces are provided. A grocery store and a boat ramp are
nearby.
Reservations, fee: No reservations; $6 fee per night.
Who to contact: Phone Shasta-Trinity National Forest at (916)246-5222.
Location: Set 12 miles southwest of Trinity Center off Highway 3 at Trinity
Lake.
Trip note: Open from May through October. Elevation 2400 feet. Trinity Lake
camping option.

Site **23**   ALPINE   ▲
                         VIEW

Campsites, facilities: There are 41 tent sites and 21 campsites for tents or motor-
homes up to 32 feet long. Piped water, flush toilets, picnic tables and fire-
places are provided.
Reservations, fee: No reservations; $5 fee per night.
Who to contact: Phone Shasta-Trinity National Forest at (916)246-5222.
Location: Set nine miles southwest of Trinity Center off Highway 3 at Trinity
Lake.
Trip note: Open from May through October. Elevation 2400 feet.

Site **24**   PINEWOOD COVE   ▲
                         CAMPGROUND

Campsites, facilities: There are 26 tent sites and 48 motorhome spaces with full
or partial hookups. Available are two laundromats, rest rooms, showers, free
movies three nights a week, game room, pinball and video machines, grocery store, ice, fishing tackle, library, boat dock with 32 slips, beach, boat
rental and sanitary dump station.
Reservations, fee: $3.50 reservation fee payable to Leisuretime Reservation Sys-
tems, Inc.: (800)822-2267; $12.50 fee per night; pets $1.
Who to contact: Phone (916)286-2201.
Location: Set 14 miles northeast of Weaverville on Trinity Lake.
Trip note: Open from April through October. Elevation 2300 feet. Reservations
advised during peak season.

Site **25**   HORSE
                               FLAT   ▲

Campsites, facilities: There are nine tent sites and 11 campsites for tents or mo-
    torhomes up to 16 feet long. No water, but vault toilets, picnic tables and
    fireplaces provided.
Reservations, fee: No reservations, no fee.
Who to contact: Phone Shasta-Trinity National Forest at (916)246-5222.
Location: Set 16 1/2 miles north of Trinity Center off Highway 3 at Eagle Lake.
Trip note: Open from June through September. Elevation 3000 feet. Eagle
    Creek Trail leads to Salmon-Trinity Alps Primitive Area. Good fishing
    spot.

Site **26**   EAGLE
                               CREEK   ▲

Campsites, facilities: There are five tent sites and 12 campsites for tents or motor-
    homes up to 22 feet long. Non-piped water, vault toilets, picnic tables and
    fireplaces are provided. A grocery store and laundromat are nearby.
Reservations, fee: No reservations, no fee.
Who to contact: Phone Shasta-Trinity National Forest at (916)246-5222.
Location: Set 16 miles north of Trinity Center off Highway 3 at Eagle Lake.
Trip note: Open from May through October. Elevation 2800 feet. Situated at
    confluence of Eagle Creek and the Trinity River. Bring a rod and reel be-
    cause there is good fishing for small rainbow trout on upper Trinity River.

Site **27**   TRINITY
                               RIVER   ▲

Campsites, facilities: There are seven campsites for tents or motorhomes up to 32
    feet long. Non-piped water, vault toilets, picnic tables and fireplaces are
    provided. A grocery store and laundromat are nearby.
Reservations, fee: No reservations; $4 fee per night.
Who to contact: Phone Shasta-Trinity National Forest at (916)246-5222.
Location: Set nine and a half miles north of Trinity Center on Highway 3.
Trip note: Open from May through October. Elevation 2600 feet. Secluded
    camp spot along upper Trinity River.

Site **28**   SCOTT
                               MOUNTAIN   🌲

Campsites, facilities: There are four tent sites and three campsites for tents or
    motorhomes up to 22 feet long. Piped water, vault toilets, picnic tables and
    fireplaces are provided.
Reservations, fee: No reservations, no fee.

Who to contact: Phone Shasta-Trinity National Forest at (916)246-5222.

Location: Set 10 miles southeast of Callahan on Highway 3.

Trip note: Open from May through October. Elevation 5400 feet. Good spot to get away from it all. Cold in spring and fall.

Site **29**   JACKASS SPRING   ▲

Campsites, facilities: There is one tent site and 20 campsites for tents or motorhomes up to 22 feet long. Piped water, vault toilets, picnic tables and fireplaces are provided.

Reservations, fee: No reservations, no fee.

Who to contact: Phone Shasta-Trinity National Forest at (916)246-5222.

Location: Set 23 miles southeast of Trinity Center on the cast shore of Trinity Lake.

Trip note: Open September through October. Elevation 2400 feet. Jackass Spring is the only camp in this region of Trinity Lake.

Site **30**   CLEAR CREEK   🌲

Campsites, facilities: There are two tent sites and six campsites for tents or motorhomes up to 16 feet long. No water, but vault toilets, picnic tables and fireplaces are provided.

Reservations, fee: No reservations, no fee.

Who to contact: Phone Shasta-Trinity National Forest at (916)246-5222.

Location: Set 17 miles north of French Gulch via Trinity Mountain and Dog Creek Roads.

Trip note: Open from May through October. Elevation 3500 feet. Situated three miles from the east shore of Trinity Lake on Clear Creek, this is a primitive option in Trinity Lake country.

Site **31**   ACKERMAN   ▲

Campsites, facilities: There are 66 campsites for tents or motorhomes up to 22 feet long. Piped water, flush toilets, picnic tables and fireplaces are provided. A grocery store and sanitary dump station are nearby.

Reservations, fee: No reservations; $5 fee per night.

Who to contact: Phone Shasta-Trinity National Forest at (916)246-5222.

Location: Set eight miles north of Lewiston at Lewiston Lake.

Trip note: Open from May through November. Elevation 2000 feet. Fishing near the Trinity Dam.

Site **32** TUNNEL
ROCK

Campsites, facilities: There are six tent sites. No water, but vault toilets, picnic tables and fireplaces are provided. A grocery store is nearby.
Reservations, fee: No reservations, no fee.
Who to contact: Phone Shasta-Trinity National Forest at (916)246-5222.
Location: Set seven miles north of Lewiston via Buckeye Creek Road.
Trip note: Open from May through November. Elevation 1900 feet. Often passed over by folks en route farther north.

Site **33** COOPER
GULCH

Campsites, facilities: There are 11 tent sites. No water, but vault toilets, picnic tables and fireplaces are provided. A grocery store and laundromat are nearby.
Reservations, fee: No reservations, no fee.
Who to contact: Phone Shasta-Trinity National Forest at (916)246-5222.
Location: Set four miles north of Lewiston at Lewiston Lake.
Trip note: Open from May through November. Elevation 1900 feet. A nice spot along Lewiston Lake, with good trout fishing on upper end of lake where current starts.

Site **34** MARY
SMITH

Campsites, facilities: There are 18 tent sites. Piped water, vault toilets, picnic tables and fireplaces are provided. A grocery store is nearby.
Reservations, fee: No reservations; $4 fee per night.
Who to contact: Phone Shasta-Trinity National Forest at (916)246-5222.
Location: Set two and a half miles north of Lewiston at Lewiston Lake.
Trip note: Open from May through November. Elevation 1900 feet. One of the prettiest spots you'll ever see, set at the shore of Lewiston Lake.

Site **35** STEEL
BRIDGE

Campsites, facilities: There are eight campsites for tents or motorhomes up to 30 feet long. No water, but vault toilets, picnic tables and fireplaces are provided. Groceries and propane gas are available nearby.
Reservations, fee: No reservations, no fee.
Who to contact: Phone (916)246-5325—A Bureau of Land Management Camp.
Location: Set seven miles northeast of Douglas City off Highway 299 on Steel Bridge Road.

Trip note: Open year around. Elevation 2000 feet. Very few campers know of this spot. Bring your own water.

Site **36** | INDIAN CREEK TRAILER PARK

Campsites, facilities: There are 20 motorhome spaces with full hookups here. Water, showers, flush toilets, picnic tables and a laundromat are provided.

Reservations, fee: $10 deposit with reservation; $10 fee per night.

Who to contact: Phone (916)623-6332.

Location: Set two miles east of Douglas City on Highway 299.

Trip note: Open year around. Elevation 1650 feet. A nice motorhome park in the heart of the Trinity River country.

Site **37** | DOUGLAS CITY

Campsites, facilities: There are 14 campsites for tents or motorhomes up to 30 feet long. Piped water, picnic tables and fireplaces are provided. Groceries and propane gas are available nearby.

Reservations, fee: No reservations; $5 fee per night.

Who to contact: Phone (916)246-5325—A Bureau of Land Management Camp.

Location: Set 1/2 mile west of Douglas City off Highway 299 on Steiner Flat Road.

Trip note: Open from May through October. Elevation 2000 feet. Good base camp for fall salmon fishing trip on Trinity River.

Site **38** | PHILPOT

Campsites, facilities: There are two tent spaces and four motorhome spaces here. Piped water, vault toilets, picnic tables and fireplaces are provided.

Reservations, fee: No reservations, no fee.

Who to contact: Phone Shasta-Trinity National Forest at (916)246-5222.

Location: Set one mile west of Peanut off Highway 3 on Plummer Lookout Road.

Trip note: Open from April through November. Elevation 2700 feet. Remote, little used campsite.

Site **39** | COLD SPRINGS

Campsites, facilities: There are two tent sites and two campsites for tents or motorhomes up to 32 feet long. Piped water, vault toilets, picnic tables and fireplaces are provided.

Reservations, fee: No reservations, no fee.
Who to contact: Phone Shasta-Trinity National Forest at (916)246-5222.
Location: Set four miles west of Peanut off Highway 3 on Rattlesnake Road.
Trip note: Open from April through November. A little-known spot. Shasta-Trinity Forest map details back-country roads, hikes.

Site **40**   HELL
                               GATE   ▲

Campsites, facilities: There are nine tent sites and seven campsites for tents or motorhomes up to 16 feet long. Piped water, vault toilets, picnic tables and fireplaces are provided. A grocery store is nearby.
Reservations, fee: No reservations; $4 fee per night.
Who to contact: Phone Shasta-Trinity National Forest at (916)246-5222.
Location: Set one mile east of Forest Glen on Highway 36.
Trip note: Open from April through November. Elevation 2300 feet. Quiet, rustic setting on National Forest.

Site **41**   FOREST
                               GLEN   ▲

Campsites, facilities: There are 15 campsites here for tents or motorhomes up to 16 feet long. Piped water, vault toilets, picnic tables and fireplaces are provided. A grocery store is nearby.
Reservations, fee: No reservations; $4 fee per night.
Who to contact: Phone Shasta-Trinity National Forest at (916)246-5222.
Location: Set in Forest Glen on Highway 36.
Trip note: Open from April through November. Elevation 2300 feet. Good layover spot in quiet forest.

Site **42**   BAILEY CANYON
                            GROUP CAMP   ▲

Campsites, facilities: There are six tent sites and 17 campsites for tents or motorhomes up to 22 feet long. Piped water, vault toilets, picnic tables and fireplaces are provided.
Reservations, fee: Reservations required; $15 group fee per night.
Who to contact: Phone Six Rivers National Forest at (707)442-1721.
Location: Set 13 miles southeast of Mad River off Highway 36 on Lower Mad River Road.
Trip note: Open from May through September. Elevation 2600 feet. Fishing, boating at nearby Ruth Lake.

Site **43**	FIR COVE	

Campsites, facilities: There are eight tent sites and 13 campsites for tents or motorhomes up to 22 feet long. Piped water, vault toilets, picnic tables and fireplaces provided.

Reservations, fee: No reservations; $4 fee per night.

Who to contact: Phone Six Rivers National Forest at (707)442-1721.

Location: Set 12 miles southeast of Mad River off Highway 36 on Lower Mad River Road.

Trip note: Open from May through October. Elevation 2600 feet. Set along Ruth Lake.

Site **44**	MAD RIVER	

Campsites, facilities: There are 15 tent sites and 25 campsites for tents or motorhomes up to 22 feet long. Piped water, vault toilets, picnic tables and fireplaces are provided.

Reservations, fee: No reservations; $3 fee per night.

Who to contact: Phone Six Rivers National Forest at (707)442-1721.

Location: Set five miles southeast of Mad River off Highway 36 on Lower Mad River Road.

Trip note: Open year around. Elevation 2500 feet. Ruth Lake provides the background.

Site **45**	WHITE ROCK	

Campsites, facilities: There are three tent sites here. No water, but vault toilets, picnic tables and fireplaces are provided.

Reservations, fee: No reservations, no fee.

Who to contact: Phone Shasta-Trinity National Forest at (916)246-5222.

Location: Set 25 miles south of Platina off Highway 36 via Stuart Gap Road.

Trip note: Open from May through October. Elevation 4800 feet. Primitive, little-known and usually empty. A good spot to really get away from it all.

Site **46**	LAKEVIEW TERRACE RESORT	

Campsites, facilities: There are 40 motorhome sites here all with full hookups. Rest rooms, hot showers, a laundromat, dump station and heated pool are on the premises. A grocery store is nearby.

Reservations, fee: Call in advance for space and rates.

Who to contact: Phone (916)778-3803.

Location: Set on Lewiston Lake, on Trinity Dam Blvd. off Highway 299.

Trip note: Close to Trinity Alps Wilderness Area, Trinity Lake, the Trinity River, Lewiston Fish Hatchery, historic gold mines, and picturesque towns. Fishing for trout, salmon, steelhead and bass is recommended.

Site **47**　　　　　TRINITY RIVER
　　　　　　　　　　　LODGE

Campsites, facilities: There are 54 motorhome sites with full hookups and 20 tent sites. Available are rest rooms, hot showers, laundromat, recreation room with movies, furnished trailer rentals, boat and trailer storage, boats, volleyball, horseshoes, badminton and croquet. Lake fishing and golfing nearby.

Reservations, fee: Call in advance for space and rates.

Who to contact: Phone (916)778-3791.

Location: Set near Lewiston Lake on Rush Creek Road via Trinity Dam Blvd. off Highway 99.

Trip note: Open year around.

Site **48**　　　　BIGFOOT CAMPGROUND　　　
　　　　　　　　　　AND RV PARK

Campsites, facilities: There are 36 motorhome sites here with full or partial hookups. From December 1 to May 1, only self-contained vehicles allowed. Laundry, grocery store, sanitary dump station and propane gas available nearby.

Reservations, fee: Call for space. Reservations desireable in September and October.

Who to contact: Phone (916)623-6088.

Location: Set three miles west of Junction City on Highway 299.

Trip note: Located on Trinity River. Among the activities available are fishing for salmon, steelhead and trout. Gold panning and rafting are also enjoyable.

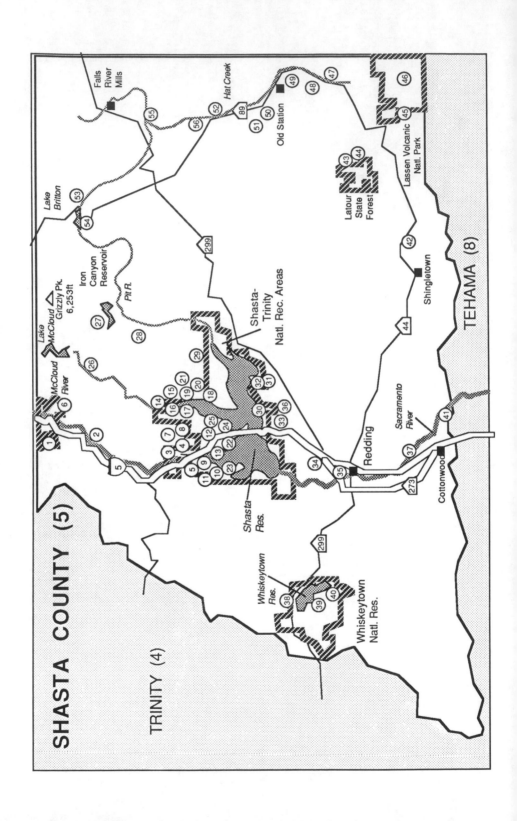

MAP FIVE

SHASTA COUNTY

◆

Site **1** | CASTLE CRAGS
STATE PARK | ▲

Campsites, facilities: There are 64 campsites for tents or motorhomes up to 27 feet. Piped water, showers, flush toilets, picnic tables and fireplaces are provided. A laundromat is nearby.
Reservations, fee: Make reservations through MISTIX by phoning (800)446-7275.
Who to contact: Call (916)235-2684.
Location: Set five miles south of Dunsmuir off Highway 5.
Trip note: Open year around. Trout fishing along two mile stretch of the Sacramento River that runs through the park. The ancient granite crags tower 6000 feet, and beyond them is Mt. Shasta. Forested with oaks and maples at lower elevations. Conifers grow at higher altitudes.

Site **2** | SIMS
FLAT | ▲

Campsites, facilities: There are 17 campsites here for tents or motorhomes to 16 feet. Non-piped water, flush toilets, picnic tables and fireplaces are provided. A grocery store is nearby.
Reservations, fee: No reservations; $5 fee per night.
Who to contact: Phone Shasta-Trinity National Forest at (916)246-5222.
Location: Set seven miles south of Castelle off Highway 5.
Trip note: Open from April through October. Elevation 1700 feet. Try trout fishing on the Sacramento River, or hike a trail along the South Fork to Tombstone Mountain or south to North Salt Creek. Visit Shiloh Mineral Springs.

Site **3** | LAKEHEAD
CAMPGROUND | ▲

Campsites, facilities: There are 20 tent sites and 30 motorhome spaces with full or partial hookups. Rest rooms, showers, dump station, store, laundromat, bike rentals, horseshoes, ping pong are available.

Reservations, fee: Reserve through Leisuretime Reservation Systems by phoning (800)822-2267. Camp fee is $10 per night.
Who to contact: Call (916)238-2671.
Location: One mile south of Lakehead on Antlers Road, off Highway 5.
Trip note: Open year around. Elevation 1200 feet. Located less than a mile from boat launch at Shasta Lake and 15 minutes from Shasta Caverns.

Site 4   ANTLER TRAILER RESORT
                   AND CAMPGROUND

Campsites, facilities: There are 30 tent sites and 77 motorhome spaces with full hookups. Rest rooms, hot showers, a playground, snack bar, grocery store, laundromat, propane gas, bikes for rent, boats for rent, houseboats, moorage and a complete marina are available.
Reservations, fee: Deposit required with reservation. $13 per night fee; pets $4.
Who to contact: Phone at (916)238-2322.
Location: Set two miles south of Lakehead off Highway 5 on Antlers Road.
Trip note: Open all year. Elevation 1215 feet. Boating, swimming and fishing at giant Lake Shasta.

Site 5   SHASTA LAKE TRAILER RESORT
                   AND CAMPGROUND

Campsites, facilities: There are 16 tent sites and 50 motorhome spaces with full hookups. Rest rooms, hot showers, a grocery store, laundromat, playground, a swimming pool and picnic tables are available. There is also a private dock with 36 boat slips.
Reservations, fee: Deposit required with reservation; $14 fee per night.
Who to contact: Phone at (916)238-2370.
Location: Set two miles south of Lakehead off Highway 5 on Lakeshore Drive.
Trip note: Open all year. Elevation 1215 feet. Boating, swimming and fishing on upper end of Lake Shasta. Shaded RV and tent sites available.

Site 6   CRAG VIEW
                   VALLEY CAMP

Campsites, facilities: There are 10 tent sites and 33 motorhome spaces with full hookups. Rest rooms, hot showers, firewood and a laundromat are available. A grocery store, propane gas and a dump station are nearby.
Reservations, fee: Call for space available.
Who to contact: Phone at (916)235-0081.
Location: Set one mile east of Highway 5 at Castella Exit.
Trip note: Here you will find wooded, secluded campsites right on the Sacramento River. Visit Castle Crags State Park.

Site 7 · ANTLERS

Campsites, facilities: There are 59 campsites for tents or motorhomes to 32 feet long. Piped water, flush toilets, picnic tables and fireplaces are provided. A grocery store and a laundromat are nearby.
Reservations, fee: No reservations; $6 fee per night.
Who to contact: Phone Shasta-Trinity National Forest at (916)246-5222.
Location: Set two miles south of Lakehead off Highway 5.
Trip note: Open year around. Swimming, boating and fishing on the northwestern inlet of Shasta Lake.

Site 8 · GREGORY CREEK

Campsites, facilities: There are five tent sites and 13 campsites for tents or motorhomes up to 16 feet long. Piped water, flush toilets, picnic tables and fireplaces are provided.
Reservations, fee: No reservations; $5 fee per night.
Who to contact: Phone Shasta-Trinity National Forest at (916)246-5222.
Location: Set seven miles southeast of Lakehead off Highway 5 via Gregory Creek Road.
Trip note: Open from May through September. Across the inlet from Antlers Campground, but more secluded on Shasta Lake.

Site 9 · LAKESHORE EAST

Campsites, facilities: There are eight tent sites and 15 campsites for tents or motorhomes up to 22 feet long. Piped water, vault toilets, picnic tables and fireplaces are provided. A grocery store and a laundromat are nearby.
Reservations, fee: No reservations; $5 fee per night.
Who to contact: Phone Shasta-Trinity National Forest at (916)246-5222.
Location: Set three miles southwest of Lakehead off Highway 5 on Lakeshore Drive.
Trip note: Open year around. A nice Forest Service campground on Shasta Lake's northern end.

Site 10 · LAKESHORE WEST

Campsites, facilities: There are 13 campsites here for tents or motorhomes up to 32 feet long. Piped water, vault toilets, picnic tables and fireplaces are provided. A grocery store and a laundromat are nearby.
Reservations, fee: No reservations; $4 fee per night.

Who to contact: Phone Shasta-Trinity National Forest at (916)246-5222.

Location: Set two and a half miles southwest of Lakehead off Highway 5 on Lakeshore Drive.

Trip note: Open year around. Elevation 1100 feet. Located at upper end of Shasta Lake.

Site **11**   OLD
                        MAN   🌲

Campsites, facilities: There are 10 tent sites here. Piped water, flush toilets, picnic tables and fireplaces are provided. A grocery store and a laundromat are nearby.

Reservations, fee: No reservations; $4 fee per night.

Who to contact: Phone Shasta-Trinity National Forest at (916)246-5222.

Location: Set eight miles southwest of Lakehead off Highway 5 on Lakeshore Road.

Trip note: Open from April through November. Situated on a secluded inlet of Lake Shasta. Backpackers will enjoy hiking the trail west from camp leading up Sugarloaf Creek. It connects with other trails that eventually end at Trinity Lake.

Site **12**   NELSON
                        POINT   ▲

Campsites, facilities: There are eight campsites here that can accommodate tents or motorhomes. Piped water, vault toilets, picnic tables and fireplaces are provided. A grocery store and a laundromat are nearby.

Reservations, fee: No reservations; $4 fee per night.

Who to contact: Phone Shasta-Trinity National Forest at (916)246-5222.

Location: Set five miles southeast of Lakehead off I-5.

Trip note: On an inlet of Lake Shasta, but very close to Highway 5.

Site **13**   OAK
                        GROVE   ▲

Campsites, facilities: There are 43 campsites for tents or motorhomes up to 22 feet long. Piped water, vault toilets, picnic tables and fireplaces are provided. A grocery store is nearby.

Reservations, fee: No reservations; $3 fee per night.

Who to contact: Phone Shasta-Trinity National Forest at (916)246-5222.

Location: Set five miles southeast of Lakehead off Highway 5.

Trip note: Open from May through September. Lake Shasta is nearby.

Site **14**   MCCLOUD
                          BRIDGE

Campsites, facilities: There are nine tent sites and 11 campsites for tents or mo-
    torhomes up to 16 feet long. Piped water, flush toilets, picnic tables and
    fireplaces provided.
Reservations, fee: No reservations; $5 fee per night.
Who to contact: Phone Shasta-Trinity National Forest at (916)246-5222.
Location: Set 20 1/2 miles east of Lakehead off Highway 5 via Gilman Road.
Trip note: Open year around. Fishing access on an inlet of Lake Shasta. A back-
    packing trail from camp leads east into the backcountry.

Site **15**   PINE
                          POINT

Campsites, facilities: There are 13 campsites for tents or motorhomes up to 22
    feet long. Piped water, vault toilets, picnic tables and fireplaces are
    provided.
Reservations, fee: No reservations; $4 fee per night.
Who to contact: Phone Shasta-Trinity National Forest at (916)246-5222.
Location: Set 19 1/2 miles east of Lakehead off Highway 5 on Gilman Road.
Trip note: Open from May through September. Fishing on Lake Shasta.

Site **16**   ELLERY
                          CREEK

Campsites, facilities: There are nine tent sites and 10 campsites for tents or mo-
    torhomes up to 22 feet long. Piped water, vault toilets, picnic tables and
    fireplaces provided.
Reservations, fee: No reservations; $4 fee per night.
Who to contact: Phone Shasta-Trinity National Forest at (916)246-5222.
Location: Set 18 1/2 miles east of Lakehead off Highway 5 on Gilman Road.
Trip note: Open from May through September. Fishing on Lake Shasta, where
    Ellery Creek empties into Lake Shasta.

Site **17**   JENNINGS
                          CREEK

Campsites, facilities: There are eight tent sites with piped water, vault toilets, pic-
    nic tables and fireplaces provided.
Reservations, fee: No reservations; $3 fee per night.
Who to contact: Phone Shasta-Trinity National Forest at (916)246-5222.
Location: Set 17 1/2 miles east of Lakehead off Highway 5 on Gilman Road.
Trip note: Open from May through September. Fishing on middle fork of Lake
    Shasta.

Site **18**   DEKKAS
                                 ROCK   ▲

Campsites, facilities: There are 10 campsites for tents or motorhomes up to 16
    feet long, with piped water, vault toilets, picnic tables and fireplaces pro-
    vided. A grocery store is nearby.
Reservations, fee: No reservations; $4 fee per night.
Who to contact: Phone Shasta-Trinity National Forest at (916)246-5222.
Location: Set 14 1/2 miles southeast of Lakehead off Highway 5 on Gilman
    Road.
Trip note: Open from May through September. Fishing on middle fork of Lake
    Shasta.

Site **19**   HIRZ
                                 BAY   ▲

Campsites, facilities: There are 48 campsites for tents or motorhomes up to 32
    feet long. Piped water, flush toilets, picnic tables and fireplaces provided.
Reservations, fee: No reservations; $6 fee per night.
Who to contact: Phone Shasta-Trinity National Forest at (916)246-5222.
Location: Set 13 miles southeast of Lakehead off Highway 5 via Gilman Road.
Trip note: Open year around. Boat ramp nearby.

Site **20**   HIRZ BAY
                                 GROUP CAMP   ▲

Campsites, facilities: There are two group campsites for motorhomes up to 32
    feet long. Piped water, vault toilets, picnic tables and fireplaces provided.
Reservations, fee: Reservations required; group fee is $45 per night.
Who to contact: Phone Shasta-Trinity National Forest at (916)246-5222.
Location: Set 13 miles southeast of Lakehead off Highway 5 via Gilman Road.
Trip note: Open from May through September. Boat launch ramp nearby.

Site **21**   MOORE
                                 CREEK   ▲

Campsites, facilities: There are 10 campsites for tents or motorhomes up to 22
    feet long. Piped water, vault toilets, picnic tables and fireplaces provided.
Reservations, fee: No reservations; $4 fee per night.
Who to contact: Phone Shasta-Trinity National Forest at (916)246-5222.
Location: Set 15 1/2 miles southeast of Lakehead off Highway 5 on Gilman
    Road.
Trip note: Open from May through September. Fishing on middle fork of Lake
    Shasta.

| Site **22** | LOWER SALT CREEK | |

Campsites, facilities: There are 12 tent sites with piped water, vault toilets, picnic tables and fireplaces provided. A grocery store is nearby.
Reservations, fee: No reservations; $3 fee per night.
Who to contact: Phone Shasta-Trinity National Forest at (916)246-5222.
Location: Set three and a half miles northwest of O'Brien off Highway 5 on Lower Salt Creek.
Trip note: Open year around. Fishing on Lake Shasta.

| Site **23** | SALT CREEK | |

Campsites, facilities: There are 43 tent sites. Piped water, flush toilets, picnic tables and fireplaces are provided. A grocery store and laundromat are nearby.
Reservations, fee: No reservations, no fee.
Who to contact: Phone Shasta-Trinity National Forest at (916)246-5222.
Location: Set four and a half miles south of Lakehead off Highway 5.
Trip note: Open from May through September. Fishing on Lake Shasta.

| Site **24** | BAILEY COVE | |

Campsites, facilities: There are 19 tent sites and five campsites for tents or motorhomes up to 16 feet long. Piped water, vault toilets, picnic tables and fireplaces are provided. A grocery store is nearby.
Reservations, fee: No reservations; $5 fee per night.
Who to contact: Phone Shasta-Trinity National Forest at (916)246-5222.
Location: Set two miles southeast of O'Brien off Highway 5.
Trip note: Open year around. Fishing on Lake Shasta.

| Site **25** | WINTOON | |

Campsites, facilities: There are 11 tent sites. No water is available, but vault toilets, picnic tables and fireplaces are provided. A grocery store is nearby.
Reservations, fee: No reservations; $3 fee per night.
Who to contact: Phone Shasta-Trinity National Forest at (916)246-5222.
Location: Set one and a half miles south of O'Brien off Highway 5 on Shasta Caverns Road.
Trip note: Open from May through September. Fishing on Lake Shasta.

Site **26**   AH-DI-NA

Campsites, facilities: There are 15 tent sites and two campsites for tents or motorhomes up to 16 feet long. Piped water, flush toilets, picnic tables and fire-
places are provided.
Reservations, fee: No reservations; $4 fee per night.
Who to contact: Phone Shasta-Trinity National Forest at (916)246-5222.
Location: Set 16 1/2 miles south of McCloud off Squaw Valley Road.
Trip note: Open from May through October. Elevation 2200 feet. Perfect base
camp for trout fishing on Lower McCloud River. Catch-and-release fishing
allowed on Wild Trout Section governed by Nature Conservancy. Pacific
Crest Trail passes through campground.

Site **27**   DEADLUN

Campsites, facilities: There are 15 tent sites and 15 campsites for tents or motorhomes up to 22 feet long. No water, but vault toilets, picnic tables and fireplaces are provided.
Reservations, fee: No reservations, no fee.
Who to contact: Phone Shasta-Trinity National Forest at (916)246-5222.
Location: Set seven miles northwest of Big Bend at Iron Canyon Reservoir.
Trip note: Open from May through November. Elevation 2700 feet. Swimming
and fishing in Iron Canyon Reservoir. Numerous trails, peaks and creeks in
area.

Site **28**   MADRONE

Campsites, facilities: There are eight tent sites and five campsites for tents or mo-
torhomes. No water, but vault toilets, picnic tables and fireplaces are
provided.
Reservations, fee: No reservations, no fee.
Who to contact: Phone Shasta-Trinity National Forest at (916)246-5222.
Location: Set 21 1/2 miles northwest of Montgomery Creek off Highway 299 via
Fenders Ferry Road.
Trip note: Open from May through October. Elevation 1200 feet. Trailhead
leads into backcountry. Numerous trails and creeks in area, all detailed on
Forest Service map.

Site **29**   CHIRPCHATTER

Campsites, facilities: There are four campsites for tents or motorhomes up to 16 feet long. No water, but vault toilets, picnic tables and fireplaces are provided.

Reservations, fee: No reservations, no fee.

Who to contact: Phone Shasta-Trinity National Forest at (916)246-5222.

Location: Set 27 1/2 miles west of Montgomery Creek off Highway 299 via Fenders Ferry Road.

Trip note: Open from May through October. Elevation 1300 feet at foot of Chirpchatter Mountain. Many trails and creeks in area.

Site **30**   MARINER'S
POINT   🔺

Campsites, facilities: There are eight tent sites with piped water, vault toilets, picnic tables and fireplaces provided. A grocery store is nearby.

Reservations, fee: No reservations; $3 fee per night.

Who to contact: Phone Shasta-Trinity National Forest at (916)246-5222.

Location: Set 13 miles north of Bella Vista via Dry Creek Road.

Trip note: Open year around. Fishing on South Shore of Lake Shasta.

Site **31**   JONES
VALLEY   🔺

Campsites, facilities: There are 27 campsites for tents or motorhomes up to 22 feet long. Piped water, vault toilets, picnic tables and fireplaces are provided. A grocery store is nearby.

Reservations, fee: No reservations; $4 fee per night.

Who to contact: Phone Shasta-Trinity National Forest at (916)246-5222.

Location: Set nine miles north of Bella Vista via Dry Creek Road.

Trip note: Open year around. Fishing near Jones Valley Resort, the Marina and on Shasta Lake's south shore. The trail to Buck Point is a scenic hike. Boat launching ramp nearby.

Site **32**   ROCKY
RIDGE   🔺

Campsites, facilities: There are 10 tent sites with piped water, vault toilets, picnic tables and fireplaces provided. A grocery store is nearby.

Reservations, fee: No reservations; $4 fee per night.

Who to contact: Phone Shasta-Trinity National Forest at (916)246-5222.

Location: Set nine and a half miles north of Bella Vista via Dry Creek Road.

Trip note: Open May through September. Elevation 1100 feet. This camp is near Jones Valley, but further from the boat ramp.

Site **33**   FAWNDALE OAKS
RV PARK

Campsites, facilities: There are 23 motorhome spaces with full hookups. Rest rooms, showers, a grocery store, snack bar, laundromat, giant water slides and two swimming pools are on the premises. A sanitary dump and propane gas station are nearby.
Reservations, fee: Reservations required with deposit; $12 fee per night.
Who to contact: Phone (916)275-5441.
Location: Set 10 miles north of Redding off Highway 5 at 8083 Fawndale Road.
Trip note: Open year around. Elevation 900 feet. Park features green grass, plenty of shade and delightful waterslides. Located near Lake Shasta.

Site **34**   KOA
OF REDDING

Campsites, facilities: There are 39 tent sites and 54 motorhome spaces with full hookups. Piped water, flush toilets, showers, a playground, a laundromat, a dump station, picnic tables and fireplaces are provided. A grocery store and propane gas are also available.
Reservations, fee: Reservation required with deposit; $10.25 fee per night.
Who to contact: Phone (916)246-0101.
Location: Set two miles northeast of Redding off Highway 5 at 280 North Boulder Drive.
Trip note: Open year around. Elevation 560 feet. Very hot in summer.

Site **35**   MARINA
MOTOR HOME PARK

Campsites, facilities: There are 86 camp and motorhome sites with full or partial hookups. Rest rooms, hot showers, a laundromat, grocery store, swimming pool and a dump station are on park grounds. Propane gas is available nearby.
Reservations, fee: Reservation fee is $3.50, payable to Leisuretime Reservation Systems, Inc.: (800)822-2267; $12.00 fee per night.
Who to contact: Phone (916)241-4396.
Location: Set in Redding at 2615 Park Marina Drive.
Trip note: Open year around. Elevation 560 feet. Swimming, fishing and boating on the Sacramento River. Miniature golf course nearby.

Site **36**   BEAR MOUNTAIN
MOTOR HOME PARK

Campsites, facilities: There are 17 tent sites and 80 motorhomes spaces with full or partial hookups. Piped water, flush toilets, a laundromat, grocery store, dump station, picnic tables and fire rings are provided. A swimming pool, recreation hall, arcade, shuffleboard court and television area are available. Nearby is a free boat launch ramp.

Reservations, fee: Call ahead for space and rates.

Who to contact: Phone (916)275-4728.

Location: Set seven miles from Redding off Highway 5 via Oasis Road to 6500 Bear Mountain Road.

Trip note: Enjoy nearby fishing, boating and skiing.

Site **37** | SACRAMENTO RIVER
MOTOR HOME PARK |

Campsites, facilities: There are 20 tent sites and 140 motorhome spaces with full hookups. Rest rooms, hot showers, a grocery store, laundromat, dump station, free satellite TV, bait and tackle shop, propane gas, a launch and slips, two tennis courts and a large swimming pool are available for campers' pleasure.

Reservations, fee: Reservation fee of $3.50 payable to Leisuretime Reservation Systems, Inc.: (800)822-2267; call for current space fees.

Who to contact: Phone (916)365-6402.

Location: Set six miles south of Redding off Highway 5 via Knighton Road to 8900 Riverland Drive.

Trip note: Open year around. You can fish in the Sacramento River or in three acre lake at campground.

Site **38** | OAK
BOTTOM |

Campsites, facilities: There are 105 tent sites and 50 motorhome spaces with piped water, flush toilets, cold showers, picnic tables, fireplaces, and a sanitary dump station provided. Groceries and propane gas are available nearby.

Reservations, fee: Reservations required; $5 camping fee per night.

Who to contact: Phone Whiskeytown National Recreation Area at (916)241-6584.

Location: Set 13 miles west of Redding off Highway 299.

Trip note: Open year around. Elevation 1250 feet. Campground is on Whiskeytown Lake, where you can enjoy boating and water skiing. There are also numerous hiking and horseback riding trails in the area. Gold panning is allowed and there are evening ranger seminars at the Oak Bottom Amphitheatre every night from mid-June through Labor Day.

Site **39** | DRY CREEK
GROUP CAMP |

Campsites, facilities: There is one large camp with piped water, pit toilets, picnic tables and fireplaces.

Reservations, fee: Reservations required; group fee is $30 per night.

Who to contact: Phone Whiskeytown National Recreation Area at (916)241-6584.

Location: Set 15 miles west of Redding off Highway 299 on Kennedy Memorial Drive.

Trip note: Open year around. Elevation 1200 feet. Same recreation options as Oak Bottom provides, plus hiking and horseback riding.

Site **40**   BRANDY
                               CREEK   🚐

Campsites, facilities: There are 35 motorhome spaces with a dump station and piped water provided. A grocery store is nearby.

Reservations, fee: No reservations, no fee.

Who to contact: Phone Whiskeytown National Recreation Area at (916)241-6584.

Location: Set 14 miles west of Redding off Highway 299 on Kennedy Memorial Drive.

Trip note: Open year around. Elevation 1250 feet. A one and a half mile hike to Whiskeytown Lake with all of the same recreational options.

Site **41**   READING
                               ISLAND   🔺

Campsites, facilities: There are eight campsites for tents or motorhomes up to 30 feet long. Piped water, vault toilets, picnic tables and fireplaces are provided. A boat ramp, groceries, propane gas and a laundromat are available nearby.

Reservations, fee: No reservations; $2 fee per night.

Who to contact: Phone (916)246-5325; a Bureau of Land Management camp.

Location: Set six miles east of Cottonwood off Highway A-17 (Balls Ferry Road) on Adobe Road.

Trip note: Open year around. Elevation 600 feet. Hiking, boating, swimming and fishing options. Boat ramp is on the Sacramento River.

Site **42**   MT. LASSEN
                               KOA   🔺

Campsites, facilities: There are 10 tent sites and 24 motorhome spaces with full or partial hookups. Piped water, flush toilets, showers and a dump station are provided. Groceries, a laundromat and propane gas are available nearby.

Reservations, fee: Deposit with reservation required; $15 fee per night.

Who to contact: Phone (916)474-3133.

Location: Set four miles east of Shingletown on Highway 44.

Trip note: Open year around. Elevation 4000 feet. On slopes of Mt. Lassen.

Site **43**   OLD COW
                              MEADOWS

Campsites, facilities: There are three campsites for tents or motorhomes. There
    is non-piped water, but no toilets. Picnic tables and fireplaces are provided.
Reservations, fee: No reservations, no fee.
Who to contact: Phone Latour State Forest at (916)225-2495.
Location: Set 15 miles east of Whitmore via Bateman Road.
Trip note: Open from June through October. Elevation 6000 feet.

Site **44**   SOUTH COW CREEK
                              MEADOWS

Campsites, facilities: There are two campsites for tents or motorhomes. Non-
    piped water available. No toilets, but picnic tables and fireplaces are
    provided.
Reservations, fee: No reservations, no fee.
Who to contact: Phone Latour State Forest at (916)225-2495.
Location: Set 14 miles east of Whitemore via Bateman Road.
Trip note: Open from June through October. Elevation 5600 feet.

Site **45**   MANZANITA
                              LAKE

Campsites, facilities: There are 179 campsites for tents or motorhomes up to 30
    feet long. Piped water, flush toilets, showers, a sanitary dump station, pic-
    nic tables and fireplaces are provided. Propane gas, groceries and a laun-
    dromat are also available nearby.
Reservations, fee: No reservations; $6 fee per night.
Who to contact: Phone Lassen Volcanic National Park at (916)595-4444.
Location: Set at Manzanita Lake on Lassen Park Road.
Trip note: Open from May through September. Elevation 5890 feet. There is
    swimming, good trout fishing with special regulations. Enjoy free ranger-led
    hikes, interpretive programs and evening discussions about Indian lore
    and other subjects. No motor boats allowed. Many inland hiking trails exist
    and maps are available at the Visitors Center.

Site **46**   SUMMIT
                              LAKE

Campsites, facilities: There are 94 campsites for tents or motorhomes up to 30
    feet long. Piped water, flush toilets, picnic tables and fireplaces are
    provided.
Reservations, fee: No reservations; $6 fee per night.
Who to contact: Phone Lassen Volcanic National Park at (916)595-4444.

Location: Set 12 miles southeast of Manzanita Lake on Lassen Park Road.
Trip note: Open from June through September. Elevation 6695 feet. Lake fishing OK. Non-powered boats only. Trails lead to lakes and wildflowers.

Site **47**   BIG
                                     PINE   ▲

Campsites, facilities: There are 19 campsites for tents or motorhomes up to 22 feet long. No water, but vault toilets, picnic tables and fireplaces are provided. A grocery store and propane gas are also available nearby.
Reservations, fee: No reservations, no fee.
Who to contact: Phone Lassen National Forest Headquarters at (916)257-2151.
Location: Set five miles southwest of Old Station off Highways 89 and 44.
Trip note: Open from May through October. Elevation 4600 feet. Camp is on Hat Creek, near Lassen National Park. Pacific Crest Trail near Big Pine.

Site **48**   HAT
                                     CREEK   ▲

Campsites, facilities: There are 73 campsites for tents or motorhomes up to 22 feet long. Piped water, flush toilets, a sanitary dump station, picnic tables and fireplaces are provided. A grocery store, laundromat, and propane gas are also available nearby.
Reservations, fee: No reservations; $5 fee per night.
Who to contact: Phone Lassen National Forest Headquarters at (916)257-2151.
Location: Set one mile south of Old Station off Highways 89 and 44.
Trip note: Open from April through October. Elevation 4400 feet. Camp on Hat Creek in Lava Bed area. Logan Lake, Devil's Half Acre, many caves and Pacific Crest Trail are nearby. Good trout fishing.

Site **49**   CAVE   ▲

Campsites, facilities: There are 12 campsites for tents or motorhomes to 22 feet long. Piped water, vault toilets, picnic tables and fireplaces are provided. A grocery store is nearby.
Reservations, fee: No reservations; $5 fee per night.
Who to contact: Phone Lassen National Forest Headquarters at (916)257-2151.
Location: Set one mile northwest of Old Station on Highway 89.
Trip note: Open from April through October. Elevation 4400 feet. Camp is on Hat Creek lava bed. Subway Cave and Devil's Half Acre are in the vicinity.

| Site 50 | ROCKY | |

Campsites, facilities: There are eight tent sites. No water, but vault toilets, picnic tables and fireplaces are provided. A grocery store and propane gas are also available nearby.

Reservations, fee: No reservations, no fee.

Who to contact: Phone Lassen National Forest Headquarters at (916)257-2151.

Location: Set three miles northwest of Old Station on Highway 89.

Trip note: Open from May through October. Elevation 4000 feet. Camp is on Hat Creek Lava Bed area near Cave, Honn and Bridge camping areas.

| Site 51 | BRIDGE | |

Campsites, facilities: There are 25 campsites here for tents or motorhomes up to 22 feet long. Piped water, flush toilets, picnic tables and fireplaces are provided. A grocery store and propane gas are also available nearby.

Reservations, fee: No reservations; $5 fee per night.

Who to contact: Phone Lassen National Forest Headquarters at (916)257-2151.

Location: Set four miles southwest of Old Station on Highway 89.

Trip note: Open from April through October. Elevation 3800 feet. Located on Hat Creek. Picnic area nearby. Good trout fishing.

| Site 52 | HONN | |

Campsites, facilities: There are six tent sites. No water, but vault toilets, picnic tables and fireplaces are provided. A grocery store, laundromat and propane gas are also available nearby.

Reservations, fee: No reservations, no fee.

Who to contact: Phone Lassen National Forest Headquarters at (916)257-2151.

Location: Set nine miles northwest of Old Station on Highway 89.

Trip note: Open from April through October. Elevation 3400 feet. Located on Hat Creek. Lava bed area on western edge.

| Site 53 | DUSTY | |

Campsites, facilities: There are six motorhome spaces here. No water, but vault toilets, picnic tables and fireplaces are provided. A grocery store and propane gas are available nearby.

Reservations, fee: No reservations, no fee.

Who to contact: Phone Lassen National Forest Headquarters at (916)257-2151.

Location: Set 18 miles northwest of Fall River Mills off Highway 89.

Trip note: Open from May through October. Elevation 3000 feet. Located on Lake Britton, near McArthur-Burney Falls Memorial State Park. Pacific Crest Trail passes by camp.

Site **54**
MCARTHUR-BURNEY FALLS MEMORIAL STATE PARK

Campsites, facilities: There are 118 campsites for tents or motorhomes up to 32 feet long. Piped water, flush toilets, a sanitary dump station, picnic tables and fireplaces are provided. A grocery store and a laundromat are also nearby.
Reservations, fee: Reservation fee of $3.75 payable to MISTIX: (800)446-7275. $6 camping fee per night; pet fee is $1.
Who to contact: Phone (916)335-2777.
Location: Set 11 miles northeast of Burney on Highway 89.
Trip note: Open year around. Elevation 3000 feet. Swimming, hiking, boating and fishing on Lake Britton. Pacific Crest Trail passes nearby. Burney Spring Mountain or Long Valley Mountain can be reached by trail. Spectacular waterfall near campground.

Site **55**
PIT RIVER

Campsites, facilities: There are 10 campsites for tents or motorhomes. No water, but vault toilets, picnic tables and fireplaces are provided. A grocery store, a laundromat and propane gas are available nearby.
Reservations, fee: No reservations, no fee.
Who to contact: Phone (916)257-5381—A Bureau of Land Management camp.
Location: Set five miles southwest of Fall River Mills off Highway 299.
Trip note: Open from May through November. Elevation 3000 feet. Located on Pit River. Pit River Falls is near site. Good trout fishing near Powerhouse No. 3.

Site **56**
HAT CREEK RANCH RV AND CAMPGROUND

Campsites, facilities: There are 42 tent sites and 38 motorhome spaces with full or partial hookups. Rest rooms, hot showers, a sanitary dump station, a laundromat, a playground and a grocery store are on the premises.
Reservations, fee: Reservations required. Call in advance for camping rates.
Who to contact: Phone (916)335-2778 or (916)335-4624.
Location: Set 16 miles southeast of Burney off Highway 299, via Highway 89 on Doty Road.
Trip note: Open from April through October. Campground set in the midst of a working cattle range. Fishing available in Hat Creek or in nearby stocked

trout pond. Sightseeing is spectacular with Burney Falls, Lassen Park and Subway Caves all within 30 miles.

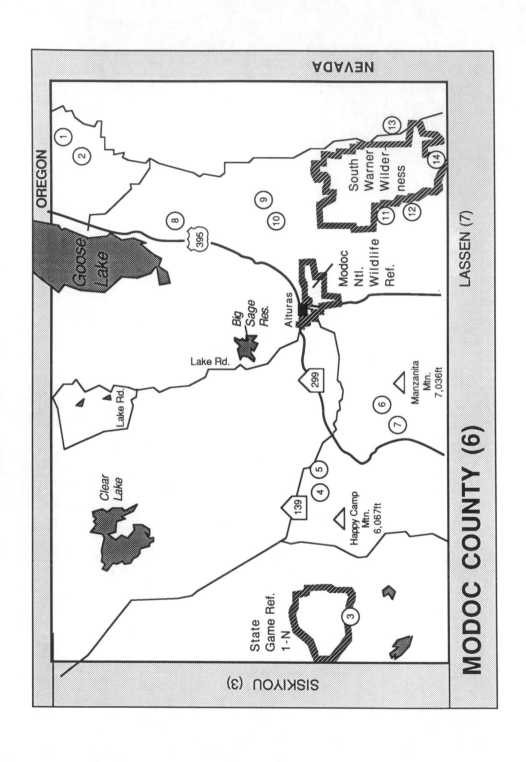

MODOC COUNTY (6)

MODOC COUNTY

◆

Site 1 | CAVE LAKE | ⏏

Campsites, facilities: There are four sites for tents and two sites for motorhomes up to 16 feet. Piped water, vault toilets, fireplace and table are provided.
Reservations, fee: No reservations, no fee.
Who to contact: Phone Modoc National Forest at (916)233-5811, or write at 411 Main Street, Alturas, CA 96101.
Location: Cave Lake is located six miles southeast of the town of New Pine Creek off Highway 395.
Trip note: Open from July through October. Elevation 6600 feet. A little-known, little-used campground hidden in Northeastern California alongside a pretty lake.

Site 2 | LILY LAKE | 🌲

Campsites, facilities: There are six tents sites, with vault toilets, picnic table and fireplace provided. No water available.
Reservations, fee: No reservations, no fee.
Who to contact: Phone Modoc National Forest at (916)233-5811.
Location: This camp is located six miles southeast of the town of New Pine Creek off of Highway 395.
Trip note: Open from July through October. Just about no one knows about this camp, but now you do. Be sure to bring water purification pump.

Site 3 | LAVA CAMP | 🌲

Campsites, facilities: There are 12 campsites for tents or motorhomes to 32 feet long. Vault toilets, tables and fireplaces are provided. No water is available, so be certain to bring your own.
Reservations, fee: No reservation, no fee.
Who to contact: Phone Modoc National Forest at (916)233-5811.
Location: Drive 21 miles northwest from the town of Lookout on Road 93/95.

Trip note: Open from May through October. Elevation 4400 feet. Set on the outskirts of Long Bell State Game Refuge and virtually unknown.

Site 4   COTTONWOOD
                             FLAT

Campsites, facilities: There are 10 sites for tents of motorhomes to 22 feet. Water, vault toilets, fireplaces and picnic tables are provided.
Reservations, fee: No reservations, no fee.
Who to contact: Phone Modoc National Forest at (916)233-5811.
Location: Drive 12 miles west of Canby off Highway 299 via Pit River Road.
Trip note: Open from June to October. Elevation 4700 feet. Rugged setting that gets very cold early or late in the season. Trout fishing nearby.

Site 5   HOWARD'S
                            GULCH

Campsites, facilities: There are 11 sites for tents or motorhomes to 22 feet long. Piped water, vault toilets, tables and fireplaces are provided. A grocery store is nearby.
Reservations, fee: No reservations, no fee.
Who to contact: Phone Modoc National Forest at (916)233-5811.
Location: Drive six miles northwest of Canby off State Route 139.
Trip note: Open from May through October. Elevation 4700 feet. A number of reservoirs are located within a five mile radius.

Site 6   UPPER RUSH
                            CREEK

Campsites, facilities: There are 13 sites for tents or motorhomes to 22 feet long. Piped water, vault toilets and tables are provided.
Reservations, fee: No reservations, no fee.
Who to contact: Phone Modoc National Forest at (916)233-5811.
Location: Drive nine miles northeast of Adin off Highway 299.
Trip note: Open from May through October. This camp sits at the foot of 7,036 foot Manzanita Mountain, a climb of 1,800 feet. Good fishing in area lakes.

Site 7   LOWER RUSH
                            CREEK

Campsites, facilities: There are five sites for tents and five sites for motorhomes to 22 feet. Piped water, vault toilets, picnic tables and fireplaces are provided.
Reservations, fee: No reservations, no fee.
Who to contact: Phone Modoc National Forest at (916)233-5811.

Location: Drive eight miles northeast of Adin off Highway 299.

Trip note: Open from May through October. Elevation 4400 feet. Good trout fishing in area. Availability of piped water makes it one of better camps in this rugged, primitive country.

Site **8**   PLUM
                          VALLEY

Campsites, facilities: There are seven sites for tents or motorhomes up to 16 feet long. Vault toilets, fireplaces and picnic tables are provided. No water is available, but a grocery store is nearby.

Who to contact: Phone Modoc National Forest at (916)233-5811.

Location: Drive four miles southeast on Road 11 from the town of Davis Creek on Highway 395.

Trip note: Open from May through October. Elevation 5600 feet. Secluded camp on the South Fork of Davis Creek. Good headquarters for quiet trout fishing trip.

Site **9**   STOUGH
                          RESERVOIR

Campsites, facilities: There are eight sites for tents or motorhomes up to 16 feet long. Piped water, vault toilets, picnic table and fireplace are provided.

Reservations, fee: No reservation, no fee.

Who to contact: Phone Modoc National Forest at (916)233-5811.

Location: Drive six miles west of Cedarville off Highway 299.

Trip note: Open from May through October. Elevation 6300 feet. This camp is tucked in the lonely Warner Mountains. Few people use this site, making it quiet even in middle of summer.

Site **10**   CEDAR
                          PASS

Campsites, facilities: There are 17 sites for tents or motorhomes. Piped water, vault toilets, picnic tables and fireplaces are provided.

Reservations, fee: No reservations, no fee.

Who to contact: Phone Modoc National Forest at (916)233-5811.

Location: Drive eight miles west of Cedarville off Highway 299.

Trip note: Open from May through October. Elevation 5900 feet. An option to Modoc County Camp No. 9, which is less than three miles away. Good trout fishing in area.

Site **11**   SOUP
                                     SPRING   ▲

Campsites, facilities: There are eight sites for tents and six sites for tents or mo-
    torhomes up to 22 feet long. Piped water, vault toilets, picnic tables and
    fireplaces are provided.
Reservations, fee: No reservations, no fee.
Who to contact: Phone Modoc National Forest at (916)233-5811.
Location: From the town of Likely, drive 18 miles east, then north on Jess Valley
    Road.
Trip note: Open from June to October. Elevation 6800 feet. Good base camp for
    wilderness backpack trip into the South Warner Wilderness. Camp set on
    Mill Creek, near Mill Creek Falls.

Site **12**   MILL CREEK
                                     FALLS   🌲

Campsites, facilities: There are 11 sites for tents and eight sites for tents or mo-
    torhomes. Piped water, vault toilets, tables and fireplaces are provided.
Reservations, fee: No reservation, no fee.
Who to contact: Phone Modoc National Forest at (916)233-5811.
Location: From the town of Likely, drive 13 miles east and then north on Jess
    Valley Road.
Trip note: Open from May through October. Elevation 5700 feet. In rugged,
    primitive setting, offers numerous hiking and fishing opportunities. Ante-
    lope herds roam the area.

Site **13**   EMERSON   🌲

Campsites, facilities: There are four tent sites. Vault toilets, tables and fireplaces
    are provided. No water is available, but a grocery store is nearby.
Reservations, fee: No reservations, no fee.
Who to contact: Phone Modoc National Forest at (916)233-5811.
Location: Drives four miles southwest from Eagleville, off Emerson Road.
Trip note: Little-used camp, in primitive setting on southeastern boundary of
    South Warner Wilderness. Good fishing in area.

Site **14**   PATTERSON   ▲

Campsites, facilities: There are five sites for tents or motorhomes to 16 feet long.
    Piped water, vault toilets, tables and fireplaces provided.
Reservations, fee: No reservations, no fee.

Who to contact: Phone Modoc National Forest at (916)233-5811.
Location: Drive 14 miles southwest of Eagleville on Patterson Sawmill Road.
Trip note: Open from July to October. Elevation 7200 feet. Very cold nights in
    spring and early fall.

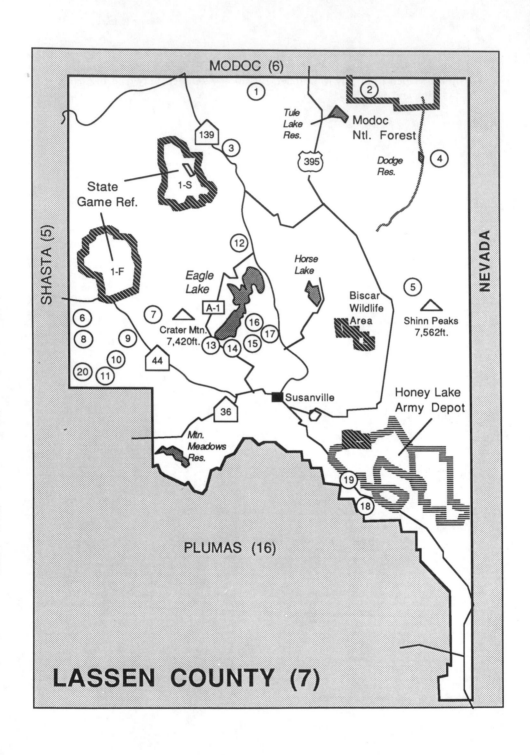

MODOC (6)

Tule Lake Res.

Modoc Ntl. Forest

Dodge Res.

State Game Ref.

1-S

139

3

395

4

SHASTA (5)

NEVADA

1-F

12

Eagle Lake

Horse Lake

Biscar Wildlife Area

5

Shinn Peaks 7,562ft.

A-1

6

7

Crater Mtn. 7,420ft.

16

17

8

9

13

14

15

10

44

20

11

Honey Lake Army Depot

36

Susanville

Mtn. Meadows Res.

19

18

PLUMAS (16)

LASSEN COUNTY (7)

LASSEN COUNTY

◆

Site 1   **ASH CREEK**   🌲

Campsites, facilities: There are seven campsites at Ash Creek which are suitable for tent campers or motorhomes no longer than 22 feet. No piped water is available, but vault toilets, tables and fireplaces are provided.
Reservations, fee: No reservations and no fee charged.
Who to contact: Phone Modoc National Forest at (916)233-5811, or write at 411 Main Street, Alturas, CA 96101.
Location: Ash Creek is located eight miles southeast of Adin off Ash Valley Road.
Trip note: Open from May through October. Elevation 4800 feet. This a remote, little-known campground. You can fish for trout on Ash Creek. It gets cold in spring.

Site 2   **BLUE LAKE**   🌲

Campsites, facilities: There are 24 tent sites and 24 additional sites that can be used for either tent camping or motorhomes. Piped water, vault toilets, tables and fireplaces are provided.
Reservations, fee: No reservations; $4 per night fee collected by the Forest Service.
Who to contact: Phone Modoc National Forest at (916)233-5811.
Location: Drive 16 miles southeast from Likely off Highway 395, via Jess Valley and Blue Lake Roads.
Trip note: This is very remote, little-known spot that gets quite cold in the spring. Fishing can be good in Parsnip Creek and Blue Lake. Elevation 6000 feet.

Site 3   **WILLOW CREEK**   ⛺

Campsites, facilities: There are eight campsites that can be used for tent camping or motorhomes up to 32 feet long. Piped water, vault toilets, tables and fireplaces are provided.

Reservations, fee: No reservations and no fee charged.
Who to contact: Phone Modoc National Forest at (916)233-5811.
Location: Drive 16 miles southeast of Adin on State Route 139.
Trip note: Open from May through October. Elevation 5200 feet. Willow Creek
    Camp is located just four miles from a State Game Refuge.

Site **4**   DODGE
                         RESERVOIR

Campsites, facilities: There are nine campsites that are suitable for tent campers
    or motorhomes. No piped water is available, but vault toilets, picnic tables
    and fireplaces are provided.
Reservations, fee: No reservations and no fee charged.
Who to contact: Contact the Bureau of Land Management at (916)257-5381.
Location: Drive 22 miles northeast of Ravendale on Tuledad Road.
Trip note: The weather turns cold in the spring and fall. Boating and fishing are
    good on Dodge Reservoir, but no swimming permitted. Elevation 5735
    feet.

Site **5**   RAMHORN
                           SPRING

Campsites, facilities: There are eight campsites suitable for either tents or motor-
    homes up to 30 feet long. Piped water, vault toilets, picnic tables and fire-
    places are provided.
Reservations, fee: No reservations, no fee charged.
Who to contact: Phone the Bureau of Land Management at (916)257-5381.
Location: Ramhorn Spring is 50 miles north of Susanville on Highway 395, then
    east two miles on Post Camp Road.
Trip note: Very remote, little known spot, with good hiking prospects. Shinn
    Peaks nearby. Elevation 5600 feet.

Site **6**   BUTTE
                            CREEK

Campsites, facilities: There are 14 campsites for either tents or motorhomes to 22
    feet long. No piped water is available. Vault toilets, fireplaces and tables are
    provided.
Reservations, fee: No reservations, no fee charged.
Who to contact: Call Lassen National Forest at (916)257-2151 or write at 707 Ne-
    vada Street, Susanville, CA 96130.
Location: Drive 13 miles southeast of Old Station off State Route 44.
Trip note: A prime, little-known spot, just three miles from northern boundary
    of Lassen Volcanic National Park, with fishing at Butte Creek and nearby
    Butte Lake.

Site 7   CRATER
LAKE   ⛺

Campsites, facilities: There are 17 campsites for tents or motorhomes up to 16
    feet long. Non-piped water is available, along with vault toilets, fireplaces
    and picnic tables.
Reservations, fee: No reservations; $4 fee per night.
Who to contact: Call Lassen National Forest at (916)257-2151.
Location: Crater Lake is 35 miles northwest of Susanville off State Route 44.
Trip note: Open from May through October. Elevation 6800 feet. Good fishing,
    swimming.

Site 8   BUTTE
LAKE   ⛺

Campsites, facilities: There are 98 campsites for tents or motorhomes up to 30
    feet long. Piped water, flush toilets, fireplaces and tables are provided.
Reservations, fee: No reservations; $6 fee per night.
Who to contact: Call Lassen Volcanic National Park at (916)595-4444.
Location: Drive 18 miles southeast of Old Station off State Route 44.
Trip note: Open from June through September. Elevation 6000 feet. A prime
    spot with hiking on a self-guiding trail or fishing in Butte Lake. Rowboats,
    canoes and other non-motored crafts are allowed on the lake.

Site 9   BOGARD   ⛺

Campsites, facilities: There are 22 campsites at Bogard that can accommodate
    tents or motorhomes up to 22 feet long. Water, vault toilets, tables and fire-
    places are provided.
Reservations, fee: No reservations; $4 per night fee.
Who to contact: Phone Lassen National Forest at (916)257-2151, or write 707
    Nevada Street, Susanville, CA 96130.
Location: Bogard Camp is located 28 miles northwest of Susanville off State
    Route 44.
Trip note: Open from May through October. Elevation 5600 feet. Fish in Pine
    Creek at the foot of Bogard Buttes (elevation 7500 feet). Cold weather in
    spring.

Site 10   ROCKY
KNOLL   ⛺

Campsites, facilities: There are seven tent sites and 11 additional campsites that
    can handle either tents or motorhomes up to 22 feet long. Piped water,
    vault toilets, fireplaces and picnic tables are provided.

Reservations, fee: No reservations; $4 fee per night.
Who to contact: Phone Lassen National Forest at (916)257-2151.
Location: Drive 20 miles northwest of Westwood via County Road A-21 and Silver Lake Road.
Trip note: Open from May through September. Elevation 6400 feet. Swimming, boating and fishing good in Silver Lake.

Site **11**   SILVER
                             BOWL   ▲

Campsites, facilities: Ten sites for tents or motorhomes are available. Piped water, vault toilets, fireplaces and picnic tables are provided.
Reservations, fee: No reservations; $4 per night fee.
Who to contact: Phone Lassen National Forest at (916)257-2151.
Location: Drive 21 miles northwest of Weswood via County Road A-21 and Silver Lake Road.
Trip note: Open from June through September. Elevation 6400 feet. The campground is set on Silver Lake where you can go fishing, swimming or boating.

Site **12**   NORTH
                             EAGLE LAKE   ▲

Campsites, facilities: There are 20 campsites that will take tents or motorhomes. A dump station, piped water, vault toilets, picnic tables and fireplaces are provided.
Reservations, fee: No reservations; $3 fee per night.
Who to contact: Phone the Bureau of Land Management at (916)257-5381.
Location: Drive 29 miles north of Susanville via State Route 139, then a half mile west on County Road A-1.
Trip note: Open from May through November. Elevation 5100 feet. Fishing, boating on North Eagle Lake, hiking on nearby trails.

Site **13**   CHRISTIE   ▲

Campsites, facilities: There are 69 campsites for tents or motorhomes up to 32 feet long. Piped water, flush toilets, fireplaces and picnic tables are provided. A grocery store and laundromat are nearby, and propane gas is available. A disposal station is two miles away at Merrill Camp.
Reservations, fee: No reservations; $5 fee per night.
Who to contact: Phone Lassen National Forest at (916)257-2151.
Location: Drive 21 miles northwest of Susanville of State Route 36 via County Road A-1.
Trip note: Open from May through September. Elevation 5100 feet. Fish for

large trout, or try boating and swimming in Eagle Lake. Windy in the afternoon, so get your fishing done early.

Site **14**   MERRILL

Campsites, facilites: There are 181 campsites for tents or motorhomes to 22 feet long. Piped water, flush toilets, picnic tables and fireplaces are provided. A grocery store, laundromat, sanitary disposal station and propane gas are available. There is access for handicapped.
Reservations, fee: No reservations; $6 fee per night.
Who to contact: Phone Lassen National Forest at (916)257-2151.
Location: Merrill Camp is 18 miles northwest of Susanville on the south shore of Eagle Lake.
Trip note: Open from May through October. Elevation 5100 feet. You can launch your boat here when fishing for the giant Eagle Lake trout.

Site **15**   WEST EAGLE
                                       GROUP CAMP

Campsites, facilities: This is a group camp for tents and motorhomes up to 22 feet long. Handicap access is provided. Piped water, flush toilets, tables and a picnic area are provided. Camp capacity is limited to 150 people.
Reservations, fee: Camping is available by reservation only; $25 fee per night.
Who to contact: For reservations call (916)257-2595.
Location: Drive 18 miles northwest of Susanville off State Route 35 via County Road A-1.
Trip note: Open May through September. Elevation 5100 feet. Boating, fishing in Eagle Lake.

Site **16**   EAGLE

Campsites, facilities: There are 50 campsites for tents or motorhomes up to 32 feet long. Piped water, flush toilets, picnic tables and fireplaces are provided. Shopping is nearby.
Reservations, fee: Reservations through Ticketron; $6 fee per night, plus a $2.25 Ticketron service charge.
Who to contact: Phone Lassen National Forest at (916)257-2151.
Location: Situated on south shore of Eagle Lake.
Trip note: Because of the facilities available, this is one of the more popular campgrounds on the southern end of Eagle Lake. However, fishing is better on northern end of lake.

| Site 17 | ASPEN GROVE | ▲ |

Campsites, facilities: There are 25 tent sites with picnic tables and fireplaces. Piped water, flush toilets, grocery store and a laundromat are nearby.
Reservations, fee: No reservations; $5 fee per night.
Who to contact: Phone Lassen National Forest at (916)257-2151.
Location: On the southern shoreline of Eagle Lake.
Trip note: Camp is located adjacent to a boat launch on Eagle Lake.

| Site 18 | LAUFMAN | ▲ |

Campsites, facilities: There are eight campsites here for tents or motorhomes up to 22 feet long. Piped water, vault toilets, tables and fireplaces are provided. Grocery store and laundromat are nearby.
Reservations, fee: No reservations; $4 fee.
Who to contact: Call Plumas National Forest at (916)283-2050, or write at 159 Lawrence Street, Quincy, CA 95971.
Location: Drive three miles southeast of Milford off Highway 395 on Milford Grade.
Trip note: Open May through October. Elevation 5100 feet. The Dixie Mountain State Game Refuge is about five miles away.

| Site 19 | HONEY LAKE | |

Campsites, facilities: There are 56 motorhome campsites with full hookups. Showers, a laundromat, grocery store and a gameroom are available for campers' use.
Reservations, fee: Call prior to planning trip.
Who to contact: Call Honey Lake Camp at (916)253-2508.
Location: Drive two miles north of Milford on Highway 395.
Trip note: A 27-acre campground overlooking Honey Lake.

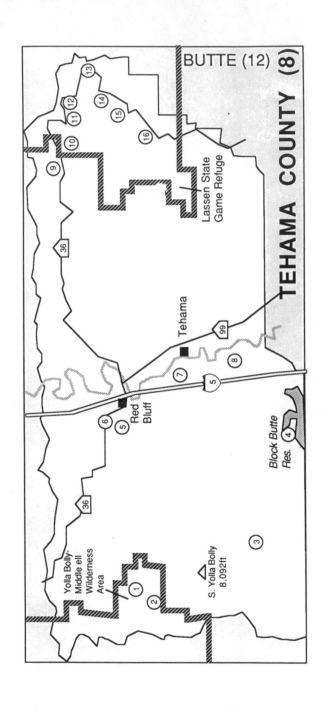

TEHAMA COUNTY (8)

Lassen State
Game Refuge

36

Tehama

99

5

8

7

Red
Bluff

6

5

Block Butte
Res.

4

36

3

Yolla Bolly-
Middle ell
Wilderness
Area

1

2

S. Yolla Bolly
8,092ft

9

10

11

12

13

14

15

16

TEHAMA COUNTY

♦

Site **1**   SADDLE
CAMP   🌲

Campsites, facilities: There are five campsites here for tents or motorhomes up to
22 feet. Piped water, vault toilets, picnic tables and fireplaces are provided.

Reservations, fee: No reservations, no fee.

Who to contact: Phone Shasta/Trinity National Forest at (916)246-5222.

Location: Drive 38 miles west of Red Bluff off State Route 36 via Cannon and
Pettyjohn roads.

Trip note: Open April through November. Elevation 3700 feet. Virtually unknown campground. Good camp for expedition into adjacent Yolla Bolly
Middle Eel Wilderness.

Site **2**   TOMHEAD
SADDLE   🌲

Campsites, facilities: There are five campsites for tents or motorhomes. No water, so bring your own. Vault toilets, picnic tables and fireplaces are
provided.

Reservations, fee: No reservations, no fee.

Who to contact: Phone Shasta/Trinity National Forest at (916)246-5222.

Location: Camp is four miles farther up the road and 2,000 feet higher than Tehama County Camp No. 1 (Saddle Camp).

Trip note: Open from April to October. Elevation 5700 feet. Really out there and
rarely visited. Located on edge of Yolla Bolly Middle Eel Wilderness area.

Site **3**   WHITLOCK   🌲

Campsites, facilities: There are five campsites for tents or motorhomes up to 22
feet long. Piped water, flush toilets, picnic tables and fireplaces are
provided.

Reservations, fee: No reservations, no fee.

Who to contact: Phone Mendocino National Forest at (916)934-3316.

Location: Set 14 miles northwest of Peskenta off Toomes Camp Road.

Trip note: Open from May through November. Elevation 4300 feet. An obscure Forest Service camp that is often empty or close to empty. Good hunting in the fall.

Site **4**   BUCKHORN

Campsites, facilities: There are 80 campsites for tents or motorhomes to 35 feet long. Piped water, picnic tables and fireplaces are provided. Flush toilets, showers and a playground are available. Nearby are a sanitary dump station, propane gas and a grocery store.
Reservations, fee: No reservations; $6 fee per night.
Who to contact: Phone Black Butte Lake campground at (916)685-4781.
Location: Set at Black Butte Lake 14 miles northwest of Orland via Road 200 and Buckhorn Road.
Trip note: Open year around. Elevation 500 feet. Good crappie fishing in Black Butte Lake in summer months. See Glenn County for more information.

Site **5**   BEND
MOBILE PARK

Campsites, facilities: There are 18 spaces for motorhomes with full or partial hookups. Piped water, showers, flush toilets, picnic tables and fireplaces are provided. A grocery store, laundromat and sanitary dump station are nearby.
Reservations, fee: An $11 deposit is required with reservation. $11 fee per night; pets allowed.
Who to contact: Phone at (916)527-6289.
Location: Set seven miles northeast of Red Bluff on Bend Ferry Road.
Trip note: Situated along the Sacramento River. Good salmon fishing from mid-August through October. Very hot weather in July and August.

Site **6**   O'NITE
PARK

Campsites, facilities: There are 15 tent sites and 60 motorhome spaces with full hookups. Piped water, flush toilets, showers, a swimming pool and laundromat are provided.
Reservations, fee: A $12 deposit is required with reservation; $12 fee per night.
Who to contact: Phone at (916)527-5868.
Location: In Red Bluff at 130 Gilmore Road.
Trip note: Located one block from the Sacramento River. Close to a supermarket and restaurants, and 45 minutes from Lassen Park.

Site 7

HIDDEN HARBOR
RV PARK

Campsites, facilities: There are 500 tent sites and 36 spaces for motorhomes with full hookups. A grocery store, laundromat and sanitary dump station are available nearby.

Reservations, fee: Call for space available, particularly for motorhome users.

Who to contact: Phone at (916)384-1800, or write at 24680 River Road, Los Molinos, CA 96055.

Location: Set on Sacramento River in Los Molinos. Turn west from Interstate 5 on Tehama and Vina Road. Follow signs.

Trip note: Open year around. Ideal spot for base camp for shad fishing trip in June or salmon trip in September. Very hot in the summer.

Site 8

WOODSON
BRIDGE

Campsites, facilities: There are 46 campsites for tents or motorhomes up to 31 feet. Piped water, picnic tables and fireplaces are provided. Showers, flush toilets, a playground and boat launch are available.

Reservations, fee: Reservations advised in summer and fall months through MISTIX by phoning (800)446-7275. $6 fee per night; pets $1.

Who to contact: Phone at (916)839-2112.

Location: Set at water's edge of the Sacramento River six miles east of Corning off County Road A-9 (South Ave.).

Trip note: Located right in middle of good shad fishing area from late May to July. Boat launch provided in park.

Site 9

BATTLE
CREEK

Campsites, facilities: There are 12 sites for tents only and 38 spaces for tents or motorhomes to 22 feet. Piped water, picnic tables, fireplaces are provided, flush toilets are available, and a grocery store, propane gas are nearby.

Reservations, fee: No reservations; $4 fee per night.

Who to contact: Phone Lassen National Forest at (916)257-2151.

Location: Two miles west of Mineral along Mill Creek on State Route 36.

Trip note: Open from May through November. Elevation 4800 feet. One of four campgrounds set on Mill Creek. Trout fishing can be good in May and June.

Site 10   HOLE-IN-THE-GROUND

Campsites, facilities: There are four sites for tents only and nine sites for tents or motorhomes. Piped water, flush toilets, picnic tables and fireplaces are provided. A grocery store is nearby.
Reservations, fee: No reservations; $4 per night fee.
Who to contact: Phone Lassen National Forest at (916)257-2151.
Location: Five miles southwest of Mill Creek off State Route 172.
Trip note: Elevation 4300 feet. Hiking and fishing in area. Map of Lassen National Forest details opportunities.

Site 11   MILL CREEK

Campsites, facilities: There are 12 campsites for tents or motorhomes to 22 feet. Non-piped water is available. Vault toilets, picnic tables and fireplaces are provided.
Reservations, fee: No reservations, no fee.
Who to contact: Phone Lassen National Forest at (916)257-2151.
Location: On State Route 172 in Mill Creek.
Trip note: Open from May through September. Elevation 4700 feet. The most primitive and least used of four campgrounds in area.

Site 12   GURNSEY CREEK

Campsites, facilities: There are 27 sites for tents, 25 spaces for tents or motorhomes to 22 feet. Piped water, flush toilets, picnic tables and fireplaces are provided. A grocery store is nearby.
Reservations, fee: No reservations; $4 fee.
Who to contact: Phone Lassen National Park at (916)257-2151.
Location: Set five miles southeast of Childs Meadow on State Route 36 and 89.
Trip note: Open from May through September. Elevation 4700 feet. Good headquarters for summer trout fishing trip with many choices in area.

Site 13   WILLOW

Campsites, facilities: There are eight sites for tents or motorhomes to 22 feet. No water is available, so bring your own. Vault toilets, picnic tables and fireplaces are provided.
Reservations, fee: No reservation, no fee.
Who to contact: Phone Lassen National Forest at (916)257-2151.
Location: Drive four miles from Deer Creek off State Route 32/State Route 89

on Lost Creek Road.

Trip note: Open from June through September. Elevation 5100 feet. Rugged setting. Bring what you need. Good hiking, fishing along Deer Creek.

Site **14**   ELAM
                                    CREEK

Campsites, facilities: There are five sites for tents and 10 sites for tents or motorhomes up to 22 feet. Piped water, flush toilets, picnic tables and fireplaces are provided.

Reservations, fee: No reservations; $4 fee per night.

Who to contact: Phone Lassen National Forest at (916)257-2151.

Location: Located 14 1/2 miles southwest of Chester via State Routes 36 and 32.

Trip note: Open from May through October. Elevation 4400 feet. Try the trout fishing in area streams.

Site **15**   ALDER
                                    CREEK

Campsites, facilities: There are five tent sites. No piped water available. Vault toilets, picnic tables and fireplaces are provided.

Reservations, fee: No reservation, no fee.

Who to contact: Phone Lassen National Forest at (916)257-2151.

Location: Four miles downriver from Tehama County Camp No. 14 (Elam Creek).

Trip note: A good alternative if other camps on Deer Creek are full. Primitive, with no piped water.

Site **16**   POTATO
                                    PATCH

Campsites, facilities: There are 20 sites for tents and 12 sites for tents or motorhomes to 22 feet. Piped water, flush toilets, picnic tables and fireplaces provided.

Reservations, fee: No reservations; $4 fee per night.

Who to contact: Phone Lassen National Forest at (916)257-2151.

Location: Set 22 miles southwest of Chester, via State Route 36 and State Route 32.

Trip note: Open from May through October. Elevation 3400 feet. Good hiking, fishing along Deer Creek.

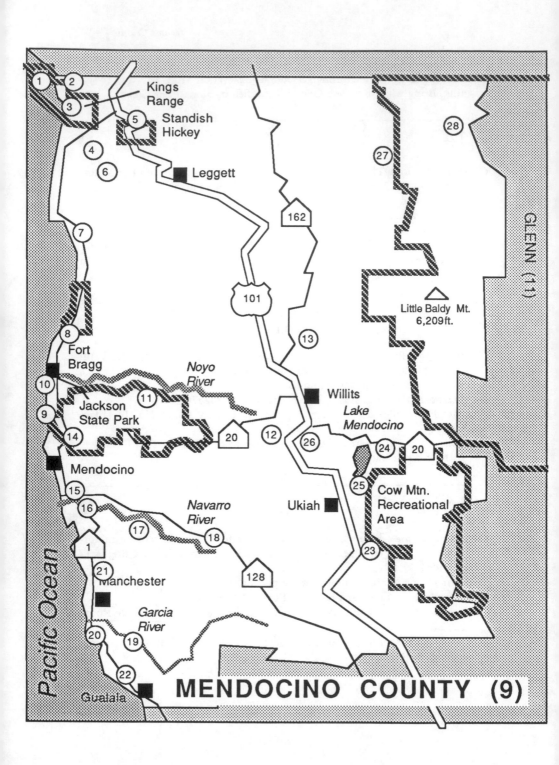

Kings
Range

Standish
Hickey

Leggett

162

101

27

28

GLENN (11)

△ Little Baldy Mt.
6,209ft.

13

Noyo
River

Fort
Bragg

Willits

Jackson
State Park

Lake
Mendocino

20

12

26

24

20

Mendocino

25

Cow Mtn.
Recreational
Area

Ukiah

Navarro
River

1

23

21 Manchester

128

Garcia
River

20

19

22

Gualala

Pacific Ocean

MENDOCINO COUNTY (9)

MENDOCINO COUNTY
♦

Site **1** | WAILAKI |

Campsites, facilities: There are 16 campsites for tents or motorhomes up to 20
  feet long. Piped water, vault toilets, picnic tables and fireplaces are pro-
  vided. A grocery store and propane gas station are nearby.
Reservations, fee: No reservations, no fee.
Who to contact: Phone (707)822-7648.
Location: Set 19 miles southwest of Briceland off Shelter Cove Road on Chemise
  Mountain Road.
Trip note: Open year around. Elevation 1840 feet. Horseback riding near the
  ocean. Enjoy the coastal beauty of the Chemise Mountain Primitive Area
  and nearby Sinkyone Wilderness State Park.

Site **2** | BOLTON'S CABANA HOLIDAY
FAMILY RESORT |

Campsites, facilities: There are 10 tent sites and 30 motorhome spaces with full
  hookups. Rest rooms, hot showers, heated pool, playground, games, store,
  laundromat, dump station and an evening campfire are among the amenities offered here.
Reservations, fee: $3.50 reservation fee payable to Leisuretime Reservation Sys-
  tems, Inc.: (800)822-2267; $12 fee per night.
Who to contact: Phone (707)925-6249.
Location: Set three miles south of Piercy on Highway 101.
Trip note: Open year around. Elevation 700 feet. Resort situated in a 20 acre
  grove of redwoods on Highway 101. A shady place to rest, explore the redwoods or fish in the Eel River. Steelhead fishing can be quite good on
  South Fork of Eel during winter months.

Site **3** | SINKYONE WILDERNESS
STATE PARK |

Campsites, facilities: At Usal Beach there are 15 walk-in campsites, each with a
  fire ring and a picnic table. There is no piped water, but there is plenty of

water on premises, provided you purify it. Pit toilets are provided. Between Bear Harbor and Jones Beach there are about 25 primitive campsites, some of which have tables, fire rings and pit toilets. You can drive to within 1/4 mile of Bear Harbor and park at Orchard Creek.

Reservations, fee: No reservations, no fee.

Who to contact: Phone (707)247-3318.

Location: Set 30 miles west of Redway on Highway 435 (Briceland Road) or 50 miles north of Ft. Bragg via Highway 1 and County Road 431 (narrow, dirt, not maintained).

Trip note: This has been called the "lost coast" because of its rugged beauty. Hiking for the experienced backpacker only. Beginning at Usal Beach there is a 17 mile trail north to Bear Harbor. This ocean front trail is steep and rugged, but beautiful as it takes you past sheer bluffs and fern meadows. There is several primitive camping sites in this area. Wheeler Creek, Bear Harbor and Usal Beach all have beach access.

Site 4   STANDISH-HICKEY   ▲

Campsites, facilities: There are 65 campsites for tents or motorhomes up to 27 feet long. Piped water, showers, flush toilets, picnic tables and fireplaces are provided. A grocery store and laundromat are nearby. There's wheelchair access to camping and picnic areas.

Reservations, fee: $3.75 reservation fee payable to MISTIX: (800)446-7275; $10 fee per night; pets $1.

Who to contact: Phone Standish-Hickey State Recreation Area at (707)946-2311.

Location: Set one mile north of Leggett off Highway 101.

Trip note: Open from May through September. Elevation 800 feet. A pretty spot in the redwoods. Reservations advised during summer. Nice layover on trip along Highway 101.

Site 5   REDWOOD

Campsites, facilities: There are 63 campsites for tents or motorhomes up to 18 feet long. Piped water, showers, flush toilets, picnic tables and fireplaces are provided. A grocery store and a laundromat are nearby. There's wheelchair access to camping and picnic areas.

Reservations, fee: $3.75 reservation fee payable to MISTIX: (800)446-7275; $10 fee per night; pets $1.

Who to contact: Phone Standish-Hickey State Recreation Area at (707)946-2311.

Location: Set one mile north of Leggett off Highway 101.

Trip note: Open from June through September. Elevation 800 feet. An option to Site No. 4.

Site **6**   ROCK
                                       CREEK

Campsites, facilities: There are 36 campsites for tents or motorhomes up to 27
   feet long. Piped water, showers, flush toilets, picnic tables and fireplaces
   are provided. A grocery store and laundromat are nearby. There's wheelchair access to camping and picnic areas.
Reservations, fee: $3.75 reservation fee payable to MISTIX: (800)446-7275; $6
   fee per night; pets $1.
Who to contact: Phone Standish-Hickey State Recreation Area at (707)946-2311.
Location: Set one mile north of Leggett off Highway 101.
Trip note: Open year around. Elevation 800 feet. An alternative to camps 4 and 5
   in same area.

Site **7**   WESTPORT UNION LANDING
                                  STATE BEACH

Campsites, facilities: There are 150 campsites for tents or motorhomes up to 35
   feet long. No water, but pit toilets, fireplaces and picnic tables are provided.
   A grocery store is nearby.
Reservations, fee: No reservations, no fee.
Who to contact: Phone (707)937-5804.
Location: Set three miles north of Westport on Highway 1.
Trip note: Open year around. Elevation 120 feet. Bring your own water. Foggy
   in summer, but clear and often warm in spring and fall.

Site **8**   MACKERRICHER
                                   STATE PARK

Campsites, facilities: There are 140 campsites for tents or motorhomes up to 35
   feet long. Piped water, showers, flush toilets, a dump station, picnic tables
   and fireplaces are provided. A grocery store, propane gas station and laundromat are available nearby. There's wheelchair access to camping, picnicking and hiking areas.
Reservations, fee: $3.75 reservation fee payable to MISTIX: (800)446-7275; $10
   fee per night; pets $1.
Who to contact: Phone (707)937-5804.
Location: Set three miles north of Fort Bragg on Highway 1.
Trip note: Open year around. Elevation 20 feet. Beautiful coastal layover on tour
   of Highway 1. Don't expect to drive anywhere fast during summer months.

Site **9**   WOODSIDE RV PARK
                       AND CAMPGROUND

Campsites, facilities: There are 34 tent sites and 70 motorhome spaces with full
   or partial hookups. On the premises there are rest rooms, showers, a recreation room, sauna, horseshoe pit, cable TV, a food store, laundromat, dump
   station and fish cleaning table. Boating and fishing access are nearby.
Reservations, fee: Call in advance for space and rates.
Who to contact: Phone (707)964-3684.
Location: Set two miles south of Fort Bragg.
Trip note: Nine acre wooded park with ocean access. Camping areas are nestled
   among woods.

Site **10**   POMO CAMPGROUND AND
                       MOTOR HOME PARK

Campsites, facilities: There are 10 tent sites and 94 motorhome spaces with full
   or partial hookups. On the premises are rest rooms, hot showers (coin-oper-
   ated), a store, laundromat, dump station, fish cleaning table, horseshoe pits
   and a large grass playing field. Picnic tables and fire rings are at each
   campsite.
Reservations, fee: Reservations accepted.
Who to contact: Phone (707)964-3373.
Location: Set two miles south of Highway 1/Highway 20 intersection on the east
   side of Highway 1.
Trip note: Seventeen acres of native tree cover along ocean.

Site **11**   JACKSON STATE
                       FOREST

Campsites, facilities: There are 44 campsites for tents or motorhomes. No water,
   but pit toilets, picnic tables and fireplaces are provided.
Reservations, fee: No reservations, no fee.
Who to contact: Phone (707)964-5674.
Location: Set 10 miles southeast of Fort Bragg off Highway 20.
Trip note: Open year around. Elevation 2000 feet. Primitive, beautiful campsite.
   Remember to bring your own drinking water.

Site **12**   KAMP SUNDOWN
                       KOA

Campsites, facilities: There are 25 tent sites and 50 motorhome spaces with partial hookups. Piped water, flush toilets, showers, picnic tables, a playground
   and a sanitary dump station are on the premises. A grocery store and laundromat are nearby.

Reservations, fee: $14 reservation deposit; $14 fee per night.
Who to contact: Phone (707)459-6179.
Location: Set one and a half miles west of Willits on Highway 20.
Trip note: Open year around. Elevation 1377 feet. Good spot to catch some sleep while traveling up Highway 101.

Site **13** SLEEPYHOLLOW
RV PARK

Campsites, facilities: There are six tent sites and 24 motorhome spaces with full or partial hookups. TV jacks are available with three stations. A grocery store, laundromat, dump station and propane gas station are all available on the premises.
Reservations, fee: $10 reservation deposit; $10 fee per night.
Who to contact: Phone (707)459-4779 or 459-2756.
Location: Set eight miles north of Willits on Highway 101 at the 55.5 mile marker (0.2 miles beyond Shimmins Ridge Road sign), turn right at the beginning of the divided four-lane highway.
Trip note: Open year around. Elevation 1300 feet. Nearby points of interest are the Skunk Train, Redwood Country Excursions, Fort Bragg, Clear Lake, Round Valley, Lake Pillsbury and Lake Mendocino.

Site **14** RUSSIAN GULCH
STATE PARK

Campsites, facilities: There are 28 campsites for tents or motorhomes up to 30 feet long. Some special sites are provided for hikers and/or bicyclists. Piped water, showers, flush toilets, picnic tables and fireplaces are provided. A grocery store, laundromat and propane gas are available nearby. Wheelchair access in camping area.
Reservations, fee: $3.75 reservation fee payable to: MISTIX: (800)446-7275.
Who to contact: Phone (707)937-5804.
Location: Set two miles northeast of Mendocino off Highway 1.
Trip note: Open year around. Elevation 50 feet. Three mile bike trail in park. Camp is set along some of California's most beautiful coast.

Site **15** MENDOCINO
CAMPGROUND

Campsites, facilities: There are 12 tent sites and 48 campsites for tents or motorhomes up to 20 feet long. Piped water, flush toilets and showers are provided.
Reservations, fee: Reservations available through Ticketron outlets. $10 fee per night; pets $1.
Who to contact: Phone (707)937-3130.

Location: Set 1/2 mile south of Mendocino on Comptche-Ukiah Road.
Trip note: Open year around. Elevation 90 feet. In the area you'll find redwood groves, botanical gardens and the Skunk Train.

Site **16**   VAN DAMME
                          STATE PARK

Campsites, facilities: There are 71 campsites for tents or motorhomes up to 35 feet long. Non-piped water, but flush toilets, showers, picnic tables and fireplaces are provided. A grocery store, laundromat and propane gas are available nearby.
Reservations, fee: $3.75 reservation fee payable to MISTIX: (800)446-7275; $10 fee per night; pets $1.
Who to contact: Phone (707)937-5804.
Location: Set three miles south of Mendocino at Little River off Highway 1.
Trip note: Open year around. Elevation 100 feet. In the park are a nature trail, designated underwater area and three mile bike trail. During winter this is a good base camp for steelhead fishing trip at Noyo River, and possible trips to Navarro, Garcia or Gualala River.

Site **17**   PAUL M. DIMMICK
                WAYSIDE CAMPGROUND

Campsites, facilities: There are 28 campsites for tents or motorhomes up to 30 feet long. No water, but pit toilets, fireplaces and picnic tables are provided.
Reservations, fee: No reservations; $3 fee per night; pets $1.
Who to contact: Phone (707)937-5804.
Location: Set five miles northwest of Navarro on Highway 128.
Trip note: Open year around. Elevation 50 feet. In winter, Navarro River gets fair steelhead run.

Site **18**   HENDY WOODS
                        STATE PARK

Campsites, facilities: There are 90 campsites here for tents or motorhomes up to 35 feet long. Non-piped water, flush toilets, showers, dump station, picnic tables and fireplaces are provided. A grocery store and propane gas station are available nearby. Wheelchair access to camping, picnicking and hiking areas.
Reservations, fee: $3.75 reservation fee payable to MISTIX: (800)446-7275; $10 fee per night; pets $1.
Who to contact: Phone (707)937-5804.
Location: Set eight miles northwest of Booneville off Highway 128.
Trip note: Open year around. Elevation 50 feet. Highway 128 to the coast makes for a nice drive.

Site 19 — MANCHESTER BEACH KOA

Campsites, facilities: There are 13 tent sites and 52 spaces for tents or motor-homes with full or partial hookups. Rest rooms, showers, heated pool, hot tub and spa, a playground, dump station, picnic tables and fireplaces are on the premises. A grocery store, laundromat, and propane gas are available nearby.

Reservations, fee: $3.50 reservation fee payable to Leisuretime Reservation Systems, Inc. $16 deposit; $16 fee per night.

Who to contact: Phone (707)882-2375.

Location: Set one and a half miles north of Pt. Arena on Kinney Road.

Trip note: Open year around. Elevation 100 feet. Easy walk to a sandy beach. Comb the beach, collect driftwood, or fish for steelhead, salmon and abalone in season.

Site 20 — MANCHESTER STATE BEACH

Campsites, facilities: There are 43 campsites for tents or motorhomes up to 30 feet long. Non-piped water, pit toilets, picnic tables and fireplaces are provided. A sanitary dump station is at the campground. A grocery store and propane gas are available nearby.

Reservations, fee: $3.75 reservation fee payable to MISTIX: (800)446-7275; $3 fee per night; pets $1.

Who to contact: Phone (707)937-5804.

Location: Set one mile north of Manchester off Highway 1.

Trip note: Open year around. Elevation 50 feet. Bring your own drinking water. Pick up supplies at Point Arena to the south. Garcia River has fair steelhead fishing during the winter months.

Site 21 — ROLLERVILLE JUNCTION

Campsites, facilities: There are seven tent sites, 15 motorhome spaces and 24 spaces for either, with full or partial hookups. Rest rooms, hot showers, a sanitary dump station, picnic tables and fireplaces are provided. There is a playground on the premises. A laundromat and propane gas can be found nearby.

Reservations, fee: $10 reservation fee; $10 fee per night.

Who to contact: Phone (707)882-2440.

Location: Set two miles north of Point Arena on Highway 1.

Trip note: Open year around. Elevation 220 feet. A quiet section of California coast.

Site **22**   ANCHOR BAY
CAMPGROUND

Campsites, facilities: There are 76 tent sites and motorhome spaces with full or
partial hookups. Rest rooms, hot showers, a sanitary dump station, picnic
tables and fireplaces are provided.
Reservations, fee: $13 reservation deposit; $13 fee per night.
Who to contact: Phone (707)884-4222.
Location: Set four miles north of Gualala on Highway 1.
Trip note: Open year around. Elevation 60 feet. In winter, Gualala River gets
steelhead run.

Site **23**   MANOR OAKS
OVERNIGHTER

Campsites, facilities: There are 54 motorhome spaces with full hookups. Rest
rooms, piped water and showers are provided. A laundromat is also on the
premises.
Reservations, fee: No reservations; $13 fee per night.
Who to contact: Phone (707)462-0529.
Location: Set in Ukiah at 700 East Gobbi Street.
Trip note: Open year around. Elevation 635 feet. Lake Mendocino nearby has
boating, skiing and average fishing for small bass or panfish.

Site **24**   BU-SHAY

Campsites, facilities: There are 171 campsites for tents or motorhomes up to 35
feet long. Rest rooms, hot showers, a playground, sanitary dump station,
picnic tables and fireplaces are provided. A grocery store, laundromat and
propane gas are available nearby.
Reservations, fee: No reservations; $6 fee per night.
Who to contact: Phone Lake Mendocino at (707)462-7581.
Location: Set 13 miles northeast of Ukiah off Highway 20.
Trip note: Open from April through September. Elevation 750 feet. Largemouth
bass and bluegill provide fair fishing on summer mornings.

Site **25**   CHE-KAKA

Campsites, facilities: There are 24 campsites for tents or motorhomes up to 35
feet long. Piped water, vault toilets, a playground, picnic tables and fireplaces are provided. A grocery store and laundromat are nearby.
Reservations, fee: No reservations, no fee.
Who to contact: Phone Lake Mendocino at (707)462-7581.

Location: Set five miles north of Ukiah off Highway 20.

Trip note: Open from April through September. Elevation 750 feet. Near upper Russian River. Clear Lake not far to the east.

Site 26 KY-EN ▲

Campsites, facilities: There are 103 campsites for tents or motorhomes up to 35 feet long. Rest rooms, hot showers, a playground, sanitary dump station, picnic tables and fireplaces are provided. A grocery store, laundromat and propane gas are available nearby.

Reservations, fee: No reservations; $6 fee per night.

Who to contact: Phone Lake Mendocino at (707)462-7581.

Location: Set 10 miles northeast of Ukiah off Highway 20.

Trip note: Open from April through September. Elevation 760 feet. Lake Mendocino, Clear Lake and Russian River provide fishing or boating options.

Site 27 EEL RIVER ▲

Campsites, facilities: There are 16 campsites for tents or motorhomes. Piped water, vault toilets, picnic tables and fireplaces are provided. A grocery store is nearby.

Reservations, fee: No reservations, no fee.

Who to contact: Phone Mendocino National Forest at (916)934-3316.

Location: Set 14 miles east of Covelo off Mendocino Pass Road.

Trip note: Open year around. Elevation 1500 feet. For rockhounds, Jadeite and Nephrite can be found along Eel River and Buttermilk Creek.

Site 28 LITTLE DOE 🌲

Campsites, facilities: There are 22 tent sites. No water, but vault toilets, picnic tables and fireplaces provided.

Reservations, fee: No reservations, no fee.

Who to contact: Phone Mendocino National Forest at (916)934-3316.

Location: Set 30 miles northeast of Covelo off Mendocino Pass Road.

Trip note: Open from June through October. Elevation 3600 feet. A primitive, little known and little used camp. Mendocino Forest map details area backcountry roads and hiking trails.

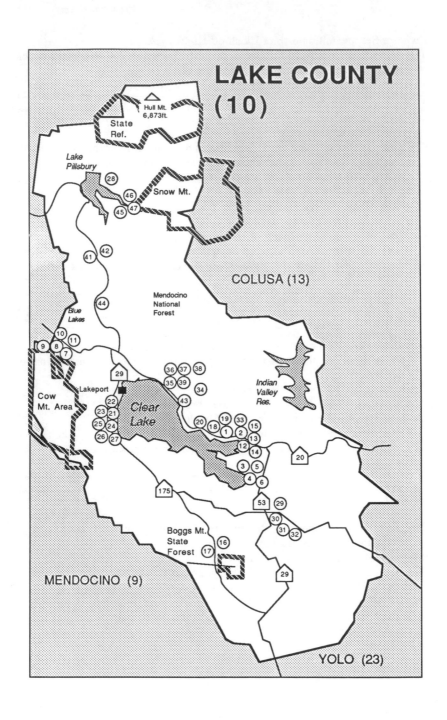

LAKE COUNTY (10)

Hull Mt. 6,873ft.

State Ref.

Lake Pillsbury

Snow Mt.

COLUSA (13)

Mendocino National Forest

Blue Lakes

Indian Valley Res.

Lakeport

Cow Mt. Area

Clear Lake

175

Boggs Mt. State Forest

MENDOCINO (9)

YOLO (23)

LAKE COUNTY

◆

Site 1   DARNELL'S
NORTHWOOD PARK

Campsites, facilities: There are 28 motorhome spaces with full hookups. Flush
toilets, showers, dump station, boat rentals, pier, boat ramp, lake frontage
sites, laundry, propane gas and groceries are available.
Reservations, fee: Call ahead for space available and fee.
Who to contact: Phone park at (707)998-3389.
Location: Drive to Clearlake Oaks, four miles west on Highway 20 from the in-
tersection of Highway 53 to 10090 East Highway 20.
Trip note: Open all year. Elevation 1320 feet. Located on the shore of Clear
Lake, the largest natural lake within California. Bass fishing is best from
March through May. Catfish, bluegill and crappie are on the bite during
the hot summer months. A prime boating lake, with 100 miles of shoreline.

Site 2   THE
BUNGALOW

Campsites, facilities: There are seven motorhome spaces with full hookups.
Flush toilets, showers, pier, lake frontage sites and laundry are available.
Boat rentals, a boat ramp, propane gas and groceries are located nearby.
Reservations, fee: Call ahead for space available and fee.
Who to contact: Phone park at (707)998-3832.
Location: Drive to Clearlake Oaks, four miles west on Highway 20 from the in-
tersection of Highway 53. Located at 10195 East Highway 20.
Trip note: See trip note for campsite No. 1.

Site 3   LAKESHORE
RESORT

Campsites, facilities: There are 14 motorhome spaces with full hookups. Flush
toilets, showers, dump station, pier, lake frontage sites and laundry are
available. Boat rental, a boat ramp, propane gas and groceries are nearby.
Reservations, fee: Call ahead for space available and fee.
Who to contact: Phone park at (707)994-8240.

Location: Drive three miles beyond the town of Lower Lake on State Route 53 to Clearlake Highlands, turn left at intersection islands and drive to 14581 Lakeshore Drive.

Trip note: See trip note for campsite No. 1.

Site **4**   LOTOWANA

Campsites, facilities: There are motorhome spaces with full hookups. Flush toilets, showers, dump station, boat rentals, pier, boat ramp, lake frontage sites, laundry, propane gas and groceries are available.

Reservations, fee: Call ahead for space and fee.

Who to contact: Phone park at (707)994-5344.

Location: Drive three miles beyond the town of Lower Lake on State Route 53 to Clearlake Highlands, turn left at intersection islands and drive to 14825 Clement Drive.

Trip note: See trip note for campsite No. 1.

Site **5**   AUSTIN'S CAMPGROUND
                        AND MARINA

Campsites, facilities: There are 80 motorhome spaces with full hookups. Flush toilets, showers, dump station, boat rentals, waterski rentals, pier, boat ramp, lake frontage sites, laundry, propane gas and groceries are available.

Reservations, fee: Call ahead for space available and fee.

Who to contact: Phone park at (707)994-6451.

Location: Drive three miles beyond the town of Lower Lake on State Route 53 to Clearlake Highlands, turn left at intersection islands and drive to 14067 Lakeshore Drive.

Trip note: See trip note for campsite No. 1.

Site **6**   GARNERS'
                              RESORT

Campsites, facilities: There are campsites and 40 motorhome spaces with full hookups. Flush toilets, showers, dump station, boat rentals, pier, boat ramp, fishing supplies, lake frontage sites, laundry, propane gas and groceries are available.

Reservations, fee: Call ahead for space and fee.

Who to contact: Phone park at (707)994-6267.

Location: Drive three miles beyond the town of Lower Lake on State Route 53 to Clearlake Highlands, turn left at intersection islands and drive to South Lakeshore Drive.

Trip note: See trip note for campsite No. 1.

Site 7
PINE ACRES
BLUE LAKE RESORT

Campsites, facilities: There are 24 motorhome spaces with full hookups. Flush toilets, showers, dump station, boat rentals, moorings, boat ramp, fishing supplies and lake frontage sites are available. Laundry, propane gas and groceries can be found nearby.

Reservations, fee: Call ahead for space available and fee.

Who to contact: Phone park at (707)275-2811.

Location: Drive seven miles west of Upper Lake via Highway 20 to 5135 West Highway 20.

Trip note: Open all year. Elevation 1400 feet. Located on the shore of Blue Lakes. Set in densely wooded hills, these lovely lakes offer numerous sports and lakeside activities, including swimming, fishing, boating, backpacking and hunting. No waterskiing is allowed.

Site 8
LE TRIANON
RESORT

Campsites, facilities: There are 400 campsites for tents or motorhome spaces with full hookups. Flush toilets, showers, dump station, boat rentals, fishing supplies, lake frontage sites, laundry, propane gas and groceries are available.

Reservations, fee: Call ahead for space and fee.

Who to contact: Phone park at (707)275-2262.

Location: Drive seven miles west of Upper Lake via Highway 20 to 5845 West Highway 20.

Trip note: Open from mid-March to mid-October. Elevation 1400 feet. Located on the shore of Blue Lakes. Set in densely wooded hills, these lovely lakes offer numerous sports and lakeside activities, including swimming, fishing, boating, backpacking and hunting. No waterskiing is allowed.

Site 9
NARROWS LODGE
RESORT

Campsites, facilities: There are 28 motorhome spaces with full hookups. Flush toilets, showers, dump station, boat rentals, pier, boat ramp, fishing supplies, lake frontage sites, laundry, propane gas and groceries are available.

Reservations, fee: Call ahead for space and fee.

Who to contact: Phone park at (707)275-2718.

Location: Drive seven miles west of Upper Lake via Highway 20, and turn on Blue Lakes Road to 5690 Blue Lakes Road.

Trip note: Open all year. Elevation 1400 feet. Located on the shore of Blue Lakes. Set in densely wooded hills, these lovely lakes offer numerous sports and lakeside activities, including swimming, fishing, boating, backpacking and hunting. No waterskiing is allowed.

Site **10**   BLUE LAKES
                      KELLY'S KAMP

Campsites, facilities: There are 75 campsites and motorhome spaces with full
   hookups. Flush toilets, showers, dump station, laundry and groceries are
   available.
Reservations, fee: Call ahead for space available and fee.
Who to contact: Phone park at (707)263-5754.
Location: Drive seven miles west of Upper Lake via Highway 20 and turn on
   Blue Lakes Road to 8220 Scotts Valley Road.
Trip note: Open all year. Elevation 1400 feet. Located near the shore of Blue
   Lakes. Set in densely wooded hills, these lovely lakes offer numerous sports
   and lakeside activities, including swimming, fishing, boating, backpacking
   and hunting. No waterskiing is allowed.

Site **11**   LAKEVIEW
                      HAVEN

Campsites, facilities: There are 46 campsites and motorhome spaces with full
   hookups. Flush toilets, showers, dump station, boat rentals, guest dock,
   fishing supplies, lake frontage sites, swimming pool, laundry, snack bar and
   restaurant are available.
Reservations, fee: Call ahead for space and fee.
Who to contact: Phone park at (707)275-2105.
Location: Drive seven miles west of Upper Lake via Highway 20 to 5178 West
   Highway 20.
Trip note: Open all year. Elevation 1400 feet. Located on the shore of Blue
   Lakes. Set in densely wooded hills, these lovely lakes offer numerous sports
   and lakeside activities, including swimming, fishing, boating, backpacking
   and hunting. No waterskiing is allowed.

Site **12**   ISLAND
                      PARK

Campsites, facilities: There are 15 motorhome spaces with full hookups. Rest
   rooms, showers, guest dock, recreation room with pool table, small private
   beach, laundromat and lake frontage sites are available. Fishing supplies,
   boat rentals, propane gas and groceries are nearby.
Reservations, fee: Reservations suggested; $12 per night.
Who to contact: Phone park at (707)998-3940.
Location: On Highway 20 drive four miles west of the intersection of Highways
   20 and 53 to 12840 Island Drive.
Trip note: This park is open all year and is on an island in the shaded lagoons
   and waterways that lead from Clear Lake into town. Enjoy fishing, swimming, boating, waterskiing and windsurfing.

Site **13**
JONES SLEEPY LAGOON
TRAILER PARK

Campsites, facilities: There are 10 motorhome spaces with full hookups. Flush toilets, showers, dump station, pier, lake frontage and a laundromat are available. Boat rentals, fishing supplies and groceries are nearby.

Reservations, fee: Call ahead for space and fee.

Who to contact: Phone park at (707)998-1466.

Location: On Highway 20 drive four miles west of the intersection of Highways 20 and 53 to 12950 Island Drive.

Trip note: This park is open all year and is on an island in the shaded lagoons and waterways that lead from Clear Lake into town. Enjoy fishing, swimming, boating, waterskiing and windsurfing.

Site **14**
M & M
CAMPGROUNDS

Campsites, facilities: There are 37 motorhome spaces with full hookups. Flush toilets, showers and lakefront sites are available. Boat rentals, pier, boat ramp, fishing supplies, laundry, propane gas and groceries are nearby.

Reservations, fee: Call ahead for space and fee.

Who to contact: Phone park at (707)998-9943.

Location: On Highway 20 drive four miles west of the intersection of Highways 20 and 53 to 13050 Island Drive.

Trip note: This park is open all year and is on an island in the shaded lagoons and waterways that lead from Clear Lake into town. Enjoy fishing, swimming, boating, waterskiing and windsurfing.

Site **15**
SUNSET
POINT

Campsites, facilities: There are nine motorhome spaces with full hookups. Flush toilets, showers, dump station, boat rentals, pier, lake frontage sites and a laundromat are available. Boat rentals, fishing supplies, propane gas and groceries are nearby.

Reservations, fee: Call ahead for space available and fee.

Who to contact: Phone park at (707)998-9933.

Location: On Highway 20 drive four miles west of the intersection of Highways 20 and 53 to 12037 East Highway 20.

Trip note: This park is open all year and is near the shaded lagoons and waterways that lead from Clear Lake into town. Enjoy fishing, swimming, boating, waterskiing and windsurfing.

Site 16   LOCH LOMOND PARK

Campsites, facilities: There are 37 motorhome spaces with full hookups. Rest
rooms, showers and a swimming pool are available. A grocery store, laundromat and propane gas are nearby.
Reservations, fee: Call ahead for space and fee.
Who to contact: Phone park at (707)928-5044.
Location: Drive 12 miles north of Middletown via State Route 175 and Loch Lomond Road.
Trip note: This park is open all year and is nestled in a green valley where there
are numerous hiking trails and clear streams. Two golf courses are nearby,
and Clear Lake is 10 miles away.

Site 17   PINE GROVE RESORT

Campsites, facilities: There are 10 motorhome spaces with full hookups. Rest
rooms and showers are available. A grocery store, laundromat and propane
gas are nearby.
Reservations, fee: Call ahead for available space and fee.
Who to contact: Phone park at (707)928-5222.
Location: Drive 10 miles north of Middletown on State Route 175.
Trip note: This park is open all year and is nestled in a green valley where there
are numerous hiking trails and clear streams. Two golf courses are nearby
and Clear Lake is 12 miles away.

Site 18   GLENHAVEN BEACH CAMPGROUND AND MARINA

Campsites, facilities: There are 21 motorhome spaces with full hookups. Rest
rooms, showers, pier and lake frontage sites are available. Boat rentals, fish-
ing supplies, laundromat, propane gas and groceries are nearby.
Reservations, fee: Call ahead for space available and fee.
Who to contact: Phone park at (707)998-3406.
Location: On Highway 20 drive eight miles west of the intersection of Highways
20 and 53 to 9625 East Highway 20.
Trip note: This campground is on a peninsula in the eastern shore of Clear
Lake. Fishing, swimming, boating, waterskiing and windsurfing all prime
activities.

Site 19   HARBOR VISTA TRAILER PARK

Campsites, facilities: There are 21 motorhome spaces with full hookups. Rest rooms, showers, a laundromat and lake frontage sites are available. Boat rentals, fishing supplies, propane gas and groceries are nearby.

Reservations, fee: Call ahead for space available and fee.

Who to contact: Phone park at (707)998-9142.

Location: On Highway 20 drive eight miles west of the intersection of Highways 20 and 53 to 19 Harbor Drive.

Trip note: This campground is on a peninsula in the eastern shore of Clear Lake. Fishing, swimming, boating, waterskiing and windsurfing are all prime activities.

Site **20**   LAKE PLACE RESORT
AND RV PARK

Campsites, facilities: There are tent sites and six motorhome spaces with full hookups. Rest rooms, showers, pier, berths, boat ramp, beach, fishing supplies and lake frontage sites are available. Boat rentals, a laundromat, propane gas and groceries are nearby.

Reservations, fee: Call ahead for space and fee.

Who to contact: Phone park at (707)998-3331.

Location: On Highway 20 drive eight miles west of the intersection of Highways 20 and 53 to 9515 Harbor Drive.

Trip note: This campground is on a peninsula in the eastern shore of Clear Lake. Fishing, swimming, boating, waterskiing and windsurfing are some of the activities you can enjoy.

Site **21**   ANTHONY'S

Campsites, facilities: There are 12 motorhome spaces with full hookups. Rest rooms, showers, boat rentals, pier, restaurant and lake frontage sites are available. Fishing supplies, laundromat, propane gas and groceries are nearby.

Reservations, fee: Call ahead for space available and fee.

Who to contact: Phone park at (707)263-4905.

Location: Drive on Highway 29 to the northwest shore of Clear Lake and Lakeport to 2509 Lakeshore Boulevard.

Trip note: Fishing, swimming, boating, waterskiing and windsurfing all prime acitivies. There is a public park nearby with picnic facilities and a children's playground. The Chateau du Lac/Kendall-Jackson Winery is just south of town.

Site **22**   AQUA
VILLAGE

Campsites, facilities: There are 18 tent and motorhome spaces with full hookups.

Rest rooms, showers, boat ramp, fuel dock, bait, pier and lake frontage sites are available. Boat rentals, fishing supplies, laundromat, propane gas and groceries are nearby.

Reservations, fee: Call ahead for space and fee.

Who to contact: Phone park at (707)263-4411.

Location: Drive on Highway 29 to the northwest shore of Clear Lake and Lakeport to 1350 South Main.

Trip note: Another nice spot on shore of Clear Lake. There is a public park nearby with picnic facilities and a children's playground. The Chateau du Lac/Kendall-Jackson Winery is just south of town.

Site **23**   GREEN
                      ANCHOR

Campsites, facilities: There are six motorhome spaces with full hookups. Rest rooms, showers, pier and lake frontage sites are available. Boat rentals, fishing supplies, laundromat, propane gas and groceries are nearby.

Reservations, fee: Call ahead for space available and fee.

Who to contact: Phone park at (707)263-5591.

Location: Drive on Highway 29 to the northwest shore of Clear Lake and Lakeport to 4680 Lakeshore Boulevard.

Trip note: See trip note for campsite No. 22.

Site **24**   HILLCREST
                       PARK

Campsites, facilities: There are 18 tent sites and motorhome spaces with full hookups. Rest rooms, showers, boat ramp, moorings, pier and lake frontage sites are available. Boat rentals, fishing supplies, laundromat, propane gas and groceries are nearby.

Reservations, fee: Call ahead for space and fee.

Who to contact: Phone park at (707)263-4516.

Location: Drive on Highway 29 to the northwest shore of Clear Lake and Lakeport to 4555 Lakeshore Boulevard.

Trip note: See trip note for campsite No. 22.

Site **25**   LUCKY FOUR
                       RESORT

Campsites, facilities: There are five motorhome spaces with full hookups. Rest rooms, showers, restaurant, and lake frontage sites are available. Boat rentals, fishing supplies, laundromat, propane gas and groceries are available nearby.

Reservations, fee: Call ahead for space available and fee.

Who to contact: Phone park at (707)263-3232.

Location: Drive on Highway 29 to the northwest shore of Clear Lake and Lakeport to 1060 North Main Street.

Trip note: See trip note for campsite No. 22.

Site **26**   U-WANNA
            CAMP

Campsites, facilities: There are 30 tent sites and motorhome spaces with full
hookups. Rest rooms, showers, dump station, laundromat and recreation
room are available. Boat rentals, fishing supplies, propane gas and groceries
are nearby.

Reservations, fee: Call for space available. $6 deposit required; $6 fee per night.

Who to contact: Phone park at (707)263-6745.

Location: Drive on Highway 29 to the northwest shore of Clear Lake and Lakeport, then two miles west via 11th Street and Riggs Road to 2699 Scotts
Creek Road.

Trip note: This campground is in a secluded location just two miles from Clear
Lake. There is a beautiful public park nearby with picnic facilities and a
children's playground in the town of Lakeport. The Chateau du Lac/Ken-
dall-Jackson Winery is just south of town.

Site **27**   WILL-O-POINT
            RESORT

Campsites, facilities: There are 65 tent sites and motorhome spaces with full
hookups. Rest rooms, showers, boat ramp, fuel dock, laundromat, boat rentals, waterski rentals, fishing supplies, LP gas restaurant, and lake frontage
sites are available. Groceries are available nearby.

Reservations, fee: Call ahead for space available and fee.

Who to contact: Phone park at (707)263-5407.

Location: Drive on Highway 29 to the northwest shore of Clear Lake and Lakeport to 1 First Street.

Trip note: See trip note for campsite No. 22.

Site **28**   LAKE PILLSBURY
            RESORT

Campsites, facilities: There are 30 motorhome spaces with full hookups. A dump
station, rest rooms, showers, boat and waterski rentals, fuel, dock, fishing
supplies, a pier and lake frontage sites are available.

Reservations, fee: Call ahead for available space and fee.

Who to contact: Phone park at (707)743-1581.

Location: Drive 19 miles east of Potter Valley on Capranas Road.

Trip note: Open from May to November. This campground is set in the heart of
Mendocino National Forest, along the shores of Lake Pillsbury. Enjoy trout

fishing in the lake and the hundreds of miles of rivers and streams in the area. Hunting is also permitted in season in the primitive areas.

Site **29**   END O' THE
              RAINBOW

Campsites, facilities: There are 25 motorhome spaces with full hookups. Rest rooms, showers, laundry, boat rentals and river frontage sites are available. Fishing supplies, propane gas and groceries are nearby.
Reservations, fee: Call ahead for space and fee.
Who to contact: Phone park at (707)994-3282.
Location: Drive 14 1/2 miles north of Middletown on Highway 29 to the intersection of Highway 53, to 7425 Old Highway 53.
Trip note: Lower Lake is one of the oldest towns in Lake County, offering numerous historic sites and Indian artifacts. It is a paradise for rockhounds. Most of the resorts are located on Cache Creek, the outlet stream for Clear Lake that flows through the area. Good catfishing outside of Cache Creek.

Site **30**   RIVER GROVE
              TRAILER PARK

Campsites, facilities: There are 33 motorhome spaces with full hookups. Rest rooms, showers, pier, laundry, dump station and river frontage sites are available. Boat rentals, fishing supplies, propane gas and groceries are nearby.
Reservations, fee: Call ahead for space and fee.
Who to contact: Phone park at (707)994-4377.
Location: Drive 14 1/2 miles north of Middletown on Highway 29 to the intersection of Highway 53. Located at 16150 Tish-a-Tang Road.
Trip note: See trip note for campsite No. 29.

Site **31**   OAKES
              WATERFRONT PARK

Campsites, facilities: There are 25 camping and motorhome spaces with full hookups. Rest rooms, showers, boat rentals, fishing supplies, boat ramp and river frontage sites are available. A laundromat, propane gas and groceries are nearby.
Reservations, fee: Call ahead for space and fee.
Who to contact: Phone park at (707)994-6255.
Location: Drive 14 1/2 miles north of Middletown on Highway 29 to the intersection of Highway 53. Located at 7669 Highway 53.
Trip note: See trip note for campsite No. 29.

Site **32**   SHAW'S
                               SHADY ACRES

Campsites, facilities: There are 16 motorhome spaces with full hookups. Rest
  rooms, showers, picr, laundry, dump station, boat rentals and river frontage
  sites are available. Boat rentals, fishing supplies, laundromat, propane gas
  and groceries are nearby.
Reservations, fee: Call ahead for space and fee.
Who to contact: Phone park at (707)994-2236.
Location: Drive 14 1/2 miles north of Middletown on Highway 29 to the intersection of Highway 53. Located at 7805 Highway 53.
Trip note: See trip note for campsite No. 29.

Site **33**   ARROW
                               TRAILER PARK

Campsites, facilities: There are 25 camping and motorhome spaces with full hookups. Rest rooms, showers, laundromat, boat rentals, moorings, fishing supplies, boat ramp, groceries, beer and wine, and ice are available.
Reservations, fee: Call ahead for space; $8 - $10 per night depending on the
  season.
Who to contact: Phone park at (707)274-7715.
Location: Drive 1/2 mile east of Lucerne on Highway 20 to 6720 East Highway
  20.
Trip note: Lucerne is noted for its harbor and its long stretch of well-kept public
  beaches along the shore of Clear Lake. The town of Lucerne offers a shopping district, restaurants and cafes.

Site **34**   BAMBOO
                               HOLLOW

Campsites, facilities: There are 39 motorhome spaces with full hookups. Rest
  rooms, showers, a laundromat, boat ramp, moorings and lake frontage sites
  are available. Groceries, boat rentals, fishing supplies and propane gas are
  nearby.
Reservations, fee: Call ahead for available space and fee.
Who to contact: Phone park at (707)274-7751.
Location: In Lucerne, drive to 5877 Lake Street off Highway 20.
Trip note: Lucerne is noted for its harbor and its long stretch of well-kept public
  beaches with barbeque facilities.

Site **35**   CALICO CAT
                               TRAILER RESORT

Campsites, facilities: There are 30 motorhome spaces with full hookups. Rest rooms, showers, pier, dump station, and lake frontage sites are available. Boat rentals, fishing supplies, laundromat, propane gas and groceries are nearby.

Reservations, fee: Call ahead for space and fee.

Who to contact: Phone park at (707)274-1950.

Location: On the north shore of Clear Lake, 18 miles north of the intersection of Highways 53 and 20, take Highway 20 to 3297 East Highway 20.

Trip note: On the shore of Clear Lake, this spot is noted for its lovely beaches dotted with large live oak, redbud and pepperwood trees. Swimming, boating, fishing, waterskiing and windsurfing are some of the pastimes you can enjoy on this large natural lake. Mendocino National Forest is nearby. Good catfishing outside of mouth of Rodman Slough.

Site **36**   NORTH SHORE RESORT
AND MARINA

Campsites, facilities: There are 26 motorhome spaces with full hookups. Rest rooms, showers, laundry, dump station, boat rentals, complete marina facilities, lake frontage sites, fishing supplies, snack bar, laundromat, propane gas, ice and groceries are available.

Reservations, fee: Call ahead for space available and fee.

Who to contact: Phone park at (707)274-7771.

Location: On the north shore of Clear Lake, 18 miles north of the intersection of Highways 53 and 20, take Highway 20 to 2345 Lakeshore Boulevard.

Trip note: See trip note for campsite No. 35.

Site **37**   SANDPIPER

Campsites, facilities: There are 28 motorhome spaces with full hookups. Rest rooms, showers, boat ramp, moorings, pier, boat rentals, lake frontage sites, fishing supplies, laundromat, propane gas, ice and groceries are available.

Reservations, fee: Call ahead for space and fee.

Who to contact: Phone park at (707)274-4448.

Location: On the north shore of Clear Lake, 18 miles north of the intersection of Highways 53 and 20, take Highway 20 to 2630 Lakeshore Boulevard.

Trip note: See trip note for campsite No. 35.

Site **38**   TALLEY'S
RESORT

Campsites, facilities: There are eight motorhome spaces with full hookups. Rest rooms, showers, pier, laundry, dump station and lake frontage sites are available. Boat rentals, fishing supplies, propane gas and groceries are available nearby.

Reservations, fee: Call ahead for space available and fee.

Who to contact: Phone park at (707)274-1177.

Location: On the north shore of Clear Lake, 18 miles north of the intersection of Highways 53 and 20, take Highway 20 to 3827 Lakeshore Boulevard.

Trip note: See trip note for campsite No. 35.

| Site **39** | TIKI
TIKI | |

Campsites, facilities: There are 29 camping and motorhome spaces with full hookups. Rest rooms, showers, boat ramp, guest dock and dump station are available. Boat rentals, fishing supplies, laundromat, propane gas and groceries are nearby.

Reservations, fee: Call ahead for space available and fee.

Who to contact: Phone park at (707)274-2576.

Location: On the north shore of Clear Lake, 18 miles north of the intersection of Highways 53 and 20, take Highway 20 to 3967 East Highway 20.

Trip note: See trip note for campsite No. 35.

| Site **40** | CLEAR LAKE
STATE PARK | |

Campsites, facilities: There are 147 campsites for tents or motorhomes. Rest rooms, showers, a dump station, boat ramp and mooring are available. A grocery store, laundromat and propane gas are nearby. The boat ramp, picnic area and some campsites are wheelchair accessible.

Reservations, fee: Phone MISTIX at (800)446-7275; $10 fee per night.

Who to contact: Phone park at (707)279-4293.

Location: Drive 1/2 mile west of Soda Bay on the south shore of Clear Lake.

Trip note: One of Clear Lake's most beautiful, inexpensive and popular campgrounds. Reservations a necessity in summer months. Good bass fishing from boats along tule-lined shoreline, and good catfishing in sloughs that run through park.

| Site **41** | BEAR CREEK
CAMPGROUND | |

Campsites, facilities: There are five tent sites and 11 campsites for tents or motorhomes. Picnic tables and fireplaces are provided, and vault toilets are available. There is no water, so bring your own.

Reservations, fee: No reservations, no fee.

Who to contact: Phone Mendocino National Forest Headquarters at (707)275-2361.

Location: Drive 25 miles northeast of Upper Lake via Elk Mountain and Bear Creek Roads.

Trip note: Open from May to October. Elevation 2000 feet. Located on Bear Creek near its confluence with Blue Slides Creek.

Site **42**   DEER VALLEY
                               CAMPGROUND   ▲

Campsites, facilities: There are 22 campsites for tents or motorhomes. Picnic tables and fireplaces are provided, and vault toilets and horseback riding facilities are available. There is no water, so bring your own.
Reservations, fee: No reservations, no fee.
Who to contact: Phone Mendocino National Forest Headquarters at (707)275-2361.
Location: Drive 11 miles north of Upper Lake on Elk Mountain Road then turn right on an unimproved road about two miles past the East Fork of Middle Creek, and drive five miles to camp.
Trip note: Open from April to November. Elevation 3700 feet. Located in Deer Valley about five miles from the East Fork of Middle Creek.

Site **43**   LAKEVIEW
                               CAMPGROUND   ▲

Campsites, facilities: There are nine campsites for tents or motorhomes. Picnic tables and fireplaces are provided, and vault toilets are available. There is no water, so bring your own.
Reservations, fee: No reservations, no fee.
Who to contact: Phone Mendocino National Forest Headquarters at (707)275-2361.
Location: Drive 10 miles northwest of Clearlake Oaks on High Valley Road.
Trip note: Open from May to October. Elevation 3400 feet. This site overlooks Clear Lake and the town of Lucerne, which are about two miles away and can be reached via a trail from camp.

Site **44**   MIDDLE CREEK
                               CAMPGROUND   ▲

Campsites, facilities: There are 12 campsites for tents or motorhomes. Piped water, picnic tables and fireplaces are provided, and vault toilets are available.
Reservations, fee: No reservations; $3 fee per night.
Who to contact: Phone Mendocino National Forest Headquarters at (707)934-3316.
Location: Drive seven miles northwest of Upper Lake via Elk Mountain Road.
Trip note: Open all year. Elevation 2000 feet. Located at the confluence of the West and East Forks of Middle Creek.

Site 45   OAK FLAT   🌲

Campsites, facilities: There are 12 campsites for tents or motorhomes. Picnic tables and fireplaces are provided, and vault toilets are available. There is no water, so bring your own.

Reservations, fee: No reservations, no fee.

Who to contact: Phone Mendocino National Forest Headquarters at (707)934-3316.

Location: Drive 21 miles northeast of Potter Valley to Lake Pillsbury.

Trip note: Open all year. Elevation 1800 feet. Located along the shore of Lake Pillsbury in the heart of Mendocino National Forest. Enjoy fishing for trout in this beautiful mountain lake or in one of the many streams in the area. Hunting is also permitted in season in the primitive areas. Trails leading into the backcountry are nearby.

Site 46   POGIE POINT   ⛰

Campsites, facilities: There are 50 campsites for tents or motorhomes. Piped water, picnic tables and fireplaces are provided, and vault toilets are available. A grocery store, laundromat and propane gas are nearby.

Reservations, fee: No reservations; $5 fee per night.

Who to contact: Phone Mendocino National Forest Headquarters at (707)934-3316.

Location: Drive 20 miles northeast of Potter Valley at Lake Pillsbury.

Trip note: Open all year. Elevation 1900 feet. Located along the shore of Lake Pillsbury in the heart of Mendocino National Forest. Enjoy fishing for trout in this beautiful mountain lake or in one of the many streams in the area. Hunting is also permitted in season in the primitive areas. Trails leading into the backcountry are nearby.

Site 47   SUNSET CAMPGROUND   ⛰

Campsites, facilities: There are 30 tent sites and 24 campsites for tents or motorhomes. Piped water, picnic tables and fireplaces are provided, and vault toilets are available. A grocery store and boat ramp are nearby.

Reservations, fee: No reservations; $5 fee per night.

Who to contact: Phone Mendocino National Forest Headquarters at (707)934-3316.

Location: Drive 22 1/2 miles northeast of Potter Valley at Lake Pillsbury.

Trip note: See trip note for campsite No. 46.

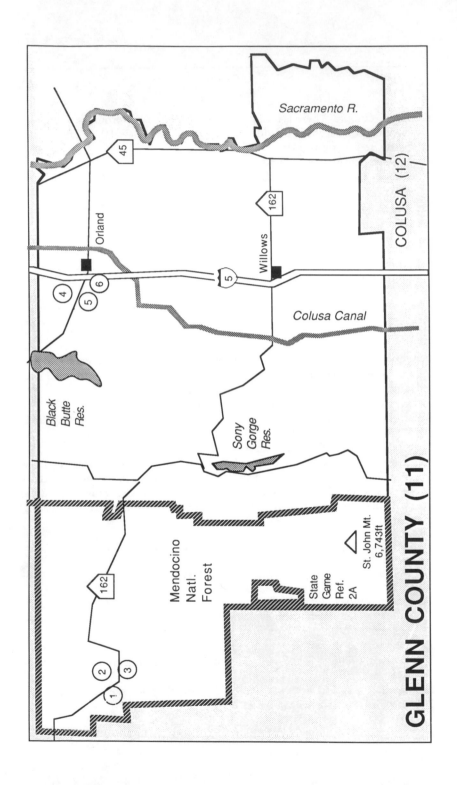

Sacramento R.

COLUSA (12)

45

162

Orland

Willows

5

Colusa Canal

Black Butte Res.

Sony Gorge Res.

162

Mendocino Natl. Forest

State Game Ref. 2A

St. John Mt. 6,743ft

GLENN COUNTY (11)

4
5
6
1
2
3

GLENN COUNTY
◆

Site 1   TELEPHONE   ▲

Campsites, facilities: There are 11 sites for tents or motorhomes to 22 feet long. Piped water, vault toilets, fireplaces and picnic tables are provided.
Reservations, fee: No reservations, no fee.
Who to contact: Call Mendocino National Forest at (916)934-3316 or write at 420 East Laurel Street, Willows, CA 95988.
Location: Drive 41 miles northwest of Elk Creek via Road 306 and Alder Springs Road.
Trip note: Open from June through October. Elevation 6800 feet. Advisable to obtain map of Mendocino National Forest. Good hiking, horseback riding potential, hunting in the fall.

Site 2   MASTERSON GROUP CAMP   ▲

Campsites, facilities: There are 20 campsites for tents only, with piped water, vault toilets, fireplaces and picnic tables provided.
Reservations, fee: Reservation required; $15 fee for group use of entire camp.
Who to contact: Phone Mendocino National Forest at (916)934-3316.
Location: The camp is located 35 miles northwest of Elk Creek via Road 306 and Alder Springs Road.
Trip note: Open from May through October. Elevation 6000 feet. Map of Mendocino National Forest details nearby streams, lakes and hiking trails.

Site 3   PLASKETT LAKE   ▲

Campsites, facilities: There are 32 campsites available for tents or motorhomes to 22 feet long. Piped water, vault toilets, fireplaces and picnic tables are provided.
Reservations, fee: No reservations; $4 per night fee.
Who to contact: Call Mendocino National Forest at (916)934-3316.
Location: Plaskett Lake is located 35 miles northwest of Elk Creek via Road 306

and Alder Springs Road.

Trip note: Open May through October. Elevation 6000 feet. Fishing for stocked trout in Plaskett Lake, hiking on adjacent Forest Service land.

Site **4**   ORLAND
                               BUTTES

Campsites, facilites: There are four tent-only campsites and 31 sites that can handle tents or motorhomes up to 35 feet long. Piped water, vault toilets, fireplaces, picnic tables and a sanitary disposal station are provided.

Reservations, fee: No reservations; $6 per night fee.

Who to contact: Phone the U.S. Army Corps of Engineers at (916)865-4781.

Location: From Orland, drive eight miles west on Road 200.

Trip note: Open from March through September. Elevation 500 feet. Good crappie fishing in Black Butte Lake in June and July. Boat launch available. Very hot in the summer.

Site **5**   KOA
                               GREEN ACRES

Campsites, facilities: There are 68 motorhome sites with partial or full hookups and 32 tent sites. A store, laundromat, sanitary dump station, barbeques, recreation room, swimming pool, ice and propane are available for visitors' use.

Reservations, fee: Call ahead to be certain room is available.

Who to contact: Phone KOA Green Acres at (916)865-9188, or write at Route 4, Box 4048, Orland, CA 95963.

Location: In Orland on Interstate 5, take the Highway 32 exit and drive a half-mile west.

Trip note: Located in the heart of the olive and almond country. Restful setting, very hot in the summer. Fishing on Sacramento River nearby, best from late July through October for big king salmon.

Site **6**   SECURITY
                           OVERNIGHT RV PARK   ▲

Campsites, facilities: There are 51 motorhome sites with partial and full hookups, and 40 tent sites. A sanitary disposal station, propane, laundromat and store are available.

Reservations, fee: Call ahead.

Who to contact: Phone at (916)865-5335, or write at Route 4, Box 4037, Orland, CA 95963.

Location: From Interstate 5 at Orland, take Black Butte Lake exit, then head one block west and turn right. Park is one block down.

Trip note: Fishing trips to nearby Black Butte Lake to the west, Sacramento River to the east can put spice in trip. Very hot in summer.

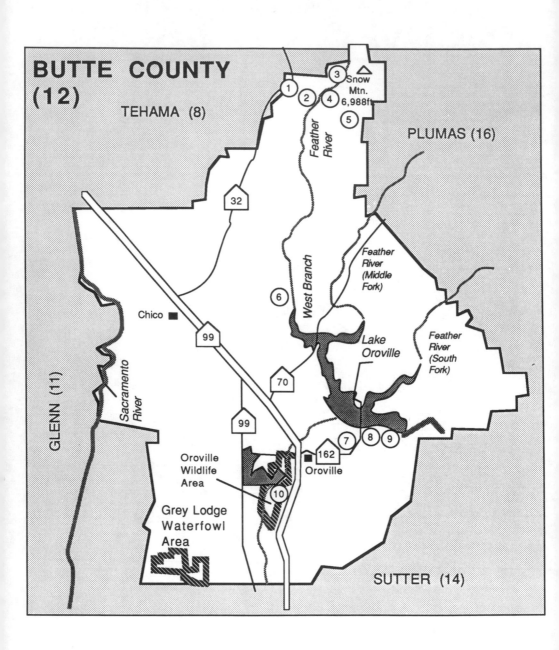

BUTTE COUNTY (12)

TEHAMA (8)

PLUMAS (16)

GLENN (11)

SUTTER (14)

Snow Mtn. 6,988ft

Feather River

Feather River (Middle Fork)

Feather River (South Fork)

West Branch

Lake Oroville

Sacramento River

Chico

Oroville

Oroville Wildlife Area

Grey Lodge Waterfowl Area

32

99

70

99

162

BUTTE COUNTY

♦

Site 1 SODA SPRINGS 🌲

Campsites, facilities: There are 10 tent sites. Tables, fireplace and vault toilets provided at each site. No water available.

Reservations, fee: No reservation, no fee.

Who to contact: Phone Lassen National Forest at (916)257-2151, or write at 707 Nevada Street, Susanville, CA 96130.

Location: Soda Springs Camp is located 29 miles northeast of Forest Ranch on State Route 32.

Trip note: Open from May through September. Elevation 3600 feet. You can camp at the confluence of Cascade and Big Chico creeks, a little-known, secluded spot. Bring a water purifier.

Site 2 BUTTE MEADOWS ⛺

Campsites, facilities: There are 12 campsites available for tents or motorhomes up to 22 feet long. Piped water, vault toilets, fireplaces, picnic tables are provided, and a grocery store is nearby.

Reservations, fee: No reservations; $4 per night fee.

Who to contact: Phone Lassen National Forest at (916)257-2151.

Location: From State Route 32, take Humboldt Road to Butte Meadows.

Trip note: Open from June through October. Elevation 4300 feet. A pretty, summer camp situated along Butte Creek. Some trout fishing.

Site 3 CHERRY HILL ⛺

Campsites, facilities: There are 13 walk-in tent spaces and 12 sites for tents or motorhomes to 22 feet long. Tables, fireplaces, piped water and vault toilets are provided. Propane gas is available.

Reservations, fee: No reservations; $4 fee.

Who to contact: Phone Lassen National Forest at (916)257-2151.

Location: Drive three miles northeast of Butte Meadows on Humboldt Road.

Trip note: A map of Lassen National Forest details the hiking and fishing potential of this area. A climb of 2000 feet in four miles will take you to Colby Mountain lookout.

Site **4**   WEST
                       BRANCH

Campsites, facilities: There are eight tent-only sites and seven sites that will accomodate tents or motorhomes to 22 feet long. Tables, fireplaces, piped water and vault toilets are provided.
Reservations, fee: No reservations; $4 fee.
Who to contact: Phone Lassen National Forest at (916)257-2151.
Location: Drive 12 miles north of Stirling City via Skyway, Humbug and Philbrook Roads.
Trip note: Open June through September. Elevation 5000 feet. A nice spot on the West Branch of the Feather River. Trout fishing can be good. Open June through September. Advisable to obtain map of Lassen National Forest.

Site **5**   PHILBROOK

Campsites, facilities: There are 10 campsites for tents or motorhomes up to 20 feet long. Tables, fireplaces, piped water and vault toilets are provided.
Reservations, fee: No reservations. Small fee charged per night.
Who to contact: Campground is run by PG&E. For information on area, contact Lassen National Forest at (916)257-2151.
Location: Drive 15 miles northeast of Stirling City via Skyway, Humbug, and Philbrook Roads.
Trip note: Open from June through September. Elevation 5500 feet. Camp situated along the shore of Philbrook Reservoir. Good trout fishing, boating.

Site **6**   PINE RIDGE
                         PARK

Campsites, facilities: There are 51 motorhome sites with full hookups. Piped water, flush toilets, showers and a laundromat are available.
Reservations, fee: Reservations can be booked through Leisuretime Reservation Systems with a $3 fee; campsites are $10 per night.
Who to contact: Phone at (916)877-0677.
Location: This motorhome park is located five miles southeast of Paradise at 5084 Pentz Magalia Highway.
Trip note: Open year around. Elevation 1700 feet. Located near the Kunkle Reservoir.

Site **7** BIDWELL CANYON

Campsites, facilities: There are 75 sites for motorhomes up to 31 feet long, all with full hookups. Piped water, flush toilets, showers, tables and fireplaces are provided. A laundromat, grocery store and propane gas are available.

Reservations, fee: Reservations advised through MISTIX by calling (800)446-7275. Reservation fee is $3.75, site fee is $12 and pet fee is $1.

Who to contact: Call the Lake Oroville State Recreation Area at (916)534-2409.

Location: Drive eight miles northeast of Oroville off State Route 162, via Kelly Ridge Road.

Trip note: Open year around. Prime trip for boating, water skiing on Lake Oroville. Fishing best in spring and fall. Very hot in mid-summer.

Site **8** LOAFER CREEK

Campsites, facilities: There are 137 campsites for tents and motorhomes up to 31 feet long. A sanitary disposal station, piped water, flush toilets, showers, fireplaces and tables are provided. Propane, grocery shopping and laundromat are available.

Reservations, fee: Reservations advised by calling MISTIX at (800)446-7275. Site fee is $6; pet fee is $1.

Who to contact: Phone Lake Oroville State Recreation Area at (916)534-2409.

Trip note: Open from April through October. Near the shores of Lake Oroville. Unique camping experience available by renting a "floating environmental campsite." Call park at (916)534-2409.

Site **9** LOAFER CREEK GROUP CAMP

Campsites, facilities: A group site with piped water, flush toilets, showers, fireplaces and picnic tables provided. A laundromat, grocery store and propane gas are available.

Reservations, fee: Can be reserved through MISTIX by phoning (800)446-7275. Site fee is $25; pets $1.

Who to contact: Phone Lake Oroville State Recreation Area at (916)534-2409.

Location: Drive eight meals east of Oroville off State Route 162.

Trip note: Open from April through October. Elevation 1000 feet. See Butte County campground No. 7 for more information.

Site **10** R&R KOA CAMPGROUND

Campsites, facilities: Sites have full hookups for motorhomes and tent circles.

Showers, swimming pool, grocery store, laundromat, horseshoe pit, volley-ball, playground, propane and sanitary dump station are available.

Reservations, fee: Reservations not required. Rates on daily, weekly, monthly basis.

Who to contact: Call at (916)533-9343, or write at Route 6, Box 2225, Oroville, CA 95965.

Location: Southbound, drive four miles south of Oroville on State Route 70, turn right at the second Pacific Heights Road turnoff and continue south to campground. Northbound on State Route 70, turn left at Palermo (Welsh) R-1 Road and continue north on Pacific Heights Road a half mile to camp.

Trip note: Adjacent to wildlife area and Feather River. Close to boating and fishing.

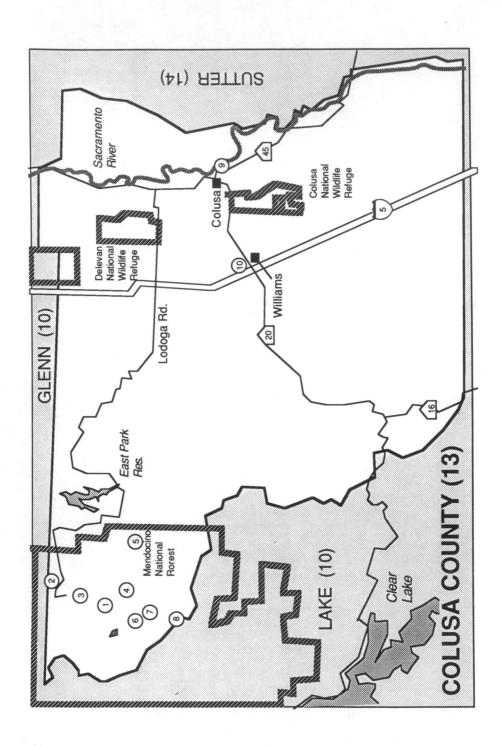

SUTTER (14)

Sacramento River

45

9

Colusa

Colusa National Wildlife Refuge

5

Delevan National Wildlife Refuge

GLENN (10)

Lodoga Rd.

10

Williams

20

East Park Res.

16

5

Mendocino National Forest

3

2

1

4

6

7

8

LAKE (10)

Clear Lake

COLUSA COUNTY (13)

COLUSA COUNTY

♦

Site **1**   MILL
CREEK

Campsites, facilities: There are five tent sites without water. Vault toilets, picnic
    tables and fireplaces are provided.
Reservations, fee: No reservations, no fee.
Who to contact: Mendocino National Forest at (916)934-3316.
Location: Set eight and a half miles west of Stonyford on Fouts Springs
    Road.
Trip note: Open year around. Elevation 1700 feet. Camp is on Mill Creek near
    Fouts Springs and Moon Glade. Several trails lead to Letts Lake, Trout
    Creek, Stoney Creek and Summit Spring.

Site **2**   NORTH
FORK

Campsites, facilities: There are six campsites here for tents or motorhomes up to
    16 feet long. Piped water, vault toilets, picnic tables and fireplaces are
    provided.
Reservations, fee: No reservations, no fee.
Who to contact: Mendocino National Forest at (916)934-3316.
Location: Set 11 1/2 miles west of Stonyford off Fouts Springs Road.
Trip note: Open from June through October. Elevation 1700 feet. Camp is on
    Fouts Creek, short distance from Happy Camp. Many hiking trails in area.

Site **3**   FOUTS

Campsites, facilities: There are seven campsites for tents or motorhomes up to 22
    feet long. No water, but vault toilets, picnic tables and fireplaces are
    provided.
Reservations, fee: No reservations, no fee.
Who to contact: Mendocino National Forest at (916)934-3316.
Location: Set nine miles west of Stonyford off Fouts Springs Road.
Trip note: Open year around. Elevation 1700 feet. Located on Fouts Creek near

Davis Flat and Fouts Springs, a short distance from Happy Camp. Hike the nearby Bathhouse and Trout Trails.

Site 4   OLD MILL   ▲

Campsites, facilities: There are eight tent sites and three campsites that will accomodate tents or motorhomes up to 16 feet long. Piped water, vault toilets, picnic tables and fireplaces are provided.
Reservations, fee: No reservations, no fee.
Who to contact: Mendocino National Forest at (916)934-3316.
Location: Set 13 1/2 miles southwest of Stonyford via Fouts Springs and John Smith Roads.
Trip note: Open from May through October. Elevation 3700 feet. Located on Trough Spring Ridge, a short walk from Mill Creek on route to Letts Lake Recreation Area.

Site 5   DIGGER PINE   🌲

Campsites, facilities: There are five campsites for tents or motorhomes. No water, but vault toilets, picnic tables and fireplaces are provided.
Reservations, fee: No reservations, no fee.
Who to contact: Mendocino National Forest at (916)934-3316.
Location: Set 10 miles southwest of Stonyford via Lodoga-Stonyford and Goat Mountain Roads.
Trip note: Open year around. Elevation 1500 feet. Secluded location on Little Stoney Creek. Frenzel Creek Research Natural Area is nearby. A trail from camp leads to Gilmore Peak.

Site 6   MILL VALLEY   ▲

Campsites, facilities: There are 15 campsites for tents or motorhomes up to 18 feet long. Piped water, vault toilets, picnic tables and fireplaces are provided.
Reservations, fee: No reservations; $3 fee per night.
Who to contact: Mendocino National Forest at (916)934-3316.
Location: Set 16 1/2 miles southwest of Stonyford via Fouts Springs and Letts Valley Roads.
Trip note: Open from April through November. Elevation 4200 feet. Located on Lilypond, a short walk from Upper Letts Lake. The area is criss-crossed with numerous creeks and trails.

Site **7**   UPPER
                              LETTS

Campsites, facilities: There are 40 campsites here that can accommodate tents or
   motorhomes. Piped water, vault toilets, picnic tables and fireplaces are
   provided.
Reservations, fee: No reservations; $5 fee per night.
Who to contact: Mendocino National Forest at (916)934-3316.
Location: Set 18 miles southwest of Stonyford via Fouts Springs and Letts Valley
   Roads.
Trip note: Open from April through November. Elevation 4500 feet. There are
   four camps around Upper Letts Lake.

Site **8**   CEDAR
                              CAMP

Campsites, facilities: There are six campsites here that can accommodate tents or
   motorhomes up to 22 feet long. No water, but vault toilets, picnic tables
   and fireplaces are provided.
Reservations, fee: No reservations, no fee.
Who to contact: Mendocino National Forest at (916)934-3316.
Location: Set 19 miles southwest of Stonyford via Fouts Springs and John Smith
   Roads.
Trip note: Open from June through October. Elevation 4300 feet. Secluded area
   near Goat Mountain.

Site **9**   COLUSA-SACRAMENTO RIVER
                     STATE RECREATION AREA

Campsites, facilities: There are five RV sites and 17 campsites for tents or motorhomes up to 28 feet long. Rest rooms, hot showers, a sanitary dump station,
   picnic tables and fireplaces are provided. A grocery store, laundromat and
   propane gas are also available nearby. A boat ramp is provided and there is
   wheelchair access for camping and picnicking.
Reservations, fee: Reservation fee of $3.75 payable to MISTIX: (800)446-7275;
   camping fee is $6 per night; pets $1 each.
Who to contact: Phone (916)458-4927.
Location: Set at the north end of Colusa off Highway 20 on 10th Street.
Trip note: Open year around. Elevation 65 feet.

Site **10**   ALMOND GROVE
                       MOBILE HOME PARK

Campsites, facilities: This is a mobile home park with a recreational vehicle section. There are 19 motorhome sites with full hookups and four tent sites. A

rest room with showers and a laundromat are provided.

Reservations, fee: Reservation fee of $3.50 payable to Leisuretime Reservation Systems, Inc. Call for additional fees.

Who to contact: Phone (916)473-5620.

Location: Set in Williams at 880 12th Street, three blocks south of Highway 20.

Trip note: About 80 miles from Highway 101.

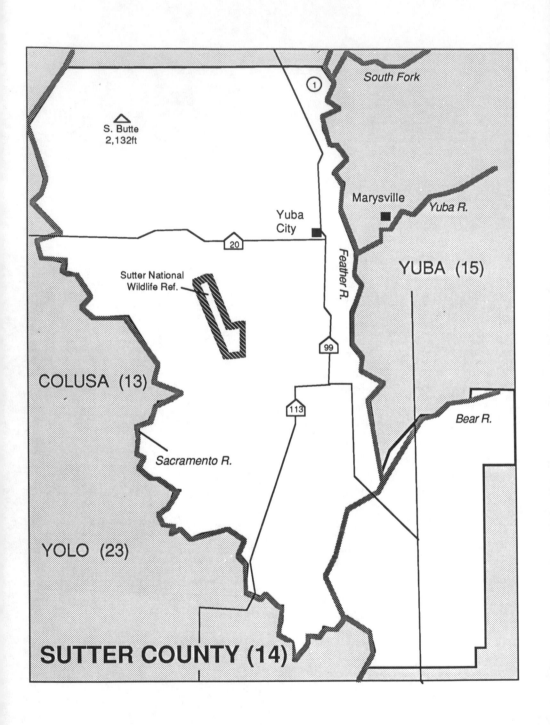

S. Butte
2,132ft

① South Fork

Marysville

Yuba City

20

Sutter National
Wildlife Ref.

Feather R.

YUBA (15)

99

COLUSA (13)

113

Bear R.

Sacramento R.

YOLO (23)

SUTTER COUNTY (14)

Yuba R.

SUTTER COUNTY

◆

Site **1** | LIVE OAK PARK | ▲

Campsites, facilities: There are 13 campsites for tents or motorhomes. Picnic tables and piped water are provided, and pit toilets are available. A grocery store, laundromat and propane gas are available nearby.

Reservations, fee: No reservations, no fee.

Who to contact: Phone park at (916)741-7407.

Location: Drive one mile west of Live Oak to 1100 Pennington Road.

Trip note: This campground is open all year and is near the confluence of the Feather and Yuba Rivers.

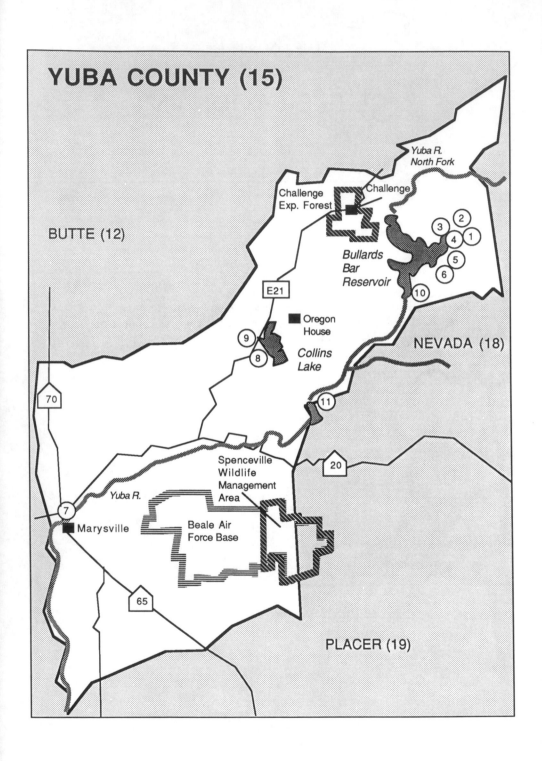

YUBA COUNTY (15)

BUTTE (12)

Yuba R.
North Fork

Challenge
Exp. Forest

Challenge

Bullards
Bar
Reservoir

③ ②
④ ①
⑤
⑥

⑩

E21

Oregon
House

⑨
⑧

Collins
Lake

NEVADA (18)

⑪

⑳

70

Spenceville
Wildlife
Management
Area

⑦

Yuba R.

Beale Air
Force Base

Marysville

65

PLACER (19)

YUBA COUNTY

♦

Site 1   SCHOOLHOUSE   ⚑

Campsites, facilities: There are 67 campsites for tents or motorhomes. Picnic tables, fireplaces and piped water are provided, and flush toilets are available. A grocery store, laundromat and propane gas are nearby.
Reservations, fee: No reservations; $4 fee per night.
Who to contact: Phone Tahoe National Forest at (916)265-4531.
Location: Drive five miles southwest of Camptonville via State Route 49 and Marysville Road.
Trip note: Open all year. Elevation 2300 feet. Located on Bullards Bar Reservoir about two miles from a three-lane concrete boat ramp at Dark Day Picnic Area. The Bullards Bar Reservoir is for fishing and water sports. It is not recommended for swimming or bank fishing due to the steep shoreline drop-offs. There are also three boat-in campgrounds around the lake.

Site 2   BURNT
BRIDGE   ⚑

Campsites, facilities: There are 15 tent sites and 15 campsites for tents or motorhomes. Picnic tables, fireplaces and piped water are provided, and vault toilets are available. Groceries are nearby.
Reservations, fee: No reservations; $3 fee per night.
Who to contact: Phone Plumas National Forest at (916)283-2050.
Location: Drive three and a half miles south of Challenge on Oregon Hill Road.
Trip note: Open from May to September. Elevation 2200 feet. Located near Bullards Bar Reservoir, about 12 miles from a three-lane concrete boat ramp on the southeast shore of the reservoir at Dark Day Picnic Area. The Bullards Bar Reservoir is for fishing and water sports. It is not recommended for swimming or bank fishing due to the steep shoreline drop-offs. There are also three boat-in campgrounds around the lake.

Site 3   HORNSWOGGLE
GROUP CAMP   ⚑

Campsites, facilities: There are five group campsites for tents or motorhomes.

Picnic tables, fireplaces and piped water are provided, and vault toilets are available. A grocery store is nearby.

Reservations, fee: Reservations requested; $20 fee per night per group.

Who to contact: Phone Tahoe National Forest at (916)265-4531.

Location: Drive five miles southwest of Camptonville via State Route 49 and Marysville Road.

Trip note: Open all year. Elevation 2300 feet. Located on Bullards Bar Reservoir about two miles from a three-lane concrete boat ramp at Dark Day Picnic Area. The Bullards Bar Reservoir is for fishing and water sports, but it is not recommended for swimming or bank fishing due to the steep shoreline drop-offs. There are also three boat-in campgrounds around the lake.

Site **4**   RIVERFRONT
PARK

Campsites, facilities: There are 70 campsites for tents or motorhomes. Picnic tables and fireplaces are provided, and flush toilets and a playground are available. There is no piped water, so bring your own. A grocery store, laundromat and propane gas are nearby.

Reservations, fee: Call ahead for available space and fee.

Who to contact: Phone park at (916)741-6666.

Location: Campground is in Marysville off State Route 70.

Trip note: The campground is set along the Yuba River where it feeds into the Feather River.

Site **5**   COLLINS LAKE
RECREATION AREA

Campsites, facilities: There are 210 campsites for tents or motorhomes. Picnic tables, fireplaces and piped water are provided. Flush toilets, dump station, showers, boat ramp, boat and motor rentals, sandy swimming beach, marina, a grocery store and propane gas are available.

Reservations, fee: Reservations recommended; $8.75 fee per night.

Who to contact: Phone campground at (916)692-1600.

Location: Drive 22 miles northeast of Marysville via Browns Valley Road and Marysville Road.

Trip note: This campground is open all year. Collins Lake is a prime lake for trout fishing, with a sprinkling of black bass a bonus.

Site **6**   MOONSHINE
CAMPGROUND

Campsites, facilities: There are 25 campsites for tents or motorhomes. Picnic tables, fireplaces, electrical connections and piped water are provided. Flush toilets, ice and firewood are available. A grocery store and propane gas are nearby.

Reservations, fee: Call ahead for available space and fee.

Who to contact: Phone campground at (916)288-3585.

Location: Drive 20 miles north of Grass Valley on State Route 49 toward Camptonville, after crossing the bridge over the Middle Fork of the Yuba River, turn left on Moonshine Road and drive 3/4 mile to campground.

Trip note: This spot is near Bullards Bar Reservoir, about seven miles from a three-lane concrete boat ramp at Dark Day Picnic Area. The Bullards Bar Reservoir is for fishing and water sports, but it is not recommended for swimming or bank fishing due to the steep shoreline drop-offs. There are also three boat-in campgrounds around the lake.

Site 7	SKIPPERS COVE

Campsites, facilities: There are 200 boat-in campsites along the shores of Englebright Lake, which stretches 11 miles up the narrow Yuba River Canyon. Boat rentals, mooring, a boat ramp, fuel dock, groceries and a cafe are available.

Reservations, fee: Call ahead for available space and fee.

Who to contact: Phone campground at (916)639-2272.

Location: Drive east on State Route 20 from Marysville to Mooney Flat Road just the other side of Smartville, and head north to the lake.

Trip note: The boat-in campgrounds around Englebright Lake are open all year. You can fish, enjoy water sports, or hike around the lake.

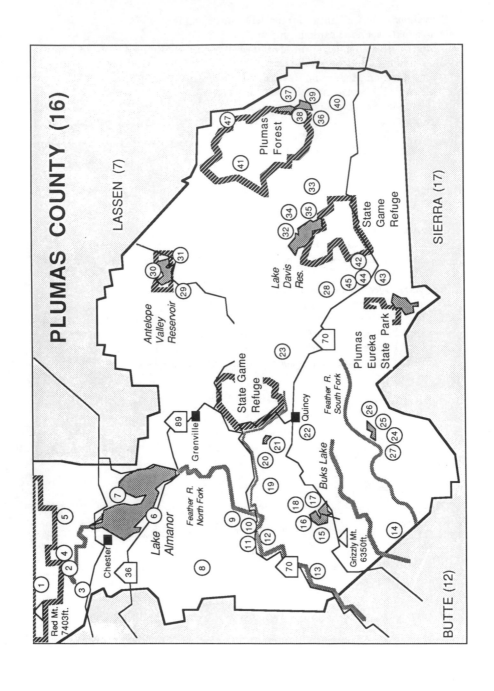

PLUMAS COUNTY (16)

LASSEN (7)

SIERRA (17)

BUTTE (12)

Red Mt.
7403ft.

Chester

Lake Almanor

Feather R.
North Fork

Grenville

State Game
Refuge

Antelope Valley
Reservoir

Plumas
Forest

Lake Davis
Res.

State Game
Refuge

Quincy

Buks Lake

Feather R.
South Fork

Plumas Eureka
State Park

Grizzly Mt.
6350ft.

PLUMAS COUNTY

♦

Site **1**   WARNER
              VALLEY   ▲

Campsites, facilities: There are 15 tent or motorhome sites in Warner Valley.
   Piped water, pit toilets, fireplaces and picnic table are provided.
Reservations, fee: No reservations; $4 fee per night.
Who to contact: Phone Lassen Volcanic National Park at (916)595-4444.
Location: Set 16 miles northwest of Chester on Chester-Warner Road.
Trip note: Open from June through September. Elevation 5650 feet. Good
   horseback riding area. Nature trail leads to various lakes, including Boiling
   Springs Lake. Camp is situated on Hot Springs Creek.

Site **2**   DOMINGO
              SPRINGS   ▲

Campsites, facilities: There are nine tent sites and nine campsites for tents or mo-
   torhomes up to 22 feet long. Piped water, vault toilets, picnic tables and
   fireplaces are provided.
Reservations, fee: No reservations; $4 fee per night.
Who to contact: Phone Lassen National Forest Headquarters at (916)257-2151.
Location: Set eight miles northwest of Chester off Warner Valley Road on Red
   Bluff Road.
Trip note: Open from June through September. Elevation 5200 feet. Lassen For-
   est map details back country trails and roads.

Site **3**   HIGH
              BRIDGE   ▲

Campsites, facilities: There are 12 campsites for tents or motorhomes up to 22
   feet long. Non-piped water, vault toilets, picnic tables and fireplaces are
   provided. Groceries and propane gas are available nearby.
Reservations, fee: No reservations, no fee.
Who to contact: Phone Lassen National Forest Headquarters at (916)257-2151.
Location: Set five miles northwest of Chester on Warner Valley Road.
Trip note: Open from June through September. Elevation 5200 feet. Situated on

North Fork of the Feather River. Good trout fishing at many streams in area.

Site 4 WARNER CREEK

Campsites, facilities: There are 11 campsites for tents or motorhomes up to 22 feet long. There is no water, but vault toilets, picnic tables and fireplaces are provided.
Reservations, fee: No reservations, no fee.
Who to contact: Phone Lassen National Forest Headquarters at (916)257-2151.
Location: Set seven miles northwest of Chester on Warner Valley Road.
Trip note: Open from June through September. Elevation 5000 feet.

Site 5 BENNER CREEK

Campsites, facilities: There are four campsites for tents or motorhomes up to 22 feet long. There is no water, but vault toilets, picnic tables and fireplaces are provided.
Reservations, fee: No reservations, no fee.
Who to contact: Phone Lassen National Forest Headquarters at (916)257-2151.
Location: Set seven miles north of Chester on Juniper Lake Road.
Trip note: Open from June through September. Elevation 5600 feet. Fishing options in area include Lake Almanor, North Fork Feather River and Butt Lake.

Site 6 ALMANOR

Campsites, facilities: There are 15 tent sites and 86 campsites for tents or motorhomes up to 22 feet long. Piped water, vault toilets, picnic tables and fireplaces are provided. A grocery store is nearby.
Reservations, fee: No reservations; $5 fee per night.
Who to contact: Phone Lassen National Forest Headquarters at (916)257-2151.
Location: Set in the town of Almanor off Highway 89.
Trip note: Open from June through October. Elevation 4600 feet. Lake Almanor has good smallmouth bass fishing in spring, trout and salmon in spring and fall.

Site 7 BIG COVE RESORT

Campsites, facilities: There are 50 motorhome sites and 12 campsites for tents or motorhomes with full or partial hookups. Piped water, flush toilets, showers, picnic tables and fireplaces are provided. A grocery store, a laundromat and propane gas station are also available.

Reservations, fee: Reservation deposit of $10.50 required. $10.50 fee per night; pets $1.

Who to contact: Phone Big Cove Resort at (916)596-3349.

Location: Set nine miles southeast of Chester at 442 Peninsula Drive.

Trip note: Open from May through October. Elevation 4500 feet. Lake Almanor is nearby.

Site **8**　　　　　　　LITTLE
　　　　　　　　　　　GRIZZLY

Campsites, facilities: There are five tent only sites. There is no water, but vault toilets, picnic tables and fireplaces are provided.

Reservations, fee: No reservations, no fee.

Who to contact: Phone Lassen National Forest Headquarters at (916)257-2151.

Location: Set 14 miles southwest of Almanor off Highway 89 via Humbug Road.

Trip note: Open from June through September. Elevation 5800 feet. Little-used, primitive camp for people who don't mind bringing water and want quiet.

Site **9**　　　　　　　QUEEN
　　　　　　　　　　　LILY

Campsites, facilities: There are 11 tent sites and one campsite for tents or motorhomes up to 16 feet long. Piped water, flush toilets, showers, fireplaces and picnic tables are provided. A grocery store and a laundromat are nearby.

Reservations, fee: No reservations; $5 fee per night.

Who to contact: Phone Plumas National Forest Headquarters at (916)283-2050.

Location: Set four miles northeast of Belden off Highway 70 on Caribou Road.

Trip note: Open from April through September. Elevation 2600 feet. Prime little hideaway with good backwoods exploring, fishing in Plumas National Forest. Forest map details hiking, back roads, lakes and streams.

Site **10**　　　　　　　NORTH
　　　　　　　　　　　FORK

Campsites, facilities: There are seven tent sites and 13 campsites for tents or motorhomes up to 32 feet long. Piped water, flush toilets, showers, fireplaces and picnic tables are provided. A grocery store and a laundromat are nearby.

Reservations, fee: No reservations; $5 fee per night.

Who to contact: Phone Plumas National Forest Headquarters at (916)283-2050.

Location: Set four miles northeast of Belden off Highway 70 on Caribou Road.

Trip note: Open from April through September. Elevation 2600 feet. Situated on

North Fork of Feather River, with good trout fishing after river clears in spring.

Site **11**   GANSNER   ▲
                                                  BAR

Campsites, facilities: There are 14 campsites for tents or motorhomes up to 32 feet long. Piped water, flush toilets, showers, fireplaces and picnic tables are provided. A grocery store and a laundromat are nearby.
Reservations, fee: No reservations; $5 fee per night.
Who to contact: Phone Plumas National Forest Headquarters at (916)283-2050.
Location: Set two miles northeast of Belden off Highway 70 on Caribou Road.
Trip note: Open from April through October. Elevation 2300 feet. Just far enough off Highway 70 to be missed by most people.

Site **12**   BELDEN   ▲

Campsites, facilities: There are nine tent sites and five campsites for tents or motorhomes up to 22 feet long. Piped water, flush toilets, showers, fireplaces and picnic tables are provided. Groceries and propane gas are available nearby.
Reservations, fee: No reservations; $5 fee per night.
Who to contact: Phone Plumas National Forest Headquarters at (916)283-2050.
Location: Set in Belden on Highway 70.
Trip note: Open from June through September. Elevation 2300 feet. Situated on Pacific Crest Trailhead. Good base camp for hiking, fishing trip.

Site **13**   JAMES   ▲
                                                  LEE

Campsites, facilities: There are 12 tent sites and 13 sites for tents or motorhomes up to 22 feet long. Piped water, flush toilets, fireplaces and picnic tables are provided. Eleven of these sites are open all year, but without piped water. Groceries are available nearby.
Reservations, fee: No reservations; $5 fee per night.
Who to contact: Phone Plumas National Forest Headquarters at (916)283-2050.
Location: Set 20 miles southwest of Belden on Highway 70.
Trip note: Open from April through October (except as indicated above in campsite info). Elevation 2000 feet. Situated on North Fork of Feather River.

Site **14**   LITTLE   ▮
                                              NORTH FORK

Campsites, facilities: There are eight campsites for tents or motorhomes up to 16 feet long. No water, but vault toilets, tables and fireplaces are provided.

Reservations, fee: No reservations, no fee.

Who to contact: Phone Plumas National Forest Headquarters at (916)283-2050.

Location: Set 15 miles northeast of Bruch Creek on Oroville-Quincy Highway. Route to site is along rough, single lane road.

Trip note: Open from May through October. Elevation 3700 feet. Primitive camp in outback that few know of.

Site **15**   GRIZZLY CREEK

Campsites, facilities: There are eight campsites for tents or motorhomes up to 22 feet long. No water, but vault toilets, picnic tables and fireplaces are provided. A grocery store and laundromat are nearby.

Reservations, fee: No reservations, no fee.

Who to contact: Phone Plumas National Forest Headquarters at (916)283-2050.

Location: Set three miles southwest of Bucks Lake on Oroville-Quincy Road.

Trip note: Open from June through October. Elevation 5400 feet. Bucks Lake nearby provides good trout fishing, especially in May.

Site **16**   SUNDEW

Campsites, facilities: There are 19 campsites for tents or motorhomes up to 22 feet long. Piped water, flush toilets, fireplaces and picnic tables are provided.

Reservations, fee: No reservations; $5 fee per night.

Who to contact: Phone Plumas National Forest Headquarters at (916)283-2050.

Location: Set six miles northwest of Bucks Lake on Bucks Lake Dam Road.

Trip note: Open from June through October. Elevation 5200 feet. Bucks Lake provides a good trout fishery. Network of back country roads take off from lake, detailed on map of Plumas National Forest.

Site **17**   WHITEHORSE

Campsites, facilities: There are 20 campsites for tents or motorhomes up to 22 feet long. Piped water, flush toilets, fireplaces and picnic tables are provided. A grocery store and laundromat are nearby.

Reservations, fee: No reservations; $4 fee per night.

Who to contact: Phone Plumas National Forest Headquarters at (916)283-2050.

Location: Set two miles east of Bucks Lake on Bucks Lake Road.

Trip note: Open from June through October. Elevation 5200 feet. Good trout fishing at Bucks Lake.

Site **18**   MILL
                                          CREEK   ▲

Campsites, facilities: There are 10 campsites for tents or motorhomes up to 22
    feet long. Piped water, flush toilets, fireplaces and picnic tables are
    provided.
Reservations, fee: No reservations; $5 fee per night.
Who to contact: Phone Plumas National Forest Headquarters at (916)283-2050.
Location: Set six miles northwest of Bucks Lake on Bucks Lake Road.
Trip note: Open from June through October. Elevation 5200 feet. Alternative
    campground if others closer to Bucks Lake are full.

Site **19**   SILVER
                                          LAKE   ▲

Campsites, facilities: There are six tent sites. Unpiped water only, but vault toi-
    lets, picnic tables and fireplaces are provided.
Reservations, fee: No reservations, no fee.
Who to contact: Phone Plumas National Forest Headquarters at (916)283-2050.
Location: Set 14 miles northwest of Quincy off Bucks Lake Road.
Trip note: Open from May through October. Elevation 5800 feet. Non-motor
    boating allowed on lake. No swimming. Sportsmen's Den in Quincy good
    source for fishing information.

Site **20**   HALLSTED   ▲

Campsites, facilities: There are five tent sites and 15 campsites for tents or motor-
    homes up to 22 feet long. Piped water, flush toilets, picnic tables and fire-
    places provided. A grocery store is nearby.
Reservations, fee: No reservations; $5 fee per night.
Who to contact: Phone Plumas National Forest Headquarters at (916)283-2050.
Location: Set 1/2 mile west of Twain on Highway 70.
Trip note: Open from May through September. Elevation 2800 feet. Situated on
    East Branch of the North Fork of the Feather River.

Site **21**   SNAKE
                                          LAKE   🌲

Campsites, facilities: There are six tent sites. No piped water, but
    vault toilets, picnic tables and fireplaces are provided.
Reservations, fee: No reservations, no fee.
Who to contact: Phone Plumas National Forest Headquarters at (916)283-2050.
Location: Set 10 miles northwest of Quincy off Highway 70.

Trip note: Open from April through October. Elevation 4200 feet. Little-known camp, primitive, good fishing.

Site **22**
DEANES
VALLEY

🌲

Campsites, facilities: There are seven sites for tents or motorhomes. No piped water, but vault toilets, picnic tables and fireplaces are provided. Dump station nearby.
Reservations, fee: No reservations, no fee.
Who to contact: Phone Plumas National Forest Headquarters at (916)283-2050.
Location: Set 11 miles southwest of Quincy off Bucks Lake Road.
Trip note: Open from April through October. Elevation 4400 feet. Situated on South Fork of Rock Creek. Remote, quiet, primitive setting.

Site **23**
BRADY'S
CAMP

🌲

Campsites, facilities: There are four tent sites. No water or toilets, but picnic tables and fireplaces are provided.
Reservations, fee: No reservations, no fee.
Who to contact: Phone Plumas National Forest Headquarters at (916)283-2050.
Location: Set eight miles east of Quincy off Highway 89 and Highway 70 on Squirrel Creek Road.
Trip note: Open from May through October. Elevation 7200 feet. Hike Argentine Rock (7209 feet) or camp on Dine Creek. Very primitive campsite, come fully prepared. Map of Plumas National Forest advised.

Site **24**
LITTLE
BEAVER

▲

Campsites, facilities: There are 60 tent sites and 60 campsites for tents or motorhomes up to 22 feet long. Piped water, flush toilets, picnic tables and fireplaces are provided. A grocery store, a sanitary dump station and a boat ramp are nearby.
Reservations, fee: No reservations, no fee.
Who to contact: Phone Plumas National Forest Headquarters at (916)283-2050.
Location: Set five miles north of La Porte off Quincy-La Porte Road via Little Grass Valley Road.
Trip note: Open from June through October. Elevation 5000 feet. Good fishing for trout in Little Grass Valley Reservoir. Trailhead for Pacific Crest Trail located at northeast end of lake.

Site **25**   RED FEATHER
GROUP CAMP

Campsites, facilities: There are 30 tent sites and 30 campsites for tents or motor-homes up to 22 feet long. This campground has group camp areas. Piped water, flush toilets, picnic tables and fireplaces are provided. A sanitary dump station, a boat ramp and a grocery store are nearby.
Reservations, fee: To reserve group camp, phone (916)675-2462; $20 fee per night.
Who to contact: Phone Plumas National Forest Headquarters at (916)283-2050.
Location: Set five and a half miles north of La Porte off Quincy-La Porte Road via Little Grass Valley Road.
Trip note: Open from June through October. Elevation 5000 feet. Optional camp to No. 24 at Little Grass Valley Reservoir.

Site **26**   RUNNING
DEER

Campsites, facilities: There are 20 tent sites and 20 campsites for tents or motor-homes up to 22 feet long. Piped water, flush toilets, picnic tables and fire-places are provided. Boat ramp, grocery store and sanitary dump station are nearby.
Reservations, fee: No reservations; $5 fee per night.
Who to contact: Phone Plumas National Forest Headquarters at (916)283-2050.
Location: Set five and a half miles north of La Porte off Quincy-La Porte Road via Little Grass Valley Road.
Trip note: Open from June through September. Elevation 5000 feet. Another good hideaway near Little Grass Valley Reservoir.

Site **27**   WYANDOTTE   ◪

Campsites, facilities: There are 15 tent sites and two campsites for tents or motor-homes up to 22 feet long. Piped water, flush toilets, picnic tables and fire-places are provided. A sanitary dump station, a boat ramp and a grocery store are nearby.
Reservations, fee: No reservations; $5 fee per night.
Who to contact: Phone Plumas National Forest Headquarters at (916)283-2050.
Location: Set four miles north of La Porte off Quincy-La Porte Road via Little Grass Valley Road.
Trip note: Open from June through October. Elevation 5000 feet. At Little Grass Valley Reservoir.

Site **28**   JACKSON
                           CREEK   ◭

Campsites, facilities: There are 15 campsites for tents or motorhomes up to 22
    feet long. Piped water, flush toilets, picnic tables and fireplaces are pro-
    vided. A grocery store is nearby.
Reservations, fee: No reservations; $5 fee per night.
Who to contact: Phone Plumas National Forest Headquarters at (916)283-2050.
Location: Set seven and a half miles northwest of Blairsden off Highways 70 and
    89.
Trip note: Open from May through October. Elevation 4500 feet. Situated on
    Jackson Creek, near Mt. Jackson (6565 feet).

Site **29**   BOULDER
                           CREEK   ◭

Campsites, facilities: There are 69 campsites for tents or motorhomes. Piped wa-
    ter, vault toilets, picnic tables and fireplaces are provided. A sanitary dump
    station, a boat ramp and a grocery store are nearby.
Reservations, fee: No reservations; $5 fee per night.
Who to contact: Phone Plumas National Forest Headquarters at (916)283-2050.
Location: Set 24 miles northeast of Taylorsville via Beckwourth and Indian
    Creek Roads.
Trip note: Open from May through October. Elevation 5000 feet. Set near pretty
    Antelope Lake.

Site **30**   LONE
                           ROCK   ◭

Campsites, facilities: There are 87 campsites for tents or motorhomes up to 22
    feet long. Piped water, vault toilets, picnic tables and fireplaces are pro-
    vided. A sanitary dump station, a boat ramp and a grocery store are nearby.
Reservations, fee: No reservations; $5 fee per night.
Who to contact: Phone Plumas National Forest Headquarters at (916)283-2050.
Location: Set 24 miles northeast of Taylorsville via Beckwourth and Indian
    Creek Roads.
Trip note: Open from May through October. Elevation 5000 feet. Set at Ante-
    lope Lake.

Site **31**   LONG
                           POINT   ◭

Campsites, facilities: There are 38 campsites for tents or motorhomes up to 32
    feet long. Piped water, vault toilets, picnic tables and fireplaces are pro-
    vided. A grocery store, boat ramp and sanitary dump station are nearby.

Reservations, fee: No reservations; $5 fee per night.
Who to contact: Phone Plumas National Forest Headquarters at (916)283-2050.
Location: Set 24 1/2 miles northeast of Taylorsville via Beckwourth and Indian Creek Roads.
Trip note: Open from May through October. Elevation 5000 feet. Nice vacation spot at Antelope Lake. Map of Plumas Forest details area hiking.

Site **32**   LIGHTNING
                            TREE

Campsites, facilities: There are 56 campsites for tents or motorhomes up to 32 feet long. No water or toilets available. A sanitary dump station, a boat ramp and a grocery store are nearby.
Reservations, fee: No reservations, no fee.
Who to contact: Phone Plumas National Forest Headquarters at (916)283-2050.
Location: Set nine miles north of Portola off Grizzly Road via Lake Davis Road.
Trip note: At Lake Davis, one of the better trout fishing lakes in Northern California. Southern end of lake is bordered by state Game Refuge.

Site **33**   CROCKER

Campsites, facilities: There are six tent sites and nine campsites for tents or motorhomes up to 32 feet long. No water, but pit toilets, picnic tables and fireplaces provided.
Reservations, fee: No reservations, no fee.
Who to contact: Phone Plumas National Forest Headquarters at (916)283-2050.
Location: Set seven miles northwest of Genessee off Beckwourth-Genessee Road.
Trip note: Open from May through October. Elevation 5800 feet. Camp two miles from Antelope Lake. Primitive alternative to more developed sites at lake.

Site **34**   GRASSHOPPER
                            FLAT

Campsites, facilities: There are 70 campsites for tents or motorhomes up to 32 feet long. Piped water, flush toilets, picnic tables and fireplaces are provided. A boat ramp, grocery store, and sanitary dump station are nearby.
Reservations, fee: No reservations; $6 fee per night.
Who to contact: Phone Plumas National Forest Headquarters at (916)283-2050.
Location: Set eight miles north of Portola off Lake Davis Road.
Trip note: Open from May through October. Elevation 5900 feet. Good fishing at Lake Davis. Mouth of Freeman Creek good for flyfishing from float tube, or trolling.

Site 35   GRIZZLY   ◣

Campsites, facilities: There are 55 campsites for tents or motorhomes up to 32 feet long. Piped water, flush toilets, picnic tables and fireplaces are provided. A boat ramp, a grocery store and a sanitary dump station are nearby.
Reservations, fee: No reservations; $6 fee per night.
Who to contact: Phone Plumas National Forest Headquarters at (916)283-2050.
Location: Set eight miles north of Portola off Lake Davis Road.
Trip note: Open from May through October. Elevation 5900 feet. One of the better developed campgrounds at Lake Davis.

Site 36   COTTONWOOD SPRINGS   ◣

Campsites, facilities: There are 20 campsites for tents or motorhomes up to 22 feet long. Piped water, flush toilets, picnic tables and fireplaces are provided. A boat ramp and sanitary dump station are nearby. There is also a group camp available.
Reservations, fee: To reserve call (916)253-2223; $5 family fee per night; $25 group fee per night.
Who to contact: Phone Plumas National Forest Headquarters at (916)283-2050.
Location: Set nine and a half miles north of Chilcoot at Frenchman Lake.
Trip note: Open from May through October. Elevation 5700 feet. Boating, swimming and fishing available. Frenchman Lake stocked regularly with rainbow trout.

Site 37   BIG COVE   ◣

Campsites, facilities: There are 38 campsites for tents or motorhomes up to 32 feet long. Two of the sites are set up for handicapped users. Piped water, flush toilets, picnic tables and fireplaces are provided. A boat ramp, sanitary dump station, grocery store and propane gas are available nearby.
Reservations, fee: No reservations; $5 fee per night.
Who to contact: Phone Plumas National Forest Headquarters at (916)283-2050.
Location: Set 10 miles north of Chilcoot at Frenchman Lake.
Trip note: Open from May through September. Elevation 5100 feet. Well developed camp along edge of Frenchman Lake.

Site 38   FRENCHMAN   ◣

Campsites, facilities: There are 25 tent sites and 37 campsites for tents or motorhomes. Piped water, vault toilets, picnic tables and fireplaces are provided.

A sanitary dump station and a boat ramp are nearby.

Reservations, fee: No reservations; $5 fee per night.

Who to contact: Phone Plumas National Forest Headquarters at (916)283-2050.

Location: Set nine miles north of Chilcoot at Frenchman Lake.

Trip note: Open from May through October. Elevation 5100 feet. Good option at Frenchman Lake.

Site **39**   SPRING
              CREEK

Campsites, facilities: There are 39 campsites for tents or motorhomes up to 22 feet long. Piped water, vault toilets, picnic tables and fireplaces are provided. A boat ramp and sanitary dump station are nearby.

Reservations, fee: No reservations; $5 fee per night.

Who to contact: Phone Plumas National Forest Headquarters at (916)283-2050.

Location: Set nine miles north of Chilcoot at Frenchman Lake.

Trip note: Open from May through October. Elevation 5700 feet. Frenchman Lake a prime spot. A short drive via Highway 395 to Reno. Good trout fishing. State Game Refuge borders northwestern end of lake.

Site **40**   CHILCOOT   ▲

Campsites, facilities: There are five tent sites and 35 campsites for tents or motorhomes up to 22 feet long. Piped water, flush toilets, picnic tables and fireplaces are provided. A boat ramp, grocery store and sanitary dump station are nearby.

Reservations, fee: No reservations; $5 fee per night.

Who to contact: Phone Plumas National Forest Headquarters at (916)283-2050.

Location: Set four miles north of the town of Chilcoot on Frenchman Lake Road.

Trip note: Open from May through October. Elevation 5400 feet. About one and a half miles from reservoir on Last Chance Creek. Trout fishing is good at Last Chance Creek just below the dam, casting small Panther Martin spinner.

Site **41**   CONKLIN
              PARK

Campsites, facilities: There are nine campsites here that can accommodate tents or motorhomes up to 22 feet long. Non-piped water, vault toilets, picnic tables and fireplaces are provided.

Reservations, fee: No reservations, no fee.

Who to contact: Phone Plumas National Forest Headquarters at (916)283-2050.

Location: Set nine miles south of Milford off Highway 395.

Trip note: Open from May through October. Elevation 5900 feet. Located on Willow Creek in State Game Refuge. Little-known, rarely-used campground. Primitive and quiet.

Site **42**
FEATHER RIVER
KOA

Campsites, facilities: There are 30 motorhome sites with full hookups and 25 tent sites. Piped water, showers, flush toilets, picnic tables and fireplaces are provided. A grocery store, laundromat, sanitary dump station, heated pool, recreation room, playground and propane gas are available.
Reservations, fee: $9 deposit with reservation; $9 fee per night.
Who to contact: Phone Feather River KOA at (916)836-2688.
Location: Set on Highway 70, 24 miles west of Highway 395, or five miles east of Highway 89.
Trip note: Open from May through October. Elevation 4954 feet. Historic Johnsville and museum nearby. Plumas Eureka State Park provides good hiking.

Site **43**
SIERRA SPRINGS
TRAILER RESORT

Campsites, facilities: There are 30 motorhome sites with full hookups. Piped water, showers, flush toilets, picnic tables and fireplaces are provided. A sanitary dump station, laundromat, playground and propane gas are available nearby.
Reservations, fee: $12 deposit with reservation; $12 fee per night.
Who to contact: Phone (916)836-2747.
Location: Set three and a half miles southeast of Blairsden on Highway 70.
Trip note: Open all year. Elevation 5000 feet.

Site **44**
LITTLE BEAR
RV PARK

Campsites, facilities: There are 20 tent sites and 59 motorhome spaces with full or partial hookups. Piped water, showers, flush toilets, picnic tables and fireplaces are provided. A grocery store, a laundromat and propane gas, a sanitary disposal station and a playground are available for campers' needs.
Reservations, fee: $13 deposit with reservation; $13 fee per night.
Who to contact: Phone (916)836-2774.
Location: Set one mile northwest of Blairsden off Highway 70 and Highway 89.
Trip note: Open year around. Elevation 4300 feet. Feather River nearby.

Site **45**
MOVIN' WEST
TRAILER RANCH

Campsites, facilities: There are 36 motorhome spaces with full or partial hook-ups. Piped water, flush toilets and showers are provided. A laundromat and propane gas are available nearby.

Reservations, fee: $12 deposit with reservation; $12 fee per night.

Who to contact: Phone (916)836-2614.

Location: Set 1/2 mile northwest of Graegle on County Road A-14.

Trip note: Open year around. Elevation 4300 feet. Good trout fishing on nearby streams, detailed on map of Plumas National Forest.

Site **46**
PLUMAS-EUREKA
STATE PARK

Campsites, facilities: There are 10 campsites for tents, 27 motorhome sites for motorhomes up to 30 feet long. Piped water, showers, flush toilets, picnic tables and fireplaces are provided. A grocery store, laundromat, a sanitary dump station and propane gas are available nearby.

Reservations, fee: $3.75 reservation fee payable to MISTIX: (800)446-7275. $8 fee per night; pets $1.

Who to contact: Phone (916)836-2380.

Location: Set five miles west of Blairsden on County Road A-14.

Trip note: Open May through September. Elevation 5200 feet. Hiking trails to numerous lakes.

Site **47**
MEADOW
VIEW

Campsites, facilities: There are six sites for tents or motorhomes. No water, but vault toilets, picnic tables and fireplaces are provided.

Reservations, fee: No reservations, no fee.

Who to contact: Phone Plumas National Forest Headquarters at (916)283-2050.

Location: Set seven and a half miles west of Doyle on Doyle Grade Road.

Trip note: Open May through October. Elevation 6100 feet. Fairly remote, primitive camp. Bring your own water.

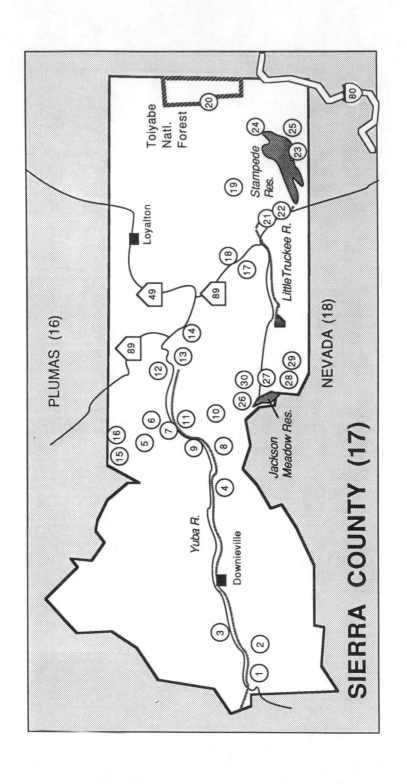

SIERRA COUNTY (17)

SIERRA COUNTY

♦

Site **1**   FIDDLE
                 CREEK

Campsites, facilities: There are 13 tent sites. No water, but vault toilets, picnic
     tables and fireplaces are provided. A grocery store and propane gas are
     available nearby.
Reservations, fee: No reservations, no fee.
Who to contact: Phone Tahoe National Forest Headquarters at (916)265-4531.
Location: Set nine and a half miles northeast of Camptonville on Highway 49.
Trip note: Open year around. Elevation 2200 feet. Situated on Yuba River in a
     quiet, primitive area. Fiddle Bow Trail leads out from camp to Halls Ranch
     Station or Indian Rock. Bring your own water.

Site **2**   INDIAN
                 VALLEY

Campsites, facilities: There are 17 campsites for tents or motorhomes up to 22
     feet long. Piped water, vault toilets, picnic tables and fireplaces are pro-
     vided. A grocery store and propane gas are available nearby.
Reservations, fee: No reservations; $4 fee per night.
Who to contact: Phone Tahoe National Forest Headquarters at (916)265-4531.
Location: Set 10 miles northeast of Camptonville on Highway 49.
Trip note: Open year around. Elevation 2200 feet. Pretty little spot set on Yuba
     River.

Site **3**   RAMS
                 HORN

Campsites, facilities: There are 16 campsites for tents or motorhomes up to 22
     feet long. Piped water, vault toilets, picnic tables and fireplaces are
     provided.
Reservations, fee: No reservations; $4 fee per night.
Who to contact: Phone Tahoe National Forest Headquarters at (916)265-4531.
Location: Set 15 miles northeast of Camptonville on Highway 49.
Trip note: Open year around. Elevation 2600 feet. Situated at confluence of

Rams Horn Creek and Yuba River. Trail leads from camp up to St. Charles Hill.

Site 4   UNION
                               FLAT   ▲

Campsites, facilities: There are 16 campsites for tents or motorhomes up to 22 feet long. Piped water, vault toilets, picnic tables and fireplaces are provided. A grocery store and propane gas are available nearby.
Reservations, fee: No reservations; $4 fee per night.
Who to contact: Phone Tahoe National Forest Headquarters at (916)265-4531.
Location: Set six miles east of Downeville on Highway 49.
Trip note: Open from May through October. Elevation 3400 feet. Situated on Yuba River, near Quartz Point and Granite Mountain. The Yuba River runs year around and provides a swimming hole next to camp.

Site 5   BERGER
                               CREEK   🌲

Campsites, facilities: There are 10 campsites for tents or motorhomes up to 22 feet long. No water, but vault toilets, picnic tables and fireplaces are provided. A grocery store is nearby.
Reservations, fee: No reservations; $6 fee per night.
Who to contact: Phone Tahoe National Forest Headquarters at (916)265-4531.
Location: Set eight and a half miles north of Sierra City off Highway 49 via Gold Lake and Packer Lake Roads.
Trip note: Open from June through October. Elevation 5900 feet. Packer Lake, Sardine Lakes, Tamarack Lakes and other nearby lakes provide good trout fishing. Primitive camp, so bring what you need, including water.

Site 6   SALMON
                               CREEK   ▲

Campsites, facilities: There are 34 campsites for tents or motorhomes up to 22 feet long. Piped water, vault toilets, picnic tables and fireplaces are provided. A grocery store, laundromat and propane gas are available nearby.
Reservations, fee: No reservations; $4 fee per night.
Who to contact: Phone Tahoe National Forest Headquarters at (916)265-4531.
Location: Set six and a half miles north of Sierra City off Highway 49 on Gold Lake Road.
Trip note: Open from June through October. Elevation 5800 feet. Situated at confluence of Packer and Salmon Creeks. There is a spectacular view of the crags that rise above the Yuba River Valley.

Site 7 — SARDINE

Campsites, facilities: There are 29 campsites for tents or motorhomes up to 22 feet long. Piped water, vault toilets, picnic tables and fireplaces are provided. A grocery store, laundromat and propane gas are available nearby.

Reservations, fee: No reservations; $4 fee per night.

Who to contact: Phone Tahoe National Forest Headquarters at (916)265-4531.

Location: Set seven miles north of Sierra City off Highway 49 via Gold Lake Road.

Trip note: Open from June through October. Elevation 5800 feet. Fishing on creek leading from nearby Sardine Lakes.

Site 8 — LOGANVILLE

Campsites, facilities: There are five tent sites and 11 campsites for tents or motorhomes up to 22 feet long. Piped water, vault toilets and picnic tables are provided. A grocery store, laundromat and propane gas are available nearby.

Reservations, fee: No reservations; $3 fee per night.

Who to contact: Phone Tahoe National Forest Headquarters at (916)265-4531.

Location: Set one and a half miles west of Sierra City off Highway 49.

Trip note: Open from May through October. Elevation 3800 feet. Situated on Yuba River.

Site 9 — SIERRA SKIES RV PARK

Campsites, facilities: There are 30 motorhome spaces with full hookups. Rest rooms, hot showers and picnic tables are provided. Propane gas is available nearby.

Reservations, fee: Reservation fee of $11; camping fee $11 per night.

Who to contact: Phone (916)862-1166.

Location: Set in Sierra City on Highway 49.

Trip note: Open from May through October. Elevation 4175 feet. Set along Yuba River.

Site 10 — WILD PLUM

Campsites, facilities: There are 47 campsites for tents or motorhomes up to 22 feet long. Piped water, vault toilets, picnic tables and fireplaces are provided. A grocery store, laundromat and propane gas are available nearby.

Reservations, fee: No reservations; $4 fee per night.

Who to contact: Phone Tahoe National Forest Headquarters at (916)265-4531.
Location: Set two miles east of Sierra City off Highway 49.
Trip note: Open from May through October. Situated on Haypress Creek, elevation 4400 feet. Haypress Trail leads out of camp past a waterfall and up to Haypress Valley. A nice, scenic spot.

Site **11**   SIERRA

Campsites, facilities: There are nine tent sites and six campsites for tents or motorhomes up to 22 feet long. No water, but vault toilets, picnic tables and fireplaces are provided. A grocery store, laundromat and propane gas are available nearby.
Reservations, fee: No reservations, no fee.
Who to contact: Phone Tahoe National Forest Headquarters at (916)265-4531.
Location: Set seven miles northeast of Sierra City on Highway 49.
Trip note: Open from June through October. Situated on Yuba River, elevation 5600 feet. A quiet and primitive spot.

Site **12**   CHAPMAN
                                         CREEK

Campsites, facilities: There are 29 campsites for tents or motorhomes up to 22 feet long. Piped water, showers, vault toilets, picnic tables and fireplaces are provided. A grocery store, laundromat and propane gas are available nearby.
Reservations, fee: No reservations; $4 fee per night.
Who to contact: Phone Tahoe National Forest Headquarters at (916)265-4531.
Location: Set 12 1/2 miles northeast of Sierra City on Highway 49.
Trip note: Open from June through October. Elevation 6000 feet. Situated at confluence of Chapman Creek and Yuba River. Chapman Creek Trail leads out of camp to Beartrap Meadow or Haskell Peak.

Site **13**   LINCOLN
                                         CREEK

Campsites, facilities: There are nine campsites here that can accommodate tents or motorhomes up to 16 feet long. No water, but vault toilets, picnic tables and fireplaces are provided. A grocery store and propane gas are available nearby.
Reservations, fee: No reservations, no fee.
Who to contact: Phone Tahoe National Forest Headquarters at (916)265-4531.
Location: Set nine and a half miles northeast of Sierra City on Highway 49.
Trip note: Open from June through October. Elevation 6200 feet. A quiet,

primitive location situated at the confluence of Lincoln Creek and Yuba River.

Site **14** YUBA
PASS ▲

Campsites, facilities: There are 20 campsites for tents or motorhomes up to 22 feet long. Piped water, vault toilets, picnic tables and fireplaces are provided. A grocery store and propane gas are available nearby.
Reservations, fee: No reservations; $3 fee per night.
Who to contact: Phone Tahoe National Forest Headquarters at (916)265-4531.
Location: Set seven and a half miles west of Sattley on Highway 49 at Yuba Pass.
Trip note: Open from June through November. Elevation 6800 feet. This site, situated at Yuba Pass, becomes a ski area in the winter.

Site **15** LAKES
BASIN 🌲

Campsites, facilities: There are 24 tent sites. Piped water, vault toilets, picnic tables and fireplaces are provided.
Reservations, fee: No reservations; $5 fee per night.
Who to contact: Phone Plumas National Forest Headquarters at (916)283-2050.
Location: Set nine miles southwest of Graeagle on Gold Lake Road.
Trip note: Open from June through October. Elevation 6400 feet. Good fishing available in area streams for rainbow and brown trout. A map of the Plumas National Forest area should be brought along.

Site **16** LAKE BASIN
GROUP CAMP ▲

Campsites, facilities: There is one group camp for tents or motorhomes. Piped water, vault toilets, picnic tables and fireplaces are provided.
Reservations, fee: No reservations; $20 group fee per night.
Who to contact: Phone Plumas National Forest Headquarters at (916)283-2050.
Location: Set nine and a half miles southwest of Graeagle on Gold Lake Road.
Trip note: Open from June through October. Elevation 2500 feet. Good fishing and hiking in area detailed on Plumas National Forest map.

Site **17** COLD
CREEK ▲

Campsites, facilities: There are 11 tent sites and six campsites for tents or motorhomes up to 22 feet long. Piped water, vault toilets, picnic tables and fireplaces are provided. A grocery store and propane gas are available nearby.
Reservations, fee: No reservations; $4 fee per night.

Who to contact: Phone Tahoe National Forest Headquarters at (916)265-4531.
Location: Set five miles southeast of Sierraville on Highway 89.
Trip note: Open from May through November. Elevation 5800 feet. This campsite is situated on Cold Creek. Nearby is Campbell Hot Springs.

Site 18   COTTONWOOD   ▲

Campsites, facilities: There are 21 tent sites and 28 campsites for tents or motorhomes up to 22 feet long. Piped water, vault toilets, picnic tables and fireplaces are provided. A grocery store and propane gas are available nearby.
Reservations, fee: No reservations; $4 fee per night.
Who to contact: Phone Tahoe National Forest Headquarters at (916)265-4531.
Location: Set five miles southeast of Sierraville on Highway 89.
Trip note: Open from May through November. Elevation 5800 feet. Hike the interpretive trail, camp on Cottonwood Creek or visit nearby Campbell Hot Springs.

Site 19   BEAR VALLEY   🌲

Campsites, facilities: There are six campsites for tents or motorhomes up to 16 feet long. Piped water, vault toilets, picnic tables and fireplaces are provided.
Reservations, fee: No reservations, no fee.
Who to contact: Phone Tahoe National Forest Headquarters at (916)265-4531.
Location: Set seven and a half miles east of Sierraville on Lemon Canyon Road.
Trip note: Open from June through November. Elevation 6700 feet. Camp is situated near the headwaters of Bear Valley Creek.

Site 20   LOOKOUT   ▲

Campsites, facilities: There are 22 campsites for tents or motorhomes up to 22 feet long. Piped water, vault toilets, picnic tables and fireplaces are provided.
Reservations, fee: No reservations, no fee.
Who to contact: Phone Toiyabe National Forest Headquarters at (702)784-5331.
Location: Set eight and a half miles northwest of Verdi via Henness Pass and Long Valley Roads.
Trip note: Open from June through October. Elevation 6700 feet. Good base camp for hikes into Toiyabe National Forest. Forest Service details hikes.

Site **21**   LOWER
                                          LITTLE TRUCKEE

Campsites, facilities: There are 12 campsites for tents or motorhomes up to 22
   feet long. Piped water, vault toilets, picnic tables and fireplaces are
   provided.
Reservations, fee: No reservations; $4 fee per night.
Who to contact: Phone Tahoe National Forest Headquarters at (916)265-4531.
Location: Set eight miles southeast of Sierraville on Highway 89.
Trip note: Open from May through November. Elevation 6200 feet. Camp on
   Little Truckee River, two miles from Stampede Reservoir.

Site **22**   UPPER
                                          LITTLE TRUCKEE

Campsites, facilities: There is one tent site and 17 campsites for tents or motor-
   homes up to 22 feet long. Piped water, vault toilets, picnic tables and fire-
   places are provided.
Reservations, fee: No reservations; $4 fee per night.
Who to contact: Phone Tahoe National Forest Headquarters at (916)265-4531.
Location: Set 10 1/2 miles southeast of Sierraville on Highway 89.
Trip note: Open from May through November. Elevation 6200 feet. Camp on
   Little Truckee River, two miles from Stampede Reservoir.

Site **23**   LOGGER

Campsites, facilities: There are 252 campsites for tents or motorhomes up to 32
   feet long. Piped water, a sanitary dump station, flush toilets, picnic tables
   and fireplaces are provided. A grocery store is nearby.
Reservations, fee: No reservations; $6 fee per night.
Who to contact: Phone Tahoe National Forest Headquarters at (916)265-4531.
Location: Set 16 miles northeast of Truckee off Highway 80 via Stampede Reservoir Road.
Trip note: Open from May through October. Elevation 5900 feet. This popular
   lakeside campground has a boat ramp on Stampede Reservoir.

Site **24**   DAVIES
                                             CREEK

Campsites, facilities: There are 10 campsites for tents or motorhomes up to 22
   feet long. No water, but vault toilets and picnic tables are provided.
Reservations, fee: No reservations, no fee.
Who to contact: Phone Tahoe National Forest Headquarters at (916)265-4531.

Location: Set 12 miles northeast of Truckee off Highway 80 via Stampede Reservoir Road.

Trip note: Open from May through October. Elevation 6000 feet. This secluded site is located on the Stampede Reservoir where Merrill and Davies Creeks empty.

Site **25**   EMIGRANT
GROUP CAMP

Campsites, facilities: There are five group campsites for tents or motorhomes up to 32 feet long. Piped water, a sanitary dump station, vault toilets, picnic tables and fireplaces are provided.

Reservations, fee: No reservations; $20 group fee per night.

Who to contact: Phone Tahoe National Forest Headquarters at (916)265-4531.

Location: Set 16 miles northeast of Truckee off Highway 80.

Trip note: Open from May through September. Elevation 5900 feet. Situated on Stampede Reservoir with boat ramp nearby.

Site **26**   ASPEN
GROUP CAMP

Campsites, facilities: There is one group campsite for tents or motorhomes up to 22 feet long. Piped water, vault toilets, a sanitary dump station, picnic tables and fireplaces are provided.

Reservations, fee: Reservation required; $20 group fee per night.

Who to contact: Phone Tahoe National Forest Headquarters at (916)265-4531.

Location: Set 33 1/2 miles northwest of Truckee off Highway 89 at Jackson Meadow Reservoir.

Trip note: Open from June through October. Elevation 6100 feet. Situated on Jackson Meadow Reservoir. Good trout fishing in early summer.

Site **27**   EAST
MEADOW

Campsites, facilities: There are four tent sites, 38 motorhome sites and eight campsites that will accommodate tents or motorhomes up to 22 feet long. Piped water, flush toilets, a sanitary dump station, picnic tables and fireplaces are provided. Boat ramp is nearby.

Reservations, fee: Reservations required; $6 fee per night.

Who to contact: Phone Tahoe National Forest Headquarters at (916)265-4531.

Location: Set 33 miles northwest of Truckee off Highway 89 at Jackson Meadow Reservoir.

Trip note: Open from June through November. Elevation 6100 feet. The Pacific Crest Trail passes near this site which is located on Jackson Meadow Reservoir.

Site 28 FINDLEY

Campsites, facilities: There are six motorhome sites and seven campsites for tents or motorhomes up to 22 feet long. Piped water, flush toilets, picnic tables and fireplaces are provided. A boat ramp is nearby.

Reservations, fee: Reservations required; $6 fee per night.

Who to contact: Phone Tahoe National Forest Headquarters at (916)265-4531.

Location: Set 35 1/2 miles northwest of Truckee off Highway 89 at Jackson Meadow Reservoir.

Trip note: Open from June through November. Elevation 6200 feet. Situated on Findley Creek near where it empties into Jackson Meadow Reservoir. A pretty and secluded spot.

Site 29 FIR TOP

Campsites, facilities: There are seven motorhome sites and four spaces for tents or motorhomes up to 22 feet long. Piped water, a sanitary dump station, flush toilets, picnic tables and fireplaces are provided. A boat ramp is nearby.

Reservations, fee: Reservations required; $6 fee per night.

Who to contact: Phone Tahoe National Forest Headquarters at (916)265-4531.

Location: Set 35 1/2 miles northwest of Truckee off Highway 89 at Jackson Meadow Reservoir.

Trip note: Open from June through November. Elevation 6200 feet. One of several campgrounds set along Jackson Meadow Reservoir. Good fishing in early summer.

Site 30 PASS CREEK AND PASS CREEK ANNEX

Campsites, facilities: There are 15 tent sites and 21 motorhomes sites that can accommodate motorhomes up to 22 feet long. Boat ramp, piped water, a sanitary dump station, vault toilets, picnic tables and fireplaces are provided.

Reservations, fee: Reservations required; $6 fee per night.

Who to contact: Phone Tahoe National Forest Headquarters at (916)265-4531.

Location: Set 33 miles northwest of Truckee off Highway 89 at Jackson Meadow Reservoir.

Trip note: Open from June through October. Elevation 6100 feet. The Pacific Crest Trail passes near this camp set along Jackson Meadow Reservoir.

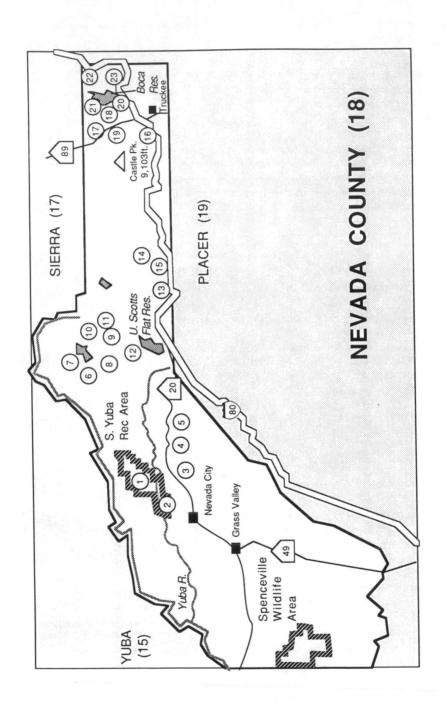

NEVADA COUNTY (18)

NEVADA COUNTY

◆

Site **1** | MALAKOFF DIGGINS
STATE HISTORICAL PARK |

Campsites, facilities: There are 30 campsites for tents or motorhomes up to 24
feet long. Piped water, flush toilets, picnic tables and fireplaces are provided. There is a grocery store in the park, and wheelchair access to camping, picnic, exhibits and fishing areas.
Reservations, fee: Reservation fee of $3.75 payable to MISTIX: (800)446-7275.
$10 camping fee per night; pets $1.
Who to contact: Phone (916)265-2740.
Location: Set 16 miles east of North San Juan off Highway 49 via Tyler Foote
Road.
Trip note: Open year around. Elevation 3400 feet. The site was formerly a gold
mining town. There are tours during the summer to numerous exhibits and
a historic Chinese settlement.

Site **2** | SOUTH
YUBA |

Campsites, facilities: There are 16 campsites for tents or motorhomes up to 30
feet long. Piped water, vault toilets, picnic tables and fireplaces are
provided.
Reservations, fee: No reservations, no fee.
Who to contact: Phone (916)985-4474—A Bureau of Land Management
Campground.
Location: Set 13 miles northeast of Nevada City off Highway 49 via Tyler Foote
Crossing Road.
Trip note: Open year around. Elevation 2600 feet. Set on upper Yuba River.

Site **3** | SCOTTS FLAT LAKE
RECREATION AREA |

Campsites, facilities: There are 150 campsites for tents or motorhomes up to 35 feet
long. Restrooms, showers and a sanitary dump station are provided. A general store, coffee shop, boat rentals, gas dock, boat ramp and bait are available.

Reservations, fee: Reservations accepted; $9.50 per night.
Who to contact: Phone (916)265-5302.
Location: Set five miles northeast of Nevada City at 23333 Scotts Flat Road.
Trip note: Open all year, weather permitting. Good trout fishing May through October at Scotts Flat Reservoir.

Site **4**   WHITE
                               CLOUD   ▲

Campsites, facilities: There are 46 campsites for tents or motorhomes up to 22 feet long. Piped water, vault toilets, picnic tables and fireplaces are provided.
Reservations, fee: No reservations; $4 fee per night.
Who to contact: Phone Tahoe National Forest Headquarters at (916)265-4531.
Location: Set 11 1/2 miles east of Nevada City on Highway 20.
Trip note: Open from May through October. Elevation 4300 feet. Tahoe National Forest map details good hiking, fishing in area.

Site **5**   SKILLMAN   ▲

Campsites, facilities: There are 16 campsites for tents or motorhomes up to 22 feet long. Piped water, vault toilets, picnic tables and fireplaces are provided.
Reservations, fee: No reservations; $3 fee per night.
Who to contact: Phone Tahoe National Forest Headquarters at (916)265-4531.
Location: Set 15 miles east of Nevada City on Highway 20.
Trip note: Open from May through October. Elevation 4400 feet. A nice spot which is often overlooked.

Site **6**   BOWMAN

Campsites, facilities: There are seven campsites for tents or motorhomes up to 22 feet long. No water, but vault toilets, picnic tables and fireplaces are provided.
Reservations, fee: No reservations, no fee.
Who to contact: Phone Tahoe National Forest Headquarters at (916)265-4531.
Location: Set 16 1/2 miles north of Emigrant Gap off Highway 80.
Trip note: Open from June through October. Elevation 5600 feet. Recreation is available at Bowman Lake and a trail leads to Pyramid Peak (6000 feet). Be sure to bring your own water.

| Site 7 | JACKSON CREEK | 🌲 |

Campsites, facilities: There are 14 campsites for tents or motorhomes up to 22 feet long. No water, but vault toilets, picnic tables and fireplaces are provided.

Reservations, fee: No reservations, no fee.

Who to contact: Phone Tahoe National Forest Headquarters at (916)265-4531.

Location: Set 17 1/2 miles north of Emigrant Gap off Highway 80.

Trip note: Open from June through October. Elevation 5600 feet. Numerous recreation options are available in Jackson Creek and Bowman Lake. A nearby trail leads to smaller lakes to the south. Bring your own water.

| Site 8 | CARR LAKE | 🌲 |

Campsites, facilities: There are four tent sites with no water, but vault toilets, picnic tables and fireplaces are provided.

Reservations, fee: No reservations, no fee.

Who to contact: Phone Tahoe National Forest Headquarters at (916)265-4531.

Location: Set 19 1/2 miles northeast of Emigrant Gap off Highway 80.

Trip note: Open from June through October. Elevation 6700 feet. A trail from camp leads to other small lakes in the vicinity. This is a virtually unknown camping spot.

| Site 9 | GROUSE RIDGE | ⛺ |

Campsites, facilities: There are nine campsites for tents or motorhomes up to 16 feet long. Piped water, vault toilets, picnic tables and fireplaces are provided.

Reservations, fee: No reservations, no fee.

Who to contact: Phone Tahoe National Forest Headquarters at (916)265-4531.

Location: Set 20 miles northeast of Emigrant Gap off Highway 80 on Grouse Ridge Road.

Trip note: Open from June through October. Elevation 7400 feet. There are numerous small lakes in area. Camp is located at the headwaters of Granite Creek.

| Site 10 | CANYON CREEK | ⛺ |

Campsites, facilities: There are nine tent sites and 11 campsites for motorhomes up to 22 feet long. Piped water, vault toilets, picnic tables and fireplaces are provided.

Reservations, fee: No reservations, no fee.

Who to contact: Phone Tahoe National Forest Headquarters at (916)265-4531.

Location: Set 19 1/2 miles north of Emigrant Gap off Highway 80.

Trip note: Open from June through October. Elevation 6000 feet. Situated on Canyon Creek between Sawmill Lake and Faucherie Lake. You can hike along trails to numerous other small lakes in the area. A good camp to use as base headquarters for a nice area trip.

Site **11**   FAUCHERIE
                      GROUP CAMP

Campsites, facilities: There is one large group camp for tents or motorhomes up to 22 feet long. No water, but vault toilets, picnic tables and fireplaces are provided.

Reservations, fee: No reservations; $20 group fee per night.

Who to contact: Phone Tahoe National Forest Headquarters at (916)265-4531.

Location: At 19 miles north of Emigrant Gap off Highway 80.

Trip note: Open from June through October. Elevation 6100 feet. Camp situated on Faucherie Lake.

Site **12**   FULLER
                       LAKE

Campsites, facilities: There are 11 tent spaces, with no water, but vault toilets, picnic tables and fireplaces are provided.

Reservations, fee: No reservations, no fee.

Who to contact: Phone Tahoe National Forest Headquarters at (916)265-4531.

Location: Set 13 miles northeast of Emigrant Gap off Highway 80.

Trip note: Open from May through October. Elevation 5600 feet. Good fishing on Fuller Lake as well as nearby Rucker and Spaulding Lakes. A primitive and quiet campsite.

Site **13**   INDIAN
                      SPRINGS

Campsites, facilities: There are seven tent sites and 35 campsites for tents or RV's up to 22 feet long. Piped water, vault toilets, picnic tables and fireplaces are provided. A grocery store and propane gas are also available nearby.

Reservations, fee: No reservations; $5 fee per night.

Who to contact: Phone Tahoe National Forest Headquarters at (916)265-4531.

Location: Set seven and a half miles northeast of Emigrant Gap off Highway 80.

Trip note: Open from May through October. Elevation 5600 feet. Forest Service map details fishing and hiking in area.

Site **14**   STERLING
                             LAKE   🌲

Campsites, facilities: There are six campsites for tents or motorhomes. No water,
   but vault toilets, picnic tables and fireplaces are provided.
Reservations, fee: No reservations, no fee.
Who to contact: Phone Tahoe National Forest Headquarters at (916)265-4531.
Location: Set 14 1/2 miles northeast of Emigrant Gap off Highway 80 via For-
   dyce Lake Road.
Trip note: Open from June through October. Elevation 7000 feet. Camp is situ-
   ated on Sterling Lake.

Site **15**   WOODCHUCK   ▲

Campsites, facilities: There are eight campsites for tents or motorhomes up to 16
   feet long. No water, but vault toilets, picnic tables and fireplaces are provided. A grocery store and propane gas are also available nearby.
Reservations, fee: No reservations; $3 fee per night.
Who to contact: Phone Tahoe National Forest Headquarters at (916)265-4531.
Location: Set 11 miles northeast of Emigrant Gap off Highway 80.
Trip note: Open from June through October. Elevation 6300 feet. Camp is situated on Rattlesnake Creek. Map of Tahoe National Forest details back
   country roads for access.

Site **16**   DONNER MEMORIAL
                            STATE PARK   ▲

Campsites, facilities: There are 153 campsites for tents or motorhomes up to 28
   feet long. Piped water, flush toilets, showers, picnic tables and fireplaces
   are provided. A grocery store, laundromat and propane gas are also available nearby.
Reservations, fee: Reservation fee of $3.75 payable to MISTIX: (800)446-7275.
   $6 fee per night; pets $1.
Who to contact: Phone (916)587-3841.
Location: Set three miles west of Truckee on Highway 80.
Trip note: Open from May through August. Elevation 5900 feet. There is a
   cross-country ski trail and nature trail. Exhibits tell the story of the ill-fated
   Donner Party.

Site **17**   SAGE HEN
                             CREEK   🌲

Campsites, facilities: There are 10 campsites for tents or motorhomes up to 16
   feet long. No water, but vault toilets, picnic tables and fireplaces are

provided.

Reservations, fee: No reservations, no fee.

Who to contact: Phone Tahoe National Forest Headquarters at (916)265-4531.

Location: Set 10 1/2 miles northwest of Truckee off Highway 89 via Sage Hen Road.

Trip note: Open from May through October. Elevation 6500 feet. Situated on Sage Hen Creek just outside of the small town of Sage Hen.

Site **18**   ANNIE MCCLOUD   ▲

Campsites, facilities: There are 10 campsites for tents or motorhomes up to 22 feet long. Vault toilets are provided. A grocery store, laundromat and propane gas are available nearby.

Reservations, fee: No reservations, no fee.

Who to contact: Phone Tahoe National Forest Headquarters at (916)265-4531.

Location: Set five and a half miles north of Truckee off Highway 89 at Prosser Creek Reservoir.

Trip note: Open from May through October. Elevation 5800 feet. Overland Emigrant Trail passes near camp.

Site **19**   LAKESIDE   ▲

Campsites, facilities: There are 40 campsites for tents or motorhomes up to 22 feet long. No water, but vault toilets and picnic tables are provided. A grocery store, laundromat and propane gas are available nearby.

Reservations, fee: No reservations, no fee.

Who to contact: Phone Tahoe National Forest Headquarters at (916)265-4531.

Location: Set five miles north of Truckee off Highway 89 at Prosser Creek Reservoir.

Trip note: Open from April through October. Elevation 5700 feet. Overland Emigrant Trail passes nearby. Good trout fishing after ice breaks up in late spring.

Site **20**   PROSSER   ▲

Campsites, facilities: There are 17 tent sites and 12 campsites for motorhomes up to 22 feet long. Piped water, vault toilets, picnic tables and fireplaces are provided. A grocery store, laundromat and propane gas are available nearby.

Reservations, fee: No reservations; $4 fee per night.

Who to contact: Phone Tahoe National Forest Headquarters at (916)265-4531.

Location: Set six miles northeast of Truckee off Highway 89.

Trip note: Open from May through October. Elevation 5800 feet. A boat ramp is available on Prosser Creek Reservoir. Swimming and fishing is allowed in lake.

Site **21**   BOCA

Campsites, facilities: There are 10 campsites for tents or motorhomes up to 16 feet long. No water, but vault toilets and fireplaces are provided.
Reservations, fee: No reservations, no fee.
Who to contact: Phone Tahoe National Forest Headquarters at (916)265-4531.
Location: Set nine miles northeast of Truckee off Highway 80 at Boca Reservoir.
Trip note: Open from May through October. Elevation 5700 feet. There is a boat ramp near camp on Boca Reservoir. A primitive, beautiful and quiet site.

Site **22**   BOYINTON
                                        MILL

Campsites, facilities: There are 10 campsites for tents or motorhomes up to 32 feet long. No water, but vault toilets and picnic tables are provided.
Reservations, fee: No reservations, no fee.
Who to contact: Phone Tahoe National Forest Headquarters at (916)l265-4531.
Location: Set 10 miles northeast of Truckee off Highway 80 via Stampede Reservoir Road.
Trip note: Open from April through October. Elevation 5800 feet. Site is near stream leading into Boca Reservoir. Bring your own water.

Site **23**   BOCA
                                        REST

Campsites, facilities: There are 25 campsites for tents or motorhomes up to 32 feet long. Piped water, vault toilets and picnic tables are provided.
Reservations, fee: No reservations, no fee.
Who to contact: Phone Tahoe National Forest Headquarters at (916)265-4531.
Location: Set nine and a half miles northeast of Truckee off Highway 80 via Stampede Reservoir Road.
Trip note: Open from April through October. Elevation 5700 feet. Boca Reservoir is in vicinity.

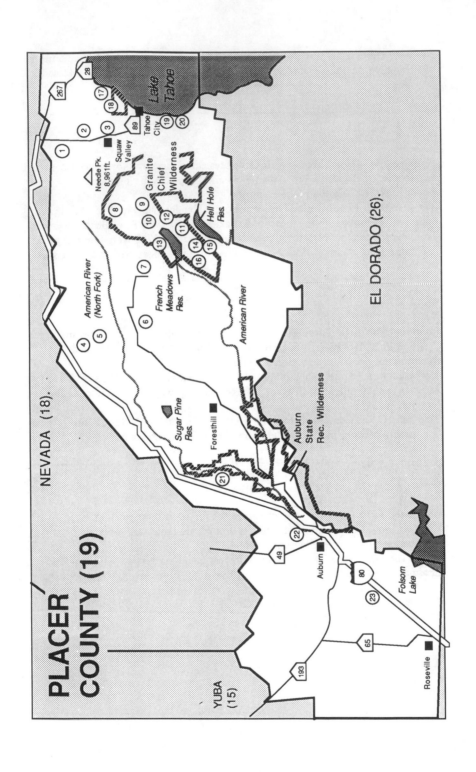

PLACER
COUNTY (19)

NEVADA (18).

YUBA
(15)

EL DORADO (26).

Lake
Tahoe

28
267
17
18
2
3
89 Tahoe
City
19
20
1

Needle Pk.
8,961 ft.

Squaw
Valley

Granite
Chief
Wilderness

Hell Hole
Res.

8
9
10
12
11
13
14
15
16
7

American River
(North Fork)

French
Meadows
Res.

American River

6
4
5

Sugar Pine
Res.

Foresthill

Auburn
State
Rec. Wilderness

21

22

49

Auburn

80

23

Folsom
Lake

65

193

Roseville

PLACER COUNTY

◆

Site 1 | GRANITE FLAT | ▲

Campsites, facilities: There are 75 campsites for tents or motorhomes to 22 feet long. Vault toilets and picnic tables are provided. No water, but a grocery store, laundromat and propane gas are available nearby.
Reservations, fee: No reservations, no fee.
Who to contact: Phone Tahoe National Forest Headquarters at (916)265-4531.
Location: Drive three miles southwest of Truckee off Highway 89.
Trip note: Open from April through October. Elevation 5900 feet. Camp is set near the Truckee River, where you can do some fishing.

Site 2 | GOOSE MEADOW | ▲

Campsites, facilities: There are 25 campsites for tents or motorhomes to 22 feet long. No water. Vault toilets and picnic tables are provided. A grocery store, laundromat and propane gas are available nearby.
Reservations, fee: No reservations, no fee.
Who to contact: Phone Tahoe National Forest Headquarters at (916)265-4531.
Location: Drive six miles southwest of Truckee on Highway 89.
Trip note: Open from May through October. Elevation 6000 feet. Camp is set near the Truckee River, where you can go fishing.

Site 3 | SILVER CREEK | ▲

Campsites, facilities: There are 21 tent spaces, and eight sites for motorhomes to 22 feet long. Piped water, vault toilets, picnic tables and fireplaces are provided. A grocery store and propane gas are available nearby.
Reservations, fee: No reservations; $4 use fee.
Who to contact: Phone Tahoe National Forest Headquarters: (916)265-4531.
Location: Drive nine miles south of Truckee on Highway 89.
Trip note: Open from May through October. Elevation 6200 feet. Fishing at confluence of Deer Creek and Truckee River. Good hiking trail up Deer Creek.

Site 4

NORTH
FORK

▲

Campsites, facilities: There are 17 campsites for tents or motorhomes to 16 feet long. Piped water, vault toilets, picnic tables and fireplaces are provided.
Reservations, fee: No reservations; $3 use fee.
Who to contact: Phone Tahoe National Forest Headquarters: (916)265-4531.
Location: Set in Onion Valley; from I-80, turn at Emigrant Gap and drive seven miles southeast on Texas Hill Road.
Trip note: Open from May through October. Elevation 4400 feet. Swimming and fishing on the North Fork of the American River.

Site 5

TUNNEL MILLS
GROUP CAMP

▲

Campsites, facilities: There are two group campsites for tents or motorhomes to 16 feet long. No water. Vault toilets, picnic tables and fireplaces are provided.
Reservations, fee: Reservations required; $20 fee for group.
Who to contact: Phone Tahoe National Forest Headquarters: (916)265-4531.
Location: From I-80, turn at Emigrant Gap and drive eight miles southeast to campground. Advisable to check Forest Service map for details of area.
Trip note: Open from June through October. Elevation 4400 feet. Swimming and fishing on the East Fork of Monumental Creek.

Site 6

SECRET
HOUSE

▲

Campsites, facilities: There are four tent spaces and two campsites for tents or motorhomes. Piped water, vault toilets, picnic tables and fireplaces are provided.
Reservations, fee: No reservations; no fee.
Who to contact: Phone Tahoe National Forest Headquarters: (916)265-4531.
Location: Drive 19 miles northeast of Foresthill via Foresthill Divide Road.
Trip note: Open from June through October. Elevation 5400 feet. Camp is set on the American River, which provides good fishing.

Site 7

ROBINSON
FLAT

🌲

Campsites, facilities: There are six tent spaces. No water. Vault toilets, picnic tables and fireplaces are provided.
Reservations, fee: No reservations, no fee.
Who to contact: Phone Tahoe National Forest Headquarters at (916)265-4531.

Location: Drive 27 miles northeast of Foresthill via Mosquito Ridge and Foresthill Divide Roads.

Trip note: Open from June through October. Elevation 6800 feet. Hiking trails to Duncan Peak and Bald Mountain. Two trails lead out from the camp southeast to French Meadows Reservoir, or southwest into the backcountry.

Site **8**   TALBOT

Campsites, facilities: There are five tent sites. No water. Vault toilets, picnic tables and fireplaces are provided.

Reservations, fee: No reservations, no fee.

Who to contact: Phone Tahoe National Forest Headquarters: (916)265-4531.

Location: From I-80, drive 20 miles south of Soda Springs via Baker Ranch and French Meadows Roads.

Trip note: Open from June through October. Elevation 5600 feet. Swimming and fishing on the American River. Camp is set at the trailhead into the Picayune Valley. French Meadows Reservoir is a hike down a gravel road.

Site **9**   AHART

Campsites, facilities: There are 17 campsites for tents or motorhomes to 22 feet long. No water. Vault toilets, picnic tables and fireplaces are provided.

Reservations, fee: No Reservations, no fee.

Who to contact: Phone Tahoe National Forest Headquarters at (916)265-4531.

Location: From I-80, drive 25 miles south of Soda Springs via French Meadows Road.

Trip note: Open from June through October. Elevation 5300 feet. Camp is near the northeastern end of French Meadows Reservoir on the American River. Swimming and fishing available on the river.

Site **10**   COYOTE
                              GROUP CAMP

Campsites, facilities: There are four group campsites for tents or motorhomes up to 22 feet long. Piped water, vault toilets, picnic tables and fireplaces are provided.

Reservations, fee: Reservations required; $20 fee for group.

Who to contact: Phone Tahoe National Forest Headquarters at (916)265-4531.

Location: Drive 43.5 miles northeast of Foresthill via Mosquito Ridge and French Meadows Roads.

Trip note: Open from June through October. Elevation 5300 feet. Camp is set on French Meadows Reservoir. Fishing and swimming on the American River. There are two trails that lead from the reservoir. One trail goes up and along the Star Ridge (or beyond to Robinson's Flat), and the other follows the American River through Picayune Valley and beyond.

Site **11**   FRENCH
                                MEADOWS   ▲

Campsites, facilities: There are 37 tent spaces and 38 campsites that will accommodate motorhomes to 22 feet long. Piped water, flush toilets, picnic tables and fireplaces are provided.
Reservations, fee: No reservations; $5 use fee.
Who to contact: Phone Tahoe National Forest Headquarters: (916)265-4531.
Location: Drive 41 miles northeast of Foresthill via Mosquito Ridge and French Meadows Roads.
Trip note: Open from June through October. Elevation 5300 feet. Camp is set on French Meadows Reservoir near a boat launch, where one can go swimming and fishing. A four-wheel drive trail leads up the ridge behind camp.

Site **12**   GATES
                                GROUP CAMP   ▲

Campsites, facilities: There are three group campsites for tents or motorhomes to 22 feet long. Piped water, vault toilets, picnic tables and fireplaces are provided.
Reservations, fee: Reservations required; $20 group fee.
Who to contact: Phone Tahoe National Forest Headquarters at (916)265-4531.
Location: Drive 43 1/2 miles northeast of Foresthill via Mosquito Ridge and French Meadows Roads.
Trip note: Open from June through October. Elevation 5300 feet. Camp is set on the American River, where one can go swimming and fishing, and is a short distance from French Meadows Reservoir. See trip note for site #10.

Site **13**   LEWIS   ▲

Campsites, facilities: There are 40 campsites for tents or motorhomes to 22 feet long. Piped water, vault toilets, picnic tables and fireplaces are provided.
Reservations, fee: No reservations; $5 use fee.
Who to contact: Phone Tahoe National Forest Headquarters at (916)265-4531.
Location: Drive 44 1/2 miles northeast of Foresthill via Mosquito Ridge and French Meadows Roads.
Trip note: Open from May through October. Elevation 5300 feet. Camp is on the north shore of French Meadows Reservoir, where swimming and fishing can be had. A boat launch is nearby. A hiking trail leads from camp up to Star Ridge and beyond into Robinson Valley.

Site 14   BIG MEADOWS   ▲

Campsites, facilities: There are nine tent spaces and 46 campsites for tents or motorhomes to 22 feet long. Piped water, vault toilets, picnic tables and fireplaces are provided.

Reservations, fee: No reservation; $4 use fee.

Who to contact: Phone El Dorado National Forest Headquarters: (916)622-5061.

Location: Drive 48 miles east of Foresthill via Mosquito Ridge and French Meadows Roads.

Trip note: Open from May through November. Elevation 5300 feet. Camp sits on the ridge between French Meadows Reservoir and Hell Hole Reservoir. Good fishing available.

Site 15   HELL HOLE   ▲

Campsites, facilities: There are 10 campsites for tents or motorhomes. Piped water, vault toilets, picnic tables and fireplaces are provided.

Reservations, fee: No reservations; $3 use fee.

Who to contact: Phone El Dorado National Forest Headquarters at (916)622-5061.

Location: Drive 46 miles east of Foresthill via Mosquito Ridge and French Meadows Roads.

Trip note: Open from May through October. Elevation 5200 feet. Camp is set on Hell Hole Reservoir, where one can go swimming and fishing. A boat launch is nearby and a four-wheel drive trail leads out from camp. Several trails go out from the reservoir in several directions into the backcountry.

Site 16   MIDDLE MEADOWS GROUP CAMP   ▲

Campsites, facilities: There are two group campsites for tents or motorhomes. Piped water, vault toilets and picnic tables are provided.

Reservations, fee: Reservations required; $15 group fee.

Location: Drive 45.5 miles east of Foresthill via Mosquito Ridge and French Meadows Roads.

Trip note: Open from June through September. Elevation 4700 feet. Fishing at Hell Hole Reservoir, about two miles away via gravel and dirt roads.

Site 17   LAKE FOREST CAMPGROUND   ▲

Campsites, facilities: There are 20 campsites for tents or motorhomes up to 22

feet long. Piped water, showers, flush toilets, picnic tables and fireplaces are provided. A grocery store, laundromat and propane gas are available nearby.

Reservations, fee: No reservations; $5 use fee.
Who to contact: Phone (916)583-5544.
Location: Drive two miles northeast of Tahoe City off Highway 28.
Trip note: Open from May through October. Elevation 6200 feet. Camp is on Lake Tahoe. A boat launch is nearby. Swimming and fishing available.

Site **18**   TAHOE STATE
                     RECREATION AREA   ▲

Campsites, facilities: There are 15 tent spaces and 22 campsites for motorhomes to 21 feet long. Piped water, showers, flush toilets, picnic tables, fireplaces and a playground are provided. A grocery store, laundromat and propane gas are available nearby.
Reservations, fee: Make reservations through MISTIX: (800)446-7275 ($3.75 fee). $6 camp use fee; $1 for pets.
Who to contact: Phone (916)583-3074.
Location: Drive 1/4 mile northeast of Tahoe City on Highway 28.
Trip note: Open from June through October. Elevation 6200 feet. Boating, swimming, horseback riding and fishing on Lake Tahoe.

Site **19**   WILLIAM
                          KENT   ▲

Campsites, facilities: There are 55 tent spaces and 40 campsites for motorhomes to 24 feet long. Piped water, flush toilets, a sanitary dump station, picnic tables and fireplaces are provided. A grocery store, laundromat and propane gas are available nearby.
Reservations, fee: No reservations; $7 use fee.
Who to contact: Phone (916)583-3642.
Location: Drive six miles south of Tahoe City on Highway 89.
Trip note: Open from June through September. Elevation 6300 feet. Camp is close to shore of Lake Tahoe, which offers swimming and fishing.

Site **20**   KASPIAN

Campsites, facilities: There are 10 tent spaces. Piped water, flush toilets, picnic tables and fireplaces are provided. A grocery store, laundromat and propane gas are available nearby.
Reservations, fee: No reservations; $3 use fee.
Who to contact: Phone (916)573-2600.
Location: Drive eight miles south of Tahoe City on Highway 89.

Trip note: Open from May through September. Elevation 6300 feet. Camp is on Lake Tahoe, which offers swimming and fishing.

Site **21**   BEAR RIVER
                           COUNTY PARK

Campsites, facilities: There are 30 tent spaces and 20 campsites for tents or motorhomes. Piped water, pit toilets, a playground, picnic tables and fireplaces are provided. A grocery store, laundromat and propane gas are available nearby.

Reservations, fee: No reservations; $4 use fee.

Who to contact: (916)823-4721.

Location: From I-80, drive three miles southwest of Colfax via Tokayana Way and Milk Ranch Road.

Trip note: Open all year. Elevation 1800 feet. Campground is little-known except to local residents.

Site **22**   AUBURN
                           KOA

Campsites, facilities: There are 23 tent or motorhome sites, and 25 motorhome only spaces with full or partial hookups. Rest rooms, a playground and a sanitary dump station are provided. A grocery store, laundromat and propane gas are available nearby.

Reservations, fee: Reservation with deposit of $12; $12 use fee.

Who to contact: Phone (916)885-0990.

Location: This campground is located 3.5 miles north of Auburn. Off Highway 49, take Rock Creek Road, then turn on KOA Way. Address is 3550 KOA Way.

Trip note: Open all year. Elevation 1250 feet. Swimming in pool at campground. Fish in the streams in the nearby Motherlode Country, or visit some of the historic sights from the gold rush days.

Site **23**   LOOMIS
                           KOA

Campsites, facilities: There are 25 tent spaces and 42 motorhome sites with full or partial hookups. Rest rooms, showers, a dump station and a playground are provided. A grocery store, laundromat and propane gas are available nearby.

Reservations, fee: Reservation with deposit of $13; $13 use fee.

Who to contact: (916)652-6737.

Location: In Loomis on Taylor Road.

Trip note: Open all year. Elevation 400 feet. In Sierra foothills, which are hot in summer.

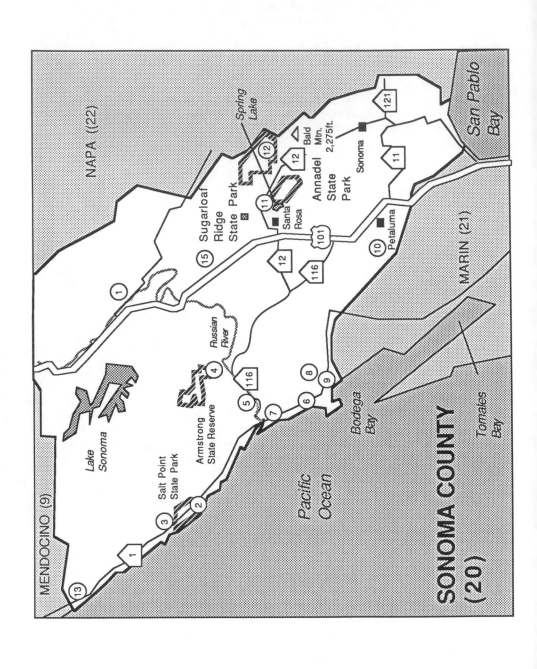

SONOMA COUNTY
(20)

SONOMA COUNTY

♦

Site **1** | CLOVERDALE
KOA |

Campsites, facilities: There are 60 tent sites and 95 motorhome spaces with full hookups. Flush toilets, showers, playground, dump station, laundry, recreation room, propane gas and groceries are available.

Reservations, fee: Call for space available. $13 deposit required; $13 fee per night.

Who to contact: Phone park at (707)894-3337.

Location: Drive six miles southeast of Cloverdale off US-101 to 26460 River Road.

Trip note: This campground is just above the Russian River in the Alexander Valley wine country. Enjoy swimming and fishing in the Russian River, or wine tasting in one of the nearby wineries.

Site **2** | STILLWATER COVE
REGIONAL PARK |

Campsites, facilities: There are four tent sites and 19 campsites for tents or motorhomes. Picnic tables, fireplaces and piped water are provided, and flush toilets, showers, dump station are available.

Reservations, fee: No reservations; $8 fee per night.

Who to contact: Phone park at (707)847-3245.

Location: Drive 16 miles north of Jenner on State Route 1.

Trip note: This campground is open all year and is on the picturesque Northern California coast.

Site **3** | SALT POINT
STATE PARK |

Campsites, facilities: There are 40 tent sites, 30 motorhome spaces and 108 campsites for tents or motorhomes. Picnic tables, fireplaces and piped water are provided. Flush toilets, showers, dump station, propane gas, groceries and horseback riding facilities are available. Picnic and some hiking trails are wheelchair accessible.

Reservations, fee: Phone MISTIX at (800)446-7275; $10 fee per night.
Who to contact: Phone park at (707)847-3221.
Location: Drive 20 miles north of Jenner on State Route 1.
Trip note: Set along the ocean, offering good abalone diving, beachcombing and sunsets.

Site **4**   AUSTIN CREEK
                STATE RECREATION AREA

Campsites, facilities: There are 24 campsites for tents or motorhomes. Picnic tables, fireplaces and piped water are provided, and flush toilets and horseback riding facilities are available.
Reservations, fee: No reservations; $10 fee per night.
Who to contact: Phone park at (707)869-2015.
Location: Drive three miles north of Guerneville on Armstrong Woods Road.
Trip note: This campground is open all year and is near the Russian River, where you can fish and swim. Nearby Armstrong Redwoods State Park provides picnic areas and hiking trails.

Site **5**   CASINI RANCH
                FAMILY CAMPGROUND

Campsites, facilities: There are 225 campsites for tents and motorhomes, some with full hookups. Flush toilets, showers, playground, dump station, laundry, cable TV, game arcade, boat and canoe rentals, propane gas and groceries are available. Horseback riding facilities are nearby.
Reservations, fee: Call for space available. $10 deposit required; $10 fee per night.
Who to contact: Phone (707)865-2255.
Location: Drive 1/2 mile east on Moscow Road off State Route 116 at Duncan Mills.
Trip note: This campground offers campsites in the sun or shade along the shores of the Russian River. Visit the redwood forests in nearby Armstrong Redwoods State Park, or drive out to the coast along the Russian River.

Site **6**   BODEGA
                DUNES

Campsites, facilities: There are 98 campsites for tents or motorhomes. Picnic tables, fireplaces and piped water are provided. Flush toilets, showers and horseback riding facilities are available. A grocery store, laundromat and propane gas are nearby.
Reservations, fee: Phone MISTIX at (800)446-7275; $10 fee per night.
Who to contact: Phone Sonoma Coast State Beach at (707)875-3483.
Location: Drive 1/2 mile north of Bodega Bay on State Route 1.

Trip note: This campground is at the south end of a beach that stretches north for several miles. Beyond that the coast becomes steep and rugged. Nearby Bodega Bay offers full marina and fishing facilities in season. Keep in mind that it is often cold and foggy along this part of the California coast in the summer, but it is nice during the fall and spring.

Site 7   WRIGHTS
BEACH

Campsites, facilities: There are 30 campsites for tents or motorhomes. Picnic tables, fireplaces and piped water are provided, and flush toilets are available. A grocery store, laundromat and propane gas are nearby.
Reservations, fee: Phone MISTIX at (800)446-7275; $10 fee per night.
Who to contact: Phone Sonoma Coast State Beach at (707)875-3483.
Location: Drive six miles north of Bodega Bay on State Route 1.
Trip note: This campground is at the north end of a beach that stretches south for several miles. The coast north of this campground becomes steep and rugged. Keep in mind that it is often cold and foggy along this part of the California coast in the summer, but it is nice during the fall and spring.

Site 8   WESTSHORE
REGIONAL PARK

Campsites, facilities: There are 47 campsites for tents or motorhomes. Piped water is provided, and flush toilets, showers and a boat ramp are available. A grocery store and propane gas are nearby.
Reservations, fee: No reservations; $8 fee per night.
Who to contact: Phone County Parks Department at (707)875-3540.
Location: Drive two miles west of Bodega Bay off State Route 1 via Bay Flat Road.
Trip note: This campground is on the west shore of Bodega Bay, which offers complete fishing and marina facilities. One of the better boat launches on the coast is near here, providing access to prime fishing waters. Salmon fishing excellent from mid-June through August.

Site 9   DORAN
REGIONAL PARK

Campsites, facilities: There are 10 tent sites and 128 campsites for tents or motorhomes. Picnic tables, fireplaces and piped water are provided. Flush toilets, showers, and a boat ramp are available. A grocery store and propane gas are nearby.
Reservations, fee: No reservations; $8 fee per night.
Who to contact: Phone County Parks Department at (707)875-3540.
Location: Drive one mile south of Bodega Bay to Doran Beach Road.
Trip note: This campground is open all year and is set along Doran Beach on

Bodega Bay, which offers complete fishing and marina facilities.

Site **10**   SAN FRANCISCO
                  NORTH/PETALUMA KOA

Campsites, facilities: There are 18 tent sites, 88 campsites for tents or motor-
homes, and 176 motorhome spaces with full hookups. Flush toilets, showers, dump station, playground, recreation rooms, swimming pool, spa, shuffleboard, laundry, propane gas and groceries are available.
Reservations, fee: Call for space available. $19.50 deposit required; $19.50 fee per
night.
Who to contact: Phone park at (707)763-1492..
Location: In Petaluma, take the Penngrove exit off US-101 and drive to 20
Rainsville Road.
Trip note: This campground is open all year and is in a rural farm setting. Near-
by are wineries, the redwoods and the Russian River.

Site **11**   SPRING LAKE
                  REGIONAL PARK

Campsites, facilities: There are three tent sites and 28 campsites for tents or mo-
torhomes. Picnic tables, fireplaces and piped water are provided. Flush toi-
lets, showers, a dump station, boat ramp (no motorboats), boat rentals, and
bike paths are available. A grocery store, laundromat and propane gas are
nearby.
Reservations, fee: No reservations; $6 fee per night.
Who to contact: Phone park at (707)539-8082.
Location: In Santa Rosa, drive three and a half miles northeast of US-101 on
Montgomery Drive, adjacent to Howarth Park and Annadel State Park.
Trip note: This campground is open all year. Spring Lake is stocked with trout.

Site **12**   SUGARLOAF RIDGE
                  STATE PARK

Campsites, facilities: There are 50 campsites for tents or motorhomes. Picnic tables, fireplaces and piped water are provided, and flush toilets and horseback riding facilities are available. Groceries are nearby.
Reservations, fee: Phone MISTIX at (800)446-7275; $10 fee per night.
Who to contact: Phone park at (707)833-5712.
Location: Drive seven miles east of Santa Rosa on Highway 12, then north three
miles on Adobe Canyon Road.
Trip note: This campground is open all year. Good hiking trails detailed on park
brochure.

Site 13   GUALALA POINT REGIONAL PARK

Campsites, facilities: There are seven tent sites and 19 campsites for tents or motorhomes. Picnic tables, fireplaces and piped water are provided. Flush toilets, dump station, propane gas, groceries and a laudromat are available.
Reservations, fee: No reservations; $8 fee per night.
Who to contact: Phone park at (707)785-2377.
Location: Drive one mile south of Gualala off State Route 1.
Trip note: This campground is open all year and is in the coastal redwoods near the ocean. Gualala River gets steelhead run in winter.

Site 14   WINDSOR LAND CAMPGROUND

Campsites, facilities: There are 10 tent sites and 56 motorhome spaces with full hookups. Flush toilets, showers, swimming pool, dump station, laundry, propane gas and groceries are available.
Reservations, fee: Call ahead for space available and fee.
Who to contact: Phone park at (707)838-4882.
Location: Drive nine miles north of Santa Rosa on US-101 to Windsor, then drive to 9290 Old Redwood Highway.
Trip note: This campground is open all year. Russian River and Lake Sonoma nearby.

Site 15   MIRABEL TRAILER PARK AND CAMPGROUND

Campsites, facilities: There are 100 tent sites and 60 motorhome spaces with full hookups. Flush toilets, showers, outdoor sports area, swimming pool, laundry, propane gas and groceries are available.
Reservations, fee: Reservations suggested; $6 per night for tent sites, $7 per night for motorhome spaces.
Who to contact: Phone park at (707)887-2383.
Location: Drive eight miles north of Sebastopol on State Route 116 to Forestville and 7600 River Road.
Trip note: This campground is open from April through October, and is near the Russian River and Armstrong Redwoods State Park.

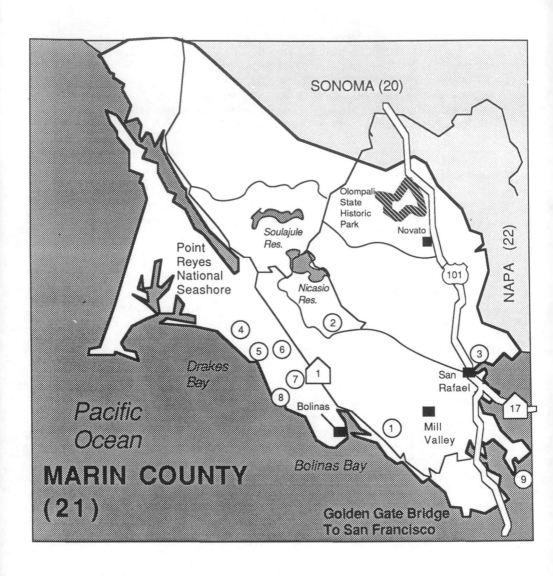

SONOMA (20)

NAPA (22)

Olompali State Historic Park

Novato

101

Soulajule Res.

Nicasio Res.

Point Reyes National Seashore

④

⑤ ⑥

② ③

San Rafael

17

Drakes Bay

⑦ 1

⑧

Bolinas

Mill Valley

①

9

Pacific Ocean

Bolinas Bay

MARIN COUNTY (21)

Golden Gate Bridge
To San Francisco

MARIN COUNTY

♦

Site 1 | MOUNT
TAMALPAIS | ⊿

Campsites, facilities: There are 16 sites for tents with piped water, toilets, fireplaces and tables provided.

Reservations, fee: Reservations can be made through MISTIX by phoning (800)446-7275; $6 fee per night.

Who to contact: Phone (415)388-2070.

Location: From Highway 101, take the Highway 1 turnoff. Make a left at the first light which will take you up Highway 1 toward the ocean. At the top of the ridge, take the Panoramic Highway turnoff to the right and continue into park.

Trip note: Good hiking with some of the best lookouts in the Bay Area. Impressive views of the bay to the east and of the ocean to the west. A magnificent mountain, with roads leading to prime vantage points.

Site 2 | SAMUEL P. TAYLOR | ⊿

Campsites, facilities: There are 20 tent sites and 45 sites for tents or motorhomes. Piped water, fireplaces and tables provided, and toilets, showers, groceries and laundromat available.

Reservations, fee: Reservation made through Mistix by phoning (800)446-7275; $6 per night fee.

Who to contact: Phone at (415)488-9897.

Location: From Highway 1, take Sir Francis Drake Blvd., then two miles northwest on Lagunitas Road.

Trip note: A well-positioned park, near famous places such as Point Reyes, Muir Woods and Mount Tamalpais. Good hiking. Open year around but quiet from September through April.

Site 3 | MARIN
RV PARK | 🚐

Campsites, facilities: There are 165 spaces for motorhomes with full hookups.

Showers, sanitary disposal station, laundromat and groceries are available.

Reservations,fee: Phone for reservations, deposit required; $22 fee per night.

Who to contact: Phone at (415)461-5199.

Location: Set near San Pablo Bay off Highway 101, two miles southeast of San Rafael at 2130 Redwood Highway.

Trip note: Good base camp for Marin County adventures, hiking, exploring Marin headlands or bay fishing trip out of Loch Lomond Marina (415-456-0321).

Site 4   SKY
                              CAMP

Campsites, facilities: There are 12 sites available in primitive walk-in setting with water. No vehicles permitted.

Reservations, fee: Reservations advised for all weekends; $6 fee per day, three-day maximum stay.

Who to contact: Call the Golden Gate National Recreation Area at (415)331-1541.

Location: Part of the Point Reyes National Seashore, Sky Camp is located on the western side of Mount Wittenberg, 2.5 miles from Bear Valley Trailhead.

Trip note: Bring backpacking gear, lightweight stove. No open fires or pets permitted. Secluded on weekdays. For free maps, write Superintendent, Point Reyes National Seashore, Point Reyes, CA 94956.

Site 5   COAST
                              CAMP

Campsites, facilities: There are 14 primitive hike-in sites. No cars permitted.

Reservations, fee: With eight-mile hike required, reservations necessary only on weekends.

Who to contact: Call park headquarters at (415)663-1092 or (415)331-1541.

Location: Set at grassy bluff 650 feet above ocean, an eight-mile hike from Bear Valley Trailhead on the Point Reyes National Seashore.

Trip note: No trees and few people. Can be windy and foggy in summer, but warm in fall and spring. Classic ocean bluff setting.

Site 6   WILDCAT
                              CAMP

Campsites, facilities: There are 12 primitive, hike-in sites. No cars permitted.

Reservations, fee: Reservations only necessary on weekends.

Who to contact: Phone (415)331-1541.

Location: Hike in six miles from Bear Valley trailhead on the Point Reyes National Seashore.

Trip note: This camp sits in a grassy meadow near a small stream that flows to the ocean. Minimum impact camping style necessary. No fires.

Site 7   GLEN
CAMP

Campsites, facilities: There are 12 primitive, hike-in sites in a primitive setting. Bring self-maintained backpacking equipment.
Reservations, fee: Reservations advised on weekends in summer.
Who to contact: Phone at (415)331-1541.
Location: Required is a five-mile hike from Bear Valley Trailhead in the Point Reyes National Seashore.
Trip note: Set in a small, wooded valley. Very quiet. Backpackers only.

Site 8   TOMALES
BAY

Campsites, facilities: A few campsites are available for bicyclists traveling along the coast. Piped water, tent sites provided.
Reservations, fee: No reservations; small fee charged.
Who to contact: Phone Tomales Bay State Park at (415)669-1140.
Location: Head four miles north of Inverness on Sir Francis Drake Blvd.
Trip note: Beautiful, secluded park on Tomales Bay with good hiking, picnicking, and during low tides, clamming.

Site 9   ANGEL
ISLAND

Campsites, facilities: Limited space at campground with piped water, toilets and tables provided. Food service available on island.
Reservations, fee: Reservations a must through MISTIX by phoning (800)446-7275; $6 fee per night.
Who to contact: Phone Angel Island State Park at (415) 435-1915.
Location: Angel Island is in northern San Francisco Bay, reached by ferry leaving from Pier 43 in San Francisco and Tiburon.
Trip note: One of the more unique campgrounds in California. A short walk to the top of Mount Livermore will provide a spectacular lookout of the Golden Gate Bridge to west, San Francisco skyline to south, and the bay and its ships in foreground.

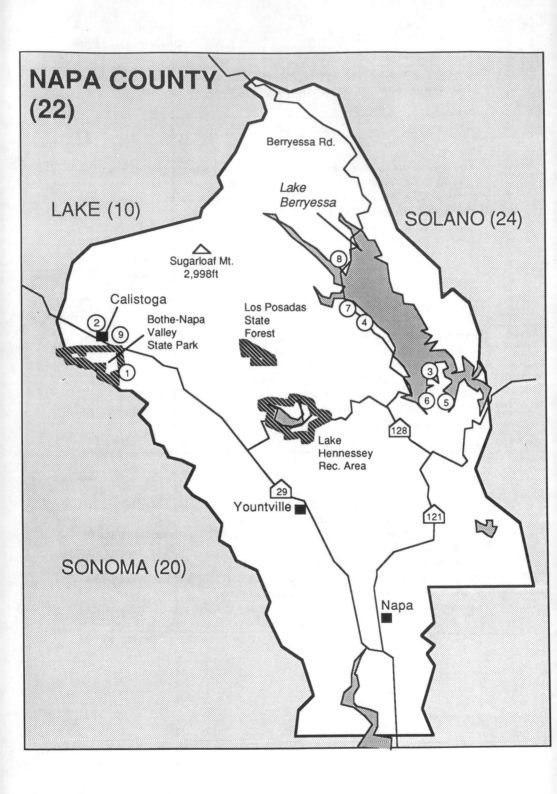

NAPA COUNTY (22)

LAKE (10)

SOLANO (24)

Berryessa Rd.

Lake Berryessa

△ Sugarloaf Mt. 2,998ft

Calistoga

Bothe-Napa Valley State Park

Los Posadas State Forest

② ⑨ ① ⑧ ⑦ ④ ③ ⑥ ⑤

Lake Hennessey Rec. Area

128

29 Yountville ■

121

SONOMA (20)

Napa ■

NAPA COUNTY
♦

Site **1** | BOTHE-NAPA VALLEY
STATE PARK |

Campsites, facilities: There are nine tent sites and 49 campsites for tents or motorhomes. Picnic tables, fireplaces and piped water are provided. Flush toilets, showers, dump station, a swimming pool (in the summer), and horseback riding facilities are available. A grocery store, laundromat and propane gas are nearby.

Reservations, fee: Phone MISTIX at (800)446-7275; $10 fee per night.

Who to contact: Phone park at (707)942-4575.

Location: Drive four miles south of Calistoga on State Route 29.

Trip note: Open year around. A hidden gem in the wine country. Some good trails in the park. There are several hot springs in the area.

Site **2** | NAPA COUNTY
FAIRGROUNDS |

Campsites, facilities: There are 49 campsites for tents or motorhomes. Piped water and electricity are provided, and a dump station is available. A nine-hole golf course is nearby.

Reservations, fee: No reservations; $7 fee per night.

Who to contact: Phone campground at (707)942-5111.

Location: Follow State Route 29 in Napa. Take Fairway and drive five blocks north of State Route 29 to 1435 Oak Street.

Trip note: At gateway to wine country.

Site **3** | SPANISH FLAT
RESORT |

Campsites, facilities: There are 123 campsites for tents or motorhomes. Picnic tables, fireplaces, piped water, and in some cases electric connections are provided. Flush toilets, boat launch, complete marina facilities, boat rentals and groceries are available. A laundromat, beauty parlor, restaurant and post office are nearby.

Reservations, fee: Phone Leisuretime Reservation Systems, Inc. at (800)822-CAMP for reservations and fee.

Who to contact: Phone park at (707)966-2101.

Location: Drive north on I-80 from Vallejo to Suisun Valley Road Overpass, then north to State Route 121. Drive 10 miles north to State Route 128 and five miles north to Berryessa-Knoxville Road, then to 4310 Knoxville Road.

Trip note: This campground is open all year and is on the shore of Lake Berryessa, the third largest man-made lake in Northern California. Here you can enjoy fishing and watersports. Trout fishing is good, whether trolling in the summer, or drifting with minnows in fall and winter.

Site **4** | LAKE BERRYESSA MARINA
RESORT |

Campsites, facilities: There are 80 tent sites and 123 motorhome spaces, some with full hookups. Flush toilets, showers, dump station, laundry, propane gas, snack bar, complete marina facilities and groceries are available.

Reservations, fee: Call ahead for space available and fee.

Who to contact: Phone park at (707)966-2161.

Location: Drive north on I-80 from Vallejo to Suisun Valley Road Overpass, then north to State Route 121. Drive 10 miles north to State Route 128, and five miles north to Berryessa-Knoxville Road. Campsite located at 5800 Knoxville Road.

Site **5** | SOUTH SHORE
RESORT MARINA |

Campsites, facilities: There are campsites for tents or motorhomes. Picnic tables, fireplaces, electricity and piped water are provided. Rest rooms, ice, restaurant, complete marina facilities, propane and groceries are available.

Reservations, fee: Reservations recommended; $10 fee per night.

Who to contact: Phone park at (707)966-2172.

Location: Drive north on I-80 from Vallejo to Suisun Valley Road Overpass, then north to State Route 121. Drive 10 miles north to State Route 128 and then head east to the south shore of the lake to 6100 Highway 128.

Trip note: See trip note for campsite No. 3.

Site **6** | STEELE
PARK |

Campsites, facilities: There are motorhome spaces with full hookups. Flush toilets, showers, playground, dump station, laundry, propane gas, complete marina facilities, waterskiing school and groceries are available.

Reservations, fee: Reservations recommended; $10 fee per night.

Who to contact: Phone park at (707)966-2123 or 255-2727.

Location: Drive 20 miles north of Napa via State Route 121 to south shore of lake and Steele Canyon Road.

Trip note: See trip note for campsite No. 3.

Site 7   RANCHO MONTICELLO
RESORT

Campsites, facilities: There are campsites for tents or motorhomes, some with
full hookups. Picnic tables, fireplaces and piped water are provided. Rest
rooms, snack bar, complete marina facilities, ice and groceries are available.

Reservations, fee: Reservations suggested; $13 fee for first night; $11 after that.

Who to contact: Phone campground at (707)966-2188.

Location: Drive north on I-80 from Vallejo to Suisun Valley Road Overpass,
then north to State Route 121. Drive 10 miles north to State Route 128,
and five miles north to Berryessa-Knoxville Road. Located at 6590 Knoxville Road.

Trip note: See trip note for campsite No. 3.

Site 8   PUTAH CREEK
PARK

Campsites, facilities: There are several motorhome spaces, some with full hookups. Rest rooms, laundry, complete marina facilities, snack bar, restaurant,
ice and groceries are available.

Reservations, fee: Reservations suggested; $10 fee per night.

Who to contact: Phone park at (707)966-2116.

Location: Drive north on I-80 from Vallejo to Suisun Valley Road Overpass,
then north to State Route 121. Drive 10 miles north to State Route 128,
and five miles north to Berryessa-Knoxville Road. Located at 7600 Knoxville Road.

Trip note: This campground is set on the northern end of Lake Berryessa. Good
bass fishing in the spring, trout trolling in the summer, and drifting minnows for trout in the winter. Water skiing popular throughout summer.

Site 9   CALISTOGA RANCH
CAMPGROUND

Campsites, facilities: There are 48 tent sites and 62 motorhome spaces with full
hookups. Flush toilets, showers, laundry, lake, swimming pool and a snack
bar are available.

Reservations, fee: Phone Leisuretime Reservation Systems, Inc. at (800)822-
CAMP for reservations and fee.

Who to contact: Phone park at (707)942-6565.

Location: Between Calistoga and St. Helena off State Route 29/128, take Lark-
mead Lane north to Silverado Trail, turn left and drive to Lommel Road,
turn right to 580 Lommel Road.

Trip note: This campground is in the heart of the wine country and near the
famous Calistoga spas and mud baths.

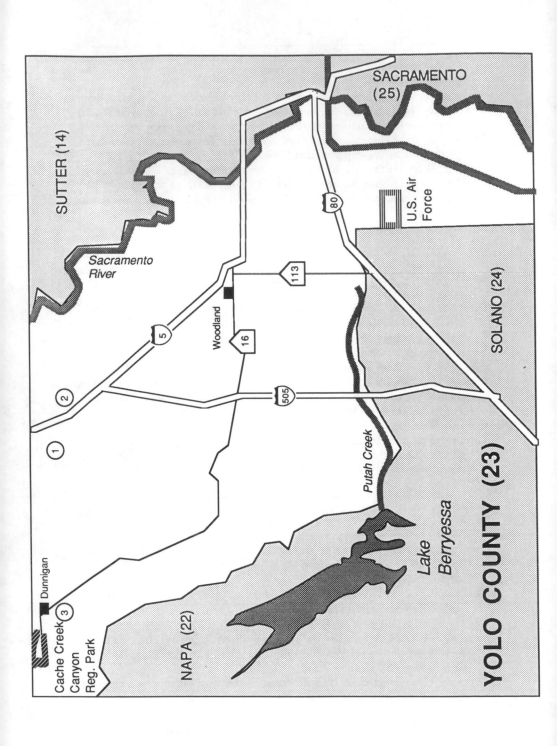

YOLO COUNTY (23)

SACRAMENTO (25)

SUTTER (14)

Sacramento River

U.S. Air Force

SOLANO (24)

Woodland

113

16

5

505

2

1

Putah Creek

Dunnigan

Cache Creek Canyon Reg. Park

NAPA (22)

Lake Berryessa

80

YOLO COUNTY

◆

Site **1**   CAMPERS
INN

Campsites, facilities: There are 13 tent sites and 59 motorhome spaces with full hookups. Flush toilets, showers, heated pool, playground, clubhouse, game room, horseshoes, dump station, laundry, propane gas, ice and groceries are available.

Reservations, fee: Phone Leisuretime Reservation Systems, Inc. at (800)822-CAMP. $13 deposit; $13 fee per night.

Who to contact: Phone park at (916)724-3350.

Location: Take the Dunnigan exit off I-5 near the 505 cut-off and drive west on County Road E-4 for one mile, then north on County Road 88 for one and a half miles.

Trip note: This campground is open all year and its rural atmosphere makes it a good layover spot before hitting the Bay Area. There is no lake close at hand, but the Sacramento River is to the east.

Site **2**   HAPPY TIME
RV PARK

Campsites, facilities: There are 30 motorhome spaces with full hookups and picnic tables. Flush toilets, showers, playground, dump station, laundry, swimming pool, restaurant and propane gas are available.

Reservations, fee: No reservations; $12 fee per night.

Who to contact: Phone park at (916)724-3336.

Location: Drive two miles southeast of Dunnigan via Road 8 and Road 99.

Trip note: This campground is open all year and is a good layover spot before hitting the Bay Area. The State Historical Park and the Railroad Museum are in Sacramento, one-half hour away. The Sacramento River is nearby.

Site **3**   CACHE CREEK CANYON
REGIONAL PARK

Campsites, facilities: There are 31 campsites for tents or motorhomes. Picnic tables, fireplaces and piped water are provided, and flush toilets and a dump station are available.

Reservations, fee: No reservations; $7 fee per night.

Who to contact: Phone the park at (916)666-8115.

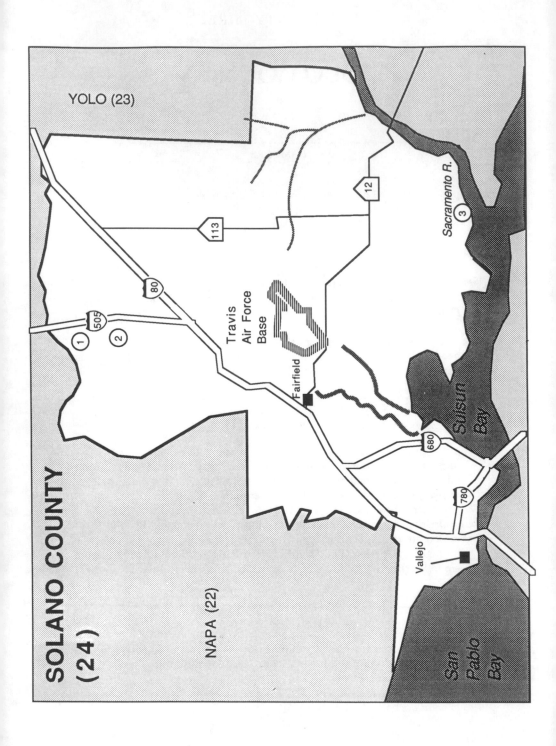

SOLANO COUNTY (24)

YOLO (23)

NAPA (22)

Travis Air Force Base

Fairfield

Vallejo

Sacramento R.

Suisun Bay

San Pablo Bay

80

113

12

3

505

680

780

1

2

SOLANO COUNTY

◆

Site 1	LAKE SOLANO	▲

Campsites, facilities: There are 50 sites for tents or motorhomes. Piped water, fireplaces and tables are provided. Sanitary disposal station, toilets, showers, groceries and laundromat available.
Reservations, fee: Call for campsite availability; $8 fee per night.
Who to contact: Call Lake Solano County Park at (707)447-0707.
Location: Set five miles southwest of Winter off State Route 128.
Trip note: Not far from Lake Berryessa. Open year around.

Site 2	GANDY DANCER	▲

Campsites, facilities: There are 20 tent sites and 70 motorhome sites with full hookups. Store, laundromat and dump station available.
Reservations,fee: Call for space available, fee charged.
Who to contact: Phone at (707)446-7679 or write at 4933 Midway Road, Vacaville, CA 95688.
Location: From the junction of Highway 80 and the Highway 505 cutoff, head three miles north on Highway 505, then east a quarter mile on Midway Road.
Trip note: Layover spot on edge of Bay Area.

Site 3	DELTA MARINA YACHT HARBOR	🚐

Campsites, facilities: There are 25 sites for motorhomes with full hookups. Store, laundromat and dump station are available.
Reservations, fee: Call for space availability; fee charged.
Who to contact: Phone at (707)374-2315 or write at 100 Marine de Rio Vista, CA 94571.
Location: Set on the shore of the Sacramento River at Rio Vista. From Highway 4, head south on Second Street to Marina Drive.
Trip note: Hot and breezy during summer months. Boat launch at harbor. Good striped bass fishing from November to March. All facilities available in town.

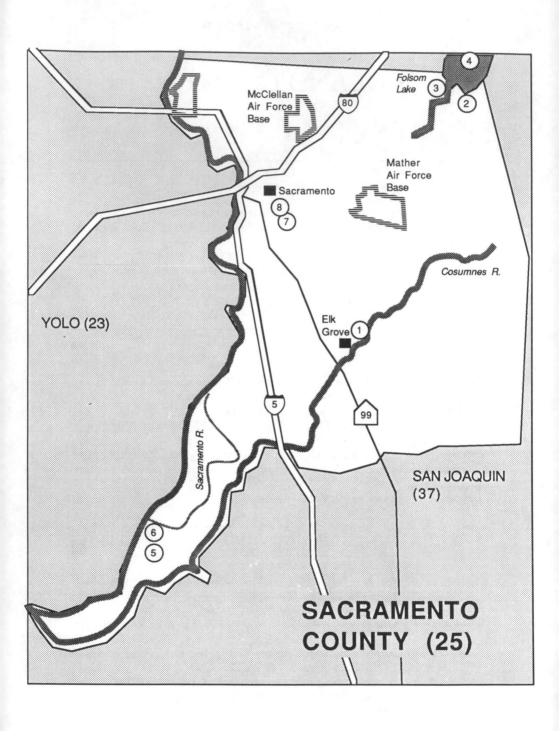

McClellan
Air Force
Base

Folsom
Lake

④
③
②

80

Mather
Air Force
Base

■ Sacramento

⑧
⑦

Cosumnes R.

YOLO (23)

Elk
Grove ①
■

5

99

Sacramento R.

SAN JOAQUIN
(37)

⑥
⑤

SACRAMENTO
COUNTY (25)

SACRAMENTO COUNTY

◆

	99	
Site **1**	TRAILER PARK	

Campsites, facilities: There are 23 motorhome spaces with full hookups, including phone. There are no separate rest room facilities. Weekly or monthly residents preferred. A grocery store, laundromat and propane gas are available nearby.

Reservations, fee: Call ahead for space available and fee.

Who to contact: Phone park at (916)423-4078.

Location: In Sacramento, take Sheldon Road exit off State Route 99 and go west to Stockton Boulevard (frontage road). Turn right and drive 1/10 of a mile to the park.

Trip note: This motorhome park is open all year and is near the Consumnes River. Most of the spaces are tree shaded.

	BEAL'S	
Site **2**	POINT	

Campsites, facilities: There are 49 campsites for tents or motorhomes. Picnic tables, fireplaces and piped water are provided. Flush toilets, showers, dump station, bike path and horseback riding facilities are available. Camping, picnicking and fishing areas are wheelchair accessible. There are boat rentals, moorings, a snack bar, ice, bait and tackle available at the Folsom Lake Marina.

Reservations, fee: Phone MISTIX at (800)446-7275; $10 fee per night.

Who to contact: Phone Folsom Lake State Recreation Area at (916)988-0205.

Location: Drive three miles north of Folsom via Folsom-Auburn Road.

Trip note: This campground is open all year and is on the shore of Folsom Lake where you can fish and enjoy watersports.

	NEGRO	
Site **3**	BAR	

Campsites, facilities: There are 20 campsites for tents or motorhomes. Picnic tables, fireplaces and piped water are provided. Flush toilets, shower, dump station and bike path are available. The camping, picnicking and fishing areas are wheelchair accessible. A grocery store and a laundromat are nearby. There are boat rentals, moorings, a snack bar, ice, bait and tackle available at the Folsom Lake Marina.

Reservations, fee: Phone MISTIX at (800)446-7275; $10 fee per night.
Who to contact: Phone Folsom Lake State Recreation Area at (916)988-0205.
Location: Drive 1/2 mile northwest of Folsom on Greenback Lane.
Trip note: This campground is open all year and is on the shore of Folsom Lake where you can fish and enjoy watersports. There is a group camp available here also with a $25 per night fee.

Site **4**   PENINSULA   ▲

Campsites, facilities: There are 100 campsites for tents or motorhomes. Picnic tables, fireplaces and piped water are provided. Flush toilets, showers and a bike path are available. The camping, picnicking and fishing areas are wheelchair accessible. There are boat rentals, moorings, a snack bar, ice, bait and tackle available at the Folsom Lake Marina.

Reservations, fee: Phone MISTIX at (800)446-7275; $10 fee per night.
Who to contact: Phone Folsom Lake State Recreation Area at (916)988-0205.
Location: Drive nine miles southwest of Pilot Hill off State Route 49 via Rattlesnake Bar Road.
Trip note: This campground is open all year and is on the shore of Folsom Lake where you can fish and enjoy watersports.

Site **5**   BRANNAN ISLAND
                    STATE RECREATION AREA   ▲

Campsites, facilities: There are 32 tent sites, 15 motorhome spaces and 102 campsites for tents or motorhomes. Picnic tables, fireplaces and piped water are provided. Flush toilets, showers, dump station, boat launch, moorings, visitor center and boats are available. A grocery store, laundromat and propane gas are nearby. The camping, picnicking, fishing, boating and visitor center are wheelchair accessible.

Reservations, fee: Phone MISTIX at (800)446-7275; $10 fee per night.
Who to contact: Phone park at (916)777-6671.
Location: Drive three and a half miles south of Rio Vista on State Route 160.
Trip note: This campground is open all year and is in the heart of the delta. Good striped bass fishing in fall and winter, good catfishing in summer.

Site **6**
EDDO'S
BOAT HARBOR

Campsites, facilities: There are 22 campsites for tents or motorhomes. Picnic tables, fireplaces and piped water are provided, and flush toilets, hot showers, launch ramp, boat storage, fuel dock, dump station, laundry and grocery store are available.

Reservations, fee: Call ahead for available space and fee.

Who to contact: Phone campground at (415)757-5314.

Location: Drive south of Rio Vista on State Route 160 to Sherman Island Levee Road, turn toward river. Camp is on river opposite light 21.

Trip note: This campground is open all year and is on the San Joaquin River. Striped bass move into immediate area during fall run.

Site **7**
SACRAMENTO-METRO
KOA

Campsites, facilities: There are 49 tent sites and 99 motorhome spaces with full hookups. Flush toilets, showers, playground, dump station, laundry, propane gas and groceries are available.

Reservations, fee: Phone Leisuretime Reservation Systems, Inc. at (800)822-CAMP. $17 deposit; $17 fee per night.

Who to contact: Phone park at (916)371-6771.

Location: In Sacramento on I-80, take the West Capitol Avenue exit and drive to 4851 Lake Road.

Trip note: This campground is open all year and is located in downtown Sacramento near the Capitol and the railroad museum.

Site **8**
STILLMAN
TRAILER PARK

Campsites, facilities: There are 50 motorhome spaces with full hookups. Flush toilets, showers and laundry are available.

Reservations, fee: Call for space available. $14 deposit required; $14 fee per night.

Who to contact: Phone park at (916)392-2820.

Location: In Sacramento, drive to 6321 Sacramento Boulevard.

Trip note: This campground is open all year and is located in downtown Sacramento near the Capitol and the railroad museum.

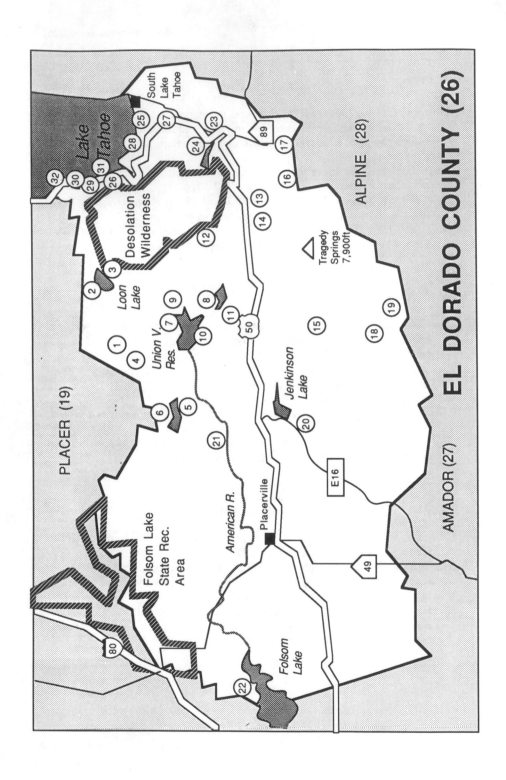

EL DORADO COUNTY (26)

EL DORADO COUNTY
◆

Site 1

GERLE
CREEK

▲

Campsites, facilities: There are 26 tent spaces and 24 campsites for tents or motorhomes to 22 feet long. Piped water, vault toilets, picnic tables and fireplaces are provided.
Reservations, fee: No reservations; $4 use fee.
Who to contact: Phone Eldorado National Forest Headquarters at (916)622-5061.
Location: From Highway 50, turn at Ice House Road and drive 31 1/2 miles northeast of Pacific House.
Trip note: Open from June through October. Elevation 5300 feet.

Site 2

WENTWORTH
SPRINGS

▲

Campsites, facilities: There are six tent spaces and two campsites for tents or motorhomes. Non-piped water, vault toilets, picnic tables and fireplaces are provided.
Reservations, fee: No reservations, no fee.
Who to contact: Phone Eldorado National Forest Headquarters at (916)622-5061.
Location: From Highway 50, drive 35 1/2 miles northeast of Pacific House via Ice House Road.
Trip note: Open from June through October. Elevation 6200 feet.

Site 3

LOON
LAKE

▲

Campsites, facilities: There are 11 tent spaces and 23 campsites for tents or motorhomes to 22 feet long. Piped water, vault toilets, picnic tables and fireplaces are provided. A boat ramp is nearby.
Reservations, fee: No reservations; $5 use fee.
Who to contact: Phone Eldorado National Forest Headquarters at (916)622-5061.
Location: From Highway 50, turn at Ice House Road and drive 33 miles northeast of Pacific House.

Site 4

SOUTH
FORK

🌲

Campsites, facilities: There are five tent spaces and 12 campsites for tents or motorhomes to 22 feet long. No piped water, but vault toilets, picnic tables and fireplaces are provided.

Reservations, fee: No reservations, no fee.

Who to contact: Phone Eldorado National Forest Headquarters at (916)622-5061.

Location: From Highway 50, turn at Ice House Road and drive 26 miles north-east of Pacific House.

Trip note: Open from June through October. Elevation 5200 feet. Camp is on the South Fork of the Rubicon River.

Site **5**   BLACK OAK
                     GROUP CAMP

Campsites, facilities: There are four group campsites for tents or motorhomes to 16 feet long. Piped water, vault toilets, picnic tables and fireplaces are provided. A boat ramp is nearby.

Reservations, fee: Reservation required; $18 group use fee.

Who to contact: For reservations call (916)333-4312.

Location: Drive 18 1/2 miles east of Georgetown via Georgetown-Wentworth Springs Road.

Trip note: Open from April through November. Elevation 4400 feet. Fishing, boating and hiking on and around Stumpy Meadows Lake.

Site **6**   STUMPY
                     MEADOWS

Campsites, facilities: There are seven tent spaces and 33 campsites for tents or motorhomes to 16 feet long. Piped water, vault toilets, picnic tables and fireplaces are provided. A boat ramp is nearby.

Reservations, fee: No reservations; $5 use fee.

Who to contact: Phone Eldorado National Forest Headquarters at (916)622-5061.

Location: Drive 21 miles east of Georgetown on Georgetown-Wentworth Springs Road.

Trip note: Open from April through November. Elevation 4400 feet. Hiking, fishing and boating on Stumpy Meadows Lake.

Site **7**   YELLOWJACKET   ▲

Campsites, facilities: There are five tent spaces and 35 campsites for tents or motorhomes to 22 feet long. Piped water, vault toilets, picnic tables and fireplaces are provided. A boat ramp is nearby.

Reservations, fee: No reservations; $5 use fee.

Who to contact: Phone Eldorado National Forest Headquarters at (916)622-5061.

Location: From Highway 50, drive 22 1/2 miles northeast of Pacific House via Ice House Road.

Trip note: Open from June through October. Elevation 4900 feet. Boating, swimming and fishing on Union Valley Reservoir.

Site **8**   ICE
                                     HOUSE   ▲

Campsites, facilities: There are 17 tent spaces and 66 campsites for tents or motorhomes to 22 feet long. Piped water, vault toilets, picnic tables and fireplaces are provided. A boat ramp and a sanitary dump station are nearby. Groceries and propane gas are available. There is wheelchair access to camping areas and pathways.

Reservations, fee: No reservations; $5 use fee.

Who to contact: Phone Eldorado National Forest Headquarters at (916)622-5061.

Location: From Highway 50, turn at Ice House Road and drive 20 miles northeast of Pacific House.

Trip note: Open from June though October. Elevation 5500 feet. Hiking, boating, swimming and fishing on Ice House Reservoir. Trout stocked early in summer.

Site **9**   WENCH
                                      CREEK   ▲

Campsites, facilities: There is one tent space and 99 campsites for tents or motorhomes to 22 feet long. There are also two group campsites. Piped water, flush toilets, vault toilets, picnic tables and fireplaces are provided. A boat ramp and a sanitary dump station are nearby.

Reservations, fee: No reservations; $5 use fee; $25 group camp fee.

Who to contact: Phone Eldorado National Forest Headquarters at (916)622-5061. For group camp reservations phone (916)644-2348.

Location: From Highway 50, drive 19 1/2 miles northeast of Pacific House via Ice House Road.

Trip note: Open from June through October. Elevation 4900 feet. Hiking, boating, swimming and fishing on Union Valley Reservoir.

Site **10**   SUNSET
                                                                       ▲

Campsites, facilities: There are 26 tent spaces and 24 campsites for tents or motorhomes to 22 feet long. Two of the campsites are big enough for two families each. A boat ramp, a sanitary dump station, piped water, vault toilets, picnic tables and fireplaces are provided. Groceries and propane gas are available nearby.

Reservations, fee: No reservations; $5 use fee.

Who to contact: Phone Eldorado National Forest Headquarters at (916)622-5061.

Location: From Highway 50, drive 18 miles northeast of Pacific House via Ice House Road.

Trip note: Open from June through October. Elevation 4900 feet. Boating, swimming and fishing on Union Valley Reservoir.

Site **11**   SILVER
                                     CREEK   🌲

Campsites, facilities: There are 11 tent spaces. No piped water, but vault toilets,
   picnic tables and fireplaces are provided. Groceries and propane gas are
   available nearby.
Reservations, fee: No reservations; no fee.
Who to contact: Phone Eldorado National Forest Headquarters at (916)622-5061.
Location: From Highway 50, drive 11 1/2 miles northeast of Pacific House via
   Ice House Road.
Trip note: Open from June through October. Elevation 5200 feet. Swimming
   and fishing in the creek or in nearby Ice House Reservoir.

Site **12**   WRIGHT'S
                                     LAKE   ▲

Campsites, facilities: There are 35 tent spaces and 36 campsites for tents or motorhomes to 22 feet long. Piped water, vault toilets, picnic tables and fire-
   places are provided.
Reservations, fee: Reservations through Ticketron and outlets in Sears stores;
   phone (213)216-6666 for outlet locations. $2.25 use fee; $5 camp use fee.
Who to contact: Phone Eldorado National Forest Headquarters at (916)622-5061.
Location: From Highway 50, drive 13 1/2 miles northeast of Kyburz.
Trip note: Open from June through October. Elevation 7000 feet. Hiking, fishing, swimming and boating on Wright's Lake, but no motorboats allowed.
   Trails lead out from camp in several directions. Two of the trails end up at
   various lakes in the Desolation Wilderness.

Site **13**   CHINA
                                     FLAT   ▲

Campsites, facilities: There is one tent space and 16 campsites for tents or motor-
   homes to 22 feet long. Piped water, vault toilets, picnic tables and fireplaces
   are provided. Groceries and propane gas are available nearby.
Reservations, fee: No reservations; $3 use fee.
Who to contact: Phone Eldorado National Forest Headquarters at (916)622-5061.
Location: Drive two miles southeast of Kyburz off Highway 50.
Trip note: Open from May through October. Elevation 4800 feet. Hiking, swim-
   ming and fishing on the Silver Fork of the American River.

Site **14**   SAND
                                     FLAT   ▲

Campsites, facilities: There are seven tent spaces and 22 campsites for tents or
   motorhomes to 22 feet long. Piped water, vault toilets, picnic tables and
   fireplaces are provided. Groceries and propane gas are available nearby.
Reservations, fee: No reservations; $5 use fee.
Who to contact: Phone Eldorado National Forest Headquarters at (916)622-5061.

Location: Drive one and a half miles southwest of Kyburz off Highway 50.
Trip note: Open all year. Elevation 3900 feet.

Site **15**   CAPPS
                          CROSSING   🌲

Campsites, facilities: There are six tent spaces. No piped water, but vault toilets,
   picnic tables and fireplaces are provided.
Reservations, fee: No reservations; no fee.
Who to contact: Phone Eldorado National Forest Headquarters at (916)622-5061.
Location: Drive 10 miles east of Grizzly Flat via Caldor Camp Road.
Trip note: Open from June through October. Elevation 5200 feet. Camp is on
   the North Fork of the Consumnes River.

Site **16**   SILVER
                            FORK   ⛺

Campsites, facilities: There are eight tent spaces and 27 campsites for tents or
   motorhomes to 22 feet long. Piped water, vault toilets, picnic tables and
   fireplaces are provided. Wheelchair access to camping areas, rest rooms and
   pathways.
Reservations, fee: No reservations; $5 use fee.
Who to contact: Phone Eldorado National Forest Headquarters at (916)622-5061.
Location: Drive eight miles southeast of Kyburz off Highway 50.
Trip note: Open from May through October. Elevation 5500 feet. Hiking, swimming and fishing on the American River.

Site **17**   KIRKWOOD
                            LAKE   ⛺

Campsites, facilities: There are 12 tent spaces here. Piped water, vault toilets,
   picnic tables and fireplaces are provided. A grocery store is nearby.
Reservations, fee: No reservations; $4 use fee.
Who to contact: Phone Eldorado National Forest Headquarters at (916)622-5061.
Location: Drive five and a half miles northeast of Kit Carson off Highway 88.
Trip note: Open from June through October. Elevation 7600 feet. Boating,
   swimming and fishing on Kirkwood Lake, but no motorboats allowed.

Site **18**   PI
                            PI   ⛺

Campsites, facilities: There are 27 tent spaces and 33 campsites for tents or mo-
   torhomes to 22 feet long. Piped water, vault toilets, picnic tables and fire-
   places are provided. Wheelchair access to camping areas, rest rooms and
   pathways.
Reservations, fee: No reservations; $4 use fee.
Who to contact: Phone Eldorado National Forest Headquarters at (916)622-5061.
Location: Drive 25 miles northeast of Pioneer off Highway 88.
Trip note: Open from May through November. Elevation 3900 feet.

Site 19   LUMBERYARD   ▲

Campsites, facilities: There are five campsites for tents or motorhomes to 16 feet long. Piped water, vault toilets, picnic tables and fireplaces are provided. A laundromat, groceries and propane gas are available nearby.
Reservations, fee: No reservations, no fee.
Who to contact: Phone Eldorado National Forest Headquarters at (916)622-5061.
Location: Drive 20 miles northeast of Pioneer off Highway 88.
Trip note: Open from June through October. Elevation 6500 feet. Camp is on a state game refuge. Nice remote spot.

Site 20   SLY PARK   ▲

Campsites, facilities: There are 182 campsites for tents or motorhomes to 30 feet long. Piped water, vault toilets, picnic tables and fireplaces are provided. Laundromat facilities, groceries and propane gas are available nearby.
Reservations, fee: No reservations; $6 use fee.
Who to contact: Phone (916)644-2545.
Location: From County Road 16, turn on Sly Park Road and drive five miles south of Pollock Pines.
Trip note: Open all year. Elevation 3500 feet. Horseback riding available.

Site 21   FINNON LAKE RESORT   ▲

Campsites, facilities: There are campsites for tents or motorhomes. Piped water, vault toilets, picnic tables and fireplaces are provided.
Reservations, fee: No reservations; $5 use fee.
Who to contact: Phone the county park at (916)622-9314.
Location: From Highway 193, turn on Rock Creek Road and drive 12 miles northeast of Placerville.
Trip note: Open all year. Elevation 2200 feet.

Site 22   PENINSULA CAMP   ▲

Campsites, facilities: There are 100 campsites for tents or motorhomes to 35 feet long. Piped water, showers, flush toilets, picnic tables and fireplaces are provided. Bicycle path, horse rentals and food service are available. Wheelchair access to camping.
Reservations, fee: Make reservations through MISTIX by phoning (800)446-7275 ($3.75 fee). $6 camp use fee; $1 for pets.
Who to contact: Phone Folsom Lake State Recreation Area at (916)988-0205.
Location: From Highway 49, drive nine miles southwest of Pilot Hill via Rattlesnake Bar Road.

Trip note: Open all year. Elevation 475 feet. Horseback riding trails and nature
trails.

Site **23**   KOA CAMPGROUND OF
SOUTH LAKE TAHOE   ▲

Campsites, facilities: There are 16 tent spaces and 52 campsites with full hookups
that will accommodate motorhomes to 30 feet long. Rest rooms and a sanitary dump station are on the premises. Laundry facilities, groceries and
propane gas are available nearby.
Reservations, fee: Reservation with $13.75 deposit; $13.75 use fee; $1.50 for pets.
Who to contact: Call (916)577-3693.
Location: Drive five miles southwest of South Lake Tahoe on Highway 50.
Trip note: Open from April through December. Elevation 6300 feet. Tahoe area
has it all, including gambling, fishing, hiking, bike rentals, and skiing.

Site **24**   TAHOE PINES CAMPGROUND
AND RV PARK   ▲

Campsites, facilities: There are 31 motorhomes spaces with full or partial hookups, and 80 campsites for tents or motorhomes to 35 feet long. Rest rooms,
a playground and a sanitary dump station are provided. Groceries and laundry facilities are available nearby.
Reservations, fee: Reserve through Leisuretime Reservation Systems, Inc. ($3.50
fee per ticket); $12.75 deposit; $12.75 camp use fee; $1.50 for pets.
Who to contact: Call (916)577-1653.
Location: From the junction of Highway 50 and Upper Truckee Road, drive five
miles south of South Lake Tahoe.
Trip note: Open from May through September. Elevation 6300 feet.

Site **25**   TAHOE VALLEY
CAMPGROUND   ▲

Campsites, facilities: There are 110 tent sites and 290 motorhome spaces with
full hookups. Rest rooms, a sanitary dump station, picnic tables, fireplaces,
laundry facilities, a heated pool, a playground, grocery store, propane gas,
ice, firewood and a recreation room are all provided on the premises.
Reservations, fee: Call ahead.
Who to contact: Phone (916)541-2222.
Location: Drive one quarter of a mile south of "Y" at the end of C Street in
South Lake Tahoe.
Trip note: Open all year. Enjoy all the recreational facilities near the campground, including snow skiing, a snow play area, five golf courses, horse-
back riding and the casinos.

Site **26**   FALLEN
LEAF   ▲

Campsites, facilities: There are 75 tent spaces and 131 campsites for tents or motorhomes to 35 feet long. Piped water, flush toilets, picnic tables and fireplaces are provided. Laundry facilities, groceries and propane gas are available nearby.

Reservations, fee: Reservations accepted through Ticketron, (213)216-6666; $10 use fee.

Who to contact: Phone California Land Management Headquarters at (916)544-0426.

Location: Drive one and a half miles southwest of Camp Richardson off Highway 89.

Trip note: Open from May through October. Elevation 6300 feet. Horseback riding.

| Site **27** | SOUTH LAKE TAHOE
EL DORADO CAMPGROUND | ▲ |

Campsites, facilities: There are 170 campsites for tents or motorhomes to 28 feet long. Piped water, flush toilets, showers, a sanitary dump station, a playground, picnic tables and fireplaces are provided. Laundry facilities, groceries and propane gas are available nearby.

Reservations, fee: Reservations accepted with deposit; $12 use fee; $1 for pets.

Who to contact: Call (916)573-2059.

Location: In South Lake Tahoe at the junction of Highway 50 and Rufus Allen Boulevard.

Trip note: Open from April through October. Elevation 6200 feet.

| Site **28** | CAMP RICHARDSON
RESORT | ▲ |

Campsites, facilities: There are 193 tent spaces and motorhome spaces, some with full hookups. Piped water, showers, flush toilets, a sanitary dump station, a playground, picnic tables and fireplaces are provided. Laundry facilities, groceries and propane gas are available nearby.

Reservations, fee: Reservations accepted with deposit; $10 use fee.

Who to contact: Phone (916)541-1801.

Location: Drive one half of a mile north of Camp Richardson off Highway 89.

Trip note: Open from June through October. Elevation 6300 feet. Horseback riding. Good trout fishing in area.

| Site **29** | CAMP
SHELLEY | ▲ |

Campsites, facilities: There are 28 campsites for tents or motorhomes to 22 feet long. No piped water, but flush toilets, showers, picnic tables and fireplaces are provided. Laundry facilities, groceries and propane gas are available nearby.

Reservations, fee: Reservations accepted; $7.50 use fee.

Who to contact: Call (415)447-7300.

Location: Drive one and a half miles west of Camp Richardson off Highway 89.

Trip note: Open from June through September. Elevation 6200 feet.

Site **30**   D.L. BLISS
STATE PARK

Campsites, facilities: There are 103 tent spaces, 33 motorhome spaces and 33
campsites for tents or motorhomes to 21 feet long. Piped water, showers,
flush toilets, picnic tables and fireplaces are provided.
Reservations, fee: Make reservations through MISTIX by phoning (800)446-7275
($3.75 fee). $10 camp use fee; $1 for pets.
Who to contact: Call (916)525-7277.
Location: Drive six miles south of Meeks Bay on Highway 89.
Trip note: Open from May through September. Elevation 6700 feet. Scenic hiking area.

Site **31**   EMERALD BAY
STATE PARK

Campsites, facilities: There are 40 tent spaces, 40 motorhome spaces and 20
campsites for tents or motorhomes to 24 feet long. Piped water, showers,
flush toilets, picnic tables and fireplaces are provided.
Reservations, fee: Make reservations through MISTIX by phoning (800)446-7275
($3.75 fee). $10 camp use fee; $1 for pets.
Who to contact: Call (916)541-3030.
Location: Drive eight miles north of South Lake Tahoe off Highway 89.
Trip note: Open from June through August. Elevation 6800 feet. Visit the exhibits and hike the trails. Beautiful spot set along Lake Tahoe.

Site **32**   SUGAR PINE POINT
STATE PARK

Campsites, facilities: There are 175 campsites for tents or motorhomes to 30 feet
long. Piped water, showers, flush toilets, a sanitary dump station, picnic tables and fireplaces are provided. A grocery store, laundromat and propane
gas are available nearby. Wheelchair access to picnic areas.
Reservations, fee: Make reservations by phoning MISTIX at (800)446-7275
($3.75 fee). $10 camp use fee; $1 for pets.
Who to contact: Call (916)525-6512.
Location: Drive one mile south of Tahoma on Highway 89.
Trip note: Open all year. Elevation 6200 feet. No showers when camping in the
winter. Visit the Pine Lodge, a grand Sierra home from the old days that
has been turned into an historical museum. It is open from noon to four
during the summer. Park is set on General Creek and Lake Tahoe, where
you can go swimming and fishing.

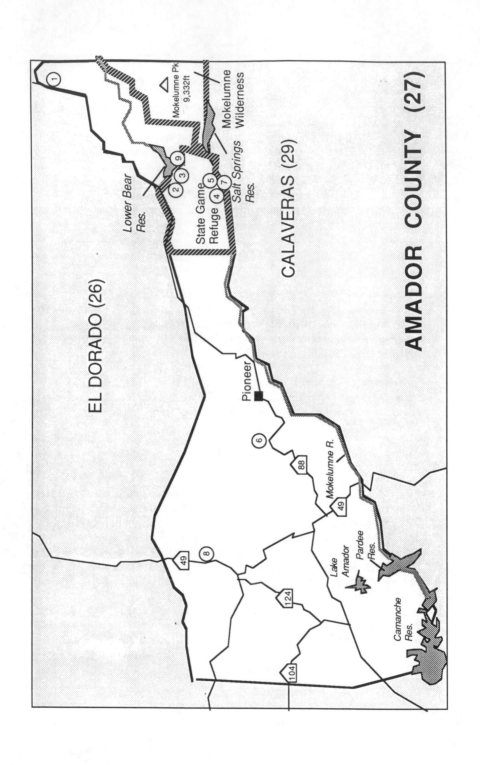

AMADOR COUNTY (27)

EL DORADO (26)

CALAVERAS (29)

Mokelumne Pk
9,332ft

Mokelumne
Wilderness

Salt Springs
Res.

Lower Bear
Res.

State Game
Refuge

Pioneer

Mokelumne R.

Lake
Amador

Pardee
Res.

Camanche
Res.

1

2

3

9

5

7

4

6

88

49

49

8

124

104

AMADOR COUNTY

♦

Site **1**   SILVER
                   LAKE   ◬

Campsites, facilities: There are 47 tent sites and 50 campsites for tents or motor-
  homes. Picnic tables, fireplaces and piped water are provided, and vault toi-
  lets and a boat ramp are available. A grocery store, laundromat, boat rentals
  and propane gas are nearby.
Reservations, fee: No reservations; $6 fee per night.
Who to contact: Phone Eldorado National Forest Headquarters at (916)622-5061.
Location: Drive 1/2 mile northeast of Kit Carson off State Route 88 at Silver
  Lake.
Trip note: Open from June to November. Elevation 7200 feet. Located on the
  shore of Silver Lake. Fishing is boosted by stocks of rainbow trout.

Site **2**   SOUTH
                   SHORE   ◬

Campsites, facilities: There are 13 tent sites and nine campsites for tents or mo-
  torhomes. Picnic tables, fireplaces and piped water are provided. Vault toilets and a boat ramp are available. A grocery store, boat rentals and propane
  gas are nearby.
Reservations, fee: No reservations; $6 fee per night.
Who to contact: Phone Eldorado National Forest Headquarters at (916)622-5061.
Location: Drive 26 miles northeast of Pioneer via State Route 88 and Bear River
  Road.
Trip note: Open from June to November. Elevation 5900 feet. Located along the
  shoreline of Lower Bear River Reservoir, where you can fish, swim, wa-
  terski and hike.

Site **3**   BEAR RIVER
                   GROUP CAMP   ◬

Campsites, facilities: There are three group campsites for tents or motorhomes.
  Picnic tables, fireplaces and piped water are provided, and vault toilets are
  available. A grocery store, boat ramp, boat rentals and propane gas are

nearby.

Reservations, fee: Reservations requested; $35 fee per night.

Who to contact: Phone Eldorado National Forest Headquarters at (916)622-5061.

Location: Drive 27 1/2 miles northeast of Pioneer via State Route 88 and Bear River Road.

Trip note: Open from June to November. Elevation 5900 feet. Located near Lower Bear River Reservoir, where you can fish, swim, waterski and hike.

Site **4**   MOKELUMNE   🌲

Campsites, facilities: There are eight tent sites. Picnic tables and fireplaces are provided, and vault toilets are available. There is no water, so bring your own.

Reservations, fee: No reservations, no fee.

Who to contact: Phone Eldorado National Forest Headquarters at (916)622-5061.

Location: Drive 29 miles northeast of Pioneer via State Route 88 and Ellis Road.

Trip note: Open from May to November. Elevation 3200 feet. Located on the North Fork of the Mokelumne River. It is a short drive to either Lower Bear River Reservoir or Salt Springs Reservoir.

Site **5**   WHITE
                             AZALEA   🌲

Campsites, facilities: There are six tent sites. Picnic tables and fireplaces are provided, and vault toilets are available. There is no water, so bring your own.

Reservations, fee: No reservations, no fee.

Who to contact: Phone Eldorado National Forest Headquarters at (916)622-5061.

Location: Drive 31 miles northeast of Pioneer via State Route 88 and Ellis Road.

Trip note: Open from May to November. Elevation 3500 feet. Located on the North Fork of the Mokelumne River. It is a short drive to either Lower Bear River Reservoir or Salt Springs Reservoir.

Site **6**   INDIAN GRINDING ROCK   ▲
                       STATE HISTORICAL PARK

Campsites, facilities: There are 21 campsites for tents or motorhomes. Picnic tables, fireplaces and piped water are provided, and flush toilets are available. A grocery store and propane gas can be found nearby.

Reservations, fee: Phone MISTIX at (800)446-7275; $6 fee per night.

Who to contact: Phone park at (209)296-7488.

Location: Drive 11 miles northeast of Jackson on State Route 88, then one and one half miles northeast on Pine Grove-Volcano Road.

Trip note: Open all year. Elevation 2500 feet. Located about three miles from

Sutter Creek. This park offers a reconstructed Miwok village with petroglyphs, bedrock mortars, cultural center and interpretive talks for groups by reservation.

Site **7** MOORE CREEK

Campsites, facilities: There are eight campsites for tents or motorhomes. Picnic tables and fireplaces are provided, and vault toilets are available. There is no water, so bring your own.
Reservations, fee: No reservations, no fee.
Who to contact: Phone Eldorado National Forest Headquarters at (916)622-5061.
Location: Drive 30 miles northeast of West Point via Lily Gap and Lookout Roads.
Trip note: Open from May to November. Elevation 3200 feet. Located on the North Fork of the Mokelumne River. It is a short drive to either Lower Bear River Reservoir or Salt Springs Reservoir.

Site **8** FAR HORIZONS 49ER TRAILER VILLAGE

Campsites, facilities: There are 329 motorhome spaces with full hookups. Flush toilets, showers, playground, recreation halls, jacuzzi, pool room, TV lounge, beauty shop, laundry, deli, propane gas and groceries are available.
Reservations, fee: Call ahead for space available and fee.
Who to contact: Phone park at (209)245-6981.
Location: Drive 1/2 mile south of Plymouth on State Route 49.
Trip note: Open all year. This motorhome park is 40 miles east of Stockton and Sacramento, in the heart of the gold country.

Site **9** BEAR RIVER LAKE RESORT

Campsites, facilities: There are 127 campsites for tents or motorhomes. Picnic tables, fireplaces and piped water are provided. Flush toilets, hot showers, dump station, boat ramp, boat rentals, firewood, ice, propane, laundry, post office, phone and grocery store are available.
Reservations, fee: Call ahead for available space and fee.
Who to contact: Phone park at (209)295-4868.
Location: Drive 29 miles northeast of Pioneer via State Route 88 and Bear River Road.
Trip note: Open all year. Elevation 6000 feet. Located on the shore of Bear River Reservoir where you can fish, waterski, swim, canoe and hike.

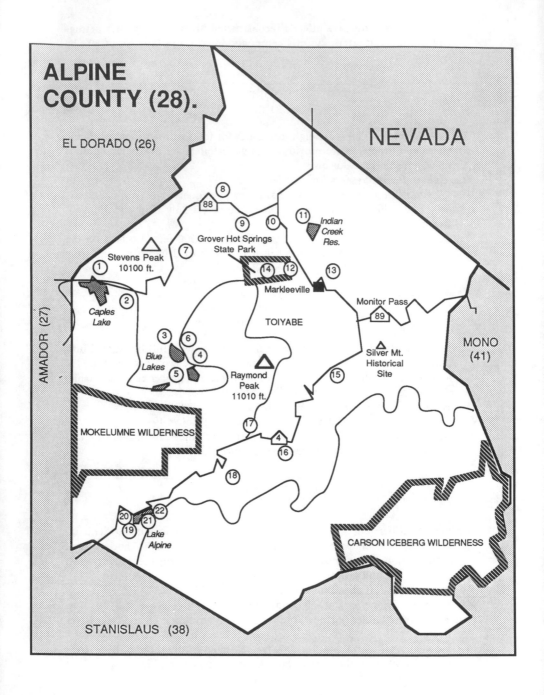

ALPINE
COUNTY (28).

EL DORADO (26)

NEVADA

⑧
[88]
⑨ ⑩
⑪ *Indian Creek Res.*
Grover Hot Springs State Park
⑦
Stevens Peak 10100 ft.
①
⑭ ⑫
⑬
Markleeville

Monitor Pass
[89]

②
Caples Lake

TOIYABE

Silver Mt. Historical Site

MONO (41)

AMADOR (27)

③ ⑥
Blue Lakes
④
⑤
Raymond Peak 11010 ft.

⑮

MOKELUMNE WILDERNESS

⑰
④
⑯

⑱

CARSON ICEBERG WILDERNESS

⑳ ㉒
⑲ ㉑
Lake Alpine

STANISLAUS (38)

MAP TWENTY-EIGHT

ALPINE COUNTY
♦

Site **1**   CAPLES
LAKE   ▲

Campsites, facilities: There are 20 campsites and 15 sites for tents or motorhomes to 22 feet long. Piped water, vault toilets, picnic tables and fireplaces are provided. Groceries, propane gas and a boat ramp are available nearby.
Reservations, fee: Reservations not required; $6 use fee.
Who to contact: Phone Eldorado National Forest at (916)622-5061.
Location: Drive six and a half miles northeast of Kit Carson on Highway 88.
Trip note: Open from June through October. Elevation 7800 feet. Good hiking trails detailed on Forest Service map.

Site **2**   WOODS
LAKE   ▲

Campsites, facilities: There are 14 campsites for tents and trailer space is available. Piped water, vault toilets, picnic tables and fireplaces are provided. Groceries and propane gas are available nearby.
Reservations, fee: Reservations not required; $4 use fee.
Who to contact: Phone Eldorado National Forest Headquarters at (916)622-5061.
Location: Drive 11 miles northeast of Kit Carson on Highway 88.
Trip note: Open from July through October. Elevation 8200 feet. Hiking trails detailed on Forest Service map.

Site **3**   UPPER BLUE LAKE
DAM   ▲

Campsites, facilities: There are 25 campsites for tents. Piped water, vault toilets, picnic tables and fireplaces are provided.
Reservations, fee: Reservations not required. Call PG&E about use fee.
Who to contact: Camp is managed by PG&E. For information call (415)972-5552.
Location: From Highway 88, drive six miles west of Carson Pass via Blue Lakes Road, or take Blue Lakes Road off Highway 88 and drive two and a half miles east of the junction of Highways 88 and 89.
Trip note: Open from June through September. Elevation 8200 feet. Good trout

fishing in May and June.

Site **4**   LOWER
                          BLUE LAKE   ▲

Campsites, facilities: There are 16 campsites for tents. Piped water, vault toilets,
    picnic tables and fireplaces are provided.
Reservations, fee: Reservations not required. Call PG&E about use fee.
Who to contact: Camp is managed by PG&E. For information call (415)972-
    5552.
Location: From Highway 88, drive six miles west of Carson Pass via Blue Lakes
    Road, or take Blue Lakes Road off Highway 88 and drive two and a half
    miles east of the junction of Highways 88 and 89.
Trip note: Open from June through September. Elevation 8100 feet. Good trout
    fishing in May and June.

Site **5**   MIDDLE
                            CREEK   ▲

Campsites, facilities: There are five campsites for tents. Piped water, vault toilets,
    picnic tables and fireplaces are provided.
Reservations, fee: Reservations not required. Call PG&E about use fee.
Who to contact: Camp is managed by PG&E. For information call (415)972-
    5552.
Location: From Highway 88, drive six miles west of Carson Pass via Blue Lakes
    Road, or take Blue Lakes Road off Highway 88 and drive two and a half
    miles east of the junction of Highways 88 and 89.
Trip note: Open from June through September. Elevation 8200 feet. Little-
    known spot with good lake and stream fishing for trout nearby.

Site **6**   UPPER
                          BLUE LAKE   ▲

Campsites, facilities: There are 32 campsites for tents. Piped water, vault toilets,
    picnic tables and fireplaces are provided.
Reservations, fee: Reservations not required. Call PG&E about use fee.
Who to contact: Camp is managed by PG&E. For information call (415)972-
    5552.
Location: From Highway 88, drive six miles west of Carson Pass via Blue Lakes
    Road, or take Blue Lakes Road off Highway 88 and drive two and a half
    miles east of the junction of Highways 88 and 89.
Trip note: Open from June through September. Elevation 8200 feet. Good trout
    fishing in early summer.

Site **7**
HOPE
VALLEY
▲

Campsites, facilities: There are 20 campsites for tents or motorhomes to 22 feet long. Piped water, vault toilets, picnic tables and fireplaces are provided. A grocery store is nearby.
Reservations, fee: Reservations not required; $4 use fee.
Who to contact: Phone Toiyabe National Forest Headquarters at (702)784-5331.
Location: Drive nine and a half miles southwest of Woodfords off Highway 88.
Trip note: Open from June through October. Elevation 7300 feet. Fishing in Red Lake Creek, Carson River. A beautiful valley.

Site **8**
KIT
CARSON
▲

Campsites, facilities: There are 12 campsites for tents or motorhomes to 22 feet long. Piped water, vault toilets, picnic tables and fireplaces are provided. A grocery store and a laundromat are nearby.
Reservations, fee: Reservations not required; $5 use fee.
Who to contact: Phone Toiyabe National Forest Headquarters at (702)784-5331.
Location: Drive five miles west of Woodfords on Highway 88.
Trip note: Open from June through October. Elevation 6900 feet. Camp is on the West Fork of the Carson River. Good trout fishing.

Site **9**
SNOWSHOE
SPRINGS
▲

Campsites, facilities: There are 13 campsites for tents or motorhomes to 16 feet long. Piped water, vault toilets, picnic tables and fireplaces are provided. A grocery store and a laundromat are nearby.
Reservations, fee: Reservations not required; $5 use fee.
Who to contact: Phone Toiyabe National Forest Headquarters at (702)784-5331.
Location: Drive four miles west of Woodfords on Highway 88.
Trip note: Open from June through October. Elevation 6600 feet. Fishing on the West Fork of the Carson River. Good trout fishing.

Site **10**
CRYSTAL
SPRINGS
▲

Campsites, facilities: There are 21 campsites for tents or motorhomes to 22 feet long. Piped water, vault toilets, picnic tables and fireplaces are provided. A grocery store and a laundromat are nearby.
Reservations, fee: Reservations not required; $5 use fee.
Who to contact: Phone Toiyabe National Forest Headquarters at (702)784-5331.
Location: Drive one and a half miles southwest of Woodfords on Highway 88.

Trip note: Open from May through October. Elevation 6000 feet. Fishing and camping on the West Fork of the Carson River.

Site **11**   INDIAN CREEK
                                  RESERVOIR

Campsites, facilities: There are 10 sites for tents and 19 campsites for tents or motorhomes to 24 feet long. Piped water, showers, flush toilets, a sanitary dump station, picnic tables and fireplaces are provided. Groceries and propane gas are available nearby.
Reservations, fee: Reservations not required; $6 use fee.
Who to contact: Camp is administered by the Bureau of Land Management. For information call (712)882-1631.
Location: Drive five miles north of Markleeville on Highway 89.
Trip note: Open from May through September. Elevation 6000 feet. Camping and fishing on Indian Creek Reservoir.

Site **12**   TURTLE ROCK
                                  PARK

Campsites, facilities: There are 25 campsites for tents or motorhomes to 30 feet long. Piped water, pit toilets, picnic tables and fireplaces are provided. Laundry facilities, groceries and propane gas are available nearby.
Reservations, fee: Reservations not required; $4 use fee.
Who to contact: Camp is administered by Alpine County Parks. For information call (916)694-2255.
Location: Drive three miles north of Markleeville on Highways 4 and 89.
Trip note: Open from May through September. Elevation 6000 feet. Trout fishing good on area streams, though fish not large.

Site **13**   MARKLEEVILLE

Campsites, facilities: There are 10 campsites for tents or motorhomes to 16 feet long. Piped water, vault toilets, picnic tables and fireplaces are provided. A laundromat and a grocery store are nearby.
Reservations, fee: Reservations not required; $5 use fee.
Who to contact: Phone Toiyabe National Forest Headquarters at (702)784-5331.
Location: Drive one mile northeast of Markleeville on Highway 89.
Trip note: Open from May through October. Elevation 5500 feet. Camping and fishing on the East Fork of the Carson River.

Site 14 — GROVER HOT SPRINGS STATE PARK ▲

Campsites, facilities: There are 26 tent sites, 13 sites for motorhomes, and 37 campsites for tents or motorhomes to 27 feet long. Piped water, flush toilets, showers, (except in the winter), hot springs pool with wheelchair access, picnic tables and fireplaces are provided. A grocery store and a laundromat are nearby.

Reservations, fee: Make reservations through MISTIX by calling (800)446-7275 ($3.75 fee). $10 camp use fee; $1 for pets.

Who to contact: Call (916)694-2248.

Location: Drive four miles west of Markleeville on Hot Springs Road.

Trip note: Open all year. Elevation 5800 feet. Hike the nature trail and enjoy the hot springs pools.

Site 15 — SILVER CREEK ▲

Campsites, facilities: There are 22 campsites for tents or motorhomes to 22 feet long. Piped water, vault toilets, picnic tables and fireplaces are provided.

Reservations, fee: Reservations not required; $5 use fee.

Who to contact: Phone Toiyabe National Forest Headquarter at (702)784-5331.

Location: Drive 12 miles south of Markleeville on Highway 4.

Trip note: Open from June through October. Elevation 6800 feet. Camping and fishing on Silver Creek.

Site 16 — BLOOMFIELD ▲

Campsites, facilities: There are 10 campsites for tents or motorhomes. No water, but vault toilets, picnic tables and fireplaces are provided. A grocery store, propane gas and a laundromat are available nearby.

Reservations, fee: No reservations, no fee.

Who to contact: Phone Stanislaus National Forest Headquarters at (209)532-3671.

Location: Drive 14 1/2 miles northeast of Lake Alpine off Highway 4.

Trip note: Open from June through September. Elevation 8000 feet. Stanislaus National Forest map details many good nearby hiking trails. Fishing can be very good for trout on Lake Alpine.

Site 17 — HERMIT VALLEY 🏕

Campsites, facilities: There are five campsites for tents or motorhomes to 16 feet long. No water, but vault toilets, picnic tables and fireplaces are provided.

Reservations, fee: No reservations, no fee.
Who to contact: Phone Stanislaus National Forest Headquarters at (209)532-3671.
Location: Drive 10 1/2 miles northeast of Lake Alpine off Highway 4.
Trip note: Open from June through September. Elevation 7500 feet. Camp is on the border of the Mokelumne Wilderness near Grouse Creek. Remote, little-known spot.

Site **18**   PACIFIC
                                      VALLEY   ▣

Campsites, facilities: There are six campsites for tents or motorhomes to 16 feet long. No water, but vault toilets, picnic tables and fireplaces are provided.
Reservations, fee: No reservations, no fee.
Who to contact: Phone Stanislaus National Forest Headquarters at (209)532-3671.
Location: Drive eight miles northeast of Lake Alpine off Highway 4.
Trip note: Open from July through September. Elevation 7600 feet. Fishing and camping on Pacific Creek.

Site **19**   LAKE
                                      ALPINE   ▲

Campsites, facilities: There are 27 campsites for tents or motorhomes to 22 feet long. Piped water, flush toilets, picnic tables, fireplaces and a boat launch are provided. A grocery store, propane gas and a laundromat are nearby.
Reservations, fee: No reservations; $6 use fee.
Who to contact: Phone Stanislaus National Forest Headquarters at (209)532-3671.
Location: At Lake Alpine off Highway 4.
Trip note: Open from June through September. Elevation 7400 feet. Boating, swimming and fishing on Lake Alpine. There are several short hikes that you can take from Lake Alpine: a one mile easy hike on a marked trail to Duck Lake, or a moderately difficult one and a half mile hike on an unmarked trail that starts at the south end of the lake and goes to Inspiration Point. Lake Alpine and the three campgrounds that follow (all of which are on or near Lake Alpine) are at a trailhead into Emigrant Wilderness.

Site **20**   SILVER
                                      TIP   ▲

Campsites, facilities: There are 23 campsites for tents or motorhomes to 22 feet long. Piped water, flush toilets, picnic tables and fireplaces are provided. The Lake Alpine boat launch is about a mile away. A grocery store, propane gas and a laundromat are nearby.

Reservations, fee: No reservations; $6 use fee.

Who to contact: Phone Stanislaus National Forest Headquarters at (209)532-3671.

Location: Drive one mile northwest of Lake Alpine off Highway 4.

Trip note: Open from June through September. Elevation 7500 feet. Hiking, boating, swimming and fishing in and around Lake Alpine. See trip note for camp No. 19.

Site **21** SILVER VALLEY

Campsites, facilities: There are 25 campsites for tents or motorhomes to 22 feet long. Piped water, flush toilets, picnic tables and fireplaces are provided. A boat launch is nearby on Lake Alpine. A grocery store, propane gas and a laundromat are nearby.

Reservations, fee: No reservations; $6 use fee.

Who to contact: Phone Stanislaus National Forest Headquarters at (209)532-3671.

Location: Drive one and a half miles northeast of Lake Alpine off Highway 4.

Trip note: Open from June through September. Elevation 7500 feet. This camp is at Lake Alpine. See trip note for camp No. 19.

Site **22** PINE MARTEN

Campsites, facilities: There are 33 campsites for tents or motorhomes up to 22 feet long. Piped water, flush toilets, picnic tables and fireplaces are provided. This camp is on Lake Alpine and the boat ramp is nearby.

Reservations, fee: No reservations; $6 use fee.

Who to contact: Phone Stanislaus National Forest Headquarters at (209)532-3671.

Location: Drive one and a half miles northeast of Lake Alpine off Highway 4.

Trip note: Evening trout rise can be worth seeing at Lake Alpine. A nice Sierra lake setting. Camp open June to September. Elevation 7400 feet. Numerous trails in adjacent back country. See trip note for camp No. 19.

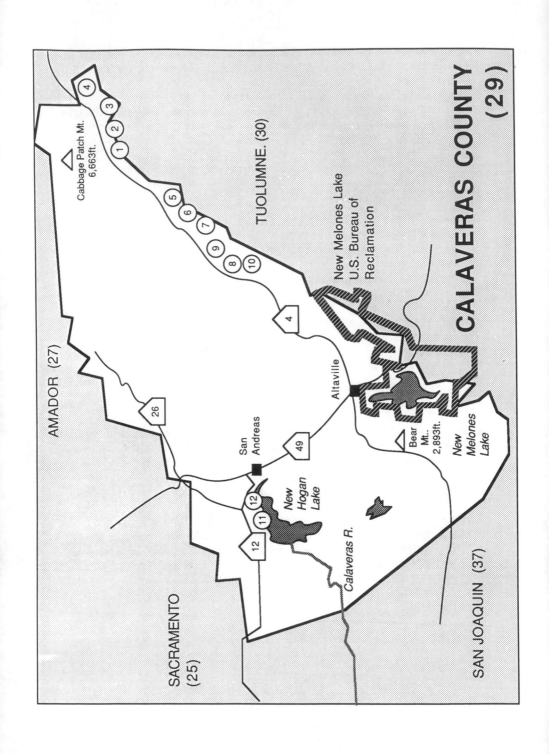

CALAVERAS COUNTY (29)

CALAVERAS COUNTY

◆

Site **1**
BIG
MEADOW
▲

Campsites, facilities: There are 68 campsites for tents or motorhomes. Piped water, fireplaces and picnic tables are provided and vault toilets are available. Groceries and propane gas are nearby.

Reservations, fee: No reservations; $6 fee per night.

Who to contact: Phone Stanislaus National Forest Headquarters at (209)532-3671.

Location: Drive nine miles southwest of Lake Alpine off State Route 4.

Trip note: Open from June to September. Elevation 6500 feet. Camp is one mile from the North Fork of the Stanislaus River. There are numerous four wheel drive trails in the area.

Site **2**
BIG MEADOWS
GROUP CAMP
▲

Campsites, facilities: There is one group campsite for tents or motorhomes. Piped water, picnic tables and fireplaces are provided, and vault toilets are available. Groceries and propane gas are nearby.

Reservations, fee: Reservations requested; $25 fee per group per night.

Who to contact: Phone Stanislaus National Forest Headquarters at (209)532-3671.

Location: Drive nine miles southwest of Lake Alpine off State Route 4.

Trip note: Open from June to September. Elevation 6500 feet. Campsite is near the North Fork of the Stanislaus River. There are numerous four wheel drive trails in the area.

Site **3**
SAND
FLAT
🌲

Campsites, facilities: There are four tent sites. Picnic tables and fireplaces are provided, while vault toilets are available. There is no water, so bring your own. Groceries and propane gas are available nearby.

Reservations, fee: No reservations, no fee.

Who to contact: Phone Stanislaus National Forest Headquarters at (209)532-3671.

Location: Drive seven miles south of Bear Valley off State Route 4.

Trip note: Open from June to September. Elevation 5800 feet. Located on the North Fork of the Stanislaus River. Map of Stanislaus National Forest details back-country roads. Primitive.

Site **4**   STANISLAUS
                          RIVER   ▲

Campsites, facilities: There are five campsites for tents or motorhomes up to 16 feet long. Fireplaces and picnic tables are provided, and vault toilets are available. There is no piped water. Groceries and propane gas are nearby.

Reservations, fee: No reservations, no fee.

Who to contact: Phone Stanislaus National Forest Headquarters at (209)532-3671.

Location: Drive eight miles south of Bear Valley off State Route 4.

Trip note: Camp is open from June to September. Elevation 5900 feet. Located on the North Fork of the Stanislaus River near the Utica and Union Reservoirs. Primitive.

Site **5**   SOURGRASS   ▲

Campsites, facilities: There are six campsites for tents or motorhomes up to 16 feet long. Piped water, fireplaces and picnic tables are provided, and vault toilets are available. Groceries and propane can be purchased nearby.

Reservations, fee: No reservations; $6 fee per night.

Who to contact: Phone Stanislaus National Forest Headquarters at (209)532-3671.

Location: Drive five miles northeast of Camp Connell off State Route 4.

Trip note: Open from April to September. Elevation 4000 feet. Located on the North Fork of the Stanislaus River. A state game refuge is nearby. Nice little spot.

Site **6**   BOARDS
                          CROSSING

Campsites, facilities: There are five tent sites. Piped water, picnic tables and fireplaces are provided, and vault toilets are available. Groceries and propane gas can be purchased nearby.

Reservations, fee: No reservations, no fee.

Who to contact: Phone Stanislaus National Forest Headquarters at (209)532-3671.

Location: Drive three miles southeast of Camp Connell of State Route 4.

Trip note: Open from April to September. Elevation 3800 feet. Located on the North Fork of the Stanislaus River. Calaveras Big Trees State Park is nearby.

Site **7**   OAK
                       HOLLOW   ▲

Campsites, facilities: There are 30 tent sites and 25 sites for motorhomes up to 27 feet long. Piped water, fireplaces and picnic tables are provided. Flush toilets and showers are available. A grocery store, laundromat, dump station and propane gas are also nearby. Campgrounds, nature trail and exhibits are wheelchair accessible.

Reservations, fee: Call MISTIX at (800)446-7275; $10 fee per night.

Who to contact: Phone Calaveras Big Trees State Park at (209)795-2334.

Location: Drive eight miles northeast of Arnold off State Route 4.

Trip note: Open from May to October. Elevation 4000 feet. This campsite has a visitor center with an herbarium, nature exhibits and lectures on the history of the area. Campfire talks and guided tours through the Big Trees are offered during the peak periods. There are cross-country skiing and snowshoeing areas.

Site **8**   NORTH
                       GROVE   ▲

Campsites, facilities: There are 30 tent sites and 44 sites for motorhomes up to 27 feet long. Piped water, fireplaces and picnic tables are provided. Flush toilets and showers are available. A grocery store, laundromat, dump station, and propane gas are nearby. Campgrounds, nature trail and exhibits are wheelchair accessible.

Reservations, fee: Call MISTIX at (800)446-7275; $10 fee per night.

Who to contact: Phone Calaveras Big Trees State Park at (209)795-2334.

Location: Drive eight miles northeast of Arnold off State Route 4.

Trip note: This camp is open all year. Elevation 4500 feet. There is a visitor center with an herbarium, nature exhibits and lectures on the history of the area. Campfire talks and guided tours through the Big Trees are offered during the peak periods and there are cross-country skiing and snowshoeing areas.

Site **9**   GROUP
                       CAMP   ▲

Campsites, facilities: There is one large group campground here that will take tents or motorhomes up to 16 feet long. Piped water, fireplaces and picnic tables are provided. Flush toilets and showers are available. A grocery store, laundromat, dump station and propane gas can be purchased nearby.

Campgrounds, nature trail and exhibits are wheelchair accessible.

Reservations, fee: Call MISTIX at (800)446-7275; $10 fee per night.

Who to contact: Phone Calaveras Big Trees State Park at (209)795-2334.

Location: Drive eight miles northeast of Arnold off State Route 4.

Trip note: Open from May to October. Elevation 5000 feet. There is a visitor center with an herbarium, nature exhibits and lectures on the history of the area. Campfire talks and guided tours through the Big Trees are offered during the peak periods. Also available are cross-country skiing and snowshoeing areas.

Site **10**　　　　　GOLDEN TORCH RV RESORT
　　　　　　　　　　　AND CAMPGROUND　　　　　▲

Campsites, facilities: There are 49 tent sites and 63 motorhome spaces. Piped water, fireplaces, picnic tables, electrical connections and sewer hookups are provided. Rest rooms, showers, a dump station, and a playground are available. A grocery store, laundromat and propane gas are nearby.

Reservations, fee: Call for space available. $16 deposit required; $16 fee per night.

Who to contact: Phone the campground at (209)795-2820.

Location: Drive six miles northeast of Arnold off State Route 4 on Golden Torch Road.

Trip note: Camp is open all year. Elevation 4900 feet. The Calaveras Big Trees State Park and the North Fork of the Stanislaus River are nearby.

Site **11**　　　　　　　　ACORN　　　　　　　　▲

Campsites, facilities: There are 122 campsites for tents or motorhomes. Piped water, fireplaces and picnic tables are provided. Flush toilets, showers, a four-lane concrete boat ramp and a sanitary dump station are available. Groceries and propane gas are nearby.

Reservations, fee: No reservations; $6 fee per night.

Who to contact: Phone New Hogan Lake at (209)772-1343.

Location: Drive three miles southeast of Valley Springs off State Route 26 via Hogan Dam Road.

Trip note: This camp is open all year and is on New Hogan Lake. Elevation 700 feet. The large lake offers abundant waterskiing opportunites. Numerous coves along the 50 miles of shoreline provide many good spots for fishing.

Site **12**　　　　　　　　OAK
　　　　　　　　　　　　　KNOLL　　　　　　　▲

Campsites, facilities: There are 53 campsites for tents or motorhomes. Piped water, fireplaces and picnic tables are provided. Vault toilets are available.

Groceries, propane gas, a sanitary dump station and a four-lane boat ramp are available nearby. (Note: There is also a small campsite area accessible by boat only.)

Reservations, fee: No reservations, no fee.

Who to contact: Phone New Hogan Lake at (209)772-1343.

Location: Drive three miles southeast of Valley Springs off State Route 26 via Hogan Dam Road.

Trip note: Open from April to October. Elevation 700 feet. Campsite is on New Hogan Lake, which was created by an Army Corps of Engineers dam project. The large lake offers abundant waterskiing opportunites. The numerous coves along the 50 miles of shoreline provide many good spots for fishing. Elevation 700 feet.

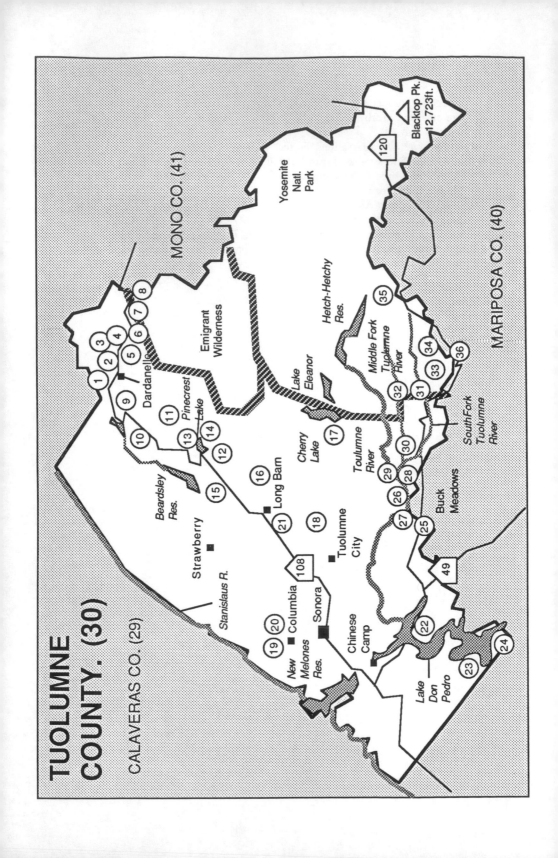

TUOLUMNE COUNTY

♦

Site **1** | BOULDER
FLAT | ⚑

Campsites, facilities: There are 23 campsites for tents or motorhomes up to 22 feet long. Fireplaces and picnic tables are provided, and vault toilets are available. There is no water, so bring your own. A grocery store, laundromat and propane gas are nearby.
Reservations, fee: No reservations; $4 fee per night.
Who to contact: Phone Stanislaus National Forest Headquarters at (209)532-3671.
Location: Drive one and a half miles northwest of Dardanelle on State Route 108.
Trip note: Open from May through October. Elevation 5600 feet. Located on the Stanislaus River.

Site **2** | BRIGHTMAN
FLAT | ⚑

Campsites, facilities: There are 30 campsites for tents or motorhomes up to 22 feet long. Fireplaces and picnic tables are provided, and vault toilets are available. There is no water, so bring your own. A grocery store, laundromat and propane gas are nearby.
Reservations, fee: No reservations, no fee.
Who to contact: Phone Stanislaus National Forest Headquarters at (209)532-3671.
Location: Drive one mile northwest of Dardanelle off State Route 108.
Trip note: Open from May to October. Elevation 5600 feet. Located on the Stanislaus River.

Site **3** | DARDANELLE | ⚑

Campsites, facilities: There are 32 campsites for tents or motorhomes up to 22 feet long. Piped water, fireplaces and picnic tables are provided, and vault toilets are available. A grocery store and propane gas are nearby.
Reservations, fee: No reservations; $3 fee per night.

Who to contact: Phone Stanislaus National Forest Headquarters at (209)532-3671.

Location: Drive to town of Dardanelle on State Route 108, camp is in town.

Trip note: This camp is open from May through October and set near the Stanislaus River. An unusual geologic formation called Columns of the Giants is accessible by a 1/4 mile trail leading out of Pidgeon Flat Campground, one mile east.

Site **4**   EUREKA
                          VALLEY   ▲

Campsites, facilities: There are 26 campsites for tents or motorhomes up to 22 feet long. Piped water, fireplaces and picnic tables are provided, and vault toilets are available. A grocery store, laundromat and propane gas are nearby.

Reservations, fee: No reservations; $3 fee per night.

Who to contact: Phone Stanislaus National Forest Headquarters at (209)532-3671.

Location: Drive three miles east of Dardanelle on State Route 108.

Trip note: Open from May to October. Elevation 6000 feet. Located on the Stanislaus River. An unusual geologic formation called Columns of the Giants is accessible by a 1/2 mile trail leading from Pidgeon Flat Campground, one mile west.

Site **5**   PIDGEON
                           FLAT   🌲

Campsites, facilities: There are six tent sites (walk-in). Fireplaces and picnic tables are provided, and vault toilets are available. There is no water, so bring your own.

Reservations, fee: No reservations, no fee.

Who to contact: Phone Stanislaus National Forest Headquarters at (209)532-3671.

Location: Drive two miles east of Dardanelle off State Route 108.

Trip note: Open from May to October. Elevation 6000 feet. Located on the Stanislaus River. Adjacent to this walk-in camp is a 1/4 mile trail to an unusual geologic formation called Columns of the Giants.

Site **6**   BAKER   ▲

Campsites, facilities: There are 44 campsites for tents or motorhomes up to 22 feet long. Piped water, fireplaces and picnic tables are provided. Vault toilets and equestrian facilities are available. A grocery store, laundromat and propane gas are nearby.

Reservations, fee: No reservations; $6 fee per night.

Who to contact: Phone Stanislaus National Forest Headquarters at (209)532-3671.

Location: Drive five and a half miles southeast of Dardanelle on State Route 108.

Trip note: This camp is open from May through October. Elevation 6200 feet. Located on the Stanislaus River.

Site **7**   DEADMAN

Campsites, facilities: There are 17 campsites for tents or motorhomes up to 22 feet long. Piped water, fireplaces and picnic tables are provided, and vault toilets are available. A grocery store, laundromat, equestrian facilities and propane gas can be found nearby.

Reservations, fee: No reservations; $5 fee per night.

Who to contact: Phone Stanislaus National Forest Headquarters at (209)532-3671.

Location: Drive six miles southeast of Dardanelle off State Route 108.

Trip note: Open from May to October. Elevation 6200 feet. Located on the Stanislaus River. A trail leaves nearby Kennedy Meadow and heads into the backcountry of the Emmigrant Wilderness. The trail forks east to Kennedy Lake or south to Relief Reservoir and beyond to many small alpine lakes.

Site **8**   CHIPMUNK
                              FLAT

Campsites, facilities: There are six campsites for tents or motorhomes up to 22 feet long. Fireplaces and picnic tables are provided, and vault toilets are available. There is no water, so bring your own.

Reservations, fee: No reservations, no fee.

Who to contact: Phone Stanislaus National Forest Headquarters at (209)532-3671.

Location: Drive 10 miles southeast of Dardanelle off State Route 108.

Trip note: Open July to September. Elevation 8400 feet. Located on Deadman Creek near Night Cap Peak (elevation 10,641 feet). Remote, quiet and primitive.

Site **9**   NIAGARA
                              CREEK

Campsites, facilities: There are five campsites for tents or motorhomes up to 22 feet long. Fireplaces and picnic tables are provided, and vault toilets are available. There is no water, so bring your own.

Reservations, fee: No reservations, no fee.

Who to contact: Phone Stanislaus National Forest Headquarters at (209)532-3671.
Location: Drive nine miles southwest of Dardanelle off State Route 108.
Trip note: Open from July through October. Elevation 6200 feet. Located on Niagara Creek. A trail from camp leads to nearby Donnell Vista picnic area which offers a spectacular view overlooking Donnell Lake.

Site **10**   CASCADE
CREEK   🌲

Campsites, facilities: There are seven campsites for tents or motorhomes up to 22 feet long. Picnic tables are provided, and vault toilets are available. There is no water, so bring your own.
Reservations, fee: No reservations, no fee.
Who to contact: Phone Stanislaus National Forest Headquarters at (209)532-3671.
Location: Drive nine miles northeast of Strawberry off State Route 108.
Trip note: Open from June to October. Elevation 6000 feet. This camp is on Cascade Creek. It is quiet and used relatively little.

Site **11**   HERRING CREEK
RESERVOIR   🌲

Campsites, facilities: There are six campsites for tents or motorhomes up to 16 feet long. Picnic tables are provided, and vault toilets are available. There is no water, so bring your own.
Reservations, fee: No reservations, no fee.
Who to contact: Phone Stanislaus National Forest Headquarters at (209)532-3671.
Location: Drive nine miles northeast of Strawberry off State Route 108.
Trip note: Open from June to October. Elevation 7400 feet. Located on Herring Creek Reservoir. A trail starts at the reservoir and follows Herring Creek for six miles passing Bloomer Lake and connecting with Eagle Creek Trail. Consult with the Forest Service for more information.

Site **12**   MEADOW
VIEW   ▲

Campsites, facilities: There are 100 campsites for tents or motorhomes up to 22 feet long. Piped water, fireplaces and picnic tables are provided. Flush toilets and equestrian facilities are available. A grocery store, laundromat, boat ramp and propane gas are nearby.
Reservations, fee: Call Ticketron at (213)216-6666 for outlet information; $6 fee per night.

Who to contact: Phone Stanislaus National Forest Headquarters at (209)532-3671.

Location: Drive one mile south of Pinecrest off State Route 108.

Trip note: Open from May to October. Elevation 5600 feet. Located one mile from Pinecrest Lake. Small boats are permitted, but the speed limit is 20 m.p.h. The Pinecrest National Recreation Trail goes around the lake and branches north for one mile to Catfish Lake.

Site **13**   PINECREST

Campsites, facilities: There are 23 motorhome spaces and 177 campsites for tents or motorhomes up to 22 feet long. Piped water, fireplaces and picnic tables are provided, and flush toilets are available. A grocery store, laundromat, equestrian facilities, a boat ramp and propane gas are available nearby.

Reservations, fee: Call Ticketron at (213)216-6666 for outlet information; $7.50 fee per night.

Who to contact: Phone Stanislaus National Forest Headquarters at (209)532-3671.

Location: Drive one mile southeast of Pinecrest off State Route 108.

Trip note: Open from May to October. Elevation 5600 feet. Located near Pinecrest Lake. Good fishing for stocked rainbow trout in early summer. Small boats are permitted and the speed limit is 20 m.p.h. The Pinecrest National Recreation Trail goes around the lake and branches north for one mile to Catfish Lake.

Site **14**   PIONEER TRAIL
GROUP CAMP

Campsites, facilities: There are three group campsites here. Piped water, picnic tables and fireplaces are provided, and vault toilets are available. A grocery store, laundromat, boat ramp and propane gas are nearby.

Reservations, fee: Call Ticketron at (213)216-6666 for outlet information; $30 per night group fee.

Who to contact: Phone Stanislaus National Forest Headquarters at (209)532-3671.

Location: Drive one mile southeast of Pinecrest off State Route 108.

Trip note: Open from May to September. Elevation 5700 feet. This camp is near Pinecrest Lake. Small boats are permitted and the speed limit is 20 m.p.h. The Pinecrest National Recreation Trail goes around the lake and branches north for one mile to Catfish Lake.

Site 15
FRASER
FLAT   ▲

Campsites, facilities: There are 17 tent sites and 21 campsites for tents or motor-
homes up to 22 feet long. Piped water, fireplaces and picnic tables are provided, and vault toilets are available. A grocery store and propane gas are
available nearby.
Reservations, fee: No reservations; $5 fee per night.
Who to contact: Phone Stanislaus National Forest Headquarters at (209)532-
3671.
Location: Drive eight miles northeast of Long Barn off State Route 108.
Trip note: Open from June to October. Elevation 4800 feet. Located on the
Stanislaus River. Beardsley Reservoir is accessible by driving west from
camp to Spring Gap and then northeast on Spring Gap Road until it connects with the main road to the reservoir, a total of nine miles. There is a
boat ramp at Beardsley Reservoir and waterskiing is allowed. One of the
better fishing lakes in the area, with good brown trout numbers.

Site 16
HULL
CREEK   ▲

Campsites, facilities: There are 11 campsites for tents or motorhomes up to 22
feet long. Fireplaces and picnic tables are provided, and vault toilets are
available. There is no piped water, so bring your own.
Reservations, fee: No reservations; $3 fee per night.
Who to contact: Phone Stanislaus National Forest Headquarters at (209)532-
3671.
Location: Drive nine miles east of Long Barn off State Route 108 on Hull Meadow Road.
Trip note: This camp is open from June to October. Elevation 5600 feet. Located on Hull Creek.

Site 17
CHERRY
VALLEY   ▲

Campsites, facilities: There are 47 campsites for tents or motorhomes up to 16
feet long. Piped water, fireplaces and picnic tables are provided, and vault
toilets are available. A boat ramp and horseback riding facilities are nearby.
Reservations, fee: No reservations; $7 fee per night.
Who to contact: Phone Stanislaus National Forest Headquarters at (209)532-
3671.
Location: Drive 22 miles northeast of Buck Meadows off State Route 120 via
Cherry Valley Road.
Trip note: Open from May to October. Elevation 4700 feet. This camp is on
Cherry Lake, where motorboats and waterskiing are allowed. A trailhead

into the Emigrant Wilderness to the north and several lakes to the northeast and east can be found on the east side of the dam at Cherry Lake. However, the trail into the Emigrant Wilderness has no water for the first 15 miles and is steep and rocky. Contact Forest Service for further information and a wilderness permit.

| Site **18** | RIVER RANCH
CAMPGROUND | |

Campsites, facilities: There are 53 campsites for tents or motorhomes. Piped water, fireplaces and picnic tables are provided, and rest rooms and a dump station are available. A grocery store, laundromat and propane gas are also nearby.

Reservations, fee: Phone Leisuretime Reservation Systems at (800)822-CAMP for fee and space available.

Who to contact: Phone park at (209)928-3708.

Location: Drive five miles northeast of Tuolumne on Buchanan Road.

Trip note: This camp is at the confluence of two rivers, which are stocked regularly by the Department of Fish and Game. Enjoy gold panning and hiking. Elevation 2700 feet.

| Site **19** | MARBLE QUARRY
RESORT | |

Campsites, facilities: There are 10 tent sites and 85 motorhome spaces. Picnic tables, piped water, electrical connections and in some cases sewer hookups are provided. Rest rooms, showers, a swimming pool, laundromat, store, dump station, clubhouse, lounge, breakfast cafe and propane gas are available.

Reservations, fee: Phone Leisuretime Reservation Systems at (800)822-CAMP. $18 deposit; $18 camp use fee.

Who to contact: Phone park at (209)532-9539.

Location: Drive 1/2 mile east of Columbia to 11551 Yankee Hill Road.

Trip note: Open all year. Elevation 2100 feet. Located just a short walk to the Columbia Historic State Park. New Melones Reservoir is nearby.

| Site **20** | 49ER
TRAILER RANCH | |

Campsites, facilities: There are 45 campsites that range from tent sites to motorhome spaces with full hookups. Piped water, picnic tables and fireplaces are provided. Rest rooms, hot showers, grocery store, propane gas, laundromat, dump station and a large barn for group activities are available.

Reservations, fee: Phone Leisuretime Reservation Systems at (800)822-CAMP for fee and space available.

Who to contact: Phone park at (209)532-9898.

Location: Drive one mile north of Columbia on Italian Bar Road to campground.

Trip note: This campground is open all year and is near Columbia State Historic Park. New Melones Reservoir is located nearby.

Site **21**   SUGARPINE
                                RV PARK

Campsites, facilities: There are 63 motorhome spaces. Picnic tables, piped water, electrical connections, cable TV and sewer hookups are provided. Rest rooms, showers, a playground, swimming pool, laundromat, store, dump station and propane gas are available.

Reservations, fee: Phone Leisuretime Reservation Systems at (800)822-CAMP for fee and space available.

Who to contact: Phone park at (209)586-4631.

Location: Drive 14 miles east of Sonora on State Route 108.

Trip note: Open all year. Good fishing in the area. Try one of the nearby golf courses, or play volleyball and horseshoes under the acres of shady trees.

Site **22**   MOCCASIN
                                POINT

Campsites, facilities: There are 65 tent sites and 15 motorhome spaces. Picnic tables and fireplaces are provided at all sites. Piped water, electrical connections and sewer hookups are provided at the motorhome spaces. Rest rooms, showers, store, dump station, propane gas, ice, snack bar, boat ramp, motorboat and houseboat rentals, fuel, moorings, and bait and tackle are available.

Reservations, fee: Reservations accepted; $12 fee per night.

Who to contact: Phone park at (209)852-2396.

Location: Drive six miles east of Chinese Camp via State Route 49 and State Route 120.

Trip note: Open all year. Elevation 850 feet. Located at the north end of Lake Don Pedro. Bass fishing can be good in the spring. Houseboating and water skiing are popular in summer.

Site **23**   BLUE
                                OAKS

Campsites, facilities: There are 197 campsites for tents or motorhomes. Piped water, fireplaces and picnic tables are provided. Flush toilets and showers are available. A grocery store, laundromat, boat ramp and propane gas are located nearby.

Reservations, fee: Reservations accepted; $12 fee per night.

Who to contact: Phone park at (209)852-2396.
Location: Drive eight miles northeast of La Grange via La Grange Road to Don
  Pedro Road.
Trip note: Open from June to August. Elevation 850 feet. Located on Lake Don
  Pedro, which is used by fishermen, water skiers and houseboaters.

Site **24**   FLEMING
MEADOWS   ▲

Campsites, facilities: There are 152 tent sites and 89 motorhome spaces. Picnic
  tables and fireplaces are provided at all sites. Piped water, electrical connections and sewer hookups are provided at the motorhome spaces. Rest
  rooms, showers and a dump station are available. Nearby are a laundromat,
  store, ice, snack bar, restaurant, tackle, bait, motorboat and houseboat rentals, boat ramp, berths, engine repairs and propane gas.
Reservations, fee: Reservations accepted; $12 fee per night.
Who to contact: Phone park at (209)852-2396.
Location: Drive 10 miles northeast of La Grange via La Grange Road to Bonds
  Flat Road.
Trip note: Open all year. Elevation 850 feet. Located on Lake Don Pedro, which
  is good for fishing, water skiing and houseboating.

Site **25**   THE
PINES   ▲

Campsites, facilities: There are 14 campsites for tents or motorhomes up to 22
  feet long. Piped water, fireplaces and picnic tables are provided, and vault
  toilets are available. A grocery store is nearby.
Reservations, fee: No reservations, no fee.
Who to contact: Phone Stanislaus National Forest Headquarters at (209)532-
  3671.
Location: Drive eight miles east of Groveland off State Route 120.
Trip note: Open all year. Elevation 3200 feet. Located one and a half miles from
  the Tuolumne River and and two miles from Buck Flat Resort.

Site **26**   LOST
CLAIM   🌲

Campsites, facilities: There are 10 tent sites. Picnic tables and fireplaces are pro-
  vided and vault toilets are available. There is no water, so bring your own.
  A grocery store is nearby.
Reservations, fee: No reservations, no fee.
Who to contact: Phone Stanislaus National Forest Headquarters at (209)532-
  3671.
Location: Drive 11 miles east of Groveland off State Route 120.

Trip note: Open from April to December. Elevation 3100 feet. Located near the South Fork of the Tuolumne River.

Site 27   LUMSDEN   [tree icon]

Campsites, facilities: There are nine tent sites. Picnic tables and fireplaces are provided, and vault toilets are available. There is no water, so bring your own.

Reservations, fee: No reservations, no fee.

Who to contact: Phone Stanislaus National Forest Headquarters at (209)532-3671.

Location: Drive seven miles northeast of Buck Meadows off State Route 120.

Trip note: Open from April to November. Elevation 1500 feet. Located on the Tuolumne River.

Site 28   SOUTH
                                       FORK   [tree icon]

Campsites, facilities: There are five tent sites. Picnic tables and fireplaces are provided, and vault toilets are available. There is no water, so bring your own.

Reservations, fee: No reservations, no fee.

Who to contact: Phone Stanislaus National Forest Headquarters at (209)532-3671.

Location: Drive seven miles northeast of Buck Meadows off State Route 120.

Trip note: Open from April to November. Elevation 1500 feet. This camp is located along the Tuolumne River.

Site 29   LUMSDEN
                                       BRIDGE   [tree icon]

Campsites, facilities: There are nine tent sites. Picnic tables and fireplaces are provided, and vault toilets are available. There is no water, so bring your own.

Reservations, fee: No reservations, no fee.

Who to contact: Phone Stanislaus National Forest Headquarters at (209)532-3671.

Location: Drive nine miles northeast of Buck Meadows off State Route 120.

Trip note: Open from April to November. Elevation 1500 feet. Located along the Tuolumne River.

Site 30   SWEETWATER   ◭

Campsites, facilities: There are 13 campsites for tents or motorhomes up to 22 feet long. Piped water, fireplaces and picnic tables are provided, and vault toilets are available. A grocery store is nearby.

Reservations, fee: No reservations; $3 fee per night.

Who to contact: Phone Stanislaus National Forest Headquarters at (209)532-3671.

Location: Drive four miles east of Buck Meadows on State Route 120.

Trip note: Open from April to November. Elevation 3300 feet. Located on the South Fork of the Tuolumne River.

Site 31   CARLTON   ◭

Campsites, facilities: There are 18 campsites for tents or motorhomes up to 16 feet long. Fireplaces and picnic tables are provided, and vault toilets are available. There is no water, so bring your own. A grocery store is nearby.

Reservations, fee: No reservations, no fee.

Who to contact: Phone Stanislaus National Forest Headquarters at (209)532-3671.

Location: Drive 13 miles northeast of Buck Meadows off State Route 120 on Evergreen Road.

Trip note: Open from May to November. Elevation 4600 feet. Located on the South Fork of the Tuolumne River.

Site 32   MIDDLE FORK   ◭

Campsites, facilities: There are 25 campsites for tents or motorhomes up to 16 feet long. Fireplaces and picnic tables are provided, and vault toilets are available. There is no water, so bring your own. A grocery store is nearby.

Reservations, fee: No reservations, no fee.

Who to contact: Phone Stanislaus National Forest Headquarters at (209)532-3671.

Location: Drive 18 miles east of Buck Meadows off State Route 120 on Evergreen Road.

Trip note: Open from April to November. Set on the Middle Fork of the Tuolumne River.

Site 33   HODGDON MEADOW   ◭

Campsites, facilities: There are 107 campsites for tents or motorhomes up to 30

feet long. Piped water, fireplaces and picnic tables are provided, and flush toilets are available. A grocery store and propane gas are nearby.

Reservations, fee: No reservations; $6 fee per night.

Who to contact: Phone Yosemite National Park Headquarters at (209)372-4461.

Location: Drive 13 miles east of Buck Meadows via State Route 120 (Big Oak Flat Road).

Trip note: Open all year. Elevation 4900 feet. Located on North Crane Creek near the South Fork of the Tuolumne River in Yosemite National Park. The Tuolumne Big Tree Grove is three miles southeast and Yosemite Valley is 25 miles from camp.

Site **34**   HODGDON MEADOW
GROUP CAMP   ▲

Campsites, facilities: There are five group campsites for tents or motorhomes up to 30 feet long. Piped water, fireplaces and picnic tables are provided, and flush toilets are available. A grocery store and propane gas are available nearby.

Reservations, fee: No reservations; $30 fee per night per group.

Who to contact: Phone Yosemite National Park Headquarters at (209)372-4461.

Location: Drive 13 miles east of Buck Meadows via State Route 120 (Big Oak Flat Road).

Trip note: Open from June to September. Elevation 4900 feet. Located on North Crane Creek near the South Fork of the Tuolumne River. The Tuolumne Big Tree Grove is five miles southeast of camp and Yosemite Valley is 25 miles from camp.

Site **35**   WHITE
WOLF   ▲

Campsites, facilities: There are 87 campsites for tents or motorhomes up to 30 feet long. Piped water, fireplaces and picnic tables are provided. Flush toilets, hot showers, horseback riding facilities and evening ranger programs are available. A grocery store is nearby.

Reservations, fee: No reservations; $6 fee per night.

Who to contact: Phone Yosemite National Park Headquarters at (209)372-4461.

Location: Drive about 35 miles east of Buck Meadows via State Route 120 (Big Oak Flat Road/Tioga Pass Road) to White Wolf Road.

Trip note: Open from June to October. Elevation 7900 feet. This camp is near the trailhead for a number of trails, including one heading east to Lukens Lake or beyond to Grant Lakes, or another (actually a dirt road) going northwest to Harden Lake. Once you arrive at Harden Lake the trail branches northwest to Smith Peak along a ridge overlooking Hetch Hetchy Reservoir, or northeast into the Grand Canyon of the Tuolumne. Get a map of the area for more details.

| Site 36 | CRANE FLAT | ▲ |

Campsites, facilities: There are 129 campsites for tents or motorhomes up to 30 feet long. Piped water, fireplaces and picnic tables are provided. Flush toilets, groceries, propane gas and evening ranger programs are available. A gasoline station is nearby.

Reservations, fee: No reservations; $6 fee per night.

Who to contact: Phone Yosemite National Park Headquarters at (209)372-4461.

Location: Drive 20 miles southeast of Buck Meadows on State Route 120 (Big Oak Flat Road).

Trip note: Open from June to October. Elevation 6200 feet. Located near the Merced and Tuolumne Groves of Big Trees about 20 miles from Yosemite Valley.

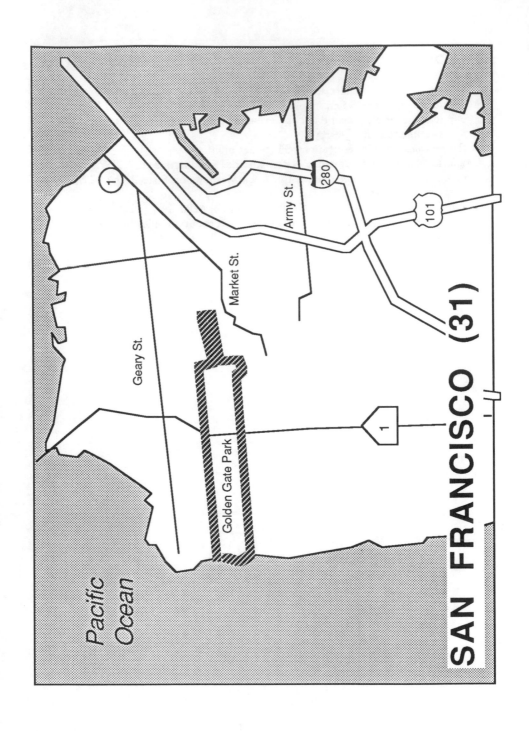

SAN FRANCISCO (31)

SAN FRANCISCO COUNTY

◆

Site 1 | SAN FRANCISCO
RV PARK

Campsites, facilities: There are 200 sites with full hookups for motorhomes. Water, barbeque and tables provided. A dump station, showers and laundromat available.

Reservations, fee: Reservations required; $18 per night fee.

Who to contact: Phone (415)986-8730 or write at 250 King Street, San Francisco, CA 94107.

Location: Set between 3rd and 4th Streets in San Francisco.

Trip note: San Francisco's only "campground," is strictly for motorhomes. A good base camp for adventuring in the West's Emerald City.

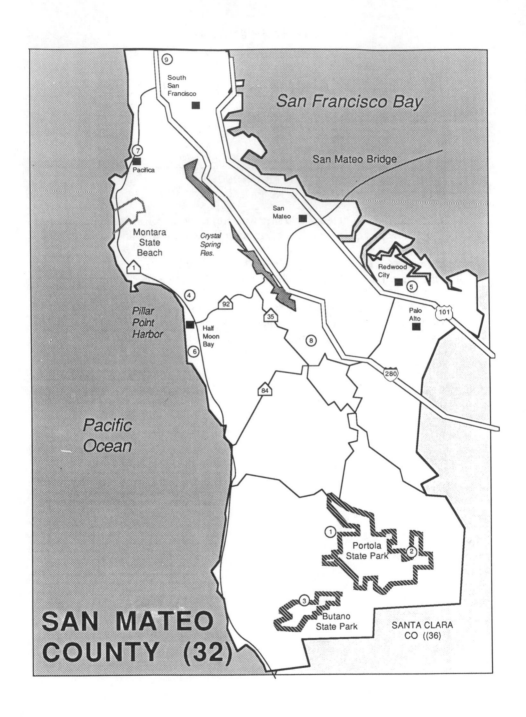

San Francisco Bay

San Mateo Bridge

South
San
Francisco

Pacifica

Montara
State
Beach

*Crystal
Spring
Res.*

San
Mateo

Redwood
City

Palo
Alto

*Pillar
Point
Harbor*

Half
Moon
Bay

*Pacific
Ocean*

Portola
State Park

Butano
State Park

SANTA CLARA
CO ((36)

SAN MATEO
COUNTY (32)

MAP THIRTY-TWO

SAN MATEO COUNTY

◆

Site 1 — MEMORIAL PARK

Campsites, facilities: There are 132 sites for tents or motorhomes. No hookups available, but fireplaces and picnic tables are provided. Showers and toilets are available.
Reservations, fee: Call for space available; $5 fee per night.
Who to contact: Phone Memorial Park at (415)879-0212.
Location: Set in the redwoods 20 miles west of Redwood City off Highway 84.
Trip note: Open year around, with plenty of space from Labor Day to Memorial Day. Crowded on summer weekends. Good hiking trails available.

Site 2 — PORTOLA STATE PARK

Campsites, facilities: There are 52 sites for tents or motorhomes. Piped water, fireplaces and tables are provided. Toilets and showers available. No motorhome hookups.
Reservations, fee: Reservations advised through MISTIX by phoning (800)446-7275. Campsite fee is $6 per night; $1 for pets.
Who to contact: Phone at (415)948-9098.
Location: Set in redwoods west of Skyline ridge. From Highway 35, turn west on Alpine Road, then south on Portola State Park Road.
Trip note: Surprisingly secluded for Bay Area parkland. Good hiking in woodlands and along Pescadero Creek. No fishing; "little trout" are actually steelhead smolts.

Site 3 — BUTANO STATE PARK

Campsites, facilities: There are 30 tent spaces, and 10 sites for tents or motorhomes. Piped water, fireplaces and picnic tables are provided with toilets available.
Reservations, fee: Reservation advised during summer season through MISTIX by phoning (800)446-7275. $6 per night fee; pets $1.

Who to contact: Phone at (415)879-0173.
Location: From Highway 1, take Pescadero Road past Pescadero, turn right at Cloverdale Road, follow sign denoting left turn to park.
Trip note: Near Pescadero on San Mateo County coast. Beautiful, secluded park with premium hikes. One hike leads to lookout of Ano Nuevo Island, others go through redwood forests and out to chaparral back country.

Site **4**   HALF MOON BAY
STATE BEACH

Campsites, facilities: There are 51 sites for tents or motorhomes. Piped water, fireplaces and tables are provided. Sanitary disposal station and toilets available.
Reservations, fee: Reservations advisable for weekends; booked well in advance on holidays. Phone MISTIX at (800)446-7275; $6 fee per night.
Who to contact: Phone at (415)726-6238.
Location: Set on the ocean just south of Half Moon Bay, west of Highway 1.
Trip note: A popular spot for vacationers driving Highway 1 in summer. Good beachcombing on low tides. Fishing trips available at Pillar Point Marina in Princeton seven miles north.

Site **5**   TRAILER
VILLA

Campsites, facilities: There are 50 spaces for motorhomes with full hookups. Water, toilets and sanitary disposal station available.
Reservations, fee: Call for space available; $16 fee per night.
Who to contact: Phone at (415)366-7880.
Location: In Redwood City, along Highway 101 at 3401 E. Bayshore Road.
Trip note: Open year around. Good holdover spot for motorhome drivers touring area. About 20 miles south of San Francisco.

Site **6**   PELICAN POINT
RV PARK

Campsites, facilities: There are 75 spaces with hookups for motorhomes. Water, toilets, showers, tables and sanitary disposal station provided.
Reservations,fee: Call for space available; $20 per night fee.
Who to contact: Phone at (415)726-9100.
Location: On the San Mateo County coast, three miles south of Half Moon Bay near the Pacific Ocean. Turn west off Highway 1 on Miramontes Point Road.
Trip note: Open year around. Rural setting near bluffs overlooking ocean on the edge of San Francisco Bay Area. All facilities nearby.

Site **7**

PACIFIC
PARK

Campsites, facilities: There are 257 sites for motorhomes with full hookups.
Heated pool, spa, groceries and cable TV available.
Reservations, fee: Call for space available; $22 fee per night.
Who to contact: Phone at (415)355-2112.
Location: Near the Pacific Ocean in Pacifica off Highway 1. From Highway 1,
take Manor/Palmetto exit. Located at 700 Palmetto Ave.
Trip note: Only 20 miles from San Francisco. Very close to golf course, coastside
restaurants, and fishing pier with good salmon fishing in July and August.

Site **8**

HUDDART
PARK

Campsites, facilities: There are 25 spaces for tents or motorhomes.
Reservations, fee: No reservations; $5 fee per night.
Who to contact: Phone Huddart County Park at (415)851-0326. If phone unat-
tended, call San Mateo County Parks and Recreation at (415)363-4020.
Location: Set in the foothills above Redwood City. From Highway 280, take
Woodside Road, then turn right on Bear Mountain Road.
Trip note: Hidden parkland on San Francisco Peninsula offers excellent hiking
opportunities. Weekdays very quiet.

Site **9**

NEW SAN FRANCISCO
TRAILER PARK

Campsites, facilities: There are 90 sites for motorhomes with hookups, toilets,
sanitary dump station, showers, laundry and supplies available.
Reservations, fee: This trailer park accepts phone reservations; $14 fee per night.
Who to contact: Phone at (415)755-5850.
Location: Located three miles south of San Francisco at 6925 Mission Street in
Daly City.
Trip note: OK spot for layover while on Bay Area tour with motorhome. A short
hop to San Francisco.

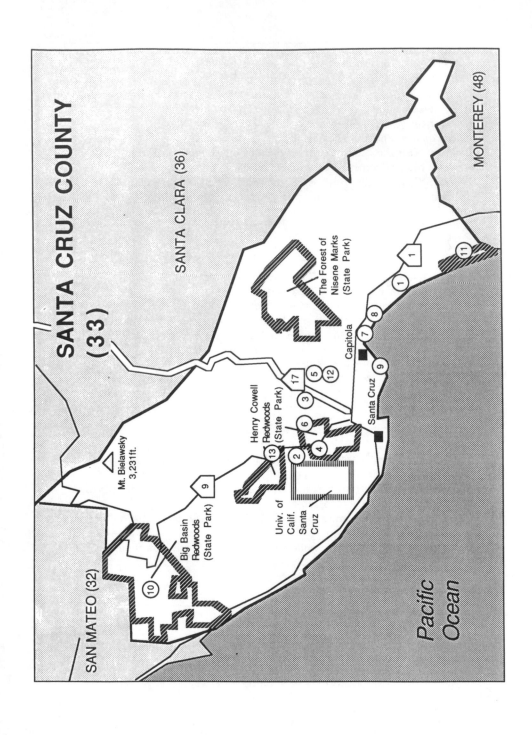

SANTA CRUZ COUNTY (33)

SAN MATEO (32)

SANTA CLARA (36)

MONTEREY (48)

Pacific Ocean

Mt. Bielawsky 3,231ft.

Big Basin Redwoods (State Park)

Henry Cowell Redwoods (State Park)

Univ. of Calif. Santa Cruz

The Forest of Nisene Marks (State Park)

Santa Cruz

Capitola

10

9

13

2

4

6

3

17

5

12

9

7

8

1

1

11

1

SANTA CRUZ COUNTY

♦

Site 1   **SANTA CRUZ**
KOA

Campsites, facilities: There are 23 sites for tents and 233 spaces for motorhomes with hookups available. Sanitary disposal station, water, toilets and showers are available.

Reservations, fee: Call for space available; motorhome fee is $18.75 per night.

Who to contact: Phone at (408)722-0551.

Location: Set 12 miles southeast of Santa Cruz off Highway 1 and Larkin Valley Road, at 1186 San Andreas Road.

Trip note: Open year around. Popular layover for motorhome tours heading up coast from Southern California.

Site 2   **COTILLION GARDENS**
RV PARK

Campsites, facilities: There are 80 sites for tents or motorhomes with hookups provided. Water and tables provided. Showers, toilets and swimming pool available.

Reservations, fee: Reservations advised; $14.50 per night fee.

Who to contact: Phone at (408)335-7669.

Location: Set in the Santa Cruz Mountains just south of Felton. From Highway 9, take Old Big Tree Road.

Trip note: This site offers the best of both worlds. It's in the redwoods yet Monterey Bay is not far away. Horseback riding available.

Site 3   **CARBONERO CREEK**
TRAILER PARK

Campsites, facilities: There are 10 sites for tents, 100 spaces for motorhomes with hookups. Water, toilets, showers and swimming pool are available.

Reservations, fee: Call for space available; $16 fee per night.

Who to contact: Phone at (408)438-1288.

Location: Set five miles northeast of Santa Cruz off Highway 17 at 4556 Scotts Valley Road.

Trip note: Just a short hop from Monterey Bay. Take a charter fishing trip in Santa Cruz, or visit one of the restaurants. Hiking trails through the redwoods at nearby state parks.

Site **4**   SMITHWOODS
              RESORT

Campsites, facilities: There are 88 spaces for motorhomes with full hookups. Disposal station, water, toilet, showers, fireplaces and playgrounds available.
Reservations, fee: Call for space available; $16 per night fee.
Who to contact: Phone at (408)335-4321.
Location: Just off Highway 9, about two miles south of Felton.
Trip note: Pretty redwood setting, redwood burl and clocks for sale in town. Not far from state parks and quality hiking trails.

Site **5**   HOLIDAY HOST
              TRAVEL PARK

Campsites, facilities: There are 152 spaces for motorhomes with full hookups. Sanitary disposal station, water, toilets, showers, fireplaces and playground available.
Reservations, fee: Call ahead for space available; $18 fee per night.
Who to contact: Phone at (408)438-1600.
Location: Set five miles northeast of Santa Cruz off Highway 17 and Granite Creek Road at 100 Santa's Village Road.
Trip note: A short drive to Monterey Bay and restaurants, fishing pier, boat charters.

Site **6**   HENRY COWELL
              REDWOODS

Campsites, facilities: There are 113 sites for tents or motorhomes up to 30 feet. Piped water, fireplaces and tables provided. Sanitary disposal station, showers and toilets available.
Reservations, fee: Reservations advisable through MISTIX by phoning (800)446-7275. $6 per night fee; pets $1.
Who to contact: Phone at (408)438-2396.
Location: Two miles north of Santa Cruz via Graham Hill Road. Follow signs from Highway 1.
Trip note: Quality redwood state park near Santa Cruz with good hiking. Some steelhead fishing during January and February on the San Lorenzo River.

Site **7** | NEW BRIGHTON BEACH

Campsites, facilities: There are 10 tent sites and 105 spaces for tents or motor-homes to 35 feet. Piped water, fireplaces and tables provided. Sanitary disposal station, toilets, showers, propane, groceries and laundromat available.
Reservations, fee: Reservations advised through MISTIX by phoning (800)446-7275. $8 fee per night; pets $1.
Who to contact: Call state park rangers at (408)475-4850.
Location: Set on Monterey Bay at the edge of Capitola, east of Highway 1.
Trip note: Enjoy beachcombing or surf fishing for perch. Dory rentals available nearby at Capitola Wharf. Good waves for surfing.

Site **8** | SEACLIFF BEACH

Campsites, facilities: There are 91 sites for tents or motorhomes up to 35 feet with hookups available. Piped water, fireplaces and tables are provided. Showers, propane, groceries and laundromat available.
Reservations, fee: Reservations advised through MISTIX by phoning (800)446-7275; $12 fee per night for motorhomes.
Who to contact: Call state park rangers at (408)688-3241, or Seacliff State Beach at (408)688-3222 (phone sometimes unattended).
Location: Set along Monterey Bay west of Highway 1 at Aptos.
Trip note: Popular layover in summer months, but best weather from mid-August to early October. Bluffs overlook Monterey Bay. Best shorefishing in Monterey Bay at old cement ship.

Site **9** | BEACH RV PARK

Campsites, facilities: There are three tent sites and 16 motorhome spaces with full hookups. Laundromat and sanitary dump station available.
Reservations, fee: Call for space available; fee charged.
Who to contact: Phone at (408)462-2505.
Location: Exit from Highway 1 at 41st Avenue and head west toward ocean, then turn right on Portola. Park is at 2505 Portola Drive.
Trip note: A short hop to beach, suntans, Monterey Bay.

Site **10** | BIG BASIN REDWOODS

Campsites, facilities: There are 188 sites for tents or motorhomes to 27 feet long. Piped water, tables and fireplaces are provided. A sanitary disposal station, showers and groceries are available.

Reservations, fee: Reservations urged through MISTIX by phoning (800)446-7275; $6 per night fee.

Who to contact: Phone Big Basin State Park at (408)338-6132.

Location: Set in heart of Santa Cruz mountain redwoods. From Santa Cruz, drive east on Highway 9, then at Boulder Creek follow signs to Highway 236, then to park.

Trip note: One of the Bay Area's best parklands. Hike to Berry Creek Falls is a winner, especially after a rain. Some giant redwoods near park headquarters.

Site **11**   SUNSET
                     STATE BEACH   ▲

Campsites, facilities: There are 90 spaces for tents or motorhomes to 35 feet long. Non-piped water, toilets, showers, fireplaces and tables are provided.

Reservations, fee: Reservations suggested through MISTIX by phoning (800)446-7275; $8 fee per night.

Who to contact: Phone park rangers at (408)688-3241.

Location: Set seven miles southwest of Watsonville off Highway 1. Follow sign.

Trip note: Good spot for Pismo clams during low tides. Sunsets look like they're imported from Hawaii.

Site **12**   SANTA VIDA
                     TRAVEL PARK   ▲

Campsites, facilities: There are 47 sites for tents or motorhomes with hookups provided. Water and fireplaces are provided. Toilets, sanitary dump station, white gas and supplies available.

Reservations, fee: Call for space available. Winter rates are $17 per night, $18 during summer. Extended stays available at $305 per month with security deposit.

Who to contact: Phone at (408)425-1945, or write at 1611 Branciforte Drive, Santa Cruz, CA 95065.

Location: Set near the ocean in Santa Cruz. Drive three miles northeast on Market Steet, then north on Branciforte Drive.

Trip note: Santa Cruz Beach Boardwalk and restaurants nearby. Charter boat fishing trips available at Santa Cruz Wharf.

Site **13**   RIVER GROVE
                     RV PARK

Campsites, facilities: Tent and motorhome sites with full hookups are provided. Tables, showers, toilets, dump station, laundromat and recreaton hall available.

Reservations, fee: Call for space available. Tent sites are $11 per night; motor-home sites $12.

Who to contact: Phone at (408)335-4511.

Location: Set in Santa Cruz Mountains on Highway 9 in Felton.

Trip note: Open year around. Nice setting in redwoods. Good hiking at nearby state parks.

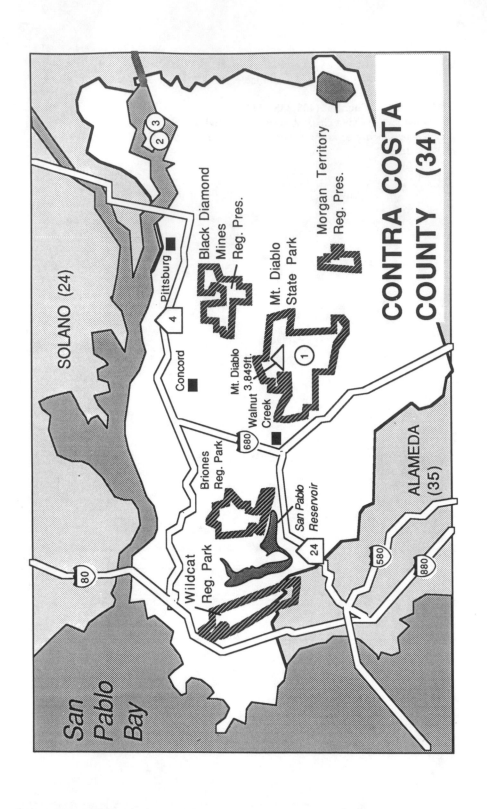

CONTRA COSTA COUNTY (34)

San Pablo Bay

SOLANO (24)

Pittsburg

Black Diamond Mines Reg. Pres.

Morgan Territory Reg. Pres.

Concord

Mt. Diablo State Park

Mt. Diablo 3,849ft.

Walnut Creek

Briones Reg. Park

San Pablo Reservoir

Wildcat Reg. Park

ALAMEDA (35)

80

680

24

580

880

4

1

2

3

CONTRA COSTA COUNTY

♦

Site 1 | MOUNT DIABLO | ▲

Campsites, facilities: There are 48 sites for tents or motorhomes with water, vault toilets, fireplaces and tables provided.

Reservations, fee: Reservations can be made through MISTIX by phoning (800)446-7275; $10 fee per night.

Who to contact: Phone Mount Diablo State Park at (415)837-2525.

Location: From Highway 680 at Danville, take Diablo Road and head east on Black Hawk Road, then turn left on South Gate Road.

Trip note: Elevation 3849 feet. Mount Diablo can provide one of the best lookouts in America. No alchohol is permitted in the park.

Site 2 | ISLAND PARK | 🚐

Campsites, facilities: There are 59 sites for motorhomes with electricity. Water and laundromat provided. Sanitary dump station and swimming pool available.

Reservations, fee: No reservations; $14 per night for two people, $15 per night for three.

Who to contact: Phone at (415)684-2144.

Location: From Highway 4 east of Oakley, take Cypress Road left to Bethel Island Bridge. Cross bridge and head north half mile to Gateway Road and make a right. Continue east a half mile to Island Park.

Trip note: On the edge of the San Joaquin Delta's boating paradise with more than 1,000 miles of waterways. Good striper fishing from November through March, catfishing, water skiing in summer.

Site 3 | DELTA RESORT | 🚐

Campsites, facilities: There are 76 sites for motorhomes with full hookups. Store, propane, laundromat and sanitary dump station available.

Reservations, fee: Reservations required. Mail in 50 percent of fee; $14 fee per night.

Who to contact: Phone at (415)684-2122 or write at P.O. Box 718, Bethel Island, CA 94511.

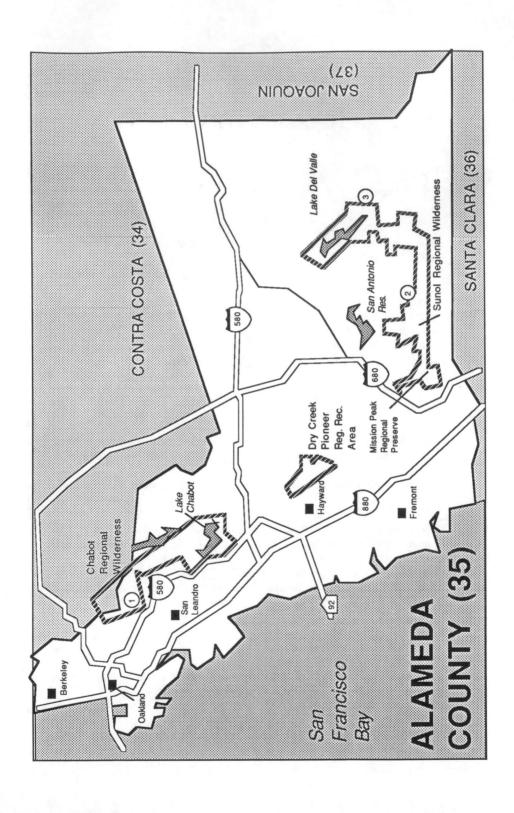

ALAMEDA COUNTY

♦

Site 1   CHABOT PARK   ▲

Campsites, facilities: There are 62 sites for tents and 12 sites for motorhomes. Piped water, fireplaces and tables are provided. Toilets, showers and sanitary disposal station are available.

Reservations,fee: No reservations; $9 fee per night.

Who to contact: For brochure, call East Bay Regional Park District at (415)531-9300; for space available, call Chabot Park at (415)881-1833.

Location: The park is located four miles west of Castro Valley off Highway 580 at Redwood Road.

Trip note: Lake Chabot provides good trout fishing from fall through spring. Boat rentals and tackle shop available.

Site 2   SUNOL REGIONAL WILDERNESS   🌲

Campsites, facilities: There are four tent sites. Piped water, tables, fireplaces and vault toilets provided.

Reservations, fee: No reservations; $6 fee per night.

Who to contact: Phone the East Bay Regional Park District at (415)531-9300, or for camp space availability, phone Sunol at (415)862-2244.

Location: Set in the golden (in summer and fall) hills of the East Bay southeast of Fremont off Highway 680.

Trip note: A little-known Bay Area park that can provide a quiet setting or nice hiking area for the few car campers who know of it.

Site 3   DEL VALLE PARK   ▲

Campsites, facilities: There are 110 sites for tents or motorhomes, 21 with full hookups. Piped water, fireplaces and tables are provided. A sanitary disposal station, toilets, showers, full marina and boat launch are available.

Reservations, fee: Reservations through Ticketron; $9 fee per night.

Who to contact: Phone the East Bay Regional Park District at (415)531-9300, or for campsite available, call the park direct at (415)443-4110.

Location: The park is set in the foothills of the East Bay 10 miles south of Livermore, via Tesla, Mines and Del Valle roads.

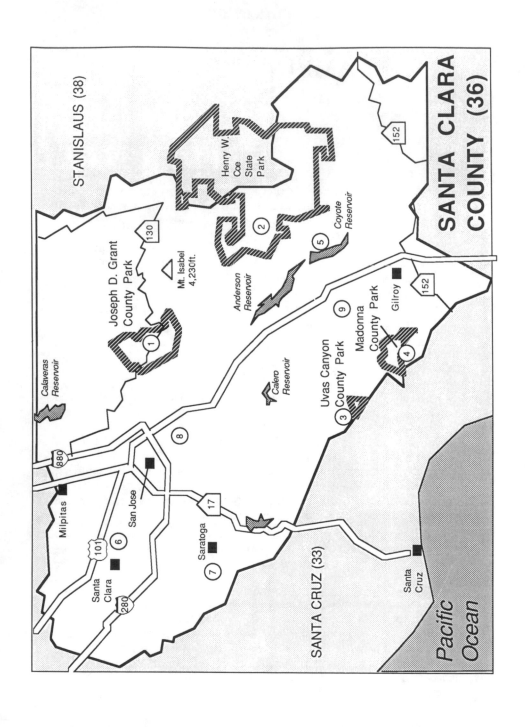

STANISLAUS (38)

SANTA CLARA COUNTY (36)

SANTA CRUZ (33)

Pacific Ocean

Henry W. Coe State Park

Joseph D. Grant County Park

Mt. Isabel 4,230ft.

Anderson Reservoir

Coyote Reservoir

Calaveras Reservoir

Calero Reservoir

Uvas Canyon County Park

Madonna County Park

Gilroy

Milpitas

San Jose

Santa Clara

Saratoga

Santa Cruz

130

152

152

880

101

280

17

SANTA CLARA COUNTY

◆

Site **1**   JOSEPH
GRANT   ▲

Campsites, facilities: Limited space for tents and motorhomes. Water, fireplaces and tables provided. Showers, toilets, groceries and laundromat available.
Reservations, fee: Phone for space available; $6 per night fee.
Who to contact: Phone Grant County Park at (408)274-6121.
Location: Set at the foot of Mount Hamilton eight miles east of San Jose on Mount Hamilton Road.
Trip note: Side trip on winding Mount Hamilton Road can take you to top of Mount Hamilton for tour of Lick Observatory. Very hot in summer.

Site **2**   HENRY
COE   ▲

Campsites, facilities: There are seven tent sites and 13 sites for tents or motorhomes. Piped water, pit toilets, fireplaces and tables are provided.
Reservations, fee: Reservations advised through Mistix by phoning (800)446-7275; $3 per night fee.
Who to contact: Phone state park rangers at (408)779-2728.
Location: Set in relative wilderness, 15 miles east of Morgan Hill off Highway 101 on East Dunne Avenue cutoff.
Trip note: Great back country fishing for bass, bluegill and crappie, but anglers must have the spirit to hike 10 miles to reach it. Bring water purifier for hikes, no piped water available. Very hot in summer and fall.

Site **3**   UVAS
CANYON   ▲

Campsites, facilities: There are 30 sites for tents and 15 spaces for tents or motorhomes. Water, fireplaces and tables provided, and toilets are available.
Reservations, fee: No reservations; $6 per night fee.
Who to contact: Call Uvas Canyon County Park at (408)358-3751.
Location: Set on the west side of the Santa Clara Valley, seven miles west of Morgan Hill. Take County Road 68 to Cray Road.

Trip note: Uvas Reservoir provides some of the better black bass and crappie fishing in the Bay Area during the spring. Call Coyote Discount Bait at (408)463-0711 for latest fishing tips.

Site **4** **MOUNT MADONNA**

Campsites, facilities: There are 117 sites for tents or motorhomes. Non-piped water, fireplaces and tables provided. Toilets and groceries available.
Reservations, fee: No reservations; $6 fee per night.
Who to contact: Call Mount Madonna County Park at (408)358-3751.
Location: Set at the top of the mountain ridgeline on Highway 152 between Watsonville and Gilroy.
Trip note: On clear days, great vistas of Monterey Bay to the west, Santa Clara Valley to the east. Horseback rentals available at Madonna Stables. Good hiking.

Site **5** **LAKEVIEW COYOTE PARK**

Campsites, facilities: There are 74 sites for tents or motorhomes. Water, tables and fireplaces are provided. Propane, groceries and landromat are available.
Reservations, fee: No reservations; $6 fee.
Who to contact: Phone for space available at (408)842-7800.
Location: Set seven miles east of Gilroy along Coyote Lake.
Trip note: Trout and bass occasionally stocked in Coyote Lake, but fishing tends to be fair. Hot, dry weather in summer. Call Coyote Bait at (408)463-0711 for free map of area lakes, directions.

Site **6** **MOBILAND MANOR**

Campsites, facilities: There are 50 motorhomes sites with full hookups provided, and laundromat available. One block to small shopping center.
Reservations, fee: Call for space available.
Who to contact: Phone at (408)773-1210, or write at 780 N. Fairoaks Ave., Sunnyvale, CA 94086.
Location: Set near Silicon Valley in Sunnyvale, not parklike setting.
Trip note: No pets permitted. A spot for a layover while in South Bay Area.

Site **7** **SARATOGA SPRINGS**

Campsites, facilities: There are 22 sites for tents and 36 sites for motorhomes, 14 with full hookups. Store, propane and laundromat available.

Reservations, fee: Call for space available.

Who to contact: Phone at (408)867-9999 or write at P.O. Box 157, Saratoga, CA 95070.

Location: Set due west of Saratoga on Highway 9.

Trip note: Country setting at creekside near Bay Area with a sense of solitude.

Site **8**   TRAILER
TEL

Campsites, facilities: There are 25 spaces for motorhomes with electricity, water, sewer, laundromat available.

Reservations, fee: Reservations suggested; phone for space available.

Who to contact: Phone at (408)293-3655.

Location: Not exactly the wilderness, but in San Jose at 1212 Oakland Road. The Oakland Road turnoff from Highway 101 is just south of Highway 17.

Trip note: No pets allowed. A layover spot en route to or from Bay Area.

Site **9**   OAK
DELL

Campsites, facilities: There are 42 spaces for motorhomes with full hookups and sanitary dump station, store, laundromat and propane available.

Reservations, fee: Call for space available.

Who to contact: Phone at (408)779-7779 or write at 12790 Watsonville Road, Morgan Hill, CA 95037.

Location: Set on edge of South Bay in Morgan Hill. From Highway 101 in Morgan Hill, drive west on Tennant Road, south on Monterey Road two blocks, then west four miles on Watsonville Road.

Trip note: Fishing, swimming and water skiing are available at nearby Lake Anderson. Recreational trout fishing at nearby Parkway Lake in Coyote.

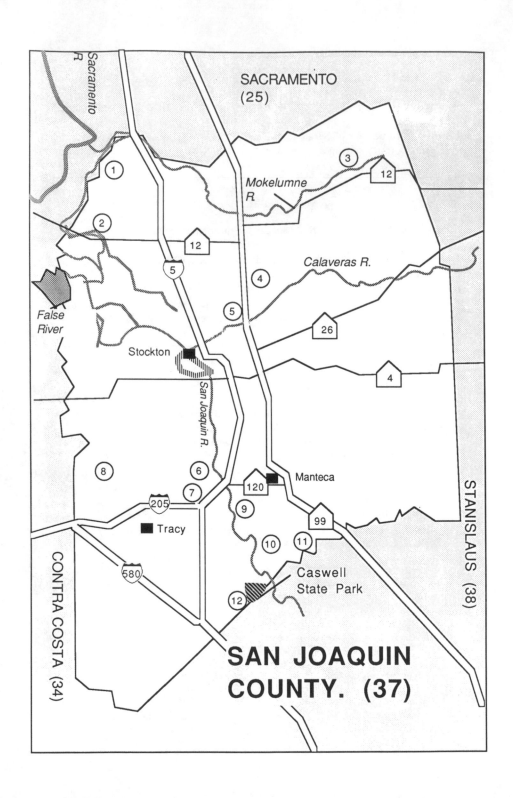

SACRAMENTO
(25)

Sacramento R.

Mokelumne R.

3

12

1

2

12

5

4

Calaveras R.

False
River

5

26

Stockton

4

San Joaquin R.

8

6

120

Manteca

7

205

9

Tracy

99

10

11

580

Caswell
State Park

12

CONTRA COSTA (34)

STANISLAUS (38)

SAN JOAQUIN
COUNTY. (37)

SAN JOAQUIN COUNTY

◆

| Site 1 | NEW HOPE LANDING | |

Campsites, facilities: There are 25 sites for tents or motorhomes. Piped water, electrical connections and some sewer hookups are provided. Rest rooms, showers, a dump station, grocery store, laundromat, propane gas and a full service marina including houseboat rentals are available.
Reservations, fee: Call ahead for space; $10.50 fee per night.
Who to contact: Phone camp at (209)794-2627.
Location: Drive 25 miles north of Stockton off I-5 via Walnut Grove Road (Thornton exit) then north 200 yards on Levy Road to the park.
Trip note: The resort is on the Mokelumne River and provides the facilities to enjoy boating and fishing in the 1100 miles of waterways that make up the California Delta system.

| Site 2 | WESTGATE LANDING PARK | |

Campsites, facilities: There are 15 campsites for tents or motorhomes. Piped water, fireplaces and picnic tables are provided. Flush toilets are available. Groceries and propane gas are nearby.
Reservations, fee: No reservations; $5 fee per night.
Who to contact: Phone County Parks Department at (209)944-2444.
Location: Drive three miles north of Terminous off State Route 12.
Trip note: Open all year. Elevation 25 feet. Located on the South Fork of the Mokelumne River.

| Site 3 | TOWER PARK MARINA AND RESORT | |

Campsites, facilities: There are 250 motorhome spaces. Picnic tables, fire places, piped water, electrical connections and sewer hookups are provided. Rest rooms, showers, a dump station, boat sales and service station, overnight boat slips, elevator boat launch, playground, laundromat, grocery store and propane gas are available.

Reservations, fee: Call for space available; $15 deposit required; $15 fee per night.
Who to contact: Phone the park at (209)369-1041.
Location: Drive 12 miles west of Lodi to 14900 West Highway 12.
Trip note: This camp is open all year and is on the Mokelumne River.

Site **4**   STOCKTON-LODI
                     KOA

Campsites, facilities: There are 14 tent sites and 80 motorhome spaces. Piped water, electrical connections and sewer hookups are provided. Rest rooms, showers, a dump station, grocery store, propane gas, laundromat, unheated pool and a playground are available.
Reservations, fee: No reservations; $16 fee per night.
Who to contact: Phone park at (209)941-2573.
Location: Drive six miles north of Stockton off State Route 99 at 2851 East 8-Mile Road.
Trip note: This camp is open all year and is about 10 miles from the Calaveras River.

Site **5**   SAHARA
                     MOBIL PARK

Campsites, facilities: There are 17 motorhome spaces. Picnic tables, fireplaces, piped water, electrical connections and sewer hookups are provided. Rest rooms, showers, recreation room, heated pool and a laundromat are available. A playground, grocery store and a donut shop are nearby.
Reservations, fee: Call for space available. $9 deposit required; $9 fee per night.
Who to contact: Phone park at (209)464-9392.
Location: Drive to 2340 Sanguinetti Lane in Stockton.
Trip note: Open all year. Elevation 14 feet. Breakfast is served at the park the first Sunday of every month. Bingo is played every Wednesday night.

Site **6**   DOS REIS PARK
                     AND PLAYGROUND

Campsites, facilities: There are 20 motorhome spaces. Piped water, electrical connections and sewer hookups are provided. Rest rooms, showers and a boat ramp are available. A grocery store, laundromat, propane gas and dump station can be found nearby.
Reservations, fee: Call ahead for space available; $8 fee per night.
Who to contact: Phone park at (209)944-2444.
Location: Drive 10 miles south of Stockton off I-5 at Lathrop, then one mile northwest to Dos Reis Road.
Trip note: The park is open all year and is on the San Joaquin River.

| Site 7 | MOSSDALE PARK | |

Campsites, facilities: There are seven campsites for tents or motorhomes. Piped water, fireplaces and picnic tables are provided. Flush toilets and a playground are available. Groceries and propane gas are nearby.

Reservations, fee: Call ahead for space available; $5 fee per night.

Who to contact: Phone County Parks Department at (209)944-2444.

Location: Drive one mile south of Lathrop via I-5 on Manthey Road.

Trip note: This camp is open all year. You can bet on hot weather in the summer.

| Site 8 | TRACY OASIS MARINA RESORT | |

Campsites, facilities: There are 30 sites for tents or motorhomes. Piped water, electrical connections and sewer hookups are provided. Rest rooms, showers, boat slips, water ski equipment rental, elevator boat launch, grocery store and propane gas are available.

Reservations, fee: Call ahead for space and fee.

Who to contact: Phone park at (209)835-3182.

Location: Drive to Tracy, take the Tracy Boulevard exit north off I-205, then turn left on Grimes Road to 12450 West Grimes Road.

Trip note: This resort is on the south Delta and has facilities and supplies for fishing and water skiing.

| Site 9 | OAKWOOD LAKE RESORT | |

Campsites, facilities: There are 87 tent sites, 116 sites for tents or motorhomes, and 194 motorhome spaces. Picnic tables and fireplaces are provided, and piped water, electrical connections and sewer hookups are provided at most sites. Rest rooms, showers, dump station, grocery store, laundromat, propane gas, swim lagoon, water slides, rampage ride, cable water skiing, rollerskating, peddle boat, canoe and wind surfing rentals, organized activities and a stocked 75-acre lake are available.

Reservations, fee: Phone Leisuretime Reservation Systems at (800)822-CAMP. $22 deposit; $22 camp use fee.

Who to contact: Phone park at (209)239-9566.

Location: Drive four miles southwest of Manteca off Arpt Way at 874 East Woodward Avenue.

Trip note: This camp is open all year. It is a 375-acre water theme park with many water related amusements and activities.

Site **10**
DURHAM FERRY RECREATION AREA
AND CAMPGROUND

Campsites, facilities: There are 75 sites for tents or motorhomes. Picnic tables, fireplaces, piped water, and in some cases electrical connections are provided. Rest rooms, hot showers, a sanitary dump station and equestrian area are available. Groceries and propane gas are nearby.

Reservations, fee: Phone Leisuretime Reservation Systems at (800)822-CAMP; $9 camp use fee.

Who to contact: Phone County Parks Department at (209)944-2444.

Location: Drive nine miles south of Manteca off Highway 120 on Airport Boulevard.

Trip note: This 176-acre park offers one and one half miles of San Joaquin River access for fishing, an equestrian area, a wilderness area, hiking trails and great bird watching.

Site **11**
CASWELL MEMORIAL
STATE PARK

Campsites, facilities: There are 65 campsites for tents or motorhomes up to 21 feet long. Piped water, fireplaces and picnic tables are provided. Flush toilets, showers, a nature trail and exhibits are available. The exhibits are wheelchair accessible.

Reservations, fee: Phone MISTIX at (800)446-7275; $6 fee per night.

Who to contact: Phone park at (209)599-3810.

Location: Drive six miles southwest of Ripon off State Route 99.

Trip note: This 258-acre park is open all year, and is on the Stanislaus River.

Site **12**
ORCHARD
RV PARK

Campsites, facilities: There are 20 tent sites and 88 motorhome spaces. Piped water, electrical connections and sewer hookups are provided. Rest rooms, showers, laundromat, dump station, swimming pool, water slides, restaurant and horseshoe pits are available. Groceries, a gift shop, propane gas, and a weekend flea market can be found nearby.

Reservations, fee: Phone Leisuretime Reservation Systems at (800)822-CAMP. $12 deposit; $12 camp use fee.

Who to contact: Phone the park at (209)836-2090.

Location: Drive three miles east of I-5 on State Route 132 to the town of Vernalis and 2701 East Highway 132.

Trip note: This camp is open all year, and offers a huge swim area with pool and water slides.

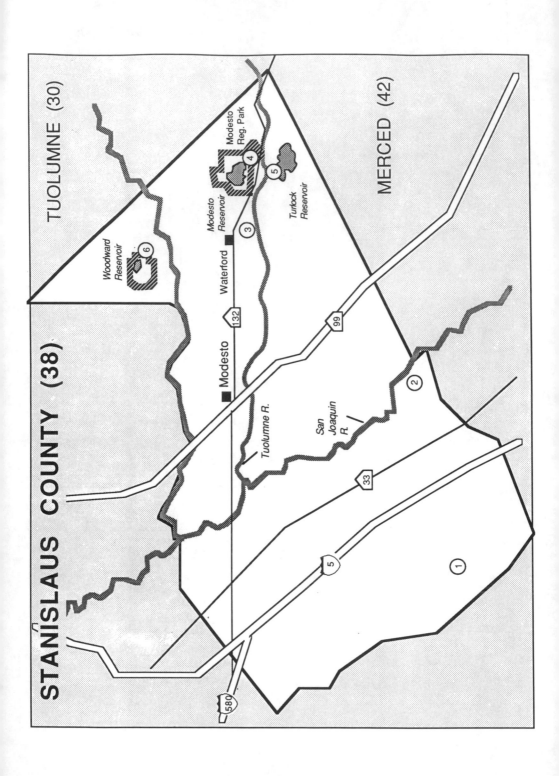

STANISLAUS COUNTY
♦

Site 1   FRANK RAINES
REGIONAL PARK

Campsites, facilities: There are 34 tent or motorhome spaces. Fireplaces, picnic
    tables, piped water, electrical connections and sewer hookups are provided.
    Rest rooms, showers, a dump station and a playground are available.
Reservations, fee: No reservations; $9 fee per night.
Who to contact: Phone park at (408)897-3127.
Location: Drive 20 miles west of Patterson off I-5 on Del Puerto Canyon Road.
Trip note: Open all year. Elevation 1300 feet. In foothills, hot in summer.

Site 2   FISHERMAN'S BEND RIVER
CAMPGROUND

Campsites, facilities: There are 10 tent sites and 28 motorhome spaces. Piped wa-
    ter, electrical connections and sewer hookups are provided. Rest rooms,
    showers, a dump station, a laundromat, boat ramp, fish cleaning station,
    TV connections and horseshoe pits are available.
Reservations, fee: Phone Leisuretime Reservation Systems at (800)822-CAMP.
    $12 deposit; $12 camp use fee.
Who to contact: Phone park at (209)862-3731.
Location: Drive four miles northeast of Newman off Hills Ferry Road at 26836
    River Road.
Trip note: Open from April to December. Elevation 90 feet. This spot offers
    shady campsites along the San Joaquin River where campers can swim and
    fish.

Site 3   BIG BEAR
PARK

Campsites, facilities: There are 100 sites for tents or motorhomes. Piped water,
    electrical connections and sewer hookups are provided. Rest rooms, show-
    ers, dump station and grocery store are available.
Reservations, fee: Call for space available. $13 deposit required; $13 fee per
    night.
Who to contact: Phone park at (209)874-1984.

Location: Drive one mile east of Waterford to 13400 Yosemite Boulevard (State Route 132).

Trip note: Open all year. Elevation 1034 feet. Located near the Tuolumne River.

Site **4**   MODESTO
                    RESERVOIR

Campsites, facilities: There are 60 campsites for tents or motorhomes. Piped water, fireplaces and picnic tables are provided. Flush toilets, dump station, showers, boat ramp, jet ski rentals, waterskiing, fishing and horseback riding facilities are available. Groceries and propane gas are located nearby.

Reservations, fee: No reservations; $9 fee per night.

Who to contact: Phone the park at (209)874-9540.

Location: Drive five miles east of Waterford off State Route 132 to 18139 Reservoir Road.

Trip note: Open all year. Elevation 220 feet. Located along shoreline of Modesto Reservoir.

Site **5**   TURLOCK LAKE
             STATE RECREATION AREA

Campsites, facilities: There are 68 campsites for tents or motorhomes up to 22 feet long. Piped water, fireplaces and picnic tables are provided. Flush toilets, showers, boat ramp, moorings, ice, grocery store, bait shop and a snack bar are available. The boat facilities, grocery store and snack bar are wheelchair accessible.

Reservations, fee: Phone MISTIX at (800)446-7275; $6 fee per night.

Who to contact: Phone park at (209)874-2008.

Location: Drive 11 miles east of Waterford off State Route 132.

Trip note: This camp is set along Turlock Lake and is open all year and provides fishing and waterskiing opportunities, some fishing. Elevation 200 feet.

Site **6**   WOODWARD
                    RESERVOIR

Campsites, facilities: There are 87 campsites for tents or motorhomes. Piped water, fireplaces and picnic tables are provided. Flush toilets, showers, a dump station, groceries, propane gas, boat ramp, mooring, boat rentals, bait and fishing licenses are available.

Reservations, fee: No reservations; $9 fee per night.

Who to contact: Phone park at (209)847-3304.

Location: Drive five miles north of Oakdale to 14528 26-Mile Road.

Trip note: Set on Woodward Reservoir. This camp is open all year, but the lake is fullest from April to October. Elevation 200 feet. The lake is used for fishing and waterskiing.

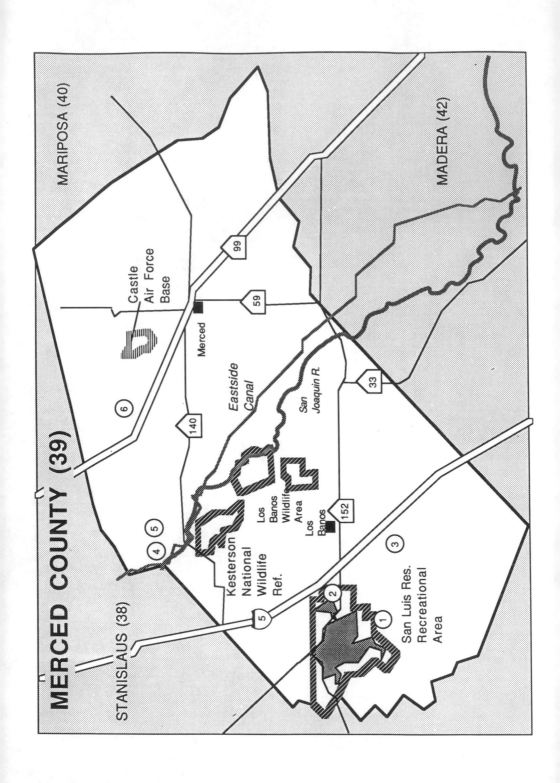

MERCED COUNTY (39)

STANISLAUS (38)

MARIPOSA (40)

MADERA (42)

Castle
Air Force
Base

Merced

99

59

6

140

33

Eastside
Canal

San
Joaquin R.

5

4

5

152

Kesterson
National
Wildlife
Ref.

Los
Banos
Wildlife
Area

Los
Banos

3

2

1

San Luis Res.
Recreational
Area

MERCED COUNTY

♦

Site **1**   BASALT   ▲

Campsites, facilities: There are 79 campsites for tents or motorhomes. Piped water, fireplaces and picnic tables are provided, and flush toilets, showers and a dump station are available. A grocery store, laundromat, propane gas, motorbike trail and boat ramp are nearby. All facilities are wheelchair accessible.

Reservations, fee: Phone MISTIX at (800)446-7275; $10 fee per night.

Who to contact: Phone San Luis Reservoir State Recreation Area at (209)826-1196.

Location: Drive 12 miles west of Los Banos off State Route 152.

Trip note: Open all year. Elevation 575 feet. Fishing for striped bass best in fall. Windy springs make for good sailboarding.

Site **2**   MADEIROS   ▲

Campsites, facilities: There are 350 campsites for tents or motorhomes. Fireplaces and picnic tables are provided, and pit toilets are available. There is no piped water, so bring your own. A grocery store, laundromat, propane gas, a motorbike trail and a boat ramp are nearby. All facilities are wheelchair accessible.

Reservations, fee: No reservations; $3 fee per night.

Who to contact: Phone San Luis Reservoir State Recreation Area at (209)826-1196.

Location: Drive 11 miles west of Los Banos off State Route 152 at O'Neill Forebay.

Trip note: Open all year. Elevation 225 feet. Enjoy swimming, fishing, waterskiing and sailboarding.

Site **3**   LOS BANOS RESERVOIR
                   STATE RECREATION AREA   ▲

Campsites, facilities: There are 25 campsites for tents or motorhomes up to 30

feet long. Fireplaces and picnic tables are provided. Pit toilets and a boat ramp are available. There is no piped water, so bring your own.

Reservations, fee: No reservations; $3 fee per night.

Who to contact: Phone park at (209)826-1196.

Location: Drive 10 miles southwest of Los Banos via State Route 165, Pioneer Road and Canyon Road (rough dirt road).

Trip note: Open all year. Elevation 400 feet. Located on a small lake set in pastureland. Enjoy fishing, sailboarding.

Site 4   **GEORGE J. HATFIELD STATE RECREATION AREA**   ◣

Campsites, facilities: There is one large group campsite for tents or motorhomes up to 32 feet long. Picnic tables, fireplaces and piped water are provided. Flush toilets and cold showers are available. A grocery store, laundromat and propane gas are nearby.

Reservations, fee: Phone MISTIX at (800)446-7275; $100 fee for group per night.

Who to contact: Phone park at (209)632-1852.

Location: Drive five miles northeast of Newman off State Route 33 via Hills Ferry Road (County Road J-18).

Trip note: Open all year. Elevation 62 feet. Located on the Merced River near where it joins the San Joaquin.

Site 5   **GEORGE J. HATFIELD STATE RECREATION AREA**   ◣

Campsites, facilities: There are 21 campsites for tents or motorhomes up to 32 feet long. Piped water, fireplaces and picnic tables are provided. Flush toilets and cold showers are available. A grocery store, laundromat and propane gas are nearby.

Reservations, fee: Phone MISTIX at (800)446-7275; $6 fee per night.

Who to contact: Phone park at (209)632-1852.

Location: Drive five miles northeast of Newman off State Route 33 via Hills Ferry Road (County Road J-18).

Trip note: Open all year. Elevation 62 feet. This spot is on the Merced River near where it joins the San Joaquin.

Site 6   **MC CONNELL STATE RECREATION AREA**   ◣

Campsites, facilities: There are 17 campsites for tents or motorhomes up to 24 feet long. Piped water, fireplaces and picnic tables are provided, and flush toilets are available. A grocery store and a laundromat are available nearby.

Reservations, fee: Phone MISTIX at (800)446-7275; $10 fee per night.

Who to contact: Phone the park at (209)394-7755.

Location: Drive five miles southeast of Delhi off State Route 99 via El Capitan Way.

Trip note: Open all year. Elevation 120 feet. Located on the Merced River. Improved salmon fishing in recent years during the fall.

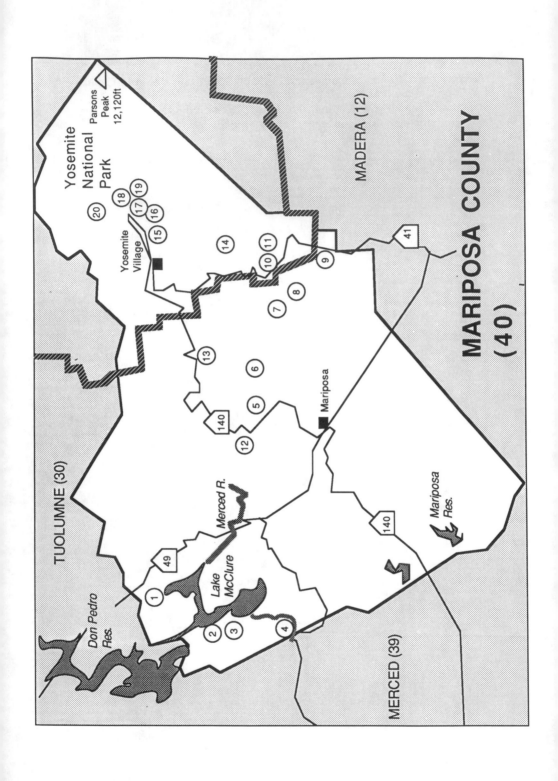

Yosemite National Park

Parsons Peak
12,120ft

20 18 19
   17 16
   15

Yosemite Village

14 11
10

7 8

9

13

6

5

140

12

Merced R.

49

1

Lake McClure

2 3

4

Don Pedro Res.

Mariposa

140

Mariposa Res.

TUOLUMNE (30)

MADERA (12)

MERCED (39)

MARIPOSA COUNTY (40)

41

MARIPOSA COUNTY

◆

Site **1** | HORSESHOE BEND
RECREATION AREA

Campsites, facilities: There are 13 tent sites and 100 tent or motorhome spaces. Piped water, electrical connections and sewer hookups are provided at some of the sites. Picnic tables and fireplaces are provided at all sites. Rest rooms, showers, a dump station, a boat ramp and a playground are available. Nearby are a grocery store, a laundromat, boat rentals and propane gas.
Reservations, fee: Call for space available. $11 deposit required; $8 fee per night.
Who to contact: Phone (800)468-8889.
Location: Drive five miles west of Coulterville off State Route 132.
Trip note: This camp and marina is open all year. Elevation 900 feet. Located on Lake McClure.

Site **2** | BARRETT COVE
RECREATION AREA

Campsites, facilities: There are 275 sites for tents or motorhomes. Piped water, electrical connections and sewer hookups are provided at some sites. Picnic tables and fireplaces are provided at all sites. Rest rooms, showers, a boat launch, a dump station and a playground are available. Nearby are a grocery store, laundromat, boat rentals and propane gas.
Reservations, fee: Call for space available. $11 deposit required; $8 fee per night.
Who to contact: Phone (800)468-8889 for information.
Location: Drive 16 miles east of La Grange off State Route 132.
Trip note: Camp and marina open all year. Elevation 900 feet. Located on Lake McClure.

Site **3** | MC CLURE POINT
RECREATION AREA

Campsites, facilities: There are 100 sites for tents or motorhomes up to 40 feet long. Piped water, electrical connections and sewer hookups are provided at most sites. Picnic tables and fireplaces are provided at all sites. Rest rooms,

showers, a boat ramp, and a dump station are available. Nearby are a grocery store, a laundromat, houseboat rentals, and propane gas.
Reservations, fee: Call for space available. $11 deposit required; $9 fee per night.
Who to contact: Phone (800)468-8889
Location: Drive 20 miles east of La Grange off State Route 132.
Trip note: This camp and marina is open all year. Elevation 900 feet. Located on Lake McClure.

Site *4*   **LAKE MC SWAIN
RECREATION AREA**

Campsites, facilities: There are 103 sites for tents or motorhomes up to 40 feet long. Piped water, electrical connections and sewer hookups are provided at most sites. Picnic tables and fireplaces are provided at all sites. Rest rooms, showers, a boat ramp, a playground and a dump station are available. A grocery store, a laundromat, boat rentals and propane gas are nearby.
Reservations, fee: Call for space available. $11 deposit required; $8 fee per night.
Who to contact: Phone (800)468-8889 for information.
Location: Drive two miles east of Merced Fall off County Road J16.
Trip note: Camp and marina open from March 1 to October 15. Elevation 700 feet. This spot is on Lake McSwain. There is no waterskiing allowed here.

Site *5*   **YOSEMITE/MARIPOSA
KOA CAMPGROUND**

Campsites, facilities: There are 40 tent sites, 30 motorhome spaces and 10 sites for tents or motorhomes. Piped water, electrical connections and sewer hookups are provided at some sites. All sites have picnic tables. Rest rooms, showers, a dump station and a playground are available, Nearby are a grocery store, laundromat and propane gas.
Reservations, fee: Call for space available. $15 deposit required; $15 fee per night.
Who to contact: Phone park at (209)966-2201.
Location: Drive seven miles northeast of Mariposa at 6323 Highway 140.
Trip note: Open all year. Elevation 2400 feet. Campsite is located 28 miles from the entrance to Yosemite National Park.

Site *6*   **JERSEYDALE**

Campsites, facilities: There are 10 campsites for tents or motorhomes up to 22 feet long. Piped water, fireplaces and picnic tables are provided, and vault toilets are available. A grocery store is nearby.
Reservations, fee: No reservations; $3 fee per night.
Who to contact: Phone Sierra National Forest Headquarters at (209)487-5155.

Location: Drive 14 miles northeast of Mariposa.

Trip note: Open from May to November. Elevation 3600 feet. Located at the beginning of a dirt road that goes west into the Chowchilla Mountains.

Site **7**   SIGNAL
                     GROUP CAMP

Campsites, facilities: There are 20 campsites for tents or motorhomes up to 22 feet long. Piped water and fireplaces are provided, and vault toilets are available.

Reservations, fee: No reservations, no fee.

Who to contact: Phone Sierra National Forest Headquarters at (209)487-5155.

Location: Drive 27 miles east of Mariposa off State Route 49 at Signal Peak (Devil Peak). The last few miles are on a dirt road.

Trip note: Open from June to October. Elevation 6400 feet. Located in the Chowchilla Mountains, ten miles from Wawona in Yosemite National Park.

Site **8**   SUMMIT
                       CAMP

Campsites, facilities: There are 10 campsites for tents or motorhomes up to 22 feet long. Piped water, fireplaces and picnic tables are provided. Vault toilets are available.

Reservations, fee: No reservations, no fee.

Who to contact: Phone Sierra National Forest Headquarters at (209)487-5155.

Location: Drive five miles southwest of Wawona off State Route 41.

Trip note: Camp is open from June to November. Elevation 5800 feet. Located three miles from Big Creek and five miles from Wawona in Yosemite National Park.

Site **9**   SUMMERDALE

Campsites, facilities: There are 21 tent sites and nine campsites for tents or motorhomes up to 22 feet long. Piped water, fireplaces and picnic tables are provided, and vault toilets are available. A grocery store is nearby.

Reservations, fee: No reservations; $6 fee per night.

Who to contact: Phone Sierra National Forest Headquarters at (209)487-5155.

Location: Drive one mile north of Fish Camp on State Route 41.

Trip note: Open from May to October. Elevation 5000 feet. Located on Big Creek, one mile from the south entrance to Yosemite National Park.

Site **10** WAWONA ▲

Campsites, facilities: There are 100 campsites for tents or motorhomes up to 30 feet long. Piped water, fireplaces and picnic tables are provided, and flush toilets are available. A grocery store, propane gas and horseback riding facilities are available nearby.
Reservations, fee: No reservations; $6 fee per night.
Who to contact: Phone Yosemite National Park Headquarters at (209)372-4461.
Location: Drive one mile northwest of Wawona on State Route 41.
Trip note: Open all year. Elevation 4000 feet. Located on the Merced River just inside the south entrance to Yosemite National Park. The Mariposa Grove of Giant Sequoias is nearby.

Site **11** WAWONA
GROUP CAMP ▲

Campsites, facilities: There is one walk-in group campsite here for tents. Picnic tables, fireplaces and piped water are provided, and flush toilets are available. A grocery store and horseback riding facilities are nearby.
Reservations, fee: Call Ticketron at (213)216-6666 for outlet information; $30 fee per night for group.
Who to contact: Phone Yosemite National Park Headquarters at (209)372-4461.
Location: Drive one mile northwest of Wawona on State Route 41.
Trip note: Open from May to September. Elevation 4000 feet. Located on the Merced River just inside the south entrance to Yosemite National Park. The Mariposa Grove of Giant Sequoias is nearby.

Site **12** MERCED RIVER
CAMP AREAS 🌲

Campsites, facilities: There are nine campsites for tents or motorhomes up to 27 feet long. Picnic tables are provided, and vault toilets are available. There is no water, so bring your own.
Reservations, fee: No reservations, no fee.
Who to contact: Phone Bureau of Land Management at (916)985-4474.
Location: Drive 15 miles north of Mariposa off State Route 140 at Briceburg and Bull Creek Road.
Trip note: Open all year. Elevation 1100 feet. Located 19 miles from the entrance to Yosemite National Park.

Site **13** INDIAN
FLAT ▲

Campsites, facilities: There are 17 campsites for tents or motorhomes up to 22

feet long. Piped water, fireplaces and picnic tables are provided, and vault toilets are available. A grocery store is nearby.

Reservations, fee: No reservations; $5 fee per night.
Who to contact: Phone Sierra National Forest Headquarters at (209)487-5155.
Location: Drive four miles southwest of El Portal on State Route 140.
Trip note: Open from June to September. Elevation 1500 feet. Located on the Merced River.

Site **14**   BRIDALVEIL
                                  CREEK

Campsites, facilities: There are 110 campsites for tents or motorhomes up to 30 feet long. Piped water, fireplaces and picnic tables are provided, and flush toilets are available.

Reservations, fee: No reservations; $6 fee per night.
Who to contact: Phone Yosemite National Park Headquarters at (209)372-4461.
Location: Drive eight miles east of Chinquapin of Glacier Point Road.
Trip note: Open from June to September. Elevation 7200 feet. Located on Bridalveil Creek in Yosemite. There are ranger programs in the evenings.

Site **15**   LOWER
                                  PINES

Campsites, facilities: There are 173 campsites for tents or motorhomes up to 30 feet long. Piped water, fireplaces and picnic tables are provided. Flush toilets and a dump station are available. Hot showers, a grocery store, laundromat, propane gas, and horse, raft, bike and cross-country ski rentals are available nearby.

Reservations, fee: Call Ticketron at (213)216-6666 for outlet information; $7 fee per night.
Who to contact: Phone Yosemite National Park Headquarters at (209)372-4461.
Location: Drive one mile east of Yosemite Village.
Trip note: Open all year. Elevation 4000 feet. Located in the Yosemite Valley. Reservations a necessity. Often full.

Site **16**   LOWER
                                  RIVER

Campsites, facilities: There are 139 campsites for tents or motorhomes up to 30 feet long. Piped water, fireplaces and picnic tables are provided. Flush toilets and a dump station are available. Hot showers, a grocery store, laundromat, propane gas, and horse, raft, bike and cross-country ski rentals are available nearby.

Reservations, fee: Call Ticketron at (213)216-6666 for outlet information; $7 fee per night.

Who to contact: Phone Yosemite National Park Headquarters at (209)372-4461.
Location: Drive to southeast end of Yosemite Village.
Trip note: Open from May to October. Elevation 4000 feet. Located in Yosemite Valley. Reservations a must.

Site **17**   NORTH
                               PINES   ▲

Campsites, facilities: There are 86 campsites for tents or motorhomes up to 30 feet long. Piped water, fireplaces and picnic tables are provided, and flush toilets are available. Hot showers, a grocery store, laundromat, a dump station, propane gas, and horse, raft, bike and cross-country ski rentals are available nearby.
Reservations, fee: Call Ticketron at (213)216-6666 for outlet information; $7 fee per night.
Who to contact: Phone Yosemite National Park Headquarters at (209)372-4461.
Location: Drive one mile east of Yosemite Village.
Trip note: Open from May to October. Elevation 4000 feet. Located in Yosemite Valley. Reservations a must.

Site **18**   UPPER
                               PINES   ▲

Campsites, facilities: There are 240 campsites for tents or motorhomes up to 30 feet long. Piped water, fireplaces and picnic tables are provided. Flush toilets and a dump station are available. Hot showers, a grocery store, laundromat, propane gas, and horse, raft, bike and cross-country ski rentals are available nearby.
Reservations, fee: Call Ticketron at (213)216-6666 for outlet information; $7 fee per night.
Who to contact: Phone Yosemite National Park Headquarters at (209)372-4461.
Location: Drive one mile southeast of Yosemite Village.
Trip note: Open from April to November. Elevation 4000 feet. Located in Yosemite Valley.

Site **19**   UPPER
                               RIVER   ▲

Campsites, facilities: There are 124 campsites for tents or motorhomes up to 30 feet long. Piped water, fireplaces and picnic tables are provided, and flush toilets are available. Hot showers, a grocery store, laundromat, propane gas, and horse, raft, bike and cross-country ski rentals are available nearby.
Reservations, fee: Call Ticketron at (213)216-6666 for outlet information; $7 fee per night.
Who to contact: Phone Yosemite National Park Headquarters at (209)372-4461.

Location: Drive southeast of Yosemite Village.

Trip note: Open from May to October. Elevation 4000 feet. Located in Yosemite Valley.

Site **20**   PORCUPINE
                                   FLAT

Campsites, facilities: There are 52 campsites for tents or motorhomes up to 30 feet long. Fireplaces and picnic tables are provided, and pit toilets are available. There is no water, so bring your own.

Reservations, fee: No reservations; $3 fee per night.

Who to contact: Phone Yosemite National Park Headquarters at (209)372-4461.

Location: Drive 16 miles west of Tuolumne Meadows off Tioga Pass Road.

Trip note: Open from June to October. Elevation 8100 feet. Trails from camp lead west to Yosemite Creek or east to Snow Creek.

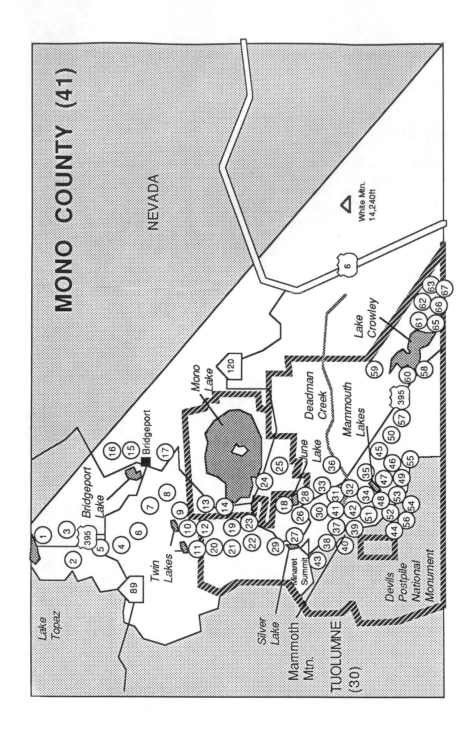

MONO COUNTY (41)

NEVADA

White Mtn.
14,240 ft

6

Lake Crowley

120

Mono Lake

Deadman Creek

Bridgeport

Bridgeport Lake

Mammoth Lakes

395

Lake Topez

89

Twin Lakes

Silver Lake

June Lake

Mammoth Mtn.

Minaret Summit

Devils Postpile National Monument

TUOLUMNE (30)

MONO COUNTY

♦

Site 1 | TOPAZ LAKE TRAILER PARK

Campsites, facilities: There are 50 motorhome spaces. Picnic tables, fireplaces, piped water, electrical connections and sewer hookups are provided. Rest rooms, showers, swimming pool, laundromat and propane gas are available.

Reservations, fee: Call for space available. $12 deposit required; $12 fee per night.

Who to contact: Phone park at (916)495-2357.

Location: Drive five miles north of Topaz on US-395.

Trip note: Open from March to October. Elevation 5000 feet. Located on Lake Topaz, which is used for watersports and fishing. The nearby Topaz Lake Marina offers a boat ramp, boat rentals, tackle rentals, a bait shop and a snack bar.

Site 2 | BOOTLEG

Campsites, facilities: There are 46 campsites for tents or motorhomes up to 22 feet long. Piped water, fireplaces and picnic tables are provided. Vault toilets are available.

Reservations, fee: No reservations; $7 fee per night.

Who to contact: Phone Toiyabe National Forest District Office at (619)932-7070.

Location: Drive 13 miles southeast of Coleville on US-395.

Trip note: Open from May to October. Elevation 6600 feet. The West Walker River is on the other side of US-395.

Site 3 | CHRIS FLAT

Campsites, facilities: There are 15 campsites for tents or motorhomes up to 22 feet long. Piped water, fireplaces and picnic tables are provided, and vault toilets are available.

Reservations, fee: No reservations; $5 fee per night.

Who to contact: Phone Toiyabe National Forest District Office at (619)932-7070.

Location: Drive 15 miles south of Coleville on US-395.
Trip note: Open from May to October. Elevation 6600 feet. This spot is adjacent to the West Walker River.

Site 4   LEAVITT
                          MEADOWS   ▲

Campsites, facilities: There are 16 campsites for tents or motorhomes up to 22 feet long. Piped water, fireplaces and picnic tables are provided. Vault toilets are available. A grocery store is nearby.
Reservations, fee: No reservations; $5 fee per night.
Who to contact: Phone Toiyabe National Forest District Office at (619)932-7070.
Location: Drive 24 miles west of Bridgeport on State Route 108.
Trip note: Open from May to October. Elevation 7000 feet. Campsite is adjacent to the West Walker River. There is a trailhead near camp that serves the upper West Walker drainage, an area which has been recommended as an addition to the Hoover Wilderness.

Site 5   SONORA
                          BRIDGE   ▲

Campsites, facilities: There are 23 campsites for tents or motorhomes up to 30 feet long. Piped water, fireplaces and picnic tables are provided. Vault toilets are available. A grocery store is nearby.
Reservations, fee: No reservations; $5 fee per night.
Who to contact: Phone Toiyabe National Forest District Office at (619)932-7070.
Location: Drive 20 miles southwest of Coleville via US-395 and State Route 108.
Trip note: Open from May to October. Elevation 6600 feet. This site is 1/2 mile from the West Walker River.

Site 6   OBSIDIAN   ▲

Campsites, facilities: There are 14 campsites for tents or motorhomes up to 30 feet long. Fireplaces and picnic tables are provided, and vault toilets are available. There is no piped water, so bring your own.
Reservations, fee: No reservations; $4 fee per night.
Who to contact: Phone Toiyabe National Forest District Office at (619)932-7070.
Location: Drive 21 miles west of Bridgeport via US-395 and turn left on an improved dirt road just before Sonora Junction. Drive four miles to campground.
Trip note: Open from May to October. Elevation 7800 feet. Campsite is adjacent to Molybenite Creek. A trailhead nearby serves the Molybenite Creek drainage and a portion of the Hoover Wilderness.

Site 7 **BUCKEYE**

Campsites, facilities: There are 69 campsites for tents or motorhomes up to 30
feet long. Piped water, fireplaces and picnic tables are provided, and flush
toilets are available. A grocery store and a laundromat are nearby.
Reservations, fee: Reservations accepted; $6 fee per night.
Who to contact: Phone Toiyabe National Forest District Office at (619)932-7070.
Location: Drive 14 west of Bridgeport off US-395 on an improved dirt road.
Trip note: Open from May to October. Elevation 7000 feet. Located near Buckeye Creek, four miles from Twin Lakes. Buckeye Hot Springs, an undeve-
loped hot springs, is two miles from camp. There is a trailhead near camp
that accesses the Hoover Wilderness through Buckeye Canyon.

Site 8 **HONEYMOON
FLAT**

Campsites, facilities: There are 47 campsites for tents or motorhomes up to 22
feet long. Piped water, fireplaces and picnic tables are provided, and vault
toilets are available. A grocery store and a laundromat are nearby.
Reservations, fee: No reservations; $5 fee per night.
Who to contact: Phone Toiyabe National Forest District Office at (619)932-7070.
Location: Drive eight miles southwest of Bridgeport on Twin Lakes Road.
Trip note: Open from May to October. Elevation 7000 feet. Campsite is adjacent
to Robinson Creek within three miles of Twin Lakes.

Site 9 **LOWER
TWIN LAKE**

Campsites, facilities: There are 17 campsites for tents or motorhomes up to 22
feet long. Piped water, fireplaces and picnic tables are provided, and vault
toilets are available. A grocery store and a laundromat are nearby.
Reservations, fee: No reservations; $5 fee per night.
Who to contact: Phone Toiyabe National Forest District Office at (619)932-7070.
Location: Drive 11 miles southwest of Brigeport on Twin Lakes Road.
Trip note: Open from May to October. Elevation 7000 feet. Located near Robinson Creek and the Twin Lakes. There are boat ramps at each of the lakes.
Motorboats are allowed if they stay within the speed limit. There is a major
trailhead at Mono Village that serves the Hoover Wilderness and accesses
the northern portion of Yosemite National Park. Lower Twin Lake holds
the state record for largest brown trout caught in California at 26 lbs., 5 oz.

Site 10   PAHA   ▲

Campsites, facilities: There are 22 campsites for tents or motorhomes up to 22
   feet long. Piped water, fireplaces and picnic tables are provided, and vault
   toilets are available. A grocery store and a laundromat are available nearby.
Reservations, fee: No reservations; $7 fee per night.
Who to contact: Phone Toiyabe National Forest District Office at (619)932-7070.
Location: Drive 10 miles southwest of Bridgeport on Twin Lakes Road.
Trip note: Open from May to October. Elevation 7000 feet. Located near Robinson Creek and the Twin Lakes. There are boat ramps at each of the lakes.
   Motorboats are allowed if they stay within the speed limit. There is a major
   trailhead at Mono Village that serves the Hoover Wilderness and accesses
   the northern portion of Yosemite National Park.

Site 11   ROBINSON   ▲
                                CREEK

Campsites, facilities: There are 54 campsites for tents or motorhomes up to 30
   feet long. Piped water, fireplaces and picnic tables are provided. Vault toilets are available. A grocery store and a laundromat are nearby.
Reservations, fee: No reservations; $7 fee per night.
Who to contact: Phone Toiyabe National Forest District Office at (619)932-7070.
Location: Drive 10 miles southwest of Bridgeport on Twin Lakes Road.
Trip note: Open from May to October. Elevation 7000 feet. Located near Robinson Creek and the Twin Lakes. Boat ramps are provided at each of the
   lakes. Motorboats are allowed if they stay within the speed limit. There is a
   major trailhead at Mono Village that serves the Hoover Wilderness and accesses the northern portion of Yosemite National Park.

Site 12   SAWMILL   ▲

Campsites, facilities: There are eight campsites for tents or motorhomes up to 22
   feet long. Piped water, fireplaces and picnic tables are provided, and vault
   toilets are available. A grocery store and a laundromat are nearby.
Reservations, fee: No reservations; $5 fee per night.
Who to contact: Phone Toiyabe National Forest District Office at (619)932-7070.
Location: Drive 11 miles southwest of Bridgeport on Twin Lakes Road.
Trip note: Open from May to October. Elevation 7000 feet. Located near Robinson Creek and the Twin Lakes. There are boat ramps at each of the lakes
   and motorboats are allowed within the speed limit. There is a major trailhead at Mono Village that serves the Hoover Wilderness and accesses the
   northern portion of Yosemite National Park.

| Site **13** | GREEN CREEK | ▲ |

Campsites, facilities: There are 11 campsites for tents or motorhomes up to 22 feet long. Piped water, fireplaces and picnic tables are provided, and vault toilets are available.

Reservations, fee: No reservations; $4 fee per night.

Who to contact: Phone Toiyabe National Forest District Office at (619)932-7070.

Location: Drive 13 miles southwest of Bridgeport off US-395 on Green Lakes Road.

Trip note: Open from May to October. Elevation 7500 feet. This spot is adjacent to Green Creek. A trailhead near camp accesses the Hoover Wilderness and the northern portion of Yosemite National Park.

| Site **14** | TRUMBULL LAKE | ▲ |

Campsites, facilities: There are 45 campsites for tents or motorhomes up to 22 feet long. Piped water, fireplaces and picnic tables are provided. Vault toilets and horseback riding facilities are available. A grocery store is nearby.

Reservations, fee: No reservations; $5 fee per night.

Who to contact: Phone Toiyabe National Forest District Office at (619)932-7070.

Location: Drive 20 miles south of Bridgeport off US-395 on Virginia Lakes Road.

Trip note: Open from June to October. Elevation 9500 feet. Campsite is adjacent to Trumball Lake. There are many other lakes in the vicinity accessible by foot or auto. The Virginia Lakes Resort is down the road and offers cabins, boat rentals and a restaurant.

| Site **15** | FALLING ROCK MARINA RV PARK | |

Campsites, facilities: There are 42 sites for tents or motorhomes. Picnic tables and fireplaces are provided at all sites, and piped water, electrical connections and sewer hookups are provided at some of them. Rest rooms, showers, laundromat, dump station, boat ramp, berths, boat rentals, bait, tackle, snack bar and propane gas are available.

Reservations, fee: No reservations; $9 fee per night.

Who to contact: Phone park at (619)932-7001.

Location: Drive two miles north of Bridgeport on State Route 182.

Trip note: Open from May to October. Elevation 6500 feet. Located on the shore of Lake Bridgeport, which offers waterskiing and sailing, and 23 miles of shoreline.

Site **16**   PARADISE SHORES
                                TRAILER PARK

Campsites, facilities: There are 10 tent sites and 36 motorhome spaces. Picnic tables, and in most cases piped water, electrical connections and sewer hookups are provided. Rest rooms, showers, dump station and propane gas are available.
Reservations, fee: No reservations; $9 fee per night.
Who to contact: Phone park at (619)932-7735.
Location: Drive two miles north of Bridgeport on State Route 182.
Trip note: Open from from April to October. Elevation 6500 feet. Located on Lake Bridgeport, which offers waterskiing and sailing, and 23 miles of shoreline. A boat ramp, berths and boat rentals are available at the nearby marina.

Site **17**   WILLOW SPRINGS
                                TRAILER PARK

Campsites, facilities: There are 20 motorhome spaces. Picnic tables, piped water, electrical connections and sewer hookups are provided. Rest rooms, showers, laundromat, store, dump station and propane gas are available.
Reservations, fee: Call for space available. $10 deposit required; $10 fee per night.
Who to contact: Phone park at (619)932-7725.
Location: Drive five miles south of Bridgeport on US-395.
Trip note: Open from May to October. Elevation 6800 feet. Located near Virginia Creek.

Site **18**   MILL
                                CREEK

Campsites, facilities: There are 100 campsites for tents or motorhomes up to 25 feet long. Vault toilets are available. There is no water, so bring your own.
Reservations, fee: No reservations; $2 fee per night.
Who to contact: Phone County Parks Department at (619)932-7415.
Location: Drive 10 miles northwest of Lee Vining off US-395 on Lundy Lake Road.
Trip note: Open from May to October. Elevation 8000 feet. Located on Mill Creek near Lundy Lake.

Site **19**   SADDLEBAG
                                LAKE

Campsites, facilities: There are 22 campsites for tents or motorhomes up to 22

feet long. Piped water, fireplaces and picnic tables are provided. Flush toilets and a boat launch are available. A grocery store is nearby.

Reservations, fee: No reservations; $5 fee per night.

Who to contact: Phone Inyo National Forest Headquarters at (619)873-5841.

Location: Drive 12 miles west of Lee Vining off State Route 120 on Saddlebag Lake Road.

Trip note: Open from June to October. Elevation 10,000 feet. This spot is on Saddlebag Lake and adjacent to Lee Vining Creek. A trailhead near camp accesses numerous lakes in the Hoover Wilderness.

Site **20**   JUNCTION   ▲

Campsites, facilities: There are 10 campsites for tents or motorhomes up to 22 feet long. Fireplaces and picnic tables are provided, and vault toilets are available. There is no water, so bring your own. A grocery store is nearby.

Reservations, fee: No reservations, no fee.

Who to contact: Phone Inyo National Forest Headquarters at (619)873-5841.

Location: Drive 10 miles southwest of Lee Vining on State Route 120.

Trip note: Open from June to October. Elevation 9600 feet. Campsite is located near Ellery and Tioga Lakes. The Tioga Tarns Nature Trail is adjacent to camp and the Hall Natural Area is nearby.

Site **21**   TIOGA
                                     LAKE   ▲

Campsites, facilities: There are 13 tent sites. Piped water, picnic tables and fireplaces are provided. Flush toilets are available. A grocery store is nearby.

Reservations, fee: No reservations; $5 fee per night.

Who to contact: Phone Inyo National Forest Headquarters at (619)873-5841.

Location: Drive 11 miles southwest of Lee Vining on State Route 120.

Trip note: Open from June to October. Elevation 9700 feet. Campsite is located on Tioga Lake. The Tioga Tarns Nature trail is adjacent to camp and the Hall Natural Area is nearby.

Site **22**   ELLERY
                                     LAKE   ▲

Campsites, facilities: There are three tent sites and 10 campsites for tents or motorhomes up to 22 feet long. Piped water, fireplaces and picnic tables are provided, and flush toilets are available. A grocery store and propane gas are nearby.

Reservations, fee: No reservations; $5 fee per night.

Who to contact: Phone Inyo National Forest Headquarters at (619)873-5841.

Location: Drive nine miles southwest of Lee Vining on State Route 120.

Trip note: Open from June to October. Elevation 9500 feet. Located on Ellery Lake, a short distance from Tioga Lake, and the Tioga Tarns Nature Trail. Saddlebag Lake is two miles from camp.

Site **23**   BIG
                                 BEND   ▲

Campsites, facilities: There are 18 campsites for tents or motorhomes up to 22 feet long. Piped water, fireplaces and picnic tables are provided, and flush toilets are available. A grocery store and propane gas are nearby.
Reservations, fee: No reservations; $5 fee per night.
Who to contact: Phone Inyo National Forest Headquarters at (619)873-5841.
Location: Drive seven miles west of Lee Vining on State Route 120.
Trip note: Open from May to October. Elevation 7800 feet. Located on Lee Vining Creek.

Site **24**   ASPEN
                                 GROVE   ▲

Campsites, facilities: There are 50 campsites for tents or motorhomes up to 20 feet long. Pit toilets are available.
Reservations, fee: No reservations; $2 fee per night.
Who to contact: Phone County Parks Department at (619)932-7415.
Location: Drive six miles west of Lee Vining on State Route 120.
Trip note: Open from May to October. Elevation 8000 feet. Located near Lee Vining Creek.

Site **25**   LEE VINING
                                 CREEK   ▲

Campsites, facilities: There are 50 campsites for tents or motorhomes up to 24 feet long. Pit toilets are available. There is no piped water, so bring your own. A grocery store, laundromat and propane gas are nearby.
Reservations, fee: No reservations; $2 fee per night.
Who to contact: Phone County Parks Department at (619)932-7415.
Location: Drive one mile south of Lee Vining off State Route 120.
Trip note: Open from April to October. Elevation 8000 feet. Located near the Mono Lake Scenic Area.

Site **26**   JUNE
                                 LAKE   ▲

Campsites, facilities: There are 22 campsites for tents or motorhomes up to 22 feet long. Piped water, fireplaces and picnic tables are provided. Flush toilets and a boat ramp are available. A grocery store, a laundromat, boat and tackle rentals, moorings and propane gas are available nearby.

Reservations, fee: No reservations; $6 fee per night.

Who to contact: Phone Inyo National Forest Headquarters at (619)873-5841.

Location: Drive 11 miles south of Lee Vining on US-395 to June Lake Junction, then take State Route 158 two miles southwest to June Lake.

Trip note: Open from May to November. Elevation 7600 feet. Located on June Lake, which is used for fishing and swimming. Good hiking nearby. Inyo Forest map details trails and area streams.

Site **27**   OH
RIDGE   ▲

Campsites, facilities: There are 148 campsites for tents or motorhomes up to 32 feet long. Piped water, fireplaces and picnic tables are provided. Flush toilets and a playground are available. A grocery store, laundromat, boat ramp, boat and tackle rentals, mooring and propane gas are available nearby.

Reservations, fee: No reservations; $6 fee per night.

Who to contact: Phone Inyo National Forest Headquarters at (619)873-5841.

Location: Drive 11 miles south of Lee Vining on US-395 to June Lake Junction, then take State Route 158 two miles to June Lake, then one mile north on Oh Ridge Road.

Trip note: Open from May to October. Elevation 7600 feet. Located on June Lake, which is used for fishing and swimming.

Site **28**   PINE CLIFF
TRAILER PARK   ▲

Campsites, facilities: There are 20 tent sites, 25 tent or motorhome sites and 154 motorhome spaces. Fireplaces, picnic tables, piped water, electrical connections and sewer hookups are provided at most sites. Rest rooms, showers, laundromat, store, dump station and propane gas are available. A boat ramp, boat and tackle rentals and fuel are available nearby.

Reservations, fee: Phone Leisuretime Reservation Systems at (800)822-CAMP. $15 deposit; $15 camp use fee.

Who to contact: Phone park at (619)648-7558.

Location: Drive two miles north of June Lake off State Route 158 on Oh Ridge Road.

Trip note: Open all year. Elevation 7800 feet. Located on June Lake, which is used for fishing and swimming.

Site **29**   SILVER
LAKE   ▲

Campsites, facilities: There are 65 campsites for tents or motorhomes up to 22 feet long. Piped water, fireplaces and picnic tables are provided, and flush toilets and horseback riding facilities are available. A grocery store, laundromat, motorboat rentals, boat ramp, bait, snack bar, boat fuel and propane gas are available nearby.

Reservations, fee: No reservations; $6 fee per night.

Who to contact: Phone Inyo National Forest Headquarters at (619)873-5841.

Location: Drive four miles west of June Lake on State Route 158.

Trip note: Open from May to October. Elevation 7200 feet. Campground is adjacent to Alger Creek on Silver Lake, where you can fish, waterski and swim. A trailhead near camp accesses numerous lakes in the Ansel Adams Wilderness and intersects with the Pacific Crest Trail.

Site **30**   GULL
                       LAKE   ▲

Campsites, facilities: There are 12 campsites for tents or motorhomes up to 22 feet long. Piped water, fireplaces and picnic tables are provided, and flush toilets are available. A grocery store, laundromat, boat ramp and propane gas are available nearby.

Reservations, fee: No reservations; $6 fee per night.

Who to contact: Phone Inyo National Forest Headquarters at (619)873-5841.

Location: Drive one mile southwest of June Lake on State Route 158.

Trip note: Open from May to November. Elevation 7600 feet. Located on Gull Lake, where you can fish and swim.

Site **31**   REVERSED
                       CREEK   ▲

Campsites, facilities: There are 17 campsites for tents or motorhomes up to 22 feet long. Piped water, fireplaces and picnic tables are provided, and flush toilets are available. A grocery store, laundromat, boat ramp and propane gas are nearby.

Reservations, fee: No reservations; $6 fee per night.

Who to contact: Phone Inyo National Forest Headquarters at (619)873-5841.

Location: Drive one mile southwest of June Lake on State Route 158.

Trip note: Open from May to October. Elevation 7600 feet. Located on Reversed Creek near Gull Lake. A trail near camp leads up to Reversed Peak (three miles) or cross country to Silver Lake (two miles).

Site **32**   HARTLEY
                       SPRINGS   ▲

Campsites, facilities: There are 20 campsites for tents or motorhomes up to 22 feet long. Fireplaces and picnic tables are provided, and vault toilets are available. There is no water, so bring your own. A grocery store is nearby.

Reservations, fee: No reservations, no fee.

Who to contact: Phone Inyo National Forest Headquarters at (619)873-5841.

Location: Drive two miles south of June Lake Junction on State Route 158, turn right on an improved dirt road and drive one and a half miles to camp.

Trip note: Open from June to October. Elevation 8400 feet. Located near Harley Springs in a primitive setting. Obsidian Dome is one and a half miles from camp on the dirt road.

Site **33**   DEADMAN   🌲

Campsites, facilities: There are 30 campsites for tents or motorhomes up to 22 feet long. Fireplaces and picnic tables are provided, and vault toilets are available. There is no water, so bring your own.

Reservations, fee: No reservations, no fee.

Who to contact: Phone Inyo National Forest Headquarters at (619)873-5841.

Location: Drive 12 miles southeast of June Lake off US-395.

Trip note: Open from June to October. Elevation 7800 feet. Located on Deadman Creek.

Site **34**   DEADMAN
                              GROUP CAMP   🌲

Campsites, facilities: There are four campsites for tents or motorhomes up to 22 feet long. Picnic tables are provided, and vault toilets are available. There is no water, so bring your own.

Reservations, fee: Reservations requested; $10 per night group fee.

Who to contact: Phone Inyo National Forest Headquarters at (619)873-5841.

Location: Drive 12 miles southeast of June Lake off US-395.

Trip note: Open from June to September. Elevation 7800 feet. Located on Deadman Creek.

Site **35**   GLASS
                              CREEK   ⛺

Campsites, facilities: There are 50 campsites for tents or motorhomes up to 22 feet long. Fireplaces and picnic tables are provided, and vault toilets are available. There is no water, so bring your own.

Reservations, fee: No reservations, no fee.

Who to contact: Phone Inyo National Forest Headquarters at (619)873-5841.

Location: Drive nine miles southeast of June Lake off US-395.

Trip note: Open from May to November. Elevation 7600 feet. This spot is located on Glass Creek. A trail leads from camp up Glass Creek, past Glass Creek Meadow to the foot of San Joaquin Mountain.

Site **36**   BIG
                                  SPRINGS   🌲

Campsites, facilities: There are 24 campsites for tents or motorhomes up to 22
    feet long. Fireplaces and picnic tables are provided, and vault toilets are
    available. There is no water, so bring your own.
Reservations, fee: No reservations, no fee.
Who to contact: Phone Inyo National Forest Headquarters at (619)873-5841.
Location: Drive 12 miles southeast of June Lake via US-395 and Owens River
    Road.
Trip note: Open from June to October. Elevation 7300 feet. Located on Dead-
    man Creek.

Site **37**   AGNEW
                                  MEADOWS   ◬

Campsites, facilities: There are 22 campsites for tents or motorhomes up to 22
    feet long. Piped water, fireplaces and picnic tables are provided. Flush toi-
    lets and horseback riding facilities are available. A grocery store is nearby.
Reservations, fee: No reservations; $4 fee per night.
Who to contact: Phone Inyo National Forest Headquarters at (619)873-5841.
Location: Drive 10 miles northwest of Mammoth Lakes off State Route 203-
    Minaret Summit Road.
Trip note: Open from June to October. Elevation 8400 feet. The Pacific Crest
    National Scenic Trail passes by camp, and a trailhead that accesses numer-
    ous lakes in the Ansel Adams Wilderness is nearby.

Site **38**   AGNEW MEADOWS
                               GROUP CAMP   ◬

Campsites, facilities: There are nine group campsites for tents or motorhomes up
    to 22 feet long. Piped water and picnic tables are provided, and flush toilets
    and horseback riding facilities are available. A grocery store is nearby.
Reservations, fee: No reservations; $30 fee per night per group.
Who to contact: Phone Inyo National Forest Headquarters at (619)873-5841.
Location: Drive 10 miles northwest of Mammoth Lakes off State Route 203-
    Minaret Summit Road.
Trip note: Open from June to October. Elevation 8400 feet. The Pacific Crest
    National Scenic Trail passes by camp, and a trailhead that accesses numer-
    ous lakes in the Ansel Adams Wilderness is nearby.

Site **39**   MINARET
                                   FALLS   ◬

Campsites, facilities: There are 27 campsites for tents or motorhomes up to 22

feet long. Piped water, fireplaces and picnic tables are provided, and flush toilets and horseback riding facilities are available. A grocery store is nearby.

Reservations, fee: No reservations; $4 fee per night.

Who to contact: Phone Inyo National Forest Headquarters at (619)873-5841.

Location: Drive 12 miles west of Mammoth Lakes off State Route 203-Minaret Summit Road.

Trip note: Open from June to October. Elevation 7600 feet. Located on the San Joaquin River near Minaret Creek. The Pacific Crest National Scenic Trail passes by camp. Nearby is a trailhead that accesses numerous lakes in the Ansel Adams Wilderness and Devil's Postpile National Monument. Devil's Postpile is less than a mile from camp.

Site **40** PUMICE FLAT ▲

Campsites, facilities: There are 17 campsites for tents or motorhomes up to 22 feet long. Piped water, fireplaces and picnic tables are provided, and flush toilets and horseback riding facilities are available. A grocery store is nearby.

Reservations, fee: No reservations; $4 fee per night.

Who to contact: Phone Inyo National Forest Headquarters at (619)873-5841.

Location: Drive 12 miles west of Mammoth Lakes off State Route 203-Minaret Summit Road.

Trip note: Open from June to October. Elevation 7700 feet. Located on the San Joaquin River. The Pacific Crest National Scenic Trail passes by camp, and a trailhead that accesses numerous lakes in the Ansel Adams Wilderness is two miles south at Devil's Postpile National Monument.

Site **41** PUMICE FLAT GROUP CAMP ▲

Campsites, facilities: There are nine group campsites for tents or motorhomes up to 22 feet long. Piped water, fireplaces and picnic tables are provided, and flush toilets and horseback riding facilities are available. A grocery store is nearby.

Reservations, fee: No reservations; $30 fee per night per group.

Who to contact: Phone Inyo National Forest Headquarters at (619)873-5841.

Location: Drive 12 miles west of Mammoth Lakes off State Route 203-Minaret Summit Road.

Trip note: Open from June to October. Elevation 7700 feet. Located on the San Joaquin River a mile from Devil's Postpile National Monument. The Pacific Crest National Scenic Trail passes near camp, and a short trail to Scotcher Lake leaves from camp. Trails which access numerous lakes in the Ansel Adams Wilderness are several miles from camp.

Site **42**   RED'S
                                    MEADOW   ◭

Campsites, facilities: There are 54 campsites for tents or motorhomes up to 22
    feet long. Piped water, fireplaces and picnic tables are provided, and flush
    toilets, showers and horseback riding facilities are available. A grocery store
    is nearby.
Reservations, fee: No reservations; $4 fee per night.
Who to contact: Phone Inyo National Forest Headquarters at (619)873-5841.
Location: Drive 14 miles southwest of Mammoth Lakes off State Route 203-
    Minaret Summit Road.
Trip note: Open from June to October. Elevation 7600 feet. Scotcher Lake, Reds
    Meadow Hot Springs and the Pacific Crest National Scenic Trail are near-
    by. Horse rentals and fishing on the upper San Joaquin River make this a
    choice spot.

Site **43**   UPPER
                                     SODA   ◭

Campsites, facilities: There are 28 campsites for tents or motorhomes up to 22
    feet long. Piped water, fireplaces and picnic tables are provided, and flush
    toilets and horseback riding facilities are available. A grocery store is
    nearby.
Reservations, fee: No reservations; $4 fee per night.
Who to contact: Phone Inyo National Forest Headquarters at (619)873-5841.
Location: Drive 11 miles west of Mammoth Lakes off State Route 203-Minaret
    Summit Road.
Trip note: Open from June to October. Elevation 7700 feet. Located on the San
    Joaquin River. The Pacific Crest National Scenic Trail passes by camp, and
    trailheads that access numerous lakes in the Ansel Adams Wilderness are
    about three miles from camp. Devil's Postpile National Monument is three
    miles to the south.

Site **44**   DEVIL'S POSTPILE
                              NATIONAL MONUMENT   ◭

Campsites, facilities: There are 26 campsites for tents or motorhomes. Piped wa-
    ter, fireplaces and picnic tables are provided. Flush toilets are available.
Reservations, fee: No reservations; $5 fee per night.
Who to contact: Phone National Park Service at (619)934-2289.
Location: Drive 13 miles west of Mammoth Lakes via State Route 203.
Trip note: Open from June to October. Elevation 7600 feet. The Pacific Crest
    National Scenic Trail passes by camp, and a trailhead that accesses numer-
    ous lakes in the Ansel Adams Wilderness is nearby.

Site **45**   NEW
                     SHADY REST   ▲

Campsites, facilities: There are 96 campsites for tents or motorhomes up to 22
  feet long. Piped water, fireplaces and picnic tables are provided. Flush toi-
  lets, dump station, playground and horseback riding facilities are available.
  A grocery store, a laundromat and propane gas are nearby.
Reservations, fee: No reservations; $6 fee per night.
Who to contact: Phone Inyo National Forest Headquarters at (619)873-5841.
Location: Drive 1/2 mile east of Mammoth Lakes off State Route 203.
Trip note: Open from May to October. Elevation 7800 feet. Located near the
  Mammoth Visitor Center.

Site **46**   OLD
                     SHADY REST   ▲

Campsites, facilities: There are 51 campsites for tents or motorhomes up to 22
  feet long. Piped water, fireplaces and picnic tables are provided. Flush toi-
  lets, dump station, playground and horseback riding facilities are available.
  A grocery store, a laundromat and propane gas are nearby.
Reservations, fee: No reservations; $6 fee per night.
Who to contact: Phone Inyo National Forest Headquarters at (619)873-5841.
Location: Drive 1/2 mile east of Mammoth Lakes off State Route 203.
Trip note: Open from June to September. Elevation 7800 feet. Located near the
  Mammoth Visitor Center.

Site **47**   PINE
                     GLEN   ▲

Campsites, facilities: There are 21 campsites for tents or motorhomes up to 22
  feet long. Piped water, fireplaces and picnic tables are provided. Flush toi-
  lets, dump station, playground and horseback riding facilities are available.
  A grocery store, a laundromat and propane gas are nearby.
Reservations, fee: No reservations; $6 fee per night.
Who to contact: Phone Inyo National Forest Headquarters at (619)873-5841.
Location: Drive 1/2 mile east of Mammoth Lakes off State Route 203.
Trip note: Open from June to September. Elevaton 7800 feet. Located near the
  Mammoth Visitor Center.

Site **48**   CAMP
                     HIGH SIERRA   ▲

Campsites, facilities: There are eight tent sites, 10 motorhome spaces and 18 sites
  for tents or motorhomes. Picnic tables, fireplaces, piped water and in some

cases electrical connections are provided. Flush toilets, showers, a playground and horseback riding facilities are available. A grocery store, a laundromat and propane gas are nearby.

Reservations, fee: Call for space available. $14 deposit required; $7 fee per night.
Who to contact: Phone camp at (619)934-2368.
Location: Drive two miles southwest of Mammoth Lakes off State Route 203.
Trip note: Open from June to September. Elevation 8400 feet. Located two miles by auto from Twin Lakes.

Site **49**　　MAMMOTH MOUNTAIN
RV PARK

Campsites, facilities: There are 10 tent sites and 80 sites for motorhomes. Piped water and electricity are provided at the motorhome sites. Rest rooms, hot showers, a dump station and a laundromat are available. A grocery store and propane gas are nearby.

Reservations, fee: Phone Leisuretime Reservation Systems at (800)822-CAMP.
Who to contact: Phone park at (619)934-3822.
Location: Drive two miles west of US-395 on State Route 203.
Trip note: This park is open all year and is across the street from the Forest Service Visitors Center, near Mammoth Creek.

Site **50**　　SHERWIN
CREEK

Campsites, facilities: There are 27 campsites for tents or motorhomes up to 22 feet long. Piped water, fireplaces and picnic tables are provided, and flush toilets and horseback riding facilities are available. A grocery store, a laundromat and propane gas are nearby.

Reservations, fee: No reservations; $4 fee per night.
Who to contact: Phone Inyo National Forest Headquarters at (619)873-5841.
Location: Drive three miles southeast of Mammoth Lakes off State Route 203 on Sherwin Lake Road.
Trip note: Open from May to October. Elevation 7600 feet. Located on Sherwin Creek. Trailheads that access Sherwin Lakes, Lost Lake and Valentine Lake in the John Muir Wilderness are a mile from camp.

Site **51**　　COLDWATER

Campsites, facilities: There are 79 campsites for tents or motorhomes up to 22 feet long. Piped water, fireplaces and picnic tables are provided. Flush toilets and horseback riding facilities are available. A grocery store is nearby.

Reservations, fee: No reservations; $6 fee per night.
Who to contact: Phone Inyo National Forest Headquarters at (619)873-5841.

Location: Drive five miles southwest of Mammoth Lakes via Lake Mary Road.

Trip note: Open from June to October. Elevation 8900 feet. Located on Cold Water Creek near Lake Mary. A trailhead adjacent to camp accesses John Muir Wilderness, the Pacific Crest Trail and several lakes.

Site **52** HORSESHOE LAKE GROUP CAMP

Campsites, facilities: There are 13 campsites for tents or motorhomes up to 22 feet long. Piped water, fireplaces and picnic tables are provided. Flush toilets are available. A grocery store is nearby.

Reservations, fee: Reservations requested; $30 per night group fee.

Who to contact: Phone Inyo National Forest Headquarters at (619)873-5841.

Location: Drive seven miles southwest of Mammoth Lakes off Lake Mary Road.

Trip note: Open from June to September. Elevation 8900 feet. Located on Horseshoe Lake. A trailhead near camp accesses the Pacific Crest Trail, John Muir Wilderness and Devil's Postpile National Monument.

Site **53** LAKE GEORGE

Campsites, facilities: There are 22 campsites for tents or motorhomes up to 16 feet long. Piped water, fireplaces and picnic tables are provided. Flush toilets and horseback riding facilities are available. Groceries and propane gas are nearby.

Reservations, fee: No reservations; $6 fee per night.

Who to contact: Phone Inyo National Forest Headquarters at (619)873-5841.

Location: Drive five miles southwest of Mammoth Lake off Lake Mary Road.

Trip note: Open from June to October. Elevation 9000 feet. Located on the shore of Lake George and near several other lakes. A trail near camp accesses Mammoth Crest.

Site **54** LAKE MARY

Campsites, facilities: There are 51 campsites for tents or motorhomes up to 22 feet long. Piped water, fireplaces and picnic tables are provided. Flush toilets and horseback riding facilities are available. A grocery store, a laundromat and propane gas are nearby.

Reservations, fee: No reservations; $6 fee per night.

Who to contact: Phone Inyo National Forest Headquarters at (619)873-5841.

Location: Drive four miles southwest of Mammoth Lake off Lake Mary Road.

Trip note: Open from June to October. Elevation 8900 feet. Located on the shore of Lake Mary. A trailhead near camp accesses the Pacific Crest Trail, the John Muir Wilderness and several other lakes.

Site 55   PINE CITY   ▲

Campsites, facilities: There are 12 campsites for tents or motorhomes up to 22 feet long. Piped water, fireplaces and picnic tables are provided. Flush toilets and horseback riding facilities are available. A grocery store, a laundromat and propane gas are available nearby.
Reservations, fee: No reservations; $6 fee per night.
Who to contact: Phone Inyo National Forest Headquarters at (619)873-5841.
Location: Drive four miles southwest of Mammoth Lake off Lake Mary Road.
Trip note: Open from June to October. Elevation 8900 feet. This spot is adjacent to Twin Lakes and near several others.

Site 56   TWIN LAKES   ▲

Campsites, facilities: There are 23 tent sites and 74 sites for tents or motorhomes up to 22 feet long. Picnic tables, fireplaces and piped water are provided, and flush toilets and horseback riding facilities are available. A grocery store, a laundromat and propane gas are nearby.
Reservations, fee: No reservations; $4 fee per night.
Who to contact: Phone Inyo National Forest Headquarters at (619)873-5841.
Location: Drive three miles southwest of Mammoth Lake off Lake Mary Road.
Trip note: Open from June to October. Elevation 8700 feet. Campsite is adjacent to Twin Lakes and near several others.

Site 57   CONVICT LAKE   ▲

Campsites, facilities: There are 88 campsites for tents or motorhomes up to 22 feet long. Piped water, fireplaces and picnic tables are provided. Flush toilets, dump station, boat ramp and horseback riding facilities are available. A grocery store is nearby.
Reservations, fee: No reservations; $6 fee per night.
Who to contact: Phone Inyo National Forest Headquarters at (619)873-5841.
Location: Drive 11 miles southeast of Mammoth Lakes via US-395 and Convict Lake Road.
Trip note: Open from April to October. Elevation 7600 feet. Located near Convict Lake. A trailhead near camp accesses several lakes in the John Muir Wilderness.

Site 58   MC GEE CREEK   ▲

Campsites, facilities: There are 34 campsites for tents or motorhomes up to 22

feet long. Piped water, fireplaces and picnic tables are provided, and flush toilets are available. A grocery store is nearby.

Reservations, fee: No reservations, no fee.

Who to contact: Phone Inyo National Forest Headquarters at (619)873-5841.

Location: Drive 10 miles southeast of Mammoth Lakes via State Route 203 and McGee Creek Road.

Trip note: This camp is open from June to October. Elevation 7600 feet.

Site **59**   BENTON CROSSING

Campsites, facilities: There is an area for tent campers. Pit toilets are available. There is no water, so bring your own.

Reservations, fee: No reservations, no fee.

Who to contact: Phone County Parks Department at (619)932-7415.

Location: Drive 11 miles east of Mammoth Lakes off US-395 on Benton Crossing Road.

Trip note: This county park is open from April to October. Elevation 7000 feet. Located near the north shore of Lake Crowley.

Site **60**   MC GEE CREEK RV PARK

Campsites, facilities: There are 30 campsites for tents or motorhomes, with partial or full hookups. Piped water, fireplaces and picnic tables are provided. Flush toilets and hot showers are available.

Reservations, fee: Call ahead for space available and fee.

Who to contact: Phone park at (619)935-4233.

Location: Drive nine miles south of Mammoth Lakes on US-395 at McGee Creek.

Trip note: Open from April to October. Elevation 7000 feet. Located near Crowley Lake where fishing, jet skiing and waterskiing can be enjoyed. Bodie Ghost Town, Devil's Postpile National Monument, Mono Lake State Reserve and many lakes and streams are nearby.

Site **61**   FRENCH CAMP

Campsites, facilities: There are six tent sites and 80 sites for tents or motorhomes up to 22 feet long. Picnic tables, fireplaces and piped water are provided, and flush toilets are available. Groceries and propane gas are nearby.

Reservations, fee: No reservations; $6 fee per night.

Who to contact: Phone Inyo National Forest Headquarters at (619)873-5841.

Location: Drive 16 miles southeast of Mammoth Lakes on US-395 to Tom's Place, then go south on Rock Creek Road for 1/4 mile.

Trip note: Open from April to October. Elevation 7500 feet. Located on Rock Creek.

Site **62**   HOLIDAY   ▲

Campsites, facilities: There are 33 campsites for tents or motorhomes up to 22 feet long. Piped water, fireplaces and picnic tables are provided, and vault toilets are available. Groceries and propane gas are nearby.
Reservations, fee: No reservations; $4 fee per night.
Who to contact: Phone Inyo National Forest Headquarters at (619)873-5841.
Location: Drive 16 miles southeast of Mammoth Lakes on US-395 to Tom's Place, then go south on Rock Creek Road for 1/2 mile.
Trip note: Open from April to November. Elevation 7500 feet. Located near Rock Creek. Enjoy fishing, jetskiing or waterskiing on nearby Lake Crowley.

Site **63**   TUFF   ▲

Campsites, facilities: There are 15 tent sites and 19 sites for tents or motorhomes up to 22 feet long. Picnic tables, fireplaces and piped water are provided, and flush toilets are available. Groceries and propane gas are nearby.
Reservations, fee: No reservations; $5 fee per night.
Who to contact: Phone Inyo National Forest Headquarters at (619)873-5841.
Location: Drive 17 miles southeast of Mammoth Lakes on US-395 just past Tom's Place.
Trip note: Open from April to November. Elevation 7000 feet. Located near Rock Creek. Enjoy fishing, waterskiing or jetskiing on nearby Lake Crowley.

Site **64**   CROWLEY
                                      LAKE   ▲

Campsites, facilities: There are 37 campsites for tents or motorhomes. Piped water, fireplaces and picnic tables are provided, and pit toilets are available. A grocery store, pack station and boat ramp are nearby.
Reservations, fee: No reservations; $4 fee per night.
Who to contact: Phone campground at (619)872-4881.
Location: Drive six miles northwest of Tom's Place off US-395.
Trip note: Open from May to October. Elevation 7000 feet. Located near the south shore of Crowley Lake. Enjoy fishing, jet skiing and waterskiing, or visit Bodie Ghost Town, Devil's Postpile National Monument or Mono Lake.

Site 65
ASPEN
GROUP CAMP

Campsites, facilities: There are five campsites for tents or motorhomes up to 16 feet long. Piped water, fireplaces and picnic tables are provided, and flush toilets are available. Groceries and propane gas are nearby.

Reservations, fee: Reservations requested; $30 per night group fee.

Who to contact: Phone Inyo National Forest Headquarters at (619)873-5841.

Location: Drive 16 miles southeast of Mammoth Lakes on US-395 to Tom's Place, then go south on Rock Creek Road for three miles.

Trip note: Open from May to October. Elevation 8100 feet. Located on Rock Creek.

Site 66
BIG
MEADOW

Campsites, facilities: There are five tent sites and six sites for tents or motorhomes up to 22 feet long. Picnic tables, fireplaces and piped water are provided, and flush toilets are available. Groceries and propane gas are nearby.

Reservations, fee: No reservations; $5 fee per night.

Who to contact: Phone Inyo National Forest Headquarters at (619)873-5841.

Location: Drive 16 miles southeast of Mammoth Lakes on US-395 to Tom's Place, then go south on Rock Creek Road for four miles.

Trip note: Camp open from May to October. Elevation 8600 feet. Located on Rock Creek.

Site 67
IRIS
MEADOWS

Campsites, facilities: There are 14 campsites for tents or motorhomes up to 22 feet long. Piped water, fireplaces and picnic tables are provided, and flush toilets are available. Groceries and propane gas are available nearby.

Reservations, fee: No reservations; $5 fee per night.

Who to contact: Phone Inyo National Forest Headquarters at (619)873-5841.

Location: Drive 16 miles southeast of Mammoth Lakes on US-395 to Tom's Place, then go south on Rock Creek Road for three miles.

Trip note: Open from May to October. Elevation 8300 feet. Located on Rock Creek at the base of Reds Mountain.

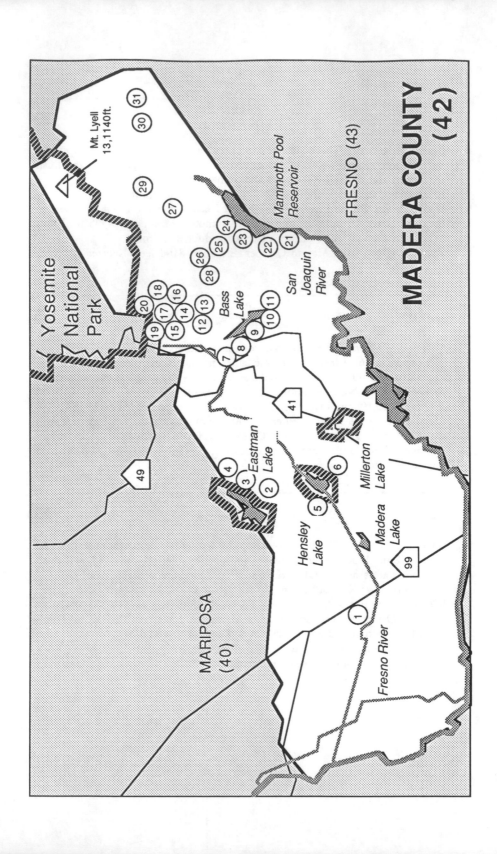

MADERA COUNTY (42)

MADERA COUNTY

◆

Site **1**   COUNTRY LIVING
RV PARK

Campsites, facilities: There are 49 motorhome spaces. Picnic tables, piped water, electrical connections and sewer hookups are provided. Rest rooms, showers, swimming pool and a grocery store are available.
Reservations, fee: Call ahead for space available; $12 fee per night.
Who to contact: Phone park at (209)674-5343.
Location: Drive two miles north of Madera off State Route 99 to 24833 Avenue 16.
Trip note: Open all year. Elevation 300 feet.

Site **2**   CORDORNIZ
RECREATION AREA

Campsites, facilities: There are 62 campsites for tents or motorhomes. Piped water, fireplaces and picnic tables are provided. Flush toilets, showers, a dump station, a playground and a boat ramp are available.
Reservations, fee: No reservations; $6 fee per night.
Who to contact: Phone the Eastman Lake at (209)689-3255.
Location: Drive 25 miles northeast of Chowchilla on County Road 29 via County Avenue 26.
Trip note: Open all year. Elevation 600 feet. Located on Eastman Lake, behind Buchanan Dam on the Chowchilla River. Enjoy swimming, waterskiing, sailboarding and fishing.

Site **3**   EASTMAN
GROUP SITE

Campsites, facilities: There are 40 tent sites and 48 motorhome spaces. Piped water, fireplaces and picnic tables are provided. Flush toilets, showers, a dump station and horseback riding facilities are available. A boat ramp is nearby.
Reservations, fee: No reservations; $25 fee for group per night.
Who to contact: Phone Eastman Lake at (209)689-3255.

Location: Drive 25 miles northeast of Chowchilla on County Road 29 via County Avenue 26.

Trip note: Open all year. Elevation 600 feet. Located on Eastman Lake, behind Buchanan Reservoir on the Chowchilla River. Enjoy swimming, waterskiing, sailboarding and fishing.

Site **4**   WILDCAT
                        RECREATION AREA

Campsites, facilities: There are 19 campsites for tents or motorhomes. Piped water, fireplaces and picnic tables are provided. Vault toilets, a dump station and a playground are available. A boat ramp is nearby.

Reservations, fee: No reservations, no fee.

Who to contact: Phone Eastman Lake at (209)689-3255.

Location: Drive 25 miles northeast of Chowchilla on County Road 29 via County Avenue 26.

Trip note: Open all year. Elevation 600 feet. Located on Eastman Lake, behind Buchanan Reservoir on the Chowchilla River. Enjoy swimming, waterskiing, sailboarding and fishing.

Site **5**   HENSLEY
                          GROUP SITE

Campsites, facilities: There are 25 campsites for tents or motorhomes. Piped water, fireplaces and picnic tables are provided. Flush toilets, showers, dump station, playground and boat ramp are available.

Reservations, fee: Reservations requested; $25 group fee per night.

Who to contact: Phone Hensley Lake at (209)673-5151.

Location: Drive 17 miles northeast of Madera on County Road 407 via County Road 400 and State Route 145.

Trip note: Open all year. Elevation 500 feet. Located on Hensley Lake, a reservoir on the Fresno River. Enjoy swimming, waterskiing, skin diving, sailboarding and fishing.

Site **6**   HIDDEN VIEW
                           CAMPGROUND

Campsites, facilities: There are 66 campsites for tents or motorhomes. Piped water, fireplaces and picnic tables are provided. Flush toilets, showers, dump station, playground and a boat ramp are available.

Reservations, fee: No reservations; $6 fee per night.

Who to contact: Phone Hensley Lake at (209)673-5151.

Location: Drive 17 miles northeast of Madera on County Road 407 via County Road 400 and State Route 145.

Trip note: Open all year. Elevation 500 feet. Located on Hensley Lake, a reservoir on the Fresno River. Enjoy swimming, waterskiing, skin diving, sailboarding, and fishing.

Site 7
DENVER
CHURCH

▲

Campsites, facilities: There are 19 tent sites, 12 motorhome spaces, and seven campsites for tents or motorhomes up to 16 feet long. Piped water, fireplaces and picnic tables are provided. Flush toilets are available. Groceries, fishing supplies, propane gas, a boat ramp and a laundromat are nearby.

Reservations, fee: Call Ticketron at (213)216-6666 for information; $8 fee per night.

Who to contact: Phone Sierra National Forest Headquarters at (209)487-5155.

Location: Drive 55 miles northeast of Fresno via State Route 41 and Road 426, campground is on northwest shore of Bass Lake.

Trip note: Open all year. Elevation 3400 feet. Located on Bass Lake, a narrow mountain lake that offers good fishing, waterskiing, sailboarding and swimming. Boats must be registered at Bass Lake observation tower after launching.

Site 8
FORKS

▲

Campsites, facilities: There are 25 tent sites and six campsites for tents or motorhomes up to 16 feet long. Piped water, fireplaces and picnic tables are provided. Flush toilets and horseback riding are available. A laundromat and a grocery store are nearby.

Reservations, fee: Call Ticketron at (213)216-6666 for outlet information; $8 fee per night.

Who to contact: Phone Sierra National Forest Headquarters at (209)487-5155.

Location: Drive 55 miles northeast of Fresno via State Route 41 and Road 426, campground is on southwest shore of Bass Lake.

Trip note: Open all year. Elevation 3400 feet. Located on Bass Lake, a narrow mountain lake that offers good fishing, waterskiing, sailboarding and swimming. Boats must be registered at Bass Lake observation tower after launching.

Site 9
LUPINE

▲

Campsites, facilities: There are 54 tent sites and 11 sites for motorhomes up to 22 feet long. Picnic tables, fireplaces and piped water are provided, and toilets are available. Groceries and a boat ramp are available nearby.

Reservations, fee: Call Ticketron at (213)216-6666 for outlet information; $8 fee per night.

Who to contact: Phone Sierra National Forest Headquarters at (209)487-5155.

Location: Drive 55 miles northeast of Fresno via State Route 41 and Road 426, campground is on southwest shore of Bass Lake.

Trip note: Open from May to November. Elevation 34 feet. Located on Bass Lake, a narrow mountain lake that offers good fishing, waterskiing, sailboarding, and swimming. Boats must be registered at Bass Lake observation tower after launching.

Site **10**   SPRING
                COVE

Campsites, facilities: There are 54 tent sites and 11 sites for tents or motorhomes up to 22 feet long. Picnic tables, fireplaces and piped water are provided, and flush toilets are available. Groceries and a boat ramp are available nearby.

Reservations, fee: Call Ticketron at (213)216-6666 for outlet information; $6 fee per night.

Who to contact: Phone Sierra National Forest Headquarters at (209)487-5155.

Location: Drive 55 miles northeast of Fresno via State Route 41 and Road 426. Campground is on southwest shore of Bass Lake.

Trip note: Camp is open from May to September. Elevation 3400 feet. Located on Bass Lake, a narrow mountain lake that offers good fishing, waterskiing, sailboarding and swimming. Boats must be registered at Bass Lake observation tower after launching.

Site **11**   WISHON
                POINT

Campsites, facilities: There are 13 tent sites, 11 motorhome spaces and 26 sites for tents or motorhomes up to 22 feet long. Picnic tables, fireplaces and piped water are provided. Flush toilets are available. Groceries and a boat ramp are nearby.

Reservations, fee: Call Ticketron at (213)216-6666 for outlet information; $8 fee per night.

Who to contact: Phone Sierra National Forest Headquarters at (209)487-5155.

Location: Drive 55 miles northeast of Fresno via State Route 41 and Road 426. Campground is on southwest shore of Bass Lake.

Trip note: Open from May to November. Elevation 3400 feet. Located on Bass Lake, a narrow mountain lake that offers good fishing, waterskiing, sailboarding and swimming. Boats must be registered at Bass Lake observation tower after launching.

Site 12   CHILCOOT

Campsites, facilities: There are eight tent sites and six sites for tents or motor-homes up to 16 feet long. Picnic tables and fireplaces are provided. Vault toilets are available, but there is no water, so bring your own. Groceries and a laundromat are available nearby.

Reservations, fee: No reservations, no fee.

Who to contact: Phone Sierra National Forest Headquarters at (209)487-5155.

Location: Drive four miles north of Bass Lake on Beasore Meadows Road.

Trip note: Open from May to September. Elevation 4600 feet. Campsite is located on Chilcoot Creek, two miles from Bass Lake. Primitive option to more developed sites at Bass Lake.

Site 13   SOQUEL

Campsites, facilities: There are 14 campsites for tents or motorhomes up to 16 feet long. Fireplaces and picnic tables are provided, and vault toilets are available. There is no water, so bring your own.

Reservations, fee: No reservations, no fee.

Who to contact: Phone Sierra National Forest Headquarters at (209)487-5155.

Location: Drive 11 miles north of Bass Lake on Beasore Meadows Road.

Trip note: Open from June to November. Elevation 5400 feet. Located on the North Fork of Willow Creek.

Site 14   GREYS MOUNTAIN

Campsites, facilities: There are eight tent sites. Picnic tables and fireplaces are provided, and pit toilets are available. No water is available, so bring your own.

Reservations, fee: No reservations, no fee.

Who to contact: Phone Sierra National Forest Headquarters at (209)487-5155.

Location: Drive eight miles north of Bass Lake on Beasore Meadows Road.

Trip note: Open from June to November. Elevation 5200 feet. This site is located on Willow Creek.

Site 15   NELDER GROVE

Campsites, facilities: There are 10 campsites for tents or motorhomes up to 16 feet long. Fireplaces and picnic tables are provided, and vault toilets are available. There is no water.

Reservations, fee: No reservations, no fee.

Who to contact: Phone Sierra National Forest Headquarters at (209)487-5155.
Location: Drive eight miles southeast of Fish Camp off State Route 41.
Trip note: Open from May to October. Elevation 5300 feet. Located in the Nelder Grove of Giant Sequoias. There is a nature trail near camp and the southern entrance to Yosemite National Park is 10 miles away.

Site **16**   TEXAS FLAT
                       GROUP CAMP   🌲

Campsites, facilities: There are four campsites for tents or motorhomes up to 16 feet long. Fireplaces and picnic tables are provided, and vault toilets are available. There is no water.
Reservations, fee: Reservations requested; $20 fee for group per night.
Who to contact: Phone Sierra National Forest Headquarters at (209)487-5155.
Location: Drive 11 miles southeast of Fish Camp off State Route 41.
Trip note: Open from June to September. Elevation 5500 feet. Located on the North Fork of Willow Creek. It is 15 miles from the south entrance to Yosemite National Forest and 15 miles north of Bass Lake.

Site **17**   FRESNO
                       DOME   🌲

Campsites, facilities: There are six tent sites and six sites for tents or motorhomes up to 16 feet long. Picnic tables and fireplaces are provided, and pit toilets are available. There is no water available, so bring your own.
Reservations, fee: No reservations, no fee.
Who to contact: Phone Sierra National Forest Headquarters at (209)487-5155.
Location: Drive eight miles southeast of Fish Camp off State Route 41.
Trip note: Open from June to November. Elevation 6400 feet. Located on Big Creek. Map of Sierra National Forest details backcountry roads, hiking trails, streams.

Site **18**   KELTY
                       MEADOW   🌲

Campsites, facilities: There are 14 campsites for tents or motorhomes up to 16 feet long. Fireplaces and picnic tables are provided, and vault toilets are available. There is no water, so bring your own.
Reservations, fee: No reservations, no fee.
Who to contact: Phone Sierra National Forest Headquarters at (209)487-5155.
Location: Drive nine miles southeast of Fish Camp off State Route 41.
Trip note: Open from June to November. Elevation 5800 feet. Located near the North Fork of Willow Creek. Fresno Dome and the Nelder Grove of Giant Sequoias are nearby. A primitive campsite.

Site **19**   BIG
                          SANDY

Campsites, facilities: There are 10 tent sites and 11 sites for tents or motorhomes
 up to 16 feet long. Picnic tables and fireplaces are provided, and vault toi-
 lets are available. There is no water available.
Reservations, fee: No reservations, no fee.
Who to contact: Phone Sierra National Forest Headquarters at (209)487-5155.
Location: Drive six miles southeast of Fish Camp off State Route 41.
Trip note: Open from June to November. Elevation 5800 feet. This spot is locat-
 ed on Big Creek and is eight miles from the south entrance to Yosemite
 National Forest.

Site **20**   LITTLE
                          SANDY

Campsites, facilities: There are 10 tent sites. Picnic tables and fireplaces are pro-
 vided, and vault toilets are available. There is no water, so bring your own.
Reservations, fee: No reservations, no fee.
Who to contact: Phone Sierra National Forest Headquarters at (209)487-5155.
Location: Drive seven miles southeast of Fish Creek off State Route 41.
Trip note: Open from June to November. Elevation 6100 feet. Located on Big
 Creek, nine miles from the south entrance to Yosemite National Forest.

Site **21**   FISH
                          CREEK

Campsites, facilities: There are seven tent sites and four sites for tents or motor-
 homes up to 16 feet long. Picnic tables are provided and vault toilets are
 available. There is no water.
Reservations, fee: No reservations, no fee.
Who to contact: Phone Sierra National Forest Headquarters at (209)487-5155.
Location: Drive 23 miles east of North Fork.
Trip note: Open from April to November. Elevation 4600 feet. Located on Fish
 Creek. A trail near camp leads north for six miles to Mammoth Pool Reser-
 voir, where there is another campground.

Site **22**   ROCK
                          CREEK

Campsites, facilities: There are 18 campsites for tents or motorhomes up to 32
 feet long. Piped water, fireplaces and picnic tables are provided. Vault toilets are available.
Reservations, fee: No reservations; $5 fee per night.
Who to contact: Phone Sierra National Forest Headquarters at (209)487-5155.

Location: Drive 27 miles northeast of North Fork.

Trip note: Open from April to November. Elevation 4300 feet. Campsite is located on Rock Creek. A trail out of camp leads southeast for one mile, then connects with a trail that goes north for five miles to Mammoth Pool Reservoir. There is another campground at Mammoth Pool.

Site **23**   MAMMOTH POOL

Campsites, facilities: There are 18 tent sites and 29 sites for tents or motorhomes up to 22 feet long. Picnic tables, fireplaces and piped water are provided. Vault toilets are available. A grocery store and a boat ramp are nearby.

Reservations, fee: No reservations; $5 fee per night.

Who to contact: Phone Sierra National Forest Headquarters at (209)487-5155.

Location: Drive 42 miles northeast of North Fork via Road 225, Minaret and Mammoth Pool Roads (narrow, winding road).

Trip note: Open from May to November. Elevation 3800 feet. Campsite located on Mammoth Pool Reservoir. Enjoy trout fishing, waterskiing and swimming on the lake.

Site **24**   SWEET WATER   ▲

Campsites, facilities: There are five tent sites and five sites for tents or motorhomes up to 16 feet long. Picnic tables and fireplaces are provided. Vault toilets are available. There is no water, so bring your own. A grocery store and a boat ramp are nearby.

Reservations, fee: No reservations, no fee.

Who to contact: Phone Sierra National Forest Headquarters at (209)487-5155.

Location: Drive 41 miles northeast of North Fork via Road 225, Minaret and Mammoth Pool Roads (narrow, winding road).

Trip note: Open from May to November. Elevation 3800 feet. Located on Chiquito Creek one mile from Mammoth Pool Reservoir.

Site **25**   PLACER   ▲

Campsites, facilities: There are seven tent sites. Piped water and picnic tables are provided, and vault toilets are available. A grocery store and a boat ramp are nearby.

Reservations, fee: No reservations; $3 fee per night.

Who to contact: Phone Sierra National Forest Headquarters at (209)487-5155.

Location: Drive 39 miles northeast of North Fork via Road 225, Minaret and Mammoth Pool Roads (narrow, winding road).

Trip note: Open from April to November. Elevation 4100 feet. Located on Chiquito Creek, three miles from Mammoth Pool Reservoir.

Site **26**   SODA
                       SPRINGS

Campsites, facilities: There are 18 campsites for tents or motorhomes up to 22 feet long. Fireplaces and picnic tables are provided, and vault toilets are available. There is no water, so bring your own. A grocery store and a boat ramp are nearby.
Reservations, fee: No reservations, no fee.
Who to contact: Phone Sierra National Forest Headquarters at (209)487-5155.
Location: Drive 37 miles northeast of North Fork via Road 225, Minaret and Mammoth Pool Roads (narrow, winding road).
Trip note: Open from April to November. Elevation 4400 feet. Located on the West Fork of Chiquito Creek, five miles from Mammoth Pool Reservoir.

Site **27**   LOWER
                       CHIQUITO

Campsites, facilities: There are seven campsites for tents or motorhomes up to 22 feet long. Fireplaces and picnic tables are provided, and vault toilets are available. There is no water, so bring your own.
Reservations, fee: No reservations, no fee.
Who to contact: Phone Sierra National Forest Headquarters at (209)487-5155.
Location: Drive 41 miles northeast of North Fork via Road 225, off Minaret Road (narrow, winding road).
Trip note: Open from May to October. Elevation 4900 feet. Located on Chiquito Creek, eight miles from Mammoth Pool Reservoir.

Site **28**   GAGGS
                       CAMP

Campsites, facilities: There are nine campsites for tents or motorhomes up to 16 feet long. Picnic tables are provided, and pit toilets are available. There is no water, but a grocery store is nearby.
Reservations, fee: No reservations, no fee.
Who to contact: Phone Sierra National Forest Headquarters at (209)487-5155.
Location: Drive 15 miles north of North Fork off Mallum Ridge Road on Central Camp Road (narrow, winding road).
Trip note: Open from June to November. Elevation 5800 feet. Located on a small creek, 15 miles from Bass Lake.

Site **29**   UPPER
                              CHIQUITO

Campsites, facilities: There are 10 tent sites and 10 sites for tents or motorhomes
    up to 22 feet long. Picnic tables and fireplaces are provided, and vault toi-
    lets are available. There is no water, so bring your own.
Reservations, fee: No reservations, no fee.
Who to contact: Phone Sierra National Forest Headquarters at (209)487-5155.
Location: Drive 16 miles northeast of Bass Lake on Beasore Meadows Road.
Trip note: Open from June to October. Elevation 6800 feet. Located on Chiquito
    Creek.

Site **30**   CLOVER
                              MEADOW

Campsites, facilities: There are seven campsites for tents or motorhomes up to 16
    feet long. Piped water and picnic tables are provided. Vault toilets are
    available.
Reservations, fee: No reservations; $3 fee per night.
Who to contact: Phone Sierra National Forest Headquarters at (209)487-5155.
Location: Drive 20 miles northeast of Mammoth Pool Reservoir off Minarets
    Road.
Trip note: Open from June to October. Elevation 7000 feet. Campsite is near
    Granite Creek. A trail from camp leads to numerous lakes in the Ansel Ad-
    ams Wilderness.

Site **31**   GRANITE
                              CREEK

Campsites, facilities: There are 10 tent sites. Picnic tables and fireplaces are pro-
    vided, and pit toilets are available. There is no water, so bring your own.
Reservations, fee: No reservations, no fee.
Who to contact: Phone Sierra National Forest Headquarters at (209)487-5155.
Location: Drive 22 miles northeast of Mammoth Pool Reservoir off Minarets
    Road.
Trip note: Open from June to October. Elevation 6900 feet. Located on Granite
    Creek. A trail from camp leads north to numerous lakes in the Ansel Ad-
    ams Wilderness.

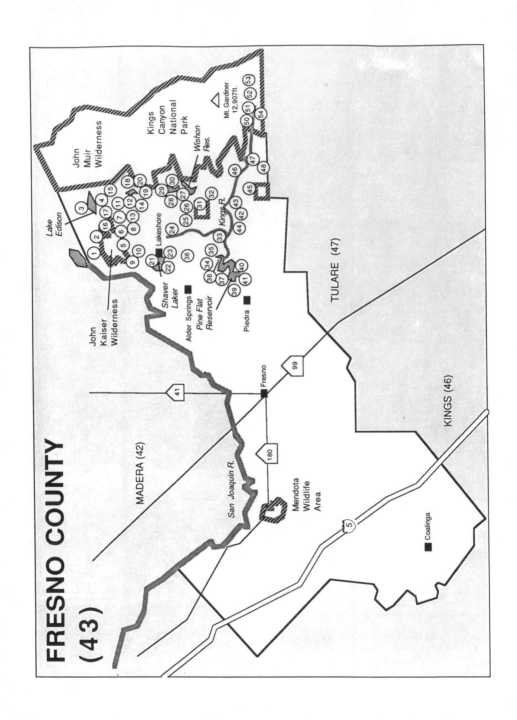

FRESNO COUNTY (43)

FRESNO COUNTY

◆

Site **1**   WEST
KAISER   🏕

Campsites, facilities: There are 10 campsites for tents or motorhomes up to 22 feet long. Picnic tables are provided and vault toilets are available. There is no water, so bring your own.

Reservations, fee: No reservations, no fee.

Who to contact: Phone Sierra National Forest Headquarters at (209)487-5155.

Location: Drive 16 miles north of Big Creek via Huntington Road and Stump Springs Road.

Trip note: Open from May to November. Elevation 5500 feet. Located on West Kaiser Creek. A trail to Mammoth Pool Reservoir can be found alongside Kaiser Creek which is about 1/2 mile northwest of camp. Go west on the trail to get to Mammoth Pool. A trailhead accessing the Kaiser Wilderness can be found at the end of a dirt road two miles south of camp.

Site **2**   SAMPLE
MEADOWS   🏕

Campsites, facilities: There are 16 campsites for tents or motorhomes up to 16 feet long. Fireplaces and picnic tables are provided. Vault toilets are available. There is no water.

Reservations, fee: No reservations, no fee.

Who to contact: Phone Sierra National Forest Headquarters at (209)487-5155.

Location: Drive 14 miles northeast of Lakeshore via Kaiser Pass Road.

Trip note: This camp is open from June to November and is on Kaiser Creek. Elevation 7800 feet. A trailhead that accesses several lakes in the Kaiser Wilderness is nearby, and another trail heads north and follows Kaiser Creek all the way to Mammoth Pool Reservoir (about 13 miles). West Kaiser campground is just off that trail near the confluence of West Kaiser Creek and Kaiser Creek.

Site **3**   VERMILLION

Campsites, facilities: There are 30 tent sites. Piped water, picnic tables and fireplaces are provided. Vault toilets are available. Horseback riding facilities, boat ramp, grocery store and a laundromat are nearby.

Reservations, fee: No reservations; $5 fee per night.

Who to contact: Phone Sierra National Forest Headquarters at (209)487-5155.

Location: Drive five miles northeast of Mono Hot Springs at Lake Edison.

Trip note: Open from June to October. Elevation 7700 feet. Located on Lake Edison. Fishing and motorboats which travel no faster than 15 m.p.h. are allowed on the lake. A trail from camp travels along the shore of Lake Edison for five miles to Quail Meadows where it intersects with the Pacific Crest Trail in the John Muir Wilderness.

Site **4**   MONO CREEK   ▲

Campsites, facilities: There are 18 tent sites and two sites for tents or motorhomes up to 22 feet long. Picnic tables, fireplaces and piped water are provided. Vault toilets are available. Horseback riding facilities, a grocery store and a boat ramp are nearby.

Reservations, fee: No reservations, no fee.

Who to contact: Phone Sierra National Forest Headquarters at (209)487-5155.

Location: Drive three miles northeast of Mono Hot Springs.

Trip note: This camp is open from June to September. Elevation 7400 feet. Located on Mono Creek near the diversion dam at Lake Edison. Lake Edison allows motorboats that travel no faster than 15 m.p.h. The Mono Hot Springs resort is three miles away and there are numerous trails nearby that access the backcountry. Good trout fishing on Mono Creek above Lake Edison.

Site **5**   CATAVEE   ▲

Campsites, facilities: There are 16 tent sites and 11 sites for tents or motorhomes up to 22 feet long. Picnic tables, fireplaces and piped water are provided. Vault toilets are available. Horseback riding facilities, laundromat and a grocery store are nearby.

Reservations, fee: No reservations; $6 fee per night.

Who to contact: Phone Sierra National Forest Headquarters at (209)487-5155.

Location: Drive 1/2 mile west of Lakeshore.

Trip note: Open from June to October. Elevation 7000 feet. Located on the shore of Huntington Lake, where you can enjoy fishing and watersports. Nearby resorts offer boat rentals and guest docks. Tackle rentals and bait are also available. A trailhead near camp accesses the Kaiser Wilderness.

Site **6**   COLLEGE   ▲

Campsites, facilities: There are 11 campsites for tents or motorhomes up to 22 feet long. Piped water, fireplaces and picnic tables are provided, and vault toilets and horseback riding facilities are available. A grocery store, a laundromat and propane gas are nearby.

Reservations, fee: No reservations; $6 fee per night.

Who to contact: Phone Sierra National Forest Headquarters at (209)487-5155.

Location: Drive 1/2 mile west of Lakeshore.

Trip note: Open from June to October. Elevation 7000 feet. Camp is located on the shore of Huntington Lake, where you can enjoy fishing and watersports. Nearby resorts offer boat rentals and guest docks. Tackle rentals and bait are also available. A trailhead near camp accesses the Kaiser Wilderness.

Site **7**   DEER CREEK

Campsites, facilities: There are 15 tent sites and 14 sites for tents or motorhomes up to 22 feet long. Picnic tables, fireplaces and piped water are provided. Vault toilets and horseback riding facilities are available. A grocery store, a laundromat and propane gas are nearby.

Reservations, fee: No reservations; $6 fee per night.

Who to contact: Phone Sierra National Forest Headquarters at (209)487-5155.

Location: Drive 1/2 mile west of Lakeshore.

Trip note: Open from June to October. Elevation 7000 feet. Located on the shore of Huntington Lake, where you can enjoy fishing and watersports. Nearby resorts offer boat rentals and guest docks. Tackle rentals and bait are also available. A trailhead near camp accesses the Kaiser Wilderness.

Site **8**   KINNIKINNICK

Campsites, facilities: There are 16 tent sites and 16 sites for tents or motorhomes up to 22 feet long. Picnic tables, fireplaces and piped water are provided. Vault toilets and horseback riding facilities are available. A grocery store and a laundromat are nearby.

Reservations, fee: No reservations; $6 fee per night.

Who to contact: Phone Sierra National Forest Headquarters at (209)487-5155.

Location: Drive 1/2 mile west of Lakeshore.

Trip note: This camp is open from June to September. Elevation 7000 feet. It is located on the shore of Huntington Lake, where you can enjoy fishing and watersports. Nearby resorts offer boat rentals and guest docks. Tackle rentals and bait are also available.

Site **9**   BILLY CREEK

Campsites, facilities: There are 20 tent sites and 24 sites for tents or motorhomes up to 22 feet long. Picnic tables, fireplaces and piped water are provided. Vault toilets are available. A grocery store is nearby.

Reservations, fee: No reservations; $6 fee per night.

Who to contact: Phone Sierra National Forest Headquarters at (209)487-5155.

Location: Drive 1/2 mile northeast of Huntington Lake.

Trip note: Open from June to October. Elevation 7000 feet. Located on the shore of Huntington Lake, where you can enjoy fishing and watersports.

Site **10**   LOWER
              BILLY CREEK

Campsites, facilities: There are eight tent sites and six sites for tents or motor-
    homes up to 16 feet long. Picnic tables, fireplaces and piped water are pro-
    vided, and vault toilets are available. A grocery store is nearby.
Reservations, fee: No reservations; $6 fee per night.
Who to contact: Phone Sierra National Forest Headquarters at (209)487-5155.
Location: Drive 1/2 mile east of Huntington Lake.
Trip note: Open from June to October. Elevation 7000 feet. Located on the
    shore of Huntington Lake where, you can enjoy fishing and watersports.
    Nearby resorts offer boat rentals and guest docks. Tackle rentals and bait
    are also available. A trailhead near camp accesses the Kaiser Wilderness.

Site **11**   BADGER
              FLAT

Campsites, facilities: There are 10 campsites for tents or motorhomes up to 22
    feet long. Fireplaces and picnic tables are provided, while vault toilets and
    horseback riding facilities are available. There is no water, so bring your
    own. A grocery store is nearby.
Reservations, fee: No reservations, no fee.
Who to contact: Phone Sierra National Forest Headquarters at (209)487-5155.
Location: Drive seven miles northeast of Lakeshore on Kaiser Pass Road.
Trip note: Open from June to October. Elevation 8200 feet. Located on Ran-
    cheria Creek. A trail that passes through camp serves Kaiser Wilderness to
    the north and Dinkey Lakes Wilderness to the south.

Site **12**   BADGER FLAT
              GROUP CAMP

Campsites, facilities: There are 10 campsites for tents or motorhomes up to 22
    feet long. Fireplaces and picnic tables are provided, and vault toilets and
    horseback riding facilities are available. There is no water, so bring your
    own. A grocery store is nearby.
Reservations, fee: Reservation with $10 deposit; $25 fee per night per group.
Who to contact: Phone Sierra National Forest Headquarters at (209)487-5155.
Location: Drive six miles northeast of Lakeshore on Kaiser Pass Road.
Trip note: Open from June to September. Elevation 8200 feet. Located on Ran-
    cheria Creek. A trail that passes through camp serves Kaiser Wilderness to
    the north and Dinkey Lakes Wilderness to the south.

Site **13**   KOKANEE EAST
              GROUP CAMP

Campsites, facilities: There are campsites for tents or motorhomes up to 22 feet
    long. Piped water, fireplaces and picnic tables are provided, and vault toi-
    lets are available. A grocery store is nearby.

Reservations, fee: Call for space available. $25 deposit required; $25 fee per night per group.

Who to contact: Phone Sierra National Forest Headquarters at (209)487-5155.

Location: Drive two miles southeast of Lakeshore off State Route 168.

Trip note: Open from June to September. Elevation 7100 feet. Camp is near Huntington Lake where you can enjoy fishing and watersports. Nearby resorts offer boat rentals and guest docks. Tackle rentals and bait are also available.

Site 14   RANCHERIA   ▲

Campsites, facilities: There are 89 tent sites and 70 sites for tents or motorhomes up to 22 feet long. Picnic tables, fireplaces and piped water are provided. Vault toilets are available. A grocery store, laundromat and propane gas are nearby.

Reservations, fee: No reservations; $6 fee per night.

Who to contact: Phone Sierra National Forest Headquarters at (209)487-5155.

Location: Drive one mile south of Lakeshore on State Route 168.

Trip note: This camp is open from June to September. Elevation 7100 feet. It is located on the shore of Huntington Lake, where you can enjoy fishing and watersports. Nearby resorts offer boat rentals and guest docks. Tackle rentals and bait are also available.

Site 15   MONO HOT SPRINGS   ▲

Campsites, facilities: There are 31 tent sites. Piped water, picnic tables and fireplaces are provided. Vault toilets are available. A grocery store is nearby.

Reservations, fee: No reservations; $5 fee per night.

Who to contact: Phone Sierra National Forest Headquarters at (209)487-5155.

Location: Drive 1/4 mile west of Mono Hot Springs.

Trip note: Open from June to September. Elevation 6500 feet. Camp is on the San Joaquin River adjacent to Mono Hot Springs Resort. There is a trail from camp that forks to Lake Edison or into the backcountry of Ansel Adams Wilderness.

Site 16   PORTAL FOREBAY   🌲

Campsites, facilities: There are nine campsites for tents or motorhomes up to 16 feet long. Picnic tables and fireplaces are provided, and vault toilets are available. There is no water, so bring your own. A grocery store is nearby.

Reservations, fee: No reservations, no fee.

Who to contact: Phone Sierra National Forest Headquarters at (209)487-5155.

Location: Drive four miles southwest of Mono Hot Springs off Kaiser Pass Road.

Trip note: Open from June to October. Elevation 7200 feet. Located on the shore of Forebay Lake. There are several trails leading from camp to Lake Edison or into the backcountry.

Site **17**   BOLSILLO   🌲

Campsites, facilities: There are four tent sites. Piped water, picnic tables and fireplaces are provided. Vault toilets are available. A grocery store is nearby.
Reservations, fee: No reservations, no fee.
Who to contact: Phone Sierra National Forest Headquarters at (209)487-5155.
Location: Drive four miles southwest of Mono Hot Springs on Kaiser Pass Road.
Trip note: Open from June to October. Elevation 7400 feet. Located on Bolsillo Creek. A trail passes through camp that heads north two miles to Mono Hot Springs or south two and a half miles to Corbett Lake.

Site **18**   WARD
                                               LAKE   🌲

Campsites, facilities: There are 17 campsites for tents or motorhomes up to 16 feet long. Picnic tables and fireplaces are provided. Vault toilets are available, but there is no water. A grocery store is nearby.
Reservations, fee: No reservations, no fee.
Who to contact: Phone Sierra National Forest Headquarters at (209)487-5155.
Location: Drive five miles southeast of Mono Hot Springs on Florence Lake Road.
Trip note: This camp is open from June to September and is on Ward Lake about two miles north of Florence Lake. Elevation 7300 feet.

Site **19**   FLORENCE
                                               LAKE   🌲

Campsites, facilities: There are 14 tent sites. Picnic tables and fireplaces are provided. Vault toilets and horseback riding facilities are available. There is no water, so bring your own. A grocery store is nearby.
Reservations, fee: No reservations, no fee.
Who to contact: Phone Sierra National Forest Headquarters at (209)487-5155.
Location: Drive seven miles southeast of Mono Hot Springs on Florence Lake Road.
Trip note: Open from June to September. Elevation 7400 feet. Camp located on Florence Lake. Motorboats are allowed on lake providing they go no faster than 15 m.p.h. The nearby Florence Lake Boathouse offers boat rentals and a ferry service. The trail around the lake ventures west and intersects with the Pacific Crest Trail in about five miles.

| Site 20 | JACKASS MEADOW | ▲ |

Campsites, facilities: There are 15 campsites for tents or motorhomes up to 16 feet long. Picnic tables and fireplaces are provided, and vault toilets are available. There is no water at this site.

Reservations, fee: No reservations; $5 fee per night.

Who to contact: Phone Sierra National Forest Headquarters at (209)487-5155.

Location: Drive seven miles southeast of Mono Hot Springs off Florence Lake Road.

Trip note: This camp is open from June to October and is on the San Joaquin River near Florence Lake. Elevation 7200 feet.

| Site 21 | CAMP EDISON | ▲ |

Campsites, facilities: There are 150 campsites for tents or motorhomes up to 22 feet long. Piped water, electrical connections, fireplaces and picnic tables are provided. Flush toilets, showers, a boat ramp, moorings and a dump station are available. A grocery store, laundromat and propane gas are nearby.

Reservations, fee: Call for space available. $20 deposit required; $8.75 fee per night.

Who to contact: Phone park at (209)841-3444.

Location: Drive one mile northeast of the town of Shaver Lake off State Route 168.

Trip note: This camp is open all year and is on the shore of Shaver Lake where you can enjoy fishing and waterskiing. Boat rentals, bait and tackle are available at the commerical marina nearby. Elevation 5400 feet.

| Site 22 | DORABELLE | ▲ |

Campsites, facilities: There are 20 tent sites, 33 motorhome spaces and 15 sites for tents or motorhomes up to 22 feet long. Picnic tables, fireplaces and piped water are provided. Vault toilets are available. A grocery store is nearby.

Reservations, fee: No reservations; $7 fee per night.

Who to contact: Phone Sierra National Forest Headquarters at (209)487-5155.

Location: Drive one mile east of the town of Shaver Lake off State Route 168.

Trip note: Open from May to October. Elevation 5400 feet. Located on the shore of Shaver Lake where you can enjoy fishing and waterskiing. Boat rentals, bait and tackle can be found at the commericial marina nearby.

| Site 23 | SWANSON MEADOW | ♣ |

Campsites, facilities: There are nine campsites for tents or motorhomes up to 22 feet long. Fireplaces and picnic tables are provided, and vault toilets are available. There is no water at this site, so bring your own. A grocery store is nearby.

Reservations, fee: No reservations, no fee.

Who to contact: Phone Sierra National Forest Headquarters at (209)487-5155.

Location: Drive three miles southeast of the town of Shaver Lake off State Route 168 on Dinkey Creek Road.

Trip note: This camp is open from May to November. Elevation 5400 feet. Located two miles from the shore of Shaver Lake where you can enjoy fishing and waterskiing. Boat rentals, bait and tackle can be found at the commerical marina at the lake.

Site **24**   DINKEY
                          CREEK   ▲

Campsites, facilities: There are 136 campsites for tents or motorhomes up to 22 feet long. Piped water, fireplaces and picnic tables are provided. Flush toilets and horseback riding facilities are available. A grocery store is nearby.

Reservations, fee: No reservations; $5 fee per night.

Who to contact: Phone Sierra National Forest Headquarters at (209)487-5155.

Location: Drive 14 miles to the end of Dinkey Creek Road off State Route 168.

Trip note: Open from May to October. Elevation 5700 feet. Camp is located on Dinkey Creek. A trail passes through camp that follows Dinkey Creek south for many miles. Taken north, the trail follows Dinkey Creek past Dinkey Dome up to Swamp Meadow, then along a dirt road for about two and a half miles to a trailhead that accesses numerous lakes in the Dinkey Lakes Wilderness.

Site **25**   GIGANTEA   🌲

Campsites, facilities: There are 11 campsites for tents or motorhomes up to 16 feet long. Picnic tables are provided, and vault toilets are available. There is no water at this site.

Reservations, fee: No reservations, no fee.

Who to contact: Phone Sierra National Forest Headquarters at (209)487-5155.

Location: Drive six miles southeast of Dinkey Creek on McKinley Grove Road.

Trip note: This camp is open from June to October and is on Dinkey Creek. Elevation 6500 feet. A trail passes through camp that follows Dinkey Creek south for many miles, or taken north follows Dinkey Creek up to the town of Dinkey Creek, where convenience and horseback riding facilities can be found.

Site **26**   BUCK
                          MEADOW   🌲

Campsites, facilities: There are 10 campsites for tents or motorhomes up to 22

feet long. Picnic tables provided and vault toilets available. There is no water, so bring your own.

Reservations, fee: No reservations, no fee.

Who to contact: Phone Sierra National Forest Headquarters at (209)487-5155.

Location: Drive eight miles southeast of Dinkey Creek on McKinley Grove Road.

Trip note: Open from June to October. Elevation 6800 feet. Camp is located on Deer Creek seven miles from Lake Wishon and five miles from Dinkey Creek.

Site **27**   WISHON
VILLAGE

Campsites, facilities: There are 25 tent sites and 97 motorhome spaces. Picnic tables, piped water, electrical connections and sewer hookups are provided. Rest rooms, showers, laundromat, store, ice, boat ramp, motorboat rentals, bait, tackle, and propane gas are available.

Reservations, fee: Phone Leisuretime Reservation Systems at (800)822-CAMP.

Who to contact: Phone park at (209)264-5361.

Location: Drive 17 miles southeast of Dinkey Creek to 54890 McKinley Grove Road.

Trip note: This camp is open from May to November and is on the north fork of the Kings River near the shore of Lake Wishon. Motorboats that travel no faster than 15 m.p.h. are allowed on this fine fishing lake. Nearby in Coolidge Meadow is a trailhead that accesses the Woodchuck Creek drainage and numerous lakes in the John Muir Wilderness. Elevation 6500 feet.

Site **28**   LILY
PAD

Campsites, facilities: There are four tent sites and 11 campsites for tents or motorhomes up to 16 feet long. Piped water, picnic tables and fireplaces are provided, and vault toilets are available. Groceries, boat rentals, boat ramp and propane gas are available nearby. This campground is wheelchair accessible.

Reservations, fee: No reservations; $6 fee per night.

Who to contact: Phone PG&E at (209)487-7250 or Sierra National Forest Headquarters at (209)487-5155.

Location: Drive 17 miles southeast of Dinkey Creek to Wishon Reservoir.

Trip note: This camp is open from June to October and is on the southwest shore of Lake Wishon. Elevation 6500 feet. Motorboats that travel no faster than 15 m.p.h. are allowed on this fishing lake. A trailhead that accesses the Woodchuck Creek drainage, and numerous lakes in the John Muir Wilderness, is nearby in Coolidge Meadow.

Site **29**   MARMOT
                                      ROCK

Campsites, facilities: There are 11 tent sites and three campsites for tents or mo-
    torhomes up to 22 feet long. Piped water, fireplaces and picnic tables are
    provided, and vault toilets and a boat ramp are available.
Reservations, fee: No reservations; $5 fee per night.
Who to contact: Phone PG&E at (209)487-7250 or Sierra National Forest Head-
    quarters at (209)487-5155.
Location: Drive 24 miles northeast of Dinkey Creek at Courtright Reservoir.
Trip note: Open from June to October. Elevation 8200 feet. Campsite is on the
    south shore of Courtright Lake. Motorboats that travel no faster than 15
    m.p.h. are allowed on this fishing lake. A trailhead on the western side of
    the lake accesses the Dinkey Lakes Wilderness, and another on the eastern
    side serves the John Muir Wilderness.

Site **30**   TRAPPER
                                      SPRINGS

Campsites, facilities: There are 30 campsites for tents or motorhomes up to 22
    feet long. Piped water, fireplaces and picnic tables are provided. Vault toi-
    lets are available. A boat ramp is nearby. This campground is wheelchair
    accessible.
Reservations, fee: No reservations; $5 fee per night.
Who to contact: Phone PG&E at (209)487-7250 or Sierra National Forest Head-
    quarters at (209)487-5155.
Location: Drive 26 miles northeast of Dinkey Creek at Courtright Lake.
Trip note: Open from June to October. Elevation 8200 feet. Campsite located on
    the shore of Cartright Lake. Motorboats that travel no faster than 15 m.p.h.
    are allowed on this fishing lake. A trailhead adjacent to camp accesses the
    Dinkey Lakes Wilderness, and another on the eastern side of the lake serves
    the John Muir Wilderness.

Site **31**   SAWMILL
                                      FLAT

Campsites, facilities: There are 15 campsites for tents or motorhomes up to 22
    feet long. Picnic tables are provided, and vault toilets are available. There is
    no water, so bring your own.
Reservations, fee: No reservations, no fee.
Who to contact: Phone Sierra National Forest Headquarters at (209)487-5155.
Location: Drive 14 miles southeast of Dinkey Creek.
Trip note: Open from June to October. elevation 6700 feet. Located on the bor-
    der of Teakettle Experimental Area, about one mile from Kings River.

Site 32   BLACK ROCK   ▲

Campsites, facilities: There are 10 campsites for tents or motorhomes up to 16 feet long. Piped water, fireplaces and picnic tables are provided. Vault toilets are available.

Reservations, fee: No reservations; $5 fee per night.

Who to contact: Phone PG&E at (209)487-7250 or Sierra National Forest Headquarters at (209)487-5155.

Location: Drive 30 miles northeast of Trimmer via Trimmer Springs Road.

Trip note: Open from May to November. Elevation 4200 feet. Located on Black Road Reservoir on the North Fork of the Kings River near the Kings River Geological Area.

Site 33   KIRCH FLAT   ▲

Campsites, facilities: There are 25 campsites for tents or motorhomes up to 22 feet long. Fireplaces and picnic tables are provided. Vault toilets are available. There is no water, so bring your own.

Reservations, fee: No reservations, no fee.

Who to contact: Phone Sierra National Forest Headquarters at (209)487-5155.

Location: Drive 18 miles east of Trimmer via Trimmer Springs Road.

Trip note: This camp is open all year, and is on the Kings River, about six miles from Pine Flat Lake. Elevation 1100 feet.

Site 34   SYCAMORE FLAT #1   ▲

Campsites, facilities: There are 12 campsites for tents or motorhomes up to 22 feet long. Piped water, fireplaces and picnic tables are provided. Vault toilets are available.

Reservations, fee: No reservations, no fee.

Who to contact: Phone Sierra National Forest Headquarters at (209)487-5155.

Location: Drive five miles east of Trimmer on Trimmer Springs Road.

Trip note: This camp is open all year. Elevation 1200 feet. Located on the shore of Pine Flat Reservoir, a large man-made lake with 67 miles of shoreline where you can fish or waterski. There are several resorts on the lake that offer boat and ski rentals, bait and tackle.

Site 35   SYCAMORE FLAT #2   ▲

Campsites, facilities: There are 20 campsites for tents or motorhomes up to 22 feet long. Piped water, fireplaces and picnic tables are provided. Vault toilets are available.

Reservations, fee: No reservations, no fee.
Who to contact: Phone Sierra National Forest Headquarters at (209)487-5155.
Location: Drive six miles east of Trimmer on Trimmer Springs Road.
Trip note: This camp is open all year. Elevation 1200 feet. Located on the shore of Pine Flat Reservoir, a man-made lake with 67 miles of shoreline. Fishing and waterskiing are allowed. There are several resorts on the lake that offer boat and ski rentals, bait and tackle.

Site **36**   BRETZ   🌲

Campsites, facilities: There are 10 campsites for tents or motorhomes up to 22 feet long. Picnic tables and fireplaces are provided, and vault toilets are available. There is no water, so bring your own.
Reservations, fee: No reservations, no fee.
Who to contact: Phone Sierra National Forest Headquarters at (209)487-5155.
Location: Drive 24 miles northeast of Trimmer off Trimmer Springs Road on Big Creek Road.
Trip note: This camp is open from March to November. Elevation 3300 feet.

Site **37**   DEER CREEK POINT GROUP SITE
                   PINE FLAT LAKE   ▲

Campsites, facilities: There are 24 campsites for tents or motorhomes. Piped water, fireplaces and picnic tables are provided. Vault toilets, a dump station and a boat ramp are available. Groceries, boat rentals and propane gas are nearby.
Reservations, fee: Reservations requested; $20 per night per group.
Who to contact: Phone U.S. Army Corps of Engineers at (209)787-2589.
Location: Drive nine miles northeast of Piedra off Trimmer Springs Road.
Trip note: Open all year. Elevation 1000 feet. Located on Pine Flat Lake, which is 21 miles long and has 67 miles of shoreline. Fishing and waterskiing are allowed. There are several resorts on the lake that offer boat and ski rentals, bait and tackle.

Site **38**   ISLAND
                                PARK   ▲

Campsites, facilities: There are 50 campsites for tents or motorhomes. Piped water, fireplaces and picnic tables are provided. Flush toilets, showers, a boat ramp and a dump station are available. Groceries, boat rentals and propane gas are nearby.
Reservations, fee: No reservations; $6 fee per night.
Who to contact: Phone U.S. Army Corps of Engineers at (209)787-2589.
Location: Drive nine miles northeast of Piedra off Trimmer Springs Road.
Trip note: Open all year. Elevation 1000 feet. Located on Pine Flat Lake, which

is 21 miles long and has 67 miles of shoreline. Fishing and waterskiing are allowed. There are several resorts on the lake that offer boat and ski rentals, bait and tackle.

Site **39**   SUNNYSLOPE CAMPGROUNDS   ▲

Campsites, facilities: There are 97 campsites for tents or motorhomes. Piped water, electrical connections, picnic tables and fireplaces are provided. Restrooms, hot showers, a laundromat and propane gas are available. Groceries, boat rentals and marinas are available nearby at Pine Lake.
Reservations, fee: Phone Leisuretime Reservation Systems at (800)822-CAMP.
Who to contact: Phone park at (209)787-2730.
Location: Drive seven miles northeast of Piedra via Trimmer Springs Road on Sunnyslope Road.
Trip note: This campground overlooks Pine Flat Lake, which is 21 miles long and has 67 miles of shoreline. Fishing and waterskiing are allowed. There are several resorts on the lake that offer boat and ski rentals, bait and tackle.

Site **40**   PINE FLAT RECREATION AREA   ▲

Campsites, facilities: There are 54 campsites for tents or motorhomes. Piped water, fireplaces and picnic tables are provided. Flush toilets, dump station, playground and horseback riding facilities are available. A grocery store, laundromat and propane gas are nearby.
Reservations, fee: No reservations; $4 fee per night.
Who to contact: Phone park at (209)488-3004.
Location: Drive three miles east of Piedra off Trimmer Springs Road on Pine Flat Road.
Trip note: This county park is open all year. Elevation 560 feet. Campsite is on Pine Flat Lake, which is 21 miles long and has 67 miles of shoreline. Fishing and waterskiing are allowed. There are several resorts on the lake that offer boat and ski rentals, bait and tackle.

Site **41**   CHOINUMNI PARK   ▲

Campsites, facilities: There are 75 campsites for tents or motorhomes up to 22 feet long. Piped water, fireplaces and picnic tables are provided. Vault toilets, dump station and playground are available. A grocery store, laundromat and propane gas are nearby.
Reservations, fee: No reservations; $4 fee per night.
Who to contact: Phone park at (209)488-3004.
Location: Drive one mile east of Piedra on Trimmer Springs Road.

Trip note: Open all year. Elevation 550 feet. Campsite is near Kings River and Pine Flat Lake, which is 21 miles long and has 67 miles of shoreline. Fishing and waterskiing are allowed. There are several resorts on the lake that offer boat and ski rentals, bait and tackle.

Site **42**   CAMP 4   🌲

Campsites, facilities: There are five campsites for tents or motorhomes up to 16 feet long. Picnic tables and fireplaces are provided, and vault toilets are available. There is no water, so bring your own.
Reservations, fee: No reservations, no fee.
Who to contact: Phone Sequoia National Forest Headquarters at (209)784-1500.
Location: Drive 14 miles southeast of Trimmer off Trimmer Springs Road.
Trip note: Open all year. Elevation 1000 feet. This spot is located on the Kings River. Map of Sequoia National Forest details back-country hiking trails.

Site **43**   MILL
                               FLAT   🌲

Campsites, facilities: There are five campsites for tents or motorhomes up to 16 feet long. Picnic tables and fireplaces are provided, and vault toilets are available. There is no water, so bring your own.
Reservations, fee: No reservations, no fee.
Who to contact: Phone Sequoia National Forest Headquarters at (209)784-1500.
Location: Drive 14 miles southeast of Trimmer off Trimmer Springs Road.
Trip note: Open all year. Elevation 1000 feet. This spot is on the Kings River at confluence of Mill Flat Creek.

Site **44**   CAMP 4 1/2   🌲

Campsites, facilities: There are five campsites for tents or motorhomes up to 16 feet long. Picnic tables and fireplaces are provided, and vault toilets are available. There is no water, so bring your own.
Reservations, fee: No reservations, no fee.
Who to contact: Phone Sequoia National Forest Headquarters at (209)784-1500.
Location: Drive 13 miles southeast of Trimmer off Trimmer Springs Road.
Trip note: Open all year. Elevation 1000 feet. This site is nestled away in a primitive area along the Kings River.

Site **45**   PRINCESS   ▲

Campsites, facilities: There are 50 tent sites and 40 sites for tents or motorhomes up to 22 feet long. Picnic tables, fireplaces and piped water are provided. Flush toilets and a dump station are available. A grocery store is nearby.

Reservations, fee: No reservations; $5 fee per night.

Who to contact: Phone Sequoia National Forest Headquarters at (209)784-1500.

Location: Drive six miles north of Wilsonia on State Route 180.

Trip note: Open from May to October. Elevation 5900 feet. Located alongside Indian Creek. Lake Hume is four miles from camp and the Grant Grove entrance to Kings Canyon National Park is six miles away.

Site **46**   HUME
                       LAKE   🔺

Campsites, facilities: There are 60 tent sites and 14 sites for tents or motorhomes up to 16 feet long. Picnic tables, fireplaces and piped water are provided, and flush toilets are available. A grocery store is nearby.

Reservations, fee: No reservations; $6 fee per night.

Who to contact: Phone Sequoia National Forest Headquarters at (209)784-1500.

Location: Drive two miles northeast of Hume to Hume Lake.

Trip note: Open from May to October. Elevation 5200 feet. Campsite is located on Hume Lake, a man-made fishing lake. The Grant Grove entrance to Kings Canyon National Park is 10 miles away.

Site **47**   LANDSLIDE   🌲

Campsites, facilities: There are four tent sites and two campsites for tents or motorhomes up to 16 feet long. Picnic tables and fireplaces are provided, and vault toilets are available. There is no water, so bring your own. A grocery store is nearby.

Reservations, fee: No reservations, no fee.

Who to contact: Phone Sequoia National Forest Headquarters at (209)784-1500.

Location: Drive three miles southeast of Hume on Hume Road of State Route 180.

Trip note: Open from May to October. Elevation 5800 feet. This site is on Landslide Creek about two miles from Lake Hume and 14 miles from the Grant Grove entrance to Kings Canyon National Park.

Site **48**   UPPER
                       TEN MILE   🌲

Campsites, facilities: There are five campsites for tents or motorhomes up to 22 feet long. Picnic tables and fireplaces are provided, and vault toilets are available. There is no water, but a grocery store is nearby.

Reservations, fee: No reservations, no fee.

Who to contact: Phone Sequoia National Forest Headquarters at (209)784-1500.

Location: Drive five miles south of Hume on Hume Road off State Route 180.

Trip note: Open from May to October. Elevation 5800 feet. Located on Ten Mile Creek about four miles from Hume Lake and 16 miles from the Grant Grove entrance to Kings Canyon National Park.

Site **49**   CRYSTAL
                               SPRINGS   ▲

Campsites, facilities: There are 57 campsites for tents or motorhomes. Piped water, fireplaces and picnic tables are provided. Flush toilets, showers, a dump station, horseback riding facilities and evening ranger programs are available. Groceries and propane gas are nearby.
Reservations, fee: No reservations; $6 fee per night.
Who to contact: Phone Kings Canyon National Park at (209)565-3341.
Location: Drive 3/4 mile north of Wilsonia off State Route 180.
Trip note: Open from May to October. Elevation 6600 feet. Beware of road and snow conditions as winter approaches. Kings Canyon is one of the deepest gorges in North America. The surrounding groves of giant sequoias are inspiring.

Site **50**   SHEEP
                               CREEK   ▲

Campsites, facilities: There are 111 campsites for tents or motorhomes. Piped water, fireplaces and picnic tables are provided. Flush toilets, showers, a dump station, horseback riding facilities and evening ranger programs are available. A grocery store, bike rentals and a laundromat are nearby.
Reservations, fee: No reservations; $6 fee per night.
Who to contact: Phone Kings Canyon National Park at (209)565-3341.
Location: Drive to 1/2 mile west of Cedar Grove in Kings Canyon National Park.
Trip note: Open from June to October. Elevation 4600 feet. Beware of road and snow conditions as winter approaches. Kings Canyon is one of the deepest gorges in North America.

Site **51**   SENTINEL   ▲

Campsites, facilities: There are 83 campsites for tents or motorhomes. Piped water, fireplaces and picnic tables are provided. Flush toilets, showers, a dump station, bike rentals and horseback riding facilities are available. A grocery store and laundromat are nearby.
Reservations, fee: No reservations; $6 fee per night.
Who to contact: Phone Kings Canyon National Park at (209)565-3341.
Location: Drive on State Route 180 to Kings Canyon National Park, campground is in the Cedar Grove area.
Trip note: Open from April to October, depending on road and snow conditions. Elevation 4600 feet.

Site **52**   CANYON
                               VIEW

Campsites, facilities: There are 37 campsites for tents or motorhomes. Piped wa-
    ter, fireplaces and picnic tables are provided. Flush toilets, showers, a dump
    station, bike rentals and horseback riding facilities are available. A grocery
    store and a laundromat are nearby.
Reservations, fee: No reservations; $6 fee per night.
Who to contact: Phone Kings Canyon National Park at (209)565-3341.
Location: Drive on State Route 180 to Kings Canyon National Park, camp-
    ground is in the Cedar Grove area.
Trip note: Open from June to September, depending on road and snow condi-
    tions. Elevation 4600 feet. Kings Canyon is one of the deepest gorges in
    North America and the surrounding groves of giant sequoias are inspiring.

Site **53**   CANYON VIEW
                            GROUP CAMP

Campsites, facilities: There are four campsites for tents or motorhomes. Piped
    water, fireplaces and picnic tables are provided, and flush toilets, showers, a
    dump station, bike rentals and horseback riding facilities are available. A
    grocery store and a laundromat are nearby.
Reservations, fee: Call ahead for reservations and fee.
Who to contact: Phone Kings Canyon National Park at (209)565-3341.
Location: Drive on State Route 180 to Kings Canyon National Park, camp-
    ground is in the Cedar Grove area.
Trip note: Open from April to September, depending on road and snow condi-
    tions. Elevation 4600 feet.

Site **54**   MORAINE
                                                                 ▲

Campsites, facilities: There are 120 campsites for tents or motorhomes. Piped
    water, fireplaces and picnic tables are provided. Flush toilets, showers, a
    dump station, bike rentals and horseback riding facilities are available. A
    grocery store and a laundromat are nearby.
Reservations, fee: No reservations; $6 fee per night.
Who to contact: Phone Kings Canyon National Park at (209)565-3341.
Location: Drive on State Route 180 to Kings Canyon National Park, camp-
    ground is in the Cedar Grove area.
Trip note: This camp is open from June to October, depending on road and
    snow conditions. Elevation 4600 feet.

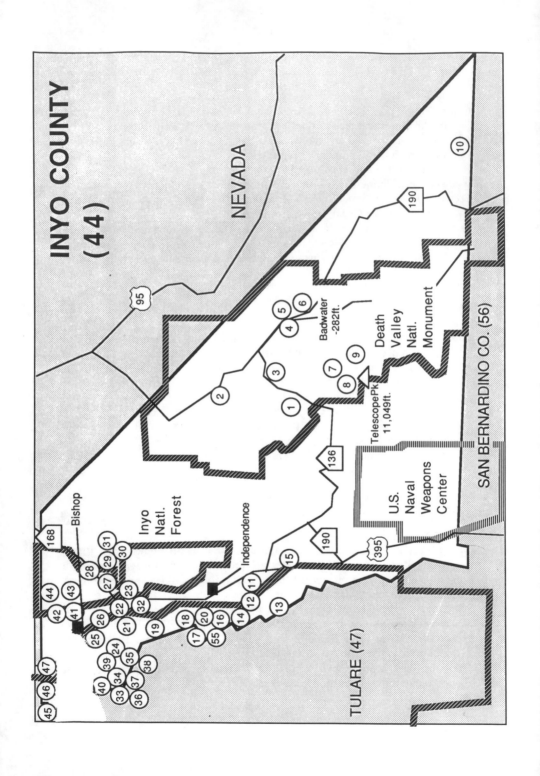

INYO COUNTY
(44)

INYO COUNTY

◆

| Site 1 | EMIGRANT | |

Campsites, facilities: There are 10 campsites for tents or motorhomes. Piped water, fireplaces and picnic tables are provided, and flush toilets are available.
Reservations, fee: No reservations, no fee.
Who to contact: Phone Death Valley National Monument at (619)786-2331.
Location: Drive nine miles southwest of Stove Pipe Wells Village on State Route 190.
Trip note: This camp is open from April to November. Elevation 2000 feet. Keep in mind that temperatures in Death Valley are commonly over 100 degrees during the summer.

| Site 2 | MESQUITE SPRINGS | |

Campsites, facilities: There are 60 campsites for tents or motorhomes. There is also one group campsite that will accommodate 35 people and nine vehicles (reservations required). Piped water, fireplaces and picnic tables are provided, and flush toilets, dump station and camp store are available. Rest rooms are wheelchair accessible.
Reservations, fee: No reservations; $5 fee per night.
Who to contact: Phone Death Valley National Monument at (619)786-2331.
Location: Drive five miles south of Scotty's Castle via State Route 267 and 190. Campground is located off State Route 190.
Trip note: Open all year. Elevation 1800 feet. Located a short distance from Scotty's Castle and the Ubehebe Crater.

| Site 3 | STOVEPIPE WELLS | |

Campsites, facilities: There are 10 tent sites and 200 campsites for tents or motorhomes. Piped water is provided and there are firegrills at the tent sites only. Flush toilets, dump station, hot showers, swimming pool, camp store, gasoline and evening ranger programs are available. The rest rooms are wheelchair accessible.

Reservations, fee: No reservations; $4 fee per night.
Who to contact: Phone Death Valley National Monument at (619)786-2331.
Location: Drive to north end of Stovepipe Wells Village on State Route 190.
Trip note: This camp is open from November through April. Located at sea level, it is near the Sand Dunes and Mosaic Canyon. A four-wheel drive road into Cottonwood and Marble Canyons is nearby.

Site **4**   BADWATER
                                  WELLS

Campsites, facilities: There are 180 campsites for tents or motorhomes. Picnic tables, fireplaces and piped water are provided. Flush toilets, dump station, swimming pool, hot showers, evening ranger programs, camp store, gasoline, laundromat and horseback riding facilities are available. The rest rooms are wheelchair accessible.
Reservations, fee: No reservations; $5 fee per night.
Who to contact: Phone Death Valley National Monument at (619)786-2331.
Location: Drive one mile north of Furnace Creek on State Route 190.
Trip note: This camp is open all year, but keep in mind that the summer temperatures commonly exceed 100 degrees. The nearby Visitors Center and Death Valley Museum offer maps and suggestions for hikes and drives in this uniquely beautiful park.

Site **5**   SUNSET

Campsites, facilities: There are 100 campsites for tents or motorhomes. Piped water, fireplaces and picnic tables are provided. Flush toilets, dump station, swimming pool, hot showers, evening ranger programs, camp store, gasoline, laundromat, and horseback riding facilities are available. There are 16 wheelchair accessible campsites near accessible rest rooms.
Reservations, fee: No reservations; $4 fee per night.
Who to contact: Phone Death Valley National Monument at (619)786-2331.
Location: Drive 1/4 mile east of Furnace Creek Ranch.
Trip note: This campground is open from November through April. Located at sea level. The nearby Visitors Center and Death Valley Museum offer maps and suggestions for hikes and drives in this uniquely beautiful park.

Site **6**   TEXAS
                                  SPRING

Campsites, facilities: There are 35 tent sites and 40 campsites for tents or motorhomes. There are also two group campsites, one that accommodates 150 people and 10 vehicles, and another that accommodates 50 people and 10 vehicles. Piped water, fireplaces and picnic tables are provided. Flush toilets, hot showers, swimming pool, dump station, evening ranger programs, camp store, gasoline, laundromat and horseback riding facilities are available.

Reservations, fee: No reservations; $5 fee per night.

Who to contact: Phone Death Valley National Monument at (619)786-2331.

Location: Drive 1/2 mile east of Furnace Creek Ranch on State Route 190.

Trip note: This campground is at sea level and is open from November through April. The nearby Visitors Center and Death Valley Museum offers maps and suggestions for hikes and drives.

Site 7   THORNDIKE

Campsites, facilities: This backcountry campground is accessible by foot or four-wheel drive and has 10 campsites for tents. Fireplaces and picnic tables are provided, and pit toilets are available. There is no water, so bring your own.

Reservations, fee: No reservations, no fee.

Who to contact: Phone Death Valley National Monument at (619)786-2331.

Location: Drive 37 miles south of Stovepipe Wells Village via State Route 190 and Panamint Valley or Emigrant Canyon Roads to Wildrose Canyon Road; drive to end of road. Note: Emigrant Canyon Road is steep, narrow and winding and not recommended for vehicles over 25 feet long.

Trip note: Open from March to October. Elevation 7500 feet. Nearby are century old charcoal kilns that were built by Chinese laborers and tended by Shoshone Indians. The trailhead that serves Telescope Peak, the highest point in Death Valley, can be found in nearby Mahogany Flat campground. It is a strenuous all-day hike.

Site 8   WILDROSE

Campsites, facilities: There are 39 campsites for tents or motorhomes. Piped water, fireplaces and picnic tables are provided, and pit toilets are available.

Reservations, fee: No reservations, no fee.

Who to contact: Phone Death Valley National Monument at (619)786-2331.

Location: Drive 30 miles south of Stovepipe Wells Village via State Route 190 and Panamint Valley or Emigrant Canyon Roads to Wildrose Canyon Road. Note: Emigrant Canyon Road is steep, narrow and winding and not recommended for vehicles over 25 feet long.

Trip note: This campground is open all year. Elevation 4100 feet. Visit the abandoned charcoal kilns or hike nearby Wildrose Peak.

Site **9**   MAHOGANY
                            FLAT

Campsites, facilities: There are 10 campsites for tents. Fireplaces and picnic tables are provided, and pit toilets are available. There is no water, so bring
  your own. The campground is accessible by foot or four-wheel drive.
Reservations, fee: No reservations; $5 fee per night.
Who to contact: Phone Death Valley National Monument at (619)786-2331.
Location: Drive 38 miles south of Stovepipe Wells Village via State Route 190
  and Panamint Valley or Emigrant Canyon Roads to Wildrose Canyon road;
  drive to end of road. Note: Emigrant Canyon Road is steep, narrow and
  winding and not recommended for vehicles over 25 feet long.
Trip note: Open from April through October. Elevation 8200 feet. The trailhead
  that accesses Bennett and Telescope Peaks leads out from camp. It is a
  strenuous all-day hike.

Site **10**   TECOPA HOT SPRINGS
                            PARK

Campsites, facilities: There are 300 campsites for tents or motorhomes. Piped
  water, fireplaces, picnic tables and in some cases electrical connections are
  provided. Flush toilets, showers, dump station, store, laundromat and propane gas are available.
Reservations, fee: No reservations; $5 fee per night.
Who to contact: Phone County Parks Department at (619)852-4264.
Location: Drive five miles south of Shoshone via State Route 127.
Trip note: Open all year. Elevation 1500 feet. The winter climate here is warm
  and dry and the mineral baths are nearby. It is a great rockhounding area,
  and a short distance to Death Valley.

Site **11**   WHITNEY
                            PORTAL

Campsites, facilities: There are 44 campsites for tents or motorhomes. Piped wa-
  ter, fireplaces and picnic tables are provided, and flush toilets are available.
  A grocery store is nearby.
Reservations, fee: No reservations; $6 fee per night.
Who to contact: Call Inyo National Forest Headquarters at (619)873-5841.
Location: Drive 13 miles west of Lone Pine on Whitney Portal Road.
Trip note: Open from May to October. Elevation 8000 feet. There is a trailhead
  in camp that accesses Mt. Whitney, the Pacific Crest Trail and numerous
  lakes in John Muir Wilderness and the backcountry of Sequoia National
  Park.

Site **12** | LONE
PINE

Campsites, facilities: There are eight tent sites and one campsite for tent or motorhome. Piped water, fireplaces and picnic tables are provided, and vault toilets and a dump station are available.
Reservations, fee: No reservations; $6 fee per night.
Who to contact: Call Inyo National Forest Headquarters at (619)873-5841.
Location: Drive seven miles west of Lone Pine on Whitney Portal Road.
Trip note: Open all year. Elevation 6000 feet. Located on Lone Pine Creek.

Site **13** | TUTTLE
CREEK

Campsites, facilities: There are 85 campsites for tents or motorhomes. Fireplaces and picnic tables are provided, and pit toilets are available. There is no water, so bring your own.
Reservations, fee: No reservations, no fee.
Who to contact: Phone Bureau of Land Management at (619)872-4881.
Location: Drive six miles southwest of Lone Pine on Tuttle Creek Road.
Trip note: Open from April to October. Elevation 5100 feet. Located on Tuttle Creek.

Site **14** | PORTAGEE
JOE

Campsites, facilities: There are 15 campsites for tents or motorhomes. Piped water, fireplaces and picnic tables are provided, and pit toilets are available. A grocery store, laundromat and propane gas are nearby.
Reservations, fee: No reservations; $4 fee per night.
Who to contact: Phone County Parks Department at (619-878-2411.
Location: Drive one mile southwest of Lone Pine on Whitney Portal Road to Tuttle Creek Road.
Trip note: Open all year. Elevation 3750 feet. It is about five miles from Diaz Lake and the Interagency Visitor Center.

Site **15** | DIAZ
LAKE

Campsites, facilities: There are 100 campsites for tents or motorhomes. Piped water, fireplaces and picnic tables are provided. Flush toilets, showers and boat ramp are available. A grocery store, laundromat and propane gas are nearby.
Reservations, fee: No reservations; $5 fee per night.
Who to contact: Phone County Parks Department at (619)878-2411.

Location: Drive two miles south of Lone Pine on US-395.
Trip note: Open all year. Elevation 3800 feet. Located on the shore of Diaz Lake.

Site **16**   ROADS
                               END   ▲

Campsites, facilities: There are 15 campsites for tents or motorhomes. Vault toilets and horseback riding facilities are available. There is no water, so bring your own.
Reservations, fee: No reservations, no fee.
Who to contact: Call Inyo National Forest Headquarters at (619)873-5841.
Location: Drive three and a half miles west of Lone Pine on Whitney Portal Road, then turn left on Horseshoe Meadows Road and drive 21 miles to the end of the road.
Trip note: This campground is at 9400 feet elevation and is open June to October.

Site **17**   ONION
                               VALLEY   ▲

Campsites, facilities: There are 17 tent sites and 12 campsites for tents or motorhomes. Piped water, fireplaces and picnic tables are provided. Flush toilets and horseback riding facilities are available.
Reservations, fee: No reservations; $5 fee per night.
Who to contact: Call Inyo National Forest Headquarters at (619)873-5841.
Location: Drive 14 miles west of Independence on Onion Valley Road.
Trip note: Open from May to September. Elevation 9200 feet. There are several trails leading out from camp that access numerous lakes in the John Muir Wilderness, Sequoia National Park and the Pacific Crest Trail.

Site **18**   INDEPENDENCE
                               CREEK   ▲

Campsites, facilities: There are 25 campsites for tents or motorhomes. Piped water and picnic tables are provided, and pit toilets are available. A grocery store, laundromat and propane gas are located nearby.
Reservations, fee: No reservations; $3 fee per night.
Who to contact: Phone County Parks Department at (619)878-2411.
Location: Drive 1/2 mile west of Independence on Onion Valley Road.
Trip note: Open all year. Elevation 3900 feet. Located on Independece Creek.

Site 19 OAK CREEK

Campsites, facilities: There are 24 campsites for tents or motorhomes. Piped water, fireplaces and picnic tables are provided, and flush toilets are available. A grocery store, laundromat and propane gas are located nearby.
Reservations, fee: No reservations; $5 fee per night.
Who to contact: Call Inyo National Forest Headquarters at (619)873-5841.
Location: Drive five miles northwest of Independence via US-395 and North Oak Creek Drive.
Trip note: This campground is open all year. Elevation 5000 feet. Located on the North Fork of Oak Creek.

Site 20 GRAY'S MEADOW

Campsites, facilities: There are 52 campsites for tents or motorhomes. Piped water, fireplaces and picnic tables are provided, and flush toilets are available. A grocery store, laundromat and propane gas are available nearby.
Reservations, fee: No reservations; $6 fee per night.
Who to contact: Call Inyo National Forest Headquarters at (619)873-5841.
Location: Drive five miles west of Independence on Onion Valley Road.
Trip note: This campground is open from April to October. Elevation 600 feet. Located on Independence Creek.

Site 21 GOODALE CREEK

Campsites, facilities: There are 62 campsites for tents or motorhomes. Fireplaces and picnic tables are provided, and pit toilets are available. There is no water.
Reservations, fee: No reservations; $3 fee per night.
Who to contact: Call Bureau of Land Management at (619)872-4881.
Location: Drive 12 miles north of Independence on US-395, then two miles west on Aberdeen.
Trip note: This campground is open from May to October. Elevation 4100 feet. Located on Goodale Creek.

Site 22 TABOOSE

Campsites, facilities: There are 45 campsites for tents or motorhomes. Fireplaces and picnic tables are provided, and non-piped water and pit toilets are available.
Reservations, fee: No reservations; $3 fee per night.

Who to contact: Phone County Parks Department at (619)878-2411.
Location: Drive 11 miles south of Big Pine on US-395, then west for a mile at Taboose Creek.
Trip note: This campground is open all year. Elevation 3900 feet. Located on Taboose Creek.

Site **23**   TINNEMAHA   ▲

Campsites, facilities: There are 45 campsites for tents or motorhomes. Fireplaces and picnic tables are provided, and non-piped water and pit toilets are available.
Reservations, fee: No reservations; $3 fee per night.
Who to contact: Phone County Parks Department at (619)878-2411.
Location: Drive seven miles south of Big Pine via US-395 and Tinnemaha Road.
Trip note: This campground is open all year. Elevation 4400 feet. It is on Tinnemaha Creek about five miles from the wildlife viewpoint at Tinnemaha Reservoir.

Site **24**   BIG PINE
                               CREEK   ▲

Campsites, facilities: There are 12 tent sites and 21 campsites for tents or motorhomes. Piped water, fireplaces and picnic tables are provided, and vault toilets and horseback riding facilities are available. A grocery store is nearby.
Reservations, fee: No reservations; $6 fee per night.
Who to contact: Call Inyo National Forest Headquarters at (619)873-5841.
Location: Drive 10 miles southwest of Big Pine on Glacier Lodge Road.
Trip note: Open from May to November. Elevation 7700 feet. There are several trails near camp that lead to numerous lakes in the John Muir Wilderness. The camp is on Big Pine Creek.

Site **25**   BAKER
                               CREEK   ▲

Campsites, facilities: There are 25 campsites for tents or motorhomes. Fireplaces and picnic tables are provided, and non-piped water and pit toilets are available. Groceries and propane gas are nearby.
Reservations, fee: No reservations; $3 fee per night.
Who to contact: Phone County Parks Department at (619)878-2411.
Location: Drive one mile northwest of Big Pine on US-395 via Baker Creek Road.
Trip note: This campground is open all year. Elevation 4100 feet. Located on Baker Creek.

Site **26**

BIG PINE
TRIANGLE

Campsites, facilities: There are 30 campsites for tents or motorhomes. Piped water, fireplaces and picnic tables are provided, and flush toilets and a playground are available. Groceries and propane gas are located nearby.
Reservations, fee: No reservations; $3 fee per night.
Who to contact: Phone County Parks Department at (619)878-2411.
Location: Drive 1/2 mile north of Big Pine on US-395.
Trip note: This campground is open from April to October. Elevation 4000 feet. Located on the Big Pine Canal.

Site **27**

FOSSIL
GROUP CAMP

Campsites, facilities: There are 11 campsites for tents or motorhomes. Picnic tables are provided and vault toilets are available. There is no water, so bring your own.
Reservations, fee: Reservations requested; $15 group fee per night.
Who to contact: Call Inyo National Forest Headquarters at (619)873-5841.
Location: Drive 13 miles northeast of Big Pine on State Route 168.
Trip note: This campground is open all year. Elevation 7200 feet. A trail leads west to Black Mountain from nearby Cedar Flat. Deep Spring Lake is 10 miles from camp via State Route 168 and primitive roads.

Site **28**

JUNIPER
GROUP CAMP

Campsites, facilities: There are five campsites for tents or motorhomes. Picnic tables are provided and vault toilets are available. There is no water, so bring your own.
Reservations, fee: Reservations requested; $15 fee per group per night.
Who to contact: Call Inyo National Forest Headquarters at (619)873-5841.
Location: Drive 13 miles northeast of Big Pine on State Route 168.
Trip note: Open all year. Elevation 7200 feet. A trail leads west to Black Mountain from nearby Cedar Flat. Deep Spring Lake is 10 miles from camp via State Route 168 and primitive roads.

Site **29**

PINYON
GROUP CAMP

Campsites, facilities: There are eight campsites for tents or motorhomes. Picnic tables are provided, and vault toilets are available. There is no water, so bring your own.
Reservations, fee: Reservations requested; $15 group fee per night.

Who to contact: Call Inyo National Forest Headquarters at (619)873-5841.
Location: Drive 13 miles northeast of Big Pine on State Route 168.
Trip note: Open all year. Elevation 7200 feet. A trail leads west to Black Mountain from nearby Cedar Flat. Deep Spring Lake is 10 miles from camp via State Route 168 and primitive roads.

Site **30**   POLETA
                             GROUP CAMP

Campsites, facilities: There are eight campsites for tents or motorhomes. Picnic tables are provided, and vault toilets are available. There is no water, so bring your own.
Reservations, fee: Reservations requested; $15 group fee per night.
Who to contact: Call Inyo National Forest Headquarters at (619)873-5841.
Location: Drive 13 miles northeast of Big Pine off State Route 168.
Trip note: Open all year. Elevation 7200 feet. A trail leads west to Black Mountain from nearby Cedar Flat. Deep Spring Lake is 10 miles from camp via State Route 168 and primitive roads.

Site **31**   GRANDVIEW

Campsites, facilities: There are six tent sites and 20 campsites for tents or motorhomes. Fireplaces and picnic tables are provided, and vault toilets are available. There is no water, so bring your own.
Reservations, fee: No reservations, no fee.
Who to contact: Call Inyo National Forest Headquarters at (619)873-5841.
Location: Drive 13 miles northeast of Big Pine off State Route 168 on White Mountain Road.
Trip note: Open from May to October. Elevation 8600 feet. A trail leads out of camp up to an old mining site and the boundary of the Ancient Bristlecone Forest is two miles away.

Site **32**   SABRINA   ▲

Campsites, facilities: There are 21 tent sites and 12 campsites for tents or motorhomes. Fireplaces and picnic tables are provided, and flush toilets and horseback riding facilities are available. There is no drinking water, so bring your own. Groceries and propane gas are nearby.
Reservations, fee: No reservations, no fee.
Who to contact: Call Inyo National Forest Headquarters at (619)873-5841.
Location: Drive 17 miles southwest of Bishop on State Route 168.
Trip note: This campground is open from May to October. Elevation 9000 feet.

It is set on Bishop Creek about 1/2 mile from Lake Sabrina. There is a trailhead at Lake Sabrina that accesses several other trails and numerous lakes in the John Muir Wilderness.

Site **33**   ASPEN
                            MEADOWS

Campsites, facilities: There are five tent sites in this walk-in campground. Fireplaces and picnic tables are provided. Vault toilets and horseback riding facilities are available. There is no water, so bring your own.
Reservations, fee: No reservations, no fee.
Who to contact: Call Inyo National Forest Headquarters at (619)873-5841.
Location: Drive 17 miles southwest of Bishop via State Route 168 and South Lake Road.
Trip note: Open from May to October. Elevation 8500 feet. It is near the South Fork of Bishop Creek and about four miles from South Lake which has a boat ramp. There are several trails near South Lake that access small lakes in the John Muir Wilderness and one that connects with the Pacific Crest Trail.

Site **34**   NORTH
                             LAKE

Campsites, facilities: There are six tent sites and five campsites for tents or motorhomes. Piped water, fireplaces and picnic tables are provided. Flush toilets and horseback riding facilities are available. Groceries and propane gas are nearby.
Reservations, fee: No reservations; $4 fee per night.
Who to contact: Call Inyo National Forest Headquarters at (619)873-5841.
Location: Drive 19 miles southwest of Bishop on State Route 168 to North Lake.
Trip note: Open from June to November. Elevation 9500 feet. It is on the North Fork of Bishop Creek near North Lake, and close to a trailhead that accesses numerous lakes in the John Muir Wilderness and eventually connects with the Pacific Crest Trail.

Site **35**   INTAKE

Campsites, facilities: There are eight tent sites and 12 campsites for tents or motorhomes. Piped water, fireplaces and picnic tables are provided. Flush toilets and horseback riding facilities are available. Groceries and propane gas are located nearby.
Reservations, fee: No reservations; $5 fee per night.
Who to contact: Call Inyo National Forest Headquarters at (619)873-5841.
Location: Drive 14 miles southwest of Bishop on State Route 168.

Trip note: Open from April to November. Elevation 7500 feet. It is set on a small reservoir on Bishop Creek about three miles from Lake Sabrina. There is a trailhead at Lake Sabrina that accesses several other trails and numerous lakes in the John Muir Wilderness.

Site **36**   BISHOP
                               PARK   ▲

Campsites, facilities: There are 10 tent sites and 10 campsites for tents or motorhomes. Piped water, fireplaces and picnic tables are provided, and flush toilets and horseback riding facilities are available. Groceries and propane gas are nearby.
Reservations, fee: No reservations; $5 fee per night.
Who to contact: Call Inyo National Forest Headquarters at (619)873-5841.
Location: Drive 15 miles southwest of Bishop on State Route 168.
Trip note: Open from May to November. Elevation 7500 feet. This site is set on Bishop Creek about two miles from Lake Sabrina. There is a trailhead at Lake Sabrina that accesses several other trails and numerous lakes in the John Muir Wilderness.

Site **37**   FOUR
                               JEFFREY   ▲

Campsites, facilities: There are 49 tent sites and 57 campsites for tents or motorhomes. Piped water, fireplaces and picnic tables are provided, and flush toilets, dump station and horseback riding facilities are available. Groceries and propane gas are nearby.
Reservations, fee: No reservations; $6 fee per night.
Who to contact: Call Inyo National Forest Headquarters at (619)873-5841.
Location: Drive 14 miles southwest of Bishop via State Route 168 and South Lake Road.
Trip note: Open April to November. Elevation 8100 feet. It is set on the South Fork of Bishop Creek about four miles from Lake Sabrina. There is a trailhead at Lake Sabrina that accesses several other trails and numerous lakes in the John Muir Wilderness.

Site **38**   FORKS

Campsites, facilities: There are nine campsites for tents or motorhomes. Piped water, fireplaces and picnic tables are provided. Flush toilets and horseback riding facilities are available. Groceries and propane gas are nearby.
Reservations, fee: No reservations; $5 fee per night.
Who to contact: Call Inyo National Forest Headquarters at (619)873-5841.
Location: Drive 13 miles southwest of Bishop on State Route 168.

Trip note: Open from May to October. Elevation 7800 feet. This site is set on Bishop Creek about four miles from Lake Sabrina. There is a trailhead at Lake Sabrina that accesses several other trails and numerous lakes in the John Muir Wilderness.

Site **39**
BIG
TREES

Campsites, facilities: There are 10 campsites for tents or motorhomes. Piped water, fireplaces and picnic tables are provided, and flush toilets and horseback riding facilities are available. Groceries and propane gas are nearby.
Reservations, fee: No reservations; $5 fee per night.
Who to contact: Call Inyo National Forest Headquarters at (619)873-5841.
Location: Drive 13 miles southwest of Bishop off State Route 168 (see Forest Service map).
Trip note: Open from April to October. Elevation 7500 feet. It is on Bishop Creek about 10 miles from both South Lake and Sabrina Lake.

Site **40**
HABEGGAR'S RESORT
AND TRAILER PARK

Campsites, facilities: There are 44 campsites for tents or motorhomes. Piped water, electrical and sewer connections are provided, and flush toilets, showers, laundromat and propane gas are available.
Reservations, fee: Reservations suggested; $13 fee per night.
Who to contact: Phone park at (619)873-4483.
Location: Drive 15 miles southwest of Bishop via State Route 168 and South Lake Road.
Trip note: Open from May to October. Elevation 8400 feet. Good trout fishing in area.

Site **41**
MILLPOND
RECREATION AREA

Campsites, facilities: There are 100 campsites for tents or motorhomes. Piped water, fireplaces and picnic tables are provided. Flush toilets, showers, playground and horseback riding facilities are available. Groceries, a laundromat and propane gas are located nearby.
Reservations, fee: Reservations suggested; $7 fee per night.
Who to contact: Phone campground at (619)873-5342.
Location: Drive seven miles north of Bishop off US-395 (see local or Forest Service map).
Trip note: Open all year. Elevation 4300 feet. McGee Creek is nearby. There is an Indian Cultural Center in Bishop.

Site 42   PLEASANT VALLEY ▲

Campsites, facilities: There are 200 campsites for tents or motorhomes. Fireplaces and picnic tables are provided, and pit toilets are available. There is no water, so bring your own.
Reservations, fee: No reservations; $4 fee per night.
Who to contact: Phone park at (619)878-2411.
Location: Drive seven miles northwest of Bishop off US-395 (see local or Forest Service map).
Trip note: This campground is at 4200 feet elevation and is open all year. The Pleasant Valley Reservoir, created by the Owens River, is nearby.

Site 43   HIGHLANDS RV PARK 🚙

Campsites, facilities: There are 103 motorhome spaces with full hookups. Piped water and picnic tables are provided, and flush toilets, showers, dump station and horseback riding facilities are available. Groceries, a laundromat and propane gas are nearby.
Reservations, fee: Reservations suggested; $12 fee per night.
Who to contact: Phone park at (619)873-7616.
Location: Drive two miles north of Bishop at 2275 North Sierra Highway.
Trip note: Open all year. Elevation 4200 feet. There is an Indian Cultural Center in Bishop, and the Pleasant Valley Reservoir is about 10 miles away.

Site 44   SHADY REST TRAILER PARK ▲

Campsites, facilities: There are 25 campsites for tents or motorhomes. Piped water, full hookups, fireplaces and picnic tables are provided. Flush toilets, showers, laundromat and horseback riding facilities are available.
Reservations, fee: Reservations suggested; $10 fee per night.
Who to contact: Phone park at (619)873-3430.
Location: In Bishop, drive to 399 East Yancy Street.
Trip note: Open all year. Elevation 4100 feet. There is an Indian Cultural Center in Bishop, and the Pleasant Valley Reservoir is about 10 miles away.

Site 45   HORTON CREEK ▲

Campsites, facilities: There are 53 campsites for tents or motorhomes. Fireplaces and picnic tables are provided, and pit toilets are available. There is no water, so bring your own.
Reservations, fee: No reservations, no fee.

Who to contact: Phone Bureau of Land Management at (619)872-4881.
Location: Drive eight miles northwest of Bishop on US-395, then go west on
Round Valley Road for five miles.
Trip note: This campground is open from May to October. Elevation 5000 feet.
It is on Horton Creek near the Inyo Mono Ecology Center.

| Site **46** | SCHOBER
LANE | ▲ |

Campsites, facilities: There are 150 campsites for tents or motorhomes. Piped
water, fireplaces and picnic tables are provided, and flush toilets are
available.
Reservations, fee: No reservations; $3 fee per night.
Who to contact: Phone County Parks Department at (619)873-5240.
Location: Drive two miles south of Bishop on US-395.
Trip note: The campground is a short distance from the Indian Cultural Center
in Bishop.

| Site **47** | SYMMES
CREEK | ▲ |

Campsites, facilities: There are 55 campsites for tents or motorhomes. Piped wa-
ter and picnic tables are provided, and flush toilets are available.
Reservations, fee: No reservations; $2 fee per night.
Who to contact: Phone the Bureau of Land Management at (619)872-4881.
Location: Drive five miles southwest of Independence on Onion Valley Road.
Trip note: The campground is near Symmes Creek and one and a half miles
from Independence Creek. Two miles from camp is a trailhead that access-
es the California Bighorn Sheep Zoological Area in Inyo National Forest,
Sequoia National Park and the Pacific Crest Trail.

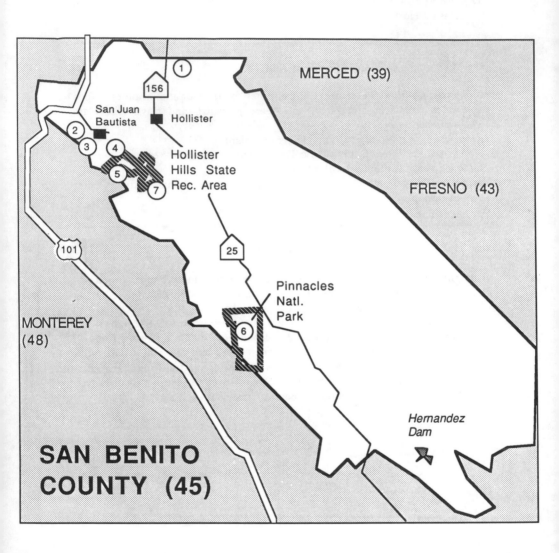

MERCED (39)

156

San Juan
Bautista

Hollister

Hollister
Hills State
Rec. Area

FRESNO (43)

101

25

Pinnacles
Natl.
Park

MONTEREY
(48)

Hernandez
Dam

**SAN BENITO
COUNTY (45)**

SAN BENITO COUNTY

◆

Site **1**   CASA DE FRUTA
             TRAVEL PARK

Campsites, facilities: There are 300 motorhome spaces with water and electric hookups. Picnic tables and fireplaces are provided. Also available are flush toilets, showers, dump station, playground, swimming pool, outdoor dance floor, horseshoes, volleyball courts, baseball diamonds, wine and cheese tasting room, candy factory, gift shop, laundry, propane gas and groceries are available.

Reservations, fee: Phone Leisuretime Reservation Systems, Inc. at (800)822-CAMP. $12 deposit; $12 fee per night.

Who to contact: Phone park at (408)842-9316.

Location: Drive 13 miles east of Gilroy or 28 miles west of Los Banos to 10031 Pacheco Pass Highway (State Route 152).

Trip note: This 80 acre park provides live country and western music and dancing on Saturdays and Sundays, and outdoor western barbeque every Sunday during the spring and summer.

Site **2**   MISSION FARM
             RV PARK

Campsites, facilities: There are 25 tent sites with water and electric hookups and 140 motorhome spaces with full hookups. Flush toilets, showers, dump station, laundry, recreation rooms, propane gas and groceries are available.

Reservations, fee: Call for space available. $15 deposit required; $15 fee per night.

Who to contact: Phone park at (408)623-4456.

Location: Drive 1/2 mile east of San Juan Bautista to 400 San Juan-Hollister Road.

Trip note: This campground is open all year and is in a walnut orchard within walking distance of the San Juan Bautista Mission.

Site 3

MONTEREY VACATION
RV PARK

Campsites, facilities: There are 88 motorhome spaces with full hookups. Flush toilets, showers, jacuzzi, dump station, laundry and propane gas are available.

Reservations, fee: Call ahead for space available and fee.

Who to contact: Phone park at (408)757-8098.

Location: On US-101 between Gilroy and Salinas drive to 1400 Highway 101 (two miles south of the State Route 156-San Juan Bautista exit).

Trip note: This campground is conveniently located minutes away from the Monterey Bay Aquarium and Fisherman's Wharf, Laguna Seca Raceway, the wine country, Mission San Juan Bautista and the Gilroy Garlic Festival.

Site 4

SAN JUAN BAUTISTA
KOA

Campsites, facilities: There are 17 tent sites, 27 campsites with partial hookups for tents or motorhomes, and 14 motorhome spaces with full hookups. Flush toilets, showers, playground, dump station, laundry, propane gas and groceries are available.

Reservations, fee: Phone Leisuretime Reservation Systems, Inc. at (800)822-CAMP. $10.75 deposit; $10.75 fee per night.

Who to contact: Phone park at (408)623-4263.

Location: On San Juan Bautista, drive to 900 Anza Road.

Trip note: This campground is open all year and is near the Mission San Juan Bautista.

Site 5

FREMONT PEAK
STATE PARK

Campsites, facilities: There are 25 primitive campsites for tents or motorhomes. Picnic tables, fireplaces and piped water are provided, and pit toilets are available.

Reservations, fee: No reservations; $3 fee per night.

Who to contact: Phone park at (408)623-4255.

Location: Drive 11 miles south of San Juan Bautista on San Juan Canyon Road.

Trip note: This campground is open all year and is adjacent to Hollister Hills State Vehicular Recreation Area.

Site 6

PINNACLES
NATIONAL MONUMENT

Campsites, facilities: There are 23 sites for tents or motorhomes up to 20 feet long. There are two wheelchair accessible sites near accessible rest rooms.

Picnic tables, fireplaces and piped water are provided, and vault toilets are available.

Reservations, fee: No reservations; $5 fee per night.

Who to contact: Phone park at (408)389-4526.

Location: Drive 11 miles northeast of Soledad via State Route 146.

Trip note: This campground is open all year. However, temperatures in the summer commonly reach 100 degrees. Shade is scarce and rattlesnakes are prevalent during warm weather. The jagged pinnacles for which this park was named were formed by the erosion of an ancient volcanic eruption. If you are planning to stay over the weekend in the spring, arrive early Friday evening to be sure you get a campsite.

Site 7   HOLLISTER HILLS
            STATE VEHICULAR RECREATION AREA

Campsites, facilities: There are 125 campsites for tents or motorhomes. Picnic tables, fireplaces and piped water are provided, and flush toilets are available. A grocery store is nearby.

Reservations, fee: Reservations suggested; $5 fee per night.

Who to contact: Phone park at (408)637-3874.

Location: Drive eight miles south of Hollister via Cienega Road.

Trip note: This park is open all year and provides 80 miles of trails for motorcycles and 40 miles of trails for four-wheel drive vehicles.

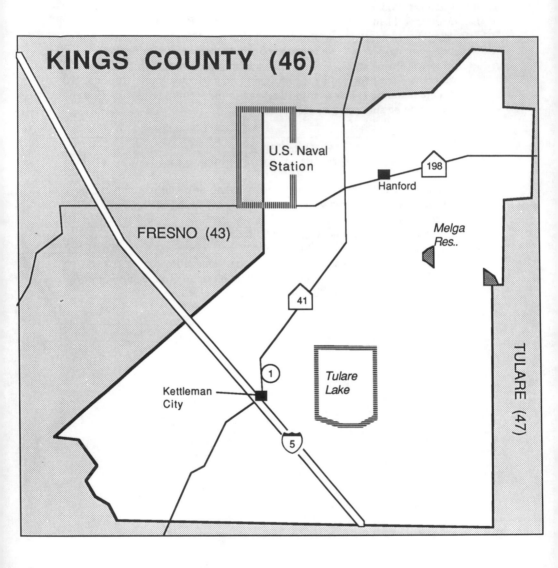

KINGS COUNTY (46)

U.S. Naval
Station

FRESNO (43)

198

Hanford

Melga
Res..

41

TULARE (47)

1

Tulare
Lake

Kettleman
City

5

KINGS COUNTY

♦

Site **1**

KETTLEMAN CITY
RV PARK

Campsites, facilities: There are 45 motorhome spaces. Picnic tables, piped water and full or partial hookups are provided. Rest rooms, showers, playgrounds, laundromat, store, dump station, dog run, restaurant, snack bar, horseback riding facilities and propane gas are available.

Reservations, fee: Call ahead for space available and fee.

Who to contact: Phone park at (209)386-4000.

Location: Take the Highway 41 exit of I-5 near Kettleman City and go northeast to 452 Cyril Place.

Trip note: This park is open all year and provides access to miles of open paths and roads for hiking or running. You can also go fishing nearby.

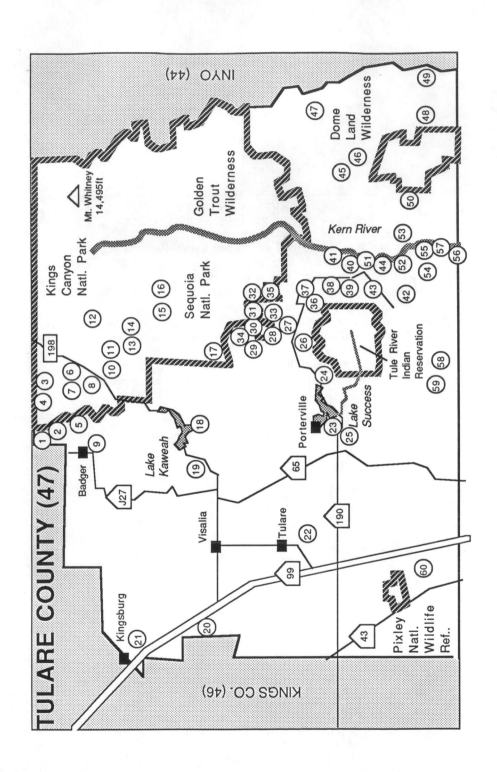

TULARE COUNTY

◆

Site 1   AZALEA   ▲

Campsites, facilities: There are 108 campsites for tents or motorhomes up to 30 feet long. Piped water, fireplaces and picnic tables are provided. Flush toilets, showers, dump station, evening ranger program and horseback riding facilities are available. The campgrounds and rest room facilities are wheelchair accessible. A grocery store and a laundromat are nearby.

Reservations, fee: No reservations; $6 fee per night.

Who to contact: Phone Kings Canyon National Park at (209)565-3341.

Location: Drive 3/4 mile north of Wilsonia on State Route 180.

Trip note: Open all year. Elevation 6600 feet.The Grant Grove of Giant Sequoias and Sequoia Lake are near camp. Visit the spectacular canyon of Kings River, one of the deepest gorges in North America.

Site 2   SUNSET   ▲

Campsites, facilities: There are 213 campsites for tents or motorhomes up to 30 feet long. Piped water, fireplaces and picnic tables are provided. Flush toilets, showers, evening ranger programs and horseback riding facilities are available. A grocery store and a laundromat are nearby.

Reservations, fee: No reservations; $6 fee per night.

Who to contact: Phone Kings Canyon National Park at (209)565-3341.

Location: Drive 1/2 mile north of Wilsonia on State Route 180.

Trip note: Open from May to October. Elevation 6600 feet. Located near the Grant Grove of Giant Sequoias and Sequoia Lake. The spectacular canyon of Kings River is one of the deepest gorges in North America.

Site 3   BIG MEADOWS   🌲

Campsites, facilities: There are 15 tent sites and 10 campsites for tents or motorhomes up to 22 feet long. Picnic tables and fireplaces are provided, and vault toilets are available. There is no water, so bring your own.

Reservations, fee: No reservations, no fee.

Who to contact: Phone Sequoia National Forest at (209)784-1500.
Location: Drive seven miles southeast of Wilsonia on Generals Highway, then make left on improved road and drive five miles to camp. See Forest Service Map.
Trip note: Open from June to October. Elevation 7600 feet. Located on Big Meadows Creek about 12 miles from Kings Canyon National Park.

Site **4**   BUCK
                              ROCK   ▣

Campsites, facilities: There are five campsites for tents or motorhomes up to 16 feet long. Picnic tables and fireplaces are provided, and vault toilets are available. There is no water, so bring your own.
Reservations, fee: No reservations, no fee.
Who to contact: Phone Sequoia National Forest at (209)784-1500.
Location: Drive seven miles southeast of Wilsonia on Generals Highway, then make left on improved road and drive four miles to camp. See Forest Service Map.
Trip note: Open from June to October. Elevation 7500 feet. Located near Big Meadows Creek about 11 miles from Kings Canyon National Park.

Site **5**   ESHOM   ▣

Campsites, facilities: There are 17 campsites for tents or motorhomes up to 22 feet long. Picnic tables and fireplaces are provided, and vault toilets are available. There is no water, so bring your own. A grocery store and a laundromat are nearby.
Reservations, fee: No reservations, no fee.
Who to contact: Phone Sequoia National Forest at (209)784-1500.
Location: Drive eight miles northeast of Badger on Red Hill Road.
Trip note: Open from May to November. Elevation 4800 feet. Located on Eshom Creek about two miles from the boundary of Sequoia National Park.

Site **6**   COVE
                       GROUP CAMPGROUND   ▲

Campsites, facilities: There is a group campsite here with piped water, picnic tables and fireplaces provided. Vault toilets are available. A grocery store, laundromat and propane gas are available nearby.
Reservations, fee: Reservations requested; $30 per night group fee.
Who to contact: Phone Sequoia National Forest at (209)784-1500.
Location: Drive 14 miles southeast of Wilsonia on Generals Highway.
Trip note: Open from May to October. Elevation 6500 feet. Located near Stony

Creek, two miles from the Kaweah River and a trailhead that serves the backcountry of Sequoia National Park.

Site 7
FIR
GROUP CAMPGROUND

Campsites, facilities: There is a group campsite here with piped water, picnic tables and fireplaces provided. Vault toilets are available. A grocery store, laundromat and propane gas are nearby.

Reservations, fee: Reservations requested with $10 deposit; $40 fee per night per group.

Who to contact: Phone Sequoia National Forest at (209)784-1500.

Location: Drive 14 miles southeast of Wilsonia on Generals Highway.

Trip note: Open from June to October. Elevation 6400 feet. Located on Stony Creek, two miles from the Kaweah River and a trailhead that leads into the backcountry of Sequoia National Park.

Site 8
STONY
CREEK

Campsites, facilities: There are 49 campsites for tents or motorhomes up to 22 feet long. Piped water, fireplaces and picnic tables are provided, and vault toilets are available. A grocery store, propane gas and a laundromat are nearby.

Reservations, fee: No reservations; $5 fee per night.

Who to contact: Phone Sequoia National Forest at (209)784-1500.

Location: Drive 13 miles southeast of Wilsonia on Generals Highway.

Trip note: Open from June to October. Elevation 6400 feet. Located on Stony Creek, one mile from the Kaweah River and a trailhead serving the backcountry of Sequoia National Park.

Site 9
SIERRA LAKES
CAMPGROUND

Campsites, facilities: There are 10 tent sites and 25 motorhome spaces. Picnic tables, fireplaces, piped water, and in most cases, electrical connections and sewer hookups are provided. Rest rooms, showers, laundromat, store, dump station and propane gas are available.

Reservations, fee: Call ahead for space available and fee.

Who to contact: Phone park at (209)337-2520.

Location: Take State Route 198 off State Route 99 and drive east through Lemon Cove, then turn left on 216 and go 1/2 mile. Turn right on Route J-21, drive 16 miles to Mountain Road 453, turn right and drive 1 1/2 miles to campground.

Trip note: This 106 acre campground has a 10 acre lake stocked with fish. They are open all year and are 30 minutes from Kings Canyon and Sequoia National Parks. There are three restaurants within three miles of camp.

Site 10   DORST

Campsites, facilities: There are 238 campsites for tents or motorhomes. Piped water, fireplaces and picnic tables are provided. Flush toilets, a dump station and evening ranger programs are available. A grocery store and a laundromat are nearby.
Reservations, fee: No reservations; $6 fee per night.
Who to contact: Phone Sequoia National Park at (209)565-3341.
Location: Drive 14 miles northwest of Giant Forest on Generals Highway.
Trip note: Open from June to September. Elevation 6700 feet. Located on Dorst Creek near a trailhead that serves the backcountry and Muir Grove.

Site 11   DORST
                    GROUP CAMP

Campsites, facilities: There is one group campsite for tents or motorhomes. Piped water, fireplaces and picnic tables are provided. Flush toilets, a dump station and evening ranger programs are available. A grocery store and a laundromat are nearby.
Reservations, fee: Call for reservations and fee.
Who to contact: Phone Sequoia National Park at (209)565-3341.
Location: Drive 14 miles northwest of Giant Forest on Generals Highway.
Trip note: Open from June to September, depending on weather and road conditions. Elevation 6700 feet. Located on Dorst Creek near a trailhead that accesses the backcountry and Muir Grove.

Site 12   LODGEPOLE

Campsites, facilities: There are 258 campsites for tents or motorhomes. Piped water, fireplaces and picnic tables are provided. Flush toilets, showers, a dump station, horseback riding facilities and evening ranger programs are available. A grocery store, propane gas and a laundromat are nearby. The campgrounds and rest room facilities are wheelchair accessible.
Reservations, fee: Call Ticketron at (213)216-6666 for outlet information; $6 fee per night.
Who to contact: Phone Sequoia National Park at (209)565-3341.
Location: Drive five miles northeast of Giant Forest on Generals Highway.
Trip note: This camp is open all year. Elevation 6700 feet. Located on the Marble Fork of the Kaweah River. Trails near camp access the backcountry, big trees and lakes of Sequoia National Park.

Site 13   POTWISHA   ▲

Campsites, facilities: There are 44 campsites for tents or motorhomes up to 16
feet long. Piped water, picnic tables and fireplaces are provided. Flush toi-
lets, a dump station and evening ranger programs are available. The camp-
grounds and rest room facilities are wheelchair accessible.
Reservations, fee: No reservations; $6 fee per night.
Who to contact: Phone Sequoia National Park at (209)565-3341.
Location: Drive three miles northeast of Ash Mountain on Generals Highway.
Trip note: Open all year. Elevation 2100 feet. Located on the Marble Fork of the
Kaweah River. Trails near camp access the backcountry and big trees of Se-
quoia National Park.

Site 14   BUCKEYE
                             FLAT   🌲

Campsites, facilities: There are 28 tent sites. Picnic tables, fireplaces and piped
water are provided. Flush toilets are available.
Reservations, fee: No reservations; $6 fee per night.
Who to contact: Phone Sequoia National Park at (209)565-3341.
Location: Drive 11 miles south of Giant Forest on Generals Highway, then turn
left to camp at the Middle Fork of the Kaweah River.
Trip note: Open from April to October, depending on road and weather condi-
tions. Elevation 2800 feet. Located on the Middle Fork of the Kaweah Riv-
er. Trails near camp provide access to the backcountry and lakes of Sequoia
National Park.

Site 15   ATWELL
                             MII L   🌲

Campsites, facilities: There are 23 tent sites. Picnic tables, fireplaces and piped
water are provided, and pit toilets are available. A grocery store is nearby.
Reservations, fee: No reservations; $4 fee per night.
Who to contact: Phone Sequoia National Park at (209)565-3341.
Location: Drive 23 miles east of Three Rivers off State Route 198 via Mineral
King Road.
Trip note: This camp is open from May to September depending on road and
weather conditions. Elevation 6650 feet. Located on Atwell Creek near the
East Fork of the Kaweah River. Trails near camp access Sequoia National
Park.

Site **16**   COLD
                               SPRINGS   🌲

Campsites, facilities: There are 37 tent sites. Picnic tables, fireplaces and piped
    water are provided, and pit toilets are available. A grocery store is nearby.
Reservations, fee: No reservations; $4 fee per night.
Who to contact: Phone Sequoia National Park at (209)565-3341.
Location: Drive 28 miles east of Three Rivers off State Route 198 via Mineral
    King Road.
Trip note: Open from May to September depending on road and weather condi-
    tions. Elevation 7500 feet. Located on the East Fork of the Kaweah River.
    Trails near camp access Sequoia National Park.

Site **17**   SOUTH
                               FORK   ⛺

Campsites, facilities: There are 12 tent sites. Picnic tables, fireplaces and piped
    water are provided, and pit toilets are available.
Reservations, fee: No reservations; $4 fee per night.
Who to contact: Phone Sequoia National Park at (209)565-3341.
Location: Drive 23 miles east of Three Rivers off State Route 198 on South Fork
    Drive.
Trip note: Open all year. Elevation 3650 feet. Located on the South Fork of the
    Kaweah River. Trails near camp access Sequoia National Park.

Site **18**   HORSE CREEK
                          RECREATION AREA   ⛺

Campsites, facilities: There are 80 campsites for tents or motorhomes. Piped wa-
    ter, fireplaces and picnic tables are provided. Flush toilets, paved boat ramp
    and a dump station are available. Nearby are a grocery store, laundromat,
    boat and waterski rental, ice, snack bar and propane gas.
Reservations, fee: No reservations; $6 fee per night.
Who to contact: Phone U.S. Army Corps of Engineers at (209)597-2301.
Location: Drive 21 miles east of Visalia via State Route 198 to the south shore of
    Lake Kaweah.
Trip note: Camp is open all year. Elevation 700 feet. Located on the south shore
    of Lake Kaweah, a man-made lake. It is open for waterskiing, fishing and
    swimming, but boats over 30 feet long are prohibited. The water level of
    the lake fluctuates a great deal during the year.

Site **19**   LEMON COVE/SEQUOIA
                              KOA   ⛺

Campsites, facilities: There are 55 sites for tents or motorhomes. Picnic tables, fireplaces, piped water, and full or partial hookups are provided. Rest rooms, showers, a playground, swimming pool, laundromat, store, dump station and propane gas are available.

Reservations, fee: Call for space available. $9.75 deposit required; $9.75 fee per night.

Who to contact: Phone park at (209)597-2346.

Location: Drive one mile southwest of Lemon Cove on State Route 198.

Trip note: Open all year. Elevation 515 feet. Located near Lake Kaweah.

Site **20**   GOSHEN/VISALIA
KOA

Campsites, facilities: There are 10 tent sites, 48 motorhome spaces and 38 sites for tents or motorhomes. Piped water and full or partial hookups are provided. Rest rooms, showers, swimming pool, laundromat, store, dump station and propane gas are available.

Reservations, fee: Call for space available. $8.50 deposit required; $8.50 fee per night.

Who to contact: Phone park at (209)651-0544.

Location: Drive five miles northwest of Visalia to 7480 Avenue 308.

Trip note: This camp is open all year and is just off US-99. Elevation 330 feet.

Site **21**   ROYAL OAK
RESORT

Campsites, facilities: There are 94 motorhome spaces. Picnic tables, piped water, and full or partial hookups are provided. Rest rooms, showers, laundromat, store, dump station, ice, firewood, boat gas and propane gas are available.

Reservations, fee: Call for space available. $3.50 deposit required; $3.50 fee per night.

Who to contact: Phone park at (209)897-2441.

Location: Drive three miles east of Kingsburg off State Route 201 to 39671 Road 28.

Trip note: The campground is open all year and the conveniences are open from May through September. Elevation 300 feet. The Kern River Park and the Kings River Golf Course are nearby. It is 55 miles to Sequoia National Park and 30 miles to Fresno.

Site **22**   SUN AND FUN
RV PARK

Campsites, facilities: There are 87 motorhome spaces. Picnic tables, fireplaces, piped water and full hookups are provided. Rest rooms, showers, dump station, playground, swimming pool, spa, laundromat, store, recreation room with color TV and billiard tables, dog run, restaurant and propane gas are available. A golf course is nearby.

Reservations, fee: Call ahead for space available and fee.

Who to contact: Phone park at (209)686-5779.

Location: Drive three miles south of Tulare on US-99 to Avenue 200 exit, then to 1000 Avenue 200.

Trip note: This motorhome park is just off US-99, exactly halfway between San Francisco and Los Angeles. Swimming pool here is a lifesaver.

Site **23**   ROCKY HILL
                     CAMPGROUND   ▲

Campsites, facilities: There are 108 campsites for tents or motorhomes up to 35 feet long. Piped water and picnic tables are provided, and vault toilets are available. A grocery store, boat ramp, boat and waterski rentals, bait, tackle and propane gas are nearby.

Reservations, fee: No reservations, no fee.

Who to contact: Phone U.S. Army Corps of Engineers at (209)784-0215.

Location: Drive five miles east of Porterville on State Route 190 to Success Lake.

Trip note: This camp is open all year and is on Lake Success where fishing and waterskiing are allowed. Elevation 655 feet.

Site **24**   TULE
                  RECREATION AREA   ▲

Campsites, facilities: There are 104 campsites for tents or motorhomes up to 35 feet long. Piped water, fireplaces and picnic tables are provided. Flush toilets, dump station and playground are available. Nearby are a grocery store, boat ramp, boat and waterski rentals, bait, tackle, and propane gas.

Reservations, fee: No reservations; $6 fee per night.

Who to contact: Phone U.S. Army Corps of Engineers at (209)784-0215.

Location: Drive 10 miles east of Porterville on State Route 190 to Success Lake.

Trip note: This camp is open all year and is on Lake Success where fishing and waterskiing are allowed. Elevation 655 feet.

Site **25**   YOKUT
                        KOA

Campsites, facilities: There are 71 motorhome spaces. Picnic tables, piped water, and full or partial hookups are provided. Rest rooms, showers, a playground, swimming pool, laundromat, store, dump station, and propane gas are available.

Reservations, fee: Call for space available. $9.50 deposit required; $9.50 fee per night.

Who to contact: Phone park at (209)784-2123.

Location: Drive five miles east of Porterville to 27798 Highway 190.

Trip note: This camp is open all year and is near man-made Lake Success where fishing and water skiing are allowed. Elevation 655 feet.

Site **26**   COFFEE
                               CAMP   △

Campsites, facilities: There are 10 tent sites. Picnic tables, fireplaces and piped water are provided, and vault toilets are available. Propane gas can be found nearby.
Reservations, fee: No reservations; $4 fee per night.
Who to contact: Phone Sequoia National Forest Headquarters at (209)784-1500.
Location: Drive five miles east of Springville on State Route 190.
Trip note: This camp is open all year and is on the Middle Fork of the Tule River. Elevation 2000 feet.

Site **27**   WISHON   △

Campsites, facilities: There are 10 tent sites and 26 sites for tents or motorhomes up to 22 feet long. Picnic tables, fireplaces and piped water are provided. Vault toilets are available. A grocery store is nearby.
Reservations, fee: No reservations; $6 fee per night.
Who to contact: Phone Sequoia National Forest Headquarters at (209)784-1500.
Location: Drive eight miles east of Springville via State Route 190 and Wishon Drive.
Trip note: Open from April to October. Elevation 4000 feet. Located on the North Fork of the Tule River. There are several trailheads near camp that lead into the backcountry.

Site **28**   BALCH
                               COUNTY PARK   △

Campsites, facilities: There are 70 campsites for tents or motorhomes up to 35 feet long. Piped water, fireplaces and picnic tables are provided, and flush toilets are available.
Reservations, fee: No reservations; $4 fee per night.
Who to contact: Phone park at (209)733-6612.
Location: Drive 20 miles northeast of Springville on Balch Park Drive.
Trip note: This camp is open from May to October. Elevation 6500 feet. Located in the middle of Mountain Home State Forest.

Site **29**   FRAZIER
                               MILL   △

Campsites, facilities: There are 50 campsites for tents or motorhomes. Piped water, fireplaces and picnic tables are provided. Vault toilets and horseback riding facilities are available.

Reservations, fee: No reservations, no fee.

Who to contact: Phone Mountain Home State Forest at (209)539-2855.

Location: Drive 22 miles northeast of Springville on Balch Park Drive.

Trip note: Open from June to October. Elevation 6000 feet. Located in Mountain Home State Forest where there are many old growth giant sequoias. There is a Forest Information Trail and the trailhead into the Golden Trout Wilderness is nearby. The Wishon Fork of the Tule River is the largest of several streams that pass through this forest.

Site **30**   HENDRICK
                                  POND   ▲

Campsites, facilities: There are 14 campsites for tents or motorhomes. Piped water, fireplaces and picnic tables are provided. Vault toilets and horseback riding facilities are available.

Reservations, fee: No reservations, no fee.

Who to contact: Phone Mountain Home State Forest at (209)539-2855.

Location: Drive 19 miles northeast of Springville on Balch Park Drive.

Trip note: Open from June to October. Elevation 6300 feet. Located in Mountain Home State Forest where there are many old growth giant sequoias. There is a Forest Information Trail and the trailhead into the Golden Trout Wilderness is nearby. The Wishon Fork of the Tule River is the largest of several streams that pass through this forest.

Site **31**   HIDDEN
                                  FALLS   🌲

Campsites, facilities: There are six tent sites. Picnic tables, fireplaces and piped water are provided. Flush toilets and horseback riding facilities are available.

Reservations, fee: No reservations, no fee.

Who to contact: Phone Mountain Home State Forest at (209)539-2855.

Location: Drive 30 miles northeast of Springville on Balch Park Drive.

Trip note: Open from June to October. Elevation 6000 feet. Located in Mountain Home State Forest where there are many old growth giant sequoias. There is a Forest Information Trail and the trailhead into the Golden Trout Wilderness is nearby. The Wishon Fork of the Tule River is the largest of several streams that pass through this forest.

Site **32**   METHUSELAH
                               GROUP CAMP   🌲

Campsites, facilities: There are campsites for tents or motorhomes. Fireplaces and picnic tables are provided, and vault toilets and horseback riding facilities are available. There is no water, so bring your own.

Reservations, fee: Reservations requested, no fee.
Who to contact: Phone Mountain Home State Forest at (209)539-2855.
Location: Drive 19 miles northeast of Springville on Balch Park Drive.
Trip note: Open from June to October. Elevation 5900 feet. Located in Mountain Home State Forest where there are many old growth giant sequoias. There is a Forest Information Trail and the trailhead into the Golden Trout Wilderness is nearby. The Wishon Fork of the Tule River is the largest of several streams that pass through this forest.

Site **33**   MOSES
GULCH

Campsites, facilities: There are 11 campsites for tents or motorhomes. Piped water, fireplaces and picnic tables are provided. Vault toilets and horseback riding facilities are available.
Reservations, fee: No reservations, no fee.
Who to contact: Phone Mountain Home State Forest at (209)539-2855.
Location: Drive 21 miles northeast of Springville on Balch Park Drive.
Trip note: Open from June to October. Elevation 6000 feet. Located in Mountain Home State Forest where there are many old growth giant sequoias. There is a Forest Information Trail and the trailhead into the Golden Trout Wilderness is nearby. The Wishon Fork of the Tule River is the largest of several streams that pass through this forest.

Site **34**   SHAKE
CAMP

Campsites, facilities: There are 11 campsites for tents or motorhomes. Piped water, fireplaces and picnic tables are provided. Vault toilets and horseback riding facilities are available.
Reservations, fee: No reservations, no fee.
Who to contact: Phone Mountain Home State Forest at (209)539-2855.
Location: Drive 22 miles northeast of Springville on Balch Park Drive.
Trip note: Open from June to October. Elevation 6500 feet. Located in Mountain Home State Forest where there are many old growth giant sequoias. There is a Forest Information Trail and the trailhead into the Golden Trout Wilderness is nearby. The Wishon Fork of the Tule River is the largest of several streams that pass through this forest.

Site **35**   SUNSET
POINT

Campsites, facilities: There are four tent sites. Picnic tables, fireplaces and piped water are provided, and flush toilets and horseback riding facilities are available.
Reservations, fee: No reservations, no fee.

Who to contact: Phone Mountain Home State Forest at (209)539-2855.

Location: Drive 22 miles northeast of Springville on Balch Park Drive.

Trip note: Open from June to October. Elevation 6000 feet. Located in Mountain Home State Forest where there are many old growth giant sequoias. There is a Forest Information Trail and the trailhead into the Golden Trout Wilderness is nearby. The Wishon Fork of the Tule River is the largest of several streams that pass through this forest.

Site 36   COY
                          FLAT   ▲

Campsites, facilities: There are 20 campsites for tents or motorhomes up to 22 feet long. Piped water, fireplaces and picnic tables are provided, and vault toilets are available.

Reservations, fee: No reservations; $4 fee per night.

Who to contact: Phone Sequoia National Forest at (209)784-1500.

Location: Drive 1/2 mile south of Camp Nelson off State Route 190.

Trip note: Open from March to October. Elevation 500 feet. Located on Coy Creek. A trail leaves from camp, goes through Belknap Camp Grove and then south along Slate Mountain.

Site 37   BELKNAP
                                                        ▲

Campsites, facilities: There are 15 campsites for tents or motorhomes up to 32 feet long. Piped water, fireplaces and picnic tables are provided. Vault toilets and horseback riding facilities are available. A grocery store is nearby.

Reservations, fee: No reservations; $4 fee per night.

Who to contact: Phone Sequoia National Forest at (209)784-1500.

Location: Drive two miles east of Camp Nelson via State Route 190 and Nelson Drive.

Trip note: Open from April to October. Elevation 5000 feet. Located on the South Middle Fork of Tule Creek near McIntyre Grove and Belknap Camp Grove. A trail leads out of camp past Wheel Meadow Grove and winds through the backcountry. It passes Forks of the Kern and accesses the Golden Trout Wilderness.

Site 38   QUAKING
                          ASPEN   ▲

Campsites, facilities: There are 32 campsites for tents or motorhomes up to 22 feet long. Piped water, fireplaces and picnic tables are provided. Vault toilets and horseback riding facilities are available. A grocery store is nearby.

Reservations, fee: No reservations; $4 fee per night.

Who to contact: Phone Sequoia National Forest at (209)784-1500.

Location: Drive 11 miles east of Camp Nelson via State Route 190.

Trip note: Open from May to October. Elevation 7000 feet. Located on Freeman Creek. A trail passes through camp that accesses other trails leading into the Golden Trout Wilderness.

Site **39**   QUAKING ASPEN
              GROUP CAMPGROUND

Campsites, facilities: There are four campsites for tents or motorhomes up to 22 feet long. Piped water, fireplaces and picnic tables are provided, and vault toilets and horseback riding facilities are available. A grocery store is nearby.
Reservations, fee: Reservations requested with $10 deposit; $20 group fee per night.
Who to contact: Phone Sequoia National Forest at (209)784-1500.
Location: Drive 11 miles east of Camp Nelson via State Route 190.
Trip note: Open from May to October. Elevation 7000 feet. Located on Freeman Creek. A trail passes through camp which accesses other trails leading into the Golden Trout Wilderness.

Site **40**   PEPPERMINT

Campsites, facilities: There are 19 campsites for tents or motorhomes up to 22 feet long. Fireplaces and picnic tables are provided, and vault toilets are available. There is no water, so bring your own. A grocery store is nearby.
Reservations, fee: No reservations, no fee.
Who to contact: Phone Sequoia National Forest at (209)784-1500.
Location: Drive 16 miles southeast of Camp Nelson via State Route 190.
Trip note: Open from May to October. Elevation 7100 feet. Located on Peppermint Creek.

Site **41**   LOWER
                      PEPPERMINT

Campsites, facilities: There are 17 campsites for tents or motorhomes up to 16 feet long. Piped water, fireplaces and picnic tables are provided, and vault toilets are available.
Reservations, fee: No reservations; $4 fee per night.
Who to contact: Phone Sequoia National Forest at (209)784-1500.
Location: Drive 32 miles northeast of California Hot Springs.
Trip note: Open from June to October. Elevation 5300 feet. Located on Peppermint Creek. There is a trailhead near camp that will take you to a trail along Rincon Fault that goes north to Forks of the Kern or south to the Kern River. A map of Sequoia National Forest details back country roads.

Site 42   HOLEY
MEADOW   ▲

Campsites, facilities: There are 10 campsites for tents or motorhomes up to 16 feet long. Piped water, fireplaces and picnic tables are provided, and vault toilets are available.
Reservations, fee: No reservations; $4 fee per night.
Who to contact: Phone Sequoia National Forest at (209)784-1500.
Location: Drive 15 miles northeast of California Hot Springs.
Trip note: Open from June to October. Elevation 6400 feet. Located on Double Bunk Creek.

Site 43   REDWOOD
MEADOW   ▲

Campsites, facilities: There are 15 campsites for tents or motorhomes up to 16 feet long. Piped water, fireplaces and picnic tables are provided, and vault toilets are available.
Reservations, fee: No reservations; $4 fee per night.
Who to contact: Phone Sequoia National Forest at (209)784-1500.
Location: Drive 18 miles northeast of California Hot Springs on Western Divide Highway.
Trip note: Open from June to September. Elevation 6500 feet. Located near Parker Meadow Creek.

Site 44   LIMESTONE   ▲

Campsites, facilities: There are 15 tent sites and seven campsites for tents or motorhomes up to 22 feet long. Fireplaces and picnic tables are provided, and vault toilets are available. There is no water, but a grocery store is nearby.
Reservations, fee: No reservations, no fee.
Who to contact: Phone Sequoia National Forest at (209)784-1500.
Location: Drive 19 miles north of Kernville on Kern River Highway.
Trip note: Open from May to October. Elevation 3800 feet. Located on the Kern River.

Site 45   TROY
MEADOW   ▲

Campsites, facilities: There are 10 tent sites and 63 campsites for tents or motorhomes up to 22 feet long. Piped water, fireplaces and picnic tables are provided. Vault toilets and horseback riding facilities are available. A grocery store is nearby.
Reservations, fee: No reservations, no fee.

Who to contact: Phone Sequoia National Forest at (209)784-1500.

Location: Drive 35 miles northwest of Brown via Nine Mile Canyon and Kennedy Meadow Roads.

Trip note: Open from June to November. Elevation 7800 feet. Located on Fish Creek. There are several designated two-wheel vehicle trails in the vicinity.

Site **46**	FISH CREEK	▲

Campsites, facilities: There are 26 campsites for tents or motorhomes up to 22 feet long. Piped water, fireplaces and picnic tables are provided, and vault toilets are available. A grocery store is nearby.

Reservations, fee: No reservations, no fee.

Who to contact: Phone Sequoia National Forest at (209)784-1500.

Location: Drive 32 miles northwest of Brown via Nine Mile Canyon and Kennedy Meadow Roads.

Trip note: Open from June to November. Elevation 7400 feet. Located at the confluence of Fish Creek and Jackass Creek. There are several designated two-wheel vehicle trails in the vicinity.

Site **47**	KENNEDY	▲

Campsites, facilities: There are 10 tent sites and 29 campsites for tents or motorhomes up to 22 feet long. Piped water, fireplaces and picnic tables are provided, and vault toilets are available. A grocery store is nearby.

Reservations, fee: No reservations, no fee.

Who to contact: Phone Sequoia National Forest at (209)784-1500.

Location: Drive 26 miles northwest of Brown via Nine Mile Canyon and Kennedy Meadow Roads.

Trip note: Open all year. Elevation 5800 feet. Located on the Pacific Crest National Scenic Trail.

Site **48**	LONG VALLEY	▲

Campsites, facilities: There are 13 campsites for tents or motorhomes up to 25 feet long. Piped water, fireplaces and picnic tables are provided, and pit toilets are available.

Reservations, fee: No reservations, no fee.

Who to contact: Phone Bureau of Land Management at (805)861-4236.

Location: Drive 15 miles northwest of Brown on Nine Mile Canyon Road. Turn left on the dirt road opposite the BLM Ranger Station, and drive 14 miles to campground.

Trip note: Open all year. Elevation 5200 feet. Located in Long Valley. A trail from camp leads two and a half miles west to the Kern River. The Pacific

Crest Trail passes about four miles from camp.

Site 49   CHIMNEY   ▲
                                 CREEK

Campsites, facilities: There are 35 campsites for tents or motorhomes up to 25
   feet long. Piped water, fireplaces and picnic tables are provided, and pit toi-
   lets are available.
Reservations, fee: No reservations, no fee.
Who to contact: Phone Bureau of Land Management at (805)861-4236.
Location: Drive 17 miles northwest of Brown via Nine Mile Canyon Road.
Trip note: Open all year. Elevation 5900 feet. Located on Chimney Creek and
   the Pacific Crest Trail.

Site 50   HORSE   ▲
                                 MEADOW

Campsites, facilities: There are 26 tent sites and 15 campsites for tents or motorhomes up to 22 feet long. Piped water, fireplaces and picnic tables are pro-
   vided, and vault toilets are available.
Reservations, fee: No reservations, no fee.
Who to contact: Phone Sequoia National Forest at (209)784-1500.
Location: Drive 38 miles northeast of Kernville off Sherman Pass Road on dirt
   road that goes along Poison Creek.
Trip note: Open from June to November. Elevation 7600 feet. Located on Salm-
   on Creek. A trail from camp goes along Salmon Creek to Salmon Creek
   Falls.

Site 51   BRUSH   ▲
                                 CREEK

Campsites, facilities: There are 12 campsites for tents or motorhomes up to 22
   feet long. Fireplaces and picnic tables are provided, and vault toilets are
   available. There is no water, but a grocery store is nearby.
Reservations, fee: No reservations, no fee.
Who to contact: Phone Sequoia National Forest at (209)784-1500.
Location: Drive 21 miles north of Kernville on Kern River Highway.
Trip note: Camp is open from May to November. Elevation 3800 feet. Located
   on the Kern River. There are several trails nearby that head into the backcountry.

Site 52   FAIRVIEW   ▲

Campsites, facilities: There are 55 campsites for tents or motorhomes up to 22

feet long. Piped water, fireplaces and picnic tables are provided, and vault toilets are available. A grocery store is nearby.

Reservations, fee: No reservations; $5 fee per night.

Who to contact: Phone Sequoia National Forest at (209)784-1500.

Location: Drive 16 miles north of Kernville to Fairview, campground is at north end of town.

Trip note: Open from May to October. Elevation 3500 feet. Located on the Kern River. There are several trails leading from camp.

Site **53**   GOLD
               LEDGE   △

Campsites, facilities: There are 37 campsites for tents or motorhomes up to 22 feet long. Piped water, fireplaces and picnic tables are provided, and vault toilets are available. A grocery store is nearby.

Reservations, fee: No reservations; $5 fee per night.

Who to contact: Phone Sequoia National Forest at (209)784-1500.

Location: Drive 10 miles north of Kernville on Kern River Highway.

Trip note: Open from May to October. Elevation 3200 feet. Located on the Kern River.

Site **54**   FROG
               MEADOW   △

Campsites, facilities: There are 10 campsites for tents or motorhomes up to 16 feet long. Piped water, fireplaces and picnic tables are provided. Vault toilets are available.

Reservations, fee: No reservations, no fee.

Who to contact: Phone Sequoia National Forest at (209)784-1500.

Location: Drive 18 miles east of Pine Flat.

Trip note: Open from June to October. Elevation 7500 feet. Located near Tobias Creek. There are several trails leading out from camp, one of which heads east to the Kern River.

Site **55**   CORRAL
               CREEK   △

Campsites, facilities: There are 15 campsites for tents or motorhomes up to 22 feet long. Fireplaces and picnic tables are provided, and vault toilets are available. There is no water, so bring your own.

Reservations, fee: No reservations, no fee.

Who to contact: Phone Sequoia National Forest at (209)784-1500.

Location: Drive eight miles northwest of Kernville on Kern River Highway.

Trip note: This camp is open all year. Elevation 3000 feet. Located on the Kern River.

Site 56   CAMP 3   ▲

Campsites, facilities: There are 52 campsites for tents or motorhomes up to 22 feet long. Piped water, fireplaces and picnic tables are provided, and vault toilets are available. A grocery store, laundromat and propane gas are nearby.
Reservations, fee: No reservations; $5 fee per night.
Who to contact: Phone Sequoia National Forest at (209)784-1500.
Location: Drive five miles northwest of Kernville on Kern River Highway.
Trip note: Open from May to October. Elevation 2800 feet. Located on the Kern River five miles north of Lake Isabella.

Site 57   HOSPITAL
                            FLAT   ▲

Campsites, facilities: There are 28 tent sites and 12 campsites for tents or motorhomes up to 22 feet long. Piped water, fireplaces and picnic tables are provided, and vault toilets are available. A grocery store is nearby.
Reservations, fee: No reservations; $5 fee per night.
Who to contact: Phone Sequoia National Forest at (209)784-1500.
Location: Drive seven miles north of Kernville on Kern River Highway.
Trip note: Open from May to October. Elevation 2800 feet. Located on the Kern River, seven miles from Lake Isabella.

Site 58   WHITE
                            RIVER   ▲

Campsites, facilities: There are eight tent sites and four campsites for motorhomes up to 16 feet long. Piped water, fireplaces and picnic tables are provided, and vault toilets are available. A grocery store and laundromat are nearby.
Reservations, fee: No reservations; $4 fee per night.
Who to contact: Phone Sequoia National Forest at (209)784-1500.
Location: Drive five miles south of Pine Flat.
Trip note: Open from May to October. Elevation 4000 feet. Located on the White River.

Site 59   LEAVIS
                            FLAT   ▲

Campsites, facilities: There are five tent sites and four campsites for motorhomes up to 16 feet long. Piped water, fireplaces and picnic tables are provided, and vault toilets are available. A grocery store, laundromat and propane gas can be found nearby.

Reservations, fee: No reservations; $4 fee per night.

Who to contact: Phone Sequoia National Forest at (209)784-1500.

Location: Drive to California Hot Springs, campground is at the west end of town.

Trip note: Open all year. Elevation 3100 feet. Located on Deer Creek.

Site **60**   ALLENSWORTH
STATE HISTORIC PARK

Campsites, facilities: There are 15 campsites for tents or motorhomes up to 35 feet long. Piped water, fireplaces and picnic tables are provided, and vault toilets are available. A grocery store is nearby.

Reservations, fee: No reservations; $6 fee per night.

Who to contact: Phone park at (805)849-3433.

Location: Drive nine miles west of Earlimart via Avenue 56 on State Route 43.

Trip note: Open all year. Elevation 240 feet. The town of Allensworth is restored as an historical park dedicated to the black pioneers who founded it with Colonel Allen Allensworth, the highest ranking army chaplin of his time. There is one museum at the school and another at the Colonel's house with a 30 minute movie on the history of Allensworth. Tours are given as requested and on the second Saturday of every month. The best weather is in the spring and fall. The campground is peaceful and the local canals provide ample fishing.

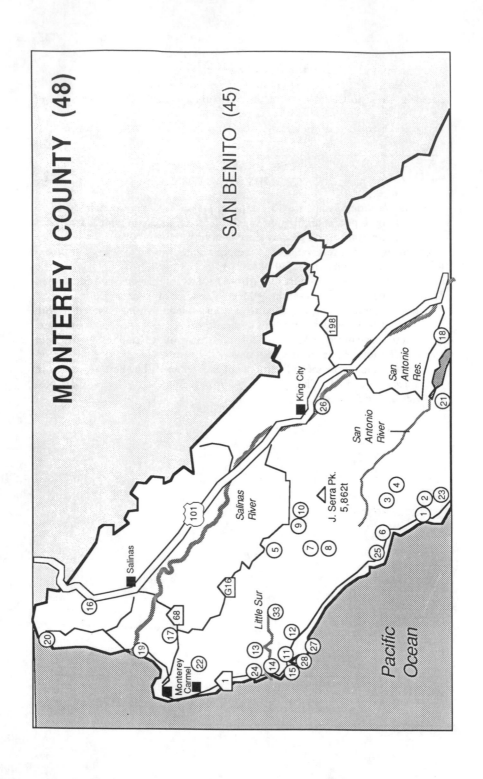

MONTEREY COUNTY (48)

SAN BENITO (45)

San Antonio Res.

San Antonio River

King City

J. Serra Pk. 5,862t

Salinas River

Salinas

Little Sur

Monterey
Carmel

Pacific
Ocean

MONTEREY COUNTY

◆

Site **1** | PLASKETT CREEK
GROUP CAMP |

Campsites, facilities: There are three group campsites for tents or motorhomes. Piped water, picnic tables and fireplaces are provided, and vault toilets are available. Groceries and propane gas are nearby.

Reservations, fee: Reservations requested; $25 group fee per night.

Who to contact: Phone Los Padres National Forest Headquarters at (408)385-5434.

Location: Drive nine and a half miles southeast of Lucia via State Route 1.

Trip note: This campground is open all year. Elevation 200 feet. Located on Plaskett Creek near the ocean.

Site **2** | PLASKETT
CREEK |

Campsites, facilities: There are 43 campsites for tents or motorhomes. Piped water, picnic tables and fireplaces are provided, and flush toilets are available. Groceries and propane gas are nearby.

Reservations, fee: No reservations; $8 fee per night.

Who to contact: Phone Los Padres National Forest Headquarters at (408)385-5434.

Location: Drive nine and a half miles southeast of Lucia via State Route 1.

Trip note: Open all year. Elevation 200 feet. Located on Plaskett Creek near the ocean.

Site **3** | NACIMIENTO |

Campsites, facilities: There are nine tent sites and eight campsites for tents or motorhomes. Piped water, picnic tables and fireplaces are provided, and vault toilets are available.

Reservations, fee: No reservations; $3 fee per night.

Who to contact: Phone Los Padres National Forest Headquarters at (408)385-5434.

Location: Drive 15 miles northwest of Jolon on Nacimiento-Fergusson Road.

Trip note: Open all year. Elevation 1600 feet. Located in Los Padres National Forest near the Ventana Wilderness and Hunter Liggett Military Reservation.

Site **4**
PONDEROSA

Campsites, facilities: There are 23 campsites for tents or motorhomes. Piped water, picnic tables and fireplaces are provided, and vault toilets are available.

Reservations, fee: No reservations; $5 fee per night.

Who to contact: Phone Los Padres National Forest Headquarters at (408)385-5434.

Location: Drive 14 miles northwest of Jolon on Nacimiento-Fergusson Road.

Trip note: Open all year. Elevation 1500 feet. Located near the Ventana Wilderness and Hunter Liggett Military Reservation.

Site **5**
WHITE
OAKS

Campsites, facilities: There are eight tent sites. Piped water, picnic tables and fireplaces are provided, and vault toilets are available.

Reservations, fee: No reservations; $3 fee per night.

Who to contact: Phone Los Padres National Forest Headquarters at (408)385-5434.

Location: Drive 19 miles southeast of Carmel Valley via Carmel Valley Road and Tassajara Road.

Trip note: Open from from May to October. Elevation 4200 feet. Located near Anastasia Creek. About a mile from camp is a trail that branches throughout the Ventana Wilderness and is dotted with backcountry campsites. Ventana Wilderness Expeditions sponsors pack trips and nature tours. For reservations call (408)659-0433.

Site **6**
KIRK
CREEK

Campsites, facilities: There are 33 campsites for tents or motorhomes. Piped water, picnic tables and fireplaces are provided, and vault toilets are available.

Reservations, fee: No reservations; $8 fee per night.

Who to contact: Phone Los Padres National Forest Headquarters at (408)385-5434.

Location: Drive four miles southeast of Lucia via State Route 1.

Trip note: Open all year. Elevation 100 feet. Located on Kirk Creek where it empties into the Pacific Ocean. A trail from camp branches north throughout the Ventana Wilderness and is dotted with backcountry campsites.

Site **7**   ESCONDIDO

Campsites, facilities: There are nine tent sites and 10 campsites for tents or motorhomes. Piped water, picnic tables and fireplaces are provided, and vault toilets are available.

Reservations, fee: No reservations; $3 fee per night.

Who to contact: Phone Los Padres National Forest Headquarters at (408)385-5434.

Location: Drive 18 miles southwest of Greenfield via Indians Road.

Trip note: Open from April to December. Elevation 900 feet. Indians Road is an unimproved dirt road, and the camp is at a trailhead that accesses numerous other trails and backcountry campsites in the Ventana Wilderness.

Site **8**   MEMORIAL PARK

Campsites, facilities: There are eight tent sites. Piped water, picnic tables and fireplaces are provided, and vault toilets are available.

Reservations, fee: No reservations; $8 fee per night.

Who to contact: Phone Los Padres National Forest Headquarters at (408)385-5434.

Location: Drive 22 miles northwest of Jolon via Indians Road.

Trip note: Open all year. Elevation 2000 feet. This campground is at a trailhead that accesses numerous other trails and backcountry campsites in the Ventana Wilderness.

Site **9**   ARROYO SECO

Campsites, facilities: There are 51 campsites for tents or motorhomes. Piped water, picnic tables and fireplaces are provided, and vault toilets are available. Groceries and propane gas are nearby.

Reservations, fee: No reservations; $5 fee per night.

Who to contact: Phone Los Padres National Forest Headquarters at (408)385-5434.

Location: Drive 19 miles southwest of Greenfield County Road G-16.

Trip note: This campground is open all year. Elevation 900 feet. Map of Los Padres National Forest details back country trails.

Site **10**   ARROYO SECO GROUP CAMP

Campsites, facilities: There is one group campsite for tents or motorhomes. Piped water, picnic tables and fireplaces are provided, and vault toilets are available. Groceries and propane gas are available nearby.

Reservations, fee: No reservations; $25 group fee per night.

Who to contact: Phone Los Padres National Forest Headquarters at (408)385-5434.

Location: Drive 19 miles southwest of Greenfield via Country Road G-16.

Trip note: This campground is open all year. Elevation 900 feet.

Site **11**   BIG SUR
CAMPGROUND

Campsites, facilities: There are 30 tent sites, 30 motorhome spaces with water and electrical hookups, and 30 campsites for tents or motorhomes. Piped water, fireplaces and picnic tables are provided. Rest rooms, showers, dump station, playground and laundromat are available.

Reservations, fee: Reservations recommended; $14 fee per night.

Who to contact: Phone park at (408)667-2322.

Location: Drive 26 miles south of Carmel on State Route 1.

Trip note: A popular spot that offers the best of all worlds. Campers can stay near redwoods, use great trails through the forest or explore nearby Pfeiffer Beach.

Site **12**   PFEIFFER BIG SUR
STATE PARK

Campsites, facilities: There are 217 campsites for tents or motorhomes. Piped water, picnic tables and fireplaces are provided. Rest rooms, showers, laundromat, groceries and propane gas are available. Campgrounds, rest room, grocery store and food service are wheelchair accessible.

Reservations, fee: Phone MISTIX at (800)446-7275; $10 fee per night.

Who to contact: Phone park headquarters at (707)667-2315.

Location: Drive 26 miles south of Carmel on State Route 1.

Trip note: This campground is open all year. Elevation 400 feet. Hike or drive to nearby Pfeiffer Beach.

Site **13**   BOTTCHER'S
GAP

Campsites, facilities: There are nine tent sites and 11 campsites for tents or motorhomes. Piped water, picnic tables and fireplaces are provided, and vault toilets are available.

Reservations, fee: No reservations; $3 fee per night.

Who to contact: Phone Los Padres National Forest Headquarters at (408)385-5434.

Location: Drive 19 miles northwest of Big Sur off State Route 1 on Palo Colorado Road.

Trip note: Open all year. Elevation 2100 feet. The Palo Colorado (red wood) Canyon is beautiful. There is also a trailhead at camp that accesses the Ventana Wilderness backcountry and numerous backcountry camps.

Site **14**   CHINA CAMP

Campsites, facilities: There are eight tent sites and five campsites for tents or motorhomes. Piped water, picnic tables and fireplaces are provided, and vault toilets are available.
Reservations, fee: No reservations; $3 fee per night.
Who to contact: Phone Los Padres National Forest Headquarters at (408)385-5434.
Location: Drive 20 miles south of Carmel Valley via Carmel Valley Road and Tassajara Road.
Trip note: Open from April to December. Elevation 4300 feet. A trailhead at camp accesses trails in the Ventana Wilderness and numerous backcountry camps. Ventana Wilderness Expeditions has pack trips and nature tours. For reservations call (408)659-0433.

Site **15**   RIVERSIDE CAMPGROUND

Campsites, facilities: There are 46 sites for tents or motorhomes, some of which have water and electrical hookups. Rest rooms, showers, dump station and a playground are available.
Reservations, fee: Reservations suggested; $13 fee per night.
Who to contact: Phone campground at (408)667-2414.
Location: Drive two miles north of Pfeiffer State Park on State Route 1.
Trip note: This campground is open from March to December and is in the redwoods. In winter, the Big Sur River attracts run of elusive steelhead.

Site **16**   CABANA HOLIDAY

Campsites, facilities: There are 96 motorhome spaces with full or partial hookups. Rest rooms, showers, picnic tables, playground, swimming pool, groceries and a laundromat are available.
Reservations, fee: Phone Leisuretime Reservation Systems, Inc. at (800)822-CAMP. $18 deposit; $18 fee per night.
Who to contact: Phone park at (408)663-2886.
Location: In Prunedale, drive to the junction of US-101 and State Route 156, then to 8710 Prunedale North Road.
Trip note: This motorhome park is open all year and is a half hour's drive from the sites in Monterey and Carmel.

Site **17**   LAGUNA SECA
                    RECREATION AREA

Campsites, facilities: There are 183 campsites for tents or motorhomes with full
or partial hookups. Picnic tables and fireplaces are provided, and rest
rooms, showers, dump station, 10 acre lake, rifle and pistol range and group
camping facilities are available. A grocery store, laundromat and propane
gas are also nearby.

Reservations, fee: No reservations; $11.50 fee per night.

Who to contact: Phone park at (408)422-6138.

Location: Drive seven miles southeast of Monterey via State Route 68.

Trip note: This campground is just minutes away from the sites in Monterey and
Carmel. It is situated in oak woodlands overlooking the world famous Laguna Seca Raceway.

Site **18**   LAKE SAN ANTONIO
                    NORTH SHORE

Campsites, facilities: There are 236 campsites for tents or motorhomes with full
or partial hookups. Piped water, fireplaces and tables are provided, and a
dump station, rest rooms, showers, boat ramp, boat rentals, playground, recreation room, laundromat and groceries are available.

Reservations, fee: Reservations accepted; $11.50 fee per night.

Who to contact: Phone resort at (805)472-2311.

Location: Drive 17 miles southeast of Lockwood off US-101.

Trip note: Enjoy swimming, waterskiing, sailboarding and fishing on this narrow
16-mile long reservoir.

Site **19**   MARINA DUNES
                    RV PARK

Campsites, facilities: There are 38 motorhome sites with full hookups. Piped water and picnic tables are provided. Rest rooms, showers, a laundromat and
groceries are available.

Reservations, fee: Reservations accepted; $19 fee per night.

Who to contact: Phone park at (408)384-6914.

Location: Drive 1/4 mile north of Marina to 3330 Dunes Drive.

Trip note: This campground is open all year and is minutes away from the sites
in Monterey and Carmel.

Site **20**   LOMA LINDA
                    TRAVEL PARK

Campsites, facilities: There are 25 motorhome spaces with full hookups. Rest
rooms, showers and propane are available.

Reservations, fee: Reservations accepted; $14 fee per night.

Who to contact: Phone park at (408)722-9311.

Location: Drive four miles south of Watsonville off State Route 1 to 890 Salinas Road.

Trip note: This campground is open all year and is minutes away from the sites in Monterey and Carmel.

Site **21** | LAKE SAN ANTONIO
SOUTH SHORE |

Campsites, facilities: There are 458 campsites for tents or motorhomes with full or partial hookups. Piped water, fireplaces and tables are provided. A dump station, rest rooms, showers, boat ramp, boat rentals, playground, recreation room, laundromat and groceries are available.

Reservations, fee: Reservations accepted; $11.50 fee per night.

Who to contact: Phone resort at (805)472-2311.

Location: Drive 24 miles south of Lockwood off US-101.

Trip note: Enjoy swimming, waterskiing, sailboarding and fishing on this narrow 16-mile long reservoir.

Site **22** | RIVERSIDE
RV PARK |

Campsites, facilities: There are 35 motorhome spaces with full hookups and cable TV. Rest rooms, showers, recreational cabana, barbecue area, horseshoes and river beach are available. A grocery store, laundromat and propane gas are available nearby.

Reservations, fee: Phone Leisuretime Reservation Systems, Inc. at (800)822-CAMP. $20 deposit; $20 fee per night.

Who to contact: Phone park at (408)624-9329.

Location: Drive five miles southeast of Carmel via Carmel Valley Road and Schulte Road to 827 Schulte Road.

Trip note: This park is open all year and is on the Carmel River, minutes away from Carmel, Cannery Row, the Monterey Aquarium, golf courses and the beach.

Site **23** | ALDER
CREEK |

Campsites, facilities: There are five tent spaces. Picnic tables and fireplaces are provided, and vault toilets are available. There is no water, so bring your own.

Reservations, fee: No reservations, no fee.

Who to contact: Phone Los Padres National Forest Headquarters at (408)385-5434.

Location: Drive 17 miles southeast of Lucia via State Route 1.
Trip note: This campground is open all year. Elevation 2300 feet. There is a trailhead in camp that accesses numerous backcountry campsites.

Site **24**   ANDREW MOLERA
                                    STATE PARK

Campsites, facilities: There are several primitive walk-in campsites here. Piped water, vault toilets and horseback riding facilities are available.
Reservations, fee: No reservations, no fee.
Who to contact: Phone park at (408)667-2315,
Location: Drive 21 miles south of Carmel on State Route 1.
Trip note: This park is open all year and is on the coast side of Highway 1. A trail from the parking area leads one mile to the beach.

Site **25**   LIMEKILN BEACH
                                    REDWOODS

Campsites, facilities: There are 28 tent sites and 60 motorhome spaces with piped water provided. Rest rooms, showers, dump station, grocery store, bait and firewood are available.
Reservations, fee: Call ahead for available space and fee.
Who to contact: Phone park at (408)667-2403.
Location: Drive 26 miles south of Big Sur on State Route 1.
Trip note: Camp on the beach or in the redwoods. Hike the trails and see the historic lime kilns.

Site **26**   SAN LORENZO
                                    REGIONAL PARK

Campsites, facilities: There are 142 campsites for tents or motorhomes with partial hookups. Tables and fireplaces are provided, and a dump station, rest rooms and showers are available.
Reservations, fee: Call ahead for available space and fee.
Who to contact: Phone park at (408)424-1971.
Location: Drive on US-101 to King City, then to 1160 Broadway.
Trip note: This park is open all year and is set on the Salinas River. It is the home of the Salinas Agricultural Historical Museum with a one room school house, exhibit barn, remodeled Spreckels house, blacksmith shop and farm equipment exhibits.

Site **27**   VENTANA
                                    CAMPGROUNDS

Campsites, facilities: There are 97 campsites for tents or motorhomes with full or partial hookups. Piped water, fireplaces and tables are provided. A dump station, rest rooms, showers, laundromat, ice and groceries are available.

Reservations, fee: Reservations accepted; $8 - $10 fee per night.

Who to contact: Phone campground at (408)667-2331.

Location: Drive one mile south of the town of Big Sur on State Route 1.

Trip note: This campground is open all year. Enjoy the spectacular coast, nearby Pfeiffer Beach and the Big Sur River.

Site **28**   FERNWOOD
                      PARK

Campsites, facilities: There are 16 tent sites and 49 motorhome spaces with fireplaces and picnic tables, some with full hookups. Rest rooms and showers are available. A grocery store, laundromat and propane gas are nearby.

Reservations, fee: Reservations accepted; $9-$10 fee per night.

Who to contact: Phone park at (408)667-2322.

Location: Drive to town of Big Sur on State Route 1.

Trip note: This campground is in the redwoods of the beautiful Big Sur coast.

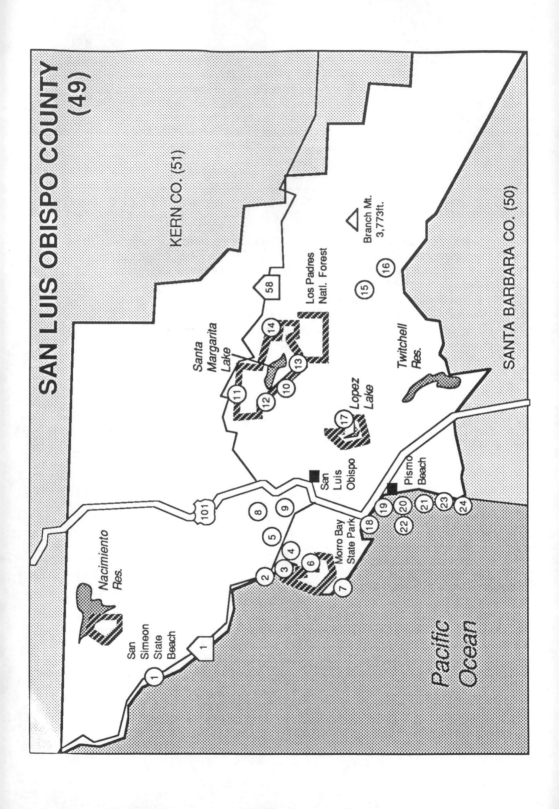

SAN LUIS OBISPO COUNTY
◆

Site **1** | SAN SIMEON
STATE BEACH

Campsites, facilities: There are 70 campsites for tents or motorhomes up to 30
feet long, and two of the sites are set up for wheelchair access. Piped water,
fireplaces and picnic tables are provided, and vault toilets and a dump station are available. A grocery store, laundromat and propane gas can be
found nearby. (Note: The Parks Department is in the process of recon-
structing a second campground of 120 sites with electrical connections and
rest rooms with showers.)
Reservations, fee: Phone MISTIX at (800)446-7275; $3 fee per night.
Who to contact: Phone park at (805)927-4509.   ~~Madonia Inn 543 3434~~   927 2035
Location: Drive three miles north of Cambria on State Route 1.
Trip note: This campground is open all year and is on the ocean. The Hearst
Castle (Hearst San Simeon State Historic Park) is 10 miles northeast of the
campground, and is open for tours on a regular basis. For tour reservations,
phone MISTIX at (800)446-7275; $8 fee per person.

Site **2** | ATASCADERO
STATE BEACH

Campsites, facilities: There are 23 tent sites and 81 motorhome spaces for motorhomes up to 24 feet long. Piped water, fireplaces and picnic tables are pro-
vided. Flush toilets and cold outdoor showers are available. A grocery store,
laundromat and propane gas are available nearby.
Reservations, fee: Phone MISTIX at (800)446-7275; $6 fee per night.
Who to contact: Phone park at (805)772-2560.
Location: Drive three miles north of Morro Bay off State Route 1.
Trip note: Open all year. Located on the ocean near Morro Bay State Park where
you may visit the Morro Bay Wildlife Refuge or the Museum of Natural
History.

Site **3** | MORRO DUNES TRAILER PARK
AND CAMPGROUND

Campsites, facilities: There are 43 tent sites and 139 motorhome spaces. Picnic
tables, fireplaces, piped water, electrical connections and in most cases sewer hookups are provided. Rest rooms, showers, a laundromat, store, and
dump station are available. Propane gas is nearby.

Reservations, fee: Call ahead for space available and fee.
Who to contact: Phone park at (805)772-2722.
Location: In Morro Bay drive west on Atascadero (Highway 41) from State Route 1 to 1700 Embarcadero.
Trip note: This campground is open all year. Enjoy deep sea fishing, clamming out of Morro Bay, or see the Hearst Castle, Montana de Oro State Park, the Museum of Natural History and the Wildlife Refuge.

Site **4**   TRATEL MORRO
                        BAY

Campsites, facilities: There are 49 motorhome spaces. Picnic tables, piped water, electrical connections and sewer hookups are provided. Rest rooms, showers, laundromat and cable TV are available. A grocery store and restaurant are nearby, and propane gas is delivered bi-weekly.
Reservations, fee: Call ahead for space available and fee.
Who to contact: Phone park at (805)772-8581.
Location: In Morro Bay drive west on Atascadero (Highway 41) from State Route 1 to 1680 Main Street.
Trip note: This adult motorhome park is open all year and is 1/2 mile from the beach. There are many services available nearby.

Site **5**   RANCHO COLINA
                        RV PARK

Campsites, facilities: There are 57 motorhome spaces. Picnic tables, piped water, electrical connections and sewer hookups are provided. Rest rooms, showers, laundromat and recreation room are available. Groceries and propane gas can be found nearby.
Reservations, fee: Call ahead for space available and fee.
Who to contact: Phone park at (805)772-8420.
Location: Drive one mile east of Morro Bay and State Route 1 on Atascadero Road (Highway 41) to 1045 Atascadero Road.
Trip note: This motorhome park is open all year. Nearby are numerous services and recreational opportunities, including state beaches, deep sea and beach fishing, a golf course, wildlife refuge and natural history museum.

Site **6**   MORRO BAY
                        STATE PARK

Campsites, facilities: There are 20 motorhome spaces with water and electrical connections and 115 campsites for tents or motorhomes up to 31 feet long. Piped water, fireplaces and picnic tables are provided. Flush toilets, dump station, laundromat, grocery store, propane gas, museum exhibits, nature walks and programs, boat ramp, mooring and food service are available. Camping, picnicking, museum and food service areas are wheelchair accessible.

Reservations, fee: Phone MISTIX at (800)446-7275; $12 fee per night.
Who to contact: Phone park at (805)772-2560.
Location: Drive to the south end of Morro Bay off State Route 1.
Trip note: Open all year. This park offers a wide range of activities and exhibits covering the natural and cultural history of the area.

Site **7**   MONTANA DE ORO

Campsites, facilities: There are 50 campsites for tents or motorhomes up to 24 feet long. Fireplaces and picnic tables are provided. Pit toilets, equestrial facilities and a nature trail are available. There is no water, so bring your own. A grocery store, laundromat and propane gas are nearby.
Reservations, fee: Phone MISTIX at (800)446-7275; $3 fee per night.
Who to contact: Phone park at (805)772-2560.
Location: Drive six miles southwest of Los Osos via Pecho Road.
Trip note: Open all year. The park encompases 7300 acres, with some of it along the coast. Within the park is Valencia Peak. Elevation 1345 feet.

Site **8**   CERRO ALTO

Campsites, facilities: There are 26 campsites for tents or motorhomes up to 16 feet long. Piped water, fireplaces and picnic tables are provided, and vault toilets are available.
Reservations, fee: No reservations; $5 fee per night.
Who to contact: Phone Los Padres National Forest Headquarters at (805)683-6711.
Location: Drive eight miles northeast of Morro Bay off State Route 41.
Trip note: Open all year. Elevation 1000 feet. Located near Morro Creek in the Santa Lucia Mountain Range.

Site **9**   EL CHORRO REGIONAL PARK

Campsites, facilities: There are 50 campsites for tents or motorhomes. Piped water, fireplaces and picnic tables are provided, and flush toilets are available. A grocery store and a laundromat are nearby.
Reservations, fee: Reservations accepted; $7 fee per night.
Who to contact: Phone park at (805)549-5219.
Location: Drive four miles north of San Luis Obispo on State Route 1.
Trip note: This park is open all year and is six miles from Morro Bay. Park is little-known among people from outside area.

Site **10** | SANTA MARGARITA LAKE CAMPGROUND

Campsites, facilities: There are 150 sites for tents or motorhomes. Picnic tables, fireplaces, piped water, and in some cases electrical connections and sewer hookups are provided. Rest rooms, showers, swimming pool, laundromat, store, dump station and propane gas are available.

Reservations, fee: Call for space available. $10 deposit required; $10 fee per night.

Who to contact: Phone camp at (805)438-5618.

Location: Drive nine miles southeast of Santa Margarita via State Route 58 on Pozo Road to 4765 Santa Margarita Lake Road.

Trip note: This camp is open all year and is in the oak woodlands. Fishing can be good in Santa Margarita Lake.

Site **11** | CIRCLE IN RANCH

Campsites, facilities: There are 20 tent sites and 25 motorhome spaces. Picnic tables, fireplaces, piped water, and in most cases electrical connections and sewer hookups are provided. Rest rooms, showers, swimming pool, laundromat, store, dump station, ice, recreation room, propane gas and a beer and wine saloon are available.

Reservations, fee: Call ahead for space available and fee.

Who to contact: Phone ranch at (805)438-5857.

Location: Drive 10 miles east of Santa Margarita on State Route 58 to Huerhuero Road.

Trip note: This campground is open all year and there is fishing at nearby Santa Margarita Lake.

Site **12** | RINCONADA CAMPGROUND

Campsites, facilities: There are 45 campsites for tents or motorhomes. Piped water, and in some cases sewer hookups and electrical connections are provided. Flush toilets, dump station and showers are available. A grocery store, laundromat and propane gas are nearby.

Reservations, fee: Call for space available. $8 deposit required; $8 fee per night.

Who to contact: Phone park at (805)438-5479.

Location: Drive nine miles southeast of Santa Margarita on Pozo Road.

Trip note: This campground is open all year and is near Santa Margarita Lake.

Site **13** | HI MOUNTAIN

Campsites, facilities: There are 11 campsites for tents or motorhomes up to 16

feet long. Piped water, fireplaces and picnic tables are provided, and vault toilets are available.

Reservations, fee: No reservations; $3 fee per night.

Who to contact: Phone Los Padres National Forest Headquarters at (805)683-6711.

Location: Drive four miles southwest of Pozo.

Trip note: Open all year. Elevation 2800 feet. This is the highest point in the Santa Lucia Wilderness. Two trails from camp lead into the Garcia Mountain area to two other camps.

Site **14**   LA PANZA   ▲

Campsites, facilities: There are 16 campsites for tents or motorhomes up to 16 feet long. Piped water, fireplaces and picnic tables are provided, and vault toilets are available.

Reservations, fee: No reservations; $3 fee per night.

Who to contact: Phone Los Padres National Forest Headquarters at (805)683-6711.

Location: Drive 12 miles northeast of Pozo.

Trip note: Open all year. Elevation 2400 feet. Located in the La Panza Range which is criss-crossed by numerous trails and streams.

Site **15**   STONY
                               CREEK   ▲

Campsites, facilities: There are 12 campsites for tents. Piped water, fireplaces and picnic tables are provided, and vault toilets are available.

Reservations, fee: No reservations, no fee.

Who to contact: Phone Los Padres National Forest Headquarters at (805)683-6711.

Location: Drive 24 miles northeast of Arroyo Grande via Huasna Road.

Trip note: Open all year. Elevation 1800 feet. Located on Stony Creek.

Site **16**   AGUA
                               ESCONDIDO   🌲

Campsites, facilities: There are three campsites for tents. Piped water, fireplaces and picnic tables are provided, and vault toilets are available.

Reservations, fee: No reservations, no fee.

Who to contact: Phone Los Padres National Forest Headquarters at (805)683-6711.

Location: Drive 31 miles northeast of Arroyo Grande via Huasna Road.

Trip note: Open all year. Elevation 2200 feet. Small and obscure. Map of Los Padres National Forest details area.

Site **17**   LOPEZ LAKE
RECREATION AREA

Campsites, facilities: There are 146 tent sites, 143 motorhome spaces, and 295 sites for tents or motorhomes up to 40 feet long. Picnic tables, fireplaces, and in many cases piped water, electrical connections and sewer hookups are provided. Rest rooms, showers, a playground, laundromat, store, ice, snack bar, boat ramp, mooring, boat fuel, propane gas, tackle and boat rentals are available.
Reservations, fee: Reservations accepted; $10 fee per night.
Who to contact: Phone park at (805)489-8019.
Location: Drive 11 miles east of Arroyo Grande off US-101.
Trip note: This campground is set among the oak woodlands next to Lopez Lake. Hiking and horseback riding trails loop through the area. The Lake is used for fishing, waterskiing and sailboarding.

Site **18**   AVILA HOT SPRINGS SPA
AND RV PARK

Campsites, facilities: There are 25 tent sites and 50 motorhome spaces. Piped water, electrical connections and sewer hookups are provided at most sites. Rest rooms, showers, swimming pool, hot mineral pool, spa, cable TV, dump station, recreation room, arcade, and group barbeque pits are available. A grocery store, laundromat, propane gas, golf course and riding stables are nearby.
Reservations, fee: Call ahead for space available and fee.
Who to contact: Phone park at (805)595-2359.
Location: Drive eight miles south of San Luis Obispo on US-101 to Avila Beach Drive exit, and go to 250 Avila Beach Drive.
Trip note: This park is open all year and is close to Avila State Beach and Pismo State Beach.

Site **19**   PISMO COAST
VILLAGE

Campsites, facilities: There are 400 motorhome spaces. Piped water, electrical connections and sewer hookups are provided. Rest rooms, showers, playgrounds, swimming pools, laundromat, store, firewood, ice, recreation room, propane gas, recreation programs, restaurant and miniature golf are available.
Reservations, fee: Call for space available. $16.50 deposit required; $16.50 fee per night.
Who to contact: Phone park at (805)773-1811.
Location: In Pismo Beach, drive to 165 South Dolliver Street.
Trip note: This park is open all year and is on the beach.

Site **20**
LE SAGE
RIVIERA

Campsites, facilities: There are 87 motorhome spaces. Picnic tables, piped water, electrical connections and sewer hookups are provided. Rest rooms, showers and a laundromat are available. Stores, restaurants and golf courses are nearby.

Reservations, fee: Call for space available. $14 deposit required; $14 fee per night.

Who to contact: Phone park at (805)489-2103.

Location: Drive two miles south of Pismo Beach via Grand Avenue or Dolliver Street to 319 North Highway 1.

Trip note: This park is open all year and is next to Pismo State Beach.

Site **21**
OCEANO
CAMPGROUND

Campsites, facilities: There are 50 campsites for tents or motorhomes. Piped water, fireplaces, picnic tables and in some cases electrical connections are provided. Flush toilets, showers, playground, horseback riding facilities, laundromat, grocery store and propane gas are available.

Reservations, fee: No reservations; $8 fee per night.

Who to contact: Phone park at (805)549-5219.

Location: In Oceano, off US-101, take Airport Road to campground.

Trip note: This campground is open from April to September and is next to Pismo State Beach.

Site **22**
NORTH BEACH
PISMO STATE BEACH

Campsites, facilities: There are 50 campsites for tents or motorhomes up to 30 feet long. Piped water, fireplaces and picnic tables are provided. Flush toilets are available. Horseback riding facilities, a grocery store, laudromat and propane gas are nearby.

Reservations, fee: Phone MISTIX at (800)446-7275; $6.50 fee per night.

Who to contact: Phone park at (805)773-2334.

Location: Drive one mile south of the town of Pismo Beach off State Route 1.

Trip note: This campground is open all year and is on the beach. Enjoy horseback riding, hiking along the dunes or fishing in the ocean.

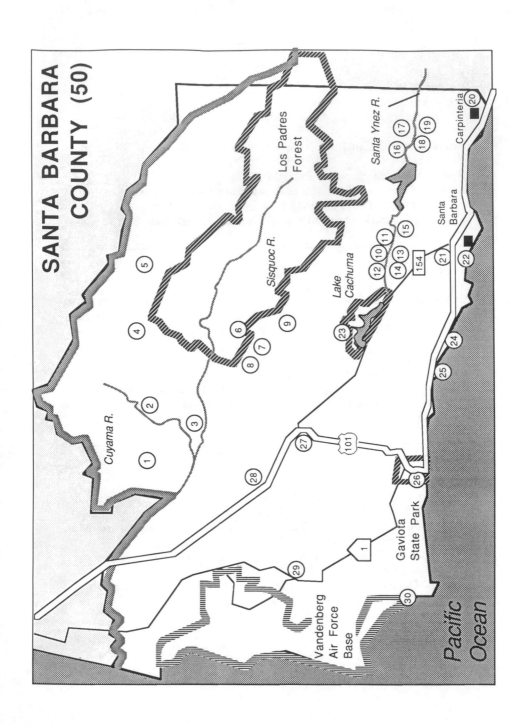

SANTA BARBARA
COUNTY (50)

SANTA BARBARA COUNTY

♦

Site **1**   COLSON   **△**

Campsites, facilities: There are seven tent sites and two campsites for tents or motorhomes up to 22 feet long. Piped water, fireplaces and picnic tables are provided, and vault toilets are available.

Reservations, fee: No reservations, no fee.

Who to contact: Phone Los Padres National Forest Headquarters at (805)683-6711.

Location: Drive 12 miles northeast of Sisquoc via Tepusquet and Colson Canyon Roads.

Trip note: Open all year. Elevation 2100 feet. Several trails lead out from camp into the backcountry of Los Padres National Forest.

Site **2**   WAGON
FLAT   **🌲**

Campsites, facilities: There are five campsites for tents or motorhomes up to 16 feet long. Fireplaces and picnic tables are provided, and vault toilets are available. There is no water, so bring your own.

Reservations, fee: No reservations, no fee.

Who to contact: Phone Los Padres National Forest Headquarters at (805)683-6711.

Location: Drive 21 miles northeast of Sisquoc via Tepusquet, Colson and La Brea Canyon Roads.

Trip note: Open all year. Elevation 1400 feet. Located on La Brea Creek. A trail out of camp goes up Kerry Canyon.

Site **3**   BARREL
SPRINGS   **🌲**

Campsites, facilities: There are six tent sites. Piped water, fireplaces and picnic tables are provided, and vault toilets are available.

Reservations, fee: No reservations, no fee.

Who to contact: Phone Los Padres National Forest Headquarters at (805)683-6711.

Location: Drive 17 miles northeast of Sisquoc via Tepusquet and Colson Canyon Roads.

Trip note: Open all year. Elevation 1000 feet. Located on La Brea Creek. A trail near camp leads into the backcountry and into the San Rafael Wilderness. There are campgrounds every ten miles along the trail.

Site **4**   BATES
                                    CANYON

Campsites, facilities: There are two tent sites and four campsites for tents or motorhomes up to 16 feet long. Piped water, fireplaces and picnic tables are provided, and vault toilets are available.
Reservations, fee: No reservations, no fee.
Who to contact: Phone Los Padres National Forest Headquarters at (805)683-6711.
Location: Drive 18 miles west of New Cuyama on Cottonwood Canyon Road.
Trip note: Open all year. Elevation 2900 feet. A little-known, little-used camp. Los Padres Forest map will open up area to you.

Site **5**   ALISO
                                    PARK

Campsites, facilities: There are 11 campsites for tents or motorhomes up to 22 feet long. Fireplaces and picnic tables are provided, and vault toilets are available. There is no water so bring your own.
Reservations, fee: No reservations, no fee.
Who to contact: Phone Los Padres National Forest Headquarters at (805)683-6711.
Location: Drive eight miles southwest of New Cuyama off State Route 166.
Trip note: Open all year. Elevation 3200 feet. A primitive and quiet campsite.

Site **6**   NIRA

Campsites, facilities: There are 12 tent sites. Fireplaces and picnic tables are provided, and vault toilets are available. There is no water, so bring your own.
Reservations, fee: No reservations, no fee.
Who to contact: Phone Los Padres National Forest Headquarters at (805)683-6711.
Location: Drive 22 miles northeast of Santa Inez off State Route 154 via Happy Canyon and Sunset Valley Roads.
Trip note: Open all year. Elevation 2100 feet. Located on Manzana Creek along the border of the San Rafael Wilderness. Trails lead from camp into the backcountry.

Site **7**   DAVY
                                    BROWN

Campsites, facilities: There are 13 campsites for tents or motorhomes up to 22

feet long. Piped water, fireplaces and picnic tables are provided, and vault toilets are available.

Reservations, fee: No reservations; $5 fee per night.

Who to contact: Phone Los Padres National Forest Headquarters at (805)683-6711.

Location: Drive 19 miles northeast of Santa Ynez via Happy Canyon Road.

Trip note: Open all year. Elevation 4000 feet. Located on Davy Brown Creek near the border of the San Rafael Wilderness. Trail from camp leads into the backcountry.

Site **8**   FIGUEROA   🔺

Campsites, facilities: There are 33 campsites for tents or motorhomes up to 22 feet long. Piped water, fireplaces and picnic tables are provided, and vault toilets are available.

Reservations, fee: No reservations; $4 fee per night.

Who to contact: Phone Los Padres National Forest Headquarters at (805)683-6711.

Location: Drive 12 miles northeast of Los Olivos on Figueroa Mountain Road.

Trip note: Open all year. Elevation 4000 feet. Located along several picnic areas near Figueroa Mountain. Nearby trails lead into the backcountry of the San Rafael Wilderness.

Site **9**   CACHUMA   🌲

Campsites, facilities: There are six tent sites. Fireplaces and picnic tables are provided, and vault toilets are available. There is no water, so bring your own.

Reservations, fee: No reservations, no fee.

Who to contact: Phone Los Padres National Forest Headquarters at (805)683-6711.

Location: Drive 16 miles northeast of Santa Ynez off State Route 154 on Happy Canyon Road.

Trip note: Open all year. Elevation 2200 feet. Dirt road south of camp follows Cachuma Creek seven miles until it empties into Lake Cachuma.

Site **10**   UPPER
                                       OSO   🔺

Campsites, facilities: There are 27 campsites for tents or motorhomes up to 22 feet long. Piped water, fireplaces and picnic tables are provided, and flush toilets are available. Horseback riding facilities are nearby.

Reservations, fee: No reservations; $5 fee per night.

Who to contact: Phone Los Padres National Forest Headquarters at (805)683-6711.

Location: Drive 22 miles northwest of Santa Barbara off State Route 154.

Trip note: Open all year. Elevation 1100 feet. Located along the Santa Ynez River. Trailhead into the San Rafael Wilderness is nearby. Once on the trail there are many rustic campsites along the way. Be sure to bring your own water.

Site 11   SAGE HILL
GROUP CAMP

Campsites, facilities: There are 62 campsites for tents or motorhomes up to 32 feet long. Piped water, fireplaces and picnic tables are provided, and flush toilets are available. Horseback riding facilities are nearby.

Reservations, fee: Reservations requested; $25 fee per group per night.

Who to contact: Phone Los Padres National Forest Headquarters at (805)683-6711.

Location: Drive 20 miles northwest of Santa Barbara off State Route 154.

Trip note: Open all year. Elevation 2000 feet. Located on the Santa Ynez River. Trail from camp leads into the San Rafael Wilderness. Once on the trail there are numerous rustic campsites. Bring your own water.

Site 12   FREMONT

Campsites, facilities: There are 15 campsites for tents or motorhomes up to 16 feet long. Piped water, fireplaces and picnic tables are provided, and flush toilets are available. Groceries and propane gas are nearby.

Reservations, fee: No reservations; $5 fee per night.

Who to contact: Phone Los Padres National Forest Headquarters at (805)683-6711.

Location: Drive 18 miles northwest of Santa Barbara off State Route 154.

Trip note: Open from April to October. Elevation 900 feet. Located near the Santa Ynez River. The eastern shore of Lake Cachuma is six miles away.

Site 13   LOS PRIETOS

Campsites, facilities: There are 38 campsites for tents or motorhomes up to 22 feet long. Piped water, fireplaces and picnic tables are provided, and flush toilets are available.

Reservations, fee: No reservations; $5 fee per night.

Who to contact: Phone Los Padres National Forest Headquarters at (805)683-6711.

Location: Drive 19 miles northwest of Santa Barbara off State Route 154.

Trip note: Open from April to October. Elevation 1000 feet. Located on the Santa Ynez River. A trail from camp leads past several other camps on its way to the San Rafael Wilderness.

Site 14   PARADISE

Campsites, facilities: There are 15 campsites for tents or motorhomes up to 22 feet long. Piped water, fireplaces and picnic tables are provided, and flush toilets are available. Horseback riding facilities, groceries and propane gas can be found nearby.

Reservations, fee: No reservations; $5 fee per night.

Who to contact: Phone Los Padres National Forest Headquarters at (805)683-6711.

Location: Drive 19 miles northwest of Santa Barbara off State Route 154.

Trip note: Open all year. Elevation 1000 feet. Located near the Santa Ynez River. Lake Cachuma is six miles to the west.

Site 15   SANTA YNEZ

Campsites, facilities: There are 34 campsites for tents or motorhomes up to 22 feet long. Piped water, fireplaces and picnic tables are provided, and vault toilets are available. Horseback riding facilities are nearby.

Reservations, fee: No reservations; $5 fee per night.

Who to contact: Phone Los Padres National Forest Headquarters at (805)683-6711.

Location: Drive 26 miles northwest of Santa Barbara off State Route 154.

Trip note: Open from April to November. Elevation 1100 feet. Located on the Santa Ynez River.

Site 16   MONO

Campsites, facilities: There are seven tent sites. Fireplaces and picnic tables are provided, and vault toilets are available. There is no water, so bring your own.

Reservations, fee: No reservations, no fee.

Who to contact: Phone Los Padres National Forest Headquarters at (805)683-6711.

Location: Drive 48 miles north of Santa Barbara off State Route 154.

Trip note: Open all year. Elevation 1500 feet. Located on Mono Creek near Gibraltar Reservoir.

Site 17   P-BAR FLAT

Campsites, facilities: There are four tent sites. Fireplaces and picnic tables are provided, and vault toilets are available. There is no water, so bring your own.

Reservations, fee: No reservations, no fee.
Who to contact: Phone Los Padres National Forest Headquarters at (805)683-6711.
Location: Drive 45 miles northeast of Santa Barbara off State Route 154.
Trip note: Open all year. Elevation 1800 feet. Located on the Santa Ynez River.

Site **18**   MIDDLE   ▲
                       SANTA YNEZ

Campsites, facilities: There are nine tent sites. Piped water, fireplaces and picnic tables are provided, and vault toilets are available.
Reservations, fee: No reservations, no fee.
Who to contact: Phone Los Padres National Forest Headquarters at (805)683-6711.
Location: Drive 44 miles northeast of Santa Barbara off State Route 154.
Trip note: Camp is open all year. Elevation 1500 feet. Located on the Santa Ynez River.

Site **19**   JUNCAL   🌲

Campsites, facilities: There are six tent sites. Fireplaces and picnic tables are provided, and vault toilets are available. There is no water, so bring your own.
Reservations, fee: No reservations, no fee.
Who to contact: Phone Los Padres National Forest Headquarters at (805)683-6711.
Location: Drive 21 miles northeast of Santa Barbara off State Route 154 via East Camino Cielo.
Trip note: Open all year. Elevation 1800 feet. Located on the Santa Ynez River.

Site **20**   CARPINTERIA   ▲
                       STATE BEACH

Campsites, facilities: There are 100 tent sites and 162 campsites for motorhomes up to 30 feet long. Piped water, fireplaces and picnic tables, and in some cases full hookups, are provided. Flush toilets, showers, playground and dump station are available. A grocery store, laundromat and propane gas are nearby. Campground, picnic areas and store are wheelchair accessible.
Reservations, fee: Phone MISTIX at (800)446-7275; $14 fee per night.
Who to contact: Phone park at (805)684-2811.
Location: Drive ten miles south of Santa Barbara off US-101 via State Route 224.
Trip note: Open all year and located on the beach.

Site **21**   EL PATIO   🚐
                       CAMPER VILLAGE

Campsites, facilities: There are 92 motorhome spaces. Piped water, picnic tables, electrical connections, sewer hookups, private patios and cable TV are provided. Rest rooms, showers, laundromat and propane delivery are available. Stores, restaurants, bowling alley, golf course, beach and deep sea fishing are nearby.

Reservations, fee: No reservations; $18 fee per night.

Who to contact: Phone park at (805)687-7614.

Location: In Santa Barbara drive northeast of the junction of US-101 and State Route 154 to 4040 Calle Real.

Trip note: This park is open all year and is five miles from El Presidio de Santa Barbara State Historical Park.

Site **22**　　SANTA BARBARA
CAMPER PARK　　

Campsites, facilities: There are 33 motorhome spaces. Picnic tables, piped water, electrical connections and sewer hookups are provided. Rest rooms, showers, and a laundromat are available. A grocery store, golf course, tennis courts and propane gas are nearby.

Reservations, fee: Call ahead for space available and fee.

Who to contact: Phone park at (805)966-9954.

Location: In Santa Barbara take the Salinas Street exit off US-101 going north, or the Milpitas Street exit off US-101 going south and follow the blue Campers signs.

Trip note: This park is open all year and is close to the beach and downtown area.

Site **23**　　LAKE
CACHUMA　　

Campsites, facilities: There are 500 campsites for tents or motorhomes. Piped water, fireplaces and picnic tables, and in some cases electrical connections and sewer hookups are provided. Flush toilets, showers, playground, horseback riding facilities, general store, swimming pool, boat ramp, mooring, boat fuel, boat rentals, ice and snack bar are available. Craft under 10 feet prohibited.

Reservations, fee: Phone Leisuretime Reservation Systems at (800)822-CAMP; $11 fee per night.

Who to contact: Phone park at (805)688-8780.

Location: Drive nine miles east of Santa Ynez off State Route 154.

Trip note: Campground is open all year. Elevation 600 feet. Located on Lake Cachuma which is set in the oak and chaparral woodlands. Big Florida bass can provide good fishing. Swimming permitted in the pool only.

Site **24**　　EL CAPITAN
STATE BEACH　　

Campsites, facilities: There are 140 campsites for tents or motorhomes up to 27

feet long. Piped water, fireplaces and picnic tables are provided. Flush toilets, showers, dump station, food service and grocery store are available. Campground, food service area, picnic grounds and grocery store are wheelchair accessible.

Reservations, fee: Phone MISTIX at (800)446-7275; $8 fee per night.

Who to contact: Phone park at (805)968-0019.

Location: Drive 20 miles northwest of Santa Barbara off US-101.

Trip note: This campground is open all year and is on the beach where you can fish and swim.

Site **25**   REFUGIO
                           STATE BEACH   ▲

Campsites, facilities: There are 85 campsites for tents or motorhomes up to 27 feet long. Piped water, fireplaces and picnic tables are provided. Flush toilets, showers, grocery store, food service and horseback riding facilities are available. Campground, food service area and grocery store are wheelchair accessible.

Reservations, fee: Phone MISTIX at (800)446-7275; $8 fee per night.

Who to contact: Phone park at (805)968-0019.

Location: Drive 23 miles northwest of Santa Barbara on US-101.

Trip note: This campground is open all year and is on the beach, where you can enjoy fishing, swimming, horseback riding and hiking.

Site **26**   GAVIOTA
                           STATE PARK   ▲

Campsites, facilities: There are 19 tent sites and 39 sites for motorhomes up to 27 feet long. Fireplaces and picnic tables are provided. Flush toilets and showers are available. There is no drinking water, so bring your own. A grocery store is nearby.

Reservations, fee: Phone MISTIX at (800)446-7275; $8 fee per night.

Who to contact: Phone park at (805)968-0019.

Location: Drive 33 miles west of Santa Barbara on US-101.

Trip note: The campground for this 2800 acre park is near the beach and there are hiking and equestrial trails in the park.

Site **27**   FLYING FLAGS
                           TRAVEL PARK   ▲

Campsites, facilities: There are 200 sites for tents or motorhomes. Picnic tables, fireplaces, piped water, and in many cases electrical connections and sewer hookups, are provided. Rest rooms with wheelchair access, showers, a playground, swimming pool, two hot therapy pools, laundromat, store, dump station, ice, recreation room, arcade, putting green and propane gas are available. A nine hole golf course is next door.

Reservations, fee: Call for space available. $14 deposit required; $14 fee per night.

Who to contact: Phone park at (805)688-3716.

Location: Drive 45 miles north of Santa Barbara on US-101 to junction with State Route 246.

Trip note: This park is open all year and is three miles from Solvang and the Santa Ynez Mission. Fishing, boating and ocean beaches are within ten miles of the park.

Site **28**   RANCHO JAMORE
                               MOTORHOME PARK   ▲

Campsites, facilities: There are 15 motorhome spaces and five sites for tents or motorhomes. Most of the sites have full hookups. Rest rooms, showers and a laundromat are available. A grocery store and propane gas are nearby.

Reservations, fee: Call for space available. $10 deposit required; $10 fee per night.

Who to contact: Phone park at (805)344-5444.

Location: Drive 18 miles south of Santa Maria to junction of State Route 135 and go to 9230 North Highway 101.

Site **29**   RIVER
                               PARK   ▲

Campsites, facilities: There are four tent sites and 32 motorhome spaces. Piped water, flush toilets, dump station, playground, grocery store, laundromat and propane gas are available.

Reservations, fee: No reservations; $5 fee per night.

Who to contact: Phone park at (805)736-6565.

Location: In Lompoc drive to the junction of State Route 246 and Sweeney Road.

Trip note: This park is open from May to September. La Purisima Mission State Historical Park is nearby.

Site **30**   JALAMA BEACH
                               COUNTY PARK   ▲

Campsites, facilities: There are 100 campsites for tents or motorhomes up to 35 feet long. Piped water, fireplaces and picnic tables are provided. Flush toilets, showers, dump station, playground, grocery store, laundromat and propane gas are available.

Reservations, fee: No reservations; $7 fee per night.

Who to contact: Phone park at (805)734-1446.

Location: Drive 20 miles southwest of Lompoc off State Route 1 on Jalama Road.

Trip note: This park is open all year. Located where Jalama Creek empties into the ocean, five miles north of Point Conception and just south of Vandenberg Air Force Base.

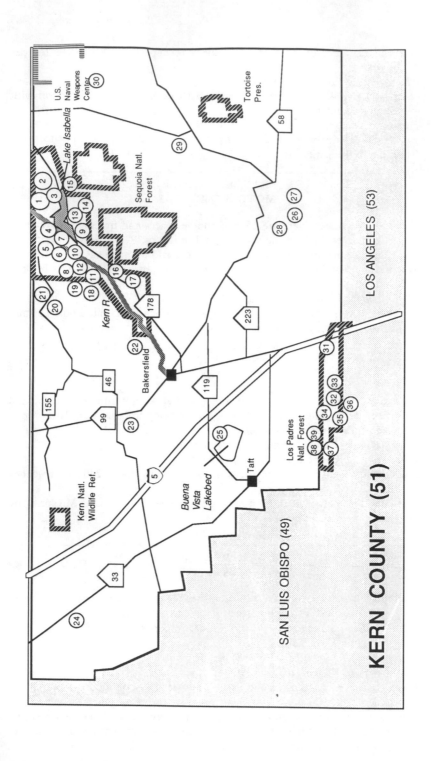

KERN COUNTY (51)

LOS ANGELES (53)

SAN LUIS OBISPO (49)

U.S. Naval Weapons Center

Tortoise Pres.

Sequoia Natl. Forest

Lake Isabella

Kern R.

Bakersfield

Kern Natl. Wildlife Ref.

Buena Vista Lakebed

Taft

Los Padres Natl. Forest

KERN COUNTY
♦

Site 1   **HEADQUARTERS**

Campsites, facilities: There are 52 campsites for tents or motorhomes up to 22 feet long. Piped water, fireplaces and picnic tables are provided. Vault toilets and horseback riding facilities are available. A grocery store, laundromat and propane gas are available nearby.
Reservations, fee: No reservations; $5 fee per night.
Who to contact: Phone Sequoia National Forest at (209)784-1500.
Location: Drive four miles northwest of Kernville on Sierra Way.
Trip note: Open from May to October. Elevation 2700 feet. Campsite is on the Kern River, five miles from Lake Isabella.

Site 2   **RIVERNOOK**
            CAMPGROUND

Campsites, facilities: There are 23 tent sites and 166 motorhome spaces. Picnic tables, piped water and full or partial hookups are provided. Rest rooms, showers and dump station are available.
Reservations, fee: Call for space available. $10 deposit required; $10 fee per night.
Who to contact: Phone park at (619)376-2705.
Location: Drive 1/2 mile north of Kernville to 14001 Sierra Way.
Trip note: This campground is open all year and is near Lake Isabella. Elevation 2665 feet. Boats for fishing or exploring the lake can be rented at one of the nearby marinas. If you want to tour the surrounding area there are many historical landmarks, including the town of Keysville, the first town to spring up on the Kern River during the gold rush. Visit Greenhorn Mountain Park and hike the trails leading to Indian petroglyphs and ritual areas.

Site 3   **EASTSIDE** ▮

Campsites, facilities: There are primitive campsites for tents or motorhomes. Picnic tables, fireplaces and piped water are provided. Flush toilets, dump station and boat launch are available. A grocery store, laundromat and propane gas are available nearby.

Reservations, fee: No reservations, no fee.

Who to contact: Phone U.S. Army Corps of Engineers at (619)379-2742.

Location: Drive five miles south of Kernville to East Shore of Isabella Lake.

Trip note: Eastside campground is open all year and is located on the shore of Lake Isabella. Elevation 2650 feet. Boats for fishing or exploring the lake can be rented at one of the marinas nearby. If you want to tour the surrounding area there are many historical landmarks, including the town of Keysville, the first town established on the Kern River during the gold rush. Visit Greenhorn Mountain Park and hike the trails leading to Indian petroglyphs and ritual areas.

Site **4**   LIVE
                              OAK   ▲

Campsites, facilities: There are 150 campsites for tents or motorhomes up to 30 feet long. Piped water, fireplaces and picnic tables are provided. Flush toilets, showers and horseback riding facilities are available. A grocery store, laundromat and propane gas are available nearby.

Reservations, fee: No reservations; $6 fee per night.

Who to contact: Phone U.S. Army Corps of Engineers at (619)379-2742.

Location: Drive 1/2 mile southwest of Wofford Heights off State Route 155.

Trip note: This camp is open from April to September, and is on Tillie Creek near the shore of Lake Isabella. Elevation 2600 feet.

Site **5**   TILLIE
                             CREEK   ▲

Campsites, facilities: There are 159 campsites for tents or motorhomes up to 30 feet long. Piped water, fireplaces and picnic tables are provided. Flush toilets, showers, dump station, playground and horseback riding facilities are available. A grocery store, laundromat and propane gas are nearby.

Reservations, fee: No reservations; $6 fee per night.

Who to contact: Phone U.S. Army Corps of Engineers at (619)379-2742.

Location: Drive one mile southwest of Wolford Heights on State Route 155.

Trip note: Open all year. Elevation 2625 feet. Located on the shore of Lake Isabella adjacent to Tillie Creek. Boats for fishing or exploring the lake can be rented at one of the marinas nearby. If you want to explore the surrounding area there are many historical landmarks, including the town of Keysville, the first town built along the Kern River during the gold rush. Visit Greenhorn Mountain Park and hike the trails leading to Indian petroglyphs and ritual areas.

Site **6**

TILLIE CREEK
GROUP CAMP

Campsites, facilities: There are group campsites for tents or motorhomes. Picnic tables, fireplaces and piped water are provided. Vault toilets, dump station and a playground are available. A grocery store, laundromat and propane gas are available nearby.

Reservations, fee: No reservations; $40 fee per night per group.

Who to contact: Phone U.S. Army Corps of Engineers at (619)379-2742.

Location: Drive one mile southwest of Wofford Heights on State Route 155.

Trip note: Tillie Creek is open all year and is on the shore of Lake Isabella. Elevation 2625 feet.

Site **7**

BOULDER
GULCH

Campsites, facilities: There are 80 campsites for tents or motorhomes up to 30 feet long. Piped water, fireplaces and picnic tables are provided. Flush toilets and showers are available. A grocery store, laundromat and propane gas are available nearby.

Reservations, fee: No reservations; $6 fee per night.

Who to contact: Phone U.S. Army Corps of Engineers at (619)379-2742.

Location: Drive four miles north of the town of Lake Isabella on State Route 155.

Trip note: Boulder Gulch is open from April to September. Elevation 2650 feet. Located on the shore of Lake Isabella. Boats for fishing or exploring the lake can be rented at one of the marinas nearby. If you want to explore the surrounding area there are many historical landmarks, including Keysville, Greenhorn Mountain Park and ancient Indian petroglyphs.

Site **8**

HUNGRY
GULCH

Campsites, facilities: There are campsites for tents or motorhomes. Piped water, fireplaces and picnic tables are provided. Flush toilets and showers are available. A grocery store, laundromat and propane gas are nearby.

Reservations, fee: No reservations; $6 fee per night.

Who to contact: Phone U.S. Army Corps of Engineers at (619)379-2742.

Location: Drive four miles north of the town of Lake Isabella on State Route 155.

Trip note: This camp is open from April to September and is near the shore of Lake Isabella. Elevation 2675 feet.

Site **9**
AUXILLIARY
DAM

Campsites, facilities: There are campsites for tents or motorhomes. Picnic tables, fireplaces and piped water are provided. Flush toilets, showers and a dump station are available. A grocery store, laundromat and propane gas are nearby.

Reservations, fee: No reservations, no fee.

Who to contact: Phone U.S. Army Corps of Engineers at (619)379-2742.

Location: Drive one mile north of the town of Lake Isabella on State Route 178.

Trip note: Auxiliary Dam is open all year. Elevation 2650 feet. Located on the shore of Lake Isabella. Boats for fishing or exploring the lake can be rented at one of the marinas nearby. The surrounding area has many historical landmarks.

Site **10**
FRENCH GULCH
GROUP CAMP

Campsites, facilities: There are campsites for tents or motorhomes. Picnic tables, fireplaces and piped water are provided. Vault toilets are available. A grocery store, laundromat and propane gas are nearby.

Reservations, fee: Reservations requested; $40 group fee per night.

Who to contact: Phone U.S. Army Corps of Engineers at (619)379-2742.

Location: Drive 2 1/2 miles northwest of the town of Lake Isabella on State Route 155.

Trip note: French Gulch is open all year. Elevation 2700 feet. Campsite is on the shore of Lake Isabella. Boats for fishing or exploring the lake can be rented at one of the marinas nearby. There are many historical landmarks to see, including the town of Keysville, Greenhorn Mountain Park and ancient Indian petroglyphs.

Site **11**
MAIN
DAM

Campsites, facilities: There are 84 campsites for tents or motorhomes up to 30 feet long. Piped water, fireplaces and picnic tables are provided. Flush toilets, a dump station and playground are available. A grocery store, laundromat and propane gas are nearby.

Reservations, fee: No reservations, no fee.

Who to contact: Phone U.S. Army Corps of Engineers at (619)379-2742.

Location: Drive one mile west of the town of Lake Isabella on State Route 155.

Trip note: Main Dam is open from April to September. Elevation 2500 feet.
This spot is on the shore of Lake Isabella. Boats for fishing or exploring the lake can be rented at one of the marinas nearby. Explore the historical

landmarks in the area including the ancient Indian petroglyphs and ritual areas.

Site **12** PIONEER POINT

Campsites, facilities: There are 77 campsites for tents or motorhomes up to 30 feet long. Piped water, fireplaces and picnic tables are provided. Flush toilets, showers and a playground are available. Nearby are a grocery store, laundromat and propane gas.

Reservations, fee: No reservations; $6 fee per night.

Who to contact: Phone U.S. Army Corps of Engineers at (619)379-2742.

Location: Drive two and a half miles north of the town of Lake Isabella on State Route 155.

Trip note: Pioneer Point is open all year. Elevation 2650 feet. Campsite is on the shore of Lake Isabella. Boats for fishing or exploring the lake can be rented at one of the marinas nearby. There are many historical landmarks to explore in the surrounding area.

Site **13** PARADISE COVE

Campsites, facilities: There are campsites for tents or motorhomes. Picnic tables, fireplaces and piped water are provided. Flush toilets and a playground are available. A grocery store, laundromat and propane gas are available nearby.

Reservations, fee: No reservations; $4 fee per night.

Who to contact: Phone U.S. Army Corps of Engineers at (619)379-2742.

Location: Drive six miles northeast of the town of Lake Isabella on State Route 178.

Trip note: Paradise Cove is open all year and is on the shore of Lake Isabella. Elevation 2600 feet. Boats for fishing or exploring the lake can be rented at one of the marinas nearby. Explore the numerous historical landmarks in the area including the ancient Indian petroglyphs and ritual areas.

Site **14** MOUNTAIN MESA TRAILER COURT

Campsites, facilities: There are 45 motorhome spaces. Picnic tables, piped water and full or partial hookups are provided. Rest rooms, showers and laundromat are available.

Reservations, fee: Call for space available. $10.50 deposit required; $10.50 fee per night.

Who to contact: Phone park at (619)379-2046.

Location: Drive six miles northeast of the town of Lake Isabella on State Route 178.

Trip note: Open all year. Elevation 2600 feet. This spot is on the shore of Lake Isabella. Boats for fishing or exploring the lake can be rented at one of the marinas nearby. If you want to explore the surrounding area there are many historical landmarks.

Site **15**

KOA
LAKE ISABELLA

▲

Campsites, facilities: There are 104 campsites for tents or motorhomes. Picnic tables, piped water and full or partial hookups are provided.
Rest rooms, showers, a playground, laundromat, store, dump station, and propane gas are available.

Reservations, fee: Call for space available. $10 deposit required; $10 fee per night.

Who to contact: Phone park at (619)378-2001.

Location: Drive 10 miles east of the town of Lake Isabella on State Route 178.

Trip note: This camp is open all year and is near Lake Isabella in the South Fork Valley. Elevation 2600 feet.

Site **16**

HOBO

▲

Campsites, facilities: There are 10 campsites for tents or motorhomes up to 16 feet long. Piped water, fireplaces and picnic tables are provided. Vault toilets, showers and a dump station are available. Nearby are a grocery store and propane gas.

Reservations, fee: No reservations; $5 fee per night.

Who to contact: Phone Sequoia National Forest at (209)784-1500.

Location: Drive five miles south of the town of Lake Isabella off State Route 178 on Kern River Road.

Trip note: Hobo is open May to October and is on the Kern River next to Miracle Hot Springs. Elevation 2300 feet.

Site **17**

BRECKENRIDGE

🌲

Campsites, facilities: There are eight tent sites. Picnic tables and fireplaces are provided and vault toilets are available.

Reservations, fee: No reservations, no fee.

Who to contact: Phone Sequoia National Forest at (209)784-1500.

Location: Drive 12 miles southwest of Havilah off Caliente Bodfish Road.

Trip note: Breckenridge is open from May to October. Elevation 7100 feet. This site is located on Mill Creek near the base of Breckenridge Mountain, a popular mountain retreat. Gold was discovered near the town of Havilah in 1864 and it became the first county seat in 1866.

Site **18**   DAVIS   ◭

Campsites, facilities: There are seven campsites for tents or motorhomes up to 20 feet long. Piped water, fireplaces and picnic tables are provided. Vault toilets are available.

Reservations, fee: No reservations, no fee.

Who to contact: Phone Sequoia National Forest at (209)784-1500.

Location: Drive 19 miles southwest of Wofford Heights off State Route 155 via Sawmill Road and Rancheria Road.

Trip note: Davis is open from May to October and is located in the Greenhorn Mountains. Elevation 5200 feet. If you want to explore the surrounding area there are many historical landmarks to see, including the town of Keysville, the first town erected on the Kern River during the gold rush. In Greenhorn Mountain Park there are trails leading to Indian petroglyphs and ritual areas.

Site **19**   EVANS
                              FLAT   🌲

Campsites, facilities: There are 12 campsites for tents or motorhomes up to 16 feet long. Fireplaces and picnic tables are provided, and vault toilets are available. There is no water at this site, so bring your own.

Reservations, fee: No reservations, no fee.

Who to contact: Phone Sequoia National Forest at (209)784-1500.

Location: Drive 14 miles southwest of Wofford Heights off State Route 155 via Sawmill Road and Rancheria Road.

Trip note: Evans Flat is open from May to October and is adjacent to Ranger Spring near the base of Woodward Peak. Elevation 6200 feet.

Site **20**   ALDER
                           CREEK   🌲

Campsites, facilities: There are 12 campsites for tents or motorhomes up to 20 feet long. Fireplaces and picnic tables are provided, and vault toilets are available. There is no water.

Reservations, fee: No reservations, no fee.

Who to contact: Phone Sequoia National Forest at (209)784-1500.

Location: Drive 11 miles east of Glennville via State Route 155 and Alder Creek Road.

Trip note: This site is open from May to November and is on Alder Creek, near Greenhorn Mountain Park. Elevation 3900 feet. There are many trails through this area leading to interesting historical landmarks and Indian cultural sites.

Site **21**   GREENHORN MOUNTAIN
PARK

Campsites, facilities: There are 91 campsites for tents or motorhomes up to 24 feet long. Piped water, fireplace and picnic table are provided. Flush toilets are available.
Reservations, fee: No reservations; $6 fee per night.
Who to contact: Phone County Parks Department at (805)861-2345.
Location: Drive 10 miles west of Wofford Heights via State Route 155.
Trip note: This county campground is open all year and is near the Shirley Meadows ski area. Elevation 6000 feet. The ski area is open on weekends, snow permitting. There are numerous trails leading to the sites of Indian petroglyphs and other natural remnants of the Indians' presence.

Site **22**   KERN RIVER
COUNTY PARK

Campsites, facilities: There are 50 campsites for tents or motorhomes. Picnic tables, fireplaces and piped water are provided. Flush toilets, showers, a dump station and a playground are available. Nearby is a grocery store.
Reservations, fee: No reservations; $8 fee per night.
Who to contact: Phone County Parks Department at (805)861-2345.
Location: Drive 12 miles northeast of Bakersfield via Mt. Vernon Avenue and Round Mountain Road.
Trip note: Open all year. Elevation 450 feet. This camp is on the Kern River a short distance from Hart Park. Enjoy Lake Ming, a boating lake which allows waterskiing, and the Foss-Kern River County Golf Course. Amusment rides are in the area.

Site **23**   KOA
CAMPGROUND

Campsites, facilities: There are 12 tent sites and 62 motorhome spaces. Picnic tables, piped water and full or partial hookups are provided. Rest rooms, showers, swimming pool, laundromat, store, dump station, and propane gas are available.
Reservations, fee: Call for space available. $15 deposit required; $15 fee per night.
Who to contact: Phone park at (805)399-3107.
Location: Drive 13 miles north of Bakersfield on State Route 99 to 32569 Lerdo Way.
Trip note: This camp is open all year and is near the town of Shafter where the

Department of Agriculture has its Experimental Farm Research Center. Elevation 415 feet.

Site 24   LOST HILLS KOA

Campsites, facilities: There are 10 tent sites and 80 motorhome spaces. Picnic tables, piped water, satellite TV, and full hookups are provided. Rest rooms, showers, swimming pool, laundromat, store, video room and propane gas are available. Restaurants are nearby.

Reservations, fee: Call ahead for space available and fee.

Who to contact: Phone park at (805)797-2719.

Location: Drive to the junction of I-5 and State Route 46.

Trip note: This campground is open all year and boasts a dry, sunny climate. It is located near the Kern National Wildlife Refuge. Tours are available by prior arrangement with refuge manager.

Site 25   BUENA VISTA

Campsites, facilities: There are 112 campsites for tents or motorhomes. Picnic tables, fireplaces, piped water and full hookups are provided. Rest rooms, showers, a playground, swimming pool, laundromat, store, dump station and propane gas are available.

Reservations, fee: No reservations; $12 fee per night.

Who to contact: Phone park at (805)763-1526.

Location: Drive 12 miles northeast of Taft on State Route 119 and take Enos Lane to campground.

Trip note: This county operated campground is open all year. It is an aquatic recreation area with one lake for fishing and another for boating. There is also a public golf course nearby. Elevation 330 feet.

Site 26   BRITE LAKE RECREATION AREA

Campsites, facilities: There are 24 campsites for tents or motorhomes up to 30 feet long. Piped water, fireplaces and picnic tables are provided. Flush toilets, dump station and a playground are available. A grocery store, laundromat and propane gas are available nearby.

Reservations, fee: No reservations; $5 fee per night.

Who to contact: Phone U.S. Army Corps of Engineers at (805)822-3228.

Location: Drive seven miles west of Tehachapi via State Route 202.

Trip note: Brite Lake camp is open from May to October and is near Tehachapi Mountain Park, a 570 acre, pine shaded alpine park. Elevation 400 feet.

Site **27** TEHACHAPI
MOUNTAIN PARK

Campsites, facilities: There are 65 campsites for tents or motorhomes up to 24
feet long. Piped water, fireplaces and picnic tables are provided. Pit toilets
and overnight corral facilities for equestrian groups are available.
Reservations, fee: No reservations; $6 fee per night.
Who to contact: Phone County Parks Department at (805)861-2345.
Location: Drive eight miles southwest of Tehachapi via Water Canyon Road.
Trip note: Tehachapi is open all year. Elevation 5700 feet. It is a 570 acre mountain wonderland in both winter and summer. Winter sports are available
when snow permits.

Site **28** INDIAN HILL
RANCH CAMPGROUND

Campsites, facilities: There are 111 sites for tents or motorhomes. Picnic tables,
piped water and full or partial hookups are provided. Rest rooms, showers,
dump station and five stocked fishing ponds are available.
Reservations, fee: Phone Leisuretime Reservation Systems at (800)822-CAMP.
Who to contact: Phone park at (805)822-6613.
Location: From State Route 58 near Tehachapi, take the Route 202 off-ramp,
turn right on Route 202 and go three and a half miles to Banducci Road.
Turn left and drive one mile to Indian Hill Road.
Trip note: This campground is open all year and offers spacious, private camp-
sites with oak trees and a view of Brite Valley. There are five ponds on the
grounds that are stocked with fish.

Site **29** REDROCK CANYON
STATE PARK

Campsites, facilities: There are 50 campsites for tents or motorhomes up to 30
feet long. Piped water, fireplaces and picnic tables are provided. Pit toilets,
dump station, exhibits and a nature trail are available. The campgrounds
are wheelchair accessible.
Reservations, fee: No reservations; $3 fee per night.
Who to contact: Phone park at (805)942-0662.
Location: Drive 25 miles northeast of Mojave on State Route 14.
Trip note: This roadside campground is open all year. Elevation 2600 feet. See
the colorful rock formations bordering State Route 14, or if you are a rock-
hound, drive up nearby Jawbone Canyon Road and explore Jawbone and
Last Chance Canyons.

Site **30** BERTRAND'S MOBILE HOME
AND RV PARK 🚐

Campsites, facilities: There are 28 motorhome spaces. Picnic tables, piped water and full hookups are provided. Rest rooms, showers, laundromat, store and a dump station are available.

Reservations, fee: Call ahead for space available and fee.

Who to contact: Phone park at (619)377-4000.

Location: Drive four miles west of Ridgecrest on State Route 178 to 4331 Inyokern Road (State Route 178).

Trip note: This campground is located near the southern entrance into Death Valley and is two hours from Los Angeles.

Site **31**   FORT TEJON TENT
AND RV CAMPGROUND

Campsites, facilities: There are 37 tent sites and 58 motorhome spaces. Picnic tables, piped water and full or partial hookups are provided. Rest rooms, showers, a playground, swimming pool, laundromat, store, dump station and propane gas are available.

Reservations, fee: Call for space available. $12.50 deposit required; $12.50 fee per night.

Who to contact: Phone park at (805)248-6145.

Location: Drive one and a half miles north of Lebec near I-5 on Lebec Road.

Trip note: The camp is open all year and is near the Fort Tejon State Historical Park, headquarters for the U.S. Army's 1st Dragoon and Camel Corps from 1854-1864. Eight miles south and west via Labec Road and Mt. Pinos Way is Frazier Mountain Park where you can fish year around. Elevation 39 feet.

Site **32**   MC GILL

Campsites, facilities: There are 73 campsites for tents or motorhomes up to 16 feet long. Piped water, fireplaces and picnic tables are provided, and vault toilets are available.

Reservations, fee: No reservations; $5 fee per night.

Who to contact: Phone Los Padres National Forest at (805)683-6711.

Location: Drive 10 1/2 miles west of Lake of the Woods via Mt. Pinos Road and Cuddy Valley Road.

Trip note: McGill is open from June to October. Elevation 7400 feet. Drive to the top of nearby Mt. Pinos and get a spectacular 360-degree view of the High Sierras, the San Joaquin Valley, the Channel Islands and Antelope Valley. You can fish year around at Frazier Mountain Park, which is about seven miles from camp.

Site **33**   MC GILL
GROUP CAMP

Campsites, facilities: There is one group campsite for tents or motorhomes up to 16 feet long. Piped water, fireplaces and picnic tables are provided, and vault toilets are available.

Reservations, fee: No reservations; $20 per group fee per night.

Who to contact: Phone Los Padres National Forest at (805)683-6711.

Location: Drive 10 1/2 miles west of Lake of the Woods via Mt. Pinos Road and Cuddy Valley Road.

Trip note: This camp is open from May to October. See trip note for campground number 32. Elevation 7400 feet.

Site **34**   MIL POTRERO
                    PARK   ▲

Campsites, facilities: There are 43 campsites for tents or motorhomes up to 30 feet long. Fireplaces and picnic tables are provided. Flush toilets, showers and a playground are available. No piped drinking water is available, so bring your own. A grocery store and laundromat are nearby.

Reservations, fee: Call for space available. $20 deposit required; $8 fee per night.

Who to contact: Phone park at (805)763-4246.

Location: Drive 11 miles west of Lake of the Woods via Cuddy Valley Road.

Trip note: This camp is open all year and is near Mt. Pinos which offers a magnificent 360 degree view from the summit. Also nearby are the Big Trees of Pleito Canyon. Elevation 5300 feet.

Site **35**   HAPPY
                    GULCH   ▲

Campsites, facilities: There are 17 campsites for tents or motorhomes up to 34 feet long. Piped water, fireplaces and picnic tables are provided. Pit toilets are available.

Reservations, fee: No reservations; $6 fee per night.

Who to contact: Phone County Parks Department at (805)861-2345.

Location: Drive 15 miles west of Lake of the Woods via Cuddy Valley Road and Mil Potrero Highway.

Trip note: Happy Gulch is open all year and is in Los Padres National Forest near Mt. Pinos. Nearby is Campo Alto Ski Tow. Elevation 6300 feet.

Site **36**   CAMPO
                    ALTO   ▲

Campsites, facilities: There are 17 campsites for tents or motorhomes up to 22 feet long. Piped water, fireplaces and picnic tables are provided. Vault toilets are available.

Reservations, fee: No reservations, no fee.

Who to contact: Phone Los Padres National Forest at (805)683-6711.

Location: Drive 24 1/2 miles west of Lake of the Woods via Cuddy Valley Road to Mil Potrero Highway, then south on Cerro Noroeste Road.

Trip note: Campo Alto is open from May to November and is on Cerro Noroeste (Mt. Abel) in Los Padres National Forest. Elevation 8200 feet.

Site **37**   TOAD
                         SPRING

Campsites, facilities: There are four tent sites and three campsites for tents or motorhomes up to 16 feet long. Fireplaces and picnic tables are provided and vault toilets are available. There is no water, so bring your own.
Reservations, fee: No reservations, no fee.
Who to contact: Phone Los Padres National Forest at (805)683-6711.
Location: Drive 15 1/2 miles west of Lake of the Woods via Cuddy Valley Road and Mil Potrero Highway.
Trip note: This camp is open from May to November. Elevation 5700 feet. A primitive, little known setting.

Site **38**   CABALLO

Campsites, facilities: There are five campsites for tents or motorhomes up to 16 feet long. Fireplaces and picnic tables are provided, and vault toilets are available. There is no water, so bring your own.
Reservations, fee: No reservations, no fee.
Who to contact: Phone Los Padres National Forest at (805)683-6711.
Location: Drive 15 1/2 miles west of Lake of the Woods via Cuddy Valley Road to Mil Potrero Highway to Cerro Noroeste Road (west).
Trip note: Caballo is open from May to November. Elevation 5800 feet. A primitive campsite.

Site **39**   MARION

Campsites, facilities: There are five campsites for tents or motorhomes up to 16 feet long. Fireplaces and picnic tables are provided and vault toilets are available. There is no water at this site.
Reservations, fee: No reservations, no fee.
Who to contact: Phone Los Padres National Forest at (805)683-6711.
Location: Drive 16 1/2 miles west of Lake of the Woods via Cuddy Valley Road to Mil Potrero Highway and off Cerro Noroeste Road.
Trip note: Marion is open from May to November and is near Brush Mountain. Elevation 6600 feet. A primitive setting.

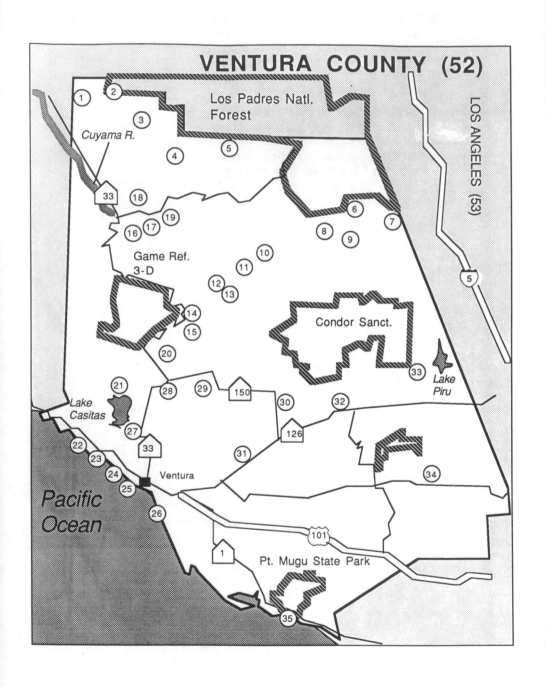

VENTURA COUNTY (52)

Los Padres Natl.
Forest

LOS ANGELES (53)

Cuyama R.

Game Ref.
3-D

Condor Sanct.

Lake
Piru

Lake
Casitas

Ventura

Pacific
Ocean

Pt. Mugu State Park

VENTURA COUNTY
♦

Site 1   BALLINGER   ▲

Campsites, facilities: There are 20 campsites for tents or motorhomes up to 32 feet long. Fireplaces and picnic tables are provided, and vault toilets are available. There is no water, so bring your own.

Reservations, fee: No reservations, no fee.

Who to contact: Phone Los Padres National Forest Headquarters at (805)683-6711.

Location: Drive 17 miles southeast of New Cuyama off State Route 33 on Ballinger Canyon Road.

Trip note: Open all year. Elevation 3000 feet. This camp is near the boundary of Los Padres National Forest. It is used mainly by four-wheel drive and motorcycle enthusiasts who come to use the off-road vehicle trails nearby.

Site 2   VALLE
 VISTA   🌲

Campsites, facilities: There are 10 campsites for tents or motorhomes up to 32 feet long. Fireplaces and picnic tables are provided, and vault toilets are available. There is no water, so bring your own.

Reservations, fee: No reservations, no fee.

Who to contact: Phone Los Padres National Forest Headquarters at (805)683-6711.

Location: Drive 21 miles south of Maricopa off State Route 33/ State Route 166 via Cerro Noroeste Road.

Trip note: Open all year. Elevation 4800 feet. This camp is near the boundary of Los Padres National Forest and offers a nice view of Bakersfield Valley. Occasionally, you can spot a rare condor here.

Site 3   NETTLE
 SPRING   ▲

Campsites, facilities: There are nine tent sites and nine campsites for tents or motorhomes up to 22 feet long. Piped water, fireplaces and picnic tables are provided, and vault toilets are available.

Reservations, fee: No reservations, no fee.

Who to contact: Phone Los Padres National Forest Headquarters at (805)683-6711.

Location: Drive 34 miles southeast of New Cuyama off State Route 33 via Apache Canyon Road.

Trip note: Open all year. Elevation 4400 feet. An infrequently maintained four-wheel drive trail leads northeast from camp and then splits after two miles. The branch that heads east connects with a backcountry trail after two more miles at the rustic campground of Mesa Spring. The trail then continues cross country passing campsites along the way. Take a map and bring water. In the fall, this campground is frequently used by hunters.

Site 4 | PINE SPRINGS | ▲

Campsites, facilities: There are 10 campsites for tents or motorhomes up to 22 feet long. Fireplaces and picnic tables are provided, and vault toilets are available. There is no water, so bring your own.

Reservations, fee: No reservations, no fee.

Who to contact: Phone Los Padres National Forest Headquarters at (805)683-6711.

Location: Drive 14 miles southwest of Lake of the Woods off Lockwood Valley Road.

Trip note: Open from May to October. Elevation 5800 feet. Located at the foot of San Guillermo Mountain (elevation 6600 feet).

Site 5 | MT. PINOS | ▲

Campsites, facilities: There are 19 campsites for tents or motorhomes up to 16 feet long. Piped water, fireplaces and picnic tables are provided, and vault toilets and horseback riding facilities are available.

Reservations, fee: No reservations; $5 fee per night.

Who to contact: Phone Los Padres National Forest Headquarters at (805)683-6711.

Location: Drive 13 miles west of Lake of the Woods on Mt. Pinos Road.

Trip note: Open from June to October. Elevation 7800 feet. Located on Mt. Pinos (8800 feet elevation), a good condor observation point.

Site 6 | KINGS CAMP | ▲

Campsites, facilities: There are three tent sites and four campsites for tents or motorhomes up to 16 feet long. Fireplaces and picnic tables are provided, and vault toilets are available. There is no water, so bring your own.

Reservations, fee: No reservations, no fee.

Who to contact: Phone Los Padres National Forest Headquarters at (805)683-6711.

Location: Drive 13 miles southwest of Gorman off I-5 via Hungry Valley Road.

Trip note: Open all year. Elevation 4200 feet. This camp is in a four-wheel drive area near Piru Creek, where there is fishing. It is five miles from the Hungry Valley State Vehicular Recreation Area.

Site 7   HARDLUCK

Campsites, facilities: There are 30 campsites for tents or motorhomes up to 22 feet long. Piped water, fireplaces and picnic tables are provided, and vault toilets are available.

Reservations, fee: No reservations; $5 fee per night.

Who to contact: Phone Los Padres National Forest Headquarters at (805)683-6711.

Location: Drive 16 miles southeast of Gorman off I-5.

Trip note: Open from April to November. Elevation 2800 feet. This camp is located on the Smith Fork of Piru Creek, three miles upstream from Pyramid Reservoir. Good fishing available. This is a four-wheel drive area. You can count on hot weather in summer and fall months.

Site 8   DUTCHMAN

Campsites, facilities: There are eight campsites for motorhomes up to 16 feet long. Vault toilets are available, but there is no piped water, so bring your own.

Reservations, fee: No reservations, no fee.

Who to contact: Phone Los Padres National Forest Headquarters at (805)683-6711.

Location: Drive 23 miles southwest of Gorman off I-5 via Alamo Mountain Road.

Trip note: Open from May to October. Elevation 6800 feet. Located at the top of Alamo Mountain. There are many four-wheel drive trails in the area.

Site 9   TWIN
                            PINES

Campsites, facilities: There are five tent sites. Fireplaces and picnic tables are provided. Vault toilets are available, but there is no water, so bring your own.

Reservations, fee: No reservations, no fee.

Who to contact: Phone Los Padres National Forest Headquarters at (805)683-6711.

Location: Drive 21 miles southwest of Gorman off I-5.

Trip note: Open from May to October. Elevation 6600 feet. Located atop Mt. Alamo. It offers a nice view.

Site 10   HALF
                           MOON   🔺

Campsites, facilities: There are 10 campsites for tents or motorhomes up to 22 feet long. Fireplaces are provided, and vault toilets are available. There is no water, so bring your own.

Reservations, fee: No reservations, no fee.

Who to contact: Phone Los Padres National Forest Headquarters at (805)683-6711.

Location: Drive 20 miles southwest of Lake of the Woods via Lockwood Valley Road and off Mutau Flat Road on a dirt road.

Trip note: Open from May to November. Elevation 4700 feet. Located near Piru Creek, where there is fishing. This campground is primarily used by motorcylists and four-wheel drive enthusiasts.

Site 11   THORN
                           MEADOWS   🌲

Campsites, facilities: There are three tent sites and one campsite for a tent or motorhome up to 16 feet long. Fireplaces and picnic tables are provided, and vault toilets are available. There is no water, so bring your own.

Reservations, fee: No reservations, no fee.

Who to contact: Phone Los Padres National Forest Headquarters at (805)683-6711.

Location: Drive 19 miles southwest of Lake of the Woods off Lockwood Valley Road on Mutau Flat Road.

Trip note: Open from May to October. Elevation 5000 feet. Located near Piru Creek, where there is fishing. This camp is used primarily by motorcycle and four-wheel drive enthusiasts.

Site 12   LION'S
                           CANYON   🔺

Campsites, facilities: There are 30 campsites for tents or motorhomes up to 16 feet long. Piped water, fireplaces and picnic tables are provided. Vault toilets and horseback riding facilities are available.

Reservations, fee: No reservations; $5 fee per night.

Who to contact: Phone Los Padres National Forest Headquarters at (805)683-6711.

Location: Drive 22 miles northeast of Ojai off State Route 33 on Sespe River Road.

Trip note: Open from April to December. Elevation 3000 feet. Located on Sespe Creek. Several hiking trails pass near or leave from this and other nearby camps. These are not off-road vehicle trails.

Site **13**   ROSE VALLEY
FALLS

Campsites, facilities: There are nine campsites for tents or motorhomes up to 16 feet long. Piped water, fireplaces and picnic tables are provided. Vault toilets and horseback riding facilities are available.

Reservations, fee: No reservations; $4 fee per night.

Who to contact: Phone Los Padres National Forest Headquarters at (805)683-6711.

Location: Drive 21 miles northeast of Ojai off State Route 33 on Sespe River Road.

Trip note: Open all year. Elevation 3400 feet. Located on Rose Valley Creek two miles from Sespe Creek, where there is fishing.

Site **14**   HOLIDAY
GROUP CAMP

Campsites, facilities: There are three campsites for tents or motorhomes up to 22 feet long. Piped water, fireplaces and picnic tables are provided, and vault toilets are available.

Reservations, fee: No reservations; fee depending on water availability.

Who to contact: Phone Los Padres National Forest Headquarters at (805)683-6711.

Location: Drive nine miles northwest of Ojai on State Route 33.

Trip note: Open from April to December. Elevation 2000 feet. Located very near the North Fork of the Matalija. A trailhead into the backcountry is nearby.

Site **15**   WHEELER
GORGE

Campsites, facilities: There are 73 campsites for tents or motorhomes up to 16 feet long. Piped water, fireplaces and picnic tables are provided, and flush toilets are available.

Reservations, fee: No reservations; $6 fee per night.

Who to contact: Phone Los Padres National Forest Headquarters at (805)683-6711.

Location: Drive nine miles northwest of Ojai on State Route 33.

Trip note: Open all year. Elevation 2000 feet. A trailhead that leads into the backcountry is nearby. The North Fork of the Matilija, a good fishing stream, runs through camp.

Site **16**   PINE
                       MOUNTAIN

Campsites, facilities: There are six tent sites. Fireplaces and picnic tables are provided, and vault toilets are available. There is no water, so bring your own.
Reservations, fee: No reservations, no fee.
Who to contact: Phone Los Padres National Forest Headquarters at (805)683-6711.
Location: Drive 35 miles north of Ojai off State Route 33 on Reyes Peak Road.
Trip note: Open from April to December. Elevation 6700 feet. This camp is set in a pretty area. From camp you can hike 1/2 mile to raspberry spring, or you can take the fishbowl trail from Pine Mountain Lodge nearby.

Site **17**   REYES
                       PEAK

Campsites, facilities: There are six tent sites. Fireplaces and picnic tables are provided, and vault toilets are available. There is no water, so bring your own.
Reservations, fee: No reservations, no fee.
Who to contact: Phone Los Padres National Forest Headquarters at (805)683-6711.
Location: Drive 36 miles north of Ojai off State Route 33 on Reyes Peak Road.
Trip note: Open from April to December. Elevation 6800 feet. A trail from nearby Pine Mountain camp leads north four miles to Ozena.

Site **18**   OZENA

Campsites, facilities: There are 12 campsites for tents or motorhomes up to 22 feet long. Piped water, fireplaces and picnic tables are provided, and vault toilets are available. Groceries and propane gas can be purchased nearby.
Reservations, fee: No reservations, no fee.
Who to contact: Phone Los Padres National Forest Headquarters at (805)683-6711.
Location: Drive 25 miles southwest of Lake of the Woods off Lockwood Valley Road.
Trip note: Open all year. Elevation 3600 feet. Located directly off the main road. It is used primarily as a roadside campground.

Site **19**   REYES
                       CREEK

Campsites, facilities: There are 23 tent sites and six campsites for tents or motorhomes up to 22 feet long. Piped water, fireplaces and picnic tables are provided, and vault toilets are available.
Reservations, fee: No reservations, no fee.

Who to contact: Phone Los Padres National Forest Headquarters at (805)683-6711.

Location: Drive 25 miles southwest of Lake of the Woods off Lockwood Valley Road.

Trip note: Open all year. Elevation 4000 feet. The camp is on Reyes Creek, which is stocked with fish in summer.

Site **20** | WHEELER GORGE CAMPGROUND |

Campsites, facilities: There are 73 campsites for tents or motorhomes. Piped water, fireplaces and picnic tables are provided, and flush toilets are available. Nearby are a phone, hot springs, laundromat, grocery store, propane gas and firewood.

Reservations, fee: Call ahead for space available and fee.

Who to contact: Phone park at (805)646-9216.

Location: Drive six miles northwest of Ojai via State Route 150 and State Route 33.

Trip note: This 15 acre park has a stream running through it with many swimming holes. There are miles of hiking trails, hunting in season, and fishing and boating at Lake Casitas nearby.

Site **21** | LAKE CASITAS RECREATION AREA |

Campsites, facilities: There are 480 campsites for tents or motorhomes up to 40 feet long. Piped water, fireplaces and picnic tables are provided. Flush toilets, showers, dump station, playground, grocery store, ice, snack bar, bait, boat ramps, laundromat and propane gas are available. Boat rentals, slips, fuel and tackle are nearby.

Reservations, fee: No reservations; $7 fee per night.

Who to contact: Phone park at (805)649-2233.

Location: Drive five miles southwest of Ojai off State Route 150.

Trip note: Open all year. Elevation 560 feet. Lake Casitas is a man-made lake for fishing and boating.Only boats between 11 and 24 feet are allowed on the lake. Swimming and waterskiing are prohibited. Casitas holds the state record for black bass.

Site **22** | HOBSON PARK |

Campsites, facilities: There are 27 campsites for tents or motorhomes up to 34 feet long. Piped water, fireplaces and picnic tables are provided. Flush toilets, showers and a grocery store are available.

Reservations, fee: Reservations accepted; $9 fee per night.

Who to contact: Phone County Parks Deptartment at (805)654-3951.

Location: Drive nine miles northwest of Ventura off US-101.

Trip note: This county park is on the ocean and is open all year. Located at the end of Rincon Parkway with easy access to the beach. Emma Wood State Beach, San Buenaventura State Beach and McGrath State Beach are all within 11 miles of the park.

Site **23**   FARIA
                                PARK   ▲

Campsites, facilities: There are 29 campsites for tents or motorhomes up to 34 feet long. Piped water, fireplaces and picnic tables are provided. Flush toilets, playground, showers and a grocery store are available.
Reservations, fee: Reservations accepted; $9 fee per night.
Who to contact: Phone County Parks Deptartment at (805)654-3951.
Location: Drive seven miles northwest of Ventura off US-101.
Trip note: Open all year. Located on the ocean. Emma Wood State Beach, San Buenaventura State Beach and McGrath State Beach are within 10 miles of the park.

Site **24**   RINCON
                                PARKWAY   🚐

Campsites, facilities: There are 112 motorhome spaces for vehicles up to 34 feet long. Vault toilets and a grocery store are available.
Reservations, fee: No reservations; $5 fee per night.
Who to contact: Phone County Parks Deptartment at (805)654-3951.
Location: Drive six miles northwest of Ventura on US-101.
Trip note: Open all year. This campground is near the ocean and there is good fishing here. Emma Wood State Beach, San Buenaventura State Beach and McGrath State Beach are all within 10 miles.

Site **25**   EMMA WOOD
                                STATE BEACH   ▲

Campsites, facilities: This is a group campground for people with tents or motorhomes up to 32 feet long. However, there are some additional sites for hikers and bicyclists. Piped water, picnic tables and fireplaces are provided. Pit toilets and showers are available. A grocery store, laundromat and propane gas are nearby.
Reservations, fee: Phone MISTIX at (800)446-7275; $30 fee per night for group site.
Who to contact: Phone park at (805)654-4611 or (805)643-7532.
Location: Drive two miles north of Ventura off US-101.
Trip note: Open all year. Located on the ocean, it is a short drive to the town of Ventura and the Mission San Buenaventura. There are tide pool tours given for groups.

| Site 26 | MCGRATH STATE BEACH | ▲ |

Campsites, facilities: There are 174 campsites for tents or motorhomes up to 34 feet long. Piped water, fireplaces and picnic tables are provided. Flush toilets, showers, dump station and playground are available. A grocery store, laundromat and propane gas are nearby.

Reservations, fee: Phone MISTIX at (800)446-7275; $10 fee per night.

Who to contact: Phone park at (805)654-4611 or (805)654-4744.

Location: Drive four miles south of Ventura off US-101 via Seaward Avenue and Harbor Boulevard.

Trip note: Open all year. This campground is located on the ocean, just a short drive to Ventura and the San Buenaventura Mission. The Santa Clara River Estuary Natural Preserve is nearby at the river mouth.

| Site 27 | FOSTER COUNTY PARK | ▲ |

Campsites, facilities: There are 55 campsites for tents or motorhomes up to 34 feet long. Piped water, fireplaces and picnic tables are provided, and flush toilets and a playground are available. A grocery store, laundromat and propane gas are nearby.

Reservations, fee: Reservations accepted; $7 fee per night.

Who to contact: Phone County Parks Deptartment at (805)654-3951.

Location: Drive six miles northeast of Ventura on State Route 33, then take Santa Ana Road to the park.

Trip note: This county park is open all year. Elevation 250 feet. There is a creek in the day use area, and the park is hilly with lots of trails.

| Site 28 | CAMP CONFORT | ▲ |

Campsites, facilities: There are 24 campsites for tents or motorhomes up to 34 feet long. Piped water, fireplaces, picnic tables, and in most cases electrical connections are provided. Flush toilets, a playground and horseback riding facilities are available. A grocery store, laundromat and propane gas are nearby.

Reservations, fee: Reservations accepted; $8 fee per night.

Who to contact: Phone County Parks Department at (805)654-3951.

Location: Drive two miles southwest of Ojai on Creek Road.

Trip note: Open all year. Elevation 1000 feet. Located on San Antonio Creek in the Ojai Valley. Lake Casitas Recreation Area is 10 miles away.

| Site 29 | EMMA WOOD COUNTY PARK | ▲ |

Campsites, facilities: There are 81 campsites including group areas for tents or motorhomes up to 34 feet long. Fireplaces are provided, and vault toilets and a dump staiton are available. All conveniences are within one mile of campground.

Reservations, fee: Reservations accepted for groups; $6 fee per night.
Who to contact: Phone County Parks Deptartment at (805)654-3951.
Location: Drive one mile north of Ventura off US-101.
Trip note: This park is open all year and is located on the beach. All campsites are beachfront. There is good surfing and fishing.

Site **30**   STECKEL
COUNTY PARK

Campsites, facilities: There are 35 campsites for tents or motorhomes up to 34 feet long. Fireplaces, picnic tables, and in most cases electrical connections are provided. Flush toilets and a playground are available. There is no piped water, so bring your own. A grocery store, laundromat and propane gas are nearby.

Reservations, fee: Reservations accepted; $8 fee per night.
Who to contact: Phone County Parks Deptartment at (805)654-3951.
Location: Drive four miles north of Santa Paula off State Route 150.
Trip note: This county park is open all year. Elevation 800 feet. Located on Santa Paula Creek.

Site **31**   MOUNTAIN VIEW
RV PARK

Campsites, facilities: There are 45 motorhome spaces. Picnic tables, piped water, electrical connections, cable TV and sewer hookups are provided. A store, laundromat, restaurant and shopping center are nearby.

Reservations, fee: Call for space available. $20 deposit required; $15 fee per night.
Who to contact: Phone park at (805)933-1942.
Location: Drive 12 miles west of Ventura off US-101 via State Route 126 and Peck Road to 710-714 West Harvard Boulevard in Santa Paula.
Trip note: This park is open all year and is 12 miles from the state beaches near Ventura and the Mission San Buenaventura. Excellent weather.

Site **32**   KENNY
GROVE

Campsites, facilities: There are 30 campsites for tents or motorhomes up to 34 feet long. Piped water, electrical connections, fireplaces and picnic tables are provided. Flush toilets and a playground are available. A grocery store, laundromat and propane gas are nearby.

Reservations, fee: Reservations accepted; $8 fee per night.
Who to contact: Phone County Parks Deptartment at (805)654-3951.
Location: Drive 28 miles northeast of Ventura off US-101 via State Route 126 and Old Telegraph Road near the town of Fillmore.

Trip note: Open all year. Elevation 120 feet. Located 12 miles from the Sespe Condor Sanctuary in Los Padres National Forest.

Site **33**
LAKE PIRU
RECREATION AREA

Campsites, facilities: There are 247 campsites for tents or motorhomes up to 35 feet long. Piped water, fireplaces, picnic tables and in some cases electrical hookups are provided. Flush toilets, showers, dump station, snack bar, ice, bait, boat ramp, temporary mooring, boat fuel and motorboat, tackle and waterski rentals are available.
Reservations, fee: No reservations; $10 fee per night.
Who to contact: Phone park at (805)521-1500.
Location: Drive 38 miles northeast of Ventura off US-101 via State Route 126 to Piru Canyon Road.
Trip note: Open all year. Elevation 1050 feet. Located on Lake Piru in Los Padres National Forest. The lake is designated for motorboats over 12 feet long. All others are prohibited. Enjoy fishing, swimming and waterskiing.

Site **34**
OAK COUNTY
PARK

Campsites, facilities: There are 20 tent sites and 35 sites for motorhomes up to 34 feet long. Piped water, electrical hookups, fireplaces and picnic tables are provided. Flush toilets, dump station, playground and horseback riding facilities are available. A grocery store, laundromat and propane gas are nearby.
Reservations, fee: Reservations accepted; $8 fee per night.
Who to contact: Phone County Parks Deptartment at (805)654-3951.
Location: Drive 23 miles east of Ventura off US-101 via State Route 126, then to State Route 118 (Los Angeles Avenue) to town of Moorpark. Campground is four miles east of Moorpark off State Route 118.
Trip note: Open all year. Elevation 1100 feet. Located in the Simi Valley. The campground is secluded in the hills and there are hiking trails.

Site **35**
LA JOLLA
STATE BEACH

Campsites, facilities: There are 100 primitive campsites for tents or motorhomes up to 31 feet long. Piped water, fireplaces and picnic tables are provided, and pit toilets are available. Propane gas can be purchased nearby. There is wheelchair access to trails, exhibits, picnic areas and Sycamore Canyon campground.
Reservations, fee: Phone MISTIX at (800)446-7275; $3 fee per night.
Who to contact: Phone Pt. Magu State Park at (818)706-1310.
Location: Drive 15 miles southeast of Oxnard on State Route 1.
Trip note: This campground is on the ocean and is part of Pt. Magu State Park which covers 14,980 acres.

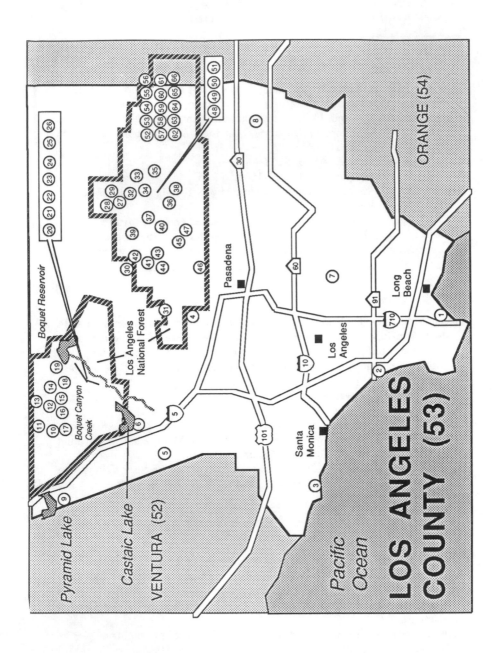

LOS ANGELES
COUNTY (53)

ORANGE (54)

VENTURA (52)

Pacific
Ocean

Pyramid Lake

Boquet Reservoir

Castaic Lake

Boquet Creek

Boquet Canyon
Creek

Los Angeles
National Forest

Pasadena

Long Beach

Los Angeles

Santa
Monica

LOS ANGELES COUNTY

◆

Site **1** | SHORELINE
RV PARK |

Campsites, facilities: There are 70 spaces for motorhomes up to 40 feet long. Picnic tables, fireplaces, piped water, electrical connections and sewer hookups are provided. Rest rooms, showers, groceries, a playground, and laundry facilities are available.

Reservations, fee: Phone Leisuretime Reservations Systems at (800)822-CAMP. $18 deposit; $18 camp use fee.

Who to contact: Phone park at (213)435-4960.

Location: Drive south on State Route 7 to downtown Long Beach and the intersection of Shoreline Drive and Pine Avenue.

Trip note: Open all year. It is 30 minutes from Disneyland, Knott's Berry Farm and Universal Studios, and five minutes from the Queen Mary and the Spruce Goose.

Site **2** | DOCKWEILER BEACH
RV PARK |

Campsites, facilities: There are 160 campsites for motorhomes up to 35 feet long. Piped water and fireplaces are provided, and flush toilets, a sanitary dump station and a playground are available. Groceries, propane gas and laundry facilities are nearby.

Reservations, fee: Phone Leisuretime Reservation Systems at (800)822-CAMP; $8 camp use fee.

Who to contact: Phone camp at (213)322-5008.

Location: Drive 12 miles southeast of Santa Monica on Vista del Mar.

Trip note: Open all year. Go swimming and fishing at the beach.

Site **3** | MALIBU BEACH
RV PARK |

Campsites, facilities: There are 40 tent sites and 125 motorhome spaces. Piped water, electrical connections and, at some sites, sewer hookups are provided. Rest rooms, showers, playground, laundry, propane, ice, cable TV and a sanitary dump station are available.

Reservations, fee: Call for space available. $26.50 deposit required; $26.50 fee per night.

Who to contact: Phone camp at (213)456-6052.

Location: Drive four miles north of Malibu on State Route 1.

Trip note: This park is open all year and is situated on a bluff overlooking the Pacific Ocean. Fish off the Malibu Pier and Paradise Cove, or drive to the attractions in Los Angeles.

Site **4**   LOS ANGELES-SAN FERNANDO VALLEY
KOA   ◭

Campsites, facilities: There are 95 tent sites and 126 motorhome spaces. Piped water, electrical connections and, at some sites, sewer hookups are provided. Rest rooms, showers, playground, swimming pool, recreation room and a sanitary dump station are available. Groceries, propane gas and laundry facilities are nearby.

Reservations, fee: Call for space available. $19.75 deposit required; $19.75 fee per night.

Who to contact: Phone camp at (818)362-7785.

Location: Drive two and a half miles northwest of San Fernando off San Fernando Road to 15900 Olden Street.

Trip note: Open all year. This campground is less than an hour's drive from all Los Angeles area attractions.

Site **5**   TRAVEL
VILLAGE

Campsites, facilities: There are 195 campsites for tents or motorhomes and 231 motorhome spaces. Piped water, fireplaces and picnic tables are provided at all sites, and electrical and sewer connections are provided at the motorhome spaces. Rest rooms, showers, dump station, cable TV, playground, two swimming pools, groceries, propane gas and laundry facilities are available.

Reservations, fee: Phone Leisuretime Reservation Systems at (800)822-CAMP. $17.50 deposit; $17.50 camp use fee.

Who to contact: Phone camp at (805)255-4222.

Location: Drive five and a half miles morthwest of Valencia off I-5 to 17946 Henry Mayo Road.

Trip note: Open all year. This campground provides a shuttle to Six Flags Magic Mountain next door. Try golfing, boating, fishing, motorcycling or horseback riding nearby.

Site **6**
CASTAIC LAKE
RV PARK

Campsites, facilities: There are 103 motorhome spaces with piped water, electrical connections and sewer hookups provided, and 50 tent sites. Rest rooms, showers, health spa, heated pool, arcade, cable TV, a playground, groceries, propane gas and laundry facilities are available. Boat rentals, stables and motorcycle trails are nearby.

Reservations, fee: Call for space available. $16 deposit required; $16 fee per night.

Who to contact: Phone camp at (805)257-3340.

Location: Drive to Castaic off I-5 to 31540 Ridge Route Road.

Trip note: Open all year. Elevation 1150 feet. Located five minutes from Magic Mountain, Lake Shore State Park, and 45 minutes from Los Angeles area attractions.

Site **7**
DEL RIO MOBILE HOME
AND RV PARK

Campsites, facilities: There are 40 motorhome spaces. Piped water, electrical connections and sewer hookups are provided. Swimming pool, groceries, propane gas and laundry facilities are available.

Reservations, fee: Call ahead for space available and fee.

Who to contact: Phone park at (213)560-2895.

Location: Drive south on I-710 (Long Beach Freeway), then west of Florence Avenue to 5246 East Florence Avenue.

Trip note: This park is 15 minutes from downtown Los Angeles, and 20 minutes from Long Beach.

Site **8**
EAST SHORE
RV PARK

Campsites, facilities: There are 25 tent sites and 426 motorhome spaces. Piped water, electrical connections and sewer hookups are provided at most motorhome sites. Rest rooms, showers, groceries, propane gas and laundry facilities are available.

Reservations, fee: Call ahead for space available and fee.

Who to contact: Phone camp at (714)599-8355.

Location: Drive five miles northwest of Pomona via I-10, take Ganesha Boulevard north one mile, then follow signs to 120 East Via Verde.

Trip note: This park is on Puddingstone Lake and offers the pleasures of a year around resort, including swimming, fishing, waterskiing, golf, horseback riding and bike trails.

Site **9**   OAK
                             FLAT   ▲

Campsites, facilities: There are 23 campsites for tents or motorhomes up to 32
   feet long. Piped water, fireplaces and picnic tables are provided, and vault
   toilets are available.
Reservations, fee: No reservations; $5 fee per night.
Who to contact: Phone Angeles National Forest Headquarters at (818)574-1613.
Location: Drive 10 1/2 miles northwest of Castaic off I-5.
Trip note: Open all year. Elevation 2800 feet.

Site **10**   ATMORE
                            MEADOWS   🌲

Campsites, facilities: There are six tent sites. Picnic tables and fireplaces are pro-
   vided, and vault toilets are available. There is no water, so bring your own.
Reservations, fee: No reservations, no fee.
Who to contact: Phone Angeles National Forest Headquarters at (818)574-1613.
Location: Drive 14 1/2 miles northwest of Lake Hughes off County Road N-2.
Trip note: Open from May to November. Elevation 4300 feet. This camp is at a
   trailhead leading into the backcountry, Bedrock Mountain and Cienega
   Canyon.

Site **11**   SAWMILL
                            MEADOWS   🌲

Campsites, facilities: There are 10 tent sites. Picnic tables and fireplaces are pro-
   vided, and vault toilets are available. There is no water, so bring your own.
Reservations, fee: No reservations, no fee.
Who to contact: Phone Angeles National Forest Headquarters at (818)574-1613.
Location: Drive 10 miles northwest of Lake Hughes. Campground is off County
   Road N-2.
Trip note: Open from May to November. Elevation 5200 feet. The camp is on
   the Pacific Crest National Scenic Trail, and one mile from the Burnt Peak
   Canyon trailhead into the backcountry.

Site **12**   LOWER
                            SHAKE   🌲

Campsites, facilities: There are five tent sites. Picnic tables and fireplaces are
   provided, and vault toilets are available. There is no water, so bring your
   own. Groceries and laundry facilities can be found nearby.
Reservations, fee: No reservations; $5 fee per night.
Who to contact: Phone Angeles National Forest Headquarters at (818)574-1613.
Location: Drive five and a half miles northwest of Lake Hughes off County Road

N-2.

Trip note: Open from May to November. Elevation 4300 feet. Camp is near the road, and the Pacific Crest National Scenic Trail passes within 1/2 mile of camp.

Site **13**   UPPER
                               SHAKE

Campsites, facilities: There are 18 campsites for tents or motorhomes up to 22 feet long. Fireplaces and picnic tables are provided, and vault toilets are available.

Reservations, fee: No reservations, no fee.

Who to contact: Phone Angeles National Forest Headquarters at (818)574-1613.

Location: Drive eight and a half miles northwest of Lake Hughes off County Road N-2.

Trip note: Open from May to November. Elevation 4300 feet. The Pacific Crest National Scenic Trail passes close to this camp.

Site **14**   COTTONWOOD

Campsites, facilities: There are 27 campsites for tents or motorhomes up to 22 feet long. Piped water, fireplaces and picnic tables are provided, and vault toilets are available. Groceries are nearby.

Reservations, fee: No reservations; $5 fee per night.

Who to contact: Phone Angeles National Forest Headquarters at (818)574-1613.

Location: Drive six and a half miles southwest of Lake Hughes on Lake Hughes Road.

Trip note: Open from May to October. Elevation 2700 feet.

Site **15**   PROSPECT

Campsites, facilities: There are 22 tent sites. Piped water, picnic tables and fireplaces are provided, and vault toilets are available.

Reservations, fee: No reservations; $6 fee per night.

Who to contact: Phone Angeles National Forest Headquarters at (818)574-1613.

Location: Drive 10 1/2 miles southwest of Lake Hughes on Lake Hughes Road.

Trip note: Open all year. Elevation 2200 feet. Camp is on Elizabeth Lake Canyon Creek.

Site **16**   WARM
                               SPRINGS

Campsites, facilities: There are 12 campsites for tents or motorhomes up to 16

feet long. Piped water, fireplaces and picnic tables are provided, and vault toilets are available.

Reservations, fee: No reservations; $5 fee per night.

Who to contact: Phone Angeles National Forest Headquarters at (818)574-1613.

Location: Drive 12 miles northeast of Castaic on Lake Hughes Road.

Trip note: Open from May to November. Elevation 2200 feet. Camp is at the base of Warm Springs Mountain. There is a trail leading out of camp to Fish Canyon.

Site **17**   CIENEGA   ♣

Campsites, facilities: There are eight tent sites and 14 campsites for tents or motorhomes up to 18 feet long. Fireplaces and picnic tables are provided, and vault toilets are available. There is no water, so bring your own.

Reservations, fee: No reservations, no fee.

Who to contact: Phone Angeles National Forest Headquarters at (818)574-1613.

Location: Drive 15 miles north of Castaic off I-5 and Castaic Canyon Road.

Trip note: Open from April to November. Elevation 2000 feet. Camp is at trailhead into the backcountry around Redrock Mountain.

Site **18**   SOUTH   ♣
                               PORTAL

Campsites, facilities: There are 11 tent sites. Picnic tables and fireplaces are provided, and vault toilets are available. There is no water, so bring your own. A grocery store is nearby.

Reservations, fee: No reservations, no fee.

Who to contact: Phone Angeles National Forest Headquarters at (818)574-1613.

Location: Drive 10 miles south of Lake Hughes off San Francisquito Canyon Road.

Trip note: Open from May to October. Elevation 2800 feet. Located on South Portal Creek.

Site **19**   SPUNKY   ▲

Campsites, facilities: There are 10 campsites for tents or motorhomes. Piped water, fireplaces and picnic tables are provided, and vault toilets are available. A grocery store is nearby.

Reservations, fee: No reservations; $5 fee per night.

Who to contact: Phone Angeles National Forest Headquarters at (818)574-1613.

Location: Drive 10 miles southeast of Lake Hughes via San Francisquito and Green Valley Roads.

Trip note: Open from April to October. Elevation 3200 feet. Located one mile from Bouquet Reservoir and three miles from Bouquet Canyon, which is stocked with rainbow trout. The Pacific Crest National Scenic Trail passes a mile north of camp.

Site **20**   CHAPARRAL

Campsites, facilities: There are seven campsites for tents or motorhomes up to 18 feet long. Fireplaces and picnic tables are provided, and vault toilets are available. There is no water, so bring your own.
Reservations, fee: No reservations, no fee.
Who to contact: Phone Angeles National Forest Headquarters at (818)574-1613.
Location: Drive 14 1/2 miles northeast of Saugus on Bouquet Canyon Road.
Trip note: Open from May to October. Elevation 2400 feet. Located on Bouquet Canyon Creek, which is stocked with rainbow trout.

Site **21**   HOLLOW
                                          TREE

Campsites, facilities: There are five tent sites. Picnic tables and fireplaces are provided, and vault toilets are available. There is no water, so bring your own. A grocery store is nearby.
Reservations, fee: No reservations, no fee.
Who to contact: Phone Angeles National Forest Headquarters at (818)574-1613.
Location: Drive 14 miles northeast of Saugus on Bouquet Canyon Road.
Trip note: Open all year. Elevation 2400 feet. Located on Bouquet Canyon Creek, which is stocked with rainbow trout.

Site **22**   THE
                                          FALLS

Campsites, facilities: There are 14 tent sites. Piped water, picnic tables and fireplaces are provided, and vault toilets are available. A grocery store is nearby.
Reservations, fee: No reservations; $5 fee per night.
Who to contact: Phone Angeles National Forest Headquarters at (818)574-1613.
Location: Drive 14 1/2 miles northeast of Saugus on Bouquet Canyon Road.
Trip note: Open all year. Elevation 2500 feet. Located on Bouquet Canyon Creek, which is stocked with rainbow trout.

Site **23**   BIG
                                          OAK

Campsites, facilities: There are nine tent sites. Piped water, picnic tables and fireplaces are provided, and vault toilets are available. A grocery store is

nearby.
Reservations, fee: No reservations; $5 fee per night.
Who to contact: Phone Angeles National Forest Headquarters at (818)574-1613.
Location: Drive 12 1/2 miles northeast of Saugus on Bouquet Canyon Road.
Trip note: Open all year. Elevation 2300 feet. Located on Bouquet Canyon Creek, which is stocked with rainbow trout.

Site **24**   BOUQUET   ♣

Campsites, facilities: There are five tent sites. Piped water, picnic tables and fireplaces are provided, and vault toilets are available.
Reservations, fee: No reservations; $5 fee per night.
Who to contact: Phone Angeles National Forest Headquarters at (818)574-1613.
Location: Drive 12 miles northeast of Saugus on Bouquet Canyon Road.
Trip note: Open all year. Elevation 2200 feet. Located on Bouquet Canyon Creek, which is stocked with rainbow trout.

Site **25**   STREAMSIDE   ♣

Campsites, facilities: There are nine tent sites. Piped water, picnic tables and fireplaces are provided, and vault toilets are available. A grocery store is nearby.
Reservations, fee: No reservations; $5 fee per night.
Who to contact: Phone Angeles National Forest Headquarters at (818)574-1613.
Location: Drive 12 1/2 miles northeast of Saugus on Bouquet Canyon Road.
Trip note: Open from April to October. Elevation 2300 feet. Located on Bouquet Canyon Creek, which is stocked with rainbow trout.

Site **26**   ZUNI   ♣

Campsites, facilities: There are nine tent sites. Piped water, picnic tables and fireplaces are provided, and vault toilets are available.
Reservations, fee: No reservations; $5 fee per night.
Who to contact: Phone Angeles National Forest Headquarters at (818)574-1613.
Location: Drive nine miles northeast of Saugus on Bouquet Canyon Road.
Trip note: Open from April to November. Elevation 1700 feet. Located on Bouquet Canyon Creek, which is stocked with rainbow trout.

Site **27**   JOSHUA
                          TREE   ▲

Campsites, facilities: There are 11 campsites for tents or motorhomes up to 18

feet long. Piped water, fireplaces and picnic tables are provided, and vault toilets are available.

Reservations, fee: No reservations; $5 fee per night.

Who to contact: Phone Angeles National Forest Headquarters at (818)574-1613.

Location: Drive eight miles southwest of Littlerock via State Route 138 and Little Rock Reservoir Road.

Trip note: Open all year. Elevation 3300 feet. This camp is on Little Rock Creek, which is stocked with rainbow trout, and is in a designated Off-Road Vehicle Area.

Site 28   JUNIPER
                                      GROVE   ▲

Campsites, facilities: There are seven tent sites. Piped water, picnic tables and fireplaces are provided, and vault toilets are available.

Reservations, fee: No reservations; $5 fee per night.

Who to contact: Phone Angeles National Forest Headquarters at (818)574-1613.

Location: Drive seven miles southwest of Littlerock via State Route 138 and Little Rock Reservoir Road.

Trip note: Open all year. Elevation 3400 feet. This camp is on Little Rock Reservoir, which is stocked with rainbow trout, and is in a designated Off-Road Vehicle Area.

Site 29   LAKESIDE   ♣

Campsites, facilities: There are six campsites for tents or motorhomes up to 18 feet long. Piped water, fireplaces and picnic tables are provided, and vault toilets are available.

Reservations, fee: No reservations; $5 fee per night.

Who to contact: Phone Angeles National Forest Headquarters at (818)574-1613.

Location: Drive seven miles southwest of Littlerock via State Route 138 and Little Rock Reservoir Road.

Trip note: Open all year. Elevation 3300 feet. This camp is on Little Rock Reservoir, which is stocked with rainbow trout, and is in a designated Off-Road Vehicle Area.

Site 30   SOLEDAD   ▲

Campsites, facilities: There are six campsites for tents or motorhomes up to 32 feet long. Piped water, fireplaces and picnic tables are provided, and vault toilets are available. A grocery store is nearby.

Reservations, fee: No reservations; $5 fee per night.

Who to contact: Phone Angeles National Forest Headquarters at (818)574-1613.

Location: Drive 10 miles east of Solemint off State Route 14.

Trip note: This camp is open all year. Elevation 2000 feet. The Pacific Crest National Scenic Trail passes within two miles of camp. There is a target shooting area nearby.

Site **31**

LIVE
OAK

Campsites, facilities: There are 10 tent sites. Piped water, picnic tables, and fireplaces are provided, and vault toilets are available. A grocery store and laundromat are nearby.
Reservations, fee: No reservations; $5 fee per night.
Who to contact: Phone Angeles National Forest Headquarters at (818)574-1613.
Location: Drive five miles southeast of Solemint on State Route 14 on Sand Canyon Road.
Trip note: Open all year. Elevation 2000 feet. Camp is on a small creek, two miles from Placerita Canyon State Park.

Site **32**

BASIN

Campsites, facilities: There are 12 tent sites, and 12 campsites for tents or motorhomes up to 16 feet long. Piped water, fireplaces and picnic tables are provided, and vault toilets are available. A grocery store is nearby.
Reservations, fee: No reservations, no fee.
Who to contact: Phone Angeles National Forest Headquarters at (818)574-1613.
Location: Drive nine miles southwest of Littlerock via State Route 138 and Little Rock Reservoir Road.
Trip note: Open from April to November. Elevation 3400 feet. This camp is on Little Rock Creek, which is stocked with rainbow trout. It is also in a designated Off-Road Vehicle Area.

Site **33**

LITTLE
SYCAMORE

Campsites, facilities: There are eight tent sites. Picnic tables and fireplaces are provided, and stream water and vault toilets are available. There is no piped water. A grocery store is nearby.
Reservations, fee: No reservations, no fee.
Who to contact: Phone Angeles National Forest Headquarters at (818)574-1613.
Location: Drive 13 miles south of Littlerock via State Route 138 and Little Rock Reservoir Road.
Trip note: Open from May to November. Elevation 3900 feet. This camp is on Little Rock Creek, which is stocked with rainbow trout. It is also in a designated Off-Road Vehicle Area.

Site **34**

LITTLE
CEDARS

Campsites, facilities: There are three tent sites. Picnic tables and fireplaces are provided, and stream water and vault toilets are available. There is no piped water.

Reservations, fee: No reservations, no fee.

Who to contact: Phone Angeles National Forest Headquarters at (818)574-1613.

Location: Drive 14 miles south of Littlerock via State Route 138 and Little Rock Reservoir Road.

Trip note: Open from May to November. Elevation 4200 feet. This camp is on Little Rock Creek, which is stocked with rainbow trout. It is also in a designated Off-Road Vehicle Area.

Site **35**

BUCKHORN

Campsites, facilities: There are 40 campsites for tents or motorhomes up to 16 feet long. Piped water, fireplaces and picnic tables are provided, and vault toilets are available.

Reservations, fee: No reservations; $6 fee per night.

Who to contact: Phone Angeles National Forest Headquarters at (818)574-1613.

Location: Drive 26 miles southwest of Wrightwood on State Route 2.

Trip note: Open from May to October. Elevation 6500 feet. The High Desert National Recreational Trail leads out from camp northward into the backcountry, over Burkhart Saddle, west around Devil's Punchbowl County Park, then south from South Fork Campground into the Islip trailhead, east past Eagle's Roost and Ridgecrest picnic areas, and goes south for the last mile back to camp. This loop is not a day hike. The distance to the halfway point at South Fork campground is 10 miles, and the hike back is about the same. There is piped water available at South Fork. For more information about South Fork, see Camground #53.

Site **36**

CRYSTAL
LAKE

Campsites, facilities: There are 232 campsites for tents or motorhomes up to 18 feet long. Piped water, fireplaces and picnic tables are provided, and flush toilets are available. A grocery store and a visitor information center are nearby.

Reservations, fee: Call Ticketron at (213)216-6666 for outlet information; $10 fee per night.

Who to contact: Phone Angeles National Forest Headquarters at (818)574-1613.

Location: Drive 25 miles north of Azuza off State Route 39.

Trip note: Open from May to October. Elevation 5700 feet. The nearby lake is stocked with rainbow trout.

Site 37
DEER FLATS
GROUP CAMP

Campsites, facilities: There are nine group campsites which will accommodate up to 300 people with tents. No motorhomes. Piped water, picnic tables, and fireplaces are provided, and vault toilets and a playground are available. A grocery store is nearby.

Reservations, fee: Reservations requested; $40 group fee per night.

Who to contact: Phone Angeles National Forest District Office at (818)335-1251.

Location: Drive 27 miles north of Azusa off State Route 39.

Trip note: Open from June to October. Elevation 6300 feet. Located one mile from Crystal Lake (See Site #36) and the visitor center. A nearby trail leads north from camp, and intersects mile with the Pacific Crest National Scenic Trail. If you take the Pacific Crest National Scenic Trail northwest for about two more miles, you arrive at the Islip trailhead for the High Desert Recreational Trail.

Site 38
COLDBROOK

Campsites, facilities: There are 14 campsites for tents or motorhomes up to 18 feet long. Piped water, fireplaces and picnic tables are provided, and vault toilets are available.

Reservations, fee: No reservations; $5 fee per night.

Who to contact: Phone Angeles National Forest Headquarters at (818)574-1613.

Location: Drive 15 miles north of Azusa off State Route 39.

Trip note: Open all year. Elevation 3300 feet. Located on the North Fork of the San Gabriel River, which is stocked with rainbow trout. About 1/4 mile from camp is a trailhead into the San Gabriel Wilderness. The six-mile trail takes you west, then south to the West Fork of the San Gabriel River.

Site 39
MOUNT
PACIFICO

Campsites, facilities: There are 10 tent sites. Picnic tables and fireplaces are provided, and vault toilets are available. There is no water, so bring your own.

Reservations, fee: No reservations, no fee.

Who to contact: Phone Angeles National Forest Headquarters at (818)574-1613.

Location: Drive 12 1/2 miles southeast of Palmdale off County Road N-3.

Trip note: Open from April to October. Elevation 7100 feet. Located on the Pacific Crest National Scenic Trail at the base of Mount Pacifico.

| Site **40** | ROUNDTOP
RIDGE | 🌲 |

Campsites, facilities: There are four tent sites. Picnic tables and fireplaces are provided, and vault toilets are available. There is no water, so bring your own.

Reservations, fee: No reservations, no fee.

Who to contact: Phone Angeles National Forest Headquarters at (818)574-1613.

Location: Drive 23 miles southeast of Plamdale off County Road N-3.

Trip note: Open from April to November. Elevation 6100 feet. Located at the base of Granite Mountain.

| Site **41** | LIGHTNING POINT
GROUP CAMP | ▲ |

Campsites, facilities: There are several group campsites here. Piped water, picnic tables and fireplaces are provided. Vault toilets are available.

Reservations, fee: Reservations requested; $15 group fee per night.

Who to contact: Phone Angeles National Forest District Office at (818)899-1900.

Location: Drive 15 miles southwest of Palmdale via County Road N-3.

Trip note: Open from April to November. Elevation 6200 feet.

| Site **42** | MESSENGER
FLATS | 🌲 |

Campsites, facilities: There are 10 tent sites. Piped water, picnic tables, and fireplaces are provided, and vault toilets are available.

Reservations, fee: No reservations; $5 fee per night.

Who to contact: Phone Angeles National Forest Headquarters at (818)574-1613.

Location: Drive 15 miles southwest of Palmdale via County Road N-3.

Trip note: Open from April to November. Elevation 5900 feet. Located on the Pacific Crest National Scenic Trail.

| Site **43** | MONTE
CRISTO | ▲ |

Campsites, facilities: There are 19 campsites for tents or motorhomes up to 32 feet long. Piped water, fireplaces and picnic tables are provided, and vault toilets are available. A grocery store is nearby.

Reservations, fee: No reservations; $5 fee per night.

Who to contact: Phone Angeles National Forest Headquarters at (818)574-1613.

Location: Drive 19 miles northeast of La Canada and Flintridge on Angeles Crest Highway.

Trip note: Open all year. Elevation 3600 feet. Located on the Middle Fork of Mill Creek. A target shooting area is nearby.

Site **44**   FALL CREEK TRAIL
GROUP CAMP

Campsites, facilities: There are several group campsites here which will accommodate up to 50 people. No motorhomes. Picnic tables and fireplaces are provided, and vault toilets are available. There is no piped water, so bring some or use the stream water. A grocery store is nearby.
Reservations, fee: Reservations requested; no fee.
Who to contact: Phone Angeles National Forest District Office at (818)899-1900.
Location: Drive 14 miles northeast of Tujunga off Big Tujunga Canyon Road.
Trip note: Open from March to November. Elevation 2400 feet. Located on the Big Tujunga River, which is stocked with rainbow trout.

Site **45**   VALLEY
FORGE

Campsites, facilities: There are 17 tent sites. Piped water, picnic tables and fireplaces are provided, and vault toilets are available.
Reservations, fee: No reservations; $3 fee per night.
Who to contact: Phone Angeles National Forest Headquarters at (818)574-1613.
Location: Drive 19 miles northeast of La Canada and Flintridge off State Route 2.
Trip note: Open from April to November. Elevation 3500 feet. Located on the West Fork of the San Gabriel River, which is stocked with rainbow trout. A National Recreation Trail passes close to camp.

Site **46**   MILLARD

Campsites, facilities: There are five tent sites. Piped water, picnic tables, and fireplaces are provided, and vault toilets are available. A grocery store, a laundromat and propane gas are nearby.
Reservations, fee: No reservations; $5 fee per night.
Who to contact: Phone Angeles National Forest Headquarters at (818)574-1613.
Location: Drive four miles north of Pasadena off Loma Alta Drive.
Trip note: Open all year. Elevation 1900 feet. Trail out of camp leads to Inspiration Point or farther to San Gabriel Peak.

Site **47**   WEST
FORK

Campsites, facilities: There are seven tent sites. Piped water, picnic tables and fireplaces are provided, and vault toilets are available.
Reservations, fee: No reservations; $4 fee per night.
Who to contact: Phone Angeles National Forest Headquarters at (818)574-1613.

Location: Drive 21 miles northeast of La Canada and Flintridge off State Route 2.

Trip note: Open from April to November. Elevation 3000 feet. Located on the West Fork of the San Gabriel River, which is stocked with rainbow trout. Two National Recreation Trails intersect near camp.

Site **48**
BANDIDO
GROUP CAMP

Campsites, facilities: There are 25 campsites for tents or motorhomes up to 16 feet long. The camp will accommodate up to 120 people. Piped water, fireplaces and picnic tables are provided. Vault toilets are available.

Reservations, fee: Reservations requested; $45 fee per night.

Who to contact: Phone Angeles National Forest District Office at (818)796-1151.

Location: Drive 32 miles northeast of La Canada and Flintridge off State Route 2.

Trip note: Open from April to December. Elevation 5100 feet. Located near the Chilao Visitor Center. Several trails into the San Gabriel Wilderness and the Pacific Crest National Scenic Trail are nearby.

Site **49**
CHILAO

Campsites, facilities: There are 110 campsites for tents or motorhomes up to 22 feet long. Piped water, fireplaces and picnic tables are provided, and vault toilets are available.

Reservations, fee: No reservations; $5 fee per night.

Who to contact: Phone Angeles National Forest Headquarters at (818)574-1613.

Location: Drive 25 miles northeast of La Canada and Flintridge off State Route 2.

Trip note: Open from May to November. Elevation 5300 feet. Camp is on a National Recreation Trail and close to the Chilao Visitor Center. Several trails into the San Gabriel Wilderness are nearby.

Site **50**
COULTER
GROUP CAMP

Campsites, facilities: There is one large campsite that will accommodate up to 50 people. No motorhomes. Piped water, picnic tables and fireplaces are provided, and vault toilets are available.

Reservations, fee: Reservations requested; $35 group fee per night.

Who to contact: Phone Angeles National Forest District Office at (818)796-1151.

Location: Drive 25 miles northeast of La Canada and Flintridge off State Route 2.

Trip note: Open from May to November. Elevation 5300 feet. Camp is in the Chilao campground (see trip note for #49).

Site 51   HORSE
           FLATS   ▲

Campsites, facilities: There are 25 campsites for tents or motorhomes up to 18 feet long. Piped water, fireplaces and picnic tables are provided, and vault toilets are available. A grocery store is nearby.
Reservations, fee: No reservations; $3 fee per night.
Who to contact: Phone Angeles National Forest Headquarters at (818)574-1613.
Location: Drive 33 miles northeast of La Canada and Flintridge off State Route 2.
Trip note: Open from May to November. Elevation 5500 feet. Camp is on a National Recreation Trail and close to the Chilao Visitor Center. Several trails into the San Gabriel Wilderness are nearby.

Site 52   SOUTH
           FORK   ▲

Campsites, facilities: There are 21 campsites for tents or motorhomes up to 22 feet long. Piped water, fireplaces and picnic tables are provided, and vault toilets are available.
Reservations, fee: No reservations; $5 fee per night.
Who to contact: Phone Angeles National Forest Headquarters at (818)574-1613.
Location: Drive 14 miles northwest of Big Pines off Big Pines Highway.
Trip note: Open from May to November. Elevation 4600 feet. Located at the trailhead for several different trails going into the wilderness. Camp is on the South Fork of Big Rock Creek.

Site 53   SOUTH FORK
           GROUP CAMP   ▲

Campsites, facilities: There is one group campsite here which will accommodate up to 50 people. Piped water, picnic tables and fireplaces are provided, and vault toilets are available. A grocery store is nearby.
Reservations, fee: Reservations requested; $35 fee per night.
Who to contact: Phone Angeles National Forest District Office at (805)944-2187.
Location: Drive 14 miles northwest of Big Pines off Big Pines Highway.
Trip note: Open from May to November. Elevation 4600 feet. Camp is on the South Fork of Big Rock Creek and at the trailhead of several trails leading into the wilderness.

Site 54   SYCAMORE
           FLAT   ▲

Campsites, facilities: There are 11 campsites for tents or motorhomes up to 22 feet long. Piped water, fireplaces and picnic tables are provided, and vault toilets are available. A grocery store is nearby.

Reservations, fee: No reservations; $5 fee per night.

Who to contact: Phone Angeles National Forest Headquarters at (818)574-1613.

Location: Drive 13 miles northwest of Big Pines off Big Pines Highway.

Trip note: Open all year. Elevation 4300 feet. Located near Devil's Punchbowl County Park.

Site 55	BIG ROCK	◭

Campsites, facilities: There are eight campsites for tents or motorhomes up to 18 feet long. Piped water, fireplaces and picnic tables are provided, and vault toilets are available.

Reservations, fee: No reservations; $5 fee per night.

Who to contact: Phone Angeles National Forest Headquarters at (818)574-1613.

Location: Drive six miles west of Big Pines off State Route 2.

Trip note: Open from June to October. Elevation 5500 feet. Camp is on Big Rock Creek and near a National Recreation Trail.

Site 56	JACKSON FLAT GROUP CAMP	◭

Campsites, facilities: There are five group campsites here which will accommodate 40 to 50 people each. Piped water, picnic tables and fireplaces are provided, and vault toilets are available.

Reservations, fee: Reservations requested, call for fee.

Who to contact: Phone Angeles National Forest District Office at (805)944-2187.

Location: Drive nine miles northwest of Wrightwood off State Route 2.

Trip note: Open from June to October. Elevation 7500 feet. Pacific Crest National Scenic Trail passes nearby. Another trail goes into Sheep Mountain Wilderness.

Site 57	APPLE TREE	◭

Campsites, facilities: There are eight tent sites. Piped water, picnic tables, and fireplaces are provided, and vault toilets are available. A grocery store is nearby.

Reservations, fee: No reservations; $5 fee per night.

Who to contact: Phone Angeles National Forest Headquarters at (818)574-1613.

Location: Drive six miles northwest of Wrightwood off State Route 2 on Big Pines Highway.

Trip note: Open from May to November. Elevation 6200 feet. Located near the Big Pines Visitor Information Center and the Table Mountain Ski Area.

Site **58**   LAKE   ◭

Campsites, facilities: There are eight campsites for tents or motorhomes up to 18
    feet long. Piped water, fireplaces and picnic tables are provided, and vault
    toilets are available.
Reservations, fee: No reservations; $5 fee per night.
Who to contact: Phone Angeles National Forest Headquarters at (818)574-1613.
Location: Drive six miles northwest of Wrightwood off State Route 2 on Big
    Pines Highway.
Trip note: Open from May to November. Elevation 6100 feet. Located on a
    small lake.

Site **59**   PEAVINE   ◭

Campsites, facilities: There are four tent sites. Piped water, picnic tables and fire-
    places are provided, and vault toilets are available. A grocery store and pro-
    pane gas are nearby.
Reservations, fee: No reservations; $5 fee per night.
Who to contact: Phone Angeles National Forest Headquarters at (818)574-1613.
Location: Drive six miles northwest of Wrightwood off State Route 2 on Big
    Pines Highway.
Trip note: Open from May to November. Elevation 6100 feet. This site is a short
    hike away from a small lake and a mile from the Pacific Crest National
    Scenic Trail.

Site **60**   GRASSY
                               HOLLOW   ◭

Campsites, facilities: There are 15 campsites for tents or motorhomes up to 18
    feet long. Piped water, fireplaces and picnic tables are provided, and vault
    toilets are available.
Reservations, fee: No reservations; $5 fee per night.
Who to contact: Phone Angeles National Forest Headquarters at (818)574-1613.
Location: Drive six miles west of Wrightwood off State Route 2.
Trip note: Open from May to November. Elevation 7400 feet. Located on the
    Pacific Crest National Scenic Trail on the border of the Sheep Mountain
    Wilderness.

Site **61**   MOUNTAIN
                               OAK   ◭

Campsites, facilities: There are 17 campsites for tents or motorhomes up to 18
    feet long. Piped water, fireplaces and picnic tables are provided, and flush

toilets are available. Groceries and propane gas are nearby.

Reservations, fee: No reservations; $6 fee per night.

Who to contact: Phone Angeles National Forest Headquarters at (818)574-1613.

Location: Drive seven miles northwest of Wrightwood off State Route 2 on Big Pines Highway.

Trip note: Open from May to October. Elevation 6200 feet. Located near a small lake, a target shooting area, and across the road from a four-wheel drive trail into the Pinyon Ridge area.

Site 62   TABLE MOUNTAIN

Campsites, facilities: There are 115 campsites for tents or motorhomes up to 22 feet long. Piped water, fireplaces and picnic tables are provided, and vault toilets are available. A grocery store, laundromat and propane gas are nearby.

Reservations, fee: No reservations; $6 fee per night.

Who to contact: Phone Angeles National Forest Headquarters at (818)574-1613.

Location: Drive five miles northwest of Wrightwood off State Route 2.

Trip note: Open from May to October. Elevation 7200 feet. Located near the Big Pine Visitor Center.

Site 63   BLUE RIDGE

Campsites, facilities: There are eight campsites for tents or motorhomes up to 18 feet long. Fireplaces and picnic tables are provided, and vault toilets are available. There is no water, so bring your own.

Reservations, fee: No reservations, no fee.

Who to contact: Phone Angeles National Forest Headquarters at (818)574-1613.

Location: Drive 10 miles southwest of Wrightwood off State Route 2 on Blue Ridge Road.

Trip note: Open from June to October. Elevation 7900 feet. Located on the Pacific Crest National Scenic Trail. A four-wheel drive route borders the Sheep Mountain Wilderness.

Site 64   CABIN FLAT

Campsites, facilities: There are 12 tent sites. Picnic tables and fireplaces are provided, and vault toilets are available. There is no water, so bring your own.

Reservations, fee: No reservations, no fee.

Who to contact: Phone Angeles National Forest Headquarters at (818)574-1613.

Location: Drive 21 miles southwest of Wrightwood off State Route 2 via Blue Ridge Road.

Trip note: Open from May to October. Elevation 5400 feet. Located on Prairie Creek near the border of Sheep Mountain Wilderness.

Site **65**   GUFFY

Campsites, facilities: There are six tent sites. Picnic tables and fireplaces are provided, and vault toilets are available. There is no water, so bring your own.
Reservations, fee: No reservations, no fee.
Who to contact: Phone Angeles National Forest Headquarters at (818)574-1613.
Location: Drive 13 miles southwest of Wrightwood off State Route 2 on Blue Ridge Road.
Trip note: Open from May to October. Elevation 8300 feet. A trail out of camp connects with the Pacific Crest National Scenic Trail.

Site **66**   LUPINE

Campsites, facilities: There are 11 tent sites. Piped water, picnic tables and fireplaces are provided, and vault toilets are available.
Reservations, fee: No reservations; $4 fee per night.
Who to contact: Phone Angeles National Forest Headquarters at (818)574-1613.
Location: Drive 18 miles northwest of Wrightwood off State Route 2 via Blue Ridge Road.
Trip note: Open from June to October. Elevation 6600 feet. Located on Prairie Fork Creek below Pine Mountain Ridge. A trail leading out from camp forks east into the Sheep Mountain Wilderness or southwest to Dawson Peak and Pine Mountain.

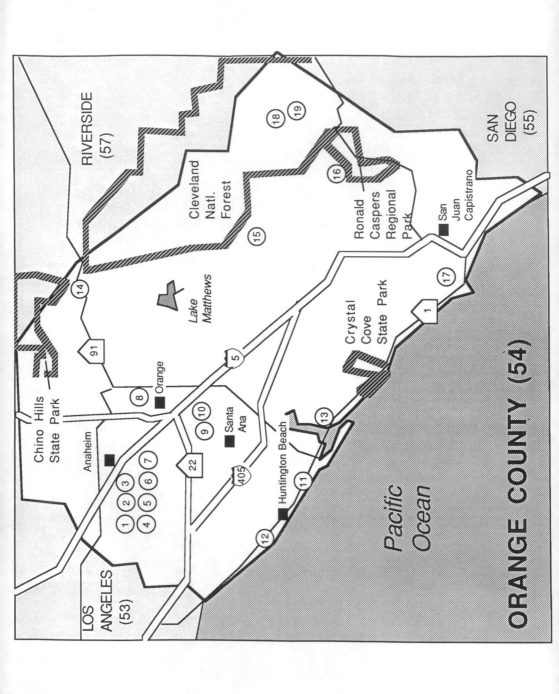

RIVERSIDE (57)

SAN DIEGO (55)

LOS ANGELES (53)

ORANGE COUNTY (54)

Pacific Ocean

Chino Hills State Park

Cleveland Natl. Forest

Lake Matthews

Ronald Caspers Regional Park

San Juan Capistrano

Crystal Cove State Park

Anaheim

Orange

Santa Ana

Huntington Beach

14

91

8

22

405

5

15

16

18 19

17

1

9 10

11

12

13

1 2 3 4 5 6 7

ORANGE COUNTY

◆

Site **1** | ANAHEIM
VACATION PARK |

Campsites, facilities: There are 222 sites for tents or motorhomes. Picnic tables, piped water, electrical connections and sewer hookups are provided. Rest rooms, showers, a playground, swimming pool, laundromat, store, ice, recreation room and propane gas are available. A grocery store is nearby.

Reservations, fee: Call for space available. $20 deposit required; $20 fee per night.

Who to contact: Phone park at (714)821-4311.

Location: In Anaheim drive to 311 N. Beach Boulevard (Highway 39).

Trip note: This park is open all year. It is walking distance from Knott's Berry Farm and a short distance from Disneyland and several beaches.

Site **2** | LINCOLN
RECREATIONAL VEHICLE PARK |

Campsites, facilities: There are 69 motorhome spaces. Picnic tables, piped water, electrical connections and sewer hookups are provided.

Rest rooms, showers, swimming pool, laundromat, dump station and propane gas are available. A grocery store is nearby.

Reservations, fee: Call for space available. $18 deposit required; $18 fee per night.

Who to contact: Phone park at (714)821-9000.

Location: In Anaheim, drive to 2651 West Lincoln Avenue.

Trip note: Open all year. Located between Knott's Berry Farm and Disneyland. Also near Universal Studios, Marineland, Lion Country and the Wax Museum.

Site **3** | ANAHEIM JUNCTION
CAMPGROUND |

Campsites, facilities: There are 124 sites for motorhomes. Picnic tables, fireplaces, piped water, electrical connections and sewer hookups are provided. Rest rooms, showers, a playground, swimming pool, laundromat, grocery store and propane gas are available.

Reservations, fee: Call for space available. $20 deposit required; $20 fee per night.

Who to contact: Phone park at (714)533-0641.

Location: Drive in Anaheim to 1230 S. West Street.

Trip note: Open all year. Located just off I-5 a short distance from Disneyland.

Site **4**   ANAHEIM
                                   KOA

Campsites, facilities: There are 221 sites for motorhomes. Picnic tables, fireplaces, piped water, electrical connections and sewer hookups are provided. Rest rooms, showers, a playground, swimming pool and rest area are available.

Reservations, fee: Call for space available. $24.75 deposit required; $24.75 fee per night.

Who to contact: Phone park at (714)533-7720.

Location: In Anaheim, drive to 1221 S. West Street.

Trip note: This park is open all year and is just off I-5 near Disneyland.

Site **5**   TRAVELERS WORLD
                               RV PARK

Campsites, facilities: There are 310 sites for tents or motorhomes. Piped water, electrical connections and sewer hookups are provided. Rest rooms, showers, a playground, swimming pool, laundromat, store, dump station, ice, recreation room, car rental and propane gas are available.

Reservations, fee: Call for space available. $19.50 deposit required; $19.50 fee per night.

Who to contact: Phone park at (714)991-0100.

Location: Drive in Anaheim to 333 West Ball Road.

Trip note: Open all year. Located 1/2 mile from Disneyland. An in-park tour bus will deliver you to Knott's Berry Farm, Movieland Wax Museum, Universal Studios, Marineland and the Queen Mary.

Site **6**   7-11 TRAVEL TRAILER PARK
                             AND MOTEL

Campsites, facilities: There are 39 sites for motorhomes. Picnic tables, piped water, electrical connections and sewer hookups are provided. Rest rooms, showers, laundromat and dump station are available.

Reservations, fee: Call ahead for space available and fee.

Who to contact: Phone park at (714)527-4394.

Location: In Anaheim, drive to 2760 W. Lincoln Avenue.

Trip note: Open all year. Located in a quiet area minutes away from Disneyland,

Knott's Berry Farm and the Anaheim Stadium.

Site **7**
DISNEYLAND HOTEL'S VACATIONLAND

Campsites, facilities: There are 60 sites for tents and 406 for motorhomes. Picnic tables, piped water, electrical connections and sewer hookups are provided. Rest rooms, showers, a playground, swimming pool, laundromat, store, ice, dump station, recreation room and propane gas are available.

Reservations, fee: Call for space available. $21.50 deposit required; $21.50 fee per night.

Who to contact: Phone park at (714)533-7270.

Location: In Anaheim, drive to 1343 S. West Street.

Trip note: This park is open all year and is within walking distance of Disneyland. Knott's Berry Farm, Movieland Wax Museum and Anaheim Stadium are nearby.

Site **8**
ORANGELAND RECREATIONAL VEHICLE PARK

Campsites, facilities: There are 212 sites for motorhomes. Picnic tables, fireplaces, piped water, electrical connections, phone hookups and sewer hookups are provided. Rest rooms, showers, a playground, video game arcade, swimming pool, therapy pool, laundromat, store, car wash, shuffleboard court, dump station, ice, recreation room and propane gas are available.

Reservations, fee: Call for space available. $18 deposit required; $18 fee per night.

Who to contact: Phone park at (714)633-0414.

Location: Drive in Orange to to 1600 W. Struck Avenue.

Trip note: This park is open all year. Located in the Orange Groves, five miles east of Disneyland.

Site **9**
C C CAMPERLAND

Campsites, facilities: There are 65 sites for tents or motorhomes. Picnic tables, piped water, electrical connections and sewer hookups are provided. Rest rooms, showers, a playground, video arcade, swimming pool, laundromat, store, dump station, ice and recreation room are available.

Reservations, fee: Call ahead for space available and fee.

Who to contact: Phone park at (714)750-6747.

Location: Drive south on Harbor Boulevard off I-5 to 12262 Harbor Boulevard.

Trip note: This park is open all year. It is nine blocks south of Disneyland and near many other sights.

Site **10**
TRATEL
RECREATIONAL VEHICLE PARK

Campsites, facilities: There are 130 sites for motorhomes. Piped water, electrical connections and sewer hookups are provided. Rest rooms, showers, a playground, swimming pool, laundromat, store, dump station, ice and propane gas are available.
Reservations, fee: Phone Leisuretime Reservation Systems at (800)822-CAMP. $17 deposit; $17 camp use fee.
Who to contact: Phone park at (714)638-4330.
Location: From State Route 22 near Garden Grove, take Harbor Boulevard 200 yards to 13190 Harbor Boulevard.
Trip note: This park is open all year. It offers a park-like setting in the midst of all the attractions, including Disneyland, Knott's Berry Farm, Anaheim Stadium and the Crystal Cathedral.

Site **11**
SUNSET
VISTA

Campsites, facilities: There are 160 campsites for tents or motorhomes up to 30 feet long. Piped water and fireplaces are provided, and flush toilets are available. A grocery store, laundromat and propane gas are nearby.
Reservations, fee: Call for space available. $10 deposit required; $10 fee per night.
Who to contact: Phone park at (714)536-5280.
Location: Drive 16 miles south of Long Beach on State Route 1 to junction with Lake Street in Huntington Beach.
Trip note: This park is open all year and is on the beach. The Bolsa Chica State Beach is nearby.

Site **12**
BOLSA CHICA
STATE BEACH

Campsites, facilities: This is an en route campsite. En route campsites are day-use parking areas where self-contained motorhomes can be parked for one night stays. En route campers must leave by 9 a.m. The beach park provides fire rings, dressing rooms, cold showers, picnic area, food service, a bicycle trail and a paved ramp for wheelchair access to the beach.
Reservations, fee: No reservations, no fee.
Who to contact: Phone park at (714)848-1566.
Location: Drive three miles (west) up the coast from Huntington Beach on State Route 1.
Trip note: This park is open all year and is on the ocean.

Site **13**   NEWPORT
                                DUNES

Campsites, facilities: There are 145 sites for tents or motorhomes. Picnic tables,
   piped water, electrical connections, and in some cases sewer hookups are
   provided. Rest rooms, showers, a playground, children's pool, laundromat,
   store, dump station, ice, recreation room and boat ramp are available.
Reservations, fee: Call ahead for space available and fee.
Who to contact: Phone park at (714)644-0510.
Location: Drive to Newport Beach off I-405 via Jamboree Road to 1131 Back
   Bay Drive.
Trip note: This park is open all year. It is located on the bay and has a sandy
   beach, a boat ramp and storage area.

Site **14**   FEATHERLY
                            REGIONAL PARK

Campsites, facilities: There are 215 campsites for tents or motorhomes up to 40
   feet long. Piped water, fireplaces and picnic tables are provided. Flush toi-
   lets, showers, dump station, playground and horseback riding facilities are
   available. A grocery store, laundromat and propane gas are nearby.
Reservations, fee: No reservations; $5 fee per night.
Who to contact: Phone park at (714)637-0210.
Location: Drive seven miles west of Corona off State Route 91.
Trip note: Open all year. Elevation 200 feet. This site is located near the Santa
   Ana River.

Site **15**   O'NEILL
                            REGIONAL PARK

Campsites, facilities: There are 183 campsites for tents or motorhomes up to 35
   feet long. Piped water, fireplaces and picnic tables are provided. Flush toilets, showers, a playground and a dump station are available. A grocery
   store is nearby.
Reservations, fee: No reservations; $5 fee per night.
Who to contact: Phone park at (714)858-9365.
Location: Drive 20 miles east of Irvine off County Road S-18.
Trip note: Open all year. Elevation 1000 feet. Several roads near this park lead to
   trailheads into the Cleveland National Forest.

Site **16**   CASPERS WILDERNESS
                                PARK

Campsites, facilities: There are 82 campsites for tents or motorhomes. Piped water, fireplaces and picnic tables are provided. Flush toilets, showers, a dump

station and a playground are available.

Reservations, fee: Call for space available. $8 deposit required; $5 fee per night.
Who to contact: Phone park at (714)831-2174.
Location: Drive eight miles northeast of San Juan Capistrano via State Route 74.
Trip note: Open all year. Elevation 500 feet. Located on San Juan Creek. The San Mateo Canyon Wilderness and San Juan Hot Springs are nearby.

Site **17**
DOHENY
STATE BEACH

Campsites, facilities: There are 120 campsites for tents or motorhomes. Piped water, fireplaces and picnic tables are provided. Flush toilets, showers, dump station, playground, exhibits and food service are available. A grocery store, laundromat and propane gas are nearby. Camping, picnicking, exhibits and food service areas are wheelchair accessible.
Reservations, fee: Phone MISTIX at (800)446-7275; $8 fee per night.
Who to contact: Phone park at (714)496-6171.
Location: Drive two miles south of San Juan Capistrano on State Route 2.
Trip note: This park is open all year and is at the entrance to Dana Point Harbor.

Site **18**
SAN CLEMENTE
STATE BEACH

Campsites, facilities: There are 157 campsites for tents or motorhomes up to 32 feet long. Piped water, fireplaces, picnic tables and in some cases full hookups are provided. Flush toilets and showers are available. A grocery store, laundromat and propane gas are nearby. The camping area is wheelchair accessible.
Reservations, fee: Phone MISTIX at (800)446-7275; $12 fee per night.
Who to contact: Phone park at (714)492-3156.
Location: Drive two miles south of San Clemente off I-5.
Trip note: This park is open all year and is on the beach where you can enjoy swimming and fishing in the warm Southern California waters.

Site **19**
BLUE
JAY

Campsites, facilities: There are eight tent sites and 43 campsites for tents or motorhomes up to 22 feet long. Piped water, fireplaces and picnic tables are provided. Vault toilets are available and a grocery store is nearby.
Reservations, fee: No reservations; $5 fee per night.
Who to contact: Phone Cleveland National Forest Headquarters at (619)293-5050.
Location: Drive 16 miles west of Lake Elsinore off State Route 74.

Trip note: Open all year. Elevation 3300 feet. The campground is at the trailhead for the San Juan Trail and the Chiquito Trail, both of which lead into the backcountry wilderness and the Santa Ana Mountains.

Site **20**   BLUE JAY
                             PRIMITIVE CAMP

Campsites, facilities: There are six tent sites. Piped water and picnic tables are provided, and vault toilets are available. A grocery store is nearby.

Reservations, fee: No reservations; $5 fee per night.

Who to contact: Phone Cleveland National Forest Headquarters at (619)293-5050.

Location: Drive 16 miles west of Lake Elsinore off State Route 74.

Trip note: Open from May to September. Elevation 3300 feet. The campground is at the trailhead for the San Juan Trail and the Chiquito Trail, both of which lead into the backcountry wilderness and the Santa Ana Mountains.

Site **21**   FALCON
                             GROUP CAMP

Campsites, facilities: There are three campsites for tents or motorhomes up to 16 feet long. Piped water, fireplaces and picnic tables are provided. Vault toilets are available. A grocery store is nearby.

Reservations, fee: Reservations requested; $35 fee per group per night.

Who to contact: Phone Cleveland National Forest Headquarters at (619)293-5050.

Location: Drive 16 miles west of Lake Elsinore off State Route 74.

Trip note: Open from May to September. Elevation 3300 feet. The campground is at the trailhead for the San Juan Trail and the Chiquito Trail, both of which lead into the backcountry wilderness.

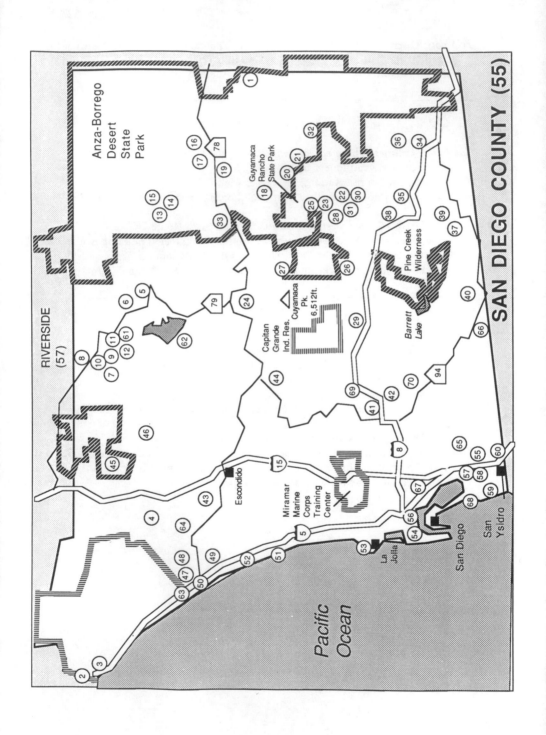

RIVERSIDE (57)

Anza-Borrego
Desert
State
Park

Guyamaca
Rancho
State Park

Capitan
Grande
Ind. Res.

Cuyamaca
Pk.
6,512ft.

Pine Creek
Wilderness

Barrett
Lake

Escondido

Miramar
Marine
Corps
Training
Center

La
Jolla

San Diego

San
Ysidro

Pacific
Ocean

SAN DIEGO COUNTY

◆

Site **1**   FISH
CREEK   🌲

Campsites, facilities: There are 15 campsites for tents or motorhomes. Pit toilets are available, but there is no water, so bring your own.
Reservations, fee: No reservations, no fee.
Who to contact: Phone Anza Borrego State Park at (619)767-5311.
Location: Drive 12 miles south of Ocotillo Wells on Split Mountain Road.
Trip note: This campground is open all year and is 12 miles from Ocotillo Wells State Vehicular Recreation Area. Primitive.

Site **2**   SAN CLEMENTE
STATE BEACH   ▲

Campsites, facilities: There are 157 campsites for tents or motorhomes. Piped water, fireplaces, picnic tables, and in some cases, full hookups are provided. Showers and flush toilets are available. A grocery store, laundromat and propane gas are nearby.
Reservations, fee: Phone MISTIX at (800)446-7275; $12 fee per night.
Who to contact: Phone campground at (714)492-3156.
Location: Drive two miles south of San Clemente on I-5.
Trip note: This campground is on the beach and is open all year. Enjoy hiking along the beach, or swimming and fishing in the warm Southern California waters.

Site **3**   SAN ONOFRE
STATE BEACH   ▲

Campsites, facilities: There are 93 motorhome spaces and 88 campsites for tents or motorhomes. Piped water, fireplaces and picnic tables are provided. Showers and flush toilets are available. A grocery store, laundromat and propane gas are nearby.
Reservations, fee: Phone MISTIX at (800)446-7275; $10 fee per night.
Who to contact: Phone campground at (714)492-4872.
Location: Drive four miles south of San Clemente on I-5.

Trip note: This campground is on the beach and is open all year. Enjoy hiking along the beach and in the park, or swimming and fishing in the warm Southern California waters. Located alongside one of California's best surfing spots and in the shadow of San Onofre Nuclear Power Plant.

Site **4**

ALL SEASONS
RV PARK

Campsites, facilities: There are 60 motorhome spaces with full hookups. Rest rooms, showers, a dump station, store and a laundromat are available.
Reservations, fee: Call ahead for available space and fee.
Who to contact: Phone park at (619)749-2982.
Location: Drive eight miles north of Escondido on I-15 to the Gopher Canyon exit and turn right, then turn left on Frontage Road to 30012 Highway 395.
Trip note: This campground is set in the country, and has a five-acre natural lake that is stocked with catfish.

Site **5**

INDIAN FLATS
CAMP

Campsites, facilities: There are 17 campsites for tents or motorhomes. Piped water, fireplaces and picnic tables are provided. Vault toilets are available.
Reservations, fee: No reservations; $5 fee per night.
Who to contact: Phone Cleveland National Forest at (619)293-5050.
Location: Drive six miles northwest of Warner Springs on State Route 79.
Trip note: Open from April to November. Elevation 3600 feet. Lake Henshaw is about 15 miles away. The lake is for fishing only and there is a resort on the south shore that has boat rentals. The Pacific Crest Trail passes about two miles from camp.

Site **6**

INDIAN FLATS
GROUP CAMP

Campsites, facilities: There are two group campsites for tents or motorhomes. Piped water, fireplaces and picnic tables are provided. Vault toilets are available.
Reservations, fee: Reservations requested; $25 per night group fee.
Who to contact: Phone Cleveland National Forest at (619)293-5050.
Location: Drive nine miles northwest of Warner Springs on State Route 79.
Trip note: Open from April to November. Elevation 3600 feet. Lake Henshaw is about 15 miles away. The lake is for fishing only and there is a resort on the south shore that has boat rentals. The Pacific Crest Trail passes about two miles from camp.

| Site 7 | FRY CREEK | ▲ |

Campsites, facilities: There are 12 tent sites and eight campsites for tents or motorhomes. Piped water, fireplaces and picnic tables are provided, and vault toilets are available. A grocery store is nearby.
Reservations, fee: No reservations, no fee.
Who to contact: Phone Cleveland National Forest at (619)293-5050.
Location: Drive two and a half miles north of Palomar Mountain on East Grade Road.
Trip note: Open from May to November. Elevation 5200 feet. Located on Fry Creek, a short distance from Palomar Observatory which houses America's largest telescope.

| Site 8 | OAK GROVE | ▲ |

Campsites, facilities: There are 81 campsites for tents or motorhomes. Piped water, fireplaces and picnic tables are provided, and flush toilets are available. Propane gas and groceries are nearby.
Reservations, fee: No reservations; $5 fee per night.
Who to contact: Phone Cleveland National Forest at (619)293-5050.
Location: Drive six and a half miles southeast of Aguanga on State Route 79.
Trip note: Open all year. Elevation 2800 feet. Located near Temecula and Chihuahua Creeks and about 15 miles from Vail Lake, a fishing lake that has a ramp and boat rentals.

| Site 9 | PALOMAR MOUNTAIN STATE PARK | ▲ |

Campsites, facilities: There are 21 tent sites and 10 motorhome spaces. Piped water, fireplaces and picnic tables are provided, and flush toilets and showers are available. A grocery store is nearby.
Reservations, fee: Phone MISTIX at (800)446-7275; $10 fee per night.
Who to contact: Phone park at (619)742-3462.
Location: Drive four miles north of Palomar Mountain on East Grade Road.
Trip note: Open all year. Elevation 4700 feet. Campground is near the Palomar Observatory which contains the largest telescope in the United States.

| Site 10 | OBSERVATORY | ▲ |

Campsites, facilities: There are 42 campsites for tents or motorhomes. Piped water, fireplaces and picnic tables are provided, and vault toilets are available. A grocery store is nearby.

Reservations, fee: No reservations; $5 fee per night.
Who to contact: Phone Cleveland National Forest at (619)293-5050.
Location: Drive two and a half miles north of Palomar Mountain on East Grade Road.
Trip note: Open from May to November. Elevation 4800 feet. Campground is on Fry Creek and near the Palomar Observatory which contains the largest telescope in the United States.

Site **11**   PALOMAR

Campsites, facilities: There are eight tent sites. Piped water, fireplaces and picnic tables are provided, and pit toilets are available. A grocery store is nearby.
Reservations, fee: No reservations; $5 fee per night.
Who to contact: Phone County Parks Department at (619)565-3600.
Location: Drive one mile east of Palomar Mountain on County Road S-7.
Trip note: Open all year. Elevation 5565 feet. It is a short drive to Palomar Observatory and Lake Henshaw (see campground #62 for facilities at Lake Henshaw).

Site **12**   CRESTLINE
                         GROUP CAMP

Campsites, facilities: There is one group campsite for tents. Piped water, fireplaces and picnic tables are provided, and vault toilets are available. A grocery store is nearby.
Reservations, fee: Reservations requested; $40 group fee per night.
Who to contact: Phone Cleveland National Forest at (619)293-5050.
Location: Drive to Palomar Mountain on County Road S-7 (see Forest Service map).
Trip note: Open from May to November. Elevation 4800 feet. It is a short drive to Palomar Observatory and Lake Henshaw (see campground #62 for facilities at Lake Henshaw).

Site **13**   ARROYO SALADO
                  PRIMITIVE CAMP AREA

Campsites, facilities: This is an open camping area in the Anza-Borrego Desert State Park. It can be used for tents or motorhomes. Open fires are not allowed and there is no water, so bring your own.
Reservations, fee: No reservations, no fee.
Who to contact: Phone Anza-Borrego Desert State Park at (619)767-5311.
Location: Drive 16 miles east of Borrego Springs on County Road S-22.
Trip note: Open all year. Elevation 880 feet. It gets very hot in the desert in the summer. Primitive.

| Site **14** | CULP VALLEY
PRIMITIVE CAMP AREA | 🌲 |

Campsites, facilities: This is an open camping area in Anza-Borrego Desert State Park. It can be used for tents or motorhomes. Open fires are not allowed and there is no water, so bring your own.
Reservations, fee: No reservations, no fee.
Who to contact: Phone Anza-Borrego Desert State Park at (619)767-5311.
Location: Drive 10 miles southwest of Borrego Springs on County Road S-22.
Trip note: Open all year. Elevation 3400 feet. The desert is hot in the summer. The Visitors Center is near the western boundary of the park on County Road S-22, and it provides exhibits and a slide show to stimulate your urge to explore park.

| Site **15** | BORREGO PALM
CANYON | ▲ |

Campsites, facilities: There are 52 motorhome spaces with full hookups and 65 campsites for tents or motorhomes. Piped water, fireplaces and picnic tables are provided. Flush toilets and showers are available. A grocery store, laundromat and propane gas are nearby.
Reservations, fee: Phone MISTIX at (800)446-7275; $12 fee per night.
Who to contact: Phone Anza-Borrego Desert State Park at (619)767-5311.
Location: Drive two and a half miles west of Borrego Springs via County Road S-22 and Palm Canyon Drive.
Trip note: Open all year. Elevation 760 feet. This spot gets hot in the summer. The Visitors Center is near the campground and provides exhibits and a slide show to stimulate your urge to explore this desert park.

| Site **16** | YAQUI PASS
PRIMITIVE CAMP AREA | |

Campsites, facilities: This is an open camping area in Anza-Borrego Desert State Park. It can be used for tents or motorhomes. Pit toilets are available. Open fires are not allowed and there is no water, so bring your own.
Reservations, fee: No reservations, no fee.
Who to contact: Phone Anza-Borrego Desert State Park at (619)767-5311.
Location: Drive eight miles south of Borrego Springs on County Road S-3 (Yaqui Pass Road).
Trip note: Open all year. Elevation 1730 feet. This spot is hot in the summer. The Visitors Center is 13 miles from camp near the western boundary of the park on County Road S-22, and it provides exhibits and a slide show.

Site 17   YAQUI WELL
                              PRIMITIVE CAMP AREA   ▣

Campsites, facilities: This is an open camping area in Anza-Borrego Desert State
    Park. It can be used for tents or motorhomes. Pit toilets are available. Open
    fires are not allowed and there is no water, so bring your own.
Reservations, fee: No reservations, no fee.
Who to contact: Phone Anza-Borrego Desert State Park at (619)767-5311.
Location: Drive 11 miles south of Borrego Springs on County Road S-3.
Trip note: Open all year. Elevation 1400 feet. This site gets hot in the summer.
    The Visitors Center is 13 miles from camp near the western boundary of
    the park on County Road S-22. It provides exhibits and a slide show.

Site 18   BLAIR VALLEY
                              ENVIRONMENTAL CAMPS   ▣

Campsites, facilities: These campsites have been developed to offer maximum se-
    clusion for the camper. The sites are walk-in and are about 100 yards from
    their parking areas. Each site has a cupboard, picnic table and pit toilet. No
    water is available, so bring your own.
Reservations, fee: Reservation requested, no fee.
Who to contact: Phone Anza-Borrego Desert State Park at (619)767-5311.
Location: Drive 11 miles northwest of Agua Caliente Springs on County Road S-
    2 near the Box Canyon Historical Area.
Trip note: Open all year. Elevation 2500 feet. The best time to visit the desert is
    in the spring. The Visitors Center is 32 miles from camp near the western
    boundary of the park on County Road S-22. It provides exhibits and a slide
    show.

Site 19   TAMARISK
                                     GROVE   ▲

Campsites, facilities: There are 27 campsites for tents or motorhomes. Piped wa-
    ter, fireplaces and picnic tables are provided, and flush toilets and showers
    are available.
Reservations, fee: Phone MISTIX at (800)446-7275; $10 fee per night.
Who to contact: Phone Anza-Borrego Desert State Park at (619)767-5311.
Location: Drive 12 miles south of Borrego Springs on County Road S-3 to the
    junction with State Route 78.
Trip note: Open all year. Elevation 1400 feet. The best time to visit the desert is
    in the spring. The Visitors Center is 13 miles from camp near the western
    boundary of the park on County Road S-22, and it provides exhibits and a
    slide show.

Site **20**
VALLECITO
COUNTY PARK

▲

Campsites, facilities: There are 50 campsites for tents or motorhomes. Fireplaces and picnic tables are provided, and flush toilets are available. There is no piped water, so bring your own.
Reservations, fee: No reservations; $5 fee per night.
Who to contact: Phone County Parks Department at (619)565-3600.
Location: Drive four miles northwest of Agua Caliente Springs on County Road S-2.
Trip note: Open from October to June. Elevation 1500 feet. Located near the Agua Caliente Hot Springs, Anza Borrego Desert State Park and about 35 miles from Cuyamaca Reservoir and Cuyamaca Rancho State Park.

Site **21**
AGUA CALIENTE
COUNTY PARK

▲

Campsites, facilities: There are 104 motorhome spaces with water and electrical hookups and in some cases sewer hookups. There are 36 campsites for tents or motorhomes. Piped water, fireplaces and picnic tables are provided. Flush toilets, showers and a playground are available. Groceries and propane gas are nearby.
Reservations, fee: Call for space available. $11 deposit required; $9 fee per night.
Who to contact: Phone County Parks Department at (619)565-3600.
Location: Drive one mile south of Agua Caliente Hot Springs off County Road S-2.
Trip note: Open all year. Elevation 1320 feet. This site gets hot in the summer. It is near the Hot Springs, Anza Borrego Desert State Park and about 35 miles from Cuyamaca Reservoir and Cuyamaca Rancho State Park.

Site **22**
HORSE HAVEN
GROUP CAMP

▲

Campsites, facilities: There are three group campsites for tents or motorhomes. Piped water, fireplaces and picnic tables are provided. Vault toilets are available. Groceries and propane gas are nearby.
Reservations, fee: Reservations requested; $35 fee per group per night.
Who to contact: Phone Cleveland National Forest Headquarters at (619)293-5050.
Location: Drive two and a half miles northwest of Mount Laguna off Sunrise Highway.
Trip note: Open from May to October. Elevation 5500 feet. It is in the Laguna Recreation Area and the Pacific Crest Trail passes near camp. Little Laguna and Big Laguna Lakes are nearby.

Site **23**
EL PRADO
GROUP CAMP   ▲

Campsites, facilities: There are five group campsites for tents or motorhomes. Piped water, fireplaces and picnic tables are provided, and vault toilets are available. A grocery store and propane gas are nearby.

Reservations, fee: Reservation requested; $10 fee per group per night.

Who to contact: Phone Cleveland National Forest Headquarters at (619)293-5050.

Location: Drive three miles northwest of Mount Laguna on Sunrise Highway.

Trip note: Open from May to October. Elevation 5500 feet. It is in the Laguna Recreation Area and near Little Laguna and Big Laguna Lakes. The Pacific Crest Trail passes nearby.

Site **24**
WILLIAM HEISE
COUNTY PARK   ▲

Campsites, facilities: There are 43 tent sites and 40 campsites for tents or motorhomes. Piped water, fireplaces and picnic tables are provided. Flush toilets, showers, dump station and playground are available. A grocery store and laundromat are nearby.

Reservations, fee: No reservations; $7 fee per night.

Who to contact: Phone County Parks Department at (619)565-3600.

Location: Drive two miles east of Pine Hills on Pine Hills Road.

Trip note: Open all year. Elevation 4200 feet.

Site **25**
LAGUNA   ▲

Campsites, facilities: There are 75 tent sites, 25 motorhome spaces and 20 campsites for tents or motorhomes. Piped water, fireplaces and picnic tables are provided, and vault toilets are available. A grocery store and propane gas are nearby.

Reservations, fee: No reservations; $5 fee per night.

Who to contact: Phone Cleveland National Forest Headquarters at (619)293-5050.

Location: Drive three miles northwest of Mount Laguna on Sunrise Highway.

Trip note: Open all year. Elevation 5500 feet. It is in the Laguna Recreation Area and near Little Laguna and Big Laguna Lakes. The Pacific Crest Trail passes nearby.

Site **26**   GREEN VALLEY
                                              FALLS

Campsites, facilities: There are 81 campsites for tents or motorhomes. Piped water, fireplaces and picnic tables are provided. Flush toilets and showers are
available. The campgrounds, picnic areas and exhibits are wheelchair accessible. A grocery store and propane gas are nearby.
Reservations, fee: Phone MISTIX at (800)446-7275; $10 fee per night.
Who to contact: Phone Cuyamaca Rancho State Park at (619)765-0755.
Location: Drive six miles northeast of Descanso on State Route 79.
Trip note: Open all year. Elevation 3900 feet. There are exhibits in the park
about Indians, gold mining and natural history of the area.

Site **27**   PASO
                                           PICACHO

Campsites, facilities: There are 85 campsites for tents or motorhomes. Piped water, fireplaces and picnic tables are provided, and flush toilets, showers and
dump station are available. The campgrounds, picnic areas and exhibits are
wheelchair accessible. A grocery store is nearby.
Reservations, fee: Phone MISTIX at (800)446-7275; $10 fee per night.
Who to contact: Phone Cuyamaca Rancho State Park at (619)765-0755.
Location: Drive 11 miles south of Julian on State Route 79.
Trip note: Open all year. Elevation 4900 feet. There are exhibits in the park
about Indians, gold mining and the natural history of the area.

Site **28**   AGUA DULCE
                                          GROUP CAMP

Campsites, facilities: There are seven group campsites for tents. Piped water,
fireplaces and picnic tables are provided, and vault toilets are available. A
grocery store is nearby.
Reservations, fee: Reservations requested, $40 fee per group per night.
Who to contact: Phone Cleveland National Forest Headquarters at (619)293-
5050.
Location: Drive three miles southwest of Mount Laguna on Sunrise Highway/
Laguna Mountain Road.
Trip note: Open from May to October. Elevation 5000 feet. It is in the Laguna
Recreation Area and near Little Laguna and Big Laguna Lakes. The Pacif-
ic Crest Trail passes nearby.

Site **29**   ALPINE
                                          RV RESORT

Campsites, facilities: There are 169 campsites for tents or motorhomes. Full or partial hookups are available. Piped water, fireplaces and picnic tables are provided, and flush toilets, showers and a laundromat are available.

Reservations, fee: Call for space available. $9 deposit required; $9 fee per night.

Who to contact: Phone park at (619)445-3162.

Location: In Alpine, drive to 5635 Willows Drive.

Trip note: Open all year. Elevation 2500 feet. It is about eight miles from Lake Jennings, a small fishing lake with boat ramp, boat rentals and supplies. The larger El Capitan Lake is about 20 miles away and provides similar services, with bass fishing very good in spring.

Site 30   BURNT
                        RANCHERIA   ▲

Campsites, facilities: There are 64 tent sites and 45 campsites for tents or motorhomes. Piped water, fireplaces and picnic tables are provided, and vault toilets and horseback riding facilities are available. A grocery store is nearby.

Reservations, fee: No reservations; $5 fee per night.

Who to contact: Phone Cleveland National Forest Headquarters at (619)293-5050.

Location: Drive 1/2 mile southeast of Mount Laguna off Laguna Mountain Road.

Trip note: Open from May to October. Elevation 6000 feet. It is in the Laguna Recreation Area near Little Laguna and Big Laguna Lakes, and is on the Pacific Crest Trail.

Site 31   WOODED HILL
                          GROUP   ▲

Campsites, facilities: There are 22 campsites for tents or motorhomes. Piped water, fireplaces and picnic tables are provided, and vault toilets are available. A grocery store is nearby.

Reservations, fee: Reservations requested; $85 group fee per night.

Who to contact: Phone Cleveland National Forest Headquarters at (619)293-5050.

Location: Drive one and a half miles southwest of Mount Laguna off Laguna Mountain Road.

Trip note: Open from May to October. Elevation 6000 feet. It is in the Laguna Recreation Area and near Little Laguna and Big Laguna Lakes. The Pacific Crest Trail passes nearby.

Site 32   BOW
                        WILLOW   ▲

Campsites, facilities: There are 14 campsites for tents or motorhomes. Piped water, fireplaces and picnic tables are provided. Pit toilets are available.

Reservations, fee: No reservations; $3 fee per night.
Who to contact: Phone Anza Borrego Desert State Park at (619)767-5311.
Location: Drive 12 miles southeast of Agua Caliente Springs off County Road S-2 at Bow Willow Canyon.
Trip note: Open all year. Elevation 950 feet. Located one mile south of camp is the Sin Nombre Canyon whose sediments contain remnants of dinosaurs. It is only accessible by four-wheel drive vehicles. Nearby is the Carrizo Badlands Overlook.

Site **33**   MOUNTAIN PALM SPRINGS
             PRIMITIVE CAMP AREA

Campsites, facilities: This is an open camping area in Anza-Borrego Desert State Park. It can be used for tents or motorhomes and pit toilets are available. Open fires are not allowed and there is no water, so bring your own.
Reservations, fee: No reservations, no fee.
Who to contact: Phone Anza-Borrego Desert State Park at (619)767-5311.
Location: Drive nine miles northwest of Ocotillo on County Road S-2 near Bow Willow Canyon.
Trip note: Open all year. Elevation 950 feet. The best time to visit the desert is in the spring. Two miles south of camp is the Sin Nombre Canyon whose sediments contain remnants of dinosaurs, but it is only accessible by four-wheel drive vehicles. Nearby is the Carrizo Badlands Overlook.

Site **34**   LARK
                   CANYON

Campsites, facilities: There are 20 campsites for tents or motorhomes. Piped water, fireplaces and picnic tables are provided, and pit toilets are available.
Reservations, fee: No reservations; $2 fee per night.
Who to contact: Phone Bureau of Land Management at (619)352-5842.
Location: Drive eight miles northeast of Boulevard off I-8 on McCain Valley Road.
Trip note: Open all year. Elevation 4000 feet. It is in the McCain Valley National Cooperative and Wildlife Management Area.

Site **35**   CIBBETS
                    FLAT

Campsites, facilities: There are 14 campsites for tents or motorhomes. Piped water, fireplaces and picnic tables are provided, and vault toilets are available.
Reservations, fee: No reservations; $5 fee per night.
Who to contact: Phone Cleveland National Forest Headquarters at (619)293-5050.
Location: Drive 12 miles south of Mount Laguna via Laguna Mountain and Kitchen Creek Roads.

Trip note: Open from May to October. Elevation 4000 feet. It is on Troy Canyon Creek less than a mile from the Pacific Crest Trail.

Site 36   COTTONWOOD

Campsites, facilities: There are 24 campsites for tents or motorhomes. Piped water, fireplaces and picnic tables are provided, and vault toilets are available.
Reservations, fee: No reservations; $2 fee per night.
Who to contact: Phone Bureau of Land Management at (619)352-5842.
Location: Drive 16 miles northwest of Boulevard off I-8 via McCain Valley Road.
Trip note: Open all year. Elevation 4000 feet. It is in the McCain Valley National Cooperative Land and Wildlife Management Area.

Site 37   LAKE MORENA
     TRAILER RESORT

Campsites, facilities: There are 42 motorhome spaces with full hookups. Picnic tables are provided, and flush toilets, showers, propane gas and a laundromat are available.
Reservations, fee: Phone Leisuretime Reservation Systems Inc. at (800)822-2267. $10 deposit; $10 fee per night.
Who to contact: Phone park at (619)478-5677.
Location: Drive five miles north of Campo via State Route 94 and County Road S-1 to 2330 Lake Morena Drive.
Trip note: Open all year. Elevation 3200 feet. Nearby Lake Morena is a large reservoir which allows fishing and swimming and has a paved ramp and rowboat rentals. A 19-pound, 2-ounce bass is the lake record.

Site 38   BOULDER
     OAKS

Campsites, facilities: There are six tent sites and 12 campsites for tents or motorhomes. Picnic tables, fireplaces and piped water are provided, and vault toilets are available. A grocery store is nearby.
Reservations, fee: No reservations; $5 fee per night.
Who to contact: Phone Cleveland National Forest Headquarters at (619)293-5050.
Location: Drive eight miles southeast of Pine Valley off I-8 on Buckman Springs Road.
Trip note: Open all year. Elevation 3500 feet. Located on the Pacific Crest Trail. Nearby Lake Morena is a large reservoir which allows fishing and swimming and has a paved ramp and rowboat rentals.

Site 39   LAKE MORENA COUNTY PARK

Campsites, facilities: There are 90 campsites for tents or motorhomes. Picnic tables, fireplaces and piped water are provided, and pit toilets and showers are available. A grocery store, boat ramp and rowboat rentals are nearby.

Reservations, fee: Call for space available. $9 deposit required; $7 fee per night.

Who to contact: Phone park at (619)565-3600 or (619)478)5473.

Location: Drive eight miles north of Campo via County Road S-1 and Lake Morena Drive.

Trip note: Open all year. Elevation 3150 feet. Located on Lake Morena, a large reservoir which allows fishing and swimming.

Site 40   POTRERO COUNTY PARK

Campsites, facilities: There are 32 campsites for tents or motorhomes. Picnic tables, fireplaces, electrical hookups and piped water are provided. Flush toilets, showers, a playground, dump station and grocery store are available.

Reservations, fee: Call for space available. $11 deposit required; $9 fee per night.

Who to contact: Phone County Parks Department at (619)565-3600.

Location: Drive two miles northeast of Potrero off State Route 94.

Trip note: Open all year. Elevation 2320 feet. Located near Tecate Mission Chapel and the Mexican Border.

Site 41   SANTEE LAKES REGIONAL PARK

Campsites, facilities: There are 50 tent sites, 50 campsites for tents or motorhomes with water and electricity, and 102 motorhome spaces with full hookups. Picnic tables and fireplaces are provided. Flush toilets, showers, dump station, boat rentals and playground are available. A grocery store, laundromat, snack bar, ice and propane gas are nearby.

Reservations, fee: Call for space available. $10 deposit required; $10 fee per night.

Who to contact: Phone park at (619)448-2482.

Location: Drive one and a half miles northwest of Santee via Carlton Hills Boulevard.

Trip note: Open all year. Elevation 400 feet. You may rent rowboats, pedal boats, canoes and fishing tackle at the lakes. It is close to Sea World, Seaport Village, the San Diego Zoo and Wild Animal Park.

Site **42**
LAKE JENNINGS
COUNTY PARK
▲

Campsites, facilities: There are 35 tent sites, 13 campsites for tents or motorhomes, and 63 motorhome spaces, most with full hookups. Picnic tables and fireplaces are provided. Flush toilets, showers, playground and dump station are available. A grocery store is nearby.

Reservations, fee: Call for space available. $11 deposit required; $9 fee per night.

Who to contact: Phone County Parks Department at (619)565-3600.

Location: Drive 20 miles northeast of San Diego via I-8 and Lake Jennings Park Road.

Trip note: Open all year. Elevation 800 feet. Lake Jennings is a small fishing lake. A boat ramp and rentals are available on the east shore of the lake.

Site **43**
DIXON LAKE
RECREATION AREA
▲

Campsites, facilities: There are 45 campsites for tents or motorhomes, some with full hookups. Picnic tables, fireplaces and piped water are provided. Flush toilets, showers, boat rentals, bait, ice, snack bar and playground are available.

Reservations, fee: Call for space available. $5 deposit required; $9 fee per night.

Who to contact: Phone park at (619)741-3328.

Location: Drive four miles northeast of Escondido to 1700 North La Honda Drive at Dixon Lake.

Trip note: Open all year. Elevation 1000 feet. This man-made reservoir is for fishing only and boating is restricted to rental boats.

Site **44**
DOS PICOS
COUNTY PARK
▲

Campsites, facilities: There are 14 tent sites and 50 motorhome spaces with full hookups. Picnic tables are provided, and flush toilets, showers, playground and dump station are available. A grocery store, laundromat and propane gas are nearby.

Reservations, fee: Call for space available. $11 deposit required; $9 fee per night.

Who to contact: Phone park at (619)565-3600.

Location: Drive five miles southwest of Ramona on State Route 67.

Trip note: Open all year. Elevation 1500 feet. San Vincente Lake is about 15 miles away. It is a fishing lake and is open Thursday through Sunday, from September through June. Boat rentals, a boat ramp, tackle, bait, ice and a snack bar are available at the lake. The Barona Ranch Indian Reservation and Barona Mission are also 15 miles from the park.

Site **45**   RANCHO
                               CORRIDO

Campsites, facilities: There are 120 campsites for tents or motorhomes. Picnic tables, fireplaces, electrical connections, piped water, and in some cases, sew-
   er connections are provided. Flush toilets, showers, dump station, play-
   ground, rifle range, propane gas and laundromat are available.
Reservations, fee: Phone Leisuretime Reservation Systems, Inc. at (800)822-
   2267. $16 deposit; $16 fee per night.
Who to contact: Phone park at (619)742-3755.
Location: Drive four miles southeast of Pala to 14715 Highway 76.
Trip note: Open all year. Elevation 750 feet. It is a short drive to Pala Indian
   Reservation and the Pala Mission.

Site **46**   WOODS VALLEY
                               KAMPGROUND

Campsites, facilities: There are 59 motorhome spaces and 30 campsites for tents
   or motorhomes. Picnic tables, fireplaces, electrical connections, piped water, and in some cases, electrical connections are provided. Flush toilets,
   showers, dump station and a playground are available. A grocery store,
   laundromat and propane gas are nearby.
Reservations, fee: Phone Leisuretime Reservation Systems, Inc. at (800)822-
   2267. $16 deposit; $16 fee per night.
Who to contact: Phone park at (619)749-2905.
Location: Drive two miles east of Valley Center to 15236 Woods Valley Road.
Trip note: Open all year. Located near San Diego Wild Animal Park and Zoo,
   Sea World, fishing lakes and golf courses.

Site **47**   PARADISE BY THE SEA
                               RV PARK

Campsites, facilities: There are 102 motorhome spaces with full hookups. Flush
   toilets, showers, cable TV hookups, swimming pool, jacuzzi, clubhouse,
   banquet room, laundry, RV supplies, telephone and mini-store are avail-
   able. Boat rentals can be found nearby.
Reservations, fee: Call for space available. $20 deposit required; $20 fee per
   night.
Who to contact: Phone park at (619)439-1376.
Location: Off I-5, take the Oceanside Boulevard exit west to 1537 South Hill
   Street in Oceanside.
Trip note: This campground is open all year with a level walk to beach. Disney-
   land, Knott's Berry Farm, San Diego Zoo, Scripps Clinic and the San
   Diego Wild Animal Park are about one hour's drive away.

Site **48**   GUAJOME
COUNTY PARK

Campsites, facilities: There are 21 motorhome spaces with full hookups. Picnic tables and fireplaces are provided. Flush toilets, showers, dump station, playground, and horseback riding facilities are available. A grocery store and propane gas are nearby.
Reservations, fee: Call for space available. $11 deposit required; $9 fee per night.
Who to contact: Phone County Parks Department at (619)565-3600.
Location: Off State Route 76 in Oceanside, drive to park via Guajome Lakes Road.
Trip note: This campground is open all year and is near the coast.

Site **49**   SOUTH CARLSBAD
STATE BEACH

Campsites, facilities: There are 225 campsites for tents or motorhomes. Picnic tables, fireplaces and piped water are provided. Flush toilets, showers and dump station are available. A grocery store and laundromat are nearby.
Reservations, fee: Phone MISTIX at (800)446-7275; $8 fee per night.
Who to contact: Phone the park at (619)438-3143.
Location: Drive five miles south of Carlsbad via County Road S-21 or I-5.
Trip note: This campground is open all year and is on the beach.

Site **50**   CASITAS POQUITAS
RV PARK

Campsites, facilities: There are 140 motorhome spaces with full hookups. Flush toilets, showers, playground, laundry, propane gas and groceries are available.
Reservations, fee: Call for space available. $16 deposit required; $16 fee per night.
Who to contact: Phone park at (619)722-4404.
Location: In Oceanside, drive to 1510 South Hill Street.
Trip note: This campground is open all year and is a short distance from the beach.

Site **51**   SURF AND TURF
TRAVEL TRAILER PARK

Campsites, facilities: There are 234 motorhome spaces with full hookups. Flush toilets, showers, playground, dump station, laundry, propane gas and groceries are available.
Reservations, fee: Call for space available. $25 deposit required; $25 fee per night.

Who to contact: Phone park at (619)755-5400.

Location: In Del Mar, drive to 15555 Turf Road.

Trip note: This campground is open all year and is on the beach. Located a short walk from Del Mar Race Track, also known as the track that Bing Crosby built. The Southern California Expo is held at the track in early July.

Site **52**   SAN ELIJO
STATE BEACH

Campsites, facilities: There are 171 campsites for tents or motorhomes. Picnic tables, fireplaces and piped water are provided. Flush toilets, showers, and a dump station are available. A grocery store, laundromat and propane gas are nearby. The campground and the store are wheelchair accessible.

Reservations, fee: Phone MISTIX at (800)446-7275, $10 fee per night.

Who to contact: Phone park at (619)753-5091.

Location: Drive 1/2 mile northwest of Cardiff by the Sea via County Road S-21.

Trip note: This campground is open all year and is on the beach.

Site **53**   CAMPLAND
ON THE BAY

Campsites, facilities: There are 705 tent and motorhome spaces with full or partial hookups. Flush toilets, showers, picnic tables, fire rings, swimming pools, jacuzzi, recreation hall, playground, dump station, laundry, propane gas, boat ramp, boat docks, boat and bike rentals, and groceries are available.

Reservations, fee: Phone Leisuretime Reservation Systems, Inc. at (800)822-2267. $35 deposit; $35 fee per night.

Who to contact: Phone park at (619)274-0601.

Location: Off I-5 southbound in San Diego, take the Balboa-Garnet exit to Olney Avenue, turn left and drive to Pacific Beach Drive, then turn left to 2211 Pacific Beach Drive.

Trip note: Open all year. Located on Mission Bay near the ocean where sailing, swimming and fishing are available.

Site **54**   SANTE FE
TRAVEL TRAILER PARK

Campsites, facilities: There are 128 motorhome spaces with full hookups. Flush toilets, showers, playground, swimming pool, dump station, laundry, propane gas and groceries are available.

Reservations, fee: Call for space available. $25 deposit required; $25 fee per night.

Who to contact: Phone park at (619)272-4051.

Location: Off I-5 southbound in San Diego, take the Balboa-Garnet exit, then turn left and drive to Santa Fe Street, make left and drive to 5707 Santa Fe Street.

Trip note: This campground is open all year and is minutes from San Diego Zoo, Sea World, golf courses, beaches, sport fishing and Tijuana.

Site 55   OTAY LAKE
COUNTY PARK

Campsites, facilities: There are 16 tent sites, eight campsites for tents or motorhomes, and 24 motorhome spaces with full hookups. Picnic tables and fireplaces are provided and flush toilets, showers, and a playground are available.

Reservations, fee: Call for space available. $11 deposit required; $9 fee per night.

Who to contact: Phone County Parks Department at (619)565-3600.

Location: Drive 12 miles southeast of Chula Vista via Telegraph Canyon Road.

Trip note: Open all year. Located at the southern tip of Lower Otay Lake. A paved boat ramp, boat rentals, tackle, snack bar and groceries are available on the west shore of the lake. The lake and facilities are open Wednesdays, Saturdays and Sundays, February through mid-October. Known for giant black bass.

Site 56   DEANZA HARBOR
RESORT

Campsites, facilities: There are 250 motorhome spaces with full hookups. Flush toilets, showers, playground, dump station, laundry, swimming pool, propane gas and groceries are available.

Reservations, fee: Call for space available. $32 deposit required; $32 fee per night.

Who to contact: Phone park at (619)273-3211.

Location: From I-5 southbound, take the Balboa-Garnet exit to Mission Bay Drive, turn left and drive to North Mission Bay Drive, turn right and drive to 2727 De Anza Road.

Trip note: This campground is open all year and is on a small peninsula that is surrounded on three sides by Mission Bay. Sea World, the San Diego Zoo, beaches and golf courses are nearby.

Site 57   SAN DIEGO
METROPOLITAN KOA

Campsites, facilities: There are 64 tent sites and 206 motorhome spaces with full hookups. Flush toilets, showers, playground, dump station, laundry, swimming pool, propane gas and groceries are available.

Reservations, fee: Phone Leisuretime Reservation Systems, Inc. at (800)822-2267. $20 deposit; $20 fee per night.

Who to contact: Phone park at (619)427-3601.

Location: In Chula Vista, drive to 111 North Second Street.

Trip note: This campground is open all year and is centrally located between Mexico and San Diego, just minutes away from the San Diego attractions and golf courses.

| Site 58 | CHULA VISTA RV PARK | |

Campsites, facilities: There are 237 motorhome spaces with full hookups. Flush toilets, showers, playground, heated pool and spa, game room, marina, fishing pier, free boat launch, free transportation to San Diego Trolley, dump station, laundry, propane gas and groceries are available.

Reservations, fee: Call for space available. $28 deposit required; $28 fee per night.

Who to contact: Phone park at (619)422-0111.

Location: In Chula Vista, drive to 460 Sandpiper Way.

Trip note: This park is open all year and is centrally located between Mexico and San Diego, just minutes away from the San Diego attractions and golf courses.

| Site 59 | INTERNATIONAL MOTOR INN RV PARK | |

Campsites, facilities: There are 42 motorhome spaces with full hookups. Flush toilets, showers, playground, swimming pool, dump station, laundry, propane gas and groceries are available.

Reservations, fee: Call for space available. $16 deposit required; $16 fee per night.

Who to contact: Phone park at (619)428-4486.

Location: Drive six miles southeast of Imperial Beach off I-5 to 190 East Calle Primero.

Trip note: This park is open all year and is near the beach, San Diego attractions and Mexico.

| Site 60 | BORDER GATE RV PARK | |

Campsites, facilities: There are 179 motorhome spaces with full hookups and individual lawns and patios. Flush toilets, showers, playground, heated pool, recreation hall, dump station, laundry, propane gas and groceries are available.

Reservations, fee: Call for space available. $20 deposit required; $20 fee per night.

Who to contact: Phone park at (619)428-4411.

Location: In San Ysidro, drive to 4141 San Ysidro Boulevard.

Trip note: This campground is open all year and is less than two miles from the Mexican border. There is a regular Mexicoach bus service from the park to downtown Tijuana and back.

Site **61**
OAK KNOLL
CAMPGROUND
▲

Campsites, facilities: There are 55 sites for tents or motorhomes with full or partial hookups. Flush toilets, showers, playground, solar heated pool, clubhouse, dump station, laundry, propane gas and groceries are available.

Reservations, fee: Call ahead for available space and fee.

Who to contact: Phone park at (619)742-3437.

Location: Drive to intersection of State Route 76 and Palomar Mountain Road.

Trip note: Open all year. Elevation 3000 feet. It is situated in the foothills among giant old California Oaks, and a short distance from the Palomar Observatory.

Site **62**
LAKE HENSHAW RESORT
RV PARK AND CAMPGROUND
▲

Campsites, facilities: There are 164 campsites for tents or motorhomes and 90 motorhome spaces with full hookups. Flush toilets, showers, swimming and therapy pools, clubhouse, playground, dump station, laundry, propane gas, boat and motor rentals, boat launch, restaurant and groceries are available. A golf course and horseback riding facilities are nearby.

Reservations, fee: No reservations; $9.50 fee per night.

Who to contact: Phone (619)782-3487 or (619)782-3501.

Location: Drive 13 miles northwest of San Ysabel on State Route 76.

Trip note: Open all year. Elevation 2700 feet. Lake Henshaw is stocked annually with 10,000 pounds of channel catfish and rainbow trout.

Site **63**
BEACH KAMPER
INN
▲

Campsites, facilities: There are 68 campsites for tents or motorhomes. Picnic tables, fireplaces, electrical connections and piped water are provided. Flush toilets, showers, dump station and a laundromat are available. A grocery store is nearby.

Reservations, fee: Call ahead for available space and fee.

Who to contact: Phone park at (619)722-5900.

Location: Off I-5 in Oceanside, take the Hill or Mission exit and drive on Sixth Street to the beach.

Trip note: This campground is open all year and is close to the beach. The attractions in San Diego are one hour's drive from the park.

Site **64**   SUNRISE TERRACE
RV PARK

Campsites, facilities: There are 30 motorhome spaces with full hookups. Flush
toilets, showers, playground, dump station, laundry, phone, cable, and propane gas are available. There is a grocery store nearby.
Reservations, fee: Call ahead for space and fee.
Who to contact: Phone park at (619)724-6654.
Location: Off I-15, take the Gopher Canyon exit to East Vista Way, turn left and
drive to Taylor Street, turn right and drive to 817 Taylor Street. Off I-5,
take State Route 76 to East Vista Way, turn right and drive to Taylor Street,
turn right and drive to 817 Taylor Street.
Trip note: This rustic county park is minutes away from the Wild Animal Park,
golf courses, tennis courts and the antique steam and gas museum.

Site **65**   OAK CREST
RV PARK

Campsites, facilities: There are 20 tent sites and 84 motorhome spaces with full
hookups, including phone. Flush toilets, showers, recreation room, dump
station, post office, and groceries are available. Riding stables and swimming are nearby.
Reservations, fee: Call ahead for space available and fee.
Who to contact: Phone park at (619)473-9040.
Location: Off I-8 (40 miles east of San Diego) take the State Route 79 exit and go
north past the turn offs for Descenso and Lake Cuyamaca, then turn east
on Olde Highway 80 and drive four miles to the park at 27521 Olde Highway 80.
Trip note: This campground is in a rustic area that is surrounded by National
Forest land. The drinking water is from a pure deep well.

Site **66**   BARRETT LAKE
TRAILER PARK

Campsites, facilities: There are 104 motorhome spaces with full hookups. Flush
toilets, showers, picnic tables, dump station, laundry, and swimming pool
are available.
Reservations, fee: Call ahead for space available and fee.
Who to contact: Phone park at (619)468-3332.
Location: Drive to the junction of State Route 94 and Barrett Lake Road, campground is at 1250 Barrett Lake Road.
Trip note: This park is a short distance from Barrett Lake and the Mexican
border.

Site **67**   SUMMIT RIDGE RESORT

Campsites, facilities: There are 150 motorhome spaces with full hookups including phone. Flush toilets, showers, swimming pool, jacuzzi, clubhouse, shade trees, and laundry are available. Propane gas and groceries are nearby.

Reservations, fee: Call ahead for space and fee.

Who to contact: Phone park at (619)264-9012.

Location: In San Diego off I-5 or I-805, drive east on Imperial Avenue to 63rd Street, then turn right and drive 1/4 mile to park.

Trip note: This 150 acre park is close to all San Diego attractions, including Sea World, San Diego Zoo, Wild Animal Park and the beach.

Site **68**   BERNARDO SHORES

Campsites, facilities: There are 120 motorhome spaces with full hookups, individual lawns and concrete patios. Flush toilets, showers, laundry, swimming pool and propane gas are available. A grocery store is nearby.

Reservations, fee: Call ahead for space available and fee.

Who to contact: Phone park at (619)429-9000.

Location: In Imperial Beach, drive south on I-5, west on Palm Avenue, then north on State Route 75 to 500 Highway 75.

Trip note: This adults-only park is near the San Diego Zoo, Wild Animal Park, beaches and Tijuana.

Site **69**   RANCHO LOS COCHES RV PARK

Campsites, facilities: There are 20 tent sites and 60 motorhome spaces with full hookups. Flush toilets, showers, dump station, laundry, propane gas and groceries are available. A grocery store is nearby.

Reservations, fee: Call ahead for space available and fee.

Who to contact: Phone park at (619)443-2025.

Location: Drive east on I-8 to Los Coches exit, then north to Olde 80, and east to park entrance at 13468 Olde Highway 80.

Trip note: This adult RV park is rural but close to all the conveniences. Fishing is available at nearby Lake Jennings. San Diego and its attractions are 20 miles away.

Site **70**   DIAMOND JACKS RV RANCH

Campsites, facilities: There are 35 tent sites and 35 motorhome spaces with full or partial hookups. Flush toilets, showers, recreation room, outdoor square dance ring, volleyball, badminton, shooting range, swimming pool and dump station are available. Propane gas and groceries are nearby.

Reservations, fee: Call ahead for space available and fee.

Who to contact: Phone park at (619)463-8938.

Location: In Jamul off State Route 94, drive east on Lyons Valley Road to 15724 Lyons Valley Road.

Trip note: This campground is in the country and there are deer, quail and rabbits on the ranch.

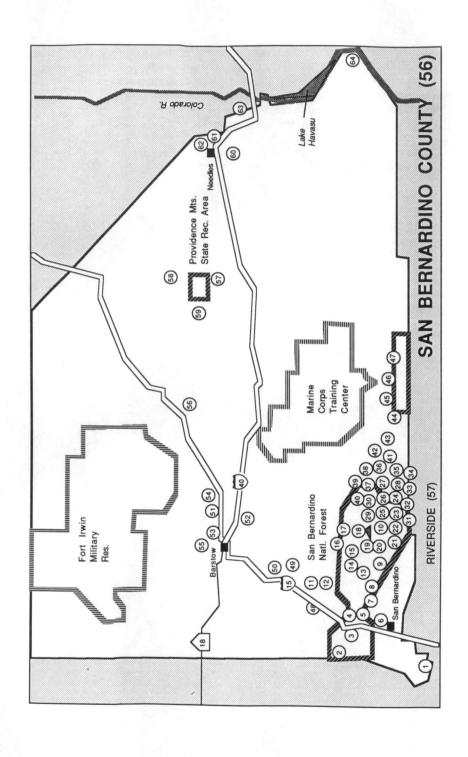

SAN BERNARDINO COUNTY
♦

Site 1   PRADO REGIONAL PARK   ◬

Campsites, facilities: There are 50 campsites for tents or motorhomes to 18 feet long. Non-piped water, flush toilets, showers, a sanitary dump station, a playground, picnic tables and fireplaces are provided. A grocery store, propane gas and a laundromat are nearby.
Reservations, fee: Reservations not required. $10 use fee; $1 for pets.
Who to contact: This is a county park. For information call (714)597-4260.
Location: Drive seven miles south of Ontario off Highway 83.
Trip note: Open all year. Elevation 550 feet. Horseback riding.

Site 2   MANKER FLATS   ◬

Campsites, facilities: There are 22 campsites for tents or motorhomes to 16 feet long. Piped water, flush toilets, picnic tables and fireplaces are provided.
Reservations, fee: Reservations not required; $5 use fee.
Who to contact: Phone Angeles National Forest Headquarters at (818)577-0050.
Location: Drive 15 miles north of Ontario via Highway 83 and Mt. Baldy Road.
Trip note: Open from April through November. Elevation 6300 feet. Good fishing in San Antonio Creek. Camp is between Cucamonga and Sheep Mountain Wilderness Areas.

Site 3   APPLE WHITE   ◬

Campsites, facilities: There are four sites for tents and 15 campsites for tents or motorhomes to 32 feet long. Piped water, flush toilets, picnic tables and fireplaces are provided. A grocery store is nearby.
Reservations, fee: Reservations not required; $6 use fee.
Who to contact: Phone San Bernardino National Forest Headquarters at (714)383-5588.
Location: Drive 1/2 mile east of Lytle Creek.
Trip note: Open all year. Elevation 3300 feet. Brushy area with fishing and

swimming nearby on Lytle Creek.

Site **4**   MESA
                    CAMPGROUND

Campsites, facilities: There are 136 campsites for tents or motorhomes to 34 feet
   long. Piped water, flush toilets, showers, a sanitary dump station, picnic tables and fireplaces are provided. Wheelchair access to campground facilities, picnic areas, fishing, hiking paths, exhibits, swimming areas, boating,
   food service and grocery store.
Reservations, fee: Make reservations through MISTIX by phoning (800)446-7275
   ($3.75 fee). $6 camp use fee; $1 for pets.
Who to contact: Phone Silverwood Lake State Recreation Area at (619)389-2303.
Location: Drive 10 miles northwest of Crestline off Highway 138.
Trip note: Open all year. Elevation 3500 feet. Enjoy lake side activities, hike the
   nature trail, or go riding on the bicycle trail.

Site **5**   WEST FORK
                    GROUP CAMPS

Campsites, facilities: There are group camps here with piped water, flush toilets,
   showers, a sanitary dump station, picnic tables and fireplaces provided. Picnic areas, fishing, hiking, swimming, boating, food service and a grocery
   store are available.
Reservations, fee: Make reservations through MISTIX by phoning (800)446-7275
   ($3.75 fee). $100 group camp use fee; $1 for pets.
Who to contact: Phone Silverwood Lake State Recreation Area at (619)389-2303.
Location: Drive 10 miles northwest of Crestline off Highway 138.
Trip note: Open from March through October. Elevation 3500 feet. Numerous
   lake side activities available, hike the nature trail, or go riding on the bicycle trail.

Site **6**   CABLE CANYON
                    KOA

Campsites, facilities: There are 136 tent and motorhome sites with full hookups.
   Piped water, flush toilets, showers and picnic tables are provided. A grocery
   store, propane gas and a laundromat are nearby.
Reservations, fee: Reservation with deposit of $14.50; $14.50 use fee.
Who to contact: Call (714)887-4098.
Location: Drive 16 miles north of San Bernardino off Highway 215. Camp locat-
   ed at 1707 Cable Canyon Road.
Trip note: Open all year. Elevation 2200 feet. OK layover on trip into nearby San
   Bernardino National Forest.

Site **7**
CRESTLINE MOUNTAIN PARK RESORT

Campsites, facilities: There are 10 tent sites and 50 motorhome spaces with full or partial hookups. Piped water, flush toilets, showers, picnic tables, fireplaces, swimming pool, recreation lodge, arcade, playground snack bar, laundromat, grocery store, propane gas, horseshoes, volley ball court, and ice are available on the premises. Within two miles are movies, shops, a waterslide, and boating and fishing facilities.

Reservations, fee: Call ahead for this information.

Who to contact: Call Crestline Mountain Park Resort at (714)338-2388.

Location: From Highway 138, drive two miles northwest of Crestline via Valley of Enchantment and the left fork of Waters Drive.

Trip note: Open all year. Nice motorhome park set near Silverwood Lake.

Site **8**
CAMP SWITZERLAND

Campsites, facilities: There are 10 campsites for tents and 30 spaces for motorhomes with full hookups. Piped water, flush toilets, showers and picnic tables are provided. Propane gas is available nearby.

Reservations, fee: Reservation with deposit of $13. $13 use fee; $1 for pets.

Who to contact: Call Camp Switzerland at (714)338-2731.

Location: Drive two miles northeast of Crestline via Highway 138 and Lake Drive at Lake Gregory.

Trip note: Open all year. Elevation 4500 feet. Swimming and fishing on Lake Gregory.

Site **9**
CANYON PARK

Campsites, facilities: There are 30 campsites for tents and 24 motorhome sites with full or partial hookups. Piped water, flush toilets, showers, picnic tables and fireplaces are provided. Horses can be boarded here.

Reservations, fee: Call ahead for this information.

Who to contact: Call (714)867-2090.

Location: Drive 12 miles northeast of San Bernardino via Highway 18, then one half mile east of the junction of Highways 18 and 330. Park is located in Running Springs at 32455 Highway 18.

Trip note: A quiet park with dirt roads. Within 10 miles of Big Bear and Lake Arrowhead.

Site **10**   HOLLOWAY'S MARINA
              AND RV PARK

Campsites, facilities: There are 66 motorhome spaces with full hookups. Piped
    water, flush toilets, showers, sanitary dump station, cable TV, snack shop,
    grocery store, ice, propane gas, a laundromat, a playground, picnic tables,
    fireplaces and a full marina with boat rentals are on the premises.
Reservations, fee: Call ahead for this information.
Who to contact: Call Holloway's Marina and RV Park at (714)866-5706.
Location: Park is at Big Bear Lake, 35 miles west of San Bernardino via Highway
    18.
Trip note: Enjoy Big Bear Lake. Good trout fishing in spring.

Site **11**   HISPERIA
              LAKES

Campsites, facilities: There are 45 campsites for tents or motorhomes. Piped wa-
    ter, vault toilets, showers, picnic tables and fireplaces are provided. A gro-
    cery store, propane gas and a laundromat are nearby.
Reservations, fee: Reservation with deposit of $8; $8 use fee.
Who to contact: Call (619)244-5951.
Location: Drive four miles southeast of Victorville off Highway 15.
Trip note: Open all year. Elevation 3250 feet. About 25 miles south to Silver-
    wood Lake.

Site **12**   MOJAVE RIVER
              FORKS

Campsites, facilities: There are 40 tent sites, 25 motorhome spaces with full hoo-
    kups, and 25 campsites for tents or motorhomes. Piped water, flush toilets,
    showers, a sanitary dump station, a playground, picnic tables and fireplaces
    are provided. A grocery store and a laundromat are nearby.
Reservations, fee: Reservations accepted; $10 use fee.
Who to contact: Call (619)389-2322.
Location: Drive eight miles southeast of Hesperia.
Trip note: Open all year. Elevation 3000 feet. About 15 minutes from Silver-
    wood Lake.

Site **13**   DOGWOOD

Campsites, facilities: There are 94 campsites for tents or motorhomes to 22 feet
    long. Piped water, flush toilets, a sanitary dump station, picnic tables and
    fireplaces are provided. A grocery store and a laundromat are nearby.
Reservations, fee: Make reservations through Ticketron ($2.25 fee) outlets in

Sears stores, or call (213)216-6666 for other outlet locations. $8 camp use fee.

Who to contact: Phone San Bernardino National Forest Headquarters at (714)383-5588.

Location: Drive three miles southwest of Lake Arrowhead off Highway 18.

Trip note: Open from May through October. Elevation 5600 feet. Set near Lake Arrowhead. Map of San Bernardino National Forest details back country.

Site **14** NORTH SHORE

Campsites, facilities: There are 24 campsites for tents and two sites for tents or motorhomes to 16 feet long. Piped water, flush toilets, picnic tables and fireplaces are provided. A grocery store and a laundromat are nearby.

Reservations, fee: Reservations not required; $6 use fee.

Who to contact: Call San Bernardino National Forest Headquarters at (714)383-5588.

Location: Drive three miles northeast of Lake Arrowhead off Highway 173.

Trip note: Open from May through September. Elevation 5300 feet. Camp is on Lake Arrowhead, where you can go swimming and fishing. Trail from camp leads to other trails in the backcountry to the east.

Site **15** TENT PEG GROUP CAMP

Campsites, facilities: There is one group camp that will accommodate 25 people and five cars. No water, but vault toilets, picnic tables and fireplaces are provided. A grocery store and a laundromat are nearby.

Reservations, fee: Reservations requested; $15 camp use fee.

Who to contact: Call San Bernardino National Forest District Office at (714)337-2444.

Location: Drive 10.5 miles north of Running Springs off Highway 18 via Crab Flat Road.

Trip note: Open from May through October. Elevation 5400 feet. Fishing in nearby Holcomb Creek. The Pacific Crest National Scenic Trail passes one mile from camp.

Site **16** HORSE SPRINGS

Campsites, facilities: There are 17 campsites for tents. No water, but vault toilets, picnic tables and fireplaces are provided.

Reservations, fee: No reservations, no fee.

Who to contact: Phone San Bernardino National Forest Headquarters at (714)383-5588.

Location: Drive 10 miles northwest of Fawnskin off Highway 38.
Trip note: Open from May through October. Elevation 5800 feet. Forest Service map shows some creeks in the area, but camp is at the origin of them.

Site **17**
BIG PINE
FLATS
▲

Campsites, facilities: There are 15 sites for tents and four campsites for tents or motorhomes to 22 feet long. Piped water, vault toilets, picnic tables and fireplaces are provided.
Reservations, fee: No reservations, no fee.
Who to contact: Phone San Bernardino National Forest Headquarters at (714)383-5588.
Location: Drive eight miles northwest of Fawnskin off Highway 38.
Trip note: Open from May through October. Elevation 6900 feet. Fairly remote, a good spot. Big Bear Lake not too far from the south.

Site **18**
IRONWOOD
GROUP CAMP
▲

Campsites, facilities: There is one group camp that can accommodate up to 25 people and five cars (no trailers or motorhomes). No water, but vault toilets, picnic tables and fireplaces are provided.
Reservations, fee: Reservation requested; $15 group use fee.
Who to contact: Phone San Bernardino National Forest District Office at (714)866-3437.
Location: Drive six and a half miles northwest of Fawnskin off Highway 38.
Trip note: Open from June through September. Elevation 6700 feet. The Pacific Crest National Scenic Trail is nearby.

Site **19**
GREEN
VALLEY
▲

Campsites, facilities: There are 27 campsites for tents or motorhomes to 22 feet long. Piped water, flush toilets, picnic tables and fireplaces are provided. A grocery store and a laundromat are nearby.
Reservations, fee: Reservations not required; $6 use fee.
Who to contact: Phone San Bernardino National Forest Headquarters at (714)383-5588.
Location: Drive seven miles northeast of Running Springs off Highway 18 via Green Valley Road.
Trip note: Open from May through October. Elevation 7000 feet. Horseback riding available. Good fishing or swimming in Green Valley Lake.

| Site **20** | SHADY COVE GROUP CAMP | |

Campsites, facilities: There is one camp that will accommodate up to 75 people and 15 cars (no trailer or motorhomes). Piped water, vault toilets, picnic tables and fireplaces are provided.

Reservations, fee: Reservations requested; $25 group use fee.

Who to contact: Phone San Bernardino National Forest District Office at (714)337-2444.

Location: Drive five and a half miles east of Running Springs off Highway 18 via Keller Peak Road.

Trip note: Open from May through September. Elevation 7500 feet. A short loop trail through the National Children's Forest is nearby.

| Site **21** | BLUFF MESA GROUP CAMP | |

Campsites, facilities: There is one group camp that will accommodate up to 40 people and 18 cars (no trailers or motorhomes). No water, but vault toilets, picnic tables, and fireplaces are provided. A grocery store and a laundromat are nearby.

Reservations, fee: Reservations requested; $15 group use fee.

Who to contact: Phone San Bernardino National Forest District Office at (714)866-3437.

Location: Drive six miles southwest of Big Bear Lake off Highway 18 via Mill Creek Road.

Trip note: Open from June through September. Elevation 7600 feet. Camp is at the trailhead of a National Recreation Trail.

| Site **22** | BOULDER GROUP CAMP | |

Campsites, facilities: There is one group camp that will accommodate up to 40 people and eight cars (limited use of trailers and motorhomes). No water, but vault toilets, picnic tables and fireplaces are provided. A grocery store and a laundromat are nearby.

Reservations, fee: Reservation requested; $15 group use fee.

Who to contact: Phone San Bernardino National Forest District Office at (714)866-3437.

Location: Drive four miles southwest of Big Bear Lake off Highway 18 via Mill Creek Road.

Trip note: Open from June through September. Elevation 7500 feet. Camp is near Metcalf Creek and Cedar Lake, and about one and a half miles from Big Bear Lake.

Site 23   COLDBROOK   ▲

Campsites, facilities: There are 32 sites for tents, and four campsites for tents or
    motorhomes to 16 feet long. Piped water, vault toilets, picnic tables and
    fireplaces are provided. A grocery store and a laundromat are nearby.
Reservations, fee: Reservations not required; $5 use fee.
Who to contact: Phone San Bernardino National Forest Headquarters at
    (714)383-5588.
Location: Drive two miles southwest of Big Bear Lake off Highway 18 via Tulip
    Lane.
Trip note: Open from May through November. Elevation 6800 feet. Camp is on
    Metcalf Creek near Big Bear Lake.

Site 24   GRAY'S PEAK   ▲
                          GROUP CAMP

Campsites, facilities: There is one group camp that will accommodate up to 40
    people and eight cars (limited use of trailers and motorhomes). No water,
    but vault toilets, picnic tables and fireplaces are provided. A grocery store
    and a laundromat are nearby.
Reservations, fee: Reservation requested; $15 group use fee.
Who to contact: Phone San Bernardino National Forest District Office at
    (714)866-3437.
Location: Drive two miles northwest of Fawnskin off Highway 38.
Trip note: Open from June through September. Elevation 7200 feet. Camp is
    about two miles from Big Bear Lake.

Site 25   HANNA   ▲
                            FLATS

Campsites, facilities: There are 69 sites for tents and 19 campsites for tents or
    motorhomes to 16 feet long. Piped water, vault toilets, picnic tables and
    fireplaces are provided. A grocery store and a laundromat are nearby.
Reservations, fee: Reservations not required; $6 use fee.
Who to contact: Phone San Bernardino National Headquarters at (714)383-5588.
Location: Drive three and a half miles northwest of Fawnskin off Highway 38.
Trip note: Open from May through September. Elevation 7000 feet. The Camp
    is two and a half miles northwest of Big Bear Lake. The Pacific Crest Na-
    tional Scenic Trail passes by one mile north.

Site 26   GROUT   ▲
                            BAY

Campsites, facilities: There are 21 sites for tents and two campsites for tents or motorhomes to 16 feet long. Piped water, flush toilets, picnic tables and fireplaces are provided. A grocery store and a laundromat are nearby.

Reservations, fee: Reservations not required; $5 use fee.

Who to contact: Phone San Bernardino National Forest Headquarters at (714)383-5588.

Location: Drive one half mile south of Fawnskin on Highway 38.

Trip note: Open from May through November. Elevation 6800 feet. Camp is set on shore of Big Bear Lake.

Site **27**
HOLCOMB
VALLEY
▲

Campsites, facilities: There are 19 campsites for tents or motorhomes to 16 feet long. No water, but vault toilets, picnic tables and fireplaces are provided.

Reservations, fee: No reservations, no fee.

Who to contact: Phone San Bernardino National Forest Headquarters at (714)383-5588.

Location: Drive five miles northwest of Big Bear City off Highway 38.

Trip note: Open from May through September. Elevation 7400 feet. Camp is near the Holcomb Valley Historic Area, and two miles north of the Pacific Crest National Scenic Trail.

Site **28**
TANGLEWOOD
GROUP CAMP
▲

Campsites, facilities: There is one group camp that will accommodate up to 40 people and eight cars (limited use of trailers or motorhomes). No water, but vault toilets, picnic tables and fireplaces are provided.

Reservations, fee: Reservation requested; $15 group use fee.

Who to contact: Phone San Bernardino National Forest District Office at (714)866-3437.

Location: Drive eight miles northwest of Big Bear City off Highway 18.

Trip note: Open from June through September. Elevation 7700 feet. Camp is on the Pacific Crest National Scenic Trail, three miles northeast of Big Bear Lake.

Site **29**
BUTTERCUP
GROUP CAMP
▲

Campsites, facilities: There is one group camp that will accommodate up to 40 people and eight cars (limited use of trailers or motorhomes). Piped water, vault toilets, picnic tables and fireplaces are provided. A grocery store and a laundromat are nearby.

Reservations, fee: Reservation requested; $15 group use fee.

Who to contact: Phone San Bernardino National Forest Headquarters at

(714)383-5588.

Location: From Highway 18, drive two and a half miles southeast of Big Bear Lake via Summit Boulevard and Bristlecone Drive.

Trip note: Open from June through September. Elevation 7000 feet. Camp is very close to Big Bear Village.

Site **30**   PINEKNOT

Campsites, facilities: There are 49 sites for tents and three campsites for tents or motorhomes to 16 feet long. Piped water, flush toilets, picnic tables, and fireplaces are provided. A grocery store and a laundromat are nearby.

Reservations, fee: Reservations not required; $6 use fee.

Who to contact: Phone San Bernardino National Forest Headquarters at (714)383-5588.

Location: From Highway 18, drive two miles southeast of Big Bear Lake via Summit Boulevard and Bristlecone Drive.

Trip note: Open from May through October. Elevation 7000 feet. Camp is very close to Big Bear Lake Village.

Site **31**   DEER
                                          GROUP CAMP

Campsites, facilities: There is one group camp that will accommodate up to 40 people and eight cars (limited use of trailers and motorhomes). No water, but vault toilets, picnic tables and fireplaces are provided.

Reservations, fee: Reservation requested; $15 group use fee.

Who to contact: Phone San Bernardino National Forest District Office at (714)866-3437.

Location: From Highway 18, drive 10 miles southwest of Big Bear Lake via Mill Creek Road.

Trip note: Open from June through September. Elevation 7600 feet. Camp is on a National Recreation Trail and is two miles from Big Bear Lake.

Site **32**   BARTON
                                          FLATS

Campsites, facilities: There are 23 sites for tents, 24 motorhome spaces, and two campsites for tents or motorhomes to 22 feet long. Piped water, vault toilets, picnic tables and fireplaces are provided.

Reservations, fee: Reservations not required; $5 use fee.

Who to contact: Phone San Bernardino National Forest Headquarters at (714)383-5588.

Location: Drive 26.5 miles northeast of Redlands off Highway 38.

Trip note: Open from May through October. Elevation 6300 feet. Camp is near

Barton Creek and Jenks Lake. A trail from camp leads into the San Gorgonio Wilderness.

Site 33   COUNCIL
GROUP CAMP   ▲

Campsites, facilities: There is one group camp that will accommodate up to 50 people and 10 cars (no trailers or motorhomes). Piped water, vault toilets, picnic tables and fireplaces are provided.

Reservations, fee: Reservation requested; $25 group use fee.

Who to contact: Phone San Bernardino National Forest District Office at (714)794-1123.

Trip note: Open from May through November. Elevation 6600 feet. Camp is near Barton Creek and Jenks Lake. A trail from camp leads into the San Gorgonio Wilderness.

Site 34   SAN GORGONIO   ▲

Campsites, facilities: There are 37 tent sites, 23 motorhome spaces and two campsites for tents or motorhomes to 24 feet long. Piped water, vault toilets, picnic tables and fireplaces are provided.

Reservations, fee: Make reservations through Ticketron or outlets in Sears stores. Call (213)216-6666 for other outlet locations ($2.25 fee). $5 camp use fee.

Who to contact: Phone San Bernardino National Forest Headquarters at (714)383-5588.

Location: Drive 28 miles northeast of Redlands off Highway 38.

Trip note: Open from May through September. Elevation 6500 feet. Camp is near Barton Creek and Jenks Lake. A trail from camp leads into the San Gorgonio Wilderness.

Site 35   SOUTH
FORK   ▲

Campsites, facilities: There are 24 campsites for tents or motorhomes to 22 feet long. Piped water, vault toilets, picnic tables and fireplaces are provided.

Reservations, fee: Reservations not required; $6 use fee.

Who to contact: Phone San Bernardino National Forest Headquarters at (714)383-5588.

Location: Drive 26 miles south of Big Bear City on Highway 38.

Trip note: Open from May through September. Elevation 6400 feet. Camp is on Lost Creek near the Santa Ana River and a short distance from a trail leading into the San Gorgonio Wilderness.

Site **36**   LOBO
                       GROUP CAMP

Campsites, facilities: There are 15 sites which will accommodate up to 75 people
   and 15 cars (limited use of trailers and motorhomes). Piped water, vault toilets, picnic tables and fireplaces are provided.
Reservations, fee: Reservation requested; $25 group fee.
Who to contact: Phone San Bernardino National Forest District Office at
   (714)794-1123.
Location: Drive 28 miles south of Big Bear City off Highway 38.
Trip note: Open from May through September. Elevation 6500 feet. Camp is on
   the Santa Ana River.

Site **37**   OSO
                       GROUP CAMP

Campsites, facilities: There are 20 campsites for tents or motorhomes to 22 feet
   long. Piped water, flush toilets, picnic tables and fireplaces are provided.
Reservations, fee: Reservations required; $45 group use fee.
Who to contact: Phone San Bernardino National District Office at (714)794-
   1123.
Location: Drive 18 miles south of Big Bear City off Highway 38.
Trip note: Open from May through October. Elevation 6600 feet. Camp is on
   the Santa Ana River.

Site **38**   GREEN CANYON
                       GROUP CAMP

Campsites, facilities: There is one group camp that will accommodate 40 people
   and eight cars (no trailers or motorhomes). No water, but vault toilets, picnic tables and fireplaces are provided.
Reservations, fee: Reservation requested; $15 group fee.
Who to contact: Phone San Bernardino National Forest District Office at
   (714)866-3437.
Location: Drive five miles southeast of Big Bear City off Highway 38.
Trip note: Open from June through September. Elevation 7200 feet. Camp is
   near a trail that goes up Green Canyon to Wild Horse Creek. There it intersects with a National Recreation Trail leading to Sugar Loaf Mountain or
   down to the Santa Ana River near Heart Bar.

Site **39**   COON CREEK
                       GROUP CAMP

Campsites, facilities: There is one group camp with 10 sites that will accommodate up to 40 people and 10 cars (no trailers or motorhomes). No water, but

vault toilets, picnic tables and fireplaces are provided.

Reservations, fee: Reservation requested; $25 group fee.

Who to contact: Phone San Bernardino National Forest District Office at (714)794-1123.

Location: Drive 17 miles southeast of Big Bear City off Highway 38.

Trip note: Open all year. Elevation 8200 feet. Camp is on the Pacific Crest National Scenic Trail and Coon Creek.

Site **40**   HEART
                          BAR

Campsites, facilities: There are 100 campsites for tents or motorhomes to 30 feet long. Piped water, vault toilets, picnic tables and fireplaces are provided.

Reservations, fee: Reservations not required; $4 use fee.

Who to contact: Phone San Bernardino National Forest Headquarters at (714)383-5588.

Location: Drive 17 miles southeast of Big Bear City off Highway 38.

Trip note: Open from May through November. Elevation 6900 feet. Camp is on the Heart Bar Creek in Big Meadows.

Site **41**   HEART BAR EQUESTRIAN
                        GROUP CAMP

Campsites, facilities: There is one group camp with 10 sites that will accommodate up to 50 people and 25 cars (limited use of trailers and motorhomes). Piped water, vault toilets, picnic tables and fireplaces are provided.

Reservations, fee: Reservation requested; $25 group fee.

Who to contact: Phone San Bernardino National Forest District Office at (714)794-1123.

Location: Drive 16 miles southeast of Big Bear City off Highway 38.

Trip note: Open from May through November. Elevation 7000 feet. Camp is on Heart Bar Creek and about three miles by dirt road to the Pacific Crest National Scenic Trail.

Site **42**   JUNIPER SPRINGS
                        GROUP CAMP

Campsites, facilities: There is one group camp that will accommodate up to 40 people and eight cars (limited use of trailers and motorhomes). Piped water, vault toilets, picnic tables and fireplaces are provided.

Reservations, fee: Reservation requested; $15 group fee.

Who to contact: Phone San Bernardino National Forest District Office at (714)866-3437.

Location: Drive 10.5 miles southeast of Big Bear City off Highway 38.

Trip note: Open from June through September. Elevation 7700 feet. Little-known camp, except to a few groups who use it yearly. Advisable to obtain map of San Bernardino National Forest.

Site **43**
ROUND VALLEY GROUP CAMP

Campsites, facilities: There is one group camp that will accommodate up to 15 people and three cars (no trailers or motorhomes). Piped water, vault toilets, picnic tables and fireplaces are provided.

Reservations, fee: Reservation requested; $15 group fee.

Who to contact: Phone San Bernardino National Forest District Office at (714)866-3437.

Location: Drive 20.5 miles southeast of Big Bear City off Highway 38.

Trip note: Open from June through September. Elevation 7000 feet. This one is out in the boondocks.

Site **44**
YUCCA PARK

Campsites, facilities: There are six campsites that can accommodate tents or motorhomes. No water, but pit toilets, picnic tables and fireplaces are provided. A grocery store, propane gas and a laundromat are nearby.

Reservations, fee: No reservations, no fee.

Who to contact: This is a county park. For information call (619)365-2376.

Location: Drive five miles west of Yucca Valley via Highway 62.

Trip note: Open all year. Elevation 3000 feet. Little-used and remote. Bring your own water.

Site **45**
INDIAN COVE CAMPGROUND

Campsites, facilities: There are 111 campsites for tents or motorhomes to 32 feet long. Drinking water is available at the Indian Cove Ranger Station. Pit toilets, picnic tables and fireplaces are provided. Gas, groceries and laundry services are in town, which is about 10 miles from camp. Wheelchair access toilets.

Reservations, fee: No reservations, no fee.

Who to contact: Phone Joshua Tree National Monument at (619)367-7511.

Location: Drive 10 miles southwest of Twentynine Palms off Highway 62 on Indian Cove Road.

Trip note: Open all year. Elevation 3200 feet. Enjoy the beauty of the desert and the stands of Joshua trees, but not in the summer when the temperature is usually over 100 degrees.

Site **46** — INDIAN COVE GROUP CAMPGROUND

Campsites, facilities: There is one group camp with three sites for tents or motorhomes up to 32 feet long. Drinking water is available at the Indian Cove Ranger Station, about a mile from camp. Pit toilets, picnic tables and fireplaces are provided. Groceries, gas and laundry facilities can be found in town, about 10 miles from camp. Wheelchair access to toilets.

Reservations, fee: Make reservations through Ticketron or outlets in Sears stores. Call (213)216-6666 for other outlet locations ($2.25 fee).

Who to contact: Phone Joshua Tree National Monument at (619)367-7511.

Location: From Highway 62, turn on Indian Cove Road and drive 10 miles southwest of Twentynine Palms.

Trip note: Open all year. Elevation 3200 feet. Very hot in summer.

Site **47** — KNOTT SKY PARK

Campsites, facilities: There are 36 motorhome spaces with full hookups. Piped water, flush toilets, showers, a sanitary dump station, a playground, picnic tables and fireplaces are provided. A grocery store and a laundromat are nearby.

Reservations, fee: Reservation requested; $5 use fee.

Who to contact: This is a county park; call (619)367-7562.

Location: Drive one mile west of Twentynine Palms off Highway 62.

Trip note: Open all year. Elevation 2000 feet. Very hot in summer.

Site **48** — DESERT WILLOW RV PARK

Campsites, facilities: There are 57 motorhome spaces with full hookups. Rest rooms, hot showers, convenience store, groceries, ice, laundry, propane gas, swimming pool, indoor spa, recreation room, library, adult lounge and cable TV are on the premises.

Reservations, fee: Reservation with deposit of $13.50; use fee $13.50.

Who to contact: Call (619)949-0377.

Location: In Hesperia at 12624 Main Street West.

Trip note: Open all year. Elevation 3500 feet. Located where the high mountains meet the desert.

Site **49** — MOJAVE NARROWS REGIONAL PARK

Campsites, facilities: There are 110 campsites for tents or motorhomes. Piped water, flush toilets, showers, a sanitary dump station, a playground, picnic tables and fireplaces are provided. A grocery store, propane gas and a laundromat are nearby.

Reservations, fee: Reservations not required; $6 use fee.

Who to contact: This a county park; call (619)245-2226 for information.

Location: In Victorville on N. Ridgecrest Road. From Highway 15, take Bear Valley Cutoff.

Trip note: Open all year. Elevation 2000 feet. Fishing in stocked pond, horseback riding facilities and trails.

Site **50**   SHADY OASIS
                   VICTORVILLE KOA

Campsites, facilities: There are 105 campsites for tents or motorhomes with full or partial hookups. Piped water, flush toilets, hot showers, a sanitary dump station, a playground, recreation room, swimming pool, picnic tables and fireplaces are provided. A grocery store, propane gas and a laundromat are nearby.

Reservations, fee: Make reservations through Leisuretime Reservation Systems, Inc. Reservation $13 (per ticket fee of $3.50); camp use fee $13.

Who to contact: Call (619)245-6867.

Location: At 16530 Stoddard Wells Road, two miles north of Victorville.

Trip note: Open all year. Elevation 3000 feet. Just minutes away from Roy Rodgers' home and museum, Edwards Air Force Base, three golf courses and Lake Silverwood, where you can fish and water ski.

Site **51**   BARSTOW CALICO
                         KOA

Campsites, facilities: There are 72 campsites for tents or motorhomes with full or partial hookups. Piped water, flush toilets, showers, sanitary dump station, playground, swimming pool, recreation room, picnic tables and fireplaces are provided. A grocery store, propane gas, ice and a laundromat are on the premises.

Reservations, fee: Reservations $12; camp use fee $12.

Who to contact: Call (619)254-2311.

Location: Drive seven miles northeast of Barstow via Highway 5 and Ghost Town Road.

Trip note: Open all year. Elevation 1960 feet. Out in the middle of nowhere.

Site **52**   DESERT DRIFTERS
                       RV PARK

Campsites, facilities: There are 29 tent sites and 49 motorhome spaces with full or partial hookups. Piped water, flush toilets, showers, a sanitary dump station, free TV, picnic tables and fireplaces are provided. Telephone hookups are available for monthly parkers. A grocery store, propane gas and a laundromat are nearby.

Reservations, fee: Reservations not required; $12 use fee.

Who to contact: Call (619)254-3200.

Location: In Deggett at 34805 Deggett Yermo Road.

Trip note: Open all year. Elevation 2400 feet. There's a lake for swimming and fishing.

Site **53**   BARSTOW STATION
          RV PARK

Campsites, facilities: There are 117 motorhome spaces here with full hookups for motorhomes to 55 feet long. Rest rooms with showers, a grocery store, laundromat, recreation room, swimming pool, spa, a pet run, complete motorhome parts and maintenance station, a restaurant, shops and a movie theater are on the premises.

Reservations, fee: Call ahead for rates and reservations.

Who to contact: Call (619)256-8282.

Location: Take the East Main Street Exit off Highway 15 or Highway 40 in Barstow.

Trip note: Open all year. Elevation 2000 feet. Visit the Calico Ghost Town.

Site **54**   CALICO GHOST TOWN
          REGIONAL PARK

Campsites, facilities: There are 114 campsites for tents or motorhomes. Piped water, fireplaces, flush toilets, showers, a sanitary dump station and picnic tables are provided. Groceries, propane gas and laundry facilities are available nearby.

Reservations, fee: Reservations requested; $6 use fee per night.

Who to contact: Phone the park at (619)254-2122.

Location: Drive one and a half miles southwest of Calico off Highway 15.

Trip note: Open all year. Elevation 2400 feet. Visit the historic Calico Ghost Town.

Site **55**   OWL
          CANYON

Campsites, facilities: There are 32 campsites for tent or motorhomes. Fireplaces, picnic tables, vault toilets and non-piped drinking water are provided.

Reservations, fee: No reservations; $2 use fee per night.

Who to contact: Phone Bureau of Land Management at (619)256-3591.

Location: From Highway 15, drive five miles north of Barstow on Camp Irwin Road, then five miles west on Fossil Beds Road.
Trip note: Open all year. Elevation 2600 feet. OK layover.

Site **56**   AFTON
                               CANYON   ▲

Campsites, facilities: There are 24 campsites for tents or motorhomes. Fireplaces, picnic tables, vault toilets and non-piped water are provided. Groceries are available nearby.
Reservations, fee: No reservations; $2 use fee per night.
Who to contact: Phone Bureau of Land Management at (619)256-3591.
Location: Drive 40 miles east of Barstow on Highway 15, then three miles south on Afton Canyon Road.
Trip note: Open all year. Elevation 1400 feet. Remote and hot in summer.

Site **57**   MID
                               HILLS   ▲

Campsites, facilities: There are 26 campsites for tents or motorhomes. Fireplaces, picnic tables, non-piped drinking water and vault toilets are provided.
Reservations, fee: No reservations; $2 use fee per night.
Who to contact: Phone Bureau of Land Management at (619)326-3896.
Location: From Highway 40 take the Essex Road exit north to the junction with Black Canyon Road, then follow the signs to the campground.
Trip note: Open all year. Elevation 5600 feet. Almost always space available here.

Site **58**   HOLE-IN-THE-WALL   🌲

Campsites, facilities: There are 10 campsites for tents or motorhomes. Fireplaces and picnic tables are provided, and vault toilets and non-piped drinking water are available.
Reservations, fee: No reservations; $2 use fee per night.
Who to contact: Phone Bureau of Land Management at (916)326-3896.
Location: From Highway 40 take the Essex Road exit north, then turn right on Black Canyon Road for 10 miles. Follow the signs to camp.
Trip note: Open all year. Elevation 5000 feet. Little-known, quiet spot.

Site **59**   TECOPA HOT SPRINGS
                              RESORT

Campsites, facilities: There are 92 motorhome sites with hookups for water, sewer and electricity. A mesa is available for tent campers. Rest rooms with hot showers, mineral bath spas, a grocery store and a laundromat are available. Propane gas can be found nearby.

Reservations, fee: Reservations recommended during the winter; $7.50 use fee per night.

Who to contact: Phone (619)852-4373.

Location: From Highway 15, take Highway 127 north to Old Spanish Trail. At Tecopa, turn on Tecopa Road and drive one and a half miles.

Trip note: Enjoy the mineral hot springs in your own personal spa. A good place for rock hounding. The resort is a short drive from Death Valley and 80 miles from Las Vegas.

Site **60**   PROVIDENCE MOUNTAINS
STATE RECREATION AREA

Campsites, facilities: There are six campsites for tents or motorhomes to 32 feet long. Piped water, fireplaces, pit toilets and picnic tables are provided.

Reservations, fee: No reservations; $3 use fee per night.

Who to contact: Phone (619)389-2281.

Location: Drive 21 miles northwest of Essex off Highway 40 onto Essex Road.

Trip note: Open all year. Elevation 4300 feet. From mid-September through mid-June, there are guided tours of Mitchell Caverns.

Site **61**   NEEDLES
KOA

Campsites, facilities: There are 55 campsites for tents or motorhomes. Piped water, electrical connections, and in some cases, sewer hookups are provided. Flush toilets and showers are available. Groceries, propane gas and laundry facilities can be found nearby.

Reservations, fee: Call for available space. A deposit of $9.50 required; camp fee $9.50.

Who to contact: Call Needles KOA at (619)326-4207.

Location: Drive one and a half miles northwest of Needles on Old National Trails Highway.

Trip note: Open all year. Elevation 500 feet. Hot and dry, but a nice place to camp. Colorado River not far away.

Site **62**   NEEDLES MARINA
PARK

Campsites, facilities: There are 75 campsites for tents and 112 spaces for motorhomes. Piped water, electrical connections and sewer hookups are provided. Rest rooms with showers, a heated pool, jacuzzi, boat ramp, boat slips, a grocery store, gas and a laundromat are available.

Reservations, fee: Call ahead for available space and fee information.

Who to contact: Call the Needles Marina Park at (619)326-2197.

Location: From Highway 40, take the "J" Street exit in Needles to Broadway. Turn left, then turn right at River Road and drive a half mile to the park.

Trip note: The campsites are on a stretch of the Colorado River that is smooth enough for water skiing. An 18-hole golf course is adjacent to the camp.

Site **63**
RAINBO BEACH RESORT
AND MARINA

Campsites, facilities: There are 60 motorhome spaces. Piped water, electrical connections, sewer hookups and picnic tables are provided. Rest rooms with showers, a laundromat and a marina are available.

Reservations, fee: Call ahead for available space. $12 deposit required; $12 use fee per night.

Who to contact: Phone Rainbo Beach Resort and Marina at (619)326-3101.

Location: Drive one and a half miles north of Needles on River Road.

Trip note: Open all year. Elevation 500 feet. Resort is on the Colorado River.

Site **64**
MOABI
REGIONAL PARK

Campsites, facilities: There are 647 campsites for tents or motorhomes. Piped water, fireplaces, picnic tables, and in some cases electrical and sewer hookups provided. Flush toilets, showers, a playground and a sanitary dump station are available. Groceries, propane gas and laundry facilities are available nearby.

Reservations, fee: Reservations accepted; $10 use fee per night.

Who to contact: Phone Moabi Regional Park at (619)326-3831.

Location: Drive 11 miles southeast of Needles off Highway 40.

Trip note: Open all year. Elevation 500 feet. Colorado River not far away.

Site **65**
EMPIRE
LANDING

Campsites, facilities: There are 20 campsites for tents and 50 spaces for motorhomes to 30 feet long. Piped water, fireplaces and picnic tables are provided. Flush toilets and a sanitary dump station are available. Groceries, propane gas and laundry facilities can be found nearby.

Reservations, fee: No reservations; $5 per night.

Who to contact: The campground is managed by the Yuma, Arizona Bureau of Land Management office. Call (602)855-8017 for information.

Location: Drive eight miles northeast of Earp off Highway 62 on Parker Dam Road.

Trip note: Open all year. Elevation 400 feet. The campground is a short distance from Lake Havasu.

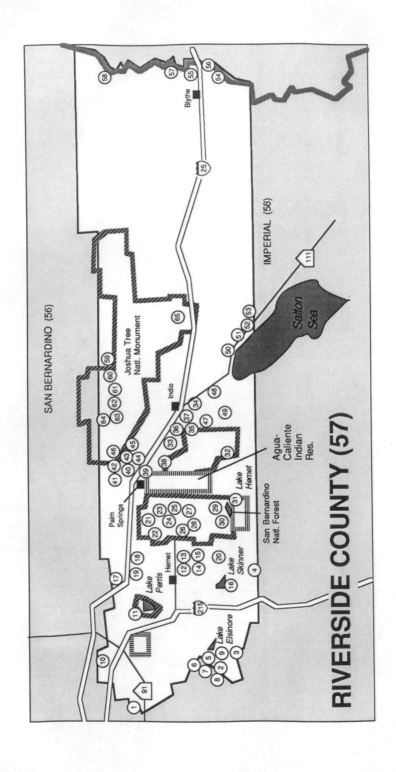

RIVERSIDE COUNTY (57)

RIVERSIDE COUNTY

◆

Site **1**
UPPER
SAN JUAN

Campsites, facilities: There are 18 campsites for tents or motorhomes up to 18 feet long. Piped water, fireplaces and picnic tables are provided. Vault toilets are available. A grocery store is nearby.

Reservations, fee: No reservations; $5 fee per night.

Who to contact: Phone Cleveland National Forest Headquarters at (619)293-5050.

Location: Drive 21 miles northeast of San Juan Capistrano on State Route 74.

Trip note: Open from April to October. Elevation 1800 feet. The campground has trailheads for hikes south into San Mateo Canyon Wilderness and north into the Santa Ana Mountains.

Site **2**
EL CARISO

Campsites, facilities: There are 10 tent sites and 39 campsites for tents or motorhomes up to 22 feet long. Piped water, fireplaces and picnic tables are provided. Vault toilets are available. A grocery store and laundromat are nearby.

Reservations, fee: No reservations; $5 fee per night.

Who to contact: Phone Cleveland National Forest Headquarters at (619)293-5050.

Location: Drive 12 miles west of Lake Elsinore on State Route 74.

Trip note: Open from April to November. Elevation 3000 feet. Located near the border of the Cleveland National Forest, overlooking Lake Elsinore.

Site **3**
TENEJA

Campsites, facilities: There are six tent sites. Piped water, picnic tables and fireplaces are provided. Vault toilets are available.

Reservations, fee: No reservations, no fee.

Who to contact: Phone Cleveland National Forest Headquarters at (619)293-5050.
Location: Drive 12 miles west of Murietta via Tenaja Road.
Trip note: Open all year. Elevation 2000 feet. Located on Tenaja Creek.

Site 4   DRIPPING
                     SPRINGS   ▲

Campsites, facilities: There are 26 campsites for tents or motorhomes up to 32 feet long. Piped water, fireplaces and picnic tables are provided. Vault toilets are available. A grocery store is nearby.
Reservations, fee: No reservations; $5 fee per night.
Who to contact: Phone Cleveland National Forest Headquarters at (619)293-5050.
Location: Drive four miles west of Redec off State Route 79.
Trip note: Open from April to November. Elevation 1500 feet. Located on Arroyo Seco Creek, three miles from Vail Lake. The Dripping Springs Trail leads from camp into the Agua Tibea Wilderness.

Site 5   ORTEGA OAKS
                     PARK   ▲

Campsites, facilities: There are 26 motorhome spaces and 59 sites for tents or motorhomes. Picnic tables, piped water, and in some cases, electrical connections and sewer hookups are provided. Rest rooms, showers, dump station, laundromat, store and propane gas are available.
Reservations, fee: Call for space available. $14 deposit required; $14 fee per night.
Who to contact: Phone park at (714)678-2949.
Location: Drive 13 miles southwest of Lake Elsinore at 34040 Ortega Highway.
Trip note: Open all year. Elevation 2000 feet. Located in Cleveland National Forest. A National Forest map details the back country.

Site 6   LAKE PARK RESORT
                     RV PARK   ▲

Campsites, facilities: There are 53 motorhome spaces. Piped water, electrical connections and sewer hookups are provided. Rest rooms, showers, swimming pool, cable TV, store, dump station, ice, recreation room, boat ramp and boat and jet-ski rentals are available.
Reservations, fee: Call for space available. $11 deposit required; $11 fee per night.
Who to contact: Phone park at (714)674-7911.
Location: Drive three miles west of I-15 on State Route 74 to 32000 Riverside Drive.

Trip note: Open all year. Elevation 1300 feet. Located next to Lake Elsinore State Recreation Area .

Site **7**	THE ROADRUNNER	

Campsites, facilities: There are 45 tent sites and 100 motorhome spaces. Picnic tables, fire rings, piped water, electrical connections, sewer hookups and cable TV connections are provided. Rest rooms, showers, a playground, swimming pool, laundromat, store, boat dock and ramp are available. Propane gas is nearby.

Reservations, fee: Call ahead for space available and fee.

Who to contact: Phone park at (714)674-4900.

Location: Drive four miles west of I-15 on State Route 74 to 32500 Riverside Drive.

Trip note: This park is open all year and is 1/2 mile from Lake Elsinore State Recreation Area.

Site **8**	ELSINORE WEST MARINA	

Campsites, facilities: There are 170 motorhome spaces. Picnic tables, piped water, electrical connections, cable TV and sewer hookups are provided. Rest rooms, showers, dump station and boat ramp are available. A grocery store, laundromat and propane gas are nearby.

Reservations, fee: Call ahead for space available and fee.

Who to contact: Phone park at (714)678-1300.

Location: Drive four miles west of I-15 on State Route 74 to 32700 Riverside Drive.

Trip note: This park is open all year and is 1/2 mile from Lake Elsinore State Recreation Area.

Site **9**	LAKE ELSINORE STATE RECREATION AREA	

Campsites, facilities: There are 175 campsites for tents or motorhomes up to 40 feet long. Piped water, electrical connections, fireplaces and picnic tables are provided. Flush toilets, showers, dump station, playground, boat launch, laundromat, grocery store and propane gas are available. The camping and picnicking areas are wheelchair accessible.

Reservations, fee: No reservations; $11.50 fee per night.

Who to contact: Phone park at (714)674-3177.

Location: Drive three miles west of I-15 on State Route 74.

Trip note: Open all year. Elevation 1250 feet. Enjoy fishing, boating, waterskiing and swimming at Lake Elsinore.

Site 10
RANCHO JURUPA
PARK

Campsites, facilities: There are 80 campsites for tents or motorhomes. Electrical connections, piped water, fireplaces and picnic tables are provided. Flush toilets, showers, dump station, playground and horseback riding facilities are available.
Reservations, fee: No reservations; $8 fee per night.
Who to contact: Phone park at (714)787-2553.
Location: Drive three miles west of Riverside on Jurupa Road.
Trip note: Elevation 780 feet. Open all year. A 20-minute drive south to Lake Mathews or Lake Perris.

Site 11
LAKE PERRIS
STATE RECREATION AREA

Campsites, facilities: There are 155 tent sites and 238 sites for tents or motorhomes up to 31 feet long. Picnic tables, fireplaces, electrical connections and piped water are provided. Flush toilets, showers, dump station, playground, grocery store, laundromat, propane gas, horseback riding facilities, boat launch, mooring and rentals are available. Exhibits, pathways, campgrounds, picnic areas and exhibits are wheelchair accessible.
Reservations, fee: Phone MISTIX at (800)446-7275; $12 fee per night.
Who to contact: Phone park at (714)657-0676.
Location: Drive 11 miles southeast of Riverside off highway 215.
Trip note: Open all year. Elevation 1600 feet. Enjoy waterskiing, fishing and swimming at Lake Perris.

Site 12
GOLDEN VILLAGE ADULT TRAVEL
TRAILER PARK

Campsites, facilities: There are 104 motorhome spaces. Picnic tables, piped water, electrical connections and sewer hookups are provided. Rest rooms, showers, pool, laundromat, recreation room and propane gas are available.
Reservations, fee: Call for space available. $17 deposit required; $17 fee per night.
Who to contact: Phone park at (714)925-2518.
Location: In Hemet, drive to 37250 West Florida Avenue.
Trip note: Open all year. Elevation 1600 feet. This site offers a recreation program with art, craft and dance classes. There are additional motorhome spaces available for long stays.

Site **13**

HEMET VALLEY
TRAVEL TRAILER PARK

Campsites, facilities: There are 95 motorhome spaces. Picnic tables, piped water, electrical connections and sewer hookups are provided. Rest rooms, showers, swimming pool, laundromat and recreation room are available. Propane gas and grocery store can be found nearby.

Reservations, fee: Call for space available. $14 deposit required; $14 fee per night.

Who to contact: Phone park at (714)658-0218.

Location: In Hemet, drive to 525 North Gilbert Street.

Trip note: Open all year. Elevation 1600 feet. This is an adults-only park, and is within an hour's drive of Palm Springs, Lake Arrowhead and the San Diego Wild Animal Park.

Site **14**

MOUNTAIN VALLEY
RECREATIONAL VEHICLE PARK

Campsites, facilities: There are 170 motorhome spaces. Piped water, cable TV, electrical connections and sewer hookups are provided. Rest rooms, showers, swimming pool, enclosed jacuzzi, laundromat, recreation room, shuffleboard and telephone hookups are available. A grocery store and propane gas are available nearby.

Reservations, fee: Phone Leisuretime Reservation Systems at (800)822-CAMP. $14.50 deposit; $14.50 camp use fee.

Who to contact: Phone park at (714)925-5812.

Location: In Hemet, drive to 235 South Lyon Avenue.

Trip note: This park is open all year. Elevation 1600 feet. Located within an hour's drive of Palm Springs, Lake Arrowhead and the San Diego Wild Animal Park.

Site **15**

ROADRUNNER
TRAVEL HOME RESORTS

Campsites, facilities: There are 358 motorhome spaces. Picnic tables, piped water, electrical connections and sewer hookups are provided. Rest rooms, showers, swimming pool and laundromat are available.

Reservations, fee: Call for space available. $15.50 deposit required; $15.50 fee per night.

Who to contact: Phone park at (714)925-2515.

Location: In Hemet drive to 2750 West Acacia Avenue.

Trip note: Open all year. Elevation 1600 feet. Located within an hour's drive of Palm Springs, Lake Arrowhead and the San Diego Wild Animal Park.

Site 16   LAKE SKINNER RECREATION AREA

Campsites, facilities: There are 41 tent sites, 216 motorhome spaces and 257 sites for tents or motorhomes. Picnic tables, fireplaces and piped water are provided at all sites. Electrical connections and sewer hookups are provided at the motorhome spaces. Rest rooms, showers, a playground, grocery store, ice, bait, dump station, boat ramp, mooring, boat rentals and propane gas are available.
Reservations, fee: Reservations requested; $10 fee per night.
Who to contact: Phone park at (714)926-1541.
Location: Drive eight miles northeast of Temecula off I-15 via Rancho California Road to 37701 Warren Road.
Trip note: Open all year. Elevation 1500 feet. Non-motorized boats under 10 feet prohibited. Good fishing.

Site 17   BOGART COUNTY PARK

Campsites, facilities: There are 65 campsites for tents or motorhomes. Piped water, fireplaces and picnic tables are provided. Flush toilets and a playground are available.
Reservations, fee: No reservations; $5 fee per night.
Who to contact: Phone park at (714)787-2553.
Location: Drive four miles north of Beaumont off I-10 via Beaumont Avenue to 14th and Cherry Streets.
Trip note: Open all year. Elevation 2800 feet. Located 35 miles from Palm Springs or San Bernardino National Forest.

Site 18   BANNING TRAVEL PARK

Campsites, facilities: There are 91 sites for tents or motorhomes. Picnic tables, piped water, electrical connections, and in most cases, sewer hookups are provided. Cable TV, rest rooms, showers, a playground, swimming pool, laundromat, store, dump station, ice, recreation room, ice cream fountain, horseshoes, video arcade and propane gas are available.
Reservations, fee: Call for space available. $12.75 deposit required; $12.75 fee per night.
Who to contact: Phone park at (714)849-7513.
Location: In Banning, drive to 1455 South San Gorgonio Avenue.
Trip note: Park is open all year. Elevation 2400 feet. Located 22 miles from Palm Springs.

| Site **19** | BREEZE LAKE
RV PARK | |

Campsites, facilities: There are 10 tent sites and 82 motorhome spaces. Picnic tables, piped water, electrical connections and sewer hookups are provided. Rest rooms, showers, a playground, swimming pool, heated whirlpool, laundromat, dump station, ice, adult recreation room, horseshoes and propane gas are available. A grocery store is nearby.

Reservations, fee: Call ahead for space available and fee.

Who to contact: Phone park at (714)845-5919.

Location: In Beaumont, take the Beaumont Avenue (Highway 79) exit off I-10 to First Street then Michigan Street to 14711 Manzanita Road.

Trip note: This park is within an hour's drive of Palm Springs, Lake Arrowhead and the San Diego Wild Animal Park.

| Site **20** | TUCALOTA SPRINGS RV PARK
AND CAMPGROUND | |

Campsites, facilities: There are 35 tent sites and 102 motorhome spaces. Picnic tables, piped water, electrical connections and sewer hookups are provided. Rest rooms, showers, a playground, bike trails, swimming pool, laundromat, store, dump station, ice, recreation room and propane gas are available. Fishing and boating nearby.

Reservations, fee: Phone Leisuretime Reservation Systems at (800)822-CAMP.

Who to contact: Phone park at (714)925-3183.

Location: Drive 13 miles south of Hemet on State Street to town of Sage, then left on Benton Road to 41601 Benton Road.

Trip note: Open all year. Elevation 2400 feet. Nestled in the hills among the oaks.

| Site **21** | BLACK MOUNTAIN
GROUP CAMP | |

Campsites, facilities: There are two group camps here for tents or motorhomes up to 22 feet long. Each has a capacity of 50 people and 16 vehicles. Piped water, picnic tables and fireplaces are provided. Vault toilets are available.

Reservations, fee: Reservations requested; $25 fee per group per night.

Who to contact: Phone San Bernardino National Forest Headquarters at (714)383-5588.

Location: Drive 16 miles northwest of Idyllwild off State Route 243.

Trip note: Open from May to October. Elevation 7500 feet. Several trails lead out from camp into the forest and Mt. San Jacinto State Park.

Site **22**   BOULDER
                                               BASIN   ▲

Campsites, facilities: There are 34 campsites for tents or motorhomes up to 22
feet long. Piped water, fireplaces and picnic tables are provided. Vault toi-
lets are available.
Reservations, fee: No reservations; $5 fee per night.
Who to contact: Phone San Bernardino National Forest Headquarters at
(714)383-5588.
Location: Drive 15 miles northwest of Idyllwild off State Route 243.
Trip note: This camp is open from May to October. Elevation 7300 feet. Near
San Jacinto Wilderness.

Site **23**   DARK
                                               CANYON   ▲

Campsites, facilities: There are 22 campsites for tents or motorhomes up to 22
feet long. Piped water, fireplaces and picnic tables are provided. Vault toilets are available.
Reservations, fee: No reservations; $7 fee per night.
Who to contact: Phone San Bernardino National Forest Headquarters at
(714)383-5588.
Location: Drive 10 miles northwest of Idyllwild off State Route 243.
Trip note: This camp is open from May to October. Elevation 5800 feet. Located
on the San Jacinto River.

Site **24**   FERN
                                               BASIN   ▲

Campsites, facilities: There are 22 campsites for tents or motorhomes up to 22
feet long. Piped water, fireplaces and picnic tables are provided. Vault toi-
lets are available.
Reservations, fee: No reservations; $6 fee per night.
Who to contact: Phone San Bernardino National Forest Headquarters at
(714)383-5588.
Location: Drive eight miles northwest of Idyllwild off State Route 243.
Trip note: Open from May to November. Elevation 6300 feet. Located near the
San Jacinto River.

Site **25**   MARION
                                              MOUNTAIN   ▲

Campsites, facilities: There are 24 campsites for tents or motorhomes up to 16
feet long. Piped water, fireplaces and picnic tables are provided. Vault toilets are available.

Reservations, fee: No reservations; $6 fee per night.
Who to contact: Phone San Bernardino National Forest Headquarters at (714)383-5588.
Location: Drive nine miles northwest of Idyllwild off State Route 243.
Trip note: This camp is open from May to September. Elevation 6400 feet. Located near the San Jacinto River.

Site **26**   STONE
                              CREEK   ▲

Campsites, facilities: There are 10 tent sites and 40 campsites for tents or motorhomes up to 24 feet long. Piped water, fireplaces and picnic tables are provided. Pit toilets are available. A grocery store, laundromat and propane gas are nearby.
Reservations, fee: Phone MISTIX at (800)446-7275; $3 fee per night.
Who to contact: Phone Mt. San Jacinto State Park at (714)659-2607.
Location: Drive five miles north of Idyllwild off State Route 243.
Trip note: Open all year. Elevation 5900 feet. Located on a state game refuge in Mt. San Jacinto State Park.

Site **27**   IDYLLWILD   ▲

Campsites, facilities: There are 11 tent sites and 22 campsites for tents or motorhomes up to 24 feet long. Piped water, fireplaces and picnic tables are provided. Flush toilets, showers and horseback riding facilities are available. A grocery store, laundromat and propane gas are nearby.
Reservations, fee: Phone MISTIX at (800)446-7275; $6 fee per night.
Who to contact: Phone Mt. San Jacinto State Park at (714)659-2607.
Location: Drive to the north end of the town of Idyllwild off State Route 243.
Trip note: Open all year. Elevation 5400 feet. Located on a state game refuge. A trail leading from camp goes into the backcountry of Mt. Jacinto State Park, Mt. Jacinto Wilderness and connects with the Pacific Crest National Scenic Trail.

Site **28**   IDYLLWILD
                          COUNTY PARK   ▲

Campsites, facilities: There are 35 tent sites, 53 motorhome spaces and 88 campsites for tents or motorhomes up to 21 feet long. Piped water, fireplaces and picnic tables are provided. Flush toilets and showers are available. A grocery store, laundromat and propane gas are available nearby.
Reservations, fee: Reservations accepted; $6 fee per night.
Who to contact: Phone park at (714)787-2553.
Location: Drive 1/2 mile west of Idyllwild off State Route 243.

Trip note: Open all year. Elevation 5300 feet. Located in a state game refuge. Mt. San Jacinto State Park, San Jacinto Wilderness and San Bernardino National Forest lands surround this park. A trail from the State Park Headquarters nearby leads into the backcountry and connects with the Pacific Crest National Scenic Trail.

Site **29**   HURKEY
                                   CREEK

Campsites, facilities: There are 300 campsites for tents or motorhomes. Piped water, fireplaces and picnic tables are provided. Flush toilets and showers are available.
Reservations, fee: Reservations accepted; $6 fee per night.
Who to contact: Phone park at (714)787-2553.
Location: Drive four miles southeast of Mountain Center off State Route 74.
Trip note: This camp is open all year. Elevation 4800 feet. Located on Hurkey Creek near Lake Hemet.

Site **30**   LAKE
                                   HEMET

Campsites, facilities: There are 500 campsites for tents or motorhomes. Piped water, fireplaces, picnic tables and in some cases electrical connections are provided. Flush toilets, showers, dump station, playground, boat ramp, boat rentals, grocery store and propane gas are available.
Reservations, fee: No reservations; $7.25 fee per night.
Who to contact: Phone camp at (714)659-2680.
Location: Drive four miles southeast of Mountain Center off State Route 243.
Trip note: Open January through November. Elevation 4300 feet. Located on the shore of Lake Hemet, a good fishing lake. Boats under 10 feet or over 18 feet are prohibited.

Site **31**   KAMP ANZA
                                   KAMP-GROUND

Campsites, facilities: There are 22 tent sites and 50 tent or motorhome spaces. Picnic tables, piped water, electrical connections and sewer hookups are provided. Rest rooms, showers, a playground, fishing pond, swim spa, horseshoe pits, laundromat, store, dump station, ice, recreation room and propane gas are available.
Reservations, fee: Phone Leisuretime Reservation Systems at (800)822-CAMP; $11 camp use fee.
Who to contact: Phone park at (714)763-4819.
Location: Drive five miles southeast of Anza off Kirby Road at 41560 Terwillinger Road.

Trip note: Open all year. Elevation 4100 feet. Hiking and jeep trails are nearby. Hemet Lake is 11 miles away.

Site **32**
PINYON
FLATS

Campsites, facilities: There are 18 campsites for tents or motorhomes up to 22 feet long. Piped water, fireplaces and picnic tables are provided. Vault toilets are available.
Reservations, fee: No reservations; $4 fee per night.
Who to contact: Phone San Bernardino National Forest Headquarters at (714)383-5588.
Location: Drive 14 miles southwest of Palm Desert on State Route 74.
Trip note: Open from October to May. Elevation 4000 feet. Located on a state game refuge near the Santa Rosa Indian Reservation. Palm Desert is 14 miles away.

Site **33**
BLUE HEAVEN
MOBILE HOME PARK

Campsites, facilities: There are 36 motorhome spaces. Piped water, electrical connections and sewer hookups are provided. Rest rooms, showers, cable TV, a swimming pool and a laundromat are available.
Reservations, fee: Call ahead for space available and fee.
Who to contact: Phone park at (619)328-1567.
Location: Drive nine miles south of Palm Springs off State Route 111 (East Palm Canyon Drive) to 39556 Peterson Road.
Trip note: This park is located midway between Palm Desert and Palm Springs and is an adults-only park.

Site **34**
INDIAN WELLS
RV ROUNDUP

Campsites, facilities: There are 381 motorhome spaces, most of which have piped water, electrical connections and sewer hookups. Rest rooms, showers, three swimming pools, two therapy pools, shuffle board courts, putting green, planned activities, ice, a barbeque, and a laundromat are available.
Reservations, fee: Call ahead for space available and fee.
Who to contact: Phone park at (619)347-0895.
Location: Drive west of Indio via State Route 111 to 47-340 Jefferson Street.
Trip note: This park is in Indio, which is midway between Palm Springs and the Salton Sea.

Site **35**　　　SUNGATE COUNTRY
　　　　　　　　　RV PARK　　　　　　　　

Campsites, facilities: There are 31 motorhome spaces. Piped water, electrical connections and sewer hookups are provided. Rest rooms, showers, swimming pool, laundromat, store and propane gas are available.
Reservations, fee: Call for space available. $16 deposit required; $16 fee per night.
Who to contact: Phone park at (714)321-2280.
Location: In Cathedral City drive to 69-333 East Palm Canyon Drive.
Trip note: Open all year. Elevation 300 feet. Located six miles from Palm Springs.

Site **36**　　DE ANZA PALM SPRINGS OASIS
　　　　　　　　　RV RESORT　　　　　　　

Campsites, facilities: There are 140 motorhome spaces. Picnic tables, piped water, electrical connections and sewer hookups are provided. Rest rooms, showers, swimming pool, laundromat, store and propane gas are available.
Reservations, fee: Call for space available. $17 deposit required; $17 fee per night.
Who to contact: Phone park at (619)328-4813.
Location: In Cathedral City drive to 36-100 Date Palm Drive.
Trip note: Open all year. Elevation 300 feet. Located six miles from Palm Springs.

Site **37**　　　　OUTDOOR
　　　　　　　　　RESORTS　　　　　　　　

Campsites, facilities: There are 602 motorhome spaces. Picnic tables, piped water, electrical connections and sewer hookups are provided. Rest rooms, showers, swimming pools, tennis courts, health club with saunas, whirlpools, 9-hole golf course, club house, snack bar, laundromat, store, shuffleboard and planned activities are available.
Reservations, fee: Call for space available. $22 deposit required; $22 fee per night.
Who to contact: Phone park at (619)324-4005.
Location: Drive two miles north of Cathedral City off Date Palm Drive to 69-411 Ramon Road.
Trip note: Open all year. Elevation 300 feet. Located four miles from Palm Springs.

Site **38**   HAPPY TRAVELER
                    RECREATIONAL VEHICLE PARK

Campsites, facilities: There are 138 motorhome spaces. Picnic tables, piped water, electrical connections and sewer hookups are provided. Rest rooms, showers, a playground, swimming pool and laundromat are available.

Reservations, fee: Call for space available. $19 deposit required; $19 fee per night.

Who to contact: Phone park at (619)325-8518.

Location: Drive one mile south of Palm Springs to 211 West Mesquite Avenue.

Trip note: Open all year. Elevation 475 feet. Large motorhome park.

Site **39**   GOLDEN SANDS
                    RV PARK

Campsites, facilities: There are 39 motorhome spaces. Picnic tables, fireplaces, piped water, electrical connections and sewer hookups are provided. Rest rooms, showers, a playground, swimming pool, jacuzzi, laundromat and recreation room are available. A grocery store is nearby.

Reservations, fee: Call for space available. $15 deposit required; $15 fee per night.

Who to contact: Phone park at (619)327-4737.

Location: In Palm Springs, drive two miles east of State Route 111 via Racquet Club Way and Sunrise Way to 1900 San Rafael Drive.

Trip note: Open all year. Elevation 450 feet. Located five minutes from the tram into Palm Springs .

Site **40**   CAREFREE
                    MOBILE VILLAGE

Campsites, facilities: There are 54 motorhome spaces. Piped water, electrical connections and sewer hookups are provided. Rest rooms, showers, swimming pool, enclosed jacuzzi, satellite TV, recreation room, billiard room, two-mile nature trail and laundromat are available.

Reservations, fee: Call for space available. $15 deposit required; $15 fee per night.

Who to contact: Phone park at (619)329-5657.

Location: Drive eight miles north of Palm Springs to 17069 North Indian Avenue.

Trip note: Open all year. Elevation 475 feet. Located near golf courses, tennis courts and the aerial tramway.

Site **41**
TWO SPRINGS RV RESORT
AND COUNTRY CLUB

Campsites, facilities: There are 60 motorhome spaces. Picnic tables, piped water, electrical connections and sewer hookups are provided. Rest rooms, showers, swimming pool, jacuzzi, tennis courts, club house, miniature golf course, fishing area, horseshoe pit, shuffleboard, billiard room, satellite TV, ping pong tables, laundromat and propane gas are available. A grocery store and boating facilities are nearby.
Reservations, fee: Call ahead for space available and fee.
Who to contact: Phone park at (619)251-1102.
Location: In North Palm Springs, drive three miles north on Indian Avenue off I-10 to 14200 North Indian Avenue.
Trip note: This adult park is eight miles north of Palm Springs and three miles from Desert Hot Springs.

Site **42**
COUNTRY SQUIRE
MOBILE HOME PARK

Campsites, facilities: There are 15 tent sites and 43 motorhome spaces. Picnic tables, piped water, electrical connections and in most cases sewer hookups are provided. Rest rooms, showers, swimming pool, jacuzzi, laundromat, dump station, recreation room and billiard room are available. A grocery store and propane gas are nearby.
Reservations, fee: Call ahead for space available and fee.
Who to contact: Phone park at (619)329-1191.
Location: Take the Palm Drive exit off I-10 and drive six miles north on Palm Drive to 66455 Dillon Road.
Trip note: This adult park is in Desert Hot Springs and 10 miles from Palm Springs.

Site **43**
SKY VALLEY
EAST

Campsites, facilities: There are 360 motorhome spaces. Picnic tables, piped water, electrical connections and sewer hookups are provided. Rest rooms, showers, swimming pools, five natural hot mineral pools, laundromat, large recreation room, social director, shuffleboard, tennis, horseshoes, crafts room and walking trails are available. A grocery store and propane gas are nearby.
Reservations, fee: Call ahead for space available and fee.
Who to contact: Phone park at (619)329-2909.
Location: Take the Palm Drive exit north off I-10 and drive 14 miles northeast via Palm Drive and Dillon Road to 74-711 Dillon Road.

Trip note: This adult park offers all the comforts while you enjoy the mineral springs and desert air.

Site **44**
SAM'S
FAMILY SPA

Campsites, facilities: There are 225 motorhome spaces. Picnic tables, piped water, electrical connections and sewer hookups are provided. Rest rooms, showers, a playground, swimming pool, hot mineral pools, sauna, laundromat, store, restaurant and propane gas are available.

Reservations, fee: No reservations; $22 fee per night.

Who to contact: Phone park at (619)329-6457.

Location: Drive nine miles southeast of Desert Hot Springs off Palm Drive to 70-875 Dillon Road.

Trip note: Open all year. Elevation 1000 feet. Located about 10 miles from Palm Springs.

Site **45**
ROYAL FOX INN
RV PARK

Campsites, facilities: There are 34 motorhome spaces. Piped water, electrical connections and sewer hookups are provided. Rest rooms, showers and swimming pool are available.

Reservations, fee: Call for space available. $15 deposit required; $15 fee per night.

Who to contact: Phone park at (619)329-4481.

Location: In Desert Hot Springs drive to 14-500 Palm Drive.

Trip note: Open all year. Elevation 1000 feet. Located eight miles from Palm Springs and 30 miles from Joshua Tree National Monument.

Site **46**
SANDS
RV COUNTRY CLUB

Campsites, facilities: There are 30 motorhome spaces. Picnic tables, fireplaces, piped water, electrical connections and sewer hookups are provided. Rest rooms, showers and swimming pool are available.

Reservations, fee: Call for space available. $15 deposit required; $15 fee per night.

Who to contact: Phone park at (619)251-1030.

Location: In Desert Hot Springs drive to 16-400 Bubbling Wells Road.

Trip note: Open all year. Elevation 1100 feet. Enjoy the desert sights at nearby Joshua Tree National Monument and Palm Springs.

Site **47**   FIESTA
                                  RV PARK

Campsites, facilities: There are 230 motorhome spaces. Picnic tables, piped wa-
    ter, electrical connections and sewer hookups are provided. Rest rooms,
    showers, swimming pool, laundromat and propane gas are available.
Reservations, fee: Call for space available. $18 deposit required; $18 fee per
    night.
Who to contact: Phone park at (619)342-2345.
Location: In Indio drive to 46-421 Madison Street.
Trip note: Open all year. Elevation 22 feet below seas level. Located near the
    state game refuge in San Bernardino National Forest. Palm Springs and the
    Salton Sea are 25 miles away in either direction.

Site **48**   BOB'S
                                RV ROUND-UP

Campsites, facilities: There are 96 motorhome spaces. Picnic tables, fireplaces,
    piped water, electrical connections and sewer hookups are provided. Rest
    rooms, showers and laundromat are available.
Reservations, fee: Call for space available. $15 deposit required; $15 fee per
    night.
Who to contact: Phone park at (619)347-9210.
Location: In Indio drive to 82-815 Avenue 42.
Trip note: Open all year. Elevation 22 feet below sea level. Located 25 miles
    from the Salton Sea and Palm Springs.

Site **49**   LAKE CAHUILLA
                                COUNTY PARK

Campsites, facilities: There are 71 motorhome spaces and 75 campsites for tent
    or motorhomes up to 21 feet long. Piped water, fireplaces and picnic tables
    are provided, and 60 of the sites have electrical connections. Rest rooms,
    showers, dump station, playground, swimming beach and unpaved boat
    ramp are available.
Reservations, fee: Reservations accepted; $8 fee per night.
Who to contact: Phone park at (619)564-4712.
Location: Drive eight miles southwest of Indio off State Route 111 via Jefferson
    Street.
Trip note: This park is at sea level and is open all year. Set among the date
    palms, this small lake is used for swimming, fishing and sailboarding. Boat-
    ers should beware of sudden winds.

Site 50
SALTON SEA
NATIONAL RECREATION AREA

Campsites, facilities: There are 25 campsites for tents or motorhomes up to 32 feet long. Piped water, fireplaces and picnic tables are provided, and 15 of the sites have electrical connections and sewer hookups. Rest rooms, showers, dump station, grocery store and propane gas are available. There is wheelchair access to camping, picnicking, boating, fishing and exhibit areas.

Reservations, fee: Phone MISTIX at (800)446-7275; $12 fee per night.

Who to contact: Phone Salton Sea National Recreation Area at (619)393-3052.

Location: Drive 10 miles southeast of Mecca off State Route 111.

Trip note: Open all year. Elevation 220 feet below sea level. You can go fishing, swimming and waterskiing in this shallow sea, but watch for underwater obstacles, sandstorms and swells from sudden winds. A red light on the northeast shore of the lake flashes when it is time to head for the nearest shore.

Site 51
MECCA
BEACH

Campsites, facilities: There are 110 campsites for tents or motorhomes up to 30 feet long. Piped water, fireplaces and picnic tables are provided. Flush toilets, showers, boat ramp, groceries and propane gas are available. There is wheelchair access to camping, picnicking, boating, fishing and exhibit areas.

Reservations, fee: No reservations; $6 fee per night.

Who to contact: Phone Salton Sea National Recreation Area at (619)393-3052.

Location: Drive 12 miles southeast of Mecca off State Route 111.

Trip note: Open all year. Elevation 220 feet below sea level. Try fishing for corvina, swimming or waterskiing. Watch for underwater obstacles, sandstorms and swells from sudden winds. A red light on the northeast shore of the lake flashes when wind warnings are up.

Site 52
CORVINA
BEACH

Campsites, facilities: There are 500 campsites for tents or motorhomes. Piped water is provided, and pit toilets, boat ramp, groceries and propane gas are available. There is wheelchair access to camping, picnicking, boating, fishing and exhibit areas.

Reservations, fee: No reservations; $3 fee per night.

Who to contact: Phone Salton Sea National Recreation Area at (619)393-3052.

Location: Drive 14 miles southeast of Mecca off State Route 111.

Trip note: Open all year. Elevation 220 feet below sea level. You can go fishing, swimming and waterskiing in this shallow sea. Watch for underwater obstacles, sandstorms and swells from sudden winds. A red light on the northeast shore of the lake flashes when wind warnings are in effect.

Site **53**   SALT CREEK
PRIMITIVE AREA

Campsites, facilities: There are 150 campsites for tents or motorhomes. Pit toilets are available, but no water is available so bring your own.
Reservations, fee: No reservations; $3 fee per night.
Who to contact: Phone Salton Sea National Recreation Area at (619)393-3052.
Location: Drive 17 miles southeast of Mecca off State Route 111.
Trip note: Open all year. Elevation 220 feet below sea level. Try fishing, swimming or waterskiing in this shallow sea. Watch for underwater obstacles, sandstorms and swells from sudden winds. A red light on the northeast shore of the lake flashes when wind warnings are in effect.

Site **54**   MC INTYRE
PARK

Campsites, facilities: There are 175 tent sites and 100 motorhome spaces. Picnic tables, piped water and electrical connections are provided. Rest rooms, showers, dump station, propane gas, snack bar, grocery store, bait, ice, boat ramp, and boat and waterski rentals are available.
Reservations, fee: No reservations; $12 fee per night.
Who to contact: Phone park at (619)922-8205.
Location: Drive seven miles south of Blythe on Intake Boulevard to the foot of 26th Avenue.
Trip note: Open all year. Elevation 270 feet. Located two miles from the Colorado River.

Site **55**   VALLEY
PALMS

Campsites, facilities: There are 37 motorhome spaces. Picnic tables, piped water, electrical connections and sewer hookups are provided. Rest rooms, showers, laundromat, store, dump station, RV service and supply business are available. Propane gas is nearby.
Reservations, fee: Call ahead for space available and fee.
Who to contact: Phone park at (619)922-7335.
Location: In Blythe, drive one block north of I-10 on Intake Boulevard (Highway 95), then go east to 8401 East Hobsonway.
Trip note: Open all year. Elevation 270 feet. Located one and a half miles from the Colorado River.

Site 56 | RIVIERA BLYTHE
MARINA

Campsites, facilities: There are 235 motorhome spaces. Picnic tables, piped water, electrical connections and sewer hookups are provided. Rest rooms, showers, swimming pool, spa, cable TV, snack bar, laundromat, store, card room, boat ramp, propane gas, and boat and waterski rentals are available. A golf course is nearby.

Reservations, fee: Phone Leisuretime Reservation Systems at (800)822-CAMP. $13 deposit; $13 camp use fee.

Who to contact: Phone park at (619)922-5350.

Location: Drive two miles east of Blythe on I-10 to 14100 Riviera Drive.

Trip note: Open all year. Elevation 250 feet. Located on the Colorado River, where you can enjoy boating, waterskiing and fishing.

Site 57 | COLLIS MAYFLOWER
COUNTY PARK

Campsites, facilities: There are 28 tent sites, 152 motorhome spaces and 152 sites that will take tents or motorhomes. Piped water and electrical connections are provided at some sites. Flush toilets, showers, dump station, playground, snack bar, groceries, ice and boat ramp are available.

Reservations, fee: Reservations accepted; $8 fee per night.

Who to contact: Phone park at (619)922-4665.

Location: From Blythe drive seven miles northeast on Intake Boulevard (Highway 95) to 6th Avenue and Colorado River Road.

Trip note: Open all year. Elevation 280 feet. Located on the Colorado River, where you can enjoy fishing, swimming and waterskiing.

Site 58 | WATER WHEEL
RECREATION AREA

Campsites, facilities: There are 50 tent sites and 50 motorhome spaces. Picnic tables, piped water, electrical connections and sewer hookups are provided. Rest rooms, showers, a playground, laundromat, grocery store, ice, bait, snack bar, propane gas, boat ramp, dry storage and boat engine repairs are available.

Reservations, fee: Call for space available. $11 deposit required; $11 fee per night.

Who to contact: Phone park at (619)922-3863.

Location: Drive 25 miles north of Blythe on US-95.

Trip note: Open all year. Elevation 260 feet. Located on the Colorado River where you can enjoy fishing.

Site 59   WHITE TANK   ▲

Campsites, facilities: There are 20 campsites here for tents or motorhomes up to 27 feet long. Picnic tables and fireplaces are provided. Pit toilets are available, but there is no water, so bring plenty along.
Reservations, fee: No reservations, no fee.
Who to contact: Phone Joshua Tree National Monument at (619)367-7511.
Location: Drive 11 miles south of Twentynine Palms via Utah Trail.
Trip note: Open from October to May. Elevation 3800 feet. Visit this area where the high desert meets the low desert and see a diversity of plants and animals.

Site 60   BELLE   ▲

Campsites, facilities: There are 20 campsites here for tents or motorhomes up to 27 feet long. Picnic tables and fireplaces are provided, and pit toilets are available. There is no water, so bring your own.
Reservations, fee: No reservations, no fee.
Who to contact: Phone Joshua Tree National Monument at (619)367-7511.
Location: Drive nine miles south of Twentynine Palms via Utah Trail.
Trip note: At 3800 feet elevation, this camp is open from October to May. Visit this unusual area where the high desert meets the low desert and see the many different plants and animals.

Site 61   JUMBO ROCKS   ▲

Campsites, facilities: There are 130 camp sites here for tents or motorhomes up to 27 feet long. Picnic tables and fireplaces are provided. Pit toilets are available. There is no water, so bring plenty along.
Reservations, fee: No reservations, no fee.
Who to contact: Phone Joshua Tree National Monument at (619)367-7511.
Location: Drive 12 miles south of Twentynine Palms off Utah Trail.
Trip note: Open all year. Elevation 4400 feet. Summer temperatures commonly exceed 100 degrees, but it is worth seeing this unique area where the high desert meets the low desert.

Site 62   SHEEP PASS GROUP CAMP   🌲

Campsites, facilities: There are six campsites here for tents. Picnic tables and fireplaces are provided, and pit toilets are available. There is no water, so bring plenty along.

Reservations, fee: Call Ticketron at (213)216-6666 for outlet information; no fee.
Who to contact: Phone Joshua Tree National Monument at (619)367-7511.
Location: Drive 16 miles south of Twentynine Palms via Monument Road.
Trip note: Open all year. Elevation 4500 feet. Summer temperatures commonly exceed 100 degrees. A unique desert habitat.

Site **63**   RYAN

Campsites, facilities: There are 27 campsites here for tents or motorhomes up to 27 feet long. Picnic tables and fireplaces are provided, and pit toilets are available. There is no water, so bring plenty along.
Reservations, fee: No reservations, no fee.
Who to contact: Phone Joshua Tree National Monument at (619)367-7511.
Location: Drive 17 miles southwest of Joshua Tree via Park Boulevard.
Trip note: Open all year. Elevation 4300 feet. Summer temperatures commonly exceed 100 degrees. Visit this unusual area where the high desert meets the low desert and see the many different plants and animals.

Site **64**   HIDDEN
                           VALLEY

Campsites, facilities: There are 62 campsites here for tents or motorhomes up to 27 feet long. Picnic tables and fireplaces are provided, and pit toilets are available. There is no water, so bring plenty along.
Reservations, fee: No reservations, no fee.
Who to contact: Phone Joshua Tree National Monument at (619)367-7511.
Location: Drive 14 miles south of Joshua Tree via Park Boulevard.
Trip note: Open all year. Elevation 4200 feet. Summer temperatures are often unbearable, exceeding 100 degrees. Visit this unusual area when it cools off and see where the high desert meets the low desert. There are many different plants and animals.

Site **65**   COTTONWOOD

Campsites, facilities: There are 62 campsites here for tents or motorhomes up to 27 feet long. Piped water, picnic tables and fireplaces are provided, and flush toilets are available.
Reservations, fee: No reservations; $5 fee per night.
Who to contact: Phone Joshua Tree National Monument at (619)367-7511.
Location: Drive 32 miles northeast of Indio off I-10 on Cottonwood Spring Road.
Trip note: Open all year. Elevation 3000 feet. Summer temperatures commonly exceed 100 degrees. Visit this unusual area where the high desert meets the low desert and see the many different plants and animals.

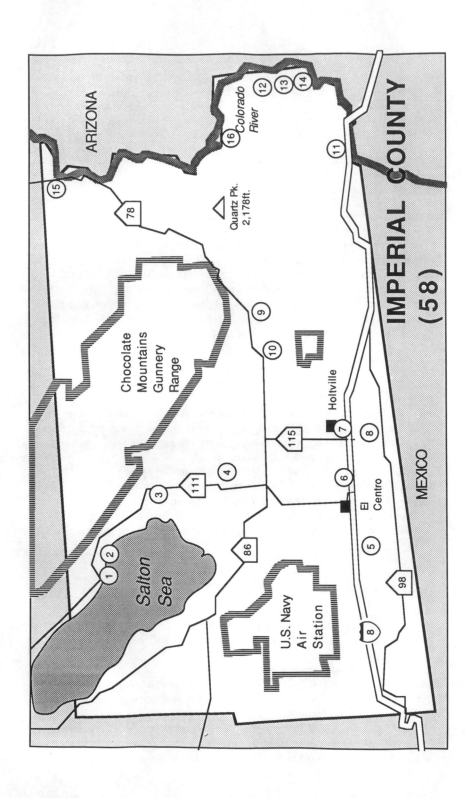

IMPERIAL COUNTY
♦

Site **1**   BOMBAY
BEACH

Campsites, facilities: There are 150 campsites for tents or motorhomes. Piped
   water is provided and pit toilets are available. A grocery store and propane
   gas are nearby.
Reservations, fee: No reservations; $3 fee per night.
Who to contact: Phone Salton Sea State Recreation Area at (619)393-3052.
Location: Drive 18 miles northwest of Niland off State Route 111.
Trip note: Open all year. This campground, on the shores of the Salton Sea, is
   actually below sea level. The northeast shore of the Salton Sea has a swimming beach and nature trails. The southern shore has salt marshes and
   freshwater ponds for migratory birds. Expect very hot weather in the
   summer.

Site **2**   FOUNTAIN OF YOUTH
SPA

Campsites, facilities: There are 400 primitive sites and 546 motorhome spaces
   with full hookups. Flush toilets, showers, natural artesian steam rooms, hy-
   drojet pools, swimming pools, recreation centers, dump stations, laundry,
   barbershop, masseur, church services, propane gas and groceries are
   available.
Reservations, fee: Call ahead for space available and fee; weekly, monthly, yearly
   rates.
Who to contact: Phone park at (619)348-1340.
Location: Drive 44 miles south of Indio or 15 miles north of Niland via State
   Route 111 on Mineral Spa Road.
Trip note: Natural artesian steamrooms a highlight.

Site **3**   RED HILL MARINA
COUNTY PARK

Campsites, facilities: There are 400 campsites for tents or motorhomes. Picnic tables, piped water, and in some cases, electrical connections are provided.

Flush toilets, showers and a dump station are available.
Reservations, fee: No reservations; $9 fee per night.
Who to contact: Phone park at (619)348-2310.
Location: Drive eight and a half miles southwest of Niland off State Route 111.
Trip note: This campground is open all year and is on the shore of the Salton Sea near the Salton Sea National Wildlife Refuge.

Site 4
WIEST LAKE
COUNTY PARK

Campsites, facilities: There are 20 tent sites and 20 motorhome spaces. Picnic tables, fireplaces, piped water and in some cases electrical connections are provided. Flush toilets and showers are available. A grocery store, laundromat and propane gas are nearby.
Reservations, fee: No reservations; $9 fee per night.
Who to contact: Phone park at (619)344-3712.
Location: Drive seven miles northeast of Brawley via State Route 111 and Rutherford Road.
Trip note: Open all year. This campground is located below sea level and is adjacent to the Imperial Wildlife Management Area.

Site 5
SUNBEAM LAKE
COUNTY PARK

Campsites, facilities: There are 200 tent sites and 200 campsites for tents or motorhomes. Picnic tables, piped water and in some cases electrical connections are provided. Flush toilets and showers are available. A grocery store, laundromat and propane gas are nearby.
Reservations, fee: No reservations; $9 fee per night.
Who to contact: Phone park at (619)352-3308.
Location: Drive eight and a half miles southwest of El Centro via Hewes Highway to intersection with Drew Road.
Trip note: This campground is open all year and is a short distance from the Mexican border and Mexicali.

Site 6
EL CENTRO
KOA

Campsites, facilities: There are 30 tent sites and 175 motorhome spaces with full hookups. Flush toilets, showers, swimming pool, spa, clubhouse, laundry, propane gas and groceries are available.
Reservations, fee: Call ahead for space available and fee.
Who to contact: Phone park at (619)353-1051.
Location: Drive 1/2 mile north of I-8 on State Route 111.

Trip note: This campground is open all year and is a short distance from the Mexican border and Mexicali.

Site **7**
WALKER
PARK
◬

Campsites, facilities: There are 50 campsites for tents or motorhomes. Picnic tables and fireplaces are provided, and flush toilets and a playground are available. There is no drinking water, so bring your own. A grocery store, laundromat and propane gas are located nearby.
Reservations, fee: Call ahead for space available and fee.
Who to contact: Phone park at (619)339-4384.
Location: Drive one mile west of Holtville on Highway 80.
Trip note: This campground is open all year and is a short drive to the Mexican border.

Site **8**
HEBER
DUNES
◬

Campsites, facilities: There are 50 tent sites and 50 motorhome spaces. Picnic tables, fireplaces and piped water are provided, and flush toilets are available. A grocery store, laundromat and propane gas are located nearby.
Reservations, fee: No reservations, no fee.
Who to contact: Phone park at (619)339-4384.
Location: Drive nine miles east of Heber via Heber Drive.
Trip note: This campground is open all year and is a short distance from the Mexican border.

Site **9**
OSBORN
PARK
◬

Campsites, facilities: There are 20 campsites for tents or motorhomes. Picnic tables and fireplaces are provided, but there is no water so bring your own.
Reservations, fee: No reservations, no fee.
Who to contact: Phone park at (619)339-4384.
Location: Drive five miles west of Glamis on State Route 78.
Trip note: This campground is open all year.

Site **10**
GECKO
◬

Campsites, facilities: There are 220 campsites for tents or motorhomes. Vault toilets are provided, but there is no water so bring your own.
Reservations, fee: No reservations, no fee.
Who to contact: Phone Bureau of Land Management at (619)352-5842.

Location: Drive 20 miles east of Brawley via State Route 78, then three miles south on Gecko Road.

Trip note: This campground is open all year. Primitive.

Site **11**   PILOT KNOB
                        CAMPGROUND

Campsites, facilities: There are 10 tent sites and 58 motorhome spaces with full hookups. Flush toilets, piped water and a laundry are available.

Reservations, fee: Call for space available. $10 deposit required; $10 fee per night.

Who to contact: Phone park at (619)572-9903.

Location: Drive eight miles west of Winterhaven to 3707 West Highway 80.

Trip note: This campground is open all year and is near the Colorado River and the Mexican border.

Site **12**   SENATOR WASH
                        RECREATION SITE

Campsites, facilities: There are 1000 campsites for tents or motorhomes. Vault toilets are provided, but there is no water so bring your own. A grocery store, laundromat and propane gas are available nearby.

Reservations, fee: No reservations, no fee.

Who to contact: Phone the Bureau of Land Management at (619)726-6300.

Location: Drive 18 1/2 miles northeast of Yuma off County Road S-24 via Senator Wash Road.

Trip note: This campground is open all year and is near the Colorado River.

Site **13**   SOUTH
                        MESA

Campsites, facilities: There are 600 campsites for tents or motorhomes. Piped water is provided, and flush toilets, a dump station and a playground are available. A grocery store and a laundromat are nearby.

Reservations, fee: No reservations, no fee.

Who to contact: Phone the Bureau of Land Management at (619)726-6300.

Location: Drive 18 1/2 miles northeast of Yuma off County Road S-24 via Senator Wash Road.

Trip note: This campground is open all year and is near the Colorado River.

Site **14**   SQUAW
                        LAKE

Campsites, facilities: There are 160 campsites for tents or motorhomes. Picnic tables and piped water are provided, and flush toilets and a playground are available. A grocery store, laundromat and propane gas are located nearby.

Reservations, fee: No reservations; $5 fee per night.

Who to contact: Phone the Bureau of Land Management at (619)726-6300.

Location: Drive 19 miles northeast of Yuma off County Road S-24 via Senator Wash Road.

Trip note: This campground is open all year and is near the Colorado River.

Site **15**   PALO VERDE
                     COUNTY PARK

Campsites, facilities: There are 25 tent sites and 25 motorhome spaces. Vault toilets and a playground are available, but there is no water so bring your own. A grocery store, laundromat and propane gas are located nearby.

Reservations, fee: No reservations, no fee.

Who to contact: Phone park at (619)339-4384.

Location: Drive three miles south of Palo Verde on State Route 78.

Trip note: This campground is set along the Colorado River, near the Cibola National Wildlife Refuge.

Site **16**   PICACHO
                   STATE RECREATION AREA

Campsites, facilities: There are 50 campsites for tents or motorhomes. Picnic tables, fireplaces and piped water are provided. Pit toilets, showers, boat rentals and boat launch are available. A grocery store is nearby. The picnic area is wheelchair accessible.

Reservations, fee: No reservations; $5 fee per night.

Who to contact: No phone.

Location: Drive 25 miles north of Winterhaven off I-8 on Picacho Road.

Trip note: This campground is open all year and is near Taylor Lake on the Colorado River.

John Storey

ABOUT THE AUTHOR

Author Tom Stienstra is recognized as one of California's premier outdoors writers. He is currently outdoors editor for the San Francisco Examiner and president of the Outdoor Writers of California.

Most importantly, Tom is an avid adventurer. He has traveled throughout the state in search of prime fishing, hiking and camping areas. Among his many adventures are several fishing expeditions for great white sharks and a month-long hunt for Bigfoot sponsored by the San Francisco Examiner. He frequently leads seminars on the subject of great white sharks.

A graduate of San Jose State, Tom joined the San Francisco Examiner in 1980 where he has won a number of writing awards, including the McQuade Award, considered Northern California's Pulitzer Prize. His articles appear regularly in Western Outdoor News and Field & Stream. Among his previous books are Salmon Magic and 101 Outdoor Adventures for the Entire Family.

In California Camping, Tom brings his entertaining style to the practical aspects of outdoor life. He reveals over 1500 camping sites across the state, from urban RV parks to primitive wilderness areas, complete with detailed maps. The result is the most complete, useful and entertaining camping guide ever written about California.